cape verde

language, literature & music

I0894225

Portuguese Literary & Cultural Studies 8

cape verde

language, literature & music

Center for Portuguese Studies and Culture
University of Massachusetts Dartmouth

This publication was made possible, in part, by a generous grant from the Luso-American Foundation of Lisbon, Portugal.

Portuguese Literary & Cultural Studies

Director: Frank F. Sousa, University of Massachusetts Dartmouth
Editor: Victor J. Mendes, University of Massachusetts Dartmouth
Guest Editor: Ana Mafalda Leite, Universidade de Lisboa
Editorial Manager: Gina M. Reis, University of Massachusetts Dartmouth
Manuscript Editor (English): Mark Streeter, University of Wisconsin Madison
Manuscript Editor (Portuguese): Isabel A. Ferreira, University of Notre Dame
Copyeditor: Richard Larschan, University of Massachusetts Dartmouth
Assistant to the Editor: Inês Paulino, University of Massachusetts Dartmouth
Graphic Designer: Spencer Ladd, University of Massachusetts Dartmouth
Art Consultant: Memory Holloway, University of Massachusetts Dartmouth
Typesetter: Inês Sena, Lisbon

Advisory Board

Vítor Manuel de Aguiar e Silva, Universidade do Minho
Onésimo Teotónio Almeida, Brown University
Abel Barros Baptista, Universidade Nova de Lisboa
Francisco Bethencourt, Universidade Nova de Lisboa
Dário Borim, University of Massachusetts Dartmouth
João Camilo dos Santos, University of California, Santa Barbara
João Cezar de Castro Rocha, Universidade do Estado do Rio de Janeiro
Luiz Costa Lima, Universidade do Estado do Rio de Janeiro
António Costa Pinto, ISCTE
Francisco Fagundes, University of Massachusetts Amherst
António M. Feijó, Universidade de Lisboa
Bela Feldman-Bianco, UNICAMP/IFCH
Ana Paula Ferreira, University of California Irvine
Fernando Gil, EHESS Paris, Universidade Nova de Lisboa
Hans Ulrich Gumbrecht, Stanford University
Anna Klobucka, University of Massachusetts Dartmouth
Ana Mafalda Leite, Universidade de Lisboa
Helder Macedo, King's College, London
António Machado Pires, Universidade dos Açores
George Monteiro, Brown University
José N. Ornelas, University of Massachusetts Amherst

Phyllis Peres, University of Maryland
Isabel Pires de Lima, Universidade do Porto
Carlos Reis, Universidade de Coimbra
A.J.R. Russell-Wood, The Johns Hopkins University
Maria Alzira Seixo, Universidade de Lisboa
Karl Erik Schøllhammer, Pontifícia Universidade Católica do Rio de Janeiro
Boaventura de Sousa Santos, Universidade de Coimbra
Miguel Tamen, Universidade de Lisboa
Nelson Vieira, Brown University
Regina Zilberman, Pontifícia Universidade Católica do Rio Grande do Sul

Portuguese Literary & Cultural Studies is a multilingual interdisciplinary peer-reviewed journal published semi-annually by the Center for Portuguese Studies and Culture at the University of Massachusetts Dartmouth. The journal addresses the literatures and cultures of the diverse communities of the Portuguese-speaking world in terms of critical and theoretical approaches.

Manuscript Policy

Portuguese Literary & Cultural Studies (PLCS) welcomes submission of original and unpublished manuscripts in English, Portuguese, or Spanish appropriate to the goals of the journal. The first page of the submission must include the following: (i), name, mailing address, e-mail address, and appropriate phone and fax numbers; (ii), a brief biography with reference to institutional affiliation, no more than three publications, and current research; (iii), a 100-word abstract of the content of the article; (iv), The article itself may not exceed 20 pages and should be submitted along with the above information in a single digital file. Reviews (no title): 800 words and, (ii), a brief biography. Review-essays (with title): 2000 words and, (ii), a brief biography. All of the information must be in the same language.

PLCS encourages submission of materials in hard copy and 3.5 diskette (in a protected envelope) by mail to:

> *Portuguese Literary & Cultural Studies*
> Center for Portuguese Studies and Culture

University of Massachusetts Dartmouth
Dartmouth, MA 02747 USA

Manuscripts should be in accordance with the *MLA Style Manual and Guide to Scholarly Publishing* (latest version) with parenthetical documentation and a list of Works Cited. The author is responsible for the accuracy of all quotations, titles, names, and dates. Notes must be manually typed out at the end of the article (before the list of Works Cited), regardless of whether they were entered as footnotes or endnotes into the word processor.

Subscription Information

The annual subscription price (2 issues) for institutions is $80.00 and $40.00 for individuals. Single issues may also be purchased for $25.00. From outside the United States add $12.00 for shipping and handling.

Inquiries should be sent to *Portuguese Literary & Cultural Studies* Subscription, Center for Portuguese Studies and Culture, University of Massachusetts Dartmouth, MA 02747 USA, or by e-mail to: greis@umassd.edu.

Advertising

Portuguese Literary & Cultural Studies accepts advertising that is of interest to scholars in the field of Portuguese, Brazilian, and Luso-African Studies and Critical Theory. Further information is available by contacting the Center for Portuguese Studies and Culture, University of Massachusetts Dartmouth.

Cover
Design: Spencer Ladd.

ISSN 1521-804X
© 2003 University of Massachusetts Dartmouth

Printed by RPI Printing, Fall River, MA

Table of Contents

xv **Introduction**
Ana Mafalda Leite

Language and the Founding Literature/ Língua e Literatura de Fundação

25 **The Construction of Natural-Geographical Space in Cape Verdean Literature**
José Maria Semedo

41 ***O Escravo*: literatura de fundação**
Francisco Salinas Portugal

61 **José Lopes and the Beginnings of Cape Verdean Literature**
Arminda Brito

79 **Bilinguismo Funcional: Assunção Descomplexada**
Manuel Veiga

87 **Escrever em crioulo: *un kaminhu lonji***
Dulce Pereira

103 *Tilôbe*, **personagem das estórias tradicionais caboverdianas**
Tânia Macedo

History, Memory and Travel/ História, Memória e Viagem

111 **(Re)claiming the Heritage: The Narratives of Manuel Veiga**
Gregory McNab

125 **Maria Isabel Barreno's *O Senhor das Ilhas*: Memory and Writing at the Threshold**
Isabel A. Ferreira

139 **Translating Trans-Atlantic Space in Two 1938 Travel Narratives to Cape Verde: Anne Morrow Lindbergh's *Listen! the Wind* and Archibald Lyall's *Black and White Make Brown***
Phyllis Peres

The Trajectories of Cape Verdean Literature – Genres, Music and Other Themes/ Percursos da Literatura Caboverdiana – Géneros, Música e Outros Temas

159 **Notes on the Historical Context of *Claridade***
Ellen W. Sapega

171 **Lugares étnicos e maravilhosos do imaginário cabo-verdiano (em *Chiquinho*, de Baltasar Lopes)**
Alberto de Carvalho

195 **A representação espacial nos contos de Gabriel Mariano**
Glória de Brito

213 **Globalização, cultura e identidade em Orlanda Amarílis**
Benjamin Abdala Junior

227 **A ficção cabo-verdiana pós-claridosa**
José Luís Hopffer Cordeiro Almada

245 **O Tema do 'Contratado' na Literatura Caboverdiana: génese e variações**
Cristina Pacheco

265 **Echoes of Cape Verdean Identity: Literature and Music in the Archipelago**
Simone Caputo Gomes

287 **Cape Verde: People and Places. Photographs**
José M. Rodrigues

Postcolonial Cape Verdean Literature/ Literatura Caboverdiana Póscolonial

303 **Projetos literários em antologias caboverdianas**
Maria Nazareth Soares Fonseca

315 **"Chronicling" from the Center of the Periphery: *Estórias Contadas (Tales Told)* by Germano Almeida**
Russell Hamilton

327 **A Busca de Adélia: Narrativa Póstuma em *Testamento do Senhor Napumoceno da Silva Araújo* de Germano Almeida**
Robert H. Moser

335 **The Beginning of the World as We Would Like It to Have Been or an Analysis Towards a Theory of Gender in Germano Almeida or ...**
Paula Gândara

353 ***A Cabeça Calva de Deus* by Corsino Fortes: Litany & Music in Praise of Cape Verde**
Ana Mafalda Leite

373 **Under the Aegis of Antigone: The Tragic Dimension of Lyrical Poetry: *O Arquipélago da Paixão* by Vera Duarte**
Carmen Lúcia Tindó Ribeiro Secco

Language Politics

393 **Literacy in Post-Colonial Cape Verde**
Donaldo Macedo

Bibliographic Appendices/Apêndices Bibliográficos

413 **A Literatura Caboverdiana: hipóteses de periodização e apêndices bibliográficos**
M. Brito-Semedo

Writing and Music/Escrita e Música

427 **Na morna! Na mazurca o trompete da evasão**
Corsino Fortes

433 **Excerpt from *O Testamento do Sr. Napumoceno da Silva Araújo* (1989)**
Germano Almeida

439 **Apeiron**
Vasco Martins

Reviews/Recensões

445 **José Vicente Lopes. *Cabo Verde: Os Bastidores da Independência.***
David Brookshaw

449 **Arménio Vieira. *No Inferno.***
Naomi James Sutcliffe de Moraes

451 **Clifford E. Landers. *Literary Translation: A Practical Guide.***
Inês da Silva Paulino

Review Essays/Recensões-ensaios

457 **Lição de crônica: *Um certo olhar* de Fátima Bettencourt sobre o mundo caboverdiano**
Simone Caputo Gomes
sobre Fátima Bettencourt. *Um certo olhar.*

463 **Light and Obscurity in *Tropical Truth***
Dário Borim Jr.
on Caetano Veloso. *Tropical Truth: A Story of Music and Revolution in Brazil.*

Other Articles/Outros Artigos

473 ***Figura Naturae*: Religion, Nature, and the Self in Miguel Torga's *Diário***
Hannes Schneider

485 **Revising the Record in Lusophone Historical Drama**
Bonnie S. Wasserman

503 **Representations of East Timor in the Poetry of Ruy Cinatti: Colonial Rule under Crossfire**
Reinaldo Francisco Silva

523 **Prefácio do livro *East Timor: Bitter Paradise*, de Elaine Briere**
Noam Chomsky

533 **Literaturas Africanas de Expressão Portuguesa – Uma História em Curso**
Ana Mafalda Leite

Introduction

Ana Mafalda Leite

Ess qu'ê nha terra, ê Cabo Verde
Terra di morna, di lua chêa
Terra di Eugénio e serenata,
Qui mar tá cantá junto d'arêa.
—Gabriel Mariano

The present volume of *Portuguese Literary & Cultural Studies* is entitled "Cape Verde: Language, Literature & Music," and the choice of title is accounted for by the very special relationship that exists between these three elements in this island-country.

In a book published in 1996 by the Instituto Caboverdiano do Livro e do Disco, *A Morna na Literatura Tradicional*, Moacyr Rodrigues and Isabel Lobo argue that the history of Cape Verdean literature can be classified by two literary currents. The first can be called "traditional literature" and precedes the appearance of a second kind of literature, the literary production in printed form that appeared towards the end of the nineteenth century. Far from being completely separate categories, the two are interconnected, and, according to Rodrigues and Lobo, at times the distinction between traditional literature and so-called high art is abolished, as is evident in a significant part of the poetic output of Eugénio Tavares, Pedro Monteiro Cardoso, some authors of *Claridade*, B. Lèza, Lela de Maninha and many others.

The relationship between music and poetry is typical of early Cape Verdean poetry; one thinks, for example, of the *mornas*/poems by Eugénio Tavares. This sort of poetry existed side-by-side with the emphatically classicist poetry that imitated the rhetorical models of the mother-country's canon, an example being the poetry of José Lopes, to whom Arminda Brito dedicates an article in the first section of this edition.

The present volume has brought together the contributions of scholars of different nationalities who have dedicated themselves to a study of the literatures in the Portuguese language, as well as those who work in other areas such as Linguistics or Comparative Literature but who have in recent years researched and published works on Cape Verdean literature. These include not only Cape Verdeans but also scholars writing from Brazil, Portugal, the United States, the United Kingdom and Galicia in Spain.

These academics bring with them different perspectives on the linguistic and literary heritage of the archipelago; this material, most of it in the form of monographs, has been organized in four sections into which similar themes have been grouped, and, whenever possible, where a chronological sequence has been observed.

This collection does not purport to be a comprehensive view of Cape Verdean literature, like that excellent bilingual publication, *Cabo Verde Insularidade e Literatura* (*Cape Verde: Insularity and Literature*), edited by Manuel Veiga in 1998; nor does it aim to have the last word on questions relating to Cape Verdean culture. If, on the one hand, this volume follows a chronological thread, another central intention was to make readers aware of certain vexing questions related to literary history, to travel themes, to the textual relationships between the former mother-country and the archipelago, to the post-colonial re-reading of Portuguese novelistic texts, to re-inventions in the form of parody and to thematic-formal qualities of Cape Verdean writing after *Claridade* and after independence.

Over and above the four central topics, there is a further section on bibliographies, which has been appended at the end of the volume. "A Literatura Caboverdiana: hipóteses de periodização e apêndices bibliográficos" ("Cape-Verdean Literature: The Possibility of Periodization and Bibliographic Appendices"), by M. Brito-Semedo, suggests alternative possibilities for the periodization of Cape Verdean literature for the period that goes from the time of the first publications in the nineteenth century to the post-independence generation. It presents as appendices bibliographical details of Cape Verdean authors and the publication of works and periodicals in the period since independence in 1975. In the final part of the journal, on "Writing and Music," is a contribution by an ethno-musicologist, the composer and writer

Vasco Martins; this section also includes texts by the writer Germano Almeida and by the poet Corsino Fortes, as well as a short section of book reviews from and about Cape Verde. The reviewers include David Brookshaw, Simone Caputo Gomes and Naomi James Sutcliffe de Moraes.

The first topic, "Language and the Founding Literature," brings together five articles. The first, written by the Cape Verdean geographer José Maria Semedo, is a foray into the topographical and mythical origins of the archipelago; the author suggests that among the literary archetypes that have been created is the mythical-historical identity that inserts the archipelago in the sphere of the legendary Hesperides. The second article, "*O Escravo*: Literatura de Fundação" ("*The Slave*: Foundational Literature"), written by Francisco Salinas Portugal, provides a comparative analysis of a text by José Evaristo de Almeida and the Cuban anti-slavery novel *Sab*, by Gertrudis Gómez de Avellaneda, published in 1841. He suggests the possibility of reading *O Escravo* in the light of the "Confederação Brasílica" (lit., "Brazilian Confederation") in the Portuguese colonies (in the 1830s) and the appearance of a proto-nationalism connected to the abolition of slavery. According to the author, even though it cannot be considered a literary masterpiece, *O Escravo*, in a manner that is possibly ambiguous, presupposes the discourse of difference insofar as it foregrounds marginality "and allows the Other to cease to be an Object in order to transform itself into a Subject."

This is followed by an article on the poetry of José Lopes, which was composed during a period that extended from the closing years of the nineteenth century through to the 1930s. This poetry was both Classical and Romantic. A close reading of this poetry reveals the "intellectual relationship" that the poet maintained with the past, which is exemplified by his appropriation of historical and mythical material derived from both Portuguese and classical sources.

The last three articles deal with the Creole language and traditional literature. In "Bilinguismo Funcional: Assunção Descomplexada" ("Functional Bilingualism: An Assumption without Complexes"), the Cape Verdean writer Manuel Veiga shows how the linguistic situation in present-day Cape Verde is one of bilingualism because of the difference in status between the Portuguese language (Lp) and the Cape Verdean language (Lcv), also known as Cape Verdean Creole. For all intents and purposes, Lp is the official language, the language of education, of administration, the media, of social discourse and of literary productions; Lcv is the language of oral traditions, of the informality of day-to-day life, of friendships, of music and is little used in literature. The article makes evident the linguistic situation that Cape Verde finds itself in at the present moment and suggests a way to a future when the linguistic situation will be better suited to the realities of the country.

In turn, Dulce Pereira in "Escrever em Crioulo: *Un Kaminhu Lonji*" ("Writing in Creole: A Long Way Away") deals with the question of writing in Creole; she stresses that when dealing with an oral-based language such as that of Cape Verde it is important not to confuse writing with its graphic transcription or even with orthography. She explains that once we have made an inventory of all words, the lexicon is precisely one of those areas that needs to be innovated. The identification of the derivational processes and of the most productive affixes both constitute—alongside other means such as word-loan—fundamental instruments for the enrichment of the Cape Verdean language; she cautions against falling into the easy trap of imitating the models of written language derived from the contact language.

Tânia Macedo's article makes a comparative analysis of Tilôbe, the greedy and unfortunate Tio Lobo ("Uncle Wolf"), a recurrent figure of traditional Cape Verdean folktales. An attempt is made to establish a parallel between this figure and other figures that occur in the oral traditions of Portuguese-speaking countries, figures such as "Pedro Malasartes," "João Grilo" ("John the Cricket") and Cancãosinho.

"History, Memory and Travel" is the title of the second section, and it includes three articles where history and the colonial relation are questioned, revisited and rewritten; the problematic nature of biographies and travel narratives is also brought into account. The first text, by Gregory McNab, is "(Re)claiming the Heritage: The Narratives of Manuel Veiga," which considers the importance of the works of this author from the point of view of the reappropriation of the Cape Verdean language and orality, as well as the dialogue between the present and the historic past. Manuel Veiga's *Odju d'Agu* and *Diário das Ilhas* constitute a specifically Cape Verdean attempt to overcome the colonial legacy. *Odju d'Agu* is rooted in the language of Cape Verde and its oral storytelling tradition; *Diário das Ilhas* is a textual itinerary of the discovery of Cape Verde. According to Gregory MacNab, "in both [...] texts, Manuel Veiga seeks to address the issue of a postcolonial identity for Cape Verde, (re)capture an historical initiative for the Cape Verdean community and (re)site Cape Verde as the locus of its own experience."

The second article, by Isabel A. Ferreira, "Maria Isabel Barreno's *O Senhor das Ilhas*: Memory and Writing at the Threshold," attempts to provide an overview of how Africa has been represented in twentieth-century Portuguese literature that deals with the colonial past. More specifically, *O Senhor das Ilhas* considers the contradictions implicit in the colonist endeavors at the same time that it establishes a dialogue with literary tradition. The colonial experience was multi-faceted and contradictory, and because of that the novel looks at it through the perspective of the colonizer, and, more specifically, through his "life-writings." In doing so, Barreno offers a "revision" of the culture of the empire.

Phyllis Peres deals with travel metaphors in "Translating Trans-Atlantic Space in Two 1938 Travel Narratives to Cape Verde: Anne Morrow Lindbergh's *Listen! the Wind* and Archibald Lyall's *Black and White Make Brown*"; she shows how these two writers write from very different positions in the economy, nation, colony, time, and memory: "The narratives that emerge from their own Cape Verdean journeys straddle discourses of travel and inform the ambivalent trans-Atlantic times and spaces between the two World Wars. It is also this traveling culture that Anne Morrow Lindbergh and Archibald Lyall invoke in their own Atlantic journeys."

The third section, "The Trajectories of Cape Verdean Literature — Genres, Music and Other Themes," begins with an article by Ellen W. Sapega, "Notes on the Historical Context of *Claridade*," which argues that it is very important to recognize the existence of *three* different avatars of the *Claridade* magazine that was so central to the development of Cape Verdean literature. They arose at three different historical moments, and each of these "series" has to be assessed in light of the specific historical context in which they appeared so that the subtle changes in direction that characterized the *Claridade* project in the twenty-four years during which it was published can be better understood. Five other articles follow, and these deal with the representation of space, with questions of genre or, still, with the appearance of certain dominant themes in Cape Verdean literature, such as music, immigration, and recruited laborers.

"Lugares Étnicos e Maravilhosos do Imaginário Cabo-verdiano (em *Chiquinho*, de Baltasar Lopes)" ("Ethnic and Marvelous Places of the Cape Verdean Imagination [in *Chiquinho* by Baltasar Lopes]"), by Alberto de Carvalho, shows how the novel *Chiquinho* by Baltasar Lopes rightly deserves to be regarded as the key text of modern Cape Verdean realist fiction, not only on account of the story it tells but also on account of the literary value of its writing, and especially the re-invention of autobiographical material. In turn, Glória de Brito's article "A Representação Espacial nos Contos de Gabriel Mariano" ("Spatial Representation in the Short Stories of Gabriel Mariano") shows how the notion of novelistic space incorporates a narrative system that combines topographical, atmospheric, cultural and chrono-biologic elements that are present at the point of historical origin and in geographical, demographic and cultural evolution. Thus, Mariano's short stories register variations of the same urban space (Mindelo), marked simultaneously by the effect of the real and of the dramatic and by the evocative weight of history, culture and ideology.

In "Globalização, Cultura e Identidade em Orlanda Amarílis" ("Globalization, Culture and Identity in Orlanda Amarílis") Benjamin Abdala Junior looks at *Cais-do-Sodré té Salamansa* by Orlanda Amarílis in the context of globalization. He highlights the nature of a kind of literature that is identified with migration, one that makes evident the "strategic senses" of community articulations (cultural communities and genre literature) that appear in the work and which resist the standardization of cultural products in the global market.

The article by José Luis Hopffer Cordeiro Almada provides an overview of Cape Verdean fiction in the period following *Claridade*; thematic changes evident in the works of some of the major writers are considered.

"O Tema do 'Contratado' na Literatura Caboverdiana: Génese e Variações" ("The Theme of the 'Hired Laborer' in Cape Verdean Literature: Genesis and Variations") is an article by Cristina Pacheco that, through a brief overview of the socio-economic and literary context of Cape Verde from the 1930s to the 60s and of the reasons that led to Cape Verdeans being recruited to work on the plantations in São Tomé and Príncipe, attempts to analyze the importance of this theme and the way it is dealt with in Cape Verdean literature.

The last article in this section, by Simone Caputo Gomes, deals with another theme, the close connection between music and literature in Cape Verde. Music is able to bring together all of the forces that are constitutive of the Cape Verdean identity: "bread, sound & phoneme." According to Gomes, "a choir of illustrious voices plays a melody (or a polyphonic composition) whose theme is the thirst for survival of the Cape Verdean people and the permanence of a Creole culture founded upon a symbolic national trilogy—corn, the discourse on music and literary discourse."

José M. Rodrigues, the author-photographer of the images that illustrate the issue, presents us with photographs of a journey he made to the ten islands of Cape Verde in 1997. Amongst the hundreds of photographs he took, the following are worth highlighting: the tombstone of Eugénio Tavares on the island of Brava, the volcano in Fogo, the black ground of magma. All in all, his photographs constitute a cultural overview of Cape Verdean day-to-day life, its music, its literature and the poetry of people and places.

"Postcolonial Cape Verdean Literature" is the fourth section, and it brings together articles on authors whose work reappropriates, sometimes in the form of parodic invention, the Cape Verdean literary inheritance prior to independence. The first text, "Projetos Literários em Antologias Caboverdianas" ("Literary Projects in Cape Verdean Anthologies") by Maria Nazareth Soares Fonseca, looks at two anthologies: the selection of *Claridade* issues edited by Manuel Ferreira in 1989, and an anthology of the more recent Cape Verdean poetry, *Mirabilis de Veias ao Sol*, which came out in 1988. The author highlights the different characteristics of the literature produced in Cape Verde in two crucial historical periods.

This is followed by three articles on Germano Almeida, one of Cape Verde's best known writers. In "'Chronicling' from the Center of the Periphery: *Estórias Contadas* (*Tales Told*) by Germano Almeida," Russell Hamilton considers the author's chronicles and their cultural implications. He reflects on how the author makes intelligent use of the *crónica*, or chronicle, which has evolved into a unique literary genre in Portuguese-speaking countries. The article focuses on several of the *crónicas* that reveal Almeida's talent for narrating the uniqueness of Cape Verdean identity and also the archipelago's paradoxically central and peripheral location in Africa, in the Portuguese-speaking world, and in the wider world.

Both of the other two articles make a comparative analysis with the work of Machado de Assis. Robert H. Moser's "A Busca de Adélia: Narrativa Póstuma em *Testamento do Senhor Napumoceno da Silva Araújo* de Germano Almeida" ("The Search for Adélia: Posthumous Narration in *The Will of Mr. Napumoceno da Silva Araújo* by Germano Almeida") looks at the short story "Galeria Póstuma" by Brazilian novelist Machado de Assis and shows how it brings to light some of the essential questions posed by a study of Germano Almeida's novel *Testamento do Senhor Napumoceno da Silva Araújo*. By offering their memoirs to posterity, these "memorialists" are in fact rehearsing their own deaths and, through the act of writing, their subsequent posthumous position. But the reconstruction of Sr. Napumoceno's life is also a collective endeavor, one that involves his memoirs, the recollections of family and friends, the manipulation of an omniscient narrator, and the inferences of readers. Paula Gândara, in turn, in her article entitled "The Beginning of the World as We Would Like It to Have Been, or an Analysis Towards a Theory of Gender in Germano Almeida, or …" shows how Germano Almeida's *Memórias de um Espírito* does justice to Machado de Assis's similarly titled work. We read in Machado's work all the traces of postmodernity—narrative fragmentation, the addressing of the reader and his inclusion in the narrative, the mixture of fiction and reality—as well as of a certain kind of feminine *écriture.*

The last two articles are about the work of two poets, Corsino Fortes and Vera Duarte. Ana Mafalda Leite is the author of "*A Cabeça Calva de Deus* by Corsino Fortes: Litany & Music in Praise of Cape Verde." The article sums up some of the major features of the three books of poetry by Corsino Fortes that were collected in the single volume *A Cabeça Calva de Deus.* It emphasizes the way the author's work can be seen as a transformation of the Cape Verdean literary tradition, the innovative nature of his poetic language, and his vocation for a kind of writing that is epic, rhetorical and sacral. It further describes the pictographic transfiguration achieved by Fortes in his poetic rendering of the cultural and historical universe that is Cape Verde. "Under the Aegis of Antigone: The Tragic Dimension of Lyrical Poetry: *O Arquipélago da Paixão* by Vera Duarte" by Carmen Lúcia Tindó Ribeiro Secco considers Vera Duarte's poetic discourse, the multiple faces and senses of passion, and in particular the tragic dimension of passion, or, in other words, "that which puts our humanness into question." Drawing inspiration from the strength of Antigone, an allegory for the unique tragic dimension of the female, Vera Duarte's *poiesis* draws up a critical inventory of the passions experienced not only by women, but also by the poets and by the people of Cape Verde.

Language and the Founding Literature/
Língua e Literatura de Fundação

The Construction of Natural-Geographical Space in Cape Verdean Literature

José Maria Semedo
Translated by
Luís R. Mitras
Revised by
Mark Streeter

Abstract. Located at a distance of five hundred kilometers off the African coast, the archipelago of Cape Verde constitutes a typical case of "distant insularity." Although Cape Verde is situated in the middle of an ocean and has a dry tropical climate, Cape Verdeans have always turned to agriculture instead of opting for fishing; they consequently depend on the uncertainty of the rain. This situation of the extreme dependency on the land made Cape Verdeans feel a profound love and connection to the land. This is manifest not only in their day-to-day life and in the temperament of Cape Verdeans, but also in their literature. In those poets and writers who came before the *Claridade* movement (Pedro Cardoso, Jorge Barbosa and José Lopes), love for land is related to their mythical vision of their country's origin. In the texts by the writers of the *Claridade* movement, the drought, the shortage of corn, and emigration were the key themes. This came of the famine that occurred as a result of the various droughts in the first half of the 20th century. In Cape Verdean literature emigration to a far-away place always had several facets, whether the desire to leave or a desire to stay and have to leave. Homesickness and the anguish of longing are at the origin of many poems, *mornas* and *funanás*. Today, in this age of globalization and quick communication, the space that separates Cape Verde from the rest of the world has become almost non-existent and literature has moved in new directions: where there is no sea, no longing, no distant country, no drought, no hunger.

1. The Cape Verde archipelago within a mythical frame

Located at a distance of five hundred kilometers off the African coast, the archipelago of Cape Verde constitutes a typical case of "distant insularity." The distance that separates it from the continent constitutes an obstacle to the spontaneous introduction of animals and vegetable species; in order to arrive at the islands, they would have to overcome the barrier of an ocean. At the same time, the volcanic origin and nature of the islands, marked by prolonged activity from the middle of the Tertiary period[1] until our present day, might have destroyed incipient vegetation or cultivated vegetation, as a result of the streams of lava and the ash emitted by the volcanoes.

To make worse this scenario of isolation and volcanic activity, the fact that Cape Verde lies within a zone of arid climates severely limited the development of vegetation and other sources of biomass capable of supporting human settlement during the prehistoric age. Even when we accept the possibility of the climatic changes possible in the last hundred thousand years, such changes in the ecosystem do not signify anything special that we will be examining for the modern-day Cape Verdean.

Volcanic insularity, the sharp relief of most of the islands, the lack of continuity, the climatic zone to which it belongs—with its arid climate and frequent and periodic droughts—are perhaps the natural characteristics most evident in the landscape of the archipelago; they are the ones with the greatest effect on the history of the people of these islands.

Studies of the flora and fauna began as far back as the fifteenth century. When these studies emphasize those species that preceded human occupation, they reveal a scarcity of vegetation and a lack of alimentary plants capable of supporting human life. Wild fauna is limited to bats, small reptiles, birds and insects—all a characteristic of a distant insularity.

For humans, it was only with the development of nautical sciences and with the ability to navigate in the high seas that people could have access to these shores. The possibility that Cape Verde could have been known about in the days before Portuguese expansion is not entirely fanciful, although it remains a mere intellectual exercise. Various possibilities have been raised about earlier visits to the islands of Cape Verde.

Duarte Pacheco Pereira, the Portuguese geographer from the fifteenth/sixteenth centuries, identifies the islands of Cape Verde as being the Hesperides, which Pliny had located south of the Canary Islands:

> pois já temos escrito do Cabo Verde, e como se antigamente se chamou aspérido promontório, assim devemos escrever das ilhas que cem léguas em mar dele estão, as quais também naquela antiguidade foram chamadas aspérida, segundo Plínio na natural história no seu sexto livro, capitulo trinta e um [...].[2]
>
> [because we already have records of Cape Verde, and, according to Pliny, in chapter thirty-one of his sixth book on natural history, because that cape was formerly designated as harsh [*aspérido*], then we should speak of those sea islands that are a hundred leagues from that cape as being the ones that were also known as harsh [*aspérida*] during antiquity (...).]

What is more, the Hesperides would be located somewhere on the southern edge of Plato's Atlantis; that is also where, according to Graeco-Roman mythology, Hercules was to find his golden apples.

If, on the one hand, the developments of the natural-historical sciences at the end of the eighteenth century and in the nineteenth century put aside the possibility of some sort of civilization in the eastern Atlantic that had vanished into the sea, it was these naturalists themselves who invented the concept of the nummulite Atlantis, temporally located in the first half of the Tertiary period, in order to explain the likeness in primitive flora and fauna verified in a group of archipelagos that lay between latitudes 15°N and 40°N; these islands would include the Azores, Madeira, the Selvagens, the Canary Islands, and Cape Verde—Macaronesia, or the Fortunate Islands, alluding to a name that navigators had originally attributed to the Canary Islands (land of dogs).[3]

Despite the fact that the two conceptions of Atlantis, the one historical, the other geological, refer to different time phases, the allure of Atlantis, including the toponymy harking back to this mythical continent, has contaminated the terminology of naturalists. It is in this context that some plant species common in Cape Verde were designated by terms such as *Artemisia gorgonum* (absinthe), *Aenonium gorgoneum* (houseleek), *Papaver gorgoneum* (Cape Verdean poppy), where the reference is to the island of the Gorgons, also known as the isle of the dead, a mythical place around lost Atlantis.

Geological studies in the first half of the twentieth century gave credence to the possibility of a nummulite Atlantis; at the same time the interest in studies of the fauna and flora of Cape Verde also subsided. However, in that same period, the Cape Verdean poets Pedro Monteiro Cardoso and José Lopes da Silva, partaking of a certain Creole patriotism (or "matriotism," as some would have it), and seeking some sort of mythical-historical identity for their Cape Verdean brothers, inserted the archipelago within the mythical framework of the legendary Hesperides. This mythical framework is a consequence of the classical education they had received at the *Seminário / Lyceu* [Seminary / Secondary School] on the island of São Nicolau. Like Camões did in his epic poem *Os Lusíadas*,[4] José Lopes da Silva dedicated *Hespéridas* to the Cape Verdean youth.[5] In his poem in praise of the islands of Cape Verde entitled "Minha Terra" ["My Land"], he traces the history of the islands from Atlantis, which "*inspira a narrativa de Platão e outros sábios, que a tinham por verdade*" ["is the inspiration behind Plato's story and that of other sages who took it for the truth"] through to the hope that the Hesperidian country will become "*a mais brilhante pérola africana*" ["the most brilliant African pearl"].

In Cape Verde, the legend of islands lost amidst the great Atlantic Ocean acquires, at times, a populist twist. In the beginning of the 1960s there was a legend circulating in the island of Santiago about the existence of an eleventh island hiding under the ocean. According to the legend, it is the largest of all the islands, and the only one that is truly green, and all that is scarce in the other island is plentiful on this one. This island symbolizes the true Cape Verde. It arises, for a fraction of a second, at midnight on the feast day of St. Sylvester, Old Year's Eve; the length of time it will linger on the surface of the water will depend on the quick glimpse cast by a sinner. If that person should glance at the horizon, no matter how discreetly, at the exact direction where it is located, even though they may know that they are doing so, in the exact moment when the New Year is born, that glimpse would rescue the population from the worldly tragedies of droughts and hunger, of the lack of water and corn—all those things that the ten "little grains of land" that were left on the surface of the water suffer from.

2. The settlement of the islands and socio-cultural evolution

A text from the end of the eighteenth century[6] makes mention of one tradition, according to which, at the time when it was discovered, the island of Santiago was inhabited by black-skinned Jalofos.[7] This position is shared by authors from the same period, such as the naturalist João Silva Feijó[8] and António Pusich[9]—who in all probability obtained this information from the document we have made mention of. Different opinions about the Jalofo settlement have been argued, but the lack of convincing documentation on this matter has rendered the debate a mere confrontation of possibilities.

What there is no doubt about is that Cape Verdeans as a people arose as a consequence of the settlement initiated in 1462, when a small group of settlers headed by António de Nole, one of the discoverers of the islands, settled in Santiago. The information we have from the period suggests that the environment was not very hospitable, and that this was the reason why [Prince] Dom Fernando, the proprietor of the islands, requested the concession of special privileges from the king in order to get people to settle in Cape Verde. The set of privileges benefited trade and navigation. Although it is not made clear, it is possible that the climatic conditions constituted an obstacle to settlement. There is a general consensus that those privileges were the principal driving force behind European settlement in the archipelago.

Taking full advantage of its geo-strategic position, the archipelago, and especially the island of Santiago, became an obligatory port-of-call for ships travelling along the sea routes between Europe, Africa, the East and, later still, America. The archipelago played an important intermediary role in trade and in the dissemination of the plants of economic interest for the tropics. It was through this process that a slave-owning society was created; it did not take too long for blacks, transported from the close-by African coast, to add their demographic weight to Cape Verdean society.

But reality is such that, whilst trade with the Americas gained in importance in the sixteenth and seventeenth centuries, trade with the islands entered into a period of decay as a result of pirate raids and as a consequence of change in the sea-trading routes.

The port city of Ribeira Grande, the main trading center, had a fast ascension in the first half of the sixteenth century; it was granted the status of city and head of a diocese in 1533, but, according to Sena Barcelos,[10] by 1545, the city, and the entire archipelago, had already fallen into decay.

The way the economy was organized, the excessive dependence on external resources connected to trade and navigation, the organization of the countryside, which was dedicated to cattle rearing in an insular-Sahelian ecosystem, quickly dragged the economy of the islands down—into long-lasting misery, with the consequent result that settlers left the country and, later, emigrants were exported to distant shores.

The decay of Ribeira Grande also manifested itself in the dispersion of the population into the rural areas and into the other islands, this in an attempt to better make use of the meager local resources. A notorious fact is the slow process of occupation of the archipelago in its totality; in the period of more than five centuries, one island (Santa Luzia) still remains uninhabited, and at least two (São Vicente and Sal) were only settled less than 200 years ago.

Turned back on its own resources, Cape Verde has had to face droughts and the progressive destruction of its island ecosystems. This is a result of the unbalanced use of the soil and overgrazing by untamed cattle which has resulted in a process of desertification; once again this upsets the equilibrium of meager resources.

Already in his day, Duarte Pacheco Pereira[11] had described the barren scenario of the islands in the first 40 years of human presence:

> e estas ilhas são esteireis porque são vizinhas ao trópico de câncer e têm muito pouco arvoredo por causa de nelas não chover mais dos ditos 3 meses; são terras altas e fragosas e serão más d'andar.[12]
>
> [and these islands are barren because they are so close to the Tropic of Cancer and they have very few trees because it does not rain for more than three months; these are high and craggy lands and are not good to walk on.]

This text quickly dispels the notion that in the first days of the occupation there was a green [*verde*] island floating on the ocean.

What is more, the consequences of the disequilibrium between population, resources and the arid scenario are well noted in the beginnings of the seventeenth century by Baltazar, who describes "*uma tão grande fome, por não chover*" ["such great hunger because it did not rain"] that "*foi necessário que desse reino viesse sustentação, e se este remedeio lhe faltara sem duvida se despovoara de todo*"[13] ["it was necessary for the Kingdom to come to the aid of the country, and if this solution were lacking then surely the entire country would have been completely depopulated"].

Hunger, its death toll, and emigration as a consequence of the drought, became so frequent that they became part of the fabric of the daily life of Cape Verdeans.

The eighteenth and nineteenth centuries were full of devastating droughts, with the consequence that the economy and the entire society, in fact, were thrown into disarray. The images of this chaos are still alive in the memory of Cape Verdeans, who continue to live with the uncertainty of rains and try to survive in an ecosystem which is subject to desertification. It is an ecosystem where, according to the poet Ovídio Martins,[14] even "*as cabras ensina-*

ram-nos a comer pedras para não perecermos" ["the goats have taught us to eat stones so that we will not perish"]. Hunger is the constant background scenario in all the Ti-lobo[15] ["Uncle Wolf"] stories (and the stories of Chibinho, Uncle Wolf's nephew) that are told to Cape Verdean children.

Some commentators found the dependence of Cape Verdeans on the land, the dominance of agriculture and the rural economy, somewhat strange. A comment in this respect by a governor at the beginning of the nineteenth century was to become famous; António Pusich asked why Cape Verdeans did not turn to the sea because, according to him, it was rich in fish (today we aware that this "richness" is not entirely correct, although there are some fish), instead of living tied to the land and the corn cob.

If hunger in Cape Verde is tied to the lack of corn, and the lack of corn to the lack of rain, it is worth asking why people on the islands, living as they did within an almost desert Sahelian ecosystem and where there was a shortage of land and irrigation, should have turned to agriculture.

The answer to this question requires that we have some knowledge of the scenario behind the consolidation of Cape Verdean identity. This insular country was dependent on the uncertain rains and on the sometimes forced cohabitation of adventurers, traders, ecclesiastical, military and administrative personnel that arrived from Europe in search of better lives, black princes curious about the lives or the wisdom of whites, African slaves and European convicts, both brought to these shores forcibly. The decline of the activities of the harbour and the loss of control over trade on the African coast forced those who stayed behind to depend on the resources of the land (the abundance of stones, lava, sand, wind, sun and sea).

The history of the islands in the seventeenth century was marked by the flight of whites (who returned to Portugal) and the disappearance of coinage. The dream of a land of business opportunities came undone; what was left was an isolated, arid land without resources and with meager potential.

If for whites the solution to the crisis was to return to Portugal, the same was not true for the native-born whites, the mulattoes, the freed blacks, the slaves; they had no choice but to adapt to the land, to live off its resources, and to depend on it.

Instead of regarding their country as an unwanted land, a warehouse for slaves, or a place where trade was stagnant, the extreme dependence on the land and the uncertainty of the rains made Cape Verdeans develop a strong bond with the islands.

3. From an Island-Sahelian World to Literature

Rather than revulsion, their extreme dependence on the land made Cape Verdeans feel more love and a deeper connection; this is manifest not only in their day-to-day life and in the temperament of Cape Verdeans, but also in their literature. The connection with the land is a recurring theme, not only among those poets and writers who were behind the *Claridade* movement, but also those who preceded them. If, on the one hand, Pedro Cardoso and José Lopes look at Cape Verde and incorporate it within the mythical frame of the Hesperides, they begin from the mythical isles in order to arrive at the real archipelago with all its daily problems. Jorge Barbosa,[16] on the other hand, created a genuine poetic geography of Cape Verde, to the point where he would highlight specific details of each of the islands or each of the rural or urban landscapes. This poetic geography is well expressed in his poem about the islands, in which the poet describes his travels around the archipelago, from Santo Antão to Brava. Interestingly, his poem ends in America, evoking the diaspora about which Eugénio Tavares had sung.

The poem "Panorama" seems to establish a link between the Hesperides of Pedro Cardoso (or those of José Lopes) and Jorge Barbosa's Archipelago—although this particular poem pays more attention to Cape Verde's great environmental problems, which are related to the drought and to hunger. He also raises questions about its origin:

Destroços de que continente,
De que cataclismos,
De que sismos,
De que mistérios?...

Ilhas perdidas
No meio do mar,
Esquecidas
Num canto do mundo,
Que as ondas embalam,
Maltratam,
Abraçam...

[Detritus from what continent,
From what cataclysm,

From what earthquakes,
From what mysteries?

Islands lost
In the middle of ocean,
Forgotten
In some corner of the world,
That is rocked by the waves,
Or else ill-treated by them,
Or embraced by them ...]

The famine that occurred as result of the successive droughts in the first half of the twentieth century, and Porto Grande's gradual decay, had an immense influence on the *Claridade* writers. Agriculture, the drought, the shortage of corn, the dependence on the rain and on the land, the migrations that took place as a result of the drought, were all transformed into recurring, almost obsessive, literary themes by the members of this literary movement.

What is interesting, and to an extent something worth inquiring about and reflecting on, is the fact that this movement was anchored on an island with meager agricultural potential. It was this movement, however, that demonstrated that Cape Verdeans were, culturally speaking, agriculturalists who lived dependent on the rain, even the intellectual class, which was not directly connected to the countryside.

This brings us back to António Pusich's observation: the theme of the sea is integral to our literature, but the sea is rarely regarded as a place of resources by our poets; at most it is that sea-lane that emigrants take to flee the drought, in other words, to flee from the failure of agriculture, or it is just an obstacle that makes the flight from the drought more difficult.

The dependency on the land, the uncertainty of the rain is dealt with by Jorge Barbosa in a poem dedicated to the writer Manuel Lopes, entitled "Terra"[17] ["Land"].

Terra fértil
Das bananeiras, das laranjeiras
Dos acajus
Dos cafeeiros, das uvas, dos batatais;
Do milho, que dá cachupa, o cuscúz,

A batanca, o gufongo;
Das canas
Que dão o grogue e o mel...
[.................................]

se não cai a chuva,
—o desalento
a tragédia da estiagem!—
—as encostas áridas, as planíceis secas,
sulcadas,
emitem rictus de uma dor profunda
e fantasiam carnes ao sol mumificadas...

—ai o drama da chuva,
ai o desalento,
o tormento
da estiagem!

[Fertile land
Of banana trees, orange trees
Cashew-trees
Coffee-trees, grapes, potato plantations;
Of corn, which gives us *cachupa*, couscous,
Batanca, gufongo;
Of sugar cane
Which gives us grog and honey...

if the rain doesn't fall
—the discouragement,
the tragedy of drought!
—the barren hillsides, the dry plains,
furrowed,
give out the rictus of a profound sorrow
and dream of flesh mummified in the sun ...

—Oh! the drama of rain,
oh the discouragement,

the torment
of the drought!]

The poem "Terra" contrasts, especially in terms of theme and meaning, with "Paisagem" ["Landscape"]. In terms of the argument we are developing, these two poems represent the two poles around which converge all the strengths and internal dynamics of the poems from the *Claridade* movement. On the one hand, we encounter hope in the rains that will eventually fall, bringing in a time of plenty, wealth and unity among all of Cape Verde's children; it will send hunger and the drought away and will stop the flow of men leaving the country and will give them a chance to remain on the land, although, towards the end, there is always the possibility that this paradisiacal scenario will be reversed. On the other hand, we are faced with human impotence against the wiles of (Sahelian) nature and all the dramatic consequences that this will have on the lives of living beings. If not, we see:

Paisagem

malditos
estes anos de seca!

Mete dó
O silencio triste
da terra abandonada
esmagada
sob o peso
do sol penetrante
[..........................]
pobres enxadas
que não servem mais!
esquecidas nos cantos dos quintais,
cobertas
de poeira e de estrume...

[Landscape

goddamned

these years of drought!

It's painful to watch
The sad silence
of the abandoned land
crushed
by the weight
of a scorching sun …

pitiful hoes
that serve no purpose anymore!
forgotten in some corner of the backyard,
covered
in dust and manure …]

Besides being one of the islands of Macaronesia, Cape Verde is also part of the Sahel, and it is precisely its Sahelian characteristics that may help us to understand the problem of drought and hunger; but it was not, however, in this African region that Cape Verdean writers found the source for their literary inspiration. Here what mattered more than anything else was language and the transportation routes. The literature of the Brazilian northeast, whose works arrived in Cape Verde thanks to the steamers that docked in Porto Grande, was taken as a point of reference: the themes of drought and of misery in rural areas suffering from the depression as well as the migrations were accepted as being similar to what was occurring in Cape Verde. In effect, for this comparison to have been made, the microclimatic scenario, at least as it was understood by the *Claridade* writers, was the most important aspect. Thus, the microcosm of islands cut off from each other by the sea was compared to the Brazilian northeast, that area on a continental scale with wide spaces and a multiplicity of landscapes; it was only in the literature that such a world could be said to resemble the small universe of the islands.

If, on the one hand, the theme of emigration from the Brazilian northeast was predominantly within the country and from a rural to an urban area, in Cape Verdean literature, on the other hand, emigration was predominantly outside the country, far from the country. In Cape Verde, emigration to a faraway place always had several facets, from the desire to leave to a desire to stay and yet have to leave. If, in the novel *Chiquinho*,[18] escape to America was seen as a desirable way-out in search of new horizons, in the *Certeza* movement, on the other hand, the dominant idea is that of wanting to stay; leaving the country is regarded as a kind of dictatorship of circumstances.

Nostalgia for the distant country and the anguish of homesickness, which were behind so many poems, *mornas* and *funanás*, perhaps have their days numbered as a result of the greater availability of telecommunications. The arrival of a letter, with a delay of months, provoked an anguish of uncertainty on the part of the sender. Having a letter in one's hand did not mean that the one who wrote it was in good health. There are cases of letters that arrived at their destination long after the person who wrote them had died. With the appearance of the telephone in rural areas letter writing became something almost old-fashioned; people could speak to each other directly, without the need of intermediaries, and those in despair no longer had to say things between the lines. The relative distance that separates any part of the world has also become the time needed to dial a number on the telephone: "If he's not in, I'll call back later."

4. New horizons for a country that lives within a global community

With the expansion of air travel the distance and time between the islands were shortened. With the revolution in telecommunications the distance that separates these places has lost significance. Thus in *Tempos da Moral moral*[19] [*In the Time of moral Morals*], the young anthropologist preferred to travel by boat because he could not bear this Helios who made him lose all notions of time and space. The sea had ceased to be that ancient obstacle to quick and immediate contact.

We live in a period where the idea of space-time has been shortened by technology. For common Cape Verdeans their country exists as much in the archipelago as it does in the communities in the diaspora, in quite specific countries in America, Europe and Africa. The community living outside the islands is a dynamic one; it promotes music and dance and the image of the islands in the world outside the archipelago; the borders of this archipelago have increasingly become almost fictional. Despite the almost obsessive opposition of many against it, annually many emigrants come back on vacation bringing deluxe cars and showing off the latest fashions of the community where they happen to live. The cellular phone permits direct contact between a rural village on the island of Santiago and Providence, or between Morrinho de Maio and Rotterdam; that is why to write letters is, to say the least, romantic and somewhat "pre-historic."

It is in the context of this new scenario, in this new conception of space, that we have to understand Cape Verdean literature. Our understanding of space is now different; the old themes have become *démodé*, as it were. The lack of rain on the islands is not reason enough to lower the consumption of rice,[20] wheat, beer, or the Mediterranean fruits that are sold everywhere. The drought is not only a climatic characteristic of the islands, it can also become a source of wealth, for the abundance of sun favors beach tourism. Regarding the theme of the sea, in other words, of fisheries as a resource, we should recall that Cape Verde's territorial waters and exclusive economic zones cover an area on the order of 700 000 Km^2.

Mr. Napumoceno[21] got rich because there was a once-off rain shower in the city of Mindelo; it was not because he sowed corn, but because he sold thousands of umbrellas that he had in his warehouse. The novels of Arménio Vieira may take place in Memphis or in Hell; the truth is that he speaks to us neither of emigration nor of whiplashes of the drought.

Faced as we are by this new space imposed on us by globalization, communication, information technology, how will our literature represent this new geographical space?

Those who wish to visit Pasárgada, as well as other things, will find this a useful link: http://www.pasarganet.com.br.

Notes

[1] Cape Verde is an archipelago of volcanic origin. The formation of the islands is associated with volcanic activity that occurred before the Miocene Epoch in the Tertiary period. On the island of Maio there is limestone from the middle of the Jurassic Period (Secondary period). It is important to state, nevertheless, that the existence of this limestone is a result of the volcanic activity that was at the origin of the formation of the island.

[2] Duarte Pachedo Pereira, *Esmeraldo de Situ Orbis*, Joaquim Barradas de Carvalho. Lisboa: Fundação Calouste Gulbenkian, 1991.

[3] The name of the Canary Islands (island or land of dogs, *cannis*) is associated with a reconnaissance trip organized by King Juba under the orders of the Roman emperor; it is on the basis of the accounts of this voyage that heraldry has symbolized this archipelago with the image of two dogs holding the arms. Surprisingly, the name of the archipelago has been more closely associated with the bird *Serinus canaries*.

[4] In Camões's days it was believed, beyond all doubt, that Cape Verde corresponded to the Hesperides.

[5] *Hespéridas Fragmentos de um Poema Perdido em Triste e Miserando Naufrágio*. Cabo Verde, Edição do Autor, 1930.

[6] Anonymous. *Noticia Corográfica e Cronológica do Bispado de Cabo Verde... 1784*. Apresentação

de António Carreira. Lisboa: ICL, 1985.

[7] The term is equivalent to the Franco-Senegalese term "Wolof."

[8] António Pusich. *Ensaio e Memórias Económicas sobre Cabo Verde (século XVIII)*. Apresentação de António Carreira. Praia: ICL, 1986.

[9] "Ensaio Físico-Político de Cabo Verde—1810," António Pusich, *Ensaio e Memórias Económicas sobre Cabo Verde (século XVIII)*. Apresentação de António Carreira. Praia: ICL, 1986.

[10] Senna Barcelos—Subsídios para a História de Cabo Verde e Guiné.

[11] Esmeraldo de Situ Orbis.

[12] Ibid.

[13] Padre Baltazar Barreira—carta anual da missão de Cabo Verde do ano de 1610 até Julho de 1611. In *Monumenta Missionária Africana (Africa Ocidental—1600-1622)* de António Brásio. Lisboa: AGU, 1968.

[14] In the poem "os flagelados do vento leste," Ovídio Martins. *Gritarei Berrarei Matarei, não vou para passargada.* Rotterdam: Edições cabo-verdianidade, n.d.

[15] The wolf is the hero of popular tales in all the islands; it plays the role of the hyena (a stupid and gluttonous animal) in stories from black Africa. The *Cannis lupus* (wolf) is not indigenous to West Africa; in Guinea-Bissau a hyena is still referred to as a "wolf."

[16] Jorge Barbosa, "Ilha," *Poesias I.* Praia: ICL, 1989.

[17] Ibid.

[18] A novel by the Cape Verdean writer Baltasar Lopes.

[19] A novel by the Cape Verdean writer Vasco Martins.

[20] Corn has ceased to be the staple food, having been supplanted by rice, something the country does not grow.

[21] In the novel by Germano Almeida.

Works Cited

Barbosa, Jorge. *Poesias I.* Praia: ICL, 1989.

Barradas de Carvalho, J. *Esmeraldo de situ orbis de Duarte Pacheco Pereira.* Lisboa: Fundação Calouste Gulbenkian, 1991.

Brásio, António. *Monumenta Missionária Africana (Africa Ocidental—1600-1622). Carta Anual da missão de Cabo Verde do ano de 1610 até Julho de 1611.* De Pe Baltazar Barreira. 1968.

Cardoso, P. *Hespéridas Fragmentos de um Poema Perdido em Triste e Miserando Naufrágio.* Cabo Verde: Private edition, 1930.

Carreira, António. *Noticia Corográfica e Cronológica do Bispado de Cabo Verde...1784.* Praia: ICL, 1985.

———. "*Ensaio Físico-Político de Cabo Verde—1810.*" António Pusich, *Ensaio e Memórias Económicas sobre Cabo Verde (século XVIII)*. Praia: ICL, 1986.

Lopes, Baltasar. *Chiquinho.* Edição Africa—literatura, arte e cultura. Lisboa: Central Distribuidora Livreira, 1984.

Lopes, José. *Hesperitanas. Poesias.* Lisboa: Livraria J. Rodrigues e Companhia, n.d.

Martins, Ovídio. *Gritarei berrarei matarei não vou para pasárgada 100 poemas.* Col. Anti-evasão. Rotterdam: Edições Caboverdianidade, n.d.

Martins, Vasco. *Tempos da Moral moral, romance.* Mindelo: Ilhéu Editora, 1993.

Senna Barcelos, C. J. *Subsídios para a História de Cabo Verde e Guiné.* Parte I, Tip. Da Academia Real das Ciências de Lisboa, 1899.

Vieira, Arménio. *O eleito do Sol.* Praia: Edição SONACOR, n.d.

———. *No Inferno.* Praia, Mindelo: Centro Cultural Português, 1999.

José Maria Semedo is a geographer and teaches at the Teachers' Training College in Cape Verde. He has co-authored *Cabo Verde — Ciclo Festivos dos Rituais da Tabanca.* He has written articles on agriculture and identity, on mourning, and on Cape Verde's name.

Luís R. Mitras is a South African at present based in Lisbon. He has published academic articles on the Lusophone literatures and has translated novels, short stories and poetry from Spanish and Portuguese. He is Adjunct Associate Professor at the European Division of the University of Maryland. E-mail: jmitras@faculty.ed.umuc.edu

O Escravo: literatura de fundação

Francisco Salinas Portugal

Resumo. O artigo apresenta a relação do texto de Almeida com o romance anti-esclavagista cubano de Gertrudis Gómez de Avellaneda, *Sab*, publicado em 1841. Põe-se em relação *O Escravo* com a Confederação Brasílica nas colónias portuguesas (década de 30 do século XIX) e coloca-se a hipótese da aparição de um sentimento proto-nacionalista ligado à abolição da escravatura. Nesse contexto, a obra cabo-verdiana contribui para "imaginar a nação" (teoria de B. Anderson) e construir o discurso da nação, nomeadamente através da elaboração do "mapa" e da reivindicação do discurso em crioulo. No artigo examina-se também o tema do estatuto do leitor implícito (recorrendo a exemplificações com as explicações etnográficas do narrador).

O (Pre)texto de uma análise

Em 1856 foi publicado em Lisboa *O Escravo* de José Evaristo de Almeida, uma obra que mais tarde aparece como folhetim no jornal *A Voz de Cabo Verde* (1916-1917). Trata-se muito provavelmente do primeiro romance cabo-verdiano, mas apenas se tornou conhecido do grande público a partir da valiosíssima edição de Manuel Ferreira em 1988, com uma segunda edição em 1989.

Pode surpreender, se não fossem os tortuosos caminhos que acompanham a difusão cultural dos antigos países colonizados, que um romance de indubitável interesse tenha passado quase despercebido entre os críticos africanistas e mais concretamente da crítica cabo-verdiana, talvez deslumbrada pelo interesse e repercurssão que para a formação e consolidação do sistema teve a escrita claridosa.

Porém, a primeira impressão do leitor, livre tanto quanto possível de preconceitos, reside na surpresa de um texto que se coloca fora das dominantes da literatura colonial (pelo menos no que à temática diz respeito) e numa época em que, naquilo que nos alcança, parece não ter existido um ambiente sócio-cultural que explique a aparição de uma obra de características, que poderíamos definir, quando menos, como surpreendentes.

Ora bem, da primeira leitura do romace de J. E. de Almeida há dois aspectos que chamaram a nossa atenção como indícios de um caminho de pesquisa que se tornou aliciante: no primeiro capítulo da obra cabo-verdiana em que se apresenta o escravo, João, este, ao contar a sua história a Maria e ao descrever como se iniciou na leitura, reconhece que "*numa ocasião deparei com a história da revolta dos negros na ilha de São Domingos*" (29), quer dizer, o protagonista dá um salto ao espaço das Caraíbas para entrar em contacto com uma realidade cujo paralelismo com aquilo que aconteceu nas ilhas de Cabo Verde é invocado numa espécie de cumplicidade com o leitor.

A partir de aqui o texto parecia indicar-nos um caminho de indagação que nos ia levar à literatura abolicionista das Caraíbas, a uma literatura surgida mais concretamente em Cuba ao calor das ideias abolicionistas e de um incipiente desejo de independência nacional. E esse caminho fez com que nos detivéssemos no romance de Gertrudis Gómez de Avellaneda (1814-1873), *Sab*, publicado em Madrid em 1841, e que é a história de um amor impossível devido à desigualdade étnica e social (Servera 49) como frequentemente tem sido definido o romance de Avellaneda.

A partir desta via de interpretação, verificamos paralelos espantosos entre os dois romances.

1. O espaço onde decorre a acção nos dois romances é um lugar afastado, longe do mundo urbano, que é em simultâneo o refúgio edénico da casa paterna ("o sítio de B..." em Almeida, o "engenho de Bellavista," propriedade de "don Carlos de B...," em Avellaneda) e que é, também, o espaço do interior do país que permite "pensar a pátria" no sentido que dá B. Anderson (1991) à "pátria imaginada":

> it is an imagined political community—and imagined as both inherently limited and sovereign. It is imagined because the members of even the smallest nation will never know most of their fellow-members, meet them, or even hear of them, yet in their minds of each lives the image of their communion. (Anderson 5-6)

2. A mulher-anjo, na tópica imagem romântica, corresponde a Carlota em *Sab* e a Maria em *O Escravo.*

Sem nos determos numa análise pormenorizada da descrição de ambas as duas mulheres, poderíamos dizer que as duas, orfãs de mãe, são muito similares e, ainda quando respondam aos *clichés* românticos val a pena compará-las no que diz respeito à sua caracterização geral e às funções romanescas que representam: Carlota esta aparece caracterizada da seguinte maneira:

> (...) el conjunto de sus delicadas facciones, y la mirada llena de alma de dos grandes y hermosos ojos pardos, daban a su fisonomía, alumbrada por la luna, un no sé qué de angélico y penetrante imposible de describir. (115, sublinhado nosso)

Por seu turno e, em paralelo, Maria, a jovem co-protagonista de *O Escravo*, apresenta-se-nos de forma similar.

> Ela, a jovem que tratava de objectos tão queridos ao seu coração, de objectos inocentes como a sua alma, puros como o seu pensar (...). (26)
> O bulir de sus lábios [de Maria] veio indicar que uma reza seráfica, uma oração fervente, levava ao céu as preces de um anjo. (90, sublinhado nosso)

Por outro lado, do ponto de vista da organização diegética, estas mulheres estabelecem relações triangulares em cujo vértice se coloca sempre o escravo: Carlota-Sab- Enrique Otway e Carlota-Sab-Teresa, no caso de *Sab* (existe um outro triângulo Carlota-Enrique Otway-Teresa, mas de menor importância e que, portanto, não vamos referir). Maria-João- Sr. Lopes e Maria-João-Luíza (no caso de *O Escravo*).

Repare-se que em ambos os romances, os escravos (Sab e João) estão em vias de alcançar a alforria (a que finalmente acedem em compensação, talvez pela não consumação dos amores respectivos); e repare-se, também, que nos dois triângulos amorosos a que fizemos referência existe um estrangeiro, embora a sua presença em termos narrativos e a sua espessura psicológica seja sensivelmente diferente: Otway, movido apenas pela ânsia de lucro em *Sab* (apesar de que exista uma atracção física de Enrique Otway por Carlota, essa atracção é menor do que o afã económico) e o Sr. Lopes, movido apenas pelo desejo libidinoso em *O Escravo*, desejo que vai unido, embora com uma certa incoerência narrativa, à necessidade compulsiva de conseguir dinheiro:

> Lopes—no seu quartel general—dava as necessárias ordens, e recebia parte do produto da rapina. Chamejavam-lhe os olhos, e na expressão do rosto notava-se-lhe uma alegria, qual a do capitão de salteadores, após a possessão de um magnífico espólio. (135)

No que diz respeito ao "estrangeiro" nestes dois triângulos, Enrique Otway (em *Sab*) tem, para além de uma funcionalidade evidente no desenvolvimento da diegese, uma caracterização psicológica de que carece a personagem do Sr. Lopes em *O Escravo*; este é também necessário para conduzir a acção ao desfecho, ideologicamente necessário, da morte de João e para introduzir o motivo anti-esclavagista da revolta dos negros, pano de fundo muito mais intenso do que na obra da Avellaneda, talvez por se tratar de uma revolta histórica qualificada de "ominosa recordação para Cabo Verde" (134), e à que o narrador alude nos seguintes termos:

> E não cuide o leitor ser isto pura ficção de romance; nem tão pouco creia haver poesia na descrição que temos feito. (133)

Porém, a caracterização da personagem de Almeida é muito esquemática, daí a sua menor importância narrativa.

Repare-se, também, que José Evaristo de Almeida introduz no segundo triângulo a figura da escrava, que participa das nobres qualidades da ama e faz com que este segundo triângulo se imponha, narrativamente falando, ao primeiro (neste sentido, a ajuda de Luíza para que João possa contemplar e tocar o seu objecto de amor, assim como a morte e o enterro conjunto de Luíza e João colocam a personagem de Luíza, assim como os valores ideológicos que esta representa, num lugar central da narrativa).

O caso do segundo triângulo, em *Sab*, é mais complexo; Teresa não é escrava mas participa da marginalidade que tem Luíza (orfandade e pobreza) e a aproximação, quase que diríamos identificação, com Carlota convertem a sua figura num *transfer* da protagonista feminina que aproveita o autor para, através dela, dar um desfecho diferente ao romance.

3. O escravo aparece caracterizado de forma similar num outro romance. João e Sab são "almas superiores," inteligentes, cultos, solidários e caridosas, mas, fundamentalmente, são amantes arrebatados.

Se quisermos procurar mais coincidências entre estes dois romances, poderíamos ainda referir a presença enigmática da mãe de cada um dos escravos: em *O Escravo*, a feiticeira, mãe biológica de João, mora no "monte chamado Vermelho—em razão do rubro da sua terra, que jamais manifestou sinal algum de vegetação—"(111, sublinhados nossos). No caso de Sab, a sua, também enigmática mãe adoptiva, Martina, mora nas "cuevas de Cubitas," terras habitadas outrora, segundo a lenda, pelo "cacique Camagüey " "que fue arrojado de la cumbre de esa gran loma y su cuerpo despedazado quedó insepulto sobre la tierra regada con su sangre. Desde entonces esta tierra tornóse roja en muchas leguas a la redonda" (168, sublinhados nossos).

Estes montes, onde moram as respectivas mães, reúnem uma carga simbólica que pode ser sublinhada a diferentes níveis: não só a cor vermelha nos põe em contacto com o símbolo do sangue que em todos os estudos do simbólico, é morte e ressurreição em simultâneo; mas, o monte também se torna na última morada dos escravos João e Sab. O cadáver do primeiro fica "entulhado de modo, que hoje, no Monte Vermelho, não há vestígio de semelhante caverna" (155) e, o segundo termina em Cubitas, aonde viera morrer ao pé da sua mãe adoptiva e onde será enterrado.

4. Nos dois romances deparamo-nos com um comportamento que, no caso de Almeida tem sido apresentado como uma marca do carácter folhetinesco da obra, que é a entrega do escravo (a escrava Luíza no caso de Almeida) para favorecer os desejos da pessoa a quem se ama. Possivelmente o facto de se tratar de um autor masculino, num caso, e de uma autora, feminina portanto, no outro, faça com que em *O Escravo* seja Luíza quem se sacrifique por João e em *Sab* seja o escravo que se sacrifique para conseguir a felicidade da pessoa que ama.

Até aqui uma série de semelhanças, que se poderia completar como forma de tematizar outras situações ou pela apresentação da descrição de alguns motivos, como, por exemplo, o "jardim," cujo significado alegórico é fundamental nos dois romances.

Achamos, portanto, que estas coincidências entre duas obras próximas no tempo e nas circunstâncias contextuais em que são produzidas, não são resultado de o simples acaso e ainda que não disponhamos de outros elementos extra-textuais que certifiquem o conhecimento que José Evaristo d'Almeida poderia ter da obra de Gertrudis Gómez de Avellaneda, a relação entre os dois textos (numa relação de modelo e cópia) é tão evidente que dificilmente se poderia negar tal hipotético desconhecimento.

À vista destas concordâncias textuais e à falta de investigações posteriores que provem realmente que foi possível o conhecimento da obra de G. Gómez de Avellaneda por parte de José Evaristo d'Almeida, podemos avançar com a hipótese que apresentamos e que justifica, cremos, uma segunda leitura da obra cabo-verdiana que se insira, como também faz a de Avellaneda, na perspectiva de um movimento de ideação da nação.

Plágio? Diálogo intertextual? Inclinamo-nos mais para a segunda das hipóteses porque as semelhanças são tão evidentes, tão descaradamente transparentes, que dificilmente o autor se veria livre de uma acusação como a primeira que sugerimos. Neste sentido, pensamos que, partindo de premissas contextuais próximas ou semelhantes e reconhecendo explicitamente um modelo, o autor tentará jogar na diferença como forma de marcar o próprio a respeito de modelos extra e inter-textuais idênticos; por outras palavras, assumir a recriação do mito calibanesco de se apropriar da fala de outrem.

Aliás, estas coincidências levam-nos a problematizar uma outra questão delas derivada: a reflexão sobre a história literária. Com efeito, em 1852, Miguel Luís Amunátegui estabelecia um modelo de periodização para todas as literaturas (González-Stephan 180). Segundo o teórico chileno, existem indubitavelmente três fases nas literaturas de qualquer país:

1ª Etapa de aprendizagem, que seria de *plágio*. Nesta fase, a literatura de outro país é inevitavelmente copiada.

2ª Período de *imitação*, em que se toma por empréstimo o pensamento, quer dizer, o fundo mas não a forma.

3ª Etapa da *originalidade*, que por volta de 1852 não teria ainda chegado à América Latina.

Esta teorização, uma das primeiras feitas para a América Latina, levar-nos-ia a perguntar se estaria a obra de José Evaristo de Almeida naquela primeira fase de plágio *tout-court*, em que temas, motivos, acção romanesca, funções, códigos ideológicos, espaço... seriam directamente tirados de outra literatura. Ou, pelo contrário, o plágio consistiria num aproveitamento de um tema e de uma organização narrativa a que só era necessário modificar uma série de referências contextuais e dotá-la de "cor local" para "nacionalizar" aqueles textos que, sendo produzidos algures, se adaptavam perfeitamente aos objectivos e à intencionalidade do autor.

Caracterização geral

Colocada a primeira questão de abertura do romance cabo-verdiano e que pretendemos aqui estudar, diríamos, em termos gerais, que a obra apresenta, numa primeira leitura, a evidência de dois temas, o amor (numa escrita que faz lembrar o romance camiliano) e a escravatura.

No que diz respeito ao primeiro, trata-se de um amor espiritualizado, que o prologuista da edição de 1988 qualifica de "saga de amor." Nesta concepção amorosa, João aproxima-se do ideal "trovadoresco e cavaleiresco da Idade Média" e Maria "tem muito do ideal romântico do século XVIII e, em certos aspectos, se confunde com o ideal de amor de um dos personagens de *La Nouvelle Heloïse* de J.J. Rousseau" (Veiga 20).

Caracterizando-se, ainda, o amor em relação a outras personagens, Luíza, a escrava, ama "sem perder a razão," enquanto que o Sr. Lopes, "não possui o romantismo de João, nem a poesia de Maria, nem o humanismo de Luiza... Trata-se de um 'amor' egoísta e venal" (Veiga 19).

O tema da escravatura leva, por sua vez, a inserir o romance na linha da ficção histórica, ficção em que, de modo geral, se conjugam elementos românticos nas histórias amorosas, com elementos realistas que produzem o "pacto de verossimillança"; para isso concorrem não só as referências geográficas e etnográficas, como a delimitação temporal.

Como indica Elsa dos Santos, num dos escassos estudos sobre *O Escravo*, "a nível da construção deste romance do século XIX conjugam-se elementos românticos muito característicos das obras de ficção desta época, com elementos realistas" (436).

A Escravatura em Cabo Verde

Quando José Evaristo d'Almeida escreve a sua obra, o sistema escravocrata em Cabo Verde está a chegar ao seu fim, pelo menos em termos político-legais.

Com efeito, se observarmos as estatísticas demográficas da Colónia, verificamos que desde os inícios do século XIX até à abolição em 1876, o número da população escrava permanece sensivelmente idêntico em números absolutos, por volta de 5.000 indivíduos (Estêvão 193) e com uma progressiva diminuição em termos percentuais: 8,8% em 1807, 6,9% em 1827, 4,8% em 1856 e a mesma percentagem em 1868.

O decreto de 1836 do Governo de Sá da Bandeira proibe o tráfico, mas permite que um colono que se translade de uma colónia a outra possa importar ou exportar escravos. Entre 1815 e 1842, surgiu "um conjunto de armadores cabo-verdianos com um número apreciável de navios, quase todos utilizados no tráfico clandestino dirigido principalmente para as Antilhas (Cuba e São Domingos). Foi a importância que Santiago voltou a ter no tráfico que permitiu a estabilização do número de escravos em Cabo Verde durante a primeira metade do século XIX" (Estêvão 195-196).

Essa relação de Cabo Verde com as Antilhas explicaria, na nossa opinião, que não seja despropositado pensarmos num certo intercâmbio literário e, em consequência, no acesso a uma literatura anti-esclavagista que estava a vingar no território americano, ligada, como já foi sido demonstrado, às incipientes ideias nacionalistas.

No caso de Cuba, por exemplo, não se pode esquecer que a percentagem de população escrava era, em 1841, de 43,3%; isto, unido à questão económica derivada da cultura açucareira, fez com que "azúcar y esclavitud son los términos unseparables en la conformacvión de la nacionalidad" (Rosell 29).

Quer dizer, o tempo da escrita de Almeida deve coincidir, por força, com os movimentos abolicionistas também em Cabo Verde, como assinala Oliveira Marques, para quem "nos começos do século XIX, encontrava-se em franco desenvolvimento uma corrente de opinião pública contrária à escravatura em geral e ao tráfico de escravos em Portugal" (Marques 166). Esse anti-esclavagismo generalizado na opinião pública deveria ter maior presença e tradução política nas colónias, como provam, para o caso do arquipélago, as notícias de sublevações (segundo informa Serra Barcelos em 1901) em que participam escravos, mas também libertos e pequenos proprietários: a revolta da Ribeira do Engenho de 1822, a sublevação de degredados e as tentativas, no mesmo sentido, dos escravos em Monte Agarro de 1835 (talvez seja esta sublevação à que se faz referência no cap. XVII da obra), ou mesmo o motim dos rendeiros de Achada Falcão de 1841.

Por outro lado, o processo de abolição do morgadio e da escravatura criou novas condições institucionais, em cujo quadro se processou o desenvolvimento da sociedade crioula e a ascensão económica da classe intermédia (Estêvão 205).

A este quadro sócio-económico soma-se a independência do Brasil em 1822, que faz com que

> Alguns indivíduos começaram a defender a ideia de que o arquipélago deveria acompanhar a colónia sul-americana na sua separação de Portugal, tornando-se assim uma província brasileira. (Oliveira 30)

Além disso, os confrontos entre liberais e miguelistas que dominam a cena política nas décadas de 20 e 30, terão o seu reflexo na política colonial e será nesse contexto que, no seio do sector liberal cabo-verdiano, apareça um movimento separatista mas, como tinha acontecido com o anterior [o de 1922 na sequência da independência do Brasil] não seria um movimento independentista (Oliveira 32). Trata-se da chamada "Confederação Brasílica" em que se integrariam, além do Brasil e Cabo Verde, outras colónias como Angola.

O miguelismo como movimento esclavagista, ou defensor das ideias esclavagistas, está reflectido na obra de Almeida pela figura do Sr. Lopes, essa personagem sobre a qual recaem as valorizações negativas do narrador e que escolheu como pretexto para a sua conquista da mulata, a via do compromisso político com D. Miguel.

> Ao começar da música, a tropa, formada no qurtel, irrompeu em um entusiasmo viva a el-rei D. Miguel I: depois saiu toda fazendo-se acompanhar da música, e levando na sua frente Lopes, elevado à categoria de comandante. (132)

Mas a tentativa de revolta, chefiada por Lopes, uma vez gorada torna-se no símbolo do insucesso do miguelismo e, por extensão, do sistema esclavagista em Cabo Verde:

> Lopes resolveu-se a partir, porque considerou que ainda mesmo que chegasse a haver às mãos a mulata, o, povo que vinha sobre a Vila lhe arrebataria a sua presa, para buscar a qual ele teria de consumir um tempo precioso. (149)

A pergunta que surge aqui é óbvia: até que ponto aquela ideia da "Confederação Brasílica" é mais do que uma simples reivindicação pontual, que demonstra um mau-estar social em termos económicos? É possível ver nela uma ideia pré-nacionalista, mesmo que seja reduzida a um grupo não muito importante da sociedade cabo-verdiana? Participaria José Evaristo de Almeida dessa ideia?

Mesmo que não tenhamos dados, por enquanto, que possam avançar uma hipótese nesse sentido, cremos que se pode pensar num certo movimento intelectual de formulação de uma ideia nacional que servisse de suporte a um hipotético movimento político de carácter nacionalitário porque, de não ser assim, dificilmente se poderia explicar, no nosso entender, uma obra isolada como *O Escravo.*

Imaginar a nação. As relações sentimentais como alegoria da pátria

Na tentativa de dar resposta às perguntas retóricas que formulámos no início deste trabalho, cremos que é possível ver as estratégias que o autor utiliza para construir a imagem da nação cabo-verdiana, embora por razões, nomeadamente de ordem política, não possa utilizar o termo nação.

É aqui que as relações sentimentais se apresentam como alegoria da nação emergente, no sentido dado por Doris Sommer:

> Love plots and political plotting keep overlapping with each other. Instead of the metaphoric parallelism, say between passion and patriotism, that readers may expect from allegory, we will see here a metonymic association between romantic love that needs to be founded on love. (41)

Quer dizer, a identificação entre uma história romântica e o destino da nação é uma das marcas distintivas dos primeiros romances latino-americanos e, portanto, não parece despropositado procurarmos também noutros contextos geográficos e culturais a utilização das mesmas estratégias.

Com efeito, ao converter o escravo João e a mestiça Maria em sujeitos românticos (até na exageração e hipervalorização das suas características como personagens datadas de acordo com uma época), as personagens de Almeida ocupam um lugar de primazia na mundividência do autor. Desta maneira são resgatas estas figuras do estranhamento em que as colocava o discurso oficial do colonialismo: um por razões de classe e ambos por razões de raça. A centralidade de ambas as figuras representa, assim, a possibilidade, como imagem especular, da recuperação da centralidade social. O autor faz com que o "contra-discurso," no significado do discurso contra a escravatura (na acepção de William Luis, em Méndez 16-17) se identifique, também, com o contra-discurso da "crioulidade."

O fracasso da "história de amor" João-Maria poderia ser visto como o fracasso-impossibilidade da alegoria nacional no sentido da possibilidade de se criar uma sociedade resultando da recuperação da centralidade do antigo escravo e da mestiça. Porém, parece-nos mais exacto vermos uma certa realização, sublimada, isso sim, na resposta final de Maria:

> Amava-o e de maneira, que, se lhe fosse possível arrancar o escravo das garras da morte, ela orgulhosa o apresentara ao mundo, como dono e senhor absoluto do seu coração; porque Maria compreendeu quanto havia de puro, delicado e sublime no amor que João lhe dedicava. (150)

Mas se é possível a união, alegoria da nação, entre um sector social importante no Cabo Verde de meados do século XIX, como o dos escravos, não o é menos o lugar primordial que a esta classe se dá pelo recurso à história de João e Luíza.

Com efeito, o escravo mulato (embora o mulatismo tenha menos importância do que a condição de escravo) e a escrava negra, Luíza, chegam a uma união também de forma simbólica, sem alterar a dinâmica da acção romântica que exige, em jeito de sacrifício ritual, a morte e permite, assim, pôr em relevo a conquista do espaço central pelos dois marginalizados que conseguem, pela via do amor que transcende a morte, prefigurar uma pátria que perdure e isto fazem-no através da imagem do Céu:

> E estes beijos que eu emprego na tua boca, em vez de se gelarem—como agora acontece sobre os teus frios beiços—terão duplicada força—serão mais ardentes, quando lá em cima os permutar pelos teus. Ah! João, pede ao Criador do mundo que me chame para si tão breve, quanto o deseja o meu coração. (155)

Possível união de classes (escravo e amo)? A união, mesmo que só seja de forma simbólica, entre João, o escravo negro e Maria, a mulata filha de um Capitão que chegou a essa posição pelos merecimentos próprios, supõe uma proposta nacionalitária como alegoria da nação possível. Nessa nação, ou se quisermos nessa nova sociedade cabo-verdiana não há porém lugar para o estrangeiro, para o colono, como se pode ver não só pelo insucesso amoroso do Sr. Lopes, como pelo facto de o homem branco (e colono) se ir embora do país.

"Pintar" a nação: A delimitação do espaço

A nação é, antes de mais, um espaço, um território a delimitar/descobrir, um mapa a ser desenhado para que os outros, os integrantes da "comunidade imaginada," tenham uma noção física de onde é que estão e que lugar ocupam no universo.

Singularizar, pois, o espaço tornou-se uma tarefa prioritária (no sentido de primeira) para os integrantes do "núcleo simbólico" da nação e, em consequência, num *leit-motif* das literaturas emergentes. Por outro lado, a paisagem, como elemento privilegiado do espaço tornou-se no lugar comum da experimentação espacial. Como indica uma estudiosa da literatura brasileira, referindo-se à literatura desse país:

> As estéticas anteriores ao romantismo mantiveram uma visão mercantil, europeia com relação à paisagem, mesmo quando o tom era de ufanismo.

> (...) o nacionalismo romântico (...) mostra, no entanto, um olhar que valoriza a paisagem como traço de identidade, o que faz desaparecer o olhar mercantil. (Ribeiro 87)

Da importância da paisagem, do espaço necessário para construir a nação, dão provas todas as literaturas africanas:

> A concepção de país releva de uma noção geográfica (o território terrestre e não só) completado por noções de unidade e totalidade (indivisibilidade da terra (...) que, mesmo assim, decorrendo da filosofia e da política, não deixam de se formar ao nível de uma certa superficialidade advinda da forte noção de realidade natural. (Laranjeira 232)

Em *O Escravo* há uma tentativa de fixar de forma claramente identificável, o espaço da acção (o mesmo que acontece com o tempo, fazendo ambos com que a narração tenha o carácter de histórica):

> O sítio de B..., pouco mais de meia légua distante da Vila da Praia da ilha de Santiago—uma das ilhas de Cabo Verde—(25).

Ao longo do texto, o autor vai desenhando o mapa de Cabo Verde, quer através dos lugares onde decorre a acção, quer através dos lugares referidos pelo narrador ou pelas personagens. Para além da ilha de Santiago que aparece como mais próxima do narrador e portanto, mais singularizada e que se apresenta como "uma das ilhas de Cabo Verde" (25), faz-se referência à personagem que "viera da ilha de Santo Antão de onde era natural" (33), ou à mãe de Maria que era "filha de um rico proprietário de São Nicolau" (33) ou do pai de Maria que "tinha ido em comissão à Guiné," lugar para onde irão, no fim do romance, a família de Maria (lembre-se que, na altura, a Guiné dependia administrativamente de Cabo Verde).

Existe, portanto, o desejo de desenhar um "mapa" do território, uma conceptualização física que permita visualizar a "nação," no sentido que lhe deu B. Anderson e que revista Moretti quando afirma:

> Los seres humanos llegan a captar de forma diferente muchos de sus habitat (...) Pero, ¿el Estado-Nación? ¿dónde está? ¿que aspecto tiene? ¿cómo se hace para verlo? (...) El Estado-Nación ha encontrado la novela y viceversa; la novela ha

> encontrado el Estado-nación. Y siendo la única forma simbólica capaz de representarlo, se ha convertido, también, en una parte esencial de nuestra cultura. (Moretti 17)

Não sendo Cabo Verde um Estado-nação, podemos, porém, presumir a ideia de um proto-nacionalismo que teria por objectivo a construção dessa nação imaginada. A nação existe porque existe a sua representação e é aí onde o mapa ultrapassa o seu carácter de motivo para se converter no eixo estruturante da narrativa. Ora bem, existem muitas maneiras de utilizar o mapa: desde o logotipo (como forma mais visível de logocização) até o estabelecimento de percursos espaciais em que a acção vai desenhando um mapa mental cuja base física existe desde o momento em que o narrador ou as personagens investem na sua conceptualização.

E se toda a Nação tem um centro, o mapa tem também um centro onde se cruzam as linhas (simbólicas) da acção e que no caso de *O Escravo* estaria "no sítio de B..." e no "monte Vermelho": um mais próximo e de efeito realista (o "efeito de real" barthesiano), e o outro mais distante e de carácter simbólico.

"O sítio de B..." é o espaço da familiaridade, o "centro" onde se projectam as emoções e as paixões das personagens; lugar de encontros e desencontros amorosos e que coloca a morte fora das suas fronteiras (e a expulsão da morte das fronteiras do espaço do aconchego matricial reveste-se, também e como parece óbvio, de um alto valor simbólico).

Por seu lado, o "monte Vermelho" é um "centro" simbólico porque aí vive Julia, a mãe de João, quem com as suas feitiçarias prediz o futuro (da nação) a que se chegará por uma acção violenta, como violento é o próprio sistema esclavagista: "Vingança! Vingança! bradou ela, Morte, maldição sobre os brancos!" (75) É, também, nesse monte onde finalmente ficam enterrados João e Luisa, quer dizer a semente de um futuro (país) que se está a construir (porque a nação é também um sonho a realizar).

Trata-se, portanto, de dois centros diferentes mas complementares conformando uma indefinição espacial que releva da indefinição que acompanha os primeiros momentos da construção (nacional) espacial instituindo-se nos eixos de uma rudimentar e incompleta cartografia.

Porém, mais interessante do que esta conceptualização, deste mapa literário, parece-nos ser a valorização de determinados elementos da paisagem, no mesmo sentido com que o fez, no seu momento, a literatura brasileira. Neste sentido, uma série de elementos simbólicos acrescenta o valor nobilitador da paisagem ou de uma certa paisagem, a começar pela importância do "jardim." e O "jardim" onde começa a acção de *O Escravo* funciona como uma espécie de *locus amoenus* onde se destaca o sentido da ordem que transmite Maria; um lugar edénico e, portanto, lugar de segurança como prolongação da pessoa que o habita:

> Em seu lugar vereis fartas laranjeiras, abundantes bananeiras, o cajueiro, o zimbrão, a norça, os tamarindos, as palmeiras altas (...). Nem faltava aí o rubicundo café (...). Não existia, é verdade, um jardim tão matizado, tñao fértuil, tão vartiado como o de hoje. (26)

Na formação das literaturas que (depois) seriam chamadas nacionais, pode predominar a ideia do elemento social e histórico (como no caso desta obra) ou uma espécie de bucolismo (a que parece remeter o micro-espaço do jardim) derivado da representação do espaço, que neste caso não está ausente.

Ora bem, a representação do espaço como marca identitária

> (Es) una referencia fácilmente manejable dentro del pensamiento letrado: lo "otro" fue convertido, en el más flagrante de los casos, en pura naturaleza o paisaje, en selva o llano, en sierra o costa; y en el menos reconvertido en cuadro de costumbres. (González-Stephan 193)

A representação do espaço em *O Escravo* segue um esquema de lugares comuns, com mais valor pelo que têm de sugestão simbólica do que pela elaboração de uma representação realista. Mesmo assim e tendo em conta que a paisagem forma parte da *check-list* identitária, ela tem alguma importância, neste sentido, na obra de Almeida, apesar do recurso à lista identitária ser o meio mais banal de representar uma nação, visto tratarem-se dos elementos mais rapidamente assimilados pelo leitor (Thiesse 18) que recorrem a uma representação espacial que não vingou na literatura "nacional" cabo-verdiana. Só vagamente se poderá reconhecer na paisagem de *O Escravo* uma paisagem nacional (embora conte com referências toponímicas e etnográficas que poderiam suprir essa ausência de identificação). Bem é verdade que a paisagem física e social na obra será facilmente reconhecível, mas aqueles elementos que acabaram por entrar no imaginário "nacional" cabo-verdiano estão ainda ausentes em *O Escravo* (a seca, o mar, a emigração, a fome).

Como assinala M. da Veiga,

> O enquadramento geográfico não deixa margem para dúvidas quanto à localização da história no espaço caboverdiano, particularmente da ilha de Santiago. Porém, se o autor se recorre à geografia como um dos elementos caracterizadores da sua história, não se esquece do húmus social que forma e enforma a sua narração. (Veiga 17)

A paisagem em *O Escravo* não configura, portanto, um espaço identitário (que encontraremos nos romances posteriores de Manuel Lopes ou Baltasar Lopes), mas, sim, um espaço simbólico e que só por essa via indirecta pode ser lido em termos de pré-figuração identitária. O espaço edénico e feliz do "sítio de B..." e o lugar terrorífico do Monte Vermelho são dois planos que se atraem e repelem a um tempo e que a personagem do escravo, através das suas deslocações espaciais, consegue unir na sua relação conflitual.

Narrador e Leitor

Para quem José Evaristo de Almeida escreve o seu romance? O problema do leitor modelo é, ao que nos parece, fulcral à hora de inserirmos o romance no início de um (novo) sistema literário em língua portuguesa, ou, pelo contrário, ao colocarmo-lo nas margens da literatura portuguesa, numa literatura de motivação africana, cabo-verdiana no caso, mas que se move numa indefinição sistémica advinda não tanto da grelha de temas e motivos que o texto actualiza, como da relação conflitual do texto numa espécie de vazio de memória literária, assim como na tensão dialéctica do texto com o seu produtor e receptor primeiros.

Cumpre, pois, atentar para o modelo de leitor que *O Escravo* actualiza e que, por razões históricas não parece que seja o cabo-verdiano. Com efeito, o autor utiliza uma série de referências etnográficas que não formam parte, ao que nos parece da "lista nacionalitária," apesar de darem uma certa "cor local," mas que têm por finalidade definir o estatuto cultural e ideológico do leitor. Assim, por exemplo, num diálogo entre o Sr. Lopes e Maria a propósito de umas plantas "que se alinham com uma perfeita igualdade," a protagonista responde:

> - Estas plantas (...) chamam-se mandioqueiras cujas raízes são neste país o pão do pobre: é delas que se faz a farinha a que vós outros chamais de pão—é delas, igualmente, que se fabrica a goma e tapioca. Além, aquele campo que se nos mostra ora verde, ora gaio—conforme as ondulações a que a brisa o força—contém a doce cana, da qual podeis extrair indistintamente o açúcar ou aguardente; esta fazendo distilar seu melífero sumo—aquela, congelando, por meio do fogo, a fluidez desse

> mesmo sumo. Este é o café saboroso; suas flores miudinhas, alvas e suavemente odoríferas, produzem multiplicidade de esféricos bagos que abrigam em sua púrpura capa cada um dois gémeos perfeitamente iguais. Aqueles arbustos que se seguram à rocha, que se inclinam de maneira a fazer persuadir que vão despenhar-se, e que vegetam com uma força espantosa (...) é a purgueira, a qual nos oferece em seu oleoso fruto azeite só próprio para alimento da luz: os pinhões, contidos em sua noz são saborossíssimos (...) Vêde ali o nespereiro, a mais copada e airosa de todas as árvores (...) Aquela é o tamarindo refrigerante (...) (43-44).

Em toda esta enumeração de verdadeiros frutos de um paraíso (esta descrição completa aquela a que já fizemos referência quando falámos do jardim), interessa sublinhar vários aspectos: o primeiro seria o facto de que descrever e explicar toda uma série de elementos da flora cabo-verdiana só tem sentido se o interlocutor é um estrangeiro, como é o caso de Lopes, mas, por esta estratégia, o autor está situando, também, o hipotético leitor (não o cabo-verdiano, é óbvio). Narradora e autor aproximam-se, uma vez que interlocutor e leitor também se aproximam porque, afinal, o texto é também um diálogo.

Mas aqui, há também uma série de oposições que merece ser frisada: o eu e o tu, o nós e o vós. Porque o emprego da primeira pessoa do plural, exigido pelo contexto da comunicação formal, sugere um plural colectivo onde se insere o eu e um plural, também colectivo, que faz referência ao estranho, ao estrangeiro ao "vós outros" cuja impossibilidade de se inserir no núcleo da personagem é manifesto.

Mais ainda, a resposta do Sr. Lopes pretende mostrar como singular e raro, o que é normal (e a análise estilística das intervenções de Maria, João, Luíza ou Júlia, na sua nivelação lingüística, põem em evidência uma unidade maior entre todos os grupos que iriam configurar a "nação emergente"). A nivelação linguística que se manifesta em todas as personagens, aí incluído o narrador, apaga as diferenças de género, raça e classe estabelecendo uma linha divisória entre nós (os caboverdianos) e vós (os portugueses), facto que explica a reacção de incredulidade de Lopes:

> - Se houvesse, senhora, de presumir o país em que estou pelo que me tendes feito notar; se tivesse que avaliar os seus habitantes pelos encantos, atractivos e superiores conhecimentos, que em vós deviso, acreditar-me-ia no país das fadas. (45)
> E eu—observou Maria—se tivesse que julgar os vossos conterrâneos pelo que vos acabo de ouvir, diria que os da Europa não são difíceis no emprego da lisonja. (45)

Se as explicações, directas ou através das personagens, de aspectos etnográficos (por exemplo as explicações sobre a dança do torno) configuram um modelo de leitor português, outro tipo de comparações seguem obviamente a mesma linha.

Assim, por exemplo, para explicar a cova onde mora Júlia, o narrador, a partir da sua omnisciência, compara-a com a serra de Sintra:

> Já atravessasteis a serra de Sintra, para visitar o conventinho dos Capuchos? Já fostes alguma vez conhecer essas pequeninas celas, para atravessar as quais seríeis constrangido a curvar-vos de modo a receardes cair? (...) havia de maravilhar-vos ainda muito mais a cova onde Santo Onofre... (111)

Tudo isto foi dito em crioulo

Se o romance que analisamos está escrito em tom realista, o autor não poderia fazer menos do que lavrar acta da peculiar situação linguística cabo-verdiana, quer dizer, da existência do crioulo.

Por razões históricas evidentes, o autor não iria utilizar outra língua que não fosse o português mas aqui interessa principalmente sublinhar que, se a nível da expressão se opera uma nivelação "estilística," o mesmo não acontece no que diz respeito ao sistema linguístico utilizado.

A partir de algumas intervenções das personagens cria-se a miragem, tão habitual nas literaturas africanas do século XX, segundo a qual as personagens falam a sua língua, embora o texto literário apareça numa espécie de tradução para línguas europeias. Num encontro entre João e Luíza os dois escravos falam em crioulo:

> Tudo isto foi dito em crioulo: nós porém não estamos senhores dessa linguagem a ponto de poder referir, no dialecto empregado pelos dois interlocutores, a conversação que vai ter lugar. Sentimo-lo pelo que respeita a Luiza; por quanto algumas das expressões dela não terão no português—que está ao nosso alcance—a força que no crioulo se lhes deve ligar. (50)

O bilinguismo aqui utilizado pelo autor pode ser interpretado de várias maneiras, mas achamos que ele pode ser uma marca de resistência, dado que só os escravos parecem utilizar o crioulo o que, para além doutras reflexões sócio-linguísticas, evidencia um mecanismo de resistência:

> le bilinguisme, loin d'être un handicap pour les rares locuteurs qui en usent, s'offre comme un exutoire et une possibilité de résistence, d'esquive et de défoulement devant la morgue et l'emprise de l'homme blanc (...). Pour les Africains, les langues africaines représentent, en face d'un colonisateur qui les ignore complètement, un facteur de complicité, une arme de défense et de résistance. La langue maternelle est un refuge; elle seule garantit la liberté au sein même de l'oppression que l'on endure. (Bokiba 30-31)

Poderíamos dizer, assim, que o autor, ao tempo que constata a existência da língua crioula, utiliza esta como uma marca de classe e, portanto, coloca-a fora da "lista identitária" a que fizemos referência dado que, como leitores, não encontramos índices textuais que nos levem a supôr que personagens como Maria utilizem essa língua.

O tema lingüístico seria, como já tem acontecido noutros casos, um magnífico lugar para a reflexão literária, mas o mérito de José Evaristo de Almeida reside, nosso entender, em ter colocado um dos temas centrais de todas as literaturas africanas: a utilização da língua e os processos de autonomização literária. Por outro lado, o autor cabo-verdiano não constrói um discurso sobre a língua e não a converte num ponto fulcral do discurso identitário, mantendo a ambiguidade que a este respeito se detecta historicamente na literatura cabo-verdiana e não só.

Conclusão

Quisemos apresentar neste trabalho uma possível linha de leitura de um romance surpreendente inserido na história literária de Cabo Verde; surpreendente e inexplicável, talvez por desconhecimento, dentro de um contexto histórico e cultural onde se encontram as raízes do Cabo Verde dos nossos dias.

O Escravo, sem ser uma obra-prima da literatura, cremos que, de uma forma certamente ambígua mas nem por isso isenta de voluntarismo, supõe uma tentativa (consciente ou não, pouco interessa), de elaborar um discurso da diferença, converter a marginalidade em centralidade, fazer com que o *Outro*, deixe de ser um *Objecto* para se converter em *Sujeito.*

O Escravo abriu-nos uma possibilidade e uma obrigação, académica e moral, de pesquisa, pôs-nos, em definitivo, perante "a necessidade de escavar o século XIX onde se poderão encontrar as sementes da nacionalidade literária" (Santos 437).

Obras Citadas

Almeida, José Evaristo de. *O Escravo*. Lisboa: ALAC, 1989.

Anderson, Benedict. *Imagined Communities: Reflections on the Origin and Spread of Nacionalism*. London & New York: Verso, 1991.

Estêvão, João. "Cabo Verde." Alexandre, Valentim e Jill Dias, (coord.). *O Império Africano (1825-1890)*. Lisboa: Editorial Estampa. 167-210.

Gómez de Avellaneda, Gertrudis. *Sab*. Madrid: Ediciones Cátedra, 1997.

González-Stephan, Beatriz. *Fundaciones: canon, historia y cultura nacional (La historiografía literaria del liberalismo hispanmoamericano del siglo XIX)*. Madrid: Iberoamericana, 2002.

Laranjeira, Pires. "A poesia da negritude africana e os conceitos de terra, povo, língua, raça, classe, nação e pátria." Cristóvão, Ferraz e Carvalho, (coord.). *Nacionalismo e Regionalismo nas Literaturas Lusófonas*. Lisboa: Edições Cosmos, 1997.

Marques, A. H. De Oliveira. *História de Portugal*. vol. III. Lisboa: Palas Editores, 1986.

Méndez Ródenas, Adriana. *Cuba en su imagen: Historia e identidad en la literatura cubana*. Madrid: Editorial Verbum, 2002.

Moretti, Franco. *Atlas de la novela europea (1800-1900)*. Madrid: Trama Editorial, 2001.

Oliveira, Joao Nobre de. *A Imprensa Cabo-Verdiana 1820-1975*. Macau: Fundação Macau, 1998.

Ribeiro, Mª Aparecida. *Literatura Brasileira*. Lisboa: Universidade Aberta, 1994.

Servera (1997). "Introducción."Gómez de Avellaneda, Gertrudis. *Sab*. Madrid: Ediciones Cátedra, 1997. 9-93.

Santos, Elsa Rodrigues dos. "O Escravo, romance do século XIX de José Evaristo de Almeida, e as primeiras marecas da nacionalidade literária caboverdiana." Cristóvão, Ferraz e Carvalho, (coord.) *Nacionalismo e Regionalismo nas Literaturas Lusófonas*. Lisboa: Edições Cosmos, 1997. 433-438.

Sommer, Doris. *Foundational Fictions: The Nacional Romances of Latin America*. Berkeley: University of California Press, 1991.

Thiesse, Anne-Marie. *A Criação das Identidades Nacionais*. Lisboa: Temas e Debates, 2000.

Francisco Salinas Portugal é licenciado em Filologia Românica e Filologia Galego-Portuguesa pela Universidade de Santiago de Compostela. Doutorou-se na mesma universidade com uma tese intitulada, "A escrita da angolanidade na narrativa de Pepetela." É Professor Titular na Universidade da Corunha (Galiza-Espanha), onde lecciona Literatura Portuguesa e Literaturas de Língua Portuguesa. Alguns dos seus trabalhos mais recentes sobre Literaturas Africanas de Língua Portuguesa são: *O Texto nas Margens. Ensaios sobre Literaturas de Língua Portuguesa* (1997), *Entre Próspero e Caliban. Literaturas Africanas de Língua Portuguesa* (1999) e *A Máscara do Sagrado. Uma leitura mitocrítica de* Mayombe (2001).

José Lopes and the Beginnings of Cape Verdean Literature

Arminda Brito
Translated by
Luís R. Mitras
Revised by
Mark Streeter

Abstract. In the period that extends from the end of the nineteenth century to the 1930s we witness the emergence of a poetry that is at once classicist and Romantic in Cape Verde; prior to this there was a total absence of a literary tradition. The foremost exponent of this kind of poetry was José Lopes, a poet who drew his inspiration from the classics. The poems that he published during his lifetime reveal the poet's penchant for themes derived from classical culture and for mythological, legendary and historical characters that would have been enjoyed as such by people living during the Renaissance. A close reading of this poetry will reveal the intellectual relationship that the poet maintained with the past, which is exemplified by his resorting to the use of historical and mythical and legendary material, be it of Portuguese origin or derived from classical antiquity, and which he transformed and absorbed into long poetic works in which he sang the historical deeds of different protagonists in different circumstances. It is precisely the proximity to Portuguese literature in those regions under Portuguese colonial domination, such as is the case of Cape Verde until independence in 1975, that permits us to seek a possible relationship between these literatures; this would include European literature. At the same time, it is important to distinguish what makes these local literatures specific or different.

One of the questions certain to be raised by those who venture to study the history of Cape Verdean literature will be the circumstances involved in the belated formation of a literature on these African islands.

History maintains that the country was discovered[1] or found in the fifteenth century; Portuguese navigators landed on its largest island in the year 1462. Historical facts are there to confirm all the theses that have been built around the mythical islands of Cape Arsinarius and the history of the formation and development of a Creole society.

It is an odd fact that only four centuries after the official recognition of the islands by the Portuguese Crown, that is to say, only in the nineteenth century, did the first signs of intellectual life appear on the horizon. We see the production and the publication of the first texts of a literary and non-literary nature, texts written mainly in prose and by Cape Verdeans—whether living within the confines of the territory or outside the country—or else by Portuguese citizens, either short-term visitors or people who came to live in Cape Verde. This does not mean that we can speak of literature in the archipelago.[2]

Most scholars of Cape Verdean literature agree that these are the signs that permit us, today, to place the beginnings of Cape Verdean letters in that century, in effect, confirming that our literary history is made up of a long period of about four hundred years marked by an intellectual vacuum and the absence of a literary tradition.

To clear up this question is the definitive position of Arnaldo França, who is categorical in affirming that

> procurar testemunhos da literatura cabo-verdiana anteriores ao inicio da segunda metade do século XIX é tarefa vã; um que outro escrito de autor ligado à terra pelo acaso do nascimento, ou mesmo com uma genealogia crioula, são insuficientes para povoar o deserto intelectual em que a ilha de Santiago se tornaria após um fugaz fausto observado por alguns no período quinhentista.[3]

> [to look for evidence of Cape Verdean literature prior to the beginning of the second half of the nineteenth century is a fruitless task; this or that bit of writing by an author connected to the country by an accident of birth or through Creole ancestors is insufficient to populate the intellectual desert that the island of Santiago had become after the fleeting grandeur that some observed in the sixteenth century.]

This scholar and critic of our literature admits the possibility that convent manuscripts could have existed prior to this date, but that unfortunately they have been lost and, for that reason, we should accept the earliest date for the beginnings of our literature to be in the middle of the 1800s. It is in that period that a support system capable of sustaining the development of an erudite literature appears: schools, the printing press and recreational associations.

In an excellent and well-grounded article, Alberto Carvalho talks about the importance of the schooling system and education in general—even though it was also elitist—as well as the proliferation of cultural institutions, such as libraries, reading rooms, museums, and others institutions of a similar nature, in the creation of a Cape Verdean intelligentsia. Especially important in this regard was the *Seminário-Lyceu* [Seminary-Secondary School] on the island of São Nicolau, which made a definitive contribution towards the formation of "*uma classe média de grande poder aglutinador*"[4] ["a middle class of great cohesive power"]. He shows that the schooling system contributed to the social and human development of Cape Verdeans, and this is vindicated by history. The introduction and development of primary schooling on the islands from 1817 onwards, the later establishment of the *Seminário-Lyceu* in São Nicolau in 1866 and the subsequent incorporation of the *Liceu* in Praia and the *Escola Principal* ["Main School"] within this institution are key events; they functioned as the driving motors behind the "*saber sobre o qual se alicerçaria a consciência da nação*"[5] ["knowledge upon which the conscience of the nation would build its foundation"].

Citizens and individuals with a solid knowledge, both literary and humanist, graduated from this *Seminário-Lyceu.* They would occupy important positions in the civil service, and in the school system.

Another aspect worthy of the attention of literary historians has to do with the fact that the appearance of literary prose in Cape Verde precedes the appearance of poetry by some years. Arnaldo França mentions several examples of prose works—either published in Cape Verde or published elsewhere by native Cape Verdeans—that reveal the first shimmering signs of a national literature, such as in the case of Guilherme Dantas. He also explains that it was the nature of the society at the time that determined why it was mainly prose that came to be written.[6] But the oldest literary work in Portuguese-speaking Africa, according to Manuel Ferreira, is a ditty by the Cape Verdean woman, Maria Antónia Pusich, entitled "Elegia à Memória das Infelizes Victímas Assassinadas por Francisco de Mattos Lobo na Noute de 25 de Junho de 1844" ["Elegy to the Memory of the Unfortunate Victims Murdered by Francisco de Mattos Lobo on the Night of June 25, 1844"] and published in Lisbon of that same year. Most of the texts, be they prose fiction or poetic texts, were published almost exclusively in the *Boletim Oficial do Governo Geral de Cabo Verde*[7] [*Official Report of the Governor-General's Office in Cape Verde*], the only means of communication available at that time, one that already came with an official literary page where the texts were published, interspersed with legal documents and journalistic texts. Symptomatic of this is the fact that a romantic love story and a historical novel by José Evaristo de Almeida entitled *O Escravo* [*The Slave*], dated 1856, was published in installments. However, it is widely accepted that the greatest prose writer to have made his appearance on the literary scene, in the period that extends from the end of the nineteenth century through to the first thirty years of the twentieth century, that is, before the appearance of the literary magazine *Claridade*, is Eugénio de Paula Tavares—a journalist, columnist, fiction author and bilingual poet. França says of him:

> Mais conhecido como poeta e nesta qualidade como autor de composições em crioulo, [...] é a prosa de Eugénio Tavares pela perfeição da forma, pela plasticidade descritiva dos ambientes, seja a paisagem marítima da fatal estrada da proa América, seja a vida dos campos da sua ilha de rusticidade sadia e fresca, pela recriação de personagens de uma ficção singela mas presa à realidade da terra, e também pelo estilo contundente, fortemente agressivo mas justo, da sua pena de jornalista.[8]

> [Better known as a poet and in his guise as the author of compositions in Creole [...] it is Eugénio Tavares's prose, for its formal perfection, for the gracefulness with which he describes different environments—the marine landscape of the fatal sea-lane of the prow *América*, the healthy freshness of rustic life in the interior of his native island—for the invention of characters who though simple fiction are grounded in the reality of that land, and also for the bruised style—strongly aggressive but just—that issued from his journalist's pen.]

It is only with the appearance of a private printing press that poetry will make its appearance, from 1877 onwards. It will acquire exceptional dimensions in the closing years of the nineteenth century and in the first thirty years of the twentieth century. It is during this time that we witness the emergence of a poetry that is at once classicist and Romantic and is best represented by Pedro Cardoso, José Lopes and Januário Leite. Oswaldo Osório, a poet and essayist, concludes his assessment of this kind of poetry with these words:

> [...] é no seu conjunto epígona da que se faz em Portugal, tematicamente exógena, academizante porque imitativa na forma e no metro; e o conteúdo, [...] é o produto de consciência fechada em um universo sem acesso ao "evoluir civilizacional" do mundo, em que a única saída reside no exercício e na aplicação do eu na escrita como forma de afirmação pessoal—poesia de sentimento, de dores e de melancolias existenciais excessivas, ambígua mesmo quando pretende o tom ser de desafio ou de recuperação da história. Poesia de herança romântica, dela não colhe, porém, na linha do romantismo iluminista, uma conduta ideológica, uma pedagogia—para se ater à sua corrente sentimental.[9]

> [(...) in broad terms, the quality is inferior to that which is made in Portugal, its themes are derived from foreign influences, and it is academic in its imitation of form and meter; as for its content (...) it is the product of a conscience that is closed off, inhabiting a universe where there is no access to the "civilizational evolution" of the world, where the only way out consisted of making use of the "I" in writing as a kind of affirmation of self—it is a poetry of sentiments, and the melancholy and pain of excessive existential self-doubts, a poetry full of ambiguities, even when the tone purports to challenge or to reclaim the past. This was the kind of poetry inherited from the Romantics, and yet it does not reap the benefits of an enlightened Romanticism: an ideological way of being, a pedagogy—it chooses, instead, to flow with the more sentimental current of Romanticism.]

He adds:

> É um período muito longo que foi ocupado por nomes mais ligados à actividade poética cujas produções se catalogam como "manifestações literárias" facilmente reivindicadas também pela literatura portuguesa.[10]

> [It was a very long period, one that was dominated by names of people linked to the production of the sort of poetry that could be classified as "literary manifestations" that could have been easily reclaimed by Portuguese literature.]

The first literary efforts of these poets, especially verse, were first printed in the *Novo Almanach de Lembranças Luso-Brasileiro*[11] [*New Luso-Brazilian Almanac of Remembrances*], a Lisbon-based publication whose principal readers were Portuguese citizens living in the four corners of the world. It made known the sort of literary and cultural initiatives carried out in the Portuguese-speaking African countries, particularly in Cape Verde, Angola and Mozambique. It was as a result of this publication, because it did bring together a large number of contributors, and significant contributions at that,[12] that these new poets could connect with the world; it guaranteed them a permanent dialogue with interlocutors from other parts and, also, credibility in the heart of the international literary community. Thus this publication has come to acquire capital importance in the study of the so-called "emergent literatures," although there is no way that this significance could have been foreseen at the time of the appearance of the publication.

The absence of a past and of a literary tradition ensured that poetry would be constructed according to a European model; it was something some of our poets could not escape from, imbued as they were with classical and humanist traditions, the result of their academic training in the then-*Seminário-Lyceu* in São Nicolau. It was here that they were exposed to the Classicist and Romantic Portuguese poets; they would acquire an easy familiarity with these poets.

Guilherme da Cunha Dantas is, admittedly, one of the first genuine poets; an ultra-Romantic in orientation, he is regarded as "*o príncipe dos poetas da minha terra*" ["the prince of poets of my country"] in the words of José Lopes, another poet who made his appearance on the literary scene at the end of the century, and who knew him personally. In an article published in *Vida Contemporânea* [*Contemporary Life*], Lopes expresses his admiration for Dantas:

> O Dantas é um romântico. Nascido e educado em plena época do romantismo, seguiu a corrente literária do tempo e foi distinto representante dessa Escola. Mas, engenho poliformo, cultivou vários géneros sem a preocupação exclusiva das chamadas Escolas Literárias.[13]

> [Dantas is a Romantic. Born and raised during the full bloom of Romanticism, he followed the literary currents of his day and was a distinguished representative of that school. But, being a man of polymorphous skills, he cultivated several genres without paying exclusive attention to any literary school.]

Two conclusions are self-evident: on the one hand, there is the absence of a literary tradition, and, on the other hand, there is the proximity of Portuguese literature. And it is precisely the proximity to Portuguese literature in those regions under Portuguese colonial domination, such as in the case of Cape Verde until independence in 1975, that permits us to seek a possible relationship between these literatures. At the same time, it is important to distinguish what makes these local literatures specific or different.

Thus it is legitimate to say that during a certain period of this "national" literature imitations of classical Portuguese texts (itself strongly influenced by classical culture) should be present, especially among the poets who wrote before the *Claridade* period. These poets admired and imitated Greek and Latin authors.

The most prominent specialists of Cape Verdean literature agree that in the work of these poets, and especially in the case of José Lopes, there is

> um anacronismo aparente que parece decorrer do seu quadro de valores e gosto e que encontra suas motivações no fundamento clássico pelas influências de ideias, trabalho de intertextualidade, atitude admirativa endereçada à alteridade, escrita literária amplificadora.[14]
>
> [an apparent anachronism that seems to stem from his set of values and tastes; the influences on his work—the intertextual allusions, the admiration he feels for the other, the exaggerated writing—find their sources in the classics.]

Alberto Carvalho affirms that

> o efeito de anacronismo que a sua irupção no século XIX pode sugerir dilui-se portanto nesta função de alicerce estabilizador, igualmente terapêutica tanto na agregação dos materiais que sincretizam a vida social como na disciplina da cena multiforme das suas variadas experiências literárias.[15]
>
> [the anachronistic effect that its appearance in the nineteenth century can suggest to us is diluted, therefore, in this function of stabilizing foundation, one that can be equally therapeutic both in the gathering of materials that synthesize social life as well as in the discipline of the multiform scene of his varied literary experiences.]

For the essayist Manuel Ferreira, it was because those poets were

> [...] prisioneiros de uma experiência oriunda do passado [e] parece terem sido incapazes de se reactualizarem, com certeza por fatalidade dos anos, do meio, do difícil acesso continuado às obras coevas, e daí a impossibilidade de motivações para a renovação estética.[16]

> [(...) prisoners of an experience that had originated in the past and seemed incapable of getting themselves up to date, surely also because of the fatalism of their advancing age, because of the environment, and because of the difficulty of getting access to work published during that time—all this explains the lack of motivation for some sort of aesthetic renewal.]

Alberto Carvalho further adds that *Hesperitanas* [*Of the Hesperides / Hesperidians*], the title of a book of poems by José Lopes, is

> aparentemente anacrónico por fazer conviver e perdurar, por enquistamento de correntes literárias, um classicismo já tardio amalgamado com tendências de escola portuguesas e europeias da segunda metade do século XIX.[17]

> [seemingly anachronistic in so far as it allows a belated classicism, already amalgamated with other tendencies in Portuguese and European literary schools of the second half of the nineteenth century, to coexist and endure besides other literary currents.]

On the other hand, maintains the same scholar,

> as suas obras (dos autores novecentistas) são exercícios de trabalho fundadores, em continuidade da escrita comunicativa e literária numa sociedade que apenas algumas décadas começara a generalizar a escolarização.

> [his works (of nineteenth-century authors) are the works of someone who was establishing a literature, and they follow directly from the sort of communicative and literary writing produced in a society where only a few decades before basic schooling had become more widespread.]

The merits of his creative efforts are open to debate.[18]

However, these same scholars also maintain that understanding this poetry aids in our understanding of Creole history. If we accept that there is a void in the tradition of writing prior to the nineteenth century, then we have to re-evaluate these authors, even though writers that have come after have questioned their intellectual stature. But they were the beginners.

The historical, cultural and literary-aesthetic context behind the poetry of these writers is certainly important. However, it is our conviction that the poetry of José Lopes, as well as that of the other poets, can take us a little farther in helping us to understand the ancestral void that was created by the fact that before they were discovered by the Portuguese there was no life on the islands. The anxiety and the anguish of an existentialist dilemma that would explain and justify the existence of the Cape Verdean as a historical and ethnic subject, a subject that, practically speaking, has no past, no memory, no history, this anxiety and the anguish assailed José Lopes throughout his life; it is also certainly evident in some of his poems. It is a legitimate existential concern.

In his search for the cultural identity and the historical origin of his "Cape Verdean brothers," the poet José Lopes wrote a long poem, included in *Hesperitanas*, a poem entitled "Minha Terra" ["My Country"], which is a poem of praise to the islands of Cape Verde. In this poem, where myth is combined with legend, José Lopes revives, from out of the far distant past, the legend of Atlantis, a legendary island that—it is believed—was located in the Atlantic, to the west of Gibraltar.

Minha Terra!
(saudação às Ilhas de Cabo-Verde)

Foi... só Deus sabe, há que milhares de anos!...
De Poseidón a Ilha ou Continente,
Maravilha dos priscos Oceanos,
Erguia sôbre o Ponto do Ocidente
Os tôpos dos seus montes soberanos.
Era imensa, formosa, viridente...
Mundo vasto, fantástico, lendário,
Segundo as mais remotas tradições,
Povoavam-na, enchiam-na milhões,
A crêrmos Diodoro de Sicília
Via-a de longe a Terra do Arsinário.

[My Country!
(praise song to the Islands of Cape Verde)

It was... only God knows, how many thousands of years ago!...
From out of Poseidon, the island or continent,

The marvel of the ancient oceans,
Raised the summits of its sovereign hills
Over the Point of the West.
It was immense, beautiful, flourishing...
A vast, fantastic, legendary world,
According to the most ancient of traditions,
It was populated, filled with millions,
And if we are to believe Diodorus Siculus
The land of Arsinarius was visible in the distance.]

This utopian island, initially mentioned by Plato, is supposed to have perished in the vast ocean during an earthquake.

The story of this mythical continent still shrouded in mystery has dazzled generations of poets and prose writers; it has become a recurrent trope in the poetic output of many. Did Atlantis really exist? Who would have inhabited this mysterious continent? How did it disappear? The more recent archaeological discoveries have not given us the definitive answer, even though clear traces of this continent have already been found and identified.[19]

It is also argued that we are not merely dealing with a lost continent. Legend has it that this was a highly advanced civilization. The islands of Cape Verde would be the remains of this mysterious continent, the heir to this thousand-year civilization. As the daughters of Hesperus they would of course be called the HESPERIDIANS, the title that J. [José] Lopes gives to his book of poetry. Or the Arsinarius islands, the island of Cape Arsinarius, so named by Strabo [Pliny—*trans.*], and by the Portuguese who changed it to Cape Verde, as is attested by Camões in *Os Lusíadas*:

Onde o Cabo Arsinário o nome perde
Chamando-se dos nossos Cabo Verde

[Where Cape Arsinarius loses its name
And which our people now call Cape Verde]
[Canto V, 7—*trans.*]

The first reference to the Hesperides occurs in Hesiod's *Theogony*; here we are told of the Hesperides, the daughters of the Night [Atlas—*trans.*], who guarded their garden in the extreme Western corner of the world; they kept watch on the golden apples that Hercules would one day come to gather.

José Lopes's knowledge of the history, myth and legend around this theme was reworked in his poem "Minha Terra," a praise poem to the islands of Cape Verde, which is none other than Atlantis "*as vastas extensões assim submersas...*" ["its vast extensions still submerged"]. He evokes the continent that thousands and thousands of years ago had succumbed "*às convulsões plutónicas*" ["to Plutonic convulsions"]; he delves into the past, and on this basis he recreates the fantastical world that had inhabited the Atlantic Ocean.

This legend is described by José Lopes in his poem in the following manner:

> Era ali o Jardim dos pomos de ouro
> (Dizem os papiros primordiais do Egipto)
> [...] Cinco ninfas, entre elas Erythea
> e Héspera, guardavam noite e dia
> O Jardim, com o auxílio de um dragão
>
> [..]
> As Hespérides, de Héspero as três filhas,
> Por essa mesma antiga tradição,
> Deram o nome às nossas, com razão
> Chamadas, pois, Ilhas Hesperitanas.
> Tambė, se denominam Arsinárias
> Pelo cabo Arsinário dos Antigos,
> Nesse mudado em Caboverdeanas.
>
> [It was there, in the garden of the golden apples
> (Or so it is said in the ancient papyri of Egypt)
> (...) Five nymphs, among them Erythea
> and Hespera, guarded the garden
> Night and day, with the help of a dragon
>
> [..]
> The Hesperides, the three daughters of Hesperus,
> According to that same ancient tradition,
> Gave the name to our isles, correctly so,
> For ours are called the Hesperidians.
> They were also named the Arsinarians

As a result of what the ancients called Cape Arsinarius,
Which has now been changed to Cape Verdean.]

José Lopes admired the classics; he would try his hand at poems in the epic mode, in the manners of Virgil and Camões. He was influenced by Camões, the greatest Portuguese epic poet, and an abiding presence in this author's work.

José Lopes dedicated a fifteen-stanza-long poem entitled "Camões"[20] to the Portuguese epic poet; here he emulates the style of the poet, develops his ideas, and portrays him as one of the greatest poets:

Entre os maiores poetas,
És o poeta maior.
Igualavas os profetas,
Sabias sentir amor!
Tu és a ave da serra
Que além das nuvens desferra
Seus vôos, longe da Terra.
Tu és a águia, o condor!

Cale-se a fama de Homero
E de Vergílio o cantar!
Camões, mais alto e sincero,
Tinha mais doce o trovar!
Era um poeta inspirado,
Tinha um génio sublimado,
Ninguém lhe foi comparado
Ninguém o pode igualar!

[Among the great poets
You are the greatest still.
You were on a par with the prophets,
You knew how to love!
You are the mountain bird
Far from the clouds
Unfolding its flights
Far from the earth.
You are an eagle, a condor!

Of no compare is Homer's fame
And Virgil's song!
Camões, loftier and more sincere,
Had the sweetest music!
He was a poet with inspiration
His skill was exalted
No one was compared to him
No one can equal him!]

Drawing on Romantic aesthetics of the nineteenth century, this author uses historical material, be it of Portuguese origin or derived from Hellenic antiquity, in long poetic works where he sings the historical deeds of different protagonists in different circumstances. The appraisal of these poems can raise the delicate problem of to which country this literature belongs. The characteristic that predominates in all of them is praise in epic proportions; he turns to European material, and to themes from Roman history, themes much in evidence in the poetic texts entitled "Úrsus e Lýgia" ["Ursus and Lygia"],[21] dated 1906, and "A Morte de César" ["Caesar's Death"], from 1910. These are poems that retell key moments in the history of ancient Rome, that is to say, (1) the time of the conspiracy that leads to the murder of the Caesar and puts an end to the dictatorship, and (2) the tumult that overwhelms the great Roman Empire as a result of the fire that razed Rome, attributed to the Emperor Nero, and the subsequent intense persecution of Christians, promoted by the emperor himself around the year 64.

In "Úrsus e Lýgia" we witness the combat between Ursus, "*o Hércules cristão, o gigantesco lygio*" ["the Christian Hercules, that gigantic Lygian"], against the ferocious lions; this occurs when he is thrown to the wild animals in the arena, in front of a "*turba-multa insana*" ["insane multitude of people"] thirsty for blood. It is an uneven combat and the tragic finale is easy to foresee. Ursus resists heroically, but his strength begins to fail him. Bloodless, he almost faints, but a miracle occurs and Ursus is able to defeat the beast and save Lygia, his protégée. The finale is a eulogy:

A turba invade o circo e arranca-os triunfantes
À arena, entre ovações e palmas retumbantes!...
Por tôda a imensa URBS as gentes aclamavam;
E, vendo-os passar, as virgens perfumavam

Os cabelos de Lygia, o meigo ser bendito,
De essências mais subtis que os bálsamos do Egipto,
Qual de um Triunfador, subindo ao Capitólio,
Na fronte majestosa o sacrossanto óleo.

[The crowd invades the circus and, amongst ovations and thundering applause,
Triumphantly drags them from the arena,
People acclaimed throughout the immense urbs;
And as they walked past virgins perfumed
Lygia's hair, that meek blessed soul,
With perfumes subtler than the balms of Egypt,
As befitting a victor, walking up the Capitol,
The sacrosanct oil on his forehead.]

The poem "A Morte de César" describes Caesar's life and that of his empire up to the time of his death. His facts, his expeditions, conquests and victories:

Foi nos idos de Março. Estava combinado
Que Bruto, Cássio e os mais matassem no Senado
A César nêsse dia. Entraram ainda cêdo.
Lenas, um Senador, aproximou-se e a mêdo
Aos ouvidos lhes disse: "*Os planos estão sabidos.*
Se hesitais um momento, estais todos perdidos...."

[It was during the ides of March. It had been arranged
That Brutus, Cassius and the rest would kill Caesar in the Senate
That day. When they arrived it was early still.
Lenas, a Senator, approached them and fearfully
Whispered in their ears: "The plans are known.
If you hesitate at all, we are all lost...."]

In sum: a more extensive study will lay bare this intellectual relationship that the poet maintained with the past, namely with Greek and Latin Antiquity. It will allow us to understand, for example, on the one hand, that underlying the classicist poetry of José Lopes are the processes of cultural *translatio*, through the transfer of elements from Graeco-Roman culture, by means of the process of *aemulatio*, and through the intellectual relationship that he maintained with classical culture, and, on the other hand, that the act of creation of his literary texts implies a confrontation with other literary texts, that is, if we situate him "in a specific tradition, be it rhetorical-stylistic, technico-literary, or thematic-literary, to which he can belong and at the same time transform or break away from."[22] A. Nascimento argues along very similar lines in an article we already have made reference to; he says that "any *translatio* is worthy of whoever performs it only if it is carried out on the basis of an *aemulatio*, so that through the *imitatio* the *melius* may be obtained. It is this agonistic attitude that characterizes the humanism of Western civilization and that which makes Quintilian (X.2.9) say that *imitari* is *contendere potius quam sequi*."[23]

Other poems by José Lopes, included among the works he published in his lifetime, reveal the poet's penchant for themes derived from classical culture. The humanism and the universality that characterize some of the poems of José Lopes, the use he makes of *imitatio*, his ease and familiarity with the great thinkers and poets of Classical antiquity, the poems in the epic mode, very much in the manner of Virgil and Camões, are all factors that permit us, without resort to any sort of subterfuge, to understand the driving lines of a poetry created at a certain time and place. Everything leads us to believe that the anachronisms were just for appearances.

Notes

[1] Even today there are some who maintain that the islands of Cape Verde were discovered and others who hold that they were found; there are arguments in favor and against the two positions. See *História Geral de Cabo Verde* 23.

[2] Ferreira, *Literaturas Africanas de Expressão Portuguesa*. In this work, the author presents an overview, as complete as possible, of the prose writers and poets who published the first texts of a literary nature, be they Cape Verdeans or Portuguese citizens of Cape Verdean origin who were either living in or outside the country.

[3] França 115. França makes reference to two writers of Cape Verdean origin, André Alvares de Almada and André Dornelas. *O Tratado Breve dos Rios da Guiné* [*Brief Treatise on the Rivers of Guinea*], dated 1594, is attributed to André Alvares de Almada, and Dornelas is credited with a description of Guinea, also from the sixteenth century. See Teixeira, A., *Dois Escritores Quinhentistas de Cabo Verde — André Alvares de Almada e André Dornelas* (Lisboa: Junta de Investigação do Ultramar, 1971).

[4] See Carvalho, "Do Classicismo ao Realismo da Claridade" 24.

[5] Carvalho, "Do Classicismo" 22.

[6] França 116.

[7] A printing press was installed in Cape Verde only in 1842, in compliance with the ordi-

nance-law of September 7, 1836. The first issue was published on August 24 of that same year. Until 1880 this government body also served the province of Guiné [Portuguese Guinea].

[8] França 120.

[9] Osório 111.

[10] Actually, these poets were never reclaimed or recovered by Portuguese literature, and their names do not figure in any history of Portuguese literature.

[11] The *Almanach de Lembranças* appeared in Lisbon around 1851, although it was made available and was read at several places where Portuguese was read and spoken. The expression "*Luso-Brasileira*" was added to the title a few years later, around 1872; this allows us to appreciate the dimension it had taken, as well as its usefulness today as a source of information about the evolution of literary and cultural forms in the countries we have referred to.

[12] See the statistical data on the peaks of greater literary production, presented by Carvalho in "Sobre o Culto de Camões, convidado das ilhas crioulas" 25.

[13] *Vida Contemporânea*, Revista mensal, nº 15 (Lisboa, Julho de 1935) 500.

[14] Carvalho, "Sobre o Culto" 35.

[15] Carvalho, "Sobre o Culto" 35.

[16] Ferreira, *Literaturas Africanas* 36.

[17] Carvalho, "Sobre o Culto" 30.

[18] Carvalho, "Sobre o Culto" 31.

[19] Recent research [1967—*trans.*] reveals the new location for Atlantis to have been Satorin (Thíra), an island in the Aegean Sea that is not much more than an arch of volcanic rock on the waters. Archaeologists have found vestiges of a highly developed society—perhaps contemporaneous with the Trojan War—in Satorin, which suddenly disappeared from Thíra some time before the largest volcanic explosion ever witnessed by the man. Today we know that an advanced society prospered on an island in Aegean Sea called Thíra... that it traded with other peoples and, all of a sudden, collapsed, the result of constant earthquakes and a devastating volcanic explosion.

[20] Lopes, *Hesperitanas* 215.

[21] This poem was reprinted in *Hesperitanas* (288), with the same title as the one with which we present it.

[22] Aguiar e Silva 34.

[23] Aguiar e Silva 34.

Works Cited

Aires, A. do Nascimento. "Os textos clássicos em período medieval: tradução como alargamento da comunidade textual." *Raízes Greco-Latinas da Cultura Portuguesa. Actas do I Congresso da APEC.* Coimbra. 1999. 35.

AAV. As Humanidades Greco-latinas e a Civilização do Universal. Actas do Congresso Internacional. Coimbra: n.p., 1988.

AAV. Revista Claridade. Praia: ICLD, 1986.

Aguiar e Silva, Vítor Manuel Pires de. *Teoria da Literatura.* Coimbra: Livraria Almedina, 1992.

Carvalho, Alberto. Prefácio. *Falucho Ancorado. Poesias.* By Manuel Lopes. Lisboa: Edições Cosmos, 1997. 11-35.

———. "Sobre o Culto de Camões, Convidado das Ilhas Crioulas." *Românica. Revista de Literatura* [Lisboa, Edições Colibri] nº 4 (1995): 25-42.

———. Do Classicismo ao Realismo da Claridade." *Camões. Revista de Letras e Culturas Lusófonas* nº1 (Abril-Junho, 1998): 20-31.

Curtius, Ernst Robert. *Literatura Europea y Edad Media Latina.* Madrid: Fondo de Cultura Economica, 1955.

Ferreira, Manuel. *A Aventura Crioula.* Lisboa: Plátano Editora, 1985.

———. *Literaturas Africanas de Expressão Portuguesa.* Lisboa: ICLP, 1986.

———. "O Mito Hesperitano ou a Nostalgia do Paraíso Perdido." *O Discurso no Percurso Africano I.* Lisboa: Plátano Editora, 1989.187-199.

———. *Reino de Caliban I.* Lisboa: Plátano Editora, 1982.

França, Arnaldo. "O Nascimento e Reconhecimento de uma Literatura em Prosa." *Cabo Verde Literatura e Insularidade.* Paris: Éditons Karthala, 1998.

História Geral de Cabo Verde. 2 vols. Lisboa: Instituto de Investigação Científica Tropical; Praia: Direcção Geral do Património Cultural de Cabo Verde [vol. 2: Lisboa: Instituto de Investigação Científica Tropical; Praia: Instituto Nacional de Cultura de Cabo Verde], 1991-1995.

Lopes, José. *Alma Arsinária.* Lisboa: n.p., 1952.

———. *Hesperitanas (Poesias).* Lisboa: Livraria J. Rodrigues, n.d. [1929?].

———. *Jardim das Hespérides.* Lisboa: Livraria J. Rodrigues, n.d. [1929?].

Osório, Oswald. "Uma Literatura Nascente: a Poesia anterior a Claridade." *Cabo Verde Literatura e Insularidade.* Paris: Éditons Karthala, 1998.

Trigo, Salvato. "Formação e Desenvolvimento das Literaturas Africanas de Língua Portuguesa." *Colóquio sobre Literaturas dos Países Africanos de Língua Portuguesa.* Lisboa: n.p., 1987.

———. "Literatura colonial/Literaturas Africanas" *Colóquio sobre Literaturas dos Países Africanos de Língua Portuguesa.* Lisboa: n.p., 1987.

Arminda Brito is a junior staff member at the Teachers' Training College in Cape Verde. She holds a bachelor's degree and is at present working on her master's degree in Comparative Literature. E-mail: britoarminda@hotmail.com

Bilinguismo Funcional: Assunção Descomplexada

Manuel Veiga

Resumo. Em Cabo Verde, a situação linguística que se vive é a de diglossia, devido ao estatuto diferenciado existente entre a língua portuguesa (Lp) e a língua caboverdiana (Lcv), a qual é reconhecida também por crioulo caboverdiano. Com efeito, a Lp é língua oficial, língua do ensino, da administração, dos mídia, do distanciamento social e das produções literárias. A Lcv, por sua vez, é língua da oralidade ambiental, do quotidiano informal, das relações de amizade, da música e com muito pouca expressão literária. O bilinguismo funcional que se pretende em Cabo Verde passa pela assunção do estatuto oficial, do uso formal e informal das duas línguas, em ambiente de inteira liberdade de opção, em paridade de circunstâncias e igualdade de oportunidades. O presente trabalho explicita a situação linguística que neste momento vigora em Cabo Verde e aponta a visão do futuro que, no campo linguístico, melhor se adequa ao País.

1. Contexto Linguístico

A formação da cultura caboverdiana processou-se num laboratório onde a presença da língua caboverdiana (Lcv) e da língua portuguesa (Lp) foi decisiva.

A identidade de que hoje nos orgulhamos resulta, pois, do confronto, dos reencontros e do labor secular destes dois importantes instrumentos de comunicação: a Lcv que emergiu do génio criador do nosso povo e a Lp que, numa determinada fase, começou por ser imposta e que agora está sendo assumida como um espaço complementar na formação e actualização do nosso ser e estar no mundo.

No longínquo século XV vieram para Cabo Verde os vários dialectos do português, sobretudo do Norte, do Sul e das ilhas adjacentes. Vieram também os vários falares da costa ocidental da África. Desde logo, verificou-se o peso numérico do contingente negro, sendo duas as circunstâncias que impediram a imposição das suas línguas. Primeiro, porque, apesar dos negros serem em grande número, muitas vezes a sua presença na ilha de Santiago, berço primeiro da Lcv, era transitória, durando, quase sempre, o tempo necessário para a ladinização, no termo do qual seguiam a rota da escravatura, umas vezes para a Europa e outras vezes para as Américas. A segunda circunstância está ligada à juventude da maioria dos escravos e à multiplicidade étnico-linguística dos mesmos. Sendo jovens, possuíam uma estrutura linguística ainda pouco cimentada e, portanto, muito susceptível a transformações ou até ao esquecimento. Pertencendo a várias etnias, em que nenhuma era maioritária,[1] seria difícil a imposição de uma das línguas étnicas.

Quanto à língua do dominador, havia em seu desfavor a fraca representatividade (o número dos brancos era reduzidíssimo, segundo o historiador A. Carreira), o baixo nível cultural dos colonos, sendo a maioria analfabeta, e ainda a ausência ou a exiguidade de instrumentos e de políticas de imposição cultural como escolas, liceus, universidades, professores, material didáctico, etc.

A finalidade primeira da dominação, sendo mais económica do que cultural, favoreceu o surgimento de uma cultura mestiça em que a língua caboverdiana é um dos elementos mais eloquentes.

Os dialectos portugueses, pelo seu lado, sem a força nem os instrumentos de imposição, foram conquistando, pouco a pouco, a unidade e construindo a sua própria estandardização, mas sem força para impor a exclusividade do seu código e da sua gramática.

É neste contexto de pluralidade étnica, de peso demográfico do negro, da diversidade dialéctica e incultura académica do dominador branco que a língua caboverdiana encontrou condições favoráveis para o seu nascimento. Nesse nascimento, porém, o recém-nascido teve, quase sempre, uma mãe africana e um pai europeu. Daí o espaço complementar que gerou a língua caboverdiana e que moldou e vem moldando a nossa cultura e a nossa identidade.

2. Estatuto da Lp

A língua portuguesa, em Cabo Verde, começou por ser, na época dos descobrimentos, um conjunto de falares dialectais que trazia o cunho das diversas regiões a que pertenciam os senhores e colonos portugueses.

Presumimos que, na altura, a expressão regional pouco contava como índice social de classe. O facto de, no século XVIII, segundo o relato de um escritor anónimo haver muitos portugueses que se acostumavam "ao estilo do falar da terra"[2] (entenda-se crioulo caboverdiano) esquecendo-se do português reinol, é uma prova inequívoca de que o peso dos falares portugueses da época contava, ao que parece, tanto quanto o das variantes do crioulo nascente.

Segundo algumas opiniões, é sobretudo a partir da criação do Seminário-Liceu de S. Nicolau, em 1886, que a língua portuguesa não só ficou mais unificada e mais consolidada, como também passou a ter um prestígio social mais relevante. Parece ser particularmente o magistério dessa altura que baptizou o português como língua de educação, de prestígio e de cultura e reconheceu o estatuto que então considerava o Crioulo como deturpação da língua de Camões, como algaraviada sem regra nem gramática e que representava um perigo para a unidade do Império.[3] Da segunda metade do século XIX até à presente data, o prestígio do português não deixou de aumentar e de se consolidar, particularmente no seio da elite: professores, escritores, comerciantes, empregados administrativos, profissionais liberais e mesmo alguns analfabetos endinheirados. A educação da época, o discurso colonial, a literatura luso-tropical, a comunicação social engajada com o sistema colonial foram os melhores instrumentos desse prestígio, em detrimento da então chamada língua de pretos, de cafres e de ignorantes.

Se até ao século XIX o português foi, em Cabo Verde, uma das línguas de comunicação, a partir dessa altura ele passou a ser, de forma exclusiva, língua de prestígio, de cultura e de civilização. Tal estatuto foi-se reforçando com a implementação da política de educação, nomeadamente com o aumento de escolas, criação de liceus e oferta de bolsas para a frequência de instituições académicas na então Metrópole. Os alunos foram estudando e o gráfico de prestígio do português sempre em notória ascendência.

Com a conquista da Independência Nacional, o prestígio do português deixa de ser uma questão apenas colonial para se transformar numa prática que tem também as bênçãos da própria Nação independente. Com efeito, o português que já era língua oficial de prestígio, durante o período de dominação, continuou com esse mesmo estatuto no pós-Independência. Muito célebre é a frase do histórico Amílcar Cabral que diz: "a melhor coisa que os tugas nos deixaram é a sua língua." Interpretando, possivelmente, de forma distorcida esta asserção de Cabral, outros homens célebres dessas nossas ilhas declararam ou têm declarado que, possuindo eles uma língua de civilização, como é o português, já não precisam, para a criação das sua obras, de uma língua como o Crioulo que não passa de um instrumento menor o qual não só limita como também restringe a comunicação, o mercado artístico, científico e cultural.

Hoje, não só a elite, mas também a grande massa do nosso povo reconhece a importância e o prestígio do português. Basta ver que os pais querem que os filhos estudem essa língua e muitos ainda desejam que os mesmos consigam uma bolsa para estudar em Portugal.

A razão de tudo isto é histórica, com certeza, mas também é conjuntural: o ensino, a administração, a comunicação social, a literatura têm particular expressão e representatividade na língua que Fernando Pessoa considerou a sua pátria e que outros cunharam como a pátria comum dos que em cinco continentes a utilizam.

Pode-se perguntar se o prestígio da língua portuguesa em Cabo Verde é um bem ou um mal. Claro que é um bem. Ninguém, minimamente informado, pode, honestamente, negar o valor comunicativo, cultural e civilizacional do português. Se algo está errado nesse processo de afirmação da língua portuguesa é a política de exclusão e de discriminação relativamente à língua caboverdiana. Como o português, também o caboverdiano é uma língua de civilização em Cabo Verde e com maior direito de cidadania, pela simples razão que é a nossa língua nacional, a língua da nossa vivência, a língua que melhor moldou e molda o que de mais profundo existe na nossa maneira de ser e de estar, a língua ainda que nasceu com o nascimento do nosso povo, "lágrima a lágrima, dor a dor, amor a amor," diria Ovídio Martins, poeta da resistência cultural e da crioulidade ambiental.

3. Estatuto da Língua Caboverdiana

Apesar da sua funcionalidade linguística e da sua utilidade (informal) abrangente, o estatuto social da língua caboverdiana teve um processo de afirmação irregular e problemático. Parece que até meados do século XIX os falantes da Lcv se preocupavam mais com a funcionalidade linguística da Lcv do que com o seu estatuto social. Talvez seja esta a razão por que os negros, os mestiços e muitos brancos tinham-na como instrumento privilegiado de comunicação. Somente alguns cultores e puristas do português tinham medo que a Lcv pudesse representar uma ameaça para a Lp. Daí a razão por que alguns de entre eles chegaram a escrever para o rei de Portugal manifestando-lhe as suas preocupações face à situação linguística reinante onde até os brancos se tinham acostumado ao "estilo da terra,"[4] esquecendo-se do português.

Porque será que até os brancos deram preferência à Lcv, a ponto de se esquecerem da sua própria língua? Só podemos encontrar a resposta na força social e comunicativa do tal falar existente, entenda-se língua caboverdiana.

Vê-se que a Lcv, pelo menos durante os primeiros tempos, tinha um estatuto linguístico de utilidade reconhecida pela maioria dos utentes. Porém, a partir da segunda metade do século XIX as coisas complicaram-se com o aumento de escolas oficiais, particularmente com a criação do Seminário-Liceu de S. Nicolau. Foi sobretudo a partir de então que o estatuto de "estilo da terra" começou a dar lugar a outros estatutos de carácter mais valorativo do que funcional. É assim que a Lcv é cada vez mais estigmatizada como deturpação da língua portuguesa, como algaraviada ridícula, sem regras nem gramática, como mixórdia de línguas africanas e do português antigo, como idioma o mais perverso e corrupto, como dialecto ridículo e atentado à unidade do Império.[5]

O estatuto de dialecto ridículo, sem regras nem gramática prevaleceu, junto de alguma elite letrada, até à Independência Nacional, ocorrida em 1975. A partir de então, com a onda do espírito nacionalista sempre crescente, a Lcv foi oficialmente declarada língua materna e nacional do povo de Cabo Verde.

Não obstante, no espírito de muitos intelectuais, cultores e puristas do português, a Lcv continua a não servir para a literatura e para as ciências. O estatuto que nela reconhecem é o de língua do amor e do coração cuja afirmação, segundo alguns ainda, afecta, negativamente, a língua portuguesa.

O estatuto da Lcv como língua de civilização foi defendida na segunda metade do século XIX por António de Paula Brito; na primeira metade do século XX por Eugénio Tavares e Pedro Cardoso; na segunda metade do século XX por alguns poetas, trovadores, compositores, músicos e investigadores.

É também no final do século XX que algumas vozes começaram a defender para a Lcv o estatuto de língua oficial, em paridade com o português. Tal reconhecimento não foi ainda alcançado. Porém, as perspectivas são encorajadoras. Com efeito, aumentou o número dos que defendem o estatuto civilizacional da Lcv; o Governo começou a tomar medidas que vão ao encontro da afirmação da Lcv, como a política do ensino (cf. Art. 3º da Resolução 8/98, BO nº 10, de 16 de Março), a aprovação experimental do alfabeto (decreto-lei nº67/98, BO nº48, de 31 de Dezembro), a criação de condições para a oficialização da Lcv constantes no Programa do Governo (BO nº12, de 30/4/96).

De igual modo, a investigação e alguns estudos universitários de nacionais e de estrangeiros têm aumentado nos últimos tempos. Refira-se, a título de exemplos, os trabalhos de Dulce Duarte, de Tomé Varela, de Donaldo Macedo, de Marlyse Baptista, de Isione Silva, de Deirdre Meintel, de Manuel Veiga e de estrangeiros como Dulce Pereira, Jügen Lang e Nicolas Quint.

Do ponto de vista político, as declarações são cada vez mais favoráveis. O PAICV tem defendido, nos últimos tempos (revisão constitucional 1999), a oficialização da língua caboverdiana e o MpD a criação de condições que permitam essa mesma oficialização.

Não há dúvidas de que a «hora» da língua caboverdiana está chegando. Todos os indicadores sociais, culturais e políticos vão neste sentido. Porém, não esperemos só para ver, como dizia o Tomé da Bíblia. Ajamos todos para que assim seja. E isto passa por aquilo que damos o nome de:

4. Construção de um Bilinguismo Funcional

Em Cabo Verde, o português tem sido língua das situações especiais. Em linguística diríamos que ele é língua das situações formais de comunicação. Com efeito, apesar do seu prestígio, ele está ainda longe de ser a língua do nosso quotidiano ambiental. O seu uso restringe-se a uma minoria da nossa população—a elite cultural e económica—e, mesmo junto dessa camada social, a comunicação em português acontece somente a determinados níveis e em determinadas circunstâncias. É assim que, a nível do ensino formal, da comunicação escrita, da literatura, da administração e dos mídia, o uso do português não só é mais frequente como também é muito mais representativo do que o da língua caboverdiana. A nível da oralidade, o emprego do português é pouco representativo, mesmo junto da elite cultural e económica. Ele restringe-se, muitas vezes, a situações de formalidade: entre pessoas desconhecidas ou de pouca familiaridade, quando se pretende exibir o nível cultural ou a superioridade da classe a que se pertence.

Mesmo somando todos os níveis de comunicação escrita e todas as situações de oralidade formal, a percentagem do uso do português não deve atingir a percentagem de 20% do quotidiano da elite cultural e económica que, como já dissemos, representa uma minoria no universo demográfico caboverdiano. Além disso, é preciso ter em conta que no seio da elite cultural e económica, o número dos que sabem fazer uso correcto do português não é elevado.

Ora, tendo o português o prestígio que tem, prestígio esse reconhecido por toda a população; ciente do seu valor instrumental e civilizacional; sabendo ainda que se trata de uma língua com mais de cinco séculos de existência em Cabo Verde e que moldou uma parte do nosso ser e estar no mundo, é de se perguntar se o estatuto que actualmente tem é o que melhor nos convém. A resposta é negativa. O estatuto apenas formal do português é demasiadamente redutor. Urge a construção de um outro estatuto mais consentâneo com a história da Lp em Cabo Verde, com o seu valor civilizacional e o seu poder instrumental.

Tudo isto para dizer que o português é uma língua em construção em Cabo Verde. Tal construção significa: alargar o seu conhecimento efectivo à população; para além do estatuto oficial e formal que já tem, conferir-lhe o estatuto de língua de oralidade informal, em paridade com o caboverdiano. Por outras palavras, trata-se da assunção descomplexada do bilinguismo através de uma política linguística sem concorrência desleal, sem discriminação, sem tentativas glotofagistas, sem a prática da diglossia.

Se a Lp se encontra na fase de construção em Cabo Verde, o mesmo se pode dizer em relação à Lcv. Porém, trata-se de níveis diferentes de construção. Enquanto a Lp precisa de rigor pedagógico, alargamento do ensino formal e de implementação do estatuto informal, a Lcv precisa da implementação do ensino formal, do reconhecimento do estatuto oficial e alargamento do seu uso formal.

Em resumo, ao português que já é língua oficial e de situações formais de comunicação, torna-se necessário alargar o seu ensino e conferir-lhe o estatuto de língua veicular e do quotidiano informal, em paridade com a Lcv. Quanto à Lcv que já é língua veicular e do quotidiano informal, há que reconhecer-lhe o estatuto oficial em paridade com a Lp, reforçar o seu uso formal e implementar o seu ensino, do primário ao universitário.

Agindo deste modo, estaremos não só a assumir como também a construir um bilinguismo funcional em Cabo Verde. Tal política linguística é uma exigência da nossa história, da nossa cultura e da nossa identidade. Ninguém pode ignorar que tanto a Lp como a Lcv, embora de formas diferentes, corporizam a nossa história, enformam a nossa cultura e moldam o nosso modo de estar no mundo. A afirmação e a valorização dessas duas línguas, mais do que um dever cívico, é uma exigência cultural e uma necessidade ambiental.

Por isso, aqui fica o nosso apelo aos governantes, aos políticos, aos professores, aos escritores e artistas, aos tradicionalistas e à população em geral: assumamos, descomplexadamente, o bilinguismo caboverdiano. Façamos da Lcv e da Lp os veículos e os suportes complementares do nosso estar e do nosso devir num mundo que se pretende cada vez mais global, mais integral e mais humano. No dizer de alguém[6], que teve grandes responsabilidades na cena política caboverdiana, isto "(...)será uma revolução, mas valerá a pena, custe o que custar e (...) não custará muito porque as vantagens serão incomensuravelmente superiores aos custos."

Notas

[1] António Carreira, *Cabo Verde—Formação e Extinção de uma Sociedade Escravocrata,* (Lisboa: Centro de Estudos da Guiné Portuguesa, 1972) 310.

[2] Idem 1, *Notícias Corográficas e Chronológicas do Bispado de Cabo Verde* (Praia: ICLD, 1985) 27.

[3] Idem 1, Ibidem 131 (NB: conf.).

[4] Idem, Ibidem 2.

[5] Manuel Ferreira, *A Aventura Crioula* (Lisboa: Plátano Editora, 1973) 27-133.

[6] Carlos Veiga, *A Semana* 394, 12 de Março de 1999.

Manuel Veiga é escritor e trabalha no Instituto Nacional de Investigação Cultural (Cabo Verde). Alguns artigos publicados: "A língua caboverdiana", em *Africana*, número especial sobre Cabo Verde, Universidade Portucalense, 1993; "La Langue des îles," em *Notre Librairie* 112, Paris, CLEF, 1993; "Morphosyntaxe des adjectifs dans le créole du Cap-Vert" em *Matériaux pour l'étude des classes grammaticales dans les langues créole* (ed. D. Véronique) Université d'Aix-en-Provence, 1996. Tem vários outros artigos publicados em revistas como: *Oceanos*, em Portugal; *Pen Internacional*, em Londres; *MI* do Museu Etnográfico de Rotterdam; *Fragmentos*, Cabo Verde; *Pré-Textos*, Cabo Verde; *Kultura*, Cabo Verde; *Cimboa*, Boston; e revista electrónica *Ciberkiosk*, Universidade de Coimbra.

Escrever em crioulo: *un kaminhu lonji*

Dulce Pereira

Resumo. É importante não confundir escrita com transcrição gráfica nem com ortografia quando se pretende definir o modo de escrever uma língua de tradição oral, como o caboverdiano. A distância em relação ao contexto situacional e a sua existência como objecto observável fazem com que a escrita obedeça a um conjunto de princípios que incluem a explicitação, a coesão e a coerência e obrigam à economia e diversidade de meios linguísticos.
O léxico é uma das áreas em que, feito o levantamento do acervo linguístico existente, é obrigatório inovar. A identificação dos processos de derivação e dos afixos mais produtivos (de que se dão exemplos) constitui, a par de outros recursos como o empréstimo, um instrumento fundamental para o enriquecimento do caboverdiano, sem se cair no excesso fácil de decalcar o modelo de escrita da língua de contacto.

Quando se fala de escrever em crioulo é muito vulgar a confusão entre representação gráfica e ortografia, por um lado, e entre ortografia e escrita, por outro. Todo o caboverdiano que tenha sido alfabetizado numa outra língua poderá transcrever a sua com um pequeno esforço de adaptação. Durante anos, e já desde o século XIX, houve em Cabo Verde tradição de escrita espontânea em crioulo. Ao mesmo tempo, particularmente após a independência, foram surgindo convenções de representação gráfica que permitiram, nomeadamente, a transcrição de documentos de tradição oral. Actualmente, existe mesmo uma ortografia definida por decreto,[1] ainda que em período experimental.

A grande diferença entre a ortografia e as outras formas de representação está na obrigatoriedade das suas convenções. O falante habituado a escrever "à sua moda," tendo como referente a língua de alfabetização (que, em Cabo Verde, é o português), sente-se em geral inseguro perante a ortografia imposta, sobretudo se não lhe forem proporcionados contextos formais de aprendizagem. Dessa insegurança resulta uma inibição que leva muitos caboverdianos alfabetizados a dizer que não sabem escrever crioulo, quando, na verdade, já frequentemente o fizeram, embora fora das normas ortográficas. No pólo oposto, estão aqueles que confundem ortografia com escrita e que, pelo simples facto de dominarem um alfabeto, julgam, apressadamente, que dominam também a escrita crioula.

Ora, como sabemos, entre a oralidade e a escrita vai uma grande distância.

A Distância

Uma das propriedades distintivas da linguagem humana actual (que a diferencia de estádios linguísticos filogeneticamente anteriores, provavelmente muito próximos em termos estruturais de um jargão e de um *pidgin*), é a sua independência do contexto: a capacidade de ***distanciação*** em relação ao aqui e agora, de referência a situações e objectos ausentes, hipotéticos ou mesmo fictícios.

Embora a escrita não seja uma faculdade biologicamente programada, mas antes uma forma facultativa e socialmente convencionada de representar a linguagem oral, tem um papel primordial no desenvolvimento dos mecanismos linguísticos de distanciação, ao mesmo tempo que produz mudanças de ordem cognitiva naqueles que a dominam.

A opção pela escrita surge, em geral, como meio de comunicar *in absentia*, o que obriga à explicitação de informações que não podem ser facultadas pelo contexto imediato. Contudo, não é tanto a necessidade de explicitação que afasta a escrita da oralidade, mas antes o grau de explicitação exigido.

Considere-se o seguinte exemplo :

Omi dja tchiga
O homem já chegou

Num contexto oral, *omi* refere-se, ou a um homem presente, ou a um homem conhecido do interlocutor. Num contexto de escrita, só a segunda hipótese é aceitável. No entanto, dado que não é possível controlar a receptividade do interlocutor, a tendência será para explicitar o que, na oralidade, fica pressuposto, identificando inequivocamente o homem em referência (*kel omi ki bu nkontra ku el na Praia, kel omi ki staba duenti...*: port.: *o homem com quem te encontraste na Praia, aquele homem que estava doente*) e, eventualmente, o local de chegada (*Purtugal, kasa* ... port.: *a Portugal, a casa*). A mesma informação é assim codificada por intermédio de um número consideravelmente maior de unidades lexicais e de estruturas gramaticais, a que vem acrescentar-se o facto de a palavra ter de suprir a informação veiculada, na oralidade, pela prosódia (entoação, intensidade da voz...).

Por outro lado, como afirma William Foley (1997: 39), "the feature of reflexivity is generally claimed to be a crucial defining feature of language and to be unique to human language." Ora, o carácter permanente da escrita torna-a, uma vez produzida, num objecto observável e criticável, pelo que a propriedade da metalinguagem é aqui activada de um modo muito especial, permitindo reflectir sobre as formas de codificação que garantem uma maior coincidência entre intenção de comunicação e interpretação e, ao mesmo tempo, estabelecer critérios de coesão e coerência textual e de ordem estética.

Um dos aspectos mais facilmente observáveis pelo escritor-leitor é o de que a explicitação se traduz em maior extensão textual e pode conduzir à redundância. Além da planificação, torna-se, pois, necessário desenvolver mecanismos que tornem o texto mais compacto e favoreçam, sem perda de clareza e de expressividade, a sua economia e fluidez.

O novo modo de comunicação verbal determina, deste modo, soluções adaptativas de carácter lexical, gramatical e textual.

Dissemos que entre oralidade e escrita ia uma grande distância. Noutra perspectiva, poderíamos afirmar o contrário, tal como Finnegan, R. (1988, 175)[2]:

> "Orality" and "literacy" are not two separate and independent things; nor (to put it more concretely) are oral and written modes two mutually exclusive and opposed processes for representing and communicating information. On the contrary they take diverse forms in differing cultures and periods, are used differently in different social contexts, and, insofar as they can be distinguished at all as separate modes rather than a ***continuum***,[3] they mutually interact and affect each other, and the relations between them are problematic rather than self-evident.

Na verdade, a fronteira entre a oralidade e a escrita nem sempre é fácil de traçar: uma *storia storia*,[4] mil vezes contada, embora sendo um texto oral, tem um grau de planificação, de explicitude e de coerência que a aproximam muito do texto escrito, tal como a mensagem breve escrita a um familiar sobre um tema rotineiro do quotidiano pouco se afasta do discurso oral. No entanto, quando se procura criar condições de passagem à escrita de uma língua de tradição oral, como o crioulo de Cabo Verde, convém, por razões metodológicas, considerar os extremos (prototípicos) do *contínuo* de modo a poder responder à questão fundamental:

> o que é que falta ao crioulo oral, do quotidiano, para poder ser escrito (e não meramente transcrito) de uma forma explícita e rigorosa, e ao mesmo tempo com fluência, economia, expressividade e diversidade estilística?

Cada um dos aspectos mencionados desdobra-se em mútiplas e complexas dimensões. A sua definição implica um trabalho meticuloso, aturado e cujo resultado deverá sempre ser sujeito ao reconhecimento social. Procuraremos abordar adiante apenas algumas dimensões de dois dos aspectos fundamentais: a economia (através da condensação) e a diversidade.

Não focaremos aqui a questão da ortografia, embora valha a pena referir que uma ortografia não é só um conjunto de grafemas e diacríticos para representar os sons da língua. Uma ortografia implica decisões de normalização, nomeadamente quanto à forma das palavras (os seus limites e a variante fónica adoptada como referente). Se há palavras que são "óbvias" como *nunka* (port.: *nunca*) ou *da* (port.: *dar*), outras são problemáticas. É o caso de *unbes* (*un bes*?). *Un bes* pode significar *uma vez* tratando-se, neste caso, indubitavelmente, de duas palavras (o artigo indefinido *un* e o substantivo *bes*). Mas a mesma expressão fónica pode ganhar um valor adverbial, significando, neste caso, *antigamente*. Será, então, mais correctamente grafada como uma palavra só. O mesmo poderíamos dizer da expressão interrogativa kuzé? que aparece frequentemente grafada como *kuz'é*? (de *kuza* é, port.: *o que é?*). E como escrever a palavra que significa *casa*, dado que existem duas variantes: *kasa* e *kaza*?

Uma vez tomadas as decisões de ordem gráfica, que implicam, não só a escolha de variantes fonéticas, mas também a análise e classificação gramatical das expressões linguísticas, para responder à questão acima formulada, relativamente à criação de condições para uma escrita plena do crioulo, é então necessário comparar os recursos existentes com os que se supõe serem necessários para a referida escrita.

Caminho *pertu*

Numa comunidade como a caboverdiana, em que o crioulo está em contacto com uma língua com largos séculos de tradição escrita (o português) que foi sempre a língua oficial e de alfabetização dos caboverdianos, é natural que haja uma tendência para tornar o *kaminhu* menos *lonji* e fazer uma transposição directa das estruturas sintácticas e do léxico (nomeadamente o de ligação textual) mais usado na escrita em português para a escrita em crioulo.

Veja-se o seguinte excerto da *Prizentason* da obra de Tomé Varela da Silva, *Na Bóka Noti* (1987: 9,10)[5]:

> *Voltandu a* (d) stórias *d'es libru* (a), k'e tirseru di kuleson "Tradisons Oral di Kauberdi," *nu kre avansa ses distribuson* (d) k'e fetu *di siginti manera* (d): [...]. *E posivi ki, na rakódjas inda pa fase, otus siklu ben raveladu* (c). *Si sin* (d), disertéza nu ta konkordadu ku el m'e mas rikéza di nos kultura oral ki ta ividensiadu.
> *Na ordenason di stórias* (a), *kirtéri ki nortia-nu* (b) e di koloka djuntu o pértu kes semelhanti. *Di li ki* (d) *nu organiza-s* (b) en kapitu y, dentu di kada kapitu, di akordu ku grau di semelhansa.

Seguindo de muito perto o texto crioulo, obtemos, como tradução:

> *Voltando às* (d) *estórias deste livro* (a), que é o terceiro da colecção "Tradições Orais de Cabo Verde," *queremos adiantar já a sua distribuição* (d), que é feita *da seguinte maneira* (d): [...]. *É possível que, nas recolhas ainda por fazer, outros ciclos venham a ser revelados* (c). *Se sim* (d), por certo se concordará que é mais uma riqueza da nossa cultura oral a ser evidenciada.
> *Na ordenação das estórias* (a), o *critério que nos norteou* (b) foi o de colocar junto ou perto as semelhantes. *Daí que* (d) as *tenhamos organizado*(b) em capítulos, de acordo com o grau de semelhança.

É fácil verificar aqui, à semelhança do que acontece com muitos textos em prosa de outros autores, que existe uma colagem entre a estrutura textual portuguesa e a crioula. O próprio léxico, em grande parte, só se diferencia pela forma fónica que a grafia deixa adivinhar (*kapitu, siklu, kuleson, distribuson, ividensiadu*). Sabemos, neste caso, que o fenómeno não decorre do processo de tradução em si, mas antes da projecção que o autor faz dos seus hábitos de escrita em português sobre a construção textual em crioulo, tal como o evidenciam as expressões sublinhadas, em que as assinaladas com (a), dizem respeito a referências ao próprio texto e à sua produção, com (b), a situações ou opções de planificação anteriores ao texto e com (c), a situações a ele subsequentes. O mesmo acontece com as expressões marcadas com (d), que fazem a ligação intratextual remetendo para pontos anteriores (*voltandu a...*), ou posteriores (*di siginti manera...*), reforçando conexões ou estabelecendo dependências lógicas (*Si sin, di li ki...*).

Poderemos considerar que a projecção da língua portuguesa, pelo menos em alguns aspectos, não foi automática e que o autor procurou recursos lexicais e de condensação textual que, aparentemente, não encontrou na sua língua. Tratar-se-ia então de uma questão de necessidade e não de mera facilidade. Na verdade, é frequente a importação, por razões funcionais e culturais, i.e., para resolver necessidades de nomeação de realidades novas (objectos e conceitos), de um léxico referencial não básico. Já nos seus *Apontamentos para a Gramática do Crioulo* que se fala na ilha de Santiago de Cabo Verde (elaborada em 1885 e publicada em 1887), A. de Paula Brito introduzia termos como *gramátika, silba, letra sijelu, letra dobradu, bogal, kõsuãti, gudu, subistãtibu, dijetibu*, fenómeno que Adolfo Coelho explicava, no prefácio, deste modo:

> Quis o senhor A. de Paula Brito redigir a sua gramática em crioulo, o que levou necessariamente a forjar diversos termos gramaticais, sem dúvida guiando-se pelas tendências de adaptação crioula, mas os quais o leitor facilmente distinguirá do que é verdadeiramente popular-crioulo.

Resta apurar "o que é verdadeiramente popular-crioulo" e, acima de tudo, quais os recursos disponíveis. Numa língua de tradição oral, como a crioula, a passagem à escrita revela sempre vazios lexicais que é necessário colmatar recorrendo, não apenas à língua de contacto, mas, sempre que possível, a processos internos à própria língua. Isto, se se considerar que a identidade e autonomia do crioulo merecem ser preservadas em algo mais que a aparência fónica.[6]

Recursos Lexicais: Diversidade e Economia

Analisemos mais de perto alguns aspectos lexicais, uma vez que o léxico (tanto referencial como gramatical) pode ser fonte da diversidade e da economia que nos propusemos tratar.

A diversidade lexical tem duas vertentes fundamentais: a sinonímia (diferentes formas de dizer *quase* o mesmo) e a extensão ou "riqueza" (quantidade de vocábulos para o mesmo campo semântico e quantidade de campos semânticos contemplados). Por outro lado, o léxico contribui para a economia no processamento verbal, uma vez que pode traduzir expressões perifrásticas numa só unidade, ao mesmo tempo que, favorecendo a sintatização (através da ligação e do encaixe de orações), permite o apagamento de informações redundantes. É o caso da palavra crioula *bador/badera* que concentra numa unidade a informação que, em português, só uma longa expressão consegue transmitir: "aquele ou aquela que tem por hábito ir."[7]

Como em todas as línguas, o crioulo caboverdiano actual tem já no seu léxico inúmeros sinónimos. Eis alguns exemplos, retirados ao acaso dos dicionários de Quint-Abrial (1998) e de Napoleão Fernandes (1990):

Andador, andexu, bágu, vunga-vunga (port.: *viajante, vagabundo, nómada); kati-kati, frutxi-frutxi:* (port.: *fadiga, afadigar-se); marlita, frunku, spinhu:* (port.: *furúnculo); txanbu, nhakri:* (port.: *provinciano, campónio, pacóvio).*

Também os encontramos no léxico gramatical, embora em menor número:

Kantu,sima (port.: *quando); pabia, pakê* (port.: *porquê); pamodi, purke* (port.: *porque); sikre, sime ki* (port.: *mesmo que).*

Uma das tendências do ser humano, na sua reflexão sobre o objecto escrito, é rejeitar a repetição excessiva ou demasiado próxima de uma mesma estrutura ou palavra (excepto quando a repetição é voluntariamente adoptada como processo retórico). A sinonímia, para além da possibilidade de codificar diferenças conotativas com valor estilístico, permite resolver esse princípio de não repetição. Um falante português tem à sua disposição, para a coordenação adversativa, os conectores *mas, porém, todavia, contudo* que poderá alternar ao longo do texto. Também na língua crioula se poderá, nas orações causais, alternar entre *pamodi* e *purke.* No entanto, nem todos os falantes dominam as diferentes variantes. Por exemplo, a forma crioula *purke* é mais antiga e normalmente pouco utilizada por falantes alfabetizados das zonas urbanas. Para garantir a diversidade, urge, pois, recuperar todas as formas ainda disponíveis na língua e consagrá-las, através da sua inclusão, descrição e classificação em léxicos e gramáticas oficiais e também através do ensino. Talvez deste modo se torne menos necessário o recurso intempestivo a formas decalcadas do português, do tipo *pur kauza di, purisu ki...* O mesmo poderíamos dizer para todos os subsistemas gramaticais, sendo o levantamento das formas crioulas existentes, neste caso, tarefa relativamente fácil, dado que o léxico gramatical, ao contrário do referencial, é um conjunto fechado.

Uma outra área a explorar é a do léxico de ligação textual que estabelece relações entre partes do texto (e não meramente entre orações) como os períodos e os parágrafos. O facto de o texto escrito ser um objecto analisável e reformulável permite, como vimos, melhorar o seu *tecido*, recorrendo a expressões de conexão. A língua portuguesa é rica em elementos deste tipo.[8] Em contrapartida, em crioulo de Cabo Verde, mesmo nos contos tradicionais (*storia storia*) que, como dissémos, são talvez as formas de discurso oral que mais se aproximam, no contínuo, do discurso escrito (apesar de, em grande parte, assumirem a forma de discurso directo e de diálogo), poucas são as expressões de ligação textual que encontramos. Por exemplo, numa das estórias transcritas em *Na Bóka Noti* (estória 38: 168-171), só pudémos encontrar quatro dessas expressões (*di maneras, agora/ago/go, dipos, anton*; port.: *de maneira que, ora/agora, depois, então*). Embora se imponha um levantamento exaustivo prévio, é de esperar que seja necessário inovar nesta área lexical.

A passagem à escrita de uma língua oral obriga também ao alargamento do léxico referencial pois, como vimos, quando escrevemos, a distância em relação ao contexto, a necessidade de explicitação, o desejo de garantir a coincidência entre a intenção comunicativa e a interpretação do leitor, a ocorrência de temas novos e o desejo de diversidade e de não repetição determinam a procura de palavras "certas" que transmitam com precisão os conceitos a veicular.

Possuirá o crioulo léxico referencial para todas estas exigências? Também aqui se impõe, tal como propõe M. C. Hazaël-Massieux (1993), um inventário e uma análise lexical, do ponto de vista das famílias de palavras, das áreas vocabulares e dos campos semânticos.

Comparemos, em dois dicionários, um português e outro crioulo, o conjunto de entradas que constituem parte da família da palavra "escrever" e da palavra "skrebe":

> Português[9]*: Escrevedor, escrevedura, escrevente, escrever, escrevinhador, escrevinhadura, escrevinhar, escriba, escribomania, escrínio, escrita, escrito, escritor, escritório, escritura, escrituração, escriturar, escriturário, escrivã, escrivania, escrivaninha, escrivão.*
> Crioulo[10]*: skrebi , skritura.*

Transcrevemos, no português, apenas as palavras derivadas por sufixação, a que poderíamos acrescentar outras, derivadas por prefixação, como *inscrever, reescrever, transcrever*, etc... Embora possam existir, tanto em crioulo como em português, outras palavras não registadas nos dicionários escolhidos,[11] e apesar de nem todas as palavras portuguesas referidas serem usadas com a mesma frequência (das 2217 palavras listadas, no *Português* Fundamental, como mais frequentes, só três se referem à escrita—*escrever, escritor e escritório*), ainda assim é óbvia a desproporção entre o léxico disponível nas duas línguas, neste domínio: a vinte e duas palavras portuguesas correspondem apenas duas crioulas, nas listas citadas.

Tudo leva a crer que o hábito de escrever em crioulo venha a desencadear a necessidade de reflectir sobre a escrita e os vários escritos, bem como de nomear os tipos de pessoas que escrevem, os meios utilizados para o fazer e as profissões que lhe estão associadas. Muitos dos conceitos veiculados pelas palavras portuguesas e que não têm ainda correspondente lexical em crioulo poderão ser expressos, de imediato, através de perífrases: "Escritor": *Kel ki ta skrebe libru* ("Aquele que escreve livros"),

"Escrevinhador: *Kel ki ta skrebe kusas kabali, kel ki ta riska papel manenti* ("Aquele que escreve coisas sem valor, aquele que está sempre a rabiscar"), "Escrivaninha": *Mesa undi ki ta skrebedu* ("Mesa em que se escreve"), mas este processo leva a uma dispersão sintagmática que, não acrescentando rigor nem capacidade de explicitação, desfavorece a economia e a velocidade de processamento (tanto do ponto de vista de quem escreve como de quem lê). Este será, pois, provavelmente, um campo semântico onde surgirão inúmeras palavras novas.

Inovação

Quando as palavras faltam, a solução pode ser, além da perífrase, o empréstimo ou o recurso a processos internos de criação de palavras (extensão semântica, abreviação, acronímia, composição, conversão, derivação). O empréstimo é um processo rápido de integração e adaptação, mas os empréstimos em massa (que começam geralmente pelo léxico, podendo afectar posteriormente a sintaxe) têm o perigo de conduzir a uma assimilação à língua fonte, em particular se houver substituição lexical e não mero acrescento.

Os processos internos, quando possível, são a solução mais aceitável, pois, além de respeitarem as regras da língua, tendem a preservar uma maior transparência de relações morfológicas e semânticas entre as várias unidades da mesma família de palavras.[12] Repare-se nas duas palavras crioulas *skrebe* e *skritura.* A palavra *skritura* foi importada directamente do português, para designar as escrituras sagradas. Dado que o verbo *skrebe* não tem flexões, não existindo, nomeadamente, nenhuma forma correspondente ao particípio passado português *escrito* (de que deriva *escritura*), a palavra *skritura* mantém com *skrebe* uma relação mais opaca do que a que liga, em português, *escrever* e *escritura.*

Para manter a transparência, em crioulo, a derivação de palavras a partir da forma verbal deverá manter a raíz do verbo e justapor-lhe os afixos (sufixos e prefixos) crioulos. Por exemplo, para criar uma palavra que expresse o mesmo que, em português, "escritor," o crioulo tem a possibilidade de

a) importar o termo directamente do português, adaptando-o fonologicamente: *skritor*[13];

b) acrescentar o sufixo crioulo —*(d) or* à raíz do verbo: *skrebedor* (sendo esta a solução mais transparente)[14].

Uma terceira possibilidade é a de criar as duas palavras, deixando que o uso determine a escolha ou as mantenha como sinónimos, especializando os significados ou os contextos de aplicação.

Se não se quiser depender em absoluto do recurso ao empréstimo, é imprescindível proceder a um inventário dos afixos crioulos (para além dos processos de formação de palavras privilegiados pelo caboverdiano) ponderando o seu grau de produtividade, de modo a que se possa, mais uma vez, nos processos de importação e de derivação, seleccionar entre afixos "mais crioulos" ou "menos crioulos." Apesar de os prefixos serem em número muito reduzido, o crioulo de Cabo Verde conta com uma lista razoável de sufixos que, embora derivados do português, estão sujeitos a regras morfológicas próprias e, em muitos casos, bastante diferenciadas das suas correspondentes na língua-fonte.[15] Basta folhear ao acaso os dicionários existentes, para nos depararmos com famílias de palavras relativamente extensas. É o caso de:

> *Dodu* (Adj, V), *doda* (V), *dodisa* (N), *dodesa* (N), *dodisada* (N) (port., respectivamente: *doido/ficar doido por; endoidecer, endoidecer de alegria; doidice; doideira; actos de doidice*); *badiu* (N e Adj), *badia* (V), *badiaji* (N), *badiason* (N) (port., respectivamente: *"badio"/natural de Santiago, vadio; vadiar; vadiagem; vadiagem*); *bedju* (Adj e N), *bedja* (V), *bedjisa* (N), *bedjosku* (N), *bedjuska* (Adj), *bedjusku* (N), *bedjusa* (N) (port., respectivamente: *velho; envelhecer; velhice; aquele que é velho; avelhentado, velhote, velharia*); *fastiu* (N), *fastia* (V), *fastios* (Adj), *fastentu* (Adj), *fastenta* (V), *fastentura* (N) (port.: *fastio, enfastiar, maçador, enfadonho, aborrecer, maçada*).

Surge, no entanto, um problema. Dado que os afixos que encontramos em crioulo derivam do português (que é simultaneamente a língua base e a língua fonte privilegiada do caboverdiano) e têm nele correspondentes directos *(-eiro, -ice, -(d)or, re-* etc...),

poderemos considerar a hipótese de terem sido importados em bloco com as palavras de que são constituintes e não serem unidades morfológicas autónomas e produtivas, em crioulo. Há casos que não suscitam dúvidas quanto a essa importação em bloco, tal como *malfetu* (port.: *feitiço*; de "malfeito"), *pazigua* (port.: *apaziguar*) ou *pintor* (port.: *pintor*). Pelo contrário, noutras palavras como *mosindadi, korida, lenbransa, fitxadura* (port., respectivamente: *mocidade, corrida, lembrança, fechadura*) é difícil determinar se estamos perante expressões importadas, como um todo, do português (pois têm nesta língua correspondentes directos) ou criadas já no crioulo, uma vez que coexistem com as palavras crioulas de que poderiam ter derivado: *mos, kore, lenbra, fitxa.*

Para garantir a real produtividade de um afixo no sistema crioulo é fundamental, pois, registar as ocorrências desse afixo em palavras sem correspondente em português. Assim, palavras como *bador/badera* (*ba + dor /dera*) (port.: *aquele ou aquela que costuma ir*) e *bendor/bendera* (*ben + dor/dera*) (port.: *aquele ou aquela que costuma vir*) são bons exemplos da autonomia dos sufixos crioulos *(d)or / (d)era.* O próprio facto de não existirem, em português, as configurações *ir+ (d)or /(d)era* e *vir + (d)or / (d)era*, afasta a hipótese de se tratar de um decalque desta língua. O mesmo se pode afirmar de *-ozu* em *artiozu* (port.: *com geito para artista*), de *-(d)ura* em *baradura* (port.: *disposição que se se dá às canas para fazer os tectos das palhotas*) ou de—*a em stanga* (port.: *indignar-se com*).

Este procedimento põe à disposição de todos aqueles que se preocupam com a escrita e com a oficialização da língua um instrumento gramatical por que poderão optar em alternativa ao mero empréstimo ou como forma de o complementar. Na certeza, porém, de que a necessidade faz o engenho, mesmo à revelia da vontade dos decisores. Uma vez que os falantes tenham condições sociais de se expressar através da escrita em crioulo, de uma forma continuada e em diferentes contextos, entram em jogo duas forças interactivas: a força reguladora dos modelos e a da criação espontânea, ambas sujeitas ao dinamismo das tensões sociais e à consagração do uso.

Tal como da oralidade à escrita, também da decisão à aceitação vai um *kaminhu lonji*, pelo que é bom não perder tempo, para dar tempo ao tempo.

Notas

[1] Cf. decreto-lei 67/98 que define as bases do alfabeto unificado para a escrita do crioulo caboverdiano.

[2] Cit. por Foley, 1997, 425.

[3] Sublinhado nosso.

[4] Estória tradicional caboverdiana, contada oralmente.

[5] Grafia adaptada.

[6] Basta analisar o texto de T. Varela, para verificarmos que B. Lopes estava demasiado optimista quando afirmava , no seu prefácio à *Aventura Crioula*, de Manuel Ferreira (1965: 22): "(...) *o crioulo tem a favor o seu profundo instinto de nobilitação, que considero a sua força mais útil e progressiva ao mesmo tempo que revela a alta sabedoria com que o dialecto se defende na concorrência idiomática: aproveitando tudo o que pode receber do português reinol, para seu aperfeiçoamento, mas não cedendo um milímetro nas suas estruturas essenciais (...)*"

[7] V. *badera di misa*, "que costuma ir à missa" (em Napoleão Fernandes, 1990).

[8] Vejam-se expressões como *paralelamente, entretanto, posto isto, então, pois, ora, deste modo, pelo que, de acordo com, na verdade, nomeadamente, a saber, em conclusão, chegados a este ponto...*

[9] Cf. *Dicionário da Língua Portuguesa* (6ª edição) da Porto Editora.

[10] Em Quint-Abrial, 1998a.

[11] Napoleão Fernandes regista ainda *escrébédo* (escrito), *escritor* (escritório) e *escrivon* (escrivão), como referiremos adiante. João Pires e J. Hutchison (1983) registam além de *skrebe* e *skrebedu*, *skritoriu* (escritório) e *skritura* (escritura; escrita).

[12] Como afirma Abrial (1998:438), "Os falantes do *badio* (crioulo santiaguense) (...) produzem muito mais activamente que os lusófonos e os francófonos palavras novas por derivação ou composição a partir de unidades lexicais já existentes em crioulo" (em francês no original). E dá alguns exemplos (439-440): "As pessoas que não têm família são **sem-pra-kenha** ... lit. "sem alguém para quem (com quem possam contar)"; **konta-tchuba** ("conta a chuva": pluviómetro); **sem-sabedu** ("sem se saber": secreto, em referência ao voto); **silera-bai** ("acelera-vai": pequenos motociclos de duas rodas).

[13] A palavra *scritor* (grafada *escritor*) aparece em Napoleão Fernandes com o significado de *escritório*, numa variante de Barlavento.

[14] À semelhança do que acontece com a forma *skrebedu* (grafada *scrèbèdo*), que encontramos também em Napoleão Fernandes com o significado de *escrito*.

[15] Eis alguns dos afixos que ocorrem mais frequentemente em Caboverdiano:

a. para a formação de nomes:

N > N

-ada: barapó> barapuada (port.: *varapau, paulada*) *batuku > batukada* (port.: *batuque, batucada*);

-eru/-era: barba> barberu (port.: *barba, barbeiro*); *batata> batatera* (port.: *batata, batatal*);

-ria: barba> barbaria (port.: *barba, barbearia*);

-ura: frida> fridura (port.: *ferida; ferimento pequeno, acto de ferir*);

Adj > N

-esa/-eza: bunitu> buniteza (port.: *bonito, boniteza*); *buru> bureza* (port.: *burro, burrice*); *runhu> runhesa* (port.: *ruim, ruindade*);

-idadi: nobu> nobidadi (port.: *novo, novidade*);

-indadi: rabes> rabesindadi (port.: *torto; maldade, carácter torcido*);

-isa: bedju> bedjisa (port.: *velho, velhice*) ; *gaiatu > gaiatisa* (port.: *brincalhão; brincadeira, graça*);

-osku: feiu> feiosku (port.: *feio, aquele que é feio*);

-ura: sabe> sabura (port.: *agradável, saboroso; bem-estar*);

V > N

-ansa: konsola > konsolansa (port.: *consolar, consolo*);

-(d)or/(d)era: badja> badjador/era (port.: *bailar, bailador/bailadeira*); *bare > baredor* (port.: *varrer, varredor*);

-(d)ura: bare> baredura (port.: *varrer, varridela*); *bua> buadura* (port.: *voar, pequeno voo*);

-son: kiria> kiriason (port.: *criar, criação*); *prendi> prendison* (port.: *aprender, aprendizagem*).

b. para a formação de adjectivos:

V > Adj

-du: buza> buzadu (port.: *abusar; abusador, atrevido*); *kunfia > kunfiadu* (port.: *confiar; convencido, confiante*);

-entu: rabolta> raboltentu (port.: *revoltar, turbulento*); *fastia> fastentu* (port.: *fartar-se, enfadonho*);

ka-: bale > kabale (port.: *valer, sem valor*);

-nti: rabida > rabidanti (port.: *revirar, voltar; revendedor*);

N > Adj

-entu: barudju> barudjentu (port.: *barulho, barulhento*): *gera> gerentu* (port.: *bulha, bulhento*); *friu> frientu* (port.: *frio, friorento*).

-eru/-era: batota> batoteru (port.: *batota, batoteiro*); *bolta>boltera* (port.: *volta, governo da casa; que sabe dar voltas, que sabe fazer a lida da casa, diligente*);

-os/-ozu: skerda> skerdos (port.: *esquerda; esquerdino, canhoto*); *arti> artiozu* (port.: *arte; artista, habilidoso*);

-udu: stangu>stangudu (port.: *estômago; que tem maus fígados, irritadiço*); *forsa>forsudu* (port.: *força, muito forte*); *boka> bokudu* (port.: *boca, inconfidente*).

c. para a formação de verbos:

V > V

dis-:prinda> disprinda (port.: *pendurar, despendurar*); *kume > diskume* (port.: *comer,ruminar*); *konche> diskonche* (port.: *conhecer; não reconhecer, esquecer*);

ra- monda> ramonda (port.: *mondar, mondar segunda vez*); *bende> rabende* (port.: *vender, revender*);

N > V

-a: batuku> batuka (port.: *batuque, batucar*); *risku > riska* (port.: *risco, riscar*); *sukuru > sukura* (port.: *escuridão, escurecer*); *musturu > mustura* (port.: *mistura, misturar*);

-ia: skerda>, skerdia (port.: *erquerda; desviar da direcção, tomar outro caminho*); *festa> festia* (port.: *festa, festejar*); *fundu> fundia* (port.: *fundo, afundar-se*);

Um outro processo de criação de verbos a partir de substantivos, muito produtivo em crioulo, consiste na elevação da vogal tónica: *fórsa, forsa* (port.: *força, forçar*); *géra, gera* (port.: *guerra, guerrear*); kóba, koba (port.: *cova, cavar*).

Adj > V

-a: bedju> bedja (port.: *velho, envelhecer*); *margos> margosa* (port.: *amargo, amargar*); *fastentu > fastenta* (port.: *enfadonho, enfastiar*);

-isi: magru>magrisi (port.: *magro, emagrecer*); *riku> rikisi* (port.: *rico, enriquecer*).

Obras Citadas

Brito, A. de Paula. "Dialectos Crioulos Portugueses. Apontamentos para a Gramática que se Fala na Ilha de Santiago de Cabo Verde." *Boletim da Sociedade de Geografia de Lisboa* 7ª série 10 (1887): 611-669.

Duarte, Dulce Almada. *Bilinguismo ou Diglossia?: As Relações de Força Entre o Crioulo e o Português na Sociedade Cabo Verdiana.* Praia: Spleen-Edições, 1998.

Finnegan, Ruth. *Literacy and Orality: Studies in the Technology of Communication.* Oxford: Blackwell, 1988.

Foley, William. *Anthropological Linguistics — An Introduction.* Oxford: Blackwell, 1997.

Hazaël-Massieux, Marie-Christine. *Écrire en Créole. Oralité et Écriture aux Antilles.* Paris: L'Harmattan, 1993.

Lang, Jürgen. *Dicionário do Crioulo da Ilha de Santiago (Cabo Verde).* Tübingen: Gunter Narr Verlag Tübingen, 2002.

Massa, Françoise, e Jean-Michel Massa. *Dictionnaire Enyiclopedique et Bilingue, Cap-Vert- Cabo Verde.* Rennes: Univ. De Haute Bretagne, 2001.

Fernandes, Armando Napoleão Rodrigues. *O Dialecto Crioulo - Léxico do Dialecto Crioulo do Arquipélago de Cabo Verde.* São Vicente: Gráfica do Mindelo, 1990.

Pereira, Dulce. "Odju ka ten Pastor ma é midjor si bu prende odja." *Actas do Forum sobre Alfabetização Bilingue.* Praia: DGEEX, Ministério da Educação, 1989a.

———. "Crioulo de Cabo Verde: Proposta de Grafia." *Revista Internacional de Língua Portuguesa* (2. Dez. de 1989): 41-48, 1989b.

———. "Fala Crioulo Papia Português." *Rev. Cultura, nº especial de comemoração dos 25 anos de Independência.* Praia: Ministério da Cultura de Cabo Verde, 2000.

Pires, Joo e John Hutchison. *Disionariu Preliminariu Kriolu.* Boston: Funkul ño Lobu, 1983.

Quint-Abrial, Nicholas. *Dicionário Caboverdiano-Português. Variante de Santiago.* Lisboa: Verbalis, 1998a.

———. Le Créole de l'Île de Santiago (République du Cap Vert). Diss. Universidade de Paris III, 1998b.

Silva, Tomé V. da. *Na Bóka Noti.* Praia: Instituto Caboverdiano do Livro, 1987.

———. *Português Fundamental – Vocabulário e Gramática.* Tomo 1. Lisboa: INIC e CLUL, 1984.

Thomason, Sarah Grey e Terrence Kaufman. *Language Contact, Creolization and Genetic Linguistics.* Berkeley & Los Angeles: University of California Press, 1988.

Veiga, Manuel. *Le Créole du Cap-Vert – É tude grammaticale descriptive et contrastive.* Paris: Karthala; Praia: IPC, 2000.

Dulce Pereira é linguista docente do Departamento de Linguística Geral e Românica da Faculdade de Letras da Universidade de Lisboa (FLUL) desde 1976, onde lecciona, actualmente, as disciplinas de Crioulos de Base Portuguesa, Sociologia da Linguagem e Linguagem e Comunicação. É membro fundador do Centro de Estudos Africanos da FLUL e da Associação de Crioulos de Base Lexical Portuguesa e Espanhola. Tem-se dedicado, desde 1980, à investigação das línguas crioulas de base portuguesa, em particular do caboverdiano (aspectos gramaticais e lexicais e efeitos sociolinguísticos do contacto com a língua portuguesa, tanto em Cabo Verde como em Portugal). Foi consultora do primeiro Projecto Experimental de Alfabetização Bilingue de adultos, em Cabo Verde, no âmbito do qual elaborou uma proposta de grafia e vários estudos de índole gramatical e lexical sobre o crioulo.

Tilôbe, personagem das estórias tradicionais caboverdianas

Tânia Macedo

Resumo. O texto realiza uma breve apresentação do guloso e azarado Tio Lobo, também conhecido por Tilôbe ou Lobo, uma figura extremamente presente nas estórias tradicionais caboverdianas. Busca-se, ao mesmo tempo, traçar um paralelo entre ele e outras personagens pertencentes aos contos da oratura dos países de língua portuguesa (Pedro Malasartes, João Grilo e Cancãosinho), sobretudo sob o aspecto da malandragem.

Manuel Rui, poeta e prosador angolano, em um texto iluminado que se intitula "Entre mim e o nómada—a flor" (1981) chama-nos a atenção, entre outros importantes elementos, para o fato de que as estórias tradicionais africanas, contadas via de regra pelos mais velhos ao pé do fogo, constituem uma semiose a que são convocados todos os sentidos a fim de instaurarem o aprendizado e o lúdico. E que, portanto, a sua tradução e/ou leitura (acrescentamos), não se constituem apenas na passagem de uma língua a outra, mas uma "quase morte do que foi oral: a oratura sem griô; sem a árvore sob a qual a estória foi contada; sem a gastronomia que condiciona a estória; sem a fogueira que aquece a estória, o rito, o ritual" (Rui 30).

A análise, portanto, de um texto da chamada oratura a partir de sua tradução escrita, corre o risco de afastar-se efetivamente da beleza e do real sentido da *voz* para agarrar-se à redução da *letra*, como bem aponta Laura Padilha:

> Na festa do prazer coletivo da narração oral, entre os grupos iletrados africanos, é pela voz do contador, do *griot,* que se põe a circular a carga simbólica da cultura

> autóctone. (...) O contador e seus ouvintes são seres em interação para quem o dito cria a necessária cumplicidade e reitera que é preciso ser, na força da diferença (...) (Padilha 14)

Ao que acrescentamos que em uma situação limite, pode induzir a uma leitura em que, à falta do gestos, dos sons e dos espaços próprios do contar, a interpretação se equivoque. É grande o risco, mas, em presença das deliciosas estórias tradicionais de Cabo Verde presentes sobretudo nas recolhas de Persons (1968) e Romano (1970), conscientemente arriscamos e propomo-nos a realizar a leitura de alguns aspectos da figura de Tilôbe (Ti-Lobo, ou Tio-Lobo).[1]

Vale ressaltar que a personagem Tilôbe está presente em variadas aventuras nas mais importantes recolhas de estórias tradicionais caboverdianas, acompanhado ou não de seu sobrinho, comumente chamado Pedro, apresentando um mesmo perfil, sobre o qual nos deteremos mais vagarosamente, ao mesmo tempo em que o aproximaremos, rapidamente, de outras personagens das estórias do mundo de língua portuguesa.

Uma figura com muita lábia

As estórias tradicionais protagonizadas por Tio Lobo via de regra iniciam com a situação de carência que, no caso dessa personagem, querem dizer sempre muita fome. E essa é uma de suas características mais evidentes: a insaciedade do Lobo. Veja-se, por exemplo, como Luis Romano (Romano, 1970: 52) nos dá o intróito de uma das estórias daquela personagem:

> Era uma vez Tipêde i Tilôbe. Tipêde ta estóde sempre guardin i Tipêde mâgrin f~ete um côbe de linha. Um dia Tilôbe ba ter c' Tipêde i el dez' el:
> A tipêde, mode quem que bô t' estóde sempre güidin i mim sempre meiguin, sem foiça pe levanta nem um ingánha de mi?
> (Era uma vez Tio-Pedro e Tio-Lobo. Tio-Pedro estava sempre gordinho e Tio-Lobo magrinho feito um cabo de linha. Um dia Tio-Lobo foi ter com Tio-Pedro e disse-lhe:
> —Ó Tio-Pedro, por que modo tu estás sempre gordinho e eu sempre magrinho, sem força para levantar um sabugo de espiga de milho?) (Tradução de Romano).

A situação de miséria e fome é, pois, o que define Tio-Lobo, já à partida, em contraste com outras personagens sempre bem alimentadas. Cremos que esse dado é importante, pois não se coloca, a princípio, a personagem com conotações negativas. Ela apenas observa os que têm e, confronta-os com sua extrema carência. E aí fará de tudo para conseguir melhorar sua situação. E será sempre a partir do convencimento, do discurso do qual não se ausentam os juramentos e os mais diversos ardis, que Ti-Lobo entrará na posse de segredos, magias, "jeitinhos" dominados por outros e que lhes garantem a abundância. Sob esse particular, o domínio do discurso para convencer o outro em franquear-lhe segredos que possibilitarão uma melhor situação, lembramo-nos de João Grilo, personagem das estórias tradicionais portuguesas. Vale aqui lembrar que João Grilo, assim como Tio-Lobo (e ao contrário de Pedro Malasartes) é franzino, uma espécie de "filho da fome":

> Porém o Grilo criou-se
> Pequeno, magro e sambudo,
> As pernas tortas e finas,
> A boca grande e beiçudo (Proença 468)

Ocorre que Tilôbe, ao contrário do "amarelo" João Grilo, herda apenas uma das vertentes do ciclo de Malasartes,[2] qual seja, o papel de bobo, tonto e estúpido, ansioso por sair-se bem das situações, mas sempre acabando por ser derrotado. Ou seja, se a nossa personagem caboverdiana tem algum parentesco com o João Grilo pequeno e magro, distancia-se dele—e de Pedro Malasartes—no que se refere à astúcia para safar-se das situações de perigo e/ou trabalho, ainda que não possamos definir Ti-Lobo como um trabalhador.

Dentre as falhas que acometem a personagem deve ser indicada a enorme ansiedade, característica importante, já que implica na sua derrota todas as vezes em que consegue alguma situação mais folgada. Veja-se, por exemplo, a estória de número 02 recolhida por Elsie Clews Parsons entre emigrantes caboverdianos nos Estados Unidos da América:

> Naquela noite o Lobo não dormiu. À meia-noite bateu à porta de Pedro. Pedro disse: 'Ó tio Lobo, vá para casa. Ainda é meia-noite. Ninguém sai a estas horas.' A uma hora o Lobo pôs-se a cantar de galo: 'Co-co-ricó! Cocoricó!Cocoricó!' Bateu à porta de Pedro. Pedro levantou-se, Pedro disse-lhe: 'Ainda é muito cedo. Vá para casa; ainda é muito cedo. É você que canta de galo! Vá para casa!' (Parsons 53-54).

Ora, apenas a idéia que haveria comida no dia seguinte, torna a noite do Lobo—e de Pedro, que lhe indicara a forma de saciar a fome—um martírio que se torna pior em razão dos ardis de que lança mão o esfomeado Lobo para tentar que o sobrinho o leve a comer o mais rápido possível. E são as tentativas falhadas da personagem que instauram o riso, dada a ingenuidade de suas artimanhas.

Mas, ao final, ou em razão de sua lábia, ou porque raia o dia, em todas as estórias Tilôbe chega a uma situação de abundância, fartando-se, o que a reiteração do verbo comer, largamente usada nos textos, indica.

Mas se o Lobo é esfomeado e ansioso, será a imprudência o que definitivamente o derrotará, já que o reino da abundância desenhado pelas estórias caboverdianas não é isento de interditos que devem ser observados, sob pena de o equilíbrio ser rompido. E aqui entra não apenas a intemperança de nossa personagem, como também o seu azar, pois parece que tudo conspira para sua perdição. Lembre-se, a respeito, uma das estórias referida por Luis Romano (1970) e por Parsons (1968), sobre como a personagem chega ao céu—atrás de alimento, obviamente—e quer voltar para sua casa na terra, solicitando ao "Nosso Senhor" o auxílio. Tudo vai bem, até que se interpõe em seu caminho mais comida e no dilema colocado entre se alimentar ou seguir as orientações divinas, o estômago ronca mais alto. E o resultado é a perdição.

Pode-se dizer, dessa maneira, que o prazer para o qual se atira com voracidade incrível Tilôbe não reconhece qualquer princípio de realidade, deixando à margem recomendações, tabus e horários, o que levará a personagem à perdição, a qual se manifestará de variadas maneiras, todas elas terríveis (morte por pauladas, por arrebentar-se contra pedras, árvores ou cacos de vidros, entre outras). E os castigos são tão cruéis, que não há como não ler aí um forte caráter pedagógico das estórias, no sentido de as mesmas quererem marcar para os ouvintes/leitores a necessidade de obedecer aos interditos e manter uma parcimônia nos atos.

E, nesse ponto, avançamos uma leitura que ilumina preferencialmente a questão da relação entre a fome, sua saciedade e os castigos infringidos a Tilôbe. Ora, ainda que a personagem cometa deslizes, como por exemplo tentar enganar Jesus Cristo, ela o faz sempre em razão da fome atroz que lhe acomete e/ou da sua gula. Em contrapartida, os castigos que lhe são dados são enormes e, não raro, conforme indicamos acima, redundam na morte da personagem. Sob esse particular, Tilôbe afasta-se tanto de Pedro Malasartes quanto de João Grilo ou de Cancãosinho (para quem, segundo o folheto de cordel de Cícero Laureano, citado por Santos, "Ninguém quer saber do bem,/Honradez não mata a fome,/Morre aquele que não come/O pão seu ou de alguém.), já que aqueles malandros populares buscam também saciar a fome e ter melhores condições de subsistência, mas ao final de suas aventuras triunfam e têm reconhecido o valor da malandragem.

Por outras palavras, Tio Lobo, ao ser comparado a outras personagens de estórias populares, sobretudo do Brasil, também elas submetidas às mesmas situações de carência, mas que obtêm vantagens, encontra-se submetido a um rígido código de conduta.

Avançamos, aqui, uma hipótese, ligando os traços acima apontados às condições de vida no Arquipélago de Cabo Verde. Segundo entendemos, dadas as difíceis condições de subsistência, em razão das severas secas que assolam o país, a questão da fome, sem dúvida, ficou indelevelmente marcada no imaginário da gente das Ilhas e, portanto, a personagem mais popular de suas histórias tem a defini-la, antes de mais nada, a carência e uma necessidade premente de ultrapassá-la. Dessa forma, a malandragem de Tio Lobo para obter alimento é vista positivamente, pois trata-se, aqui, de fazer valer a malícia e a esperteza para escapar de uma situação limite como a fome.

Se sobreviver é preciso, precaver-se para tempos difíceis que, certamente em razão do clima, virão, é ainda mais necessário. E é aqui que vemos o papel didático que as punições de Tio-Lobo possuem no imaginário, especialmente das crianças. Tratar-se-ia de apontar, de forma veemente, a necessidade não apenas de obedecer aos interditos, mas, sobretudo, de manter a parcimônia, para que o alimento sempre exista e a sobrevivência esteja garantida. Por isso o nosso pobre malandro não é vitorioso e a gula é severamente punida.

É muito provável que nossa leitura da personagem e suas estórias seja passível de outros sentidos ainda e, malandramente, Tilôbe esconda muitos truques e traquejos de linguagem que nos tenham escapado. Mas, assim como nas estórias tradicionais brasileiras, diríamos: "entrou por uma porta, saiu pela outra, quem quiser que conte outra."

Notas

1 Como as estórias consultadas usam indistintamente as três maneiras de nomear a personagem, também as utilizaremos.

2 Conforme nos alerta Braúlio do Nascimento em "Pedro Malasartes na tradição luso-brasileira" "(...) em Portugal, Pedro Malasartes é um tolo e raramente um velhaco; na Espanha, Pedro Urdemales é tolo e também pícaro; na Itália, Giufá é o tolo e ocasionalmente o trapaceiro. Atravessando o Atlântico, o tipo adquire caráter definido" (Alban 47).

Obras Citadas

Nascimento, Bráulio. "Pedro Malasartes na tradição luso-brasileira." Albán, Maria Del Rosário. Org. de *Revista internacional de língua portuguesa* 9 (Julho 1993): 43-56.

Padilha, Laura Cavalcante. *Entre voz e letra: o lugar da ancestralidade na ficção angolana do século XX.* Niterói: EDUFF, 1995.

Parsons, Elsie Clews. *Folclore do Arquipélago de Cabo Verde.* (Introd. Fernando Castro Pires de Lima). Lisboa: Agência-geral do Ultramar, 1968.

Proença, Manoel Cavalcanti. (Seleção, Introdução e Comentários). *Literatura popular em verso: antologia.* São Paulo: Editora da Universidade de São Paulo; Rio de Janeiro: Fundação Casa de Rui Barbosa, 1986.

Romano, Luís. *Cabo Verde — Renascença de uma civilização no Atlântico médio.* 2 ed. Lisboa: Revista Ocidente, 1970.

Rui, Manuel. "Entre mim e o nómada—a flor." *Teses angolanas.* Luanda: União dos escritores angolanos, 1981. 29-34.

Santos, Idelette Muzart Fonseca dos. "Pícaros e malandros no cordel: uma galeria de tipos." Albán, Maria Del Rosário. Org. de *Revista internacional de língua portuguesa* 9 (Julho 1993): 121-136.

Tânia Macedo é Professora de Literaturas de Língua Portuguesa na UNESP—campus de Assis e Professora Visitante na USP, na Área de Pós-graduação em Estudos Comparados de Literaturas de Língua Portuguesa. Publicou, entre outros, "Caminhos da escrita de uma cidade," Milton, H. C. & SPERA, J. M., *Estudos de literatura e lingüística* (Assis: Unesp--Assis Publicações, 2001) 35-56; "Visões do mar na literatura angolana contemporânea," Quataert, A. & Afonso, M. F., org., *La lusophonie-Voies/Voix oceaniques* (Bruxelas: Universidade Livre de Bruxelas, 2000) 257-265; "Uma guerra, várias escritas," *Letras*: 23 (Santa Maria: Universidade Federal de Santa Maria, 2001) 115-119. E-mail: taniamacedo@uol.com.br e macedotc@femanet.com.br

History, Memory and Travel/ História, Memória e Viagem

(Re)claiming the Heritage: The Narratives of Manuel Veiga

Gregory McNab

Abstract. Manuel Veiga's concern in *Odju d'Agu* and *Diário das Ilhas* is a specific Cape Verde to replace the colonial legacy. *Odju d'Agu* is a textual prescription for becoming Cape Verdean. It is rooted in the language and approach of Cape Verde's oral storytelling tradition and framed with a tale-telling session to show that the tradition can serve to (dis)articulate the hierarchies of the past and point the way to a progressive future. *Diário das Ilhas* is a textual itinerary for the discovery of Cape Verde. It imaginatively and poetically (re)invents a past for the archipelago that showcases the importance of Cape Verde's African heritage and gives voice to Jorge Barbosa and a number of other Cape Verdean poets. In both of those texts, Manuel Veiga seeks to address the issue of a postcolonial identity for Cape Verde, (re)capture an historical initiative for the Cape Verdean community and (re)site Cape Verde as the locus of its own experience.

Manuel Veiga has always vigorously advocated the unique features of Cape Verdean culture. Anyone who studies the *Diskrison Strutural di Lingua Kaboverdianu* and the *Introducção à Gramática do Crioulo*; probes the essays in *A Sementeira* and in *África, Voz di Povo, Fragmentos, Pré-Textos,* and other periodicals; takes note of his work with the Instituto Nacional de Cultura and the Associação de Escritores Caboverdianos, or follows his progress in the National Assembly knows this. This essay will argue that *Odju d'Agu* and *Diário das Ilhas* contribute by structuring a historically and linguistically specific Cape Verde to supplant colonialism's construct.

An unfamilar toponymy in both is an obvious sign. Goltarpu and Kukuli are Veiga's terms for Portugal and Africa. The *baías* of Milho, Algodão, Cana Sacarina, Palmeiras, Dragoeiro, Flores, Chacina, Santa Maria, and Porto Grande are Veiga's names for the islands of Santiago, Fogo, Santo Antão, Boa Vista, São Nicolau, Brava, Maio, Sal, and São Vicente. If it is correct that "to name a place is to announce discursive control over it by the very act of inscription" (Ashcroft, Griffiths and Tiffin 1998: 183), then what Veiga does is make those places Cape Verdean.

That having been noted, let us now turn to *Odju d'Agu*, which should be read as a textual prescription for being reborn Cape Verdean. Veiga's text is rooted in Cape Verde's oral storytelling tradition. Its language, the tales it tells, its narrative approach, and its endorsement of the presence of an audience all acknowledge a veneration for the Cape Verdean storytelling tradition. But Veiga does not merely pay lip service to the format; he shows how the tradition can be mobilized to dismantle the colonialist, classist hierarchies of power that mark Cape Verde for much of its lifetime and to map out the direction to a properly Cape Verdean future.

In a 1996 study, George Lang felt compelled to cite *Odju d'Agu* as "[t]he most ambitious work in the [Cape Verdean] Crioulo canon and one of [the] few sustained works in creoles world-wide" (58). That Lang felt obligated to point out Veiga's work as so singular, because it used Cape Verdean, requires us to probe the importance of Veiga's choice of language. In its hybridity the Cape Verdean language is representative of Cape Verdeanity's more than five-hundred-years-old process of development. Everyone in Cape Verde is proficient in Cape Verdean (see Lesourd and Réaud-Thomas 108). Veiga's composition of *Odju d'Agu* in Cape Verdean denies the monopoly of literary expression to the Portuguese language (see Ashcroft, Griffiths and Tiffin 1989: 38). *Odju d'Agu* confirms the validity of Cape Verdean as a literary language as much as does the *Diskrison Strutural di Lingua Kaboverdianu* the worth of Cape Verdean as a legitimate vehicle for scholarly writing.

The casting of *Odju d'Agu* in Cape Verdean is also a speech act to increase the prestige of the language in the eyes of its detractors and proponents. Veiga and others who have sought to contribute to Cape Verdean literature through the medium of the national language have had to face a centuries-old disdain for it. Chelmicki called Cape Verdean "idioma o mais perverso, corrupto e imperfeito, sem construcção, sem gramática, e que não se pode escrever" (2: 331). Costa said that it is "um legado do escravo boçal e inculto que não pôde aprender melhor o português dos antigos senhores" (25). As Veiga himself has observed: "Durante muitos séculos o nosso inimigo procurou convencer-nos de que a nossa língua não era um facto cultural. Durante muito tempo, ser culto, era saber imitar o colonizador. Imitar a sua língua, a sua filosofia, a sua religião, a sua maneira de pensar e sentir" (1994: 198).

It is especially important to note the use of the Cape Verdean language in *Odju d'Agu* as a commitment to authenticity. This shows that the dramas of the Cape Verdean experience can be constructed in a Cape Verdean way. Moreover, the overwhelming use of the Sotavento variant from Santiago, the one most removed from formerly imperial Portuguese and the one associated with the earliest settled part of the Cape Verdean archipelago where the African presence is most marked, represents a zeal to find the most exclusively Cape Verdean mode of doing so. As Veiga has expressed it: "O facto é que para transmitir a mensagem de Odju d'Agu, a melhor língua em que eu a podia exprimir era em crioulo—nada mais—porque é uma vivência moldada em crioulo" (Laban 2: 589).

In the tales that it tells, Manuel Veiga's book is about the (re)constitution of Cape Verde in a post-colonial context. It does not organize an emplotment of the (re)constitution process itself but rather presents four stories that exemplify some of the issues that must be resolved before the shaping of an authentically Cape Verdean Cape Verde is possible. People from three of them undertake a quest for an appropriate place in the Cape Verde being born at the time of independence; the fourth person tells the story of the quest of each of the other three.

The first of these accounts is the tale of Zé di Béba, the son of an *assimilado*, absentee, landowning family with holdings on Santiago and Fogo. Zé di Béba's story is a lesson in how to unassimilate from the colonial master's standards and overcome cultural alienation. He must learn how to do without the comforts of wealth, how to leave the life of a *branku* behind, and how to be humble. To discover what it is to be Cape Verdean, he must learn that returning to Cape Verde is not a facile, romantic journey.

The second is the tale of Pedrinhu, the son of a tenant of Zé di Béba's family. Pedrinhu's story is a lesson in how to learn the best way to help build the nation. Although early on he hears the messages of anticolonialism and antiapartheid, it takes him some time to feel free enough to apply the benefits of his education to the betterment of his people. When he does, although having committed himself to enter the priesthood, Pedrinhu finds his vocation is service to the people outside of the church. He comes to understand that his independent way of being and seeing is incompatible with the church, which seems more an extension of colonialist authoritarianism than a refuge and nurturer for all the people.

The third tale is of Rejina, the daughter of a prominent family from Fogo, who had been in love with Pedrinhu. Rejina represents the potential of the priviledged to see the inequities of a system that benefits her class and to work to disassemble it. With Mamadú, an African and probably Guinean, she must unassimilate from a colonialist imposition of Afrophobia, without moving to Afrophilia. The story of Mamadú and Rejina is a lesson in defining a relationship with Africa. They wind up discovering that it is possible to appreciate Europe without having to submit themselves to it, that it is possible to be oriented by Africa without having to abandon what in Cape Verde is not purely African. They succeed in perceiving that even though Cape Verde is not Africa, Africa is in Cape Verde.

In those three tales, each person's process of learning is precipitated by a sense of alienation arising from the colonial experience. Each one's decision to return to Cape Verde is a move toward the dismantling of class barriers and signifies a rejection of the colonialist teaching that a colonized people could only be civilized if they are assimilated into the colonizers' culture. It also indicates a recognition of the value and presence of an African heritage in Cape Verde, as well as a commitment to active participation in building an authentically Cape Verdean nation. This discovery involves, as Veiga has said elsewhere, the notion that "o centro para todas essas personagens, a terra-mãe, é mesmo Cabo Verde" (Laban 2: 564).

Palu di Djodja, the presenter of Veiga's tales, is a traditional storyteller, who has in him the collective wisdom of society (Lang 58). His own story is also part of the fabric of Veiga's work. In point of fact, what frames the book is the story of what happens to him, to his family and to those in the audience who listen to him tell his tale. The absence of the parents of Djon di Mana, Palu's grandson, casts Palu and Djon in roles of the Cape Verdean drama, which is as much theirs as of the characters in the tales Palu tells. While those tales are about those who come home, Palu's and Djon's is the drama of those at home who wait for the emigrants' return. That final ingathering is what allows Veiga to conclude his story.

All of that acknowledges a veneration for the Cape Verdean storytelling tradition exemplified in the texts collected by Tomé Varela da Silva and by

Elsie Clews Parsons. That storytelling aspect of *Odju d'Agu*, which is the center of some dozen of the book's fifty chapters, has not always been recognized, and if recognized, not studied. Laban's interview of Veiga does not confront it, nor do Semedo (1987) and Romano (1988) in their essays. Whatever the recognition of the narrational mode of *Odju d'Agu*, it is usually limited to an acknowledgement of that aspect of Manuel Veiga's book. That is as far as Duarte (1987: 11; 1998: 175) and Lang (59) go.

Veiga's narrative frame, however, does more than acknowledge the fact of traditional Cape Verdean storytelling. For one thing, it presents that art as discourse vital to Cape Verde's progress in a modern world. The onset of the storytelling is instigated by a younger generation of students, who are the audience, particularly by Djon di Mana. Those young people had decided to recover the traditional story, about which they had been told by their school teacher and of which he said that it was at risk of disappearing in the face of more technologically complex forms of entertainment. When the tale-telling begins, the traditional opening formula for the traditional story is kept for the opening of the real and historical story of Zé di Béba: "Kusa ma kusa [...] éra un bes un rapasinhu ki txomaba Zé di Béba" (12). What Manuel Veiga gives us, however, is not the traditional narrative in the sense of generalized content. Its telling begins on a specific day, its characters have specific histories, and they travel to specific places.

Of course the specificity is deliberate. Palu di Djódja's response, in which he insists that he will tell "un storia diferenti" (11), clearly underlines that intent. Yet, this "stória diferenti" offers more than a mere narrative of people, places and events that could be part of the historical world of Palu's audience. While the primary purpose of the traditional story is to entertain and to enliven a difficult life, the active and engaged reaction of Palu's audience indicates that the purpose of his narrative is to stimulate and provoke. Naturally the members of this audience interact with each other. They comment on the stories Palu gives them. They tell him when they like his tale and when they have trouble with it. They tell him what they want to hear more about. They remind him where he left off when it is time to continue after an interval in the telling.

More importantly, however, the students who are Palu's audience take what Palu gives them in his tale and explore what it means for them and their lives. They reveal a critical and questioning impulse. Their enthusiasm is so strong that when they are in school their teacher suggests that they put on a play to dramatize what they have heard as well as to interpret and explore their reactions. The play consists, however, not of an adaptation but of their continuation. With their play, the youths contribute to the richness and the potentiality of the old man's material and prove themselves potential contributers to the well-being of their country in its first moments of freedom. "Stória éra diferenti, Ka so kel ki Palu di Djódja konta, mas tanbe kel ki mininus prende y sa ta prende ku independénsa di ses txon, ku liberdadi di ses povu y pugresu di ses téra" (54).

In the pedagogical process that allows for that kind of active involvement, freedom must be accompanied by discipline and patience. We note that the young people in Palu's audience react unfavorably to parts of Pedrinhu's story, perhaps because, as Moser speculates, something is "above the heads of [Palu's] young listeners" (713). Thus, it is important to note that, here, through Palu, Veiga suggests that in addition to being a joy, learning is also a challenge: "Sabi e kunpanhéru di kasabi. Pa nhos xinti sabi, nhos ten ki konxe kasabi, nhos ten ki sabe ma kasabi di oxi pode ser sabi de manhan, ma kasabi di un pode ser sabi di out" (91).

Much of what we observe in Veiga's configuration of the young students in the learning process related in *Odju d'Agu* is reminiscent of the thinking of Paulo Freire, who did share his view with Cape Verdean educators in the 1970s. The interactive and dialogic pedagogy between Palu and his audience in Veiga's book seems to be what is described in these words from *Pedagogy of the Oppressed*: "The students—no longer docile listeners—are now critical co-investigators in dialogue with the teacher. The teacher presents the material to the students for their re-consideration and re-considers her earlier considerations as the students express their own" (81).

If *Odju d'Agu* should be read as a textual prescription for being reborn Cape Verdean, then *Diário das Ilhas* should be read as a textual itinerary for the (re)discovery of Cape Verde's roots. It is a kind of ship's log that, although plotting the trajectory of Cape Verdean history from its beginning, sets a course different from that which had been operative during the time of the colony. It accumulates relevant factors, presents the impact of those factors on Cape Verdean history and explores the ways those factors shaped contemporary Cape Verde. It also articulates those facts through a distinctively Cape Verdean voice.

Given the PAIGC's publication of its history before independence, and, more recently, Elisa Andrade's release of her account, considering the scholarly project to put together a history of Cape Verde since the coming of independence leading to the appearance of the first two volumes of the *História Geral de Cabo Verde*, and keeping in mind his own interest in this kind of undertaking as president of the Instituto Nacional de Cultura in the early 1990s and as a scholar himself, it is only natural that Manuel Veiga should decide to articulate his own version of the Cape Verdean past. It seems evident, however, that his intent in *Diário das Ilhas* was to serve other needs. Recall that the coverage field of the PAIGC's account was broader than what Viega had in mind. Cape Verde and Guinea-Bissau had each been going its own way since late 1980; it is possible that the tale of Rejina and Mamadú in *Odju d'Agu* alludes to those separate directions. Remember also that the *História Geral de Cabo Verde* depended on archival and secondary material from primarily Portuguese sources. A cursory glance at the contents of the two volumes of the *História Geral de Cabo Verde: Corpo Documental* and at the bibliography to each volume of the *História Geral de Cabo Verde* itself confirms such a reliance. That debt might suggest to some that no matter how heavily involved the Cape Verdean scholars were in the project, the tilt of any scholarly account will inevitably be Eurocentric. As Bernabé, Chamoiseau and Confiant point out through a citation from Eduard Glissant in their little book, from which Veiga takes one of *Diário das Ilhas*'s epigraphs, the methodology of historians gives the post-colonial writer access only to the colonial chronicle, which reveals that which supports the colonialist viewpoint. There is then, we may extrapolate from them, no anticolonial chronicle. Therefore, only the imagination or a poetic knowledge can lead to what the colonial chronicle does not reveal. "Seule la connaissance poétique, la connaissance romanesque, la connaissance artistique, pourra nous déceler, nous percevoir, nous ramener évanescents aux réanimations de la conscience" (38). It is in that kind of alternative context that *Diário das Ilhas* should be viewed: as a narrative that elaborates a portrait of its own Cape Verde, supplanting the authoritarian vision left to us by the colonialist discourse of a bygone era and recognizing the contribution of a formerly marginalized originating people to the formation of Cape Verde.

Veiga's most important objective in *Diário das Ilhas* is to reassess the importance of the African contribution to Cape Verde. The way he does this is to go back to the moment in time when the African and European forebearers of Cape Verde first encountered each other, taking a direction that colonial historians and chroniclers did not follow. He affirms the predominance of Africanness in the story of Cape Verde and its people over the

Europeanness, even during the colonial era. Pedro Monteiro Cardoso's "Ode a África" is the text that defines the esteem for Africa that underlies that position.

To begin with, Veiga establishes the African forebearers of today's Cape Verdeans as the protagonists of the story. We may note, for example, that when the first Portuguese arrive on the coast of Africa it is they whom the text considers strange, not the Africans. Clearly, the text judges Africans morally superior at that moment of transition from a stage of freedom in their *história milenária* to another of captivity. In contrast to colonialist history, the text acknowledges the value of the culture and society of Africa and argues that its people have never been at odds with it, but rather have worked symbiotically within it.

Veiga's text also seeks to convert the Africans's impotence in a new existence into an inherent power. It affirms that enslaved Africans were the foundation on which colonial Cape Verde sat. Even though they seemed to be onlookers, not actors, in the drama of the nature and the exercise of hegemony in pre-independence Cape Verde, it argues that they were the strength at the base of the social triangle that had to carry the weight of the crown and its vassals. The "'poder' da base era o mais significativo" (118).

In addition, Veiga's text reconfigures the cultural losses the enslaved Africans suffered and makes it clear that they were the segment of the populace in the early days with the greater capacity for adaptation to new circumstances. One area was in religion. Here, "procuraram, lá onde era possível, harmonizar a palavra da Bíblia com a da sua própria Tradição" (113). A new language is also an organic part of the new culture. It is a vehicle for the expression of the physical suffering and the existential anguish of the descendants of Africa. It forms aphorisms that analyze their reality. It is the tool that allows them to understand the tasks they need to undertake. It is the expression of the unfolding culture.

Veiga's text also rejects a *pathos* of the tragedy of loss in favor of an admiration for the spirit of resistence in the face of that loss. To underline the nature of the deprivation, the text gives a litany of the outrages suffered: uprooting, destruction, coercion, sacrifice, subservience, etc. It compensates them for their pain with a notation of the acts of resistence: a display of bravado when the Europeans showed up on the coast of Africa for the first enslavements, suicide on the way from Africa, sabotage whenever possible, escape into the interior of the new land, an Africanization of the environment and Portuguese culture and language, and ultimately the creation of a new society.

In contrast to *Odju d'Agu*, *Diário das Ilhas* is in Portuguese, and, so, very much as Ashcroft, Griffiths and Triffin might have remarked, in "the process of capturing and remoulding the language to new usages" (1989: 38). Veiga commandeers the Portuguese language to deny the colonialist a major role in the construction of Cape Verde's history as he works to make the main trunk of its past a link to an ancestral Africa. Since Veiga makes use of the colonizer's language to reach his goal, it would not be surprising to see that he uses some of the colonizer's narrative traditions as well, especially those most associated with the texts of the early years of the expansion. In some cases, what he does seems to be to replace some components of the Portuguese tradition with elements of his own. For example, Veiga's title, *Diário das Ilhas*, seems to allude to a title such as *Diário da Viagem de Vasco da Gama.* Any mention of Vasco da Gama will, of course, conjure up Luís de Camões, who used the voyage of Vasco da Gama as a pretext to elaborate a history of Portugal. Manuel Veiga also uses the motif of the voyage to frame his text and, in truth, as the metaphor for Cape Verdean history. His pretext is Jorge Barbosa's posthumously published 1966 poem "Relato da Nau," which, because it relates and recuperates a first and emblematic voyage of a slave ship from the African continent, must truly be considered the portal through which we all have to pass to access that past hidden by versions of the colonialist narrative.

A second point of contact is Jorge's vision from the Pico de António. His contemplation of the geologic establishment of the islands, seeing them passed in review before him, with a catalog of features associated with each island has to remind us of the "Ilha dos Amores" segment in *Os Lusíadas* (X: 76 ff.), where Gama is priviledged to see the consequences of his 1497 voyage for Portugal's future history. The difference between those two visions is, of course, that Gama's is a sort of textual reward for his *ousadia* while Jorge Barbosa's is part of the process of anointing him.

In a remarkable instance, Veiga seeks to contest rather than replace something of the colonialist account, recalling a similar contestation in Virgílio Pires's "Titina." In this case, what Veiga does is conjure up an ironic (re)awakening of consciousness for Diogo Gomes, one of the original discoverers of Cape Verde and the only one who remains present there, in the form of a statue overlooking Praia's harbor from a vantage point high on the Platô. In his presentation, Veiga juxtaposes Diogo Gomes's recollection of the rivalries between himself, António da Nóli, and Cadamosto to the presence in his,

Gomes's mind of the putative ideology of crusade and discovery, and what he forgot or might not ever have known about Cape Verde. The words Veiga assigns to the hovering consciousness he creates for his Diogo Gomes make it clear that Gomes articulates an attitude of callous and petty cynicism about the Portuguese overseas adventure. Reduced to its human and petty aspirations, this profile of the *navegador* transforms the officialized panegyric verbiage of the speech (quoted in part by Veiga) with which the statue was unveiled in 1958 into the discourse of burlesque.

To imbue his story with plausibility, Veiga articulates it through another Cape Verdean, a poet of course, Jorge Barbosa. As the one founder of modern Cape Verdean literature who was almost exclusively a poet, Jorge Barbosa was one of the poets who have most acutely explored the factors contributing to a Cape Verdean identity, and, as Veiga has noted, the poet in whom he reads himself (1994: 26). Veiga gives his readers an indirect paraphrase of what Barbosa would have perhaps uttered if he had elaborated on his poems about Cape Verde, intersecting his material with many of Barbosa's own poems; with poems by Eugénio Tavares, Pedro Cardoso, António Nunes and Amílcar Cabral; with citations from the *História Geral de Cabo Verde* and from manuscripts relevant to Cape Verde's past; and with references to Palu di Djódja, *Odju d'Agu*'s tale-teller.

Understandably, a noticeable portion of Veiga's text is occupied with a process of weaving Jorge Barbosa into the fabric of the narrative, as was the case with Palu di Djódja in *Odju d'Agu*. One sign of this process is Jorge's previously mentioned ascent up the Pico de António, practically the center of Santiago, Cape Verde's largest, most populated, longest populated and first populated island. If the visit to the Pico de António integrates Jorge into the landscape of Cape Verde, his visit to Nhô Nacho, the traditionalist teller of tales and oracle of the people, after he comes down from the Pico de António, represents Jorge's integration into its popular culture. Their conversation in the scenario of rustic, rural, unmechanized Cape Verde in the interior of Santiago touches on the recurring themes of Cape Verdean existence: hunger and want in the times of drought, forced emigration to São Tomé, departure to America in search of the dollar, and the possibilities of Europe.

This legitimization of Jorge as narrator empowers him to be the filter of the story that Veiga presents to his readers. Jorge is, however, not to be the ur-narrator of the Cape Verdean story. Rather, he is a transitional narrator, a successor to Pálu di Djodja. Significantly, just before Jorge begins his work, he reads the concluding words of Palu's narrative, where Palu tells his audience that he is tired and his story incomplete. Those remarks seem to mark Jorge's as a complementary narrative to Palu's. Yet Jorge's time as the narrator will also come to an end when his work is done and his energy spent. As the chronology of the story of Cape Verde he projects draws closer to his present, the poet, tired of "tanto escrever sobre a história sem História" (1997: 215), and doubting he can keep on with the saga and the future, gives his work over to a popular prophet who recites lines from António Nunes's "Poema de amanhã," "contando [the better future that] a oratura ainda não sabe ou não pode escrever" (217). This passing on of a narrative legacy suggests that neither learned nor popular culture alone can completely articulate the discourse of Cape Verde and that as Veiga himself reminds us in the epilogue to *Diário das Ilhas*, there is a third voice yet to be heard from.

Inasmuch as that third voice has yet to speak, this would be an appropriate juncture to recall what the first two voices have offered up. For one thing they have put forward an impressive demonstration of language's possibilities, whether it be to show the worth of the national one, or whether it be to adapt the one left by colonialism to national uses. For another, they have spoken from the point of view of the people from whom they come. Thirdly, they have told the people's stories. And, finally, they have left the way open for those stories to be continued.

It is not just that there will be new storytellers, perhaps Djon di Mana among them. It is that with the recovery of what had been cast aside or fallen by the wayside and with the return to the wellspring of those who had departed, the groundwork has been laid for Cape Verdeans to apply their inner resources and the resources of their heritage to the building of their own future Cape Verde. Certainly that appears to be the hope contained in the imaginative retelling of a different Cape Verdean past and in the pedagogic dynamism of the new traditional tale-telling. Perhaps Veiga's third storyteller is only waiting to see what that future will be like before beginning another *stória.*

Works Cited

Andrade, Elisa Silva. *Les îles du Cap-Vert de la «Découverte» à l'Indépendence Nationale (1460-1975)*. Paris: L'Harmattan, 1996.

Ashcroft, Bill, Gareth Griffiths and Helen Tiffin. *The Empire Writes Back: Theory and Practice in Post-Colonial Literatures.* London and New York: Routledge, 1989.

———. *Key Concepts in Post-Colonial Studies.* London and New York: Routledge, 1998.

Barbosa, Jorge. "Relato da Nau." *Poesia Inédita e Dispersa.* Lisboa: ALAC, 1993. 149-151.

Bernabé, Jean, Patrick Chamoiseau and Raphaël Constant. *Éloge de la Créolité.* Paris: Gallimard, 1989.

Camões, Luís de. *Os Lusíadas.* Oxford: Clarenden Press, 1973.

Cardoso, Pedro Monteiro. "Ode a África." *Jardim das Hespérides.* Cabo Verde: n.p., 1926. 11-14.

Chelmicki, José Conrado Carlos de. *Corographia Cabo-Verdiana, ou Descripção Geographico-Historica da Provincia das Ilhas de Cabo-Verde e Guiné.* [Vol. 2 by Chelmicki and Francisco Adolfo de Varnhagen.] Lisboa: Typ. de L.C. da Cunha, 1841-43.

Costa, José Maria da. "Devemos Evitar o Crioulo." *Cabo Verde* 4.43 (1953): 24-25.

Diário da Viagem de Vasco da Gama. 2 vols. Porto: Civilização, 1945.

Duarte, Dulce Almada. *Bilinguismo ou Diglossia.* Praia: Spleen, 1998.

———. "*Odju d'Agu* de Manuel Veiga: Uma Proposta de Leitura." *Voz di Povo* 23 May 1987: 11, 12.

Freire, Paulo. *Pedagogy of the Oppressed.* Trans. Myra Bergman Ramos. New York: Continuum, 2000.

História Geral de Cabo Verde. 2 vols. Lisboa: Instituto de Investigação Científica Tropical; Praia: Direcção Geral do Património Cultural de Cabo Verde [vol. 2: Lisboa: Instituto de Investigação Científica Tropical; Praia: Instituto Nacional de Cultura de Cabo Verde], 1991-1995.

História Geral de Cabo Verde Corpo Documental. 2 vols. Lisboa: Instituto de Investigação Científica Tropical; Praia: Direcção Geral do Património Cultural de Cabo Verde, 1988-1990.

Laban, Michel. "[Interview with] Manuel Veiga." *Cabo Verde: Encontro com Escritores.* [Porto]: Fundação Eng. António de Almeida, [1992]. 2: 557-607.

Lang, George. "Literary *Crioulo* since Independence in São Tomé, Guiné-Bissau and Cape Verde." *Luso-Brazilian Review* 33 (1996): 53-63.

Lesourde, Michel and Guilène Réaud-Thomas. "Le fait créole dans la formation de l'identité nationale en republique du Cap-Vert." *Îles tropicales: Insularité, insularisme. Actes du colloque organizé à Bordeaux-Talence.* Talence: Université de Bordeaux III, 1987. 107-124.

Moser, Gerald. "[Review of *Odju d'Agu*]." *World Literature Today* 62 (1988): 713.

Nunes, António. "Poema de Amanhã." *Poemas de Longe.* Lisboa: Emp. Nacional de Publicidade, 1945.

Parsons, Elsie Clews, ed. *Folk-Lore from the Cape Verde Islands.* 2 vols. Cambridge, MA and New York: American Folk-Lore Society, 1923.

Partido Africano para a Independência da Guiné e Cabo Verde. *História da Guiné e Ilhas de Cabo Verde.* Porto: Afrontamento, 1974.

Pires, Virgílio. "Titina." *Claridade* 9 (1960): 10-12.

Romano, Luís. "*Odju d'Agu*: Ficção Caboverdiana de Manuel Veiga." *Fragmentos* 1.3-4 (1988): 5-7.

Semedo, Manuel Brito. "[Review of] *Odju d'Agu*." *Voz di Povo* 9 May 1987: 4, 5.

Silva, T[omé] V[arela] da, ed. *Na Bóka Noti.* [Praia]: Institutu Kauberdianu di Libru, 1987.

Veiga, Manuel. *Diário das Ilhas.* [Praia]: Spleen, 1997.

———. *Diskrison Strutural di Lingua Kabuverdianu.* [Praia]: Institutu Kabuverdianu di Livru, [1987].

———. *Introdução à Gramática do Crioulo*. [Praia]: Instituto Caboverdiano do Livro e do Disco; Instituto Nacional de Cultura, 1995.

———. *Odju d'Agu*. Praia: Instituto Caboverdiano do Livro, 1987.

———. *A Sementeira*. Linda-a-Velha: ALAC, [1994].

Gregory McNab is Professor Emeritus of Portuguese at the University of Rhode Island. He has been a contributor to the Modern Language Association's *International Bibliography* and to *Encyclopedia of World Literature in the Twentieth Century*, as well as a translator of texts by Orlanda Amarílis, António Aurélio Gonçalves, José Dias de Melo, José Rodrigues Miguéis and Sérgio Sant'Ana. His essays have been published in *África*, *Brasil / Brazil*, *Colóquio-Letras*, the *Luso-Brazilian Review*, the *Revista Letras*, *Romance Notes*, *Seara Nova*, and *Vértice*. His research interests include literature from Africa in Portuguese, the contemporary Portuguese novel, the historical novel and historiography.
E-mail: McNab@uri.edu

Maria Isabel Barreno's *O Senhor das Ilhas*: Memory and Writing at the Threshold*

Isabel A. Ferreira

Abstract. This paper is composed of two parts. The first provides an overview of representations of Africa in the twentieth-century Portuguese literature that revisits the colonial experience, paying particular attention to the relationship between history, memory and fiction, and to the novel of the 1990s as a counter-narrative of belonging. This segment assesses the problematic displacement of the Portuguese colonial self and locates the emergence of new groups in literary representations of empire. The second part addresses Maria Isabel Barreno's portrayal of Cape Verde's colonial past in the historical novel *O Senhor das Ilhas*. This final segment examines both the act of writing the colonizer's fictional (auto)biography, and the relationship between travel, writing and empire.

Qual o meu exacto lugar nesse mundo dele?
(*O Senhor das Ilhas* 18)

Mas é verdade também que na história e nos feitos que se narram sobre aqueles que de algum modo conquistaram a fama, estão mais presentes os motivos de quem narra do que as acções do herói da história.
(*O Senhor das Ilhas* 152-153)

In the decade marking the twentieth anniversary of the Portuguese revolution and the independence of the former colonies of Cape Verde, Mozambique, Angola and Guinea-Bissau, writers persuasively revisited and re-imagined the

Portuguese presence in the former empire. Although literary representations of Africa are far from being a recent invention, revisions of the colonial experience have been a particularly recurrent tendency in the post-revolutionary fiction published in Portugal. Envisioned paradoxically as a space of both regeneration and disenchantment in the post-revolutionary literature, Africa signifies above all a space of return, a place revisited through memory and writing. This is specifically the case with the Portuguese fiction of the 1990s that reflects on the colonial past, stressing the prolonged impact of colonialism through depictions of colonizers and multigenerational families in works that elude the dividing lines between history, memory and fiction.[1]

While contemporary critics have focused primarily on the theme of colonial war and the final collapse of the African empire in post-1974 fiction, none has examined the literary representation of the agents of empire—officials, missionaries, entrepreneurs, uprooted migrants, expatriates and outcasts—and the particular worldviews of those who traveled, settled in colonial outposts, and were born overseas. Dominated by the viewpoint of the Portuguese born and raised in Cape Verde, Maria Isabel Barreno's novel *O Senhor das Ilhas*[2] questions the very dualism that divided colonizer from colonized, as well as metropolis from colony, in order to understand the fundamental contradictions inherent in colonial projects and the internal *tensions of empire*, as the seminal writings of scholars like Ann Laura Stoler, Frederick Cooper, John L. Comaroff and others emphasize.[3] Adopting the perspective of the colonizer's offspring, Maria Isabel Barreno's work reinvents the colonial past at the threshold,[4] from a point of view situated at the crossroads of the Cape Verdean archipelago, and between the colony and the metropolis.

O Senhor das Ilhas demonstrates, on the one hand, how the "civilizing mission" produced sites of appropriation, tension, complicity and resistance in the colony. On the other hand, this historical novel traces the role that colonial Africa has played in the reconfiguration of Portuguese identity at home, showing how metropolis and colony were interconnected through a web of cultural influences. Part of a *macro-corpus* of literature that promotes a dialogue between the past and present, the post-revolutionary fictional representations of empire found in writers as diverse as António Lobo Antunes, Maria Isabel Barreno, Teolinda Gersão, Helder Macedo and others expose the fragments of a culture trying to come to terms with its colonial heritage. At the end of the millennium, this *macro-corpus* thus contributes to the "dialogues of identity" in contemporary Portuguese society.[5]

This paper is composed of two parts. The first provides an overview of representations of Africa in the twentieth-century Portuguese literature that revisits the colonial experience, paying particular attention to the relationship between history, memory and fiction, and to the novel of the 1990s as a counter-narrative of belonging. This segment assesses the problematic displacement of the Portuguese colonial self and locates the emergence of new groups in literary representations of empire. The second part addresses Maria Isabel Barreno's portrayal of Cape Verde's colonial past in the historical novel *O Senhor das Ilhas.* This final segment examines both the act of writing the colonizer's fictional (auto)biography, and the relationship between travel, writing and empire.

I.

Although images of Africa have proliferated since the voyages of Portuguese explorers, it is mainly after the Independence of Brazil that Africa gains extensive literary projection in Portuguese fiction. Published in the late nineteenth century, Eça de Queirós's novels *Os Maias* and *A Ilustre Casa de Ramires,* for example, invented Africa as a place of adventure and redemption that allowed the protagonists to escape from the nation's crisis. Standing in sharp contrast to the dangerous Cape of Torments described by Camões, such a view of earthly paradise attempted to compensate for the country's decline and the anxiety over the loss of Brazil. Viewed as an exotic place, in Eça's novels Africa awaits development by the Portuguese, who dreamed of a "New Brazil" in Africa.[6]

Literary representations of Africa abounded in Portugal during the military dictatorship and the New State. The prolific literary production of this period and the effort to propagate an imperial mystique both in Portugal and overseas were largely attributed to the Colonial Literary Prizes, the Colonial Exhibitions, and the "Colonial Weeks."[7] The New State's investment in disseminating an image of Africa as a desirable destination for Portuguese settlers was twofold: it promoted emigration to the colonies and reinforced the notion of Portugal as a transcontinental nation. For the most part, Portuguese colonial authors[8] not only voiced official visions of imperial rule, but also represented an effort to normalize the subjugation of Africans. They often explored a series of themes centered on parental imagery primarily articulated in masculine terms, and invested in the history of male European heroism. The rhetorical celebration of the family in paternalistic tones served to consolidate the relationship between metropolis and colony by emphasizing the idea of a benevolent Portuguese tutelage. Written for a wide audience, the colonial adventure tale provided a way to dramatize the colonizers' experience of founding a home in exotic, often described as feminized, lands. Intended to celebrate Portugal's "civilizing mission," imperial narratives drew upon familial metaphors to reinforce the normalcy of colonial power overseas.

To be sure, Africa became the object of a different literary approach with the advent of colonial war literature. A major genre in the twentieth century, colonial war literature is primarily a literature of catharsis[9] and denunciation. This genre, which has strong autobiographical resonances, not only recreates the chaos of war, thus avoiding the erosion of memory, but also searches for the redemption of the Portuguese self. Accounts of travel and texts about personal journeys, colonial war novels narrate the soldier's and the individual's dilemma when faced with the agony of the unresolved military conflict and an increasing awareness of colonialism. Incorporating partial visions of war in an attempt to autopsy the Portuguese nation in crisis, colonial war fiction voices the "Other," who does not principally embody the African, but rather the Portuguese soldier, who finds himself changed, "Other," as the war progresses.

Read primarily as fictions of historical failure and as postcolonial narratives,[10] colonial war literature and the novel of the 1990s question Portugal's mission overseas and stage the imperial decline, the twilight of the African empire. Assessing the founding symbols of the Portuguese past, the novel of the 1990s draws special attention, however, to the culture of colonialism as a culture of contamination. By placing the relations between agents of empire and the intercultural contact between colonizer and colonized at the center of their narratives, these writers also display a keen awareness of the problematic displacement of the Portuguese colonial self. Focusing mainly on multigenerational family sagas, the novel of the 1990s functions as a counterpoint to the colonial narrative. Whereas in the colonial adventure tale longing for the appropriation of "exotic" subjects, cultures and lands lies at the heart of its fantasies and idealized depictions, in the Portuguese novel of the 1990s belonging stands at the center of the narrative.

By bringing to light the colonizers' ambivalent positioning between center and periphery, the Portuguese novel of the 1990s examines the struggle for colonial identity and, above all, raises questions of belonging to both a colonial heritage and a society dislocated from the metropolis while still alienated from the autochthonous populations. If the tensions within and against the binaries of metropolis-colony and colonizer-colonized evoke the colonizers' ambivalent and displaced identity, it is hardly surprising that the subaltern nature of Portuguese colonialism also contributes to the colonizers' problem of self-representation. In "Entre Prospero e Caliban: Colonialismo, pós-colonialismo e inter-identidade,"[11] Boaventura de Sousa Santos offers an excellent assessment of the subaltern nature of Portuguese colonialism:

> No domínio dos discursos coloniais, a subalternidade do colonialismo português reside no facto de, a partir do século XVII, a história do colonialismo ter sido escrita em inglês e não em português. Isto significa que o colonizador português tem um problema de auto-representação algo semelhante ao do colonizado pelo colonialismo britânico. [...] Aplicado ao colonizador português, este problema traduz-se na necessidade de definir o colonialismo português em termos de especificidade em relação ao colonialismo hegemónico, o que significa a impossibilidade ou dificuldade em o definir em termos que não reflictam essa subalternidade [...]. (27)

Boaventura de Sousa Santos identifies the colonizers' dual problem of self-representation and identity as it follows:

> A identidade do colonizador português não se limita a conter em si a identidade do outro, o colonizado por ele. Contém ela própria a identidade do colonizador enquanto colonizado por outrem. [...] O Prospero português não é apenas um Prospero calibanizado, é um Caliban quando visto da perspectiva dos Super-Prosperos europeus. A identidade do colonizador português é, assim, duplamente dupla. É constituída pela conjunção de dois outros: o outro que é o colonizado e o outro que é o próprio colonizador enquanto colonizado. Foi esta duplicidade de alta intensidade que permitiu ao português ser emigrante, mais do que colono, nas "suas" próprias colónias. (42)

Although the phenomenon of "staging history" and the dialogue between history and fiction are not recent in Portugal, the valorization of competing versions and alternative angles from which to recreate the country's past is a persistent feature found in recent works. These narratives clearly exhibit a commitment to revisions of national identity in Portugal's semi-peripheral culture. Thus the need to dialogue with the past[12] has resulted, on the one hand, in a critical investigation of the nation's collective self-image, and, on the other, in a process of reassessment of major aspects of Portuguese history (i.e., the colonization of Africa, the emigration to the colonies, *decolonization*, and the post-colonial transformations of Portuguese identity).

Displaying a profound interest in the marginalized and often forgotten agents of history, post-revolutionary writers have expressively incorporated their experiences as a way of accounting for the heterogeneity of Portuguese identity and the manifold contradictions in Portugal's social and cultural configurations. Despite its controversy, the emergence of "new" colonial groups and categories from the past attests to this crucial aspect. Within this vein, the novel of the 1990s identifies competing colonial agendas (based primarily on gender and class stratification, but also on race) to observe how these agendas shaped the politics of expansion and colonization overseas.

The insertion of "marginal" voices into the colonial project, especially the inclusion of children and women in representations of empire (i.e., women's interaction with colonized peoples, particularly with African women, as well as their complicity with imperial consolidation and downfall, or resistance to it) attests to a critical perspective on colonialism that several novels of the 1990s clearly share. That is specifically the case of Maria Isabel Barreno's *O Senhor das Ilhas*. Rejecting the notion of the colony primarily as a male setting, *O Senhor das Ilhas* examines not only the role Portuguese colonial women played in *domesticating the empire*,[13] but also the complex interconnections between family, domesticity and colonialism.

II.

Among Portugal's most prominent writers, Maria Isabel Barreno (born in Lisbon, 1939) is well known for co-authoring *Novas Cartas Portuguesas*[14] with Maria Teresa da Horta, and Maria Velho da Costa. Published during the Caetano regime and banned immediately after its publication, the book's radicalism captured the attention of readers and critics both in Portugal and abroad. Composed of a collection of essays, letters, excerpts from diaries, and poems, this fragmented and multiform work explored new modes of writing to express the condition of Portuguese women and contest Portugal's dominant culture.[15] In this regard, it is important to emphasize one of the most illuminating aspects of Maria Isabel Barreno's work: her interest in voices of dissidence, which has been particularly present since 1968, upon publication of her first novel.

In recent years, the writer has skillfully examined key moments in twentieth-century Portuguese history (i.e. the end of the monarchy, Salazar's dictatorship, the colonial wars, and the revolution and its aftermath) in *A Crónica do Tempo* (1990), a multigenerational family novel dealing with the relationship between family, memory and the national past.[16] In *O Senhor das Ilhas,* Barreno readopts the family chronicle/saga,[17] a sub-genre of the historical novel, to resurrect the past of the Martins family, and the author's Cape Verdean ancestry.[18]

Intertwining the historical novel, the family chronicle, the fictional biography/autobiography, and the travel narrative, *O Senhor das Ilhas* recreates not only the private life of the clan, but also Cape Verdean colonial society of the late 1800s. It describes the nature of race relations and slavery, the role of the *creole* elite in the archipelago, and particularly the effects of colonial rule on the marginalized and often illegitimate *mestiço,* at the time of the rise of the emancipation movements. Although the work concentrates on the complex and often paradoxical role of the patriarch's "civilizing mission" in Cape Verde, it clearly attempts to bring into view those who were left unspoken in the histories/fictions of empire.

Written from the youngest generation's perspective, *O Senhor das Ilhas* relates the offspring's dispute over the act of remembering and writing the fictional biography of their dead father. Throughout this first-person, retrospective narrative, the reader is confronted with the question of who represents the voice most authorized to retell and imagine the life and mission of the family's leading member, Manuel António Martins. The unresolved tension between Manuel Maria, "marginal" protagonist, "author" and narrator who inherits his mother's voice, and Marta, who intervenes and appropriates the narration on several occasions, is never overcome and is a central aspect of the novel.[19] This tension clearly expresses the opposite forces behind the desire to memorialize and the need to unveil the "true" image of the paternal figure.

Writing is a privileged theme that *O Senhor das Ilhas* explores in many directions. Alluding to the existence of a manuscript or "original matrix" granting historical "authenticity" to *O Senhor das Ilhas,* the novel's introduction raises the problem of representing the past and shows how private history can only be unveiled through fiction and invention:

> O manuscrito que a seguir se publica foi encontrado por um descendente da família Martins, na ilha Brava, em 1993. Tratava-se de uma colecção de cadernos de capa preta, bastante maltratados pelo tempo e pelas mãos humanas. [...] como se alguém quisesse preservar-lhes a intimidade, ou afirmar que a história privada

> não pode ser contada, e que qualquer tentativa de a contar a transforma fatalmente em ficção.
>
> Dever-se-á também supor, dadas todas estas interferências no manuscrito deixado pelo primeiro autor e que se terão sucedido ao longo de várias gerações, que alterados ou inventados foram todos os episódios que não possam ser verificados em fontes históricas. (13)

Informed by the first-person narrator's viewpoint, both in close proximity and distant from the events, Manuel Maria's memorial to the colonizer[20] reinvents the colonial sites of familial memory mainly through imagination:

> Para relatar as histórias dos meus, e a minha, as linhas que vieram determinando e colorindo nossas existências e também essas escuras cavernas do tempo que a memória não consegue explorar, recorrerei a todos os relatos que ouvi e li. Mas usarei sobretudo a minha imaginação, porque só essa luz de cada um de nós ressuscita os mortos e as sombras do passado. (20)

As a novel that mimics life-writing, *O Senhor das Ilhas* blurs the distinction between a fictional biographical reconstruction of the father and a fictional autobiography of the son. From the very beginning, the narrative brings into question the authority surrounding the fictional author, the motivation for writing lives and the biographer's responsibility to truthfulness. Both a scribe of memory and a chronicler of a parent's death, Manuel Maria's version of the past embodies, nevertheless, failure, omission and distortion.

Biographical writing—a genre indigenous to the Western world and associated developmentally with the spread of empire—serves, on the one hand, to commemorate and immortalize life against death and, on the other, to demystify illusions.[21] Primarily a demythologizing form that strives to correct or reinterpret false or distorted accounts of the subject, biography nevertheless can, as Ira Bruce Nadel points out in *Biography: Fiction, Fact & Form*,[22] both destroy and create myths.

Does Manuel Maria's narrative contribute to forging a colonial identity (as a fiction of empire) or does it revise the myth of the "patriarch's mission" (as a fiction against empire)? In other words, does the novel, written from the perspective of the colonizer's offspring, overtly destabilize the myths surrounding the father's authority, thus unmasking his construction and unsettling the entire colonial order? In Manuel Maria's own words:

> Olho as páginas que escrevi, e muitas dúvidas me assaltam, tanto nas razões como nos resultados. Terei esclarecido e acrescentado a figura e o destino do meu pai, ou terá sido o meu destino que cumpri? Tão obstinadamente me opus a herdar suas empresas, que acabei unindo minha rota à sua. Nossas acções não se definem por nossos propósitos, mas sim por seus resultados. (363-364)

Resonating throughout the novel, Manuel Maria's question, "Qual o meu exacto lugar nesse mundo dele?" (18), reflects the narrator's quest for personal identity and shows how identity is defined in relation to the father figure and his legacy. Thus it is the father-son relation that constructs the frame through which we read the private history of colonialism. As both an act of revision of the paternal figure—as "meio de tornar claro o [seu] caminho" (19)—and a reinvention of the self performed in the writing of the other, writing unveils the tension between father-son, patrimony-identity.[23]

A hybrid form and an amalgam of biography, autobiography and history, Manuel Maria's narrative challenges the myth of autonomy in life-writing, suggesting that all forms of self-representation are relational and generated by the tension between self and other.[24] The opening, founding proposition of the novel—"Talvez a meu pai eu empreste meus sonhos, meus amores e minhas paixões" (17)—attests to the relational dimension of identity. Thus, Manuel Maria's revisionist project comprises the recovery of the self and the offspring's story of colonialism, told as the story of the colonizer and the Martins clan. Seen as "the history of a becoming," while providing the "account of an undoing," the autobiographer's narrative charts a journey outwards.[25]

Travel is a constant motif throughout the work and is associated with writing and belonging. The novel, which dialogues with classic sagas of the Western literary tradition, presents the narrator's search for identity and meaning with regard to his own culture. The novel also explores travel writing as a form emphasizing the self-reflexivity of the journey,[26] which allows for the production of the self in the course of the act of writing while traveling. In Barreno's novel the association of travel writing and empire, which normally suggests the consolidation of the imperial power, is subverted. In *O Senhor das Ilhas*, travel means transgression, for Manuel Maria and Marta search for the "real" paternal figure through writing during their voyage from Cape Verde to the metropolis.[27] In this vein, their voyage inverts the Portuguese colonizer's typically European direction of travel from the imperial center to the colonial periphery.[28] In sum, *O Senhor das Ilhas* offers a fictional rewriting of canonized types of travelogues and displays the offspring's marginal perspective on the imperial center.

Travel also means displacement, which the image of Manuel Maria's boat wandering incessantly from coast to coast accentuates. Manuel Maria, simultaneously protagonist, narrator and fictional author of the colonizer's (auto)biography, represents the figure of the wanderer, a subject that cannot be fixed and has nowhere to return. A product of "o mundo que o português criou" or "do mundo que criou o português," Manuel Maria "é esse português, criado por tal mundo, que hoje peregrina em simbólicas viagens à procura de si mesmo através dos outros e dos outros através de si mesmo," as Eduardo Lourenço aptly reminds us in "Errância e busca num imaginário lusófono" (112).[29]

A wandering figure in search of a place and time to belong to, Manuel Maria personifies nostalgia, which, as Svetlana Boym argues in *The Future of* Nostalgia,[30] "attempts a transhistorical reconstruction of the lost home," and "dwells on the ambivalences of human longing and belonging" (xviii). Nostalgia, emphasizes Boym, "is not always for the ancient regime or fallen empire but also for the unrealized dreams of the past and visions of the future that became obsolete" (xvi). The final image of the shipwrecked boat, in which the narrator dies, suggests not only the fragmentation of the self, but, above all, the failure of the Portuguese colonial project in Africa. Written by the colonizer born in Cape Verde, who challenges the assumed centrality of the Portuguese perspective as well as European representations of travel, Manuel Maria's fictional narrative questions, from the African margin, notions of home, culture, identity and belonging.

Maria Isabel Barreno's compelling novel not only revisits the colonial sites of familial memory, but also re-inscribes Africa as a focal point for reflection about individual and national identity. Published in the 1990s, *O Senhor das Ilhas* examines the contradictions inherent in colonial projects, while dialoging with the literary tradition. Given the diversity of experiences of colonialism, the novel privileges the representation of the colonizer's problematic identity in life-writing and revises the cultures of empire. At the turn of the millennium, as the twilight settles around the memories of colonialism, literature promotes a generational dialogue between past and present, as well as among cultures, and continues to search for the haunting meanings of the past while asking what it means to be back at home, what it means to belong to a post-imperial nation.

Notes

* I am grateful to Lisa Beth Voigt and Naomi Parker for their gracious help in editing this paper. This article draws on sections of my Brown University dissertation, especially Chaper I, "Colonos, Família e Registo da Memória Colonial em *O Senhor das Ilhas* de Maria Isabel Barreno."

[1] For representations of colonialism in the Portuguese novel of the 1990s, see, for instance, Teolinda Gersão, *A Árvore das Palavras* (Lisboa: Publicações Dom Quixote, 1997); António Lobo Antunes, *O Esplendor de Portugal* (Publicações Dom Quixote, 1997); Helder Macedo, *Partes de África* (Lisboa: Editorial Presença, 1991); and *Pedro e Paula* (Lisboa: Editorial Presença, 1998). Onésimo T. Almeida refers to this recent body of fiction as "romance de revisitação africana."

[2] (Lisboa: Editorial Caminho, 1994).

[3] Frederick Cooper and Ann Laura Stoler, ed., *Tensions of Empire, Colonial Cultures in a Bourgeois World* (Berkeley: U of California P, 1997).

[4] This term evokes a way of reading and writing the cultures of empire at the threshold. *O Senhor das Ilhas* embodies this liminal location: it is a novel both about Cape Verde and from Cape Verde.

[5] Luís de Sousa Rebelo, "Os Diálogos da Identidade no Fim do Século," *Tesserae* 1 (1994-95).

[6] Valentim Alexandre, "The Colonial Empire," António Costa Pinto, ed. *Modern Portugal* (Palo Alto, Calif.: Society for the Promotion of Science and Scholarship, 1998) 41.

[7] Alexandre, "The Colonial Empire" (49), and "África no Imaginário Português (séculos XIX-XX)," *Penélope* 15 (1995):39-52.

[8] For studies on colonial literature, see Pires Laranjeira, "La Littérature Coloniale Portugaise," Jean Sévry, ed., *Regards sur les literatures coloniales, Afrique anglophone et lusophone*, Tome III (Paris: L'Harmattan, 1999) 231-258; Inocência Mata, "Reflexões em torno de um conceito de literatura colonial—Haverá uma estética colonial?," *Pelos Trilhos da Literatura Africana em Língua Portuguesa* (Braga: Cadernos do Povo, 1992) 11-18; Manuel Ferreira, "Uma perspectiva do romance colonial vs. literaturas africanas," *Discurso no percurso africano I* (Lisboa: Plátano, 1989) 231-259; and Salvato Trigo, "Literatura Colonial, Literaturas Africanas," *Ensaios de Literatura Comparada Afro-Lusa-Brasileira* (Lisboa: Vega, 1986) 129-146. Also see Elleke Boehmer, *Colonial & Postcolonial Literature* (Oxford: Oxford UP, 1995) 2-4.

[9] Rui de Azevedo Teixeira, *A Guerra Colonial e o Romance Português* (Lisboa: Notícias Editorial, 1998) 99.

[10] I use the term "postcolonial" here not primarily as a historical periodization, but as a self-reflexive system of knowledge and its narratives, a particular form of enquiry and analysis that contests both colonial domination and colonialist perspectives. See Catherine Hall, "Introduction: thinking the postcolonial, thinking the empire," *Cultures of Empire: A Reader, Colonizers in Britain and the Empire in the Nineteenth and Twentieth Centuries* (New York: Routledge, 2000) 3-5; Elleke Boehmer (3); and Ania Loomba, *Colonialism/Postcolonialism* (New York: Routledge, 1998) 12.

[11] In Maria Irene Ramalho e António Sousa Ribeiro, org., *Entre Ser e Estar: Raízes, Percursos e Discursos da Identidade* (Porto: Edições Afrontamento, 2001).

[12] I employ here LaCapra's concept of dialogue with the past: "[...] to employ the notion of 'dialogue' to designate one's relation to the past (including its texts) is obviously to employ a metaphor. A text cannot literally answer one back in an 'I-thou' relation in the manner in which a face-to-face conversation presumably allows. [...] The more basic sense of dialogue is conveyed by *dia-logos*—a divergence or dehiscence in the logos that itself enables anything like an 'I-thou' rapport to emerge in a face-to-face encounter." See Dominick LaCapra, *History, Politics and the Novel* (Ithaca: Cornell UP, 1987) 10.

13 For an excellent collection of essays on the intersection between race, gender, family and colonialism, see Julia Clancy-Smith and Frances Gouda (ed.), *Domesticating the Empire. Race, Gender, and Family Life in French and Dutch Colonialism* (Charlottesville: UP of Virginia, 1998).

14 (Lisboa: Editorial Futura, 1972).

15 Maria Isabel Barreno's interest in the recording and interpretation of women's reality is parallel to her interest in the social and historical memory of the nation. See Álvaro Manuel Machado, *Dicionário de Literatura Portuguesa* (Lisboa: Editorial Presença, 1996): "A leitura do conjunto da obra de Isabel Barreno põe em evidência a formação de uma voz comprometida com a chamada 'escrita feminina' [...] e com a memória histórico-social do país. Desse modo, desde o seu primeiro romance até um dos mais recentes, não por acaso intitulado *Crónica do Tempo* [...] é explícita a preocupação da autora com o tempo, tanto na sua dimensão individual, como na sua dimensão histórica, elevando muitas vezes, à condição de tema a própria reflexão sobre a passagem do tempo" (51).

16 For a study of the novel, see Isabel Allegro de Magalhães, "Os Tempos de três gerações," *Jornal de Letras, Artes e Ideias* 11: 456 (Abril 2-8, 1991).

17 For an elaboration on the family saga as a sub-genre of the historical novel—a particularly recurrent trend in the Portuguese literature published in the last twenty years—see Maria de Fátima Marinho, *O Romance Histórico em Portugal* (Porto: Campo das Letras, 1999). On Barreno's novel, the critic writes: "*O Senhor das Ilhas* é, pois, um romance sobre a História de Cabo Verde, na sua íntima ligação com a de Portugal, História contada através da vida, costumes, sentimentos e afazeres de uma família, que poderemos considerar como paradigmática de um tempo, lugar e classe social demarcados" (167).

In the preface to the Cape Verdean edition of *O Senhor das Ilhas* (Praia: Centro Cultural Português, 1998), António Leão Correia e Silva identifies the author's contribution to the inauguration of the historical novel in Cape Verde as follows: "Sendo a história de Cabo Verde de grande potencialidade ficcional causa estranheza não se ter produzido no arquipélago, até data recente, romances históricos. *O Senhor das Ilhas* da escritora Isabel Barreno é por isso para a literatura sobre Cabo Verde, a inauguração de um género, a abertura de um novo território. Ele instaura um começo. Por esta razão, mais do que propriamente pela sua inquestionável qualidade literária, trata-se de um marco. O género foi aberto com chave de ouro" (iii).

18 On Maria Isabel Barreno's Cape Verdean background and comments on *O Senhor das Ilhas* as an "archeological search for dreams and feelings," as well as "an alternative history of colonialism," see "Nota da Autora"in the Cape Verdean edition.

19 In his review of *O Senhor das Ilhas* in *Quadrant* 13 (1996), Paulo Alexandre Jorge dos Santos refers to this tension as a game (alluding to the game of backgammon) embodying the narrative's central force: "[...] nous pouvons presque dire que le personnage le plus important n'est autre que le jeu. [...] Le jeu est déjà le grand moteur de la fiction qui provoque des doutes chez le lecteur: qui écrit le roman? Combien de personnages sont vraiment des narrateurs? Est-ce que Marta a un role important dans la formulation du récit?" (266-267).

On the mediation between the (implicit/explicit) author, the narrator and Marta, David Mourão-Ferreira argues in "A ressurreição dos antepassados," that "Muito aliás haveria a dizer sobre o intrínseco relacionamento entre a autora explícita (ou implícita) e o narrador masculino sobre cujos ombros recai a responsabilidade da narração. Não me parece fruto do acaso a circunstância de existir, entre tal autora e narrador, a mediação de uma feminina personagem—a irmã mais velha, Marta—nem o facto de a própria narração se desenvolver sob o olhar vigilante, e mesmo interventor, desta figura carismática, a seu modo e para o seu tempo inquietantemente emancipada," *Jornal de Letras, Artes e Ideias* (Dezembro 21, 1994): 23.

20 My use of "memorial" oscillates between a book of remembrances and a memorial to the dead. Manuel Maria's fictional writing is initiated at sea, while on a mission to the metropolis

to obtain a stone for his father's mausoleum. Standing as a controversial memorial to the colonizer, Manuel Maria's narrative not only reflects on past experiences, but also on memory and writing, reminding us, as James E. Young points out, that "the motives of memory are never pure" (2). His narrative is less a metaphorical monument than a memorial. Different from monuments, which are celebratory and embody the myths of beginnings, argues Young, memorials indicate the twilight of ends, educate future generations, and can be conceived as expiations of guilt (3). For an elaboration on memorials and monuments, see James E. Young, *The Texture of Memory* (New Haven: Yale UP, 1993).

21 See Catherine Park, *Biography. Writing Lives* (New York: Twayne, 1996) 22.

22 *Biography: Fiction, Fact & Form* (New York: St. Martin's, 1984) 176, 181.

23 In *Bequest & Betrayal, Memoirs of a Parent's Death* (New York: Oxford UP, 1996), Nancy K. Miller identifies patrimony both as what we inherit by birth and comes after a parent's death, and what haunts our identity (31). I employ here Miller's notion of "patrimony."

24 See Paul John Eakin, "Relational Selves, Relational Lives: Autobiography and the Myth of Autonomy" (43), In *How our lives become stories: Making selves* (Ithaca: Cornell UP, 1999).

25 Nancy Miller 39, 53-54.

26 On travel narrative and empire, see Steve Clark, ed., *Travel Writing and Empire: Postcolonial Theory in Transit* (London: Zed Books, 1999).

27 Manuel Maria's (travel) narrative subverts the traditional fiction of empire since it consists of an inquiry into his father's identity and (unknown) origins. In *The Appropriated Voice* (Ann Arbor: The U of Michigan P, 1990), Bette London states: "The fiction of empire cannot withstand much inquiry into origins, since it premises itself on eternal omnipresence [...]. To investigate origins is to bring imperial power into a provisional realm, to reveal it as a human construct and not an unalterable act of God. And it is to reveal the shaky logic at its core, for the purported cause of colonial power" (75).

28 For a detailed study of postcolonial travel writing in the twentieth century and inverted patterns of travel, see Barbara Korte, *English Travel Writing, From Pilgrimages to Postcolonial Explorations* (New York: St. Martin's, 2000).

29 *A Nau de Ícaro seguido de Imagem e Miragem da Lusofonia* (Lisboa: Gradiva, 1999).

30 (New York: Basic Books, 2001). For a detailed study of this theme in the novel, see Piero Ceccucci's article "La memoria e il sogno, o la nostalgia delle proprie radici in *O Senhor das Ilhas* di Maria Isabel Barreno," Françoise Massa, org., *Les Îles Atlantiques: Realites et Imaginaire*, Actes du colloque organize par l'équipe ERILAR, 1999.

Isabel A. Ferreira is a Ph.D. candidate in the Department of Portuguese & Brazilian Studies at Brown University (RI, USA), Fellow of The Helen Kellogg Institute for International Studies and of the Nanovic Institute for European Studies, and Director of the Portuguese Language Program at the University of Notre Dame (IN, USA). Her research and teaching interests include: autobiography and immigrant literature from Brazil and Portugal, post-revolutionary Portuguese fiction, war literature, and postcolonial literature from Lusophone Africa. Ferreira has published on the twentieth-century Portuguese novel and diary, and is currently finishing her doctoral dissertation on family, empire and memory in the recent fiction of three Portuguese authors. E-mail: ferreira.5@nd.edu

Translating Trans-Atlantic Space in Two 1938 Travel Narratives to Cape Verde: Anne Morrow Lindbergh's *Listen! the Wind* and Archibald Lyall's *Black and White Make Brown*

Phyllis Peres

As we came nearer we could see they were not round knobs of equal height protruding from the sea. Light clouds, which were not visible before, hovered over the islands and covered some of the volcanic peaks, making them appear to be of the same height. Their shores, too, far from sloping gently into the ocean, were cut up, ragged, and irregular, scattered with rocks and ledges as though indicating a constant struggle with the elements around them. [...] It was unrelated to any country I could remember. These islands—what were they like? I groped in my mind for something comparable. They were just islands, suspended in the Atlantic, lost islands, jumping-off places.
—Anne Morrow Lindbergh, 1938

It was our first warm, sunny day and the flying fish were gliding like silver swallows over the calm blue mirror of the sea when we caught the first glimpse of Africa. [...] The islands have been likened to a fleet of petrified galleons riding at anchor, and certainly the skyline was almost too fantastic to be true. The peaks and pinnacles and cliffs chequered the horizon like the backcloth of a modernist theater. As we came nearer, Santo Antão showed itself as a mass of naked rock, crinkled and crumpled as though by the same sun which had singed off whatever vegetation might have sprung up after the last rains. When the purser said that Santo Antão was reputed to be the most fertile of all the islands, I began to wonder whether I was not going to spend the next month or two on a sort of open-air geological museum.
—Archibald Lyall, 1938

I. Atlantic Space and Metaphors of Travel

Anne Morrow Lindbergh's *Listen! the Wind* recounts the last ten days of an almost six-month Atlantic air journey undertaken in 1933. Morrow Lindbergh (1906-2001) and her husband Charles traversed thirty thousand miles in a single engine Lockheed aircraft baptized the Tingmissartoq from the Greenlander cry—"one who flies like a big bird"—on the sighting of a plane (Lindbergh vi). This was the same plane that had set a 1930 continental record from California to New York, although the later journey was not intent on breaking aviation barriers in the same sense. Rather, it was one of geographic and economic exploration, to survey the Atlantic and chart potential routes for commercial airlines. Morrow Lindbergh's text relates the story of the homeward route of the journey and opens with the air approach to Cape Verde and the subsequent landing and short stay at the French seaplane base in the port of Praia on the island of Santiago (São Tiago).

Three years later, Archibald Lyall departed on a very different type of Atlantic journey by means of a series of ships that carried him first to Portugal, onto Cape Verde, between islands, and finally to then Portuguese Guinea. Lyall (1904-1964), who studied at Oxford, was at times a barrister, served as an Intelligence Corps officer during the Second World War, and for a short period directed the Public Information Office of the Allied British-United States Zone of Trieste. First and foremost though, he was a traveler. Lyall's published accounts of his trips span more than thirty years and fall into two discrete sets; the first recounts travels of the 1930s and the second dates from 1956 until his death. The journeys themselves are quite distinct, from the early ones to the Balkans, Russia, Cape Verde, and Portuguese Guinea undertaken when Lyall was in his late twenties and early thirties to the later ones to Rome, southern France, Madrid, and Tuscany in the 1950s and 60s that resulted in intimate travel guides for the discerning English tourist.

At the time of his travels to Cape Verde and Portuguese Guinea, Archibald Lyall was already a well-known eccentric in a sector of 1930s London society and likened by a close friend of his to an early novel by Evelyn Waugh into which "Archie fitted like a hand in a glove" (Clarke and Footman 15). Ostensibly, Lyall traveled to Portuguese Guinea in the employ of a chemical laboratory to investigate an herbal drug reportedly used by locals as an oral contraceptive. The circle of Archie's English friends, however, conjectured that the real purpose of the journey was to look into the rumors that the Germans were building submarine bases in the Guinean Bissagos Islands (Clarke and Footman 17). Lyall, however, hints only vaguely at espionage activity in the text of his 1936 journey, *Black and White Make Brown: An Account of a Journey to the Cape Verde Islands and Portuguese Guinea* (Lyall 252). Published in the same year as Morrow Lindbergh's travel account of the homeward journey from Lisbon through the South Atlantic, Lyall's narrative moves away from home and into the unknown. Both recount journeys of rediscovery and exploration in the sea paths of fifteenth-century Portuguese travelers of sorts whose own voyages through the Atlantic charted it with real, not illusory islands (Johnson 27). If both Morrow Lindbergh and Lyall interpolate Portuguese journeys of empire, their own very different travels further participate in the renewed cartographic project of what Fernández-Armesto, writing of medieval Atlantic exploration, cites as the "one authentic discovery of transcendent importance," that of Atlantic space (56).

To speak of fifteenth-century Portuguese explorers, Morrow Lindbergh, and Lyall all as "travelers" recognizes, even briefly, how recent critical debate has expanded the tropes of travel beyond the more accepted dislocations of European leisure travel in the late eighteenth and nineteenth centuries. While some critics such as Mary Louise Pratt include narratives of science, anthropology, and discovery among travel texts, others such as James Clifford and Caren Kaplan argue for mobility narratives to encompass those of slavery, marronnage, captivity, migration, and immigration.

Intrinsically rooted in discourses of othering, the culture of modern travel narrative has a richness that can be applied well before the post-18th century second period of colonialism and, indeed, to the discourses of the very beginnings of modern colonial encounters, the first period that began, in one version, when Columbus attempted to narrate his travels to a New World in, as Stephen Greenblatt argues, a rhetoric of wonder to compensate for the failure to discover a set of metaphors adequate to his experience. In contrast, José Rabasa, in *Inventing America*, contends that Columbus is a prime example of a practitioner of a new type of travel discourse to describe a New World, one that both borrows from existing medieval forms of travel rhetoric, but transforms and reinvents that narrative as a new form of Renaissance scripture. Rabasa's own reading is indebted to Michel de Certeau's *The Writing of History* and his theory of a Renaissance scriptural economy whose most salient feature is the transformation from a medieval scripture that purports to narrate exemplary lives—*exemplum fidei*—and chronicle events to a scripture that seeks to valorize an individual subject and provide a record of the appropriation and transformation of a territory or social body.

It is this traveling culture to which the Portuguese not only belong, but, indeed, inform, through the ambiguous narrations that accompany the late medieval and modern opening of Atlantic space. Even an introduction to the highly complex Portuguese culture of travel would necessarily study the textual locations where bodies meet, engage, and struggle for power over space and are transformed by the series of encounters. It is also this traveling culture that Anne Morrow Lindbergh and Archibald Lyall invoke in their own Atlantic journeys. If that former culture is poised between de Certeau's notion of medieval scripture and the dynamic Renaissance scriptural economy, it is also one that produces discourses of power to incorporate and ultimately colonize encountered spaces and bodies. And, above all, early Portuguese travel narratives inscribe the economy of Atlantic spaces as locations of hegemonical, imperial, colonial and capitalist exchanges. As Morrow Lindbergh and Lyall retrace the paths of fifteenth-century Portuguese travelers through Atlantic oceanic and island spaces, they, too, write from specific and very different locations of economy, nation, colony, time, and memory. The narratives that emerge from their own Cape Verdean journeys straddle discourses of travel and inform the ambivalent trans-Atlantic times and spaces between the two World Wars.

II. Traveling Home: Anne Morrow Lindbergh's *Listen! the Wind*

> These bare, brown broken-off scraps of the African continent are two hundred miles nearer to South America than the closest part of Africa.
>
> —Anne Morrow Lindbergh

Of the historic six-month journey through the Atlantic that Anne Morrow Lindbergh made in 1933 with her pioneering aviator husband Charles, she chose to narrate the travels of the last week and a half of the accidental homeward leg. Theirs had been a journey to survey the three "natural" North Atlantic air routes, which Lindbergh designates the northern Greenland Route, the southern Azores Route, and the center "Great Circle Route" (Lindbergh vi). Traveling from Lisbon, the Lindberghs arrive at the Azores too late in the year to complete the Southern Route and are forced to move farther south to begin the flight home along the equator separating the north and south Atlantic. At the start of her narrative in the moments prior to sighting Cape Verde, Morrow Lindbergh retraces their travels of the past few days:

> Last night outside the tents of the Moors on that dry spit of desert Africa; the night before at Las Palmas in the Canary Islands, among the bazaars and shops, the docks and markets of that old crossroad of the east and west. One jump back from Las Palmas and we had been at the Azores, stepping stones in the Atlantic. One jump before that, Lisbon (Morrow Lindbergh 3).

And, of course, before her lay those pieces of Africa, whose only redemption is their location two hundred miles closer to Brazil.

In this short passage that begins *Listen! the Wind*, Anne Morrow Lindbergh manages to both resonate and disrupt a culture of travel established some five hundred years before her own air voyage. Unlike the narratives of sea voyages, however, her travel through this part of the Atlantic consists of staccato-like jumps from space to space in an island itinerary of entrepots, interstitial locations, and take-off points that foreshadow the dislocation of the postmodern traveler. Travel writing, however, is inherently ambivalent, so that Morrow Lindbergh's text plays these intermediary island spaces off against those continental ones inscribed with almost metaphorical Moors, viewed as pieces of the colonial and barren landscape. But even on the continent, there is a transience of tents, a station on a larger Atlantic journey. This textual ambiguity in the opening passages of Morrow Lindbergh's narrative is not unrelated to what David Spurr terms "the anxiety of colonial discourse," particularly in the relationship between author and text (11). At the end of a long endeavor to chart the commercial routes of air exchanges across the Atlantic, Morrow Lindbergh immerses herself in the discourse of travel and pins an ambivalent colonial gaze on landscapes and subjects as she sets her sights on home.

In the passage that opens my text, Anne Morrow Lindbergh's first view of Cape Verde in many ways echoes the initial sightings of land in the travel narratives of late medieval and Renaissance explorers who wonder at the otherness of the landscape, of course with an important difference; this is not a sighting across the horizon, but rather one from above. The strangeness of the Cape Verdean topography is untranslatable and ultimately is expressed in the islands' description as suspended and lost, mere "jumping-off spaces." This strangeness is compounded by the almost impossible landing conditions of strong winds and rough waves, though the safe haven appears in the sighting of the harbor, a crane, and a hangar. The Lindberghs manage to land the Tingmissartoq at the French seaplane base at Praia and are greeted by a rowboat of islanders, the French mechanic in a sun helmet, and "two Negroes" who moor the plane with a single anchor. For Morrow Lindbergh, the irony is that to be at a jumping-off space means that one first has to land; to journey home, one first must start out from some other place, even if that place is intermediary.

Once on land, Morrow Lindbergh's sense of the "unrecognizability" of Cape Verde and of Cape Verdeans themselves increases as she meets and interacts with the chief of the seaplane base and his wife in a sphere of cultural strangeness not unlike that of the geographical one. David Spurr's work on colonial discourse and imperial rhetoric is illuminating here particularly in the ways in which Morrow Lindbergh's travel narrative of Atlantic space reverberates with earlier Atlantic narratives of conquest and contemporary ones of colonization. Morrow Lindbergh, though only passing through the islands, interacts in the colonial society and participates in the writings of self-inscription "onto the lives of people who are conceived as an extension of the landscape" (Spurr 7). She first sights the Cape Verdean couple in shadow by the pier and adjusts her gaze to the new island light:

> I put my hand up to shade my face and looked at them. They were both young and both in sun helmets. The man was a Negro. No—perhaps not. […] But he was very dark, with almost a blue tinge to his skin. And he was so thin and long that his nicely cut and brushed dark suit hung on him listlessly as though on a rack, and showed no trace of the figure beneath. Why, he might be just poles underneath, I thought, a scarecrow.
>
> The girl was thin also and wore a clumsy sun helmet on her head which looked as though it might extinguish her like the snuffer of a candle. It was probably a man's sun helmet, too heavy for her sweet sallow little face, for that flimsy cotton print dress flapping listlessly in the wind against bare brown legs, for those narrow feet showing dusty through the openwork sandals. (19)

Not unlike the early chroniclers of Atlantic encounters, Morrow Lindbergh's descriptions of the "natives" move from that which they are not, particularly in terms of racial categories. Was the man a "Negro," and if not, what was he other than very dark with blue overtones? In later sections of the narrative, Morrow Lindbergh labors to discern the woman's race, and only at the end of her stay does she learn her identity as Italian, but island-born. She is fascinated with their bodies, or rather, the ways in which their bodies are erased and made listless beneath the European attire; they are extinguished or transformed, devoid of life. Throughout their brief appearance in the travel narrative, the couple are never referred to by their birth names, but only by the names given them by Morrow Lindbergh—"Chef" and "his wife" or "the girl." Her name for the base chief is a bit of linguistic mockery since at their first meeting he speaks to her in halting English and identifies himself as the "chef," undoubtedly using the Portuguese word *chefe* as a false cognate. Her amusement, however, quickly turns to disdain when the "Chef" turns to his more fluent French and she realizes that one of her roles on Santiago will be that of translator, a task that she cannot fulfill, not even in the most rudimentary sense.

It is in this forced intermediary role that Morrow Lindbergh passes through various sectors of Cape Verdean society to secure the shackles that her husband requests to reinforce the plane's sole anchor, to obtain fuel for the trans-Atlantic flight, to arrange for their lodging in Praia, and to linger for a few hours in Santiago's colonial haute culture. These ventures lead her to the center of town, as well as to various commercial establishments, the Governor's house, and to the home of Chef and his wife, who attempt to interact with the Lindberghs. Morrow Lindbergh's trip to Praia puts her in the midst of the local women, most of whom she notes are pregnant, and with the swollen-bellied children who run out to look at her. She, of course, looks back with the fascinated, horrified gaze of a traveler:

> A large crowd had gathered in the hot street, men, women, and children, their black faces shining with perspiration. The women had limp babies, like wilting poppy buds, drooping on their backs. Some of them had baskets on their heads, balanced on red bandannas. They raised their hands and waved at us. The men shouted in broken English. We pushed our way through the hot, pressing bodies. Here was something waving that was not an arm. It was a claw, opening and shutting rhythmically, in the middle of those black hands. I stopped and stared at it, horrified, fascinated. It was a chicken's foot, torn off, held in the hand of a small boy who was manipulating it, pulling the tendons. He gave a delighted leer at my startled face. (36-37)

As in the case of the scarecrow-like Chef, Morrow Lindbergh narrates the vitality out of the Cape Verdean subjects, instead creating broken, incomprehensible, dehumanized and animal bodies whose own gaze in return, even in the face of a child, becomes a mocking leer.

Furthermore, Morrow Lindbergh's colonial anxiety of the public space finds no relief in the house of Chef and his wife. An entire chapter—"Where

Would We Sleep?"—follows the Lindbergh's search for an adequate place to spend the night. The former chief's bungalow, filthy and atop a treacherous hill becomes a colonial emblem of the forgotten island port: "There were newspapers on the bare floor, French ones, old and yellowing [...]. And none of those things mattered now. [...] I wondered how much they ever mattered to Porto Praia" (41). In the ambivalence of the traveler, however, Morrow Lindbergh cannot bring herself to accept the Cape Verdean couple's offer to use their own bedroom, even after learning that the alternative spaces are contaminated with tuberculosis or infested with bed bugs. The Lindberghs end up sleeping in their plane, choosing the certain space, par excellence, of the travelers, rather than the uncertainty of Cape Verdean space. Upon seeing their hosts the next morning, in yet another "untranslate-able" moment, the Lindberghs assume an air of "blank British cheerfulness," with no words to excuse the poverty and the dirt (Morrow Lindbergh 70).

If there is one Cape Verdean island space that Morrow Lindbergh approaches with some assurance, it is the house of the Portuguese Governor where she and Charles eat a long leisurely lunch. Here, she finds a bathroom with unused scented soap, purple hand towels, women in silk, men in uniform, a world that she deems "easy, comfortable, and completely unreal" (81). Here, Morrow Lindbergh learns the history and geography of the islands, told to her in "beautiful French." The Governor brings out the maps of the Islands, "neatly contoured and marked, set in a flawless paper sea" (82), which, too, cannot translate the wind and waves that halt the journey home. The maps are useless, but Morrow Lindbergh longs to linger—"If only it were something else we wanted: facts about the early slave traffic from Africa, sisal or eucalyptus oil, baobab trees or coffee" (83). The harsh colonial locations of Cape Verdean histories are lures away from that which would take her home; for Morrow Lindbergh they are unreal stories told in an unreal place and she turns towards the harbor, the plane, and the wind, all of which signify departure.

Ultimately, the departure becomes not only the journey towards home, but also away from Cape Verde. If Morrow Lindbergh fails as an intermediary in Santiago, the island as well fails as an adequate trans-Atlantic space. The strong winds make it impossible for the plane to take off with a full load of fuel sufficient to cross the ocean, and the Lindberghs are forced to return to Africa. With a yellow fever epidemic raging in Dakar, they turn to Bathurst in the British Gambia as their next jumping-off point. Morrow Lindbergh narrates their departure as an escape from the perceived timelessness of the island, from an intermediary dimension that is not measured in Western time:

> Of course, we had gone by time. There were our chronometers to be wound every morning. But they did not seem to have any connection with the time on the island. They were arbitrary instruments that we had brought with us from another world. [...] How long had we been here? Could it be measured in weeks, days, or hours. (91-92)

Even in her farewells to Chef and his wife, Morrow Lindbergh only can relate the immutability of Cape Verdean island space expressed in the couple's "appalling stillness" (Morrow Lindbergh 112). And in her final gaze at the two people whose human-ness escapes her, she casts her eyes towards an unchanging landscape:

> Such stillness [...] I have only felt in a waiting train, standing in a country station. Another train goes by, clickety-click, clickety-click. The sound of rattling cars, the rush of wind, the kaleidoscopic pattern of passing faces and windows, light and darkness, give you the illusion that you too are moving. Then, with a rattle and swish of wind, the train is gone. You are suddenly faced again with the same stark landscape; the still roadbed covered with oil and cinders, the still tracks, the still water tank, the telegraph poles, the ditch, the fence. It was the same landscape I saw now in the faces opposite me. (112-113)

It is this gaze that Morrow Lindbergh maintains as the plane struggles to take off in the rush of water from the harbor at Praia. As she watches from the cockpit window, Chef and his wife wave their "miniature arms" and lose all importance in Morrow Lindbergh's world view as they quickly become a "dim and dreamlike memory, an old nightmare" (Morrow Lindbergh 118). There are not even any photos to carry away—in contrast to the small girl who asks to snap a picture of the Lindberghs as they leave—but only the faint crackle of the radio as the last contact is made and lost. And in a wonderfully pre-postmodern moment, Morrow Lindbergh watches the Atlantic island landscape recede as the plane ascends and "space became time in that instant" (118). In that moment of dislocation-location she moves from an island space without Western time to a new measure of time that utterly merges with space towards the ordered space and time of British colonialism—

forested, paved, whitewashed, and wired: "A British colony, of course. We would be all right here" (Morrow Lindbergh 122).

III. Traveling Away: Archibald Lyall's *Black and White Make Brown*

> I had only met one man who had ever been to Portuguese Guinea; and he found himself there more or less by accident. He was an American novelist named Norman Matson who I ran across in Lisbon in 1929. He had just come up from Guinea and was waiting for a boat back to New York. Matson had lived in Provincetown, Massachusetts, which I gathered from his description was a sort of an American St. Ives; a little town of writers, painters and fishermen perched at the end of Cape Cod. Portuguese fishermen from the Azores and mulatto fishermen from the Cape Verde Islands went there every year in large numbers, he said, and he had made friends with some of the Capverdians and persuaded them to take him back to their native islands with them. So he had crossed the Atlantic in a big sailing ship manned by seventy "niggers" and been becalmed for a month in mid-ocean and arrived in the end at Praia, the miniature capital of Cape Verde. He had stayed there for a while, and then sailed on with his dusky friends when they crossed to the mainland of Guinea. In Guinea apparently, against a Darkest African background of jungle and savagery, he found himself in a highly sophisticated society of Portuguese exiles from the Dictatorship. They were all doctors and lawyers and poets from Lisbon, and they lived there in Guinea with beautiful mulatto mistresses and talked about Paris and never saw a stranger from one year to another. He was the first tourist who had ever been heard of there. So I made up my mind to go to these almost unvisited colonies as soon as I had the opportunity, and suddenly the opportunity came along. (Lyall 1-2)

Thus begins Archibald Lyall's travel narrative of his own journey to Cape Verde and Portuguese Guinea—with the tale of another traveler. As a framing device, Matson's complex tale is the lure that draws Lyall, already a seasoned traveler, first to the Atlantic islands and then to continental Africa. What is the lure, or in this case, the series of lures for Lyall? The Atlantic voyage? The island space? The tale of the Portuguese exile community set in the savage jungle? The mulatto women who help sustain the dreams of Paris?

In many ways, Matson's story is the perfect take-off device for Lyall's narrative journey as it seamlessly interweaves the tales of many travelers and their worldviews—those of Matson himself, the Azorean and Cape Verdean fishermen to Massachusetts, the sailors' return to the islands and then to Guinea, the exiled Portuguese revolutionaries, and the promise of Lyall's own Atlantic travels. And the lure? For Lyall the only one that really matters: to visit the unvisited colonies. And so, seven years after hearing Matson's tale, Lyall sets off for Cape Verde and Portuguese Guinea, not as a modern African wanderer who "depended for prestige very largely on the dangers and difficulties they had surmounted," nor as an "anthropologist, sportsman nor explorer," but as a traveler and thus "interested as much in the white and brown men as in the black" (Lyall 3). What Lyall does claim, however, from the contemporary anthropologist, at least, is the fascination with the "field." James Clifford's telling assessment of Lyall's contemporaries, that generation of Franz Boas anthropologists who spoke and wrote with seriousness about the field as laboratory finds its expression in the title of Lyall's narrative, and its suggested reports of the racial mingling and mixing of Portuguese colonial laboratories (Clifford 21). If, as the text that opens this present work suggests, Lyall's first impressions of Cape Verdean topography are those of a museum, he quickly sets about attempting to catalogue and archive racial and cultural topographies for exhibit in his travel narrative.

For Lyall, however, this space that he deems as creolized is not the controlled anthropological laboratory where his own mobility is contrasted with the static and centered native dwelling place or field. In sharp contrast to Anne Morrow Lindbergh, whose gaze imprisoned Cape Verdean subjects at least as much as she perceived her own imprisonment on Santiago and who fled in fascinated horror from the impossibility of translation, Archibald Lyall revels in translation, whether that be linguistic, cultural, or material. Where Morrow Lindbergh pins her subjects to the static landscape, Lyall narrates mobility, oftentimes privileging others' travel over his own, and in so doing positions Cape Verde as that space that ultimately does translate the Atlantic as ambivalent, interstitial, colonized, dynamic, and decadent. Where Morrow Lindbergh's narrative recognizes dislocation only in the impossibility of home, order, and time in the Cape Verdean location and marks the frontier between travelers and locals with a swift gaze from above, Archibald Lyall's narrative, like his gaze, wanders among the possibilities of location and dislocation. Where Morrow Lindbergh denies the realities of colonial histories, economies, and hegemonies, Lyall is the consummate translator of their cultural expressions in the bodies and landscapes of numerous travelers both historical and contemporary.

Lyall's journey begins in London in a Portuguese conversation class where, after a dozen lessons, he can make himself understood in a "vile Portuguese-Spanish *patois*" of his own (4). Once in Lisbon proper, he collects introductions and letters to carry to Cape Verde and Guinea and, while waiting for his boat to sail, indulges in a side trip to the Algarve. No ordinary jaunt, this is a pilgrimage to Sagres and Lagos, the holy sites of the Infante Dom Henrique, where Lyall provides the Prince's exemplary life narration. This is itself a travel narrative within a travel narrative, not only Lyall's or of the landlubber Infante, of course, but that of the traveling Portuguese nation. As he reaches Cape St. Vincent, "the uttermost end of Europe," he looks out on the sea and begins his true Atlantic voyage at the "suddenest place in all the world" (18).

Of his own Atlantic voyage, Lyall recounts little, but instead devotes the narrative space to a detailed history of Cape Verde that situates the archipelago as trans-Atlantic space, an obligatory port of call for the slave trade, treasure-ships from India and, with the rise of ocean liners at the end of the nineteenth century, as a (imported) coal refueling station for luxury ships. To these narratives of mobility, Lyall weaves those of the emigrants as well, particularly those of Brava, who were before the first World War the economic saviors of a colony beset by famine and, between the Wars, all but forgotten by the metropolis: "The average Portuguese knows Cape Verde solely from the recurring newspaper headline 'Famine in Cape Verde,' which is to him what 'Revolution in Cuba' or 'Floods in China' are to us. The Islands have been forgotten for centuries and they are still forgotten" (32).

Once in Praia, at the Hotel Vasconcelos, Lyall immerses himself in another traveling group, a trio of expatriate Europeans who for assorted reasons have ended up in Santiago. With them, Lyall forms the "English-speaking colony of Praia" (45). From his hotel base, Lyall studies the "human cocktail-shaker" racial laboratory of the island and, in addition to the inventory of color, his narrative catalogues the labor practices, diseases, dress, and class structure of the island capital. He declares the Cape Verdeans to be "bohemians" since they do not possess "a sense that everything ought to serve a particular purpose and no other" (39). Thus, petrol tins become showerheads or flower pots, kerosene packing cases turn into lavatory seats, and empty flour-cloth sacks are reinvented as shirts or sails. Always the consummate modernist reader and viewer in his writing of racialized and gendered bodies, Lyall recognizes, albeit incompletely, a thoroughly different type of "translate-ability" that informs the very basis of Cape Verdean creole culture, as if those very bodies were sites of trans-Atlantic hybrid practices.

If Lyall catalogues, he also collects, and at the center of his Cape Verdean narrative is a chapter devoted to "The Creole Poets." The chapter opens with Lyall's account of meeting José Lopes da Silva for whom Lyall admits a certain fascination as an autodidact who taught himself English by reading Shakespeare, Byron, Spenser and Milton (90). The traveler reproduces stanzas from Lopes's "Ode on England" on Lord Nelson and the Battle of Jutland, undoubtedly an intriguing and ambiguous relic for Lyall's future English audience. Indeed, the three Cape Verdean writers who Lyall most cites in this chapter—Lopes, Pedro Cardoso, and Eugénio Tavares—all belong to what Manuel Ferreira has termed the "generation of ambiguity" (Ferreira xlv).

David Brookshaw well situates this generation within the social and political context of Cape Verde and, in particular, within the early decades of the twentieth century with a liberal Portuguese Republic that decentralized the colonial administration, as well as with the aforementioned relative economic boom due to trans-Atlantic shipping and American dollars from Cape Verdean emigrants (Brookshaw 183). The new centralizing colonial policies of Salazar's *Estado Novo* combined with the world economic crisis to drastically change the interstitial island space and economy as well as its literary-cultural practices. Lyall, who writes extensively both in this chapter and elsewhere in the narrative about the political and economic decadence of the islands, recognizes the ambiguity of trans-Atlantic cultural expressions, most particularly in his cataloguing and rudimentary analysis of contemporary Cape Verdean verse. He writes of Pedro Cardoso as a versatile poet who "competes with José Lopes in producing ornate poems in classical Portuguese" but who also writes *mornas* in Fogo Creole (97). Lyall even translates some of the verses and *mornas* of the Brava poet Eugénio Tavares and offers a basic lesson in the grammar and historical linguistics of Creole. Most telling here is Lyall's translation of Tavares's "Morna de Despedida," (as "The Morna of Farewell"), a traveling song of economic exile and departure.

Even more telling is Lyall's coincidence in Cape Verde in 1936 with the publication of the first number of *Claridade*, a name that the English traveler deems somewhat unwarranted (93). Citing Jorge Barbosa, Manuel Lopes, Osvaldo Alcantara, Baltasar Lopes da Silva and the artist Jaime Figueiredo as the chief proponents, Lyall comments on the *claridosos*' "intensely local" poetics: "Their subjects are almost always the islands of Cape Verde, their mountains and seas, their rains and droughts, and the hardships of their people" (93). He includes a translation of Jorge Barbosa's "Islands," from the 1935 collection *Archipelago*, a poem that travels throughout the archipelago and expresses the movements of dance, music, politics, emigration, and the market places in the islands.

As a translator, Lyall himself recognizes his always-distanced subjectivity from the creole and ambiguous expressions of *caboverdianidade*. Lyall may, as he put it, "amuse myself trying to translate [...] whenever I could find someone to help me"; he may, in fact assay to explain *sodade* in terms of exile and longing; but, ultimately, he cannot convey the creole memory that is not part of his own cultural landscape (99, 104). Does he, as James Clifford suggests, engage then in the dual edge of translation and betrayal that extends to all those who travel and inscribe, if we regard travel as a translation term: "Travel [...] offers a good reminder that all translation terms used in global comparison—get us some distance and fall apart. *Tradittore, traduttore*. In the kind of translation that interests me most, you learn a lot about peoples, cultures, and histories different from your own, enough to begin to know what you're missing" (Clifford 39). For Archibald Lyall, travel to Cape Verde signifies translations of locations of class, race, and even literariness. If these inscriptions of Cape Verdean cultural, literary, material, and historical landscapes are necessarily marked by that which is lacking, a discursive absence, so to speak, they also are marked by that which is present in terms of both strategies and contingencies.

IV. Home and Away: Translating Trans-Atlantic Space

> Every story is a travel story, a spatial practice.
>
> —Michel de Certeau, *The Practice of Everyday Life*

A travel narrative, as a spatial practice, is mobility itself, as it moves between locations and the strategic discursive practices that transform them. That travel narratives are always contingent underscores the ambiguities and betrayals of cultural comparisons. Anne Morrow Lindbergh's mobile narrative of travel seemingly finds its direction between away and home as an anxious discursive charting of the direct air routes of Atlantic exchanges. Part of that dynamic process of exchange relies on the transformative practices of her own narration, even in her translations of home and away. As Van den Abbeele argues, the concept of home is itself mediated through travel and the spatialization of time (xix). For Morrow Lindbergh, the air voyage makes this problematic, at the very least, for in that take-off moment in which space and time converge, there is also a discursive convergence of that which is future with memories of home and away. Home, in her travel narrative, is both prospective and retrospective, as the "away" of Cape Verde is forgotten, and she inscribes this absence through the writing of the islands and the islanders as both static and timeless. At one end of her narrative journey, Morrow Lindbergh imposes home on the Atlantic approach to Brazil, in fact to that city which signifies home, Natal:

> Only an hour to go, an hour was nothing. An hour could be measured easily. [...] Down the driveway and around the curve—such a bad curve—go slow there. Past the entrance with the silver birches all leaning out to meet you, the corner of the big Brinkerhoff place, now deserted, windows gutted out, and a forest of young shoots where there used to be lawn. [...] The first dim line of land was pushing up over the horizon—South America. It was then, I realized, for the first time, that we were on the other side. [...] Nevertheless, I gave up driving from Englewood to New York and kept my eye on that dim line [...]. (257-258)

If Morrow Lindbergh's travel narrative ends with a translation of home and away, so does Archibald Lyall's but in a very different sense. Unlike Morrow Lindbergh who inscribes home in the memory of that which is still away, Lyall returns to Europe and declares his trip a "successful one beyond my wildest expectations" and basks in the "happy memory" of his visit to "these little twin first-born of Henry the Navigator" (302). He counters the claustrophobic Guinean coastal space with a ten-day stay on a balcony in Gibraltar where he can gaze at the harbor, the ultimate ambiguous traveler who watches the "warships gliding in and out like slim, grey sea-birds" (302). His sojourn in Gibraltar, at once both home and away for Lyall, however, does not end the narrative. Rather, he closes his mobile tale in a Spanish prison cell in the midst of a civil war and his memories:

> [...] I found myself thinking nostalgically of the Dark Continent I had left behind me, where peace and tolerance and friendliness were virtues highly prized, and to kill one's neighbors for a point of politics would have been looked on as the work of an uncivilised savage. (303)

In the colonial writing of Africa as the "Dark Continent," Lyall's closing evokes the repeated tale of Norman Matson that opened his own travel narrative. Here, he frames that narrative through the translations of African coastal and trans-Atlantic space once again into locations of nostalgia, almost, but never *sodade.* And in this transformative discursive practice, Lyall inscribes the memory of the trans-Atlantic away almost as longingly as Morrow Lindbergh maps her trans-Atlantic home.

Works Cited

Brookshaw, David. "Cape Verde." *The Portcolonial Literature of Portuguese Speaking Africa.* Ed. Patrick Chabal. Evanston: Northwestern UP, 1996.

Certeau, Michel de. *The Practice of Everyday Life.* Berkeley: U of California P, 1984.

_____. *The Writing of History.* New York: Columbia UP, 1988.

Clarke, Patricia and David Footman, eds. *In Memoriam Archie 1904-1964.* Cambridgeshire: Fordham Printing Works, 1966.

Clifford, James. *Routes: Travel and Translation in the Late Twentieth Century.* Cambridge: Harvard UP, 1997.

Fernández-Armesto, F. "Medieval Exploration: The Evidence of Maps." *Portugal the Pathfinder: Journeys From the Medieval Toward the Modern World.* Ed. George Winius. Madison: Hispanic Seminary of Medieval Studies, 1995. 40-70.

Ferreira, Manuel. *Literaturas Africanas de Expressão Portuguesa.* Lisbon: Instituto de Cultura Portuguesa, 1977.

Greenblatt, Stephen. *Marvelous Possession: The Wonder of the New World.* Chicago: U of Chicago P, 1991.

Johnson, Donald. *Phantom Islands of the Atlantic.* New York: Avon Books, 1994.

Kaplan, Caren. *Questions of Travel.* Durham: Duke UP, 1996.

Lindbergh, Charles. Foreward. Anne Morrow Lindbergh. *Listen! the Wind.* New York: Harcourt, Brace, 1938.

Lyall, Archibald. *Black and White Make Brown: An Account of a Journey to the Cape Verde Islands and Portuguese Guinea.* London: William Heinemann, Ltd, 1938.

Pratt, Mary Louise. *Imperial Eyes: Travel Writing and Transculturation.* London: Routledge, 1992.

Rabasa, José. *Inventing America.* Norman: U of Oklahoma P, 1993.

Spurr, David. *The Rhetoric of Empire: Colonial Discourse in Journalism, Travel Writing, and Imperial Administration.* Durham: Duke UP, 1993.

Van den Abbeele, G. *Travel as Metaphor.* Minneapolis: U of Minnesota P, 1993.

Phyllis Peres is Associate Dean of Undergraduate Studies at the University of Maryland, College Park, where she holds a joint faculty appointment in Portuguese and Latin American Studies. Her scholarly research focuses on the Portuguese and Hispanic Atlantic. She has published widely on the literatures of Portuguese-speaking Africa, African Brazilian literatures and cultures, and Portuguese colonial and postcolonial discourses. Her book *Transculturation and Resistance in Lusophone African Literatures* was published in 1997 by the University Press of Florida. She is currently working on a new book on Angolan literature of the 1950s. E-mail: pb59@umail.umd.edu

The Trajectories of Cape Verdean Literature — Genres, Music and Other Themes/ Percursos da Literatura Cabo Verdiana — Géneros, Música e Outros Temas

Notes on the Historical Context of *Claridade*

Ellen W. Sapega

Abstract. This essay takes its starting point from the premise that a single coherent project for the publication of *Claridade* never existed, either in terms of the review's contents or of its actual physical layout. After demonstrating that three very different incarnations of *Claridade* appeared at three distinct historical moments (1936-7; 1947-49; 1959-60), I set about examining each "series" in light of the specific date in which it appeared. Paying particular attention to the selection and treatment of texts written in Creole, I identify several clear-cut changes in the placement and framing of these texts that occurred between the first and the second series. This, in turn, indicates that the purpose and reception of *Claridade* changed significantly over the course of its publication, as the editors sought different solutions to the problem of how to provide a metaphoric entry of Cape Verdean culture into the "Portuguese" text.

The literary review *Claridade* has undoubtedly received more critical attention than any other single publication in the history of Cape Verdean literature. As it occupies a central, yet ambiguous, place in the literature of the archipelago, *Claridade* has been the object of much praise; yet, at the same time it has received its equal share of negative critical responses. The review's founders were among the first to investigate the specificity of Cape Verdean experience, basing their studies on carefully documented customs, traditions and cultural practices of the islands, and the initial publication of *Claridade* in 1936 clearly marks an important historical moment in the process of imagining Cape Verdean identity as unique and autonomous from that of metropolitan Portugal. For *Claridade*'s critics, nonetheless, much of its contents have been judged disappointing since its contributors never venture so far as to issue a proclamation of political independence, or to affirm the centrality of an African component in Cape Verdean cultural identity.

This latter position, which took the *claridosos* to task for their emphasis on the twin themes of drought and emigration, was first staked out by the generation of nationalist writers who appeared on the Cape Verdean literary scene in the 1950s and 60s. Influenced by the philosophies of Négritude or by pan-African theories of liberation, writers such as Manuel Duarte ("Caboverdianidade e africanidade" [1954]) and Onésimo Silveira (*Conscien-cialização na literatura caboverdiana* [1963]) accused the review's founders of grounding their literary project on a simplistic and escapist critique of the problems facing the Cape Verdean population.[1] Attempting to insert a model of Cape Verdean experience into a more generalized debate regarding the independence of Portugal's African colonies, this later generation also faulted the *claridosos* for having committed the unpardonable error of having placed too much emphasis on the European origins of the Creole culture and language that they wished to promote.[2]

While these accusations may appear a bit extreme today, they accurately reflect the polemical nature of the debate regarding *Claridade*'s significance that took place in the decades prior to Cape Verdean independence.[3] It is difficult, however, to interpret these negative criticisms as directed at the final issues of the review, published in 1959 and 1960. Appearing at a moment when the idea of independence had begun to circulate in Portugal's *províncias ultramarinas*, these issues contained material that was far less problematic for the younger generation. Indeed, several of *Claridade*'s collaborators at this point were also associated with the fight against Portuguese colonialism.[4] In the same vein, it is also very unlikely that the movement's detractors were addressing the first three issues of *Claridade*, published in 1936 and 1937. At that early date, it would have been nearly impossible to attempt more than a simple revindication of Cape Verdean political and cultural autonomy. In contrast, the decade of the 1940s represents an important transitional period, both in the history of the review and in the history of Portugal's colonial empire. At that time, some ten years after the appearance of *Claridade*'s inaugural issues, its founders' cultural project was to undergo several important transformations.

In order to accurately assess these transformations, it is essential to return the review to its original socio-historical context and to examine each issue of

Claridade in light of the specific moment in which it appeared. Only through an analysis that takes into account the attendant conditions surrounding *Claridade*'s publication will it be possible to identify and understand the subtle changes to the project that took place over the twenty-four year period that the review was published. As I shall demonstrate in the analysis that follows, it is not a coincidence that the most controversial issues of *Claridade* (numbers four to seven) are those that were published between 1947 and 1949. Presenting a view of Cape Verdean culture that was less engaged in a thoroughly defined political project, these are undoubtedly the most problematic issues when viewed from a pro-independence perspective. These issues appeared at a time when the Portuguese empire in Africa was undergoing significant structural changes that resulted in new concrete demands and more subtle ideological shifts. In keeping with these shifts, the pages of *Claridade* register at this time a seemingly more ambivalent response to the hegemonic discourses that aimed to justify the continued existence of the Portuguese empire in Africa.

A preliminary step to understanding the choices and restrictions that the *claridosos* were forced to confront in the 1940s entails the recognition that a single coherent project for the publication of *Claridade* never existed, either in terms of the review's content or of its actual physical layout. While not explicitly identified as belonging to different series, three very different incarnations of the review appeared at three different historical moments. There are, of course, several elements that remained constant throughout *Claridade*'s existence: it was always published in Mindelo, on the Island of São Vicente; after the fourth issue the director remained the same;[5] and each issue also contained work by at least two of three figures considered as the movement's founders—Baltasar Lopes, Manuel Lopes and Jorge Barbosa. However, some notable changes to the physical layout of the review did take place between the first and the second series. When the review reappeared in 1947, after ten years of silence, the initial length of eight to ten pages was extended to an average of forty-five pages. In a similar fashion, the number of collaborators increased from less than half a dozen to almost double that number. Moreover, in the second series, *Claridade*'s original subtitle of "Revista de arte e letras" was modified to include the notice in parentheses, "não periódica," and the actual physical size of the pages was reduced in size by more than half.

While the third series of the review maintained a layout similar to the second, the final two issues that comprise this group (published in May 1959 and December 1960) continued the practice of adding new voices and new materials. Containing seventy-five and eighty-two pages, respectively, the number of contributors increased at this time to twelve, in issue number eight, and fifteen in the final issue. In both cases, Manuel Lopes's name is absent; by this time he had left the archipelago, moving first to the Azores in 1944, then to Lisbon. As a final note to this brief overview of *Claridade*'s material features, it is intriguing that only the last issue used a graphic design on its cover: in the place of the customary poetic text that was used to open the previous issues, the cover of this final issue contains an unsigned drawing of five women on a dock clustered around a fisherman.[6]

As these simple facts suggest, *Claridade* opened up its pages to new voices in the second and third phases of its publication. Logically, these new contributors were younger and brought with them new social and aesthetic concerns. Bearing in mind that it was also inevitable that the review's founders were to modify their views in light of the specific context of the moment, it becomes evident that each phase or series of the review consisted of a rereading and reformulation of the earlier issues. Turning our attention to the contents of *Claridade*, it is curious to note, however, that the changes that occurred between the first and second series seem, at least initially, to be slight. Besides the greater number of pages and contributors that mark the second series, the division of material into specific genres is maintained.

It is possible, on one hand, to identify modernist-inspired poetry that covers topics ranging from the social to the existential as well as literary prose written in Portuguese but inspired by the popular culture of the islands (good examples of this are excerpts from *Chiquinho* by Baltasar Lopes and various short stories by Manuel Lopes). On the other hand, we find essays that attempt to interpret the Cape Verdean experience already alluded to in the fiction and poetry from a sociological point of view. In this vein, a recurring topic is the study of Creole carried out by Baltasar Lopes that deals, in particular, with its origins and status as a language, and not just as a mere dialect of Portuguese. As a complement to this linguistic study, it was natural that the pages of the review also contained transcriptions of compositions from Cape Verdean popular music, such as *finaçons*, *batuques* and *mornas*, in which the original Creole language was maintained. It is only in the sixth issue of *Claridade*, nonetheless, published in July 1948, that there begin to appear original poems written in Creole and attributed to Gabriel Mariano, Mário Macedo Barbosa, Jorge Pedro, and Sérgio Frusoni.

While several of the poems and stories written in Portuguese refer to concrete social situations, it is in the varying selection and treatment of texts written in Creole that the different socio-political contexts of the first and second series of *Claridade* really come to the fore. By looking specifically at the placement and framing of these texts, it will become clear that their purpose and reception changes significantly over the course of *Claridade*'s publication. Following on Ashcroft *et al.*'s observation that language variance is metonymic of cultural difference (52) and that in the post-colonial text it is the writing itself, dwelling at the intersection of a vast array of cultural conditions, that sets the scene for a constitution of meaning (59), my analysis of the specific instances of inclusion of Creole texts in the pages of *Claridade* will show the varying, and perhaps divergent, ways in which the editors sought to provide a metaphoric entry of Cape Verdean culture into the "Portuguese" text.

On the cover of the very first issue of *Claridade*, a "lantuna & 2 motivos de finaçom" are transcribed and identified as taken from *batuques* of the Island of Santiago.[7] Several critics have called attention to the importance of this cover as presenting a strong statement of the group's project. For Pierre Rivas, "é um manifesto em ato, provocador no seu laconismo e revelador de seu espírito duplamente manifesto e dissimulado" (40).[8] By presenting these songs without commentary or translation, *Claridade* begins its publication with a strong and sure affirmation of the importance of the Creole language and of cultural practices that are African in origin. After this moment, however, this gesture is never repeated—while the cover of the following issue also transcribes a text written in Creole, it is a *morna*, not a *finaçom*. The third issue of *Claridade* is then opened with the "Poema de quem ficou" by Manuel Lopes, and the covers of all the following issues, with only two exceptions, also present original poems written in Portuguese rather than Creole.[9]

If the material chosen for the cover of the inaugural issue constituted a challenge to prevalent ideas about Cape Verdean cultural identity by proclaiming a radical difference from Portuguese and European models, the choice of a *morna* for the cover of the second issue is already indicative of a move away from a cultural model inspired by African artistic practices. Although it is also written in Creole, this is not an anonymously authored text. On the contrary, the *morna* entitled "Venus" is identified as written by Xavier da Cruz, a prominent composer popularly known as B. Leza. At least one step away from the anonymous oral tradition that inspired the *batuques* of Santiago, the *morna* also belongs to a more ethnically mixed popular tradition than the *finaçom*. In this way, B. Leza's lyrics for the issue's cover are representative of the cultural politics of miscegenation that would inspire a great deal of the literary and theoretical works produced by the *Claridade* generation. Finally, and in marked contrast to the inaugural issue, the text chosen for the cover of the third issue of the review—Manuel Lopes's "Poema de quem ficou"—represents a return to European Modernist-inspired literary values. Besides incorporating a dynamic constructed around the opposites *eu-tu* and *cá-lá*, this text privileges subjective intimate experience as a means to knowledge: "… O mundo não é maior / que a pupila dos teus olhos: / tem a grandeza / da tua inquietação e das tuas revoltas."

The other four poems appearing on the cover of *Claridade* do not differ significantly from this particular example. Although they sometimes present veiled images of an economically difficult situation that is experienced by the community as a whole, they do not directly address the culturally miscegenated aspects of Cape Verdean experience.[10] A composition written in Creole will never again serve as the review's opening text; when the Creole language does reappear in issues 6 and 7 (July 1948; December 1949), the transcribed *finaçons* and *batuques* are followed by literal translations and explanatory notes about the forms and vocabulary employed.[11] As this tendency to translate and interpret is then carried over to the poems written in Creole that are published by contemporary authors, it becomes abundantly clear that the relation between *Claridade*'s editors and its readers has changed greatly in the review's second series. Initially, if *Claridade*'s intended audience was not made up exclusively of Cape Verdean readers (and I believe it was not), its readers had, at least, to accept the responsibility of having some reading knowledge of the Creole language and being able to recognize popular art forms. In the case of the second series, however, the review's editorial board took it upon itself to present and interpret Cape Verdean culture to an audience that was unfamiliar with the language and with cultural practices like the *batuque* or the *finaçom*.

This move from an openly provocative stance to a more didactic position in regard to the material presented indicates the editors' response to certain changes in the political situation. Even if this response was unconscious, it attests to new restrictions that were to affect the editors' and contributors' freedom of expression. Perhaps the earliest and clearest instance of these new limitations can be found in the editors' refusal to submit the first issue for inspection by the censors. Indeed, the fact that the infamous phrase "Visado pela censura" does not appear anywhere in the inaugural issue of *Claridade* emphasizes the daring and independent-minded atitude that was behind this intellectual project. It is evident, nonetheless, that the authorities soon caught wind of this project and became ever more vigilant—in all the following issues it is impossible to ignore the censors' mark, as the words "Visado pela censura" always appear in bold capital letters.[12]

The concrete demands imposed by the Salazar regime's censorship authority do not serve, however, to explain all the changes that occur after the first series in regard to the editors' view of Cape Verdean culture. A wider view of the social and political context will also help to account for other transformations that took place during the 1930s and 40s. *Claridade* appeared at an important historical juncture characterized by the rapid consolidation of the Estado Novo's repressive structures and the changes made to the structure of the regime greatly altered various aspects of daily life in both the *metrópole* and the colonies. The extremely difficult local conditions in Cape Verde have been well documented in both literary and historical texts. São Vicente in 1936 was still facing many of the problems portrayed in Baltasar Lopes's novel *Chiquinho*. While the action of this novel took place more than a decade earlier, several chapters of this book were published in the first issues of *Claridade* and the crisis to which it referred continued to shape daily life in Mindelo. Traffic in the port declined precipitously as the result of fierce competition from Dakar and Las Palmas. Moreover, the traditional escape from poverty via emigration to the US was also closed off, as Jorge Barbosa reminds us in the poem "Irmão," which also appears in the inaugural issue of *Claridade*.

While the fate of abandonment resulted in an exacerbated sense of isolation from the world that is subsequently denounced in the literature produced during the 1930s, it should also be noted that this isolation created unique opportunities for writers to express their plight from a freer and more autonomous position. As Alfredo Margarido has pointed out in an essay on *Chiquinho*, the paucity of references to Portugal in this novel affirms that "já a metrópole, já Portugal, são apenas um lugar distante e vazio, que envia autoridades incompetentes e incapazes" (459). This leads Margarido to conclude that Lopes's book is in effect a "decolonized text" in which the Portuguese are excluded from any discussion regarding the destiny of the islands and their inhabitants (460). This tendency to neglect the colonies was coming to an end though, exactly at the moment when *Claridade*'s founders were preparing to launch the review. It was at this very moment that such paramilitary groups as the *Mocidade Portuguesa* and the *Legião Portuguesa* were created in the *metrópole*. We should also remember that in April of 1936, just months before the first issue of *Claridade* appeared, the Tarrafal prison camp opened on the Cape Verdean island of Santiago. In response to the outbreak of the Spanish Civil War, the Estado Novo regime began to extend its direct control over the metropolitan and colonial populations by tightening its grip on censorship, by giving new and greater powers to the PIDE and by investing more resources and energy to the project of cultural control through propaganda (Oliveira Marques 649-650). One can only imagine that it was difficult, if not impossible, for *Claridade*'s contributors to ignore these important structural changes to the regime. It is likely, in fact, that these changes contributed to the rapid disappearance of the review after the publication of only three issues.

When *Claridade* reappeared after an interval of ten years, there is little doubt that the review's interlocutors had changed greatly, as evidenced in the editors' decision to translate and gloss the Creole texts included in its pages. While the Salazar regime would maintain the practice of political and social neglect for years to come, the colonialist ideology it was predicated on had begun to undergo some important transformations. Cape Verde's position in the imperial system would not be significantly reconfigured as a consequence, but the concept of the Empire as a privileged space for a uniquely Portuguese model of colonial development did begin to acquire new currency in the metropolitan imagination. This was due, in part, to heightened interest in the work of Gilberto Freyre. While it is not within the scope of the present essay to enter into a detailed analysis of the complex relationship between *Claridade*'s founders and the Brazilian sociologist, it is worth remembering that Freyre's influence was of great use to the government in Portugal during the post-War years. As most Western powers began to accept the inevitability of decolonization, the Brazilian's theories of Luso-tropicalism, with its emphasis on the "acção civilizadora lusitana," became an important tool for the Salazar regime's justification of its continued presence in Africa.

In the opening number of the second series of *Claridade*, several issues before the appearance of transcriptions or original poems in Creole, Baltasar Lopes published the first part of his treatise on the origins and structure of Creole. Entitled "Uma experiência românica nos trópicos," this essay laid out an argument in favor of the language's predominantly European influences. While Lopes's theories in this essay are grounded on the work of a wide spectrum of respected linguists, he uses the ideas of Gilberto Freyre first and foremost to justify the need for such a study. In addition to the explicit allusion to Freyre's work contained in the essay's title, the author uses the opening paragraphs to map out a method of inquiry that departs from the Brazilian's thesis that the politics of *mestiçagem* united those living in the "Mundo que o português criou." While in this instance it may appear that Lopes, by citing Freyre's theories as inspiration for his research, was participating in the newly sanctioned state-sponsored project to glorify the impact of the Portuguese on Cape Verdean culture, it should be noted that his interest in Gilberto Freyre goes well beyond that of mere political opportunism. In fact, Freyre's ideas had also had a great impact on the selection of material for the three issues of *Claridade* that were published in the 1930s. At that time, the Estado Novo's project of imperial renewal did not coincide with Freyre's culturalist views regarding race (Vale de Almeida 166) and recourse to these views could be construed as representative of a challenge to the prevailing notions of European superiority.[13]

We may conclude, nonetheless, that Baltasar Lopes in the 1940s would certainly have been more aware of the new importance that certain politicians in the *metrópole* were ascribing to Freyre's theories. It is possible, in fact, that Lopes at this moment saw in Freyre an opportunity to establish a dialogue with the Portuguese authorities. Like any dialogue, of course, the objective would be to initiate and maintain an exchange of ideas, and not just defend a specific fixed position. Judging from the ideas developed in Lopes's essay and from the diversity of Creole texts contained in the issues of *Claridade* that were published in the 1940s, it is evident that he and his colleagues expected this dialogue to be about the need to continue to value and investigate such cultural forms as the *batuque* and the *finaçom.* This dialogue would also entail the active promotion of Creole as a viable language, capable of serving as the vehicle for original literary compositions.

From our historical perspective, it is evident that Baltasar Lopes's efforts in this direction had scant result. The failure of this dialogue may well explain the return to a challenging and contestatory stance that characterizes the two final issues of *Claridade* published in the late 1950s. In the context of the previous decade, however, the options pursued by Lopes and the review's other collaborators made more sense. Through the translations and glosses of the

Creole texts, together with his academic investigations into the linguistics of Creole, Baltasar Lopes continued his project of valorizing the language spoken by all Cape Verdeans, calling attention to its richness and its vital importance as a cultural practice. In this manner, he remained firm in relation to his project of the earlier decade, even while recognizing that the cultural context had changed significantly in the intervening years.

Notes

[1] According to Silveira, this escapism was revealed in an "atitude espiritual" that attempted a "tradução intelectual do problema da emigração do ilhéu." By focusing on the problems behind the need to emigrate, the *claridosos* "acabaram por simplificar, arbitrariamente, este complexo problema e por oferecer uma imagem estereotipada do homem caboverdiano" (10).

[2] While he cited the importance of the group associated with *Claridade* for its "tarefa colectiva e histórica de enraizar as letras caboverdianas," Manuel Duarte criticizes those who "supõem não deverem os novos outra coisa fazer senão seguir na esteira daqueles" (643). As he had earlier denounced "o recalcamento social e individual do que [no caboverdiano de cor] existe de negro-africano" (642), Duarte's project of promoting Creole as an instrument of agency and change was clearly predicated on valorizing Cape Verde's cultural ties to Africa.

[3] For an extended discussion and contribution to the debate surrounding European and African influences on Cape Verdean cultural production that took place prior to independence, see Hamilton, pp. 233-257; Brookshaw, for his part, observes that Germano Almeida's post-independence "parody of the themes dear to the '*Claridosos*' is evidence enough that the fundamental ethic of the earlier generation had survived the years and political changes, even if adapted to new circumstances" (199).

[4] A contributor himself to *Claridade*'s issue number eight (May 1958), Onésimo de Silveira recognized in it a "clave de denúncia e protesto" (17).

[5] Manuel Lopes is identified as the director of the first two issues; with the publication of issue number three, João Lopes assumed that role.

[6] This change in the format of the cover may be a further indication of the new directions that were to characterize the final series of *Claridade*. Also, the move to include elements of visual culture may speak to the printer's access to technical procedures for reproducing images that were previously unavailable.

[7] A *finaçom* usually appears as the final part of a *batuque*. This musical genre, from the island of Santiago, is associated with the *badio* culture of the island's interior. It is the Cape Verdean musical tradition most closely tied to traditional African music and rhythms. Performed by women who keep the rhythm by clapping their hands or beating on rolled up loincloths held between their thighs, the *batuque* accompanies such ritual celebrations as birth or marriage, and is also associated with religious festivals and the reception of important guests. The *finaçom* is a long poetic improvisation sung by a woman of high authority whose wisdom is used to teach the members of the community.

[8] Pires Laranjeira, on the other hand, calls attention to the "arranjo gráfico leve, acessível, anti-académico, quase juvenil" of the review, noting that the typewritten font used on this cover "lhe dá um realce, uma clareza, inabituais em revistas dessa década" (12).

[9] Besides the drawing on the cover of issue number nine, the cover of number five (September 1947) presents the second part of Baltasar Lopes's essay, "Uma experiência românica nos trópicos." I make reference to this essay in my conclusion.

[10] See, for example, "Poema do rapaz torpedeado," de Osvaldo Alcântara (Baltasar Lopes), that appears on the cover of issue six (Julho de 1948).

[11] See: No. 6, pp. 36-37 and No. 7 pp. 38-39.

[12] It is interesting to note, in this sense, that this same declaration appears much more discretely in the final two issues of *Claridade*, an indication that, by the end of the 1950s, the Salazar regime wished to downplay (but not abandon) its interventions in the sphere of cultural production.

[13] In the same vein, it is worth remembering that Freyre only began to use the term "Lusotropicalism" in 1951, when he was travelling around the Portuguese Empire at the invitation of the Minister of the Overseas Provinces (Vale de Almeida 164). Ironically, on this same trip he visited Cape Verde for the first time. His quite negative impressions of the archipelago are collected in the volume *Aventura e Rotina*. For a response to Freyre, see Baltasar Lopes, "Cabo Verde visto por Gilberto Freyre."

Works Cited

Almeida, Miguel Vale de. *Um Mar da Cor da Terra: Raça, Cultura e Política da Identidade.* Oeiras: Celta, 2000.

Ashcroft, Bill, Gareth Griffiths and Helen Tiffen. *The Empire Writes Back: Theory and Practice in Post-Colonial Literatures.* London and New York: Routledge, 1989.

Brookshaw, David. "Cape Verde." *The Postcolonial Literature of Lusophone Africa.* Evanston: Northwestern UP, 1996. 179-233.

Claridade. Edição facsimilada. Linda a Velha: A.L.A.C. (África, Literatura, Arte e Cultura, Lda.), 1986.

Duarte, Manuel. "Caboverdianidade e africanidade." *Vértice* XIV, 134 (1954): 639-644.

Freyre, Gilberto. *Aventura e Rotina.* Lisboa: Livros do Brasil, n.d.

Hamilton, Russell G. *Voices from an Empire: A History of Afro-Portuguese Literature.* Minneapolis: U Minnesota P, 1975.

Laranjeira, Pires. "As certezas da *Claridade* e influências na sombra." *Ponto & Vírgula* 15 (1985): 11-19.

Lopes, Baltasar. "Cabo Verde visto por Gilberto Freyre." Praia: Divisão de Propaganda da Imprensa Nacional, 1956. Rprt. in *Anais da Academia de Estudos de Culturas Comparadas* 1.2 (1999): 137-154.

Margarido, Alfredo. "*Chiquinho*: um romance não português ou antiportuguês?" *Estudos sobre a literatura das nações africanas de língua portuguesa.* Lisboa: A Regra do Jogo, 1980.

Marques, A.H. de Olivera. *Breve História de Portugal.* Lisboa: Presença, 1995.

Rivas, Pierre. "*Claridade*: emergência e diferenciação de uma literatura nacional." *Estudos Portugueses e Africanos* 14 (Julho/Dezembro 1989): 39-47.

Silveira, Onésimo. *Consciencialização na literatura caboverdiana.* Lisboa: Casa dos Estudantes do Império, 1963.

Ellen W. Sapega is Associate Professor of Spanish and Portuguese at the University of Wisconsin-Madison. She received her Ph.D. in Spanish and Portuguese from Vanderbilt University in 1987. A specialist in the Modernist Movement in Portugal, she has published articles on Fernando Pessoa, Mário de Sá-Carneiro and José de Almada Negreiros, as well as on the contemporary Portuguese novel. She is the author of a book-length study on Almada Negreiros (*Ficções Modernistas: Um estudo da obra em prosa de José de Almada Negreiros* [Lisbon: ICALP, 1992]). Sapega is currently at work on a project that examines public memory and visual culture in Portugal during the 1930s and 40s. She is co-editor of the *Luso-Brazilian Review*. E-mail: ewsapega@facstaff.wisc.edu

Lugares étnicos e maravilhosos do imaginário cabo-verdiano (em *Chiquinho*, de Baltasar Lopes)

Alberto de Carvalho

Resumo. O romance *Chiquinho*, de Baltasar Lopes, merece com toda a justiça ser considerado uma referência capital na moderna ficção realista cabo-verdiana, quer devido à história que nele se narra, quer ao valor literário da sua escrita. Mas, ao ser uma referência notável de identificação entre o homem crioulo e o protagonista, aquele valor tende a ser desvalorizado na proporção do seu ganho em popularidade. Com pouco de contador de histórias, Baltasar Lopes investe no texto toda uma estética de entendimento da vida, e toda uma poética que só se revelam pela análise minuciosa não apenas da história e do mundo crioulo que a envolve, da interpretação dos aspectos menos visíveis do texto mas, sobretudo, dos processos que Mestre Baltasar Lopes designava por oficina da escrita. A esta luz descritiva, de análise, interpretação e síntese, tanto se atingem melhores eixos de sentido, como os valores humanos mais genuínos, ocultos pelas realidades empíricas da vida (a seca, a emigração, a falta de perspectivas de futuro), como se esclarecem todos os percursos que envolveram a génese e composição do romance.

(...) não posso também negar que eu me sentia cativado pelos seus modos de velha dona, apesar dos cabelos: não estavam penteados, ela não esperava visitas àquela hora. Pormenor que notei porque Mamãe tinha sempre as suas tranças penteadas, com pente de cágado ou trancinha, e eu não podia conceber outra ordem além da que Mamãe respirava para mim. (Baltasar Lopes, "Muminha vai para a Escola" 47)

Era uma vez um boi. Um boi grande, um *boiona* que se chamava Blimundo. Blimundo, filho das rochas, possante, calmo e sabedor do mundo, amante da vida e da liberdade, era boi respeitado por todos os seus iguais, e não só, pelas ribeiras, campos e vertiginosas montanhas. (Leão Lopes, *A História de Blimundo* 9)

1. Intenções/Intencionalidades

Com justiça considerado um marco de referência na modernidade literária iniciada pela revista *Claridade*,[1] o romance *Chiquinho*[2] deu motivo a pequenas histórias que, em determinados aspectos elucidadas, poderão ajudar à compreensão da sua escrita e da intencionalidade que nele se coordena. Algumas vezes homóloga da intenção do Autor, outras idêntica ou afim, a intencionalidade de um texto pode ser identificada por uma série de linhas semânticas de valor dominante, em toda a sua extensão ligadas à da vontade significante dos processos em acção, no geral animadas por códigos, estruturas e processos retóricos responsáveis pela unidade do conjunto. Assim sumariamente definida, não será difícil colocar a hipótese limite de a intenção de um autor ser contrariada pela intencionalidade do seu texto ou, em situação muito mais benigna, como convém ao romance *Chiquinho*, distinguir e salvaguardar a parte devida a cada instância, à do Autor (Baltasar Lopes) com a sua intenção de escrita do livro, e à do narrador (de Chiquinho, Francisco Soares) que nele conta a (sua) história.

Um dos efeitos semânticos mais aparentes do texto, devido ao jogo entre intenção e intencionalidade, consiste na derrapagem realista que cria a confusão de instâncias por redução da ficção literária ao documentalismo. Num dos sentidos leva à identificação da matéria de *Chiquinho* (do livro) com a individualidade própria de Baltasar Lopes e, no oposto, por motivos de projecção literária, reconhece em Chiquinho (personagem) um valor de alcance simbólico, generalizado portanto à representação do cabo-verdiano de determinado período social. Num outro plano de maior alcance, mas que com estes se prende directamente, a ambiguidade mal compreendida desta ficção foi ainda a causa próxima para uma crítica da década de 1940 afirmar que o romance não chegava a contar uma história, por falta de urdidura de uma teia de nexos lógicos, ficando-se por um encadeamento de pequenas histórias que, apesar de tudo, tiravam do protagonismo de Chiquinho o princípio unificador do texto.

Pode-se de facto, em aparência, dizer que se acumulam elementos de convergência a favor da identificação entre o protagonista e o autor, nomeadamente os suscitados pelo lugar de origem e pelo percurso escolar. Como Chiquinho no romance, também Baltasar Lopes nasceu no Caleijão

(23/4/1907) e aí frequentou a Escola Primária. Mas, excluindo esta coincidência indutora, nada de especial valoriza a similaridade das duas restantes etapas, do Seminário-Lyceu da Vila da Ribeira Brava e do Liceu de Mindelo. Além de constituir um itinerário comum a tantos outros meninos, condicionado até pela falta de alternativas de escolha de outras Escolas, a distribuição do percurso de estudos do autor mais acentua as diferenças do que as afinidades com o de Chiquinho. Tendo concluído na Escola Primária de Caleijão apenas o 1º Grau, entre 1913 e 1916 (1ª-3ª Classe), foi já no Seminário-Lyceu que o autor realizou o 2º grau (4ª Classe) bem como o 1º Ciclo (1º-3º Anos), entre 1916 e 1920. Representando o Liceu de Mindelo a sua etapa seguinte, ela corresponde apenas ao 2º Ciclo (4º e 5º Anos), concluído entre 1920 e 1922.

Na lógica da narrativa que regula o percurso de Chiquinho, a conclusão do 7º Ano no Liceu de Mindelo constitui então uma alternativa que rasura ostensivamente, por via ficcional, a realidade dos factos, assim postulando a auto-suficiência das instituições de Cabo Verde, ou seja, a encenação textual da sua independência numa matéria sensível como a formação exclusiva de um jovem orientada como instrumento de trabalho. Que Chiquinho finalmente emigre para a América, para junto do pai, mais não faz do que confirmar a regra do fazer ficcional conduzido agora por dois paradigmas conjugados, o sociológico e o ideológico. No primeiro, é plausível que emigre para a América (facto social comum sobretudo em Sotavento), mas fictício é ir ao encontro do pai (que nunca foi emigrante). No segundo, é plausível a necessidade afirmativa de independência face ao colonizador (à ideologia imperial do Estado Novo), mas é fictícia quanto ao percurso estudantil notável de B. Lopes. Saindo tardiamente de S. Nicolau para Lisboa (perdido o barco de carreira por motivo de doença), embarcaria depois a 17/10/1922 (no Carvalho Araújo entregue ao Comandante Cisneiros) e, já sem possibilidade de escolher no Liceu Camões a alínea de Medicina, faz por junto os 6º e 7º Anos, em 1922/23, orientado para Direito, Curso que realiza de 1923/24 a 1927/28, numa parte do tempo (desde 1926/27) em conjunto com o de Românicas que termina em 1929/30.

Considerando estes elementos biográficos, dir-se-á que a composição do romance obedece a um programa ambivalente, de intenção autorial clara. Da rasura do percurso de elite cumprido por B. Lopes em favor do perfil mais comum de Chiquinho sobressai o protagonismo de identificação popular que sustenta a projecção simbólica do crioulo em Chiquinho. Adensam-na ainda alguns tópicos recorrentes na última parte da obra, como a incerteza das chuvas, o espectro da seca, as fomes e as mortes calamitosas e o recurso à emigração, de grande efeito existencial e étnico. Sob a pressão emocional do dramatismo em que a contingência das chuvas mergulha o destino dos camponeses, o esteticismo realista tende a converte-se na intenção documental e em armadilha que anula aquilo que na ambivalência do programa romanesco pertence à intencionalidade do texto e do autor, simultaneamente.

2. Re-escrita autobiográfica

No plano discursivo, esta junção de intencionalidades ambiguiza-se com evidência na enunciação dominada pela primeira pessoa verbal, por definição genológica própria do autobiografismo, em registos de escrita que tendem sempre a reforçar o conceito de verdade (verídica ou verosímil) dos conteúdos veiculados mediante relações várias. Em primeiro lugar, a identificação entre o narrador e a personagem e, depois, o crédito que daí decorre, quanto à fiabilidade do testemunho pessoal respeitante a todos os aspectos ligados ao conhecimento em causa própria, respondem com grande força de persuasão ao sentido de autenticidade da história.

Ao sujeito do discurso que diz "eu"-narrador, nos tempos verbais de presente, que pode falar de si como personagem em acção no passado, adere uma força de persuasão medida pela credibilidade da confissão pessoal de experiência directa. Toda a escrita de *Chiquinho* obedece a esse programa de efeitos expressivos, modulando de tonalidades várias jamais neutras, umas vezes eufóricas, outras disfóricas, outras elegíacas, outras dramáticas ou trágicas, os acontecimentos que acabam por dissimular toda a produção fictícia sob a impressão do documento vivenciado. Dois momentos do romance são a este respeito especialmente sugestivos, o que estabelece os protocolos de abertura da narrativa e o que demarca o princípio do seu fim. Em "Como quem ouve uma melodia muito triste, recordo a casinha em que nasci no Caleijão"[3] implicam-se as linguagens verbal (dos conteúdos da lembrança), que objectiva a realidade das coisas, e a musical (melodia) que as tonaliza de nostalgia directamente referida à subjectividade do "eu" narrador.

E assim também no anúncio da morte de nho Chic'Ana, antepenúltimo capítulo do fechamento do romance:

> Pimpinha é que levou a notícia. Logo depois do almôço eu estava sentado na cadeira-de-balanço (...) a ouvir Mamãe-Velha (...) nhô Chic'Ana tinha morrido.

> (...) Saí um instante para fora. Relancei os olhos pelos arredores, até ao alcance da vista. Hortas secas, côr cinzenta, vegetação rala da carestia. Voltei para a salinha. (...) Mamãe-Velha mandou gente à casa do morto. (...) Fez a Pimpinha o elogio de nhô Chic'Ana. Velho direito, muito amigo dos familiares da nossa casa (...) Com Chiquinho, então, era uma cegueira. (...) Deixei Mamãe-Velha e as suas evocações e fui direito à casa do morto.(...) Uma angústia profunda tomava conta de mim, nhô Chic'Ana morreu de fome. Senti vontade de gritar, para que todos ouvissem. Nhô Chic'Ana morreu de fome. À direita, à esquerda, a vista era a mesma. As mesmas hortas, nuas no seu chão de barro e comidas pelos gafanhotos. Na casa do morto já havia muita gente.[4]

Na situação de catástrofe generalizada, a recepção da notícia, a visão desoladora da paisagem e a partida para a casa do defunto conjugam-se num registo discursivo em que as frases curtas aliam o olhar incisivo ao sentimento da precaridade da vida. Exprimem ao mesmo tempo o bloqueio da lucidez descritiva e narrativa sob o efeito dramático da situação agravada pelo inesperado da morte do amigo, ficando-se a dever a esta escrita na primeira pessoa verbal o mais importante das suas modulações de perplexidade e de angústia. Através da expressão confessional as repetições avolumam o tom de desabafo dos sentimentos no íntimo de Chiquinho, a inquietação e revolta contra a injustiça das mortes que só o absurdo pode justificar. A escrita na primeira pessoa é, com efeito, o lugar específico da completa eclosão da subjectividade que, no caso deste fragmento do texto, se dá a ver plenamente comprometida com os afectos pessoais na verdade dos enleios de solidariedade, reveladores da sofrida participação na morte do velho.

Fica de modo convincente explicado o alcance de um tal tipo de escrita se ela for submetida ao cotejo com o que se admite ter constituído a sua forma primeira, assim também iluminando outro elemento do referido historial da composição de *Chiquinho*. Com efeito, com data de 6ª feira, 16/8/1935, publica o "Suplemento literário" do *Diário de Lisboa*, sob organização de Augusto Casimiro, um texto designado "O drama da terra," da autoria de Baltazar Lopes, apresentado como capítulo do romance inédito *Expansão*, de facto correspondente ao que viria a ser o Cap. 18 da terceira parte, "As-Águas," o acima referido antepenúltimo de *Chiquinho*. E dado que B. Lopes publicou logo no primeiro número da revista *Claridade* (Março de 1936), na sua segunda página, o texto "Bibia," "excerto do romance inédito "chiquinho," num outro registo discursivo, inserido no livro como Cap. 24 da primeira parte "Infância," parece poder-se admitir com esta soma de factos que em cerca de seis meses (de Agosto de 1935 a Março de 1936), B. Lopes teria reordenado todo o seu programa autorial de planificação estética e, mesmo, de estratégia de romancista.

Quanto a este segundo aspecto, as mudanças não são surpreendentes. Se os planos do romance *Expansão* se convertiam entretanto em *Chiquinho*, também neste se anuncia o título "Ponta de Praia," romance "a seguir," projecto depois substituído por outro de título *Acushnet Avenue* que as restrições políticas impediriam de concretizar, posto que implicava uma deslocação do autor à América para recolha de material. Dos sentidos aparentes daqueles títulos, e do que por informação do autor conhecemos de *Acushnet Avenue* dedicado ao cabo-verdiano (Chiquinho) emigrante na América, deduz-se que *Chiquinho* consubstancia um recentramento de escrita que, para melhor atingir o cerne da identidade crioula esteticamente enraizada, não poderia deixar de adoptar o rumo poético ilustrado no fragmento acima transcrito, muito mais nitidamente expressivo do dramatismo do momento do que o seguinte, na forma primeira incluída em *Expansão*:

> Pimpinha é que levou a notícia. Logo depois do café Chico estava sentado na cadeira de balanço (...) a ouvir mamãe-velha (...) Nhô Chic'Ana tinha morrido. *? Como, como, nhô Chic'Ana morreu? -Ah-home, coitado de nhô Chic'Ana!* Francisco levantou-se. *Que diabo lhe bulia dentro da alma?* Relanceou os olhos pelos arredores, até ao alcance da vista- e nada: hortas secas, côr cinzenta, vegetação rala da carestia. Voltou para dentro. (...) *O barrete de Chico estava sobre o baú do outro quarto, Francisco saiu.* Mamãe-velha mandou gente para ir descobrir a casa do morto. (...) Coitado de nhô Chic'Ana. Homem agradável muito amigo dos familiares da casa de Mamãe-velha. (...) Com Chiquinho, então, era uma cegueira. (...) Francisco foi direito a casa do morto. (...) *E aquela guisa parecia-lhe coisa nova. Era nhô Chic'Ana que choravam?* (...) *Mas Francisco não podia compreender que aquela guisa fosse por morte de nhô Chic'Ana. Havia qualquer coisa naquele choro que excedia nhô Chic'Ana. De que teria morrido nhô Chic'Ana?* (...) *Nhô Chic'Ana morreu de fome.* Uma angústia profunda invadiu a alma do moço. Nhô Chic'Ana morreu de fome. Sentiu vontade de gritar para que todos ouvissem. Nhô Chic'Ana morreu de fome. Á direita, á esquerda, a vista era a mesma. As mesmas hortas, nuas no seu chão de barro, amaninhadas *pela seca e pelas mandíbulas* dos gafanhotos (...) *As sementeiras tinham-se perdido. Nhô Chic'Ana morreu de fome. Na casa do morto já havia muita gente.*[5]

Excluindo a alusão aos movimentos do protagonista dentro de casa, que infectam aliás o estilo de perda de concisão, as características dominantes do regime de escrita derivam todas da utilização do modo narrativo clássico. Ao dizer "ele," a respeito de Francisco/Chico, o narrador permanece formalmente destacado do contexto, alheio aos factos e ao envolvimento pessoal na história visto que, por definição estrutural, deverá preservar a objectividade do relato. Da objectividade do seu olhar depende o coeficiente de fidelização da reportagem e a conformidade dela aos acontecimentos, bem como a lucidez racional (cf. passagens em itálico) para formular questões, indagar, comentar, dar opiniões, generalizar ou, em sentido oposto, tonalizar o discurso de colorações emocionais, tudo favorecido pelo atributo narrativo da omnisciência.

Entretanto expurgados do texto de *Chiquinho* (como se observa na transcrição mais acima) é nos fragmentos em itálico que se encontram alguns dos aspectos narrativos de menor coerência lógica. Com o dom de omnisciência, o narrador pode dizer-saber tudo, acompanhar "Francisco (que) saiu" e saber-informar, mesmo depois de ter partido, que "Mamãe-Velha mandou gente para ir descobrir a casa do morto." Mas, por outro lado, não usa essa omnisciência para sondar as perplexidades de Francisco ("Que diabo lhe bulia dentro da alma?"), alibi de narrador para, em vez de "explicar o quê," poder "mostrar como" a personagem realiza a descoberta das motivações do choro ("E aquela guisa parecia-lhe coisa nova. Era nhô Chic'Ana quem choravam?"). E, neste caso específico, substituir a "explicação directa" pelo "dar a ver o como" Francisco acede à verdade (que interpretamos na letra do texto: as pessoas chorariam nhô Chic'Ana, mas chorariam também a situação que o excedia, as mortes calamitosas pela fome, o absurdo das mortes sofridas passivamente e, logo, a injustiça do Poder e o bem fundado direito do povo à revolta no "levante no S. João," no capítulo que, em *Chiquinho*, precede o da morte de nhô Chic'Ana, etc.) cabe inteiramente na retórica da ideologia, da pedagogia e da ameaça da demagogia muito comum em algum realismo social.

3. Retrato crioulo

Embora publicado em 1947, num tempo de rápidas mutações dominadas por fortes realismos de causas bélicas e outras, o ideário de *Chiquinho* identifica-se no entanto por inteiro com o tempo próprio do grupo da *Claridade*, na primeira fase (década de 1930), de objectivos mais tarde resumido nas consabidas teses de Baltasar Lopes ("pensar no *nosso problema*"[6] e de Manuel Lopes.[7]) Sintomático de tal ideário em esboço no começo dos anos trinta é o artigo[8] do jovem Manuel Lopes, incitando os conterrâneos a libertarem-se do marasmo em que dormiam e a passarem à acção orientada para novos ideais e novas directrizes. Nesse reagir ao marasmo juvenil parecem inscrever-se a obstinação de Mané Quim em manter os "pés fincados no chão," recusando emigrar[9] e o "pensar no problema" do crioulo pelo jovem Chiquinho (e Andrézinho),[10] segundo dois campos de acção que se situam em níveis complementares, empírico o primeiro, e intelectual o segundo. Em conjunto, conotam uma determinada forma de empenhamento da literatura na representação compreensiva dos factos e na experiência da vida e dos valores, como modo de assumir a consciência do real e do crioulo descrito no interior da realidade cabo-verdiana, em exclusivo, ou seja, "em si mesmo" e na "relação do seu corpo com o mundo" das ilhas.[11]

Ora, no plano lógico, concebe-se (Merleau-Ponty) como verdade operatória que o "conhecimento de si (crioulo) e do seu mundo (cabo-verdiano) para si" constitui uma fase de auto-identificação, absolutamente preliminar ao estabelecimento da relação com o "outro," um outro qualquer, facto que, por certo involuntária mas oportunamente, é demonstrado pela sequência da obra poética publicada por Jorge Barbosa. Se em "Arquipélago" (1935) se situa, identifica e resume a territorialidade das ilhas atlânticas, e em "Ambiente" (1941) ela se preenche das substâncias (a dita "cabo-verdianidade") específicas do "ser em si" da humanidade crioula, em *Caderno de um Ilhéu* (1956) já pode ser apresentada a plenitude da sua personalidade, ágil de múltiplas aptidões, de camponês, citadino (cronista, festivo, crítico), marinheiro, emigrante, mas sobretudo de autor-poeta, interlocutor em evasão para o encontro que, finalmente, o leva a se expor (a dizer-se, dar-se a conhecer) no afrontamento face a "outrem."

No caso de B. Lopes, tudo se passa como se a reescrita de *Expansão* na sua forma final de *Chiquinho* correspondesse a uma utilização da sequência lógica que se acaba de resumir, para dela representar o correspondente aos dois primeiros momentos lógicos, a imagética do "arquipélago" e o "ambiente" em que o crioulo forma o seu ser, sem curar de o comunicar a "outrem" (p. ex., ao colonizador, de facto de nome rasurado no texto, apenas referido pela função "Ministro das Colónias," "S. Ex.ª o Governador" ou pela gíria, "Sexa"[12]). Interpretados os fragmentos sublinhados pelo lado das causas imediatas (nhô Chic'Ana morreu de fome), permanece-se na esfera dos factos que integram aqueles dois primeiros momentos lógicos, mas pode-se sair dela imediatamente pela insinuação das causas próximas (nhô Chic'Ana morreu de fome por causa da falta de medidas de emergência, logo, por causa do colonizador). Mas, implicar o colonizador na causalidade é, insiste-se, considerá-lo nos termos exactos de "o outro" que detém o Poder, submete, condiciona, decide, absolutamente incompatível com as fases de plena afirmação de si (Merleau-Ponty, J. Barbosa; na idealização elaborada por este a balizagem temporal é clara sobre os limites da auto-afirmação do exclusivamente cabo-verdiano, "territorialidade—ambiente" [1935 - 1941]). A fase de afrontamento face ao "Outro" de *Caderno de um Ilhéu,* pertence já aos anos cinquenta (1956), como a poética do "Suplemento Cultural."[13]

Evitar a insinuação das causas próximas consiste em excluir das mensagens as verdades não isentas de demagogia. Como mostram certas obras, nem só o colonizador seria causa próxima (cf. os comerciantes Artur: "Cada um sabe o que pensa e o que deseja" "Negócios são negócios, não é?,"[14] e Sr. Silva: "Estou vendo nhâ Chica Clara (...) Mas vou fazer um jeitinho para acomodar você... Olhe, dou-lhe cinquenta escudos..."[15]; o narrador: "Houve um grande levante no S. João (...) Um cavalheiro de gravata deteve-a a inquirir: - É Lela que foi apanhar farinha em loja de gente (...)."[16] Na exacta verdade dos factos bons[17] os que morrem e os que têm fome, e os outros, colonizador e comerciantes (estes decerto não oriundos do país colonizador) acabam por serem todos vítimas de uma muito mais vasta causa remota, circunstancial, geográfica, climatológica (que, obviamente, não anula, embora condicione fortemente, a causa político-administrativa).

Graças à reescrita de *Expansão,* a causalidade remota converte-se (em *Chiquinho)* em realidade primeira que tudo condiciona em Cabo Verde, no circunstancialismo do espaço-"chão" (do "Arquipélago") e nos "problemas" (do "Ambiente") avolumados pelo tempo histórico que imprimiu nos homens uma substância própria que funde o étnico no sócio-cultural. E, como defende Käte Hamburger, contra a narrativa na terceira pessoa que se identifica em absoluto com a ordem do fictício e com o fechamento do símbolo referencial, ficará reservada à linguagem na primeira pessoa o sistema do sujeito--de-enunciação lírico que, por definição, obriga o signo referencial a uma abertura através da qual os contextos e os factos se submetem à filtragem pela subjectividade do sujeito que os vivencia.[18] Nesta forma discursiva que atribui a Chiquinho a narração e o protagonismo da história no lapso de vida em que emerge e se instala na vida, entre cerca dos cinco e vinte anos, se compõe a representação autobiográfica do texto que os manuais de teoria literária definem como "romance de formação."

Também por aqui se explica a rasura, na versão final de *Chiquinho*, dos fragmentos em itálico (da transcrição acima) que sustentavam a pedagogia da razão interpretativa. Não seria verosímil num romance que representa a formação de um jovem até à entrada na vida adulta o saber de experiência feito para o exercício racional do mundo, para o interpretar e sensatamente o julgar. No bem pensado da sua arte, em vez da entrega da atitude judicativa-ideológica a uma personagem (Francisco/Chico), o autor delega-a no narrador (em Chiquinho-adulto, na América) que a infiltra no próprio modo narrativo dominado pela descrição, em sentido lato, deixando assim ao destinatário (e ao leitor) a liberdade de interpretação do universo em que a personagem surge, cresce, se move, aprende, age e reage. Sem sairem directamente da fala de outrem, da personagem ou do narrador, as anotações críticas retida pelo destinatário emergem do seu ver todo pessoal a personagem em acção nos diferentes contextos que a condicionam, onde descobrir e experimentar obedecem à pedagogia formativa por esforço de descoberta e compreensão do aparecer da realidade e do seu lugar nela:

> O meu primeiro contacto com a minha gente foi quási dolorosa (...). Por que não sentiria eu ainda o frémito de entusiasmo heróico que me possuia quando Mamãe-Velha recordava a figura do marido morto tão novo? (...) Para quê? A revolta surda que eu sentia contra aqueles que me puseram na prenda, para fazerem de mim *homem grande, homem de capacidade* (...).[19]

Como Francisco/Chico no texto de *Expansão*, também Chiquinho se interroga aqui mas com duas diferenças capitais. Naquele o narrador dá ver Francisco interrogando-se para insinuar uma questão para a qual tem logo resposta. Neste o narrador, muitos anos depois descreve (dá a ver) a personagem surpreendida por problemas que lhe tolhiam os movimentos e as expectativas, para os quais não tinha resposta, por isso os formulava: a) a iniciação no saber que desloca e afasta do estatuto anterior; b) o saber de formação profissional que nem sempre tem um emprego compatível, ou nem sequer tem emprego; c) mais grave ainda, como no mito adâmico, a lucidez que provém do acesso ao saber por vezes mata (em Adão a inocência, no homem a ingenuidade). E, conforme postulam as regras do género na versão clássica europeia, aliás também comum à estética de raiz tradicional africana onde predomina a ordem dos mais velhos, este desencanto que torna infeliz Chiquinho faz parte integrante da diegese do romance de formação que termina em disforia, em contextos onde o social predomina sobre o individual.

Por pertencerem à ordem dos ideais "irrealizáveis," os projectos de idade juvenil acabam sempre frustrados pelas circunstâncias práticas da vida, a todos os níveis na de Chiquinho, a) no amor, cujas "esperanças de casamento (com Nuninha) [...] foram emoção ocasional de uma tarde de S. Vicente"[20] ; b) nos contactos humanos com mundo que o fizeram "viver a experiência de S. Vicente, em que o arquipélago desemboca com as suas ilusões, imediatamente seguidas de desencantamento?"[21]; c) na carreira de professor em que Mamãe "ficou desiludida com a minha colocação no Morro Braz. A sua ambição de me ver leccionando (...) no Caleijão, não pôde ser satisfeita. Escrevi uma carta furiosa a Andrézinho."[22] Entre as forças em jogo no texto, de inovação (Chiquinho, Euclides Varanda, Tio Joca, Chico Zepa, Andrèzinho, José Lima) e de conservação (os gravatas, o povo e outros), o predomínio teria de pertencer a estas, sustentadas pelo mais velho simbólico, Mamãe-Velha, que fez "ouvir a voz da razão. Para que havia eu de me insurgir contra os governos do destino? Ela ensinou-me a lição das gerações que me produziram."[23]

Sendo dado no texto que o sociologismo dos novos não reconhece utilidade no providencialismo de Mamãe-Velha, a crítica de Chiquinho-personagem não precisa de ser expressa para, pedagogicamente, Chiquinho-narrador guiar o destinatário quanto à boa interpretação. Face à informação sobre as reacções, a "carta furiosa a Andrèzinho" e a aceitação da verdade da avó, a contradição parece evidente. Ao optar pela reprodução da fala dela, sem resumo nem comentário manipulador, o discurso impregna-se de ironia enquanto expõe a questão das "verdades boas" (A. Schaft) que são consoante a ordem dos factos. Na praxiológica, não é respeitoso responder a um velho nos termos da "carta furiosa" e, na gnoseológica, um velho não tem culpa de deter a "voz da razão" feita de sabedoria. Se for justa a máxima de Amadou Hampaté Bâ, "quando morre um velho é uma biblioteca que arde," então a fala tradicional do velho é factor de "autenticidade" por conservar genuinos valores mas, porque conservadora, bloqueia o progresso.

Sob a aparência da descrição e da explicação que demonstram a solução disfórica da história, o autor vai no entanto instilando ao longo da narrativa um mecanismo lógico que se resolve pela subversão da forma autobiográfica clássica, de matriz europeia. Por um lado, a história da formação de Chiquinho ordenada pelo projecto do pai termina de maneira conforme, com o seu desemprego após o encerramento da Escola de Morro Braz, um final infeliz. Por outro, emigrar com o patrocínio intelectual e ético de Euclides Varanda constitui uma solução de grande alcance estético. De acordo com a tese do velho, partir não é sair de Cabo Verde, porque "As ilhas vivem é na alma de cada um de nós."[24] Se a personagem não emigrar e permanecer em Cabo Verde, de facto, fica prisioneira do final disfórico, virtualmente no horizonte do grogue, a exemplo de Tio Joca. Se partir motivado pela tese de E. Varanda tudo se passa como se não emigrasse, não saísse de Cabo Verde, mas subsiste o final disfórico porque, apesar disso, vai contrariado "querendo ficar" junto dos seus.

Assim, sob o conforto de tal filosofia, partir constitui o mal menor, posto que nesse tal Cabo Verde que "vive na alma de cada um" a esperança de realização pessoal parece ser maior. Mas, como quer que se interpretem os dados da história, emigrar será sempre um dado da tópica "evasionista" que acerta o realismo do texto pela verdade histórica do crioulo, fundamentando-se assim a subversão que em *Chiquinho* se faz das regras do género, cabo-verdianizando-o. Em vez de o discurso terminar e obrigar a história a ficar na sua disforia absoluta, o discurso termina de facto mas não sem antes reabrir a história e a encaminhar para a América, com o beneplácito de Tio Joca, de José Lima, de Euclides Varanda e de vários dos mais velhos notáveis, nhô João Joana, nhô Roberto Tomásia, e certamente nhô Chic'Ana se não tivesse acabado de morrer.

4. Refundição genológica

Dois elementos de inovação se podem portanto rastrear no texto, modificadores do "romance de formação" por aculturação do género à estética do ideário da *Claridade* que propõe a inauguração de um ideologema de dupla entrada. Sem negar a solução lógica da castração juvenil que obriga o protagonista a submeter-se à disforia final, para se integrar no sistema vigente, é admissível contrariá-la em *Chiquinho*, como se viu, pelo reinício da história a cumprir fora do âmbito daquela ordem, para também conceder às gerações novas o direito de tentarem realizar-se em euforia. E, como se deduz do exposto, o ideologema inclui o patrocínio da própria esfera de acção dos gerontocratas que, muito naturalmente, se distribuem por grupos opostos, um centrífugo, dos homens que ou incitam ou aceitam a partida de Chiquinho, em nome da necessidade emigrante e da expectativa de modificação do sistema, outro centrípeto, representado pelas mulheres que exprimem os avatares étnicos e culturais que fixam o homem à terra.

Como se anotou já, a soma de esforços económicos, expectativas e frustrações do percurso de formação escolar direcciona-se entre espaços que, substancialmente, não divergem dos paradigmas comuns, propiciando os tais efeitos de índole projectiva de leitores que encontram em Chiquinho uma referência simbólica de identificação pessoal. E insiste-se na linha interpretativa de que promover a descrição identitária do homem crioulo na sociedade activa das ilhas, e identificar-se com ele na matéria que compõe o romance, pertence de facto à intencionalidade do autor e do romance, bem explícita no sub-título da primeira edição "romance caboverdeano," revelador aliás de um plano autenticador de muito mais vasto alcance.

Com efeito, aceitando que a lógica narrativa da autobiografia canonizada pelo género, de solução disfórica, responde taxativamente à problemática da escrita realista europeia (e africana tradicional), ela representa a verdade da ordem da vida nos exactos parâmetros de um tempo determinado (a época colonial). Mas, com a inovação autorial que relança a finalidade lógica da história para a abertura emigrante, que tem como consequência a formação do novo ideologema, é também o cânone que fica obrigado a adaptar-se ao específico realismo das ilhas, em condições que permitem equacionar uma nova relação de homologia entre os dois trajectos de Chiquinho e de Cabo Verde.

Sob este ponto de vista, para que se realize, em plenitude semântica, a intenção autorial grafada em "romance caboverdeano" são necessárias duas condições básicas, que o percurso de formação e o seu final infeliz se reconheça serem semelhante à ordem dominante nas ilhas, e que o programa de estudos dessa formação e a situação que aí se vive, ou se sofre, sejam próprios de Cabo Verde. Com a revisão do programa de vida, sob proposta do pai, "com as notícias que lhe iam chegando, perguntou-me se eu queria ir para a América. Toi Joca apoiou imediatamente. Mamãe lamentou o destino que me obrigava a largar a minha terra,"[25] o que era uma função terminal mal sucedida transforma-se em função interméria do que iria ser o prolongamento da história na América, mas também conotador do desejável desenvolvimento positivo da situação colonial em Cabo Verde. Dois eixos lógicos paralelos de evolução salutar se poderão assim formular, o actancial da história de Chiquinho e o prospectivo da História que em boa causalidade teriam de concluir em soluções eufóricas, os estudos universitários de Chiquinho ("José Lima deu-me indicações úteis. A minha fôrça em inglês era um grande trunfo (...) De noite, operário nas fábricas (...) de-dia era o estudante universitário"[26] e a aquisição da soberania por Cabo Verde.

Aceitando-se a analogia entre as histórias (de Chiquinho // de Cabo Verde), todas as qualidades de "romance caboverdeano" que Baltasar Lopes quis para *Chiquinho* são também comuns ao "romance" protagonizado por Cabo Verde, personagem colectiva que subsume a intencionalidade do texto e da *Claridade* a que ele pertence. E é deste modo que melhor se pode entender o alcance dos sentidos implícitos nos testemunhos cautelosos (de 1963) de Manuel Lopes, Teixeira de Sousa e Arnaldo França e que Gabriel Mariano enuncia expressamente afirmando que "o ciclo claridoso ainda não se fechou."[27] Ainda aberto em 1963, o ciclo claridoso entendido ao nível ético dos ideais de um autor e estético dos seus escritos terminaria então com o fechamento do ciclo colonial (em 1974-1975).

Em migração por entre os factores que sustentam a intencionalidade polissémica desta identificação "romance caboverdeano" subsiste o poder ordenador, estruturante e semântico, de alguns tópicos mais referidos na dinâmica da acção para assegurarem a unidade das três partes, "Infância," "S. Vicente" e "As-Águas." Nesta última se situam os factos de maior poder motivador das leituras desviantes que interpretam a calamidade da seca como intenção ideológica de denúncia crítica. Embora justas e importantes, tais leituras obliteram por completo a ironia dramática (mas também trágica no âmbito da gnoseologia das personagens que crêem no destino) desencadeada pelo título, de "As-Águas" que não chegaram a acontecer. Na ordem empírica dos factos as mortes são uma das consequências da falta das chuvas (causa lógica suficiente) mas na intencionalidade do texto e na interpretação que a ela se ajusta a falta das chuvas e as suas consequências de mortandade constituem também outras coisas, como se referiu em mais de um lugar, devendo agora ser tomadas, como sequência catastrófica (falta de chuvas, seca, mortes), na função de causa radicalmente necessária (mas não suficiente) para a consequente partida contrariada da personagem.

Já adulto, ser empurrado para a América e juntar-se ao pai (e aí padecer a castração edipiana que faltou em tempo útil) não é por isso visto por Chiquinho, nos derradeiros dias, pelo ângulo essencial dos objectivo a atingir, mas pelo das circunstâncias de valor acessório, "infantilmente," como tempo de retomar "o caminho de Vovô (...) novamente Chiquinho, o Chiquinho de Mamãe-Velha e de nhâ Rosa Calita. Companheiro de Tói Mulato nas viagens desvairadas (...).[28] Inteligência contraditória, portanto, que foge das coisas práticas em progresso no espaço e se refugia no regresso à infância e às recordações amáveis desses tempos. Em aparência infantil, este facto capital merece ser esclarecido à luz do modelo estruturante do perfil da personagem mais intimamente subjectivo, tendo em atenção o aspecto iterativo de tais ocorrências.

I. No início da estadia em casa de nhâ Cidália, estudante no Liceu de Mindelo, sentindo que a paixão o descentrava:

> Eu não concebia o amor por Nuninha abundantemente nutrido às garfadas largas. Na minha cabeça cantavam as velhas canções sentimentais que celebravam heróis magros e pálidos, do tempo em que Mamãe-Velha era rapariguinha nova.[29]

II. Dois anos depois, no regressso a S. Nicolau já formado, cedendo aos receios de falta de horizontes onde coubessem as suas ambições de futuro, como que se refugia na segurança do passado:

> Titio Joca veio logo da Praia Branca ver-me. Com o seu jeito estranho de dizer as coisas, começou por me dar os pêsames. E os seus pêsames cairam-me como a própria verdade, no côro alvoroçado dos homens de enxada (...) para quem o saber é a maior riqueza deste mundo, e que iam salvar elegremente o menino *esperto* que tinha tanta prenda na cabeça (...) Lela e Nanduca continuavam gostando dos casos de nhâ Rosa Calita. Ela aparecia sempre, com o seu farol apagado e as suas histórias. E eu era da mesma idade dos meus irmãos mais novos, ao ouvir aqueles casos todos de Roldão, de Brancaflor, de Galalão. E Tio Lôbo enganado por Chibinho.[30]

III. A natureza profunda destes motivos como que se dá a ver em equação antes da partida para Mindelo, como sintomatologia do apego:

> Agora eu seguiria para S. Vicente estudar o 6º e o 7º ano no Liceu. Papai deu ordem e Mamãe e Mamãe-Velha concordaram (...) Ficavam-me para trás os campos em que me criei e os companheiros da minha infância. Mas tinha vontade de conhecer S. Vicente. Era a ilha que eu sentia da Praia Branca (...) S. Vicente era para mim a terra em que a civilização passa em desfile (...) Queria ver o mundo. Eu não sentia o ímpeto inquieto de Cico Zepa, de embarcar fugido num vapor (...) mas possuía espírito de aventura suficiente para ir até S. Vicente. De lá adivinhava o que o mar escondia aos meus olhos e podia ouvir a voz da minha gente, chamando-me.[31]

IV. Aprisionado por tais motivações, parece ser uma personagem destituída de carácter amadurecido para enfrentar as realidade, como que se desviando delas escudado nas fantasias do imaginário etéreo. Os exactos contornos do seu perfil, longe no entanto desta interpretação simplista, esclarecem-se com a lucidez que revela no momento final dos estudos no Seminário-Lyceu:

> Passei cinco anos estudando no Seminário as matérias do liceu. (...) Fui descobrindo que o mundo não se limitava ao universo de nhâ Rosa Calita e à lenda misteriosa de Totone Menga Menga [...] O Chiquinho que a cultura liceal ia modelando não era substancialmente diferente daquele que namorava as estrelas, pedia varinhas-de-condão à lua e desejava ter o braço tatuado, como nhô João Joana. Eu era matéria plástica que se moldava a todas as experiências.

5. Imaginário e identidade

Entre outras significações mais subtis, a deslocação para o imaginário e o retorno ao mundo familiar são uma expressão sub-consciente da busca de segurança. Mas, por orientação secante, também representam de maneira exacta uma forma de fidelização à origem, por efeito da tenacidade dos valores étnicos que, substancialmente, definem a identidade cabo-verdiana em circulação no texto. E esse é o processo que se encontra posto em cena na primeira unidade, "Infância," onde o Caleijão também figura como personagem colectiva (como B. Lopes e Maria de Lourdes Belchior estimavam dizer). Aí, na primeira etapa de modelagem ao longo dos Cap. 1-21, desde cerca dos cinco anos até à conclusão da Escola Primária, a dominante espacial centra-se naturalmente no mundo familiar, em rigorosa ordem (expressão/conteúdo), dispondo em contraponto, de um lado, a casa, as mulheres, o trabalho, o interior doméstico, o essencial e o nocturno e, do outro, a rua e outros sítios, os jogos de brincadeira, os homens, o mar oceano, o circunstancial e o diurno/a noite pública.

A Mamãe e a Mamãe-Velha pertencem os cuidados com os meninos no ritual que faz a passagem do dia para a noite, espécie de matriarcado substituto do patriarcado que a ausência do pai na América decapitou. E porque é ao serão que se contam histórias, não na rua, mas em casa (sublinhe-se este facto), são as mulheres (sublinhe-se ainda) que desempenham essa função, as velhas, que detêm a maior sabedoria. Primeiro, as orações da avó (sublinhe-se ainda), de celebração pelas Graças recebidas, entregam a família aos desígnios da Divina Providência.[33] Logo depois, a função fática de nhâ Rosa Calita somente retoma as coisas da ordem da vida comum para logo promover uma descolagem dela, com histórias onde irrompem os mundos compensadores do real fantástico-teúrico, enfeitiçante, demoníaco, cosmogónico, lendário, maravilhoso, mítico, de bruxedos e almas penadas. Associados ao fabulário, à alegoria e à parábola, fazem o itinerário do conto universal, europeu de origem carolíngia e céltica, e africano da região sudanesa, até chegarem ao maravilhoso, ao fantástico e ao fabulário autóctones que dirigem o encantamento para a pedagogia:

> Mas muitas vezes nhâ Rosa buscava casos que contivessem lições de vida moral para nosso ensinamento. Os exemplos que ela botava vinham vestidos daquela lábia pitoresca com que as palavras, saídas da sua boca mocha de dentes, se animavam de vida real. Eram verdadeiras cenas abertas à curiosidade atenta da meninência.[34]

Se a nhâ Rosa Calita pertence o papel de contadeira de histórias que desenvolvem a fantasia e permitem sonhar outros mundos para além dos espaços estreitos das ilhas, a Mamãe-Velha cabe protagonizar ainda o saber não imaginativo que consubstancia a realidade historiográfica. Oriunda da família do velho "Joaquim Naninho, da nação de Gaída Branca,"[35] e com toda a autoridade ética e moral de "Gente direita e com quê de seu" (id., ibid), ela é a personagem que, vinda de fora, "daquela gente de nhâ Rosa Maria Antiga, da Ribeira dos Calhaus,"[36] encarna a representação etno-histórica do crioulo particularizado numa genealogia que se instala, com o vigor do seu sangue novo chegado ao Caleijão, para inaugurar um espaço e um tempo outros. Ao seu discurso aflui por isso a dialéctica regida por conexões entre o presente e o passado, a terra e o mar, já esvaziadas de produtividade social e cultural actuante, mas portadoras de substância histórica essencial tendo por balizas de passado os anos de má memória da "Ventona" e da "Cólera."[37]

Da sua voz narradora da História, alicerce da autenticação étnica, destaca-se em primeiro lugar a calamidade da peste, enorme no terror pânico que suscitava, tanto que deixava cega a razão dos homens e que, não sem ironia, incentivava o nivelamento social, levando o "senhor" por "pavor perante a ideia de morte (...) (a livrar os escravos) dos trabalhos suados das plantações."[38] Distintos deste relato de conteúdos por ela testemunhados directamente, outros ainda do seu tempo, mas mais gerais, respeitam ao esclavagismo com indexação de três tópicos: a) dos negreiros e das suas crueldades[39]; b) da vingança de escravos pelas afrontas recebidas dos Senhores[40]; c) do trato familiar dos escravos e sua festas[41]; d) da alforria dos escravos e seus efeitos económicos[42], e ao mistério dos "pateados" no tempo do Dr. Júlio.[43] Outros porém são já muito mais antigos, caso dos "cartajanas" que pirateavam e mantinham em sobressalto as povoações da costa.[44] Por junto, a voz de Mamãe-Velha representa as duas versões comuns da cronística, a reelaborada pelo romantismo que trata dos casos da vida com repercussões no presente, e a mais antiga que sustenta a memória historiográfica ancestral. Reunidas, asseguram e dão fundamento, com emocionantes situações, ao acidentado destino da colectividade e à realidade nacional em processo formativo.

Também contribui para adensar as significações da casa o lugar privilegiado que ocupa na abertura do romance. Longe dela e no presente da enunciação (na América) elementos evocadores particulares são a distância espacial (América/Cabo Verde) e a passagem dos anos (adulto, hoje/jovem, passado), agindo como operadores semânticos que impregnam de valores simbólicos e míticos o conteúdo sígnico da marração:

> E lá toda a minha gente se fixou. Ela povoou-se das imagens que enchiam o nosso mundo. O nascimento dos meninos. O balanço da criação. O trabalho das hortas e a fadiga de mandar comida para os trabalhadores. A partida de Papai para a América. A ansiedade quando chegavam cartas. Os melhoramentos a pouco e pouco introduzidos com os dólares que recebíamos. Mamãe deslisava como uma sombra silenciosa no trafêgo da casa. Mamãe-Velha não parava (…).[45]

Se da mulher Mamãe-Velha, a única a merecer genealogia, provém a substância que confere espessura à mitologia fundadora da origem e a voz narrativa que impregna de densidade o tempo histórico, do marido, marinheiro que o mar matou cedo, irrompe o tempo sócio-económico da fundação da "morada coberta de telha francesa e emboçada de cal por fora (...) com dinheiro ganho de-riba da água do mar."[46] No lugar de terceira geração, Chiquinho ocupa nesta narrativa da terra e crónica da linhagem o ponto alto enobrecido pela sua "boa cabeça," "novelista oficial do Grémio,"[47] na sucessão onde os avós são a imagem ordenadora do mito e da história, fundamento para a actancialidade do pai e da mãe, criadores da riqueza da casa, "pequena realeza" no meio da pobreza do Caleijão[48] que não deixa de exercer o seu mecenato acolhendo nhâ Rosa Calita no papel difusor cultura tradicional.

Na pedagogia desta velha a imaginação infantil fertiliza-se com encantamentos, casos demoníacos, bruxedos, que naturalizam a oposição "Deus /Diabo (aquele homem)."[49] Na da avó o entendimento prepara-se para as coisas da vida com narrativas de historicidade garantida pela vida real, narrativas que não deixam afinal de implicar o terreno do fértil imaginário popular, ao darem relevo à justiça de Deus que condena as "almas errantes" a pagarem depois da morte pelos seus pecados. Mas, como se encena no Cap. 24, a crença no penar das almas ainda se justifica pela necessidade de responder ao problema da morte por "destino" imprevisto a que nenhum marinheiro é alheio, e à humana solidariedade de lhe satisfazer a última vontade para seu eterno descanso.

Com o alicerce intelectual estruturado pela função feminina, a espiral concêntrica que daí progressivamente se alarga começa em nhô Chic'Ana que com Mamãe-Velha deambulava sobre as sedutoras "recordações dos tempos antigos (...) (arrependido de ter deixado) a vida de marinheiro."[50] Ele, como nenhuma outra personagem, representa a ambiguidade crioula assente na junção do apego à terra e do desejo do mar, em histórias de façanhas e de lance sedutores que aguçavam a fantasia para as regiões oceânicas. Contra as histórias que prenderam os meninos à terra estas alargam-se no sonho dos horizontes que tocam os mistérios do grande mar, exemplarmente expressos por Tói Mulato que na vida de marinheiro encontrava a sua vocação absoluta.

O mar nefasto, de onde emergiam os "cartajanas" que pilhavam a terra, nos tempos da saga dos colonizadores africanos e europeus, e o mar profícuo dos tempos modernos laboriosos (do avô, de nhô Chic'Ana, de nhô João Joana, de Chico Zepa), são as duas versões de "o mesmo" mar de pura memória para Chiquinho. Nefasto, para o feminino que gera a vida, profícuo para o masculino que a arrisca, algures, como o avô com quem Chiquinho se assemelha, mas não para ser marinheiro como ele. Na letra do texto, este narrador autobiográfico que não queria ser marinheiro como Chico Zepa,[51] nem recusa nem aceita a oposição "nefasto/profícuo"//mar/terra. Como nos tópicos que se referem o esclavagismo, e em muitos outros, os factos dão-se a ver na complexidade da dialéctica que os anima à vista do destinatário. O mar "nefasto" que matou o marido de Mamãe-Velha foi o mesmo, "profícuo," que lhe permitiu ganhar dinheiro para a morada da famíla. Nhô Chic'Ana, nhô João Joana e Chico Zepa marinheiros que a terra sedutora fez desembarcar, deslocaram a sua vivência para as recordações da memória.

Mas, porque o processo é dialéctico a inversa também é verdadeira com Tói Mulato "o mais puro de todos,"[52] auditor das histórias nhô João Joana, que brincava com barquinhos de purgueira imaginando o seu futuro de adulto. E é na injunção do destinos destes dois amigos que a dialéctica se desenvolve por disjunção produtiva. Depois que Chiquinho regressa com o seu curso liceal a S. Nicolau, Tói Mulato parte como marinheiro na "cabotagem das ilhas."[53] Finalmente quando parte emigrante para a América, Tói Mulato embarca como "marinheiro de longo curso. Do 'Vitória' passou para um quatro-mastros que filhos da Brava compraram na América."[54] Cada uma protagoniza um lado da mesma saga contraditória, um dando continuidade ao historial do emigrante em terra, o outro ao dos homens viris, para quem o mar "tem caprichos de mulher."[55]

Embora resolvida no texto com a repartição pelos protagonismos distintos de Tói Mulato e de Chiquinho, o somatório das relações contraditórias "terra/mar/ficar/partir" aponta para outros despistes do ideologema geral. Se o velho nhô Chic'Ana e o menino exemplar Tói Mulato situam a admiração de Chiquinho, a sua idolatria activa orienta-se para Chico Zepa, marinheiro que permanecia preso à terra depois de visitar a mãe, mas sempre desejoso de embarcar. Fascinando todos com a sua lábia de basofo, a que não resistiam as namoradas alheias, Chico Zepa representa textualmente, contra o saber de experiência livresca (do mindelense Andrèzinho), a versão crítica daquele que detém a pura experiência de quem já viu muito mundo, que recusa o destino e em tempo de fome se rebela contra as injustiças dos homens:

> Nhô Roberto duvidada/ - Cale a boca, homem sem fé! Fé em Deus é que salva a criatura./ - E se fé em Deus não nos der chuva?/ - Destino, homem.../ Chico Zepa revoltou-se:/ - Qual destino, velho! Destino é cair de rocha... Se fôr preciso brigarei com o destino.../ - Deus não deixou isto à criatura. Só uma pessoa venceu o destino, Totone Menga Menga.../ - Explique como Totone venceu o destino.../ - Ninguém sabe, Chico.[56]

> Houve um grande levante no S. João (...) Aparece Chico Zepa com o seu passo coxeante. Soube do que se passava, e vinha brigar. Quando o viram aproximar-se foi uma grita de todo o mundo:/ - Chico Zepa é que é filho-macho de verdade.../ Chico mostra a êstes vacões que não foste criado a abóbora...Chico Zepa adiantou-se:/ - Povo tem fome, Sr. Administrador!... A pouco e pouco todos se foram retirando. Chico Zepa ficou lamentando:/ - Pobre é como filho de gafanhoto. Nasce com as asas verdes, mas depois vira cinzento, côr de nada... Pobreza é escarrador de todo mundo...[57]

Completam a galeria de referências admirativas de Chiquinho a casa distante de Tio Joca, em Praia Branca, lugar de experiência iniciática patriarcal, e a casa aureolada de mistério de Totone Menga Menga no Chamiço, o "saibo" que "venceu o destino," lugar de benedição. Englobando todo este mundo é pela retórica da sinédoque que a narrativa compõe a personagem humana do Caleijão impregnada de mais variados sincretismos. Actante de múltiplos actores reunidos em cena no Cap. 24- "Bibia estava com alma," aí representavam o espectáculo da grande pedagogia:

> Os dois velhos, afastados do caso contemporâneo de Bibia Ludovina, mergulhavam nas recordações da mocidade. Todos nós ficávamos atentos, embebidos na narração dos velhos. Eu largava tudo para os ouvir. Nos dias em que sabia que eles iriam depois da ceia para a Água do Canal, engulia a cachupa à pressa e não sossegava enquanto não me via no caminho da Combota. Era sempre guerra certa com Mamãe-Velha. Minha avó não compreendia que era ela, nhâ Rosa, nhô Chic'Ana, todos os velhos, que, com as histórias que a sua experiência tinha depositado, iam modelando minha alma de menino. E era extraordinário o seu talento de narradores. As cenas apareciam na nossa frente, vivendo."[58]

Concluindo

Nas noites da Água de Canal, coração da terra, o povo faz a crónica da vida da personagem Caleijão, tal como em toda essa primeira parte do romance o autor relata a "Infância" de Chiquinho, tal como o professor interino do Liceu de Mindelo, Baltasar Lopes, feito etnólogo na primeira metade da década de 1930, recolhia histórias contadas pelo povo, durante as suas férias passadas em Lajedos, para as recontar transfiguradas pela ficção.[59]

Notas

[1] 1 (March 1936).

[2] (S. Vicente: Edições "Claridade," Outubro 1947).

[3] Chiquinho, *id.*, 11.

[4] *id.*, 282-283.

[5] "Suplemento literário" do *Diário de Lisboa.* 16/8/1935, 3-4 (itálicos nossos A. C.).

[6] Baltasar Lopes, *Cabo Verde Visto por Gilberto Freyre* (Praia: Imp. Nacional, 1956), 5.

[7] Manuel Lopes, "O programa da *Claridade* era fincar os pés na terra cabo-verdiana", *Diário Ilustrado* 22/8/1959.

[8] *id.*, "A Mocidade Caboverdiana," *Notícias de Cabo Verde* (Mindelo: S.I., 1931).

[9] *id.*, *Chuva Braba* (Lisboa: Edições 70, 1982).

[10] Baltasar Lopes, *Chiquinho, id.*

[11] Maurice Merleau-Ponty, *Phénomenologie de la perception* (Paris: Gallimard, 1945).

[12] Baltasar Lopes, *Chiquinho*, 270, 155, 158.

[13] *Boletim Cabo Verde* 1 (Outubro 1958).

[14] Manuel Lopes, *Chuva Braba*, id., 119-120.

[15] Gabriel Mariano, "Ti Lobo." *Vida e morte de João Cabafume* (Lisboa: Vega, s.d.), 100.

[16] Baltasar Lopes, *Chiquinho*, *id.*, 278.

[17] Adam Schaft, *Verdade e História* (Lisboa: Estampa, 1977).

[18] Käte Hamburger, *A Lógica da Criação Literária* (S. Paulo: Ed. Perspectiva, 1975).

[19] Baltasar Lopes, *Chiquinho*, 210.

[20] *id.*, 213.

[21] *id.*, 210.

[22] *id.*, 260.

[23] *id.*, 260.

[24] *id.*, 234.

[25] *id.*, 289.

[26] *id.*, 294.

[27] "Suplemento 'Quinta feira à tarde.'" N° 329, 330, 334, 332, in *Diário Popular*, N° 7382, 7389, 7414 e 7413, Ano XXI, Lisboa, Maio-Jun./1963.

28 Baltasar Lopes, *Chiquinho*, 295.

[29] *id.*, 129.

[30] *id.*, 211.

[31] *id.*, 116.

[32] *id.*, 115.

[33] *id.*, 21.

[34] *id.*, 23.

[35] *id.*, 114.

[36] *id. ibid.*

[37] *id.* 35.

[38] *id.*, 36.

[39] *id.*, 36.

[40] *id.*, 37.

[41] *id.*, *ibid.*

[42] *id.*, 37.

[43] José Dias; *id.*, 38-39.

[44] *id.*, 39.

[45] *id.*, 11.

[46] *id.*, 11.

[47] *id.*, 116, 290.

[48] *id.*, 113, 249.

[49] *id.*, 38.

[50] *id.*, 28-29.

[51] *id.*, 116.

[52] *id.*, 33.

[53] *id.*, 244.

[54] *id.*, 293.

[55] *id.*, 245.

[56] *id.*, 107-108.

[57] *id.*, 278-282.

[58] *id.*, 87.

[59] cf. nhô Manuel Antoninho, "Os trabalhos e os dias." in Arnaldo França (dir), *Raízes* 5-6 (1978) ou Egídio de "Egídio e Job." *Claridade.* 9 (Dezembro 1960).

Alberto Carvalho é Doutorado em Literatura Cabo-Verdiana pela Faculdade de Letras da Universidade de Lisboa. Docente de Literaturas Africanas de Língua Portuguesa da FLUL, nos níveis de Licenciatura e de Mestrado. Algumas publicações (respeitantes a Cabo Verde) incluem: "Baltasar Lopes, a Obra e o Autor do seu Tempo." *Arquivos do Centro Cultural Português,* Vol. XXIX (Lisboa-Paris: Fund. Calouste Gulbenkian, 1991); "Evasionismo, configuração existencial da insularidade caboverdiana." *Coscienza Nazionale Nelle Letterature Africane Di Lingua Portoghese* (Roma, Bulzoni: 1995); "Apresentação." Manuel Lopes. *Falucho Ancorado* (Lisboa: Cosmos, 1997); "A narrativa cabo-verdiana, nacionalidade e nacionalismo." *La narrativa en lengua portuguesa de los últimos cinquenta años, Revista de Filologia Românica. Anejos* (Madrid: Universidad Complutense, 2001).

A representação espacial nos contos de Gabriel Mariano

Glória de Brito

Resumo. Os contos "Caduca" e "O Rapaz doente ou a conjura" de Gabriel Mariano inscrevem variantes do mesmo espaço urbano (Mindelo), marcado simultaneamente pelo efeito de real e de dramaticidade, e por uma carga evocativa histórica, cultural e ideológica. Os lugares inseridos nos universos ficcionais dos dois contos contêm relações numa dupla perspectiva sincrónica e diacrónica. Portadores de memória dos acontecimentos passados, reveladores das percepções das personagens, os lugares assumem funções e graus de tonalidades afectivas e atmosféricas, propondo múltiplos sentidos e significações.

Os espaços representados e os signos identificatórios

Vida e Morte de João Cabafume,[1] constitui a primeira obra completa de Gabriel Mariano (1928-2002), publicada em 1976, embora já fosse autor destacado de poemas, ensaios e contos dispersos em jornais e revistas, nomeadamente na *Claridade*[2] e no *Suplemento Cultural*.[3] Posteriormente, o escritor reuniu igualmente os seus ensaios no volume *Cultura Caboverdeana*,[4] prefaciado por Alberto de Carvalho, e os poemas numa publicação com o título *Ladeira Grande*.[5]

No seu conjunto, os contos de Gabriel Mariano retratam uma grande variedade de personagens ligadas a uma não menos significativa variedade de contextos espácio-temporais, actualizando, simultaneamente, uma diversidade de temas e de formas narrativas. O processo de abordagem dos espaços e ambientes revela-se bastante próximo das marcas do realismo humanista,[6] próprio dos *claridosos,* no qual o "telurismo serve de textura literária ao homem cabo-verdiano em comunhão com o seu meio ambiente" (Almada 175). O processo de integração realista é ainda acentuado pela ancoragem das personagens em lugares cujos topónimos são atestados do ponto de vista geográfico ou histórico, ou em lugares comuns que reenviam para referentes reais (a baía, o cais, o mercado, o Grémio, o porto, a praia, o hospital, o liceu...), "convocando um conjunto de semas com valor denotativo e conotativo, que estruturam a organização espacial de um grupo social" (Gardies 54). A propósito da relação entre o homem e o seu meio ambiente, J. M. Thorberg escreve:

> Alors, les lieux seront l'expression de la manière dont chaque génération construit l'ouverture—et l'isolement—entre la réalité intérieure et la réalité extérieure, et entre le sentiment et la pensée, aboutissant à son propre équilibre logique et psychologique.[7]

Estas afirmações revelam que os espaços constituem um lugar de troca e de continuidade das experiências vividas e herdadas. Eles fornecem indicações sobre a existência de uma consciência associada ao comportamento e às actividades físicas e culturais. "L'homme tend à identifier sa propre image avec celle de l'espace qu'il habite," afirma E. Hall (219).

A noção de espaço romanesco engloba, por conseguinte, um sistema narrativo que combina elementos topográficos, atmosféricos, culturais e cronobiológicos que se inserem numa ascendência histórica e numa evolução geográfica, demográfica e cultural. H. Mitterrand (83), num estudo sobre a obra de Emile Zola, afirma que o espaço romanesco "est conçu non seulement pour satisfaire aux exigences de la *mimesis,* pour faire connaître des sites réels, mais aussi pour servir la logique et la dynamique d'une action dramatique, avec ses personnages, ses situations et ses péripéties."

A insularidade e a continentalidade constituem dois elementos de diferenciação na concepção do espaço, na produção literária africana. Segundo Manuel Veiga (9), a insularidade cabo-verdiana não se reduz aos sentimentos de solidão ou de nostalgia que emergem do espaço geográfico reduzido das ilhas. Ela incorpora outros aspectos que se prendem com a dialéctica do mar circundante e imenso, face à pequenez das ilhas e de cada ilha. Esta oposição dialéctica funda alguns dos paradigmas estéticos que sustentam as temáticas literárias cabo-verdianas, assumindo configurações diferentes em cada escritor que, na opinião de Pierre. Rivas (293) se desdobram em estruturas em espelho: a evasão no espaço do exílio, partir e ficar, a ilha como mundo pequeno que procura a libertação na dimensão do universal. Manuel Lopes poetizou esta concepção em vários poemas.[8] Parece-nos, por conseguinte, que a percepção da limitação e da dimensão do espaço geográfico gerou fenómenos sociais e temáticas culturais que os reflectem: evasão, exílio, partida, emigração, regresso e até identidade Mar/Mãe no caso de Baltasar Lopes[9] (Rivas 293), exploradas na poesia, na ficção e igualmente nas composições musicais, em particular, na *morna.*

Se, por um lado, a insularidade, o clima, a topografia acidentada, a dispersão do território e, por outro, os factores históricos e culturais condicionaram o desenvolvimento do arquipélago, naturalmente eles modelaram a idiossincrasia e a originalidade do cabo-verdiano que, ao longo dos tempos, teve que encontrar múltiplas formas de superação e de compensação. Estas são descritas por Gabriel Mariano (*Cultura* 70) do seguinte modo:

> Acomodação às condições do clima, de mesologia, de insularidade; acomodação às vicissitudes do cultivo do solo; ao regime das chuvas. Acomodação, principalmente às necessidades de contacto e de aproveitamento do escravo negro. Acomodação sobre todos os aspectos: de economia animal e vegetal como cultural.

Considera ainda o autor que, em relação às outras sociedades colonizadas pelos Portugueses, o caso de Cabo Verde é particular. Na sua perspectiva "foram os negros e os mulatos os responsáveis directos na estruturação da sua sociedade," testemunhada no "funco" e no "sobrado," dois elementos reveladores da cultura material reflectida na organização do espaço.

Passando do ensaio para a ficção de Gabriel Mariano, verificamos que nos seus contos (e até na poesia), os lugares da acção e as atmosferas que envolvem as personagens testemunham uma "acomodação," ou seja, influências recíprocas, especificadas por diferentes processos narrativos, como iremos demonstrar oportunamente.

Os contos de Gabriel Mariano enraízam no contexto insular cabo-verdiano (à excepção do "Titia" e "A conta do café") e traçam facetas do meio natural e de ambientes físicos e sociais que assumem configurações e idiossincrasias particulares, inspirando-se em contextos da sua história familiar e do itinerário pessoal, características que também se verificam na sua poesia. Naturalmente, os espaços descritos ou sugeridos nas suas narrativas reenviam para S.

Nicolau, sua ilha natal, S. Vicente, ilha onde estudou e finalmente Lisboa, onde completou os estudos. Três contos ("Filho Primogénito," "Família," e "O Intruso") introduzem o tema da infância, decorrendo os dois primeiros no contexto rural e marítimo de S. Nicolau e o último, "O Intruso," num espaço interior, semi-urbano do Mindelo. Numa entrevista dada a Michel Laban (348), Gabriel Mariano admite que em "Família" e "Filho Primogénito" existem marcas autobiográficas, que confeririam alguma verosimilhança.

Os contos "Caduca," "O rapaz doente ou a conjura," Vida e morte de João Cabafume" e "Ti Lobo" decorrem em S. Vicente, tendo como pano de fundo a cidade do Mindelo. Constroem situações dramáticas e imagens da vida quotidiana dos anos quarenta e põem em cena diferentes lugares, carregados de informações e índices históricos e culturais. Os contos "Titia" e "A conta do café" passam-se em Lisboa, introduzindo o espaço da diáspora. Em função das realidades descritas, alguns dos espaços, descritos ou evocados nos vários contos, impregnam-se de qualidades e sentimentos que lhes são inerentes: sonho, desolação, desespero, medo, revolta...

Assim, as singularidades das personagens, geradas pelos diferentes meios, integram na estrutura narrativa os signos que testemunham um tipo de ambiente físico, social, psicológico e até mítico, e as tonalidades afectivas que os envolvem.

Onirismo, antropomorfismo e realismo em "Caduca"

Debrucemo-nos com mais detalhe no conto "Caduca." Este conto, muito curto, tem como cenários a baía e os ambientes nocturnos da cidade do Mindelo, apresentando uma forma próxima da prosa poética.[10] Caduca, o protagonista, homónimo da narrativa, é descrito como uma figura semi-humana e semi-marinha, resultado da influência que o mar exerce sobre ele. Os seus traços físicos definem-se por propriedades comuns às do seu espaço circundante que lhe incrusta, também, determinados sentimentos e lhe molda o carácter.

Caduca vive na baía, dorme na areia e conhece os segredos marinhos. Durante a noite, mergulha nas profundezas do mar, munido de um saco, para roubar três bocados de carvão, nas lanchas ancoradas no porto, para vender mais tarde. De manhã, ajuda os pescadores a deslizar os botes na água, mantendo com eles conversas sobre a crise do Porto Grande e sobre as carências do povo em geral, que assumem um tom político e até filosófico.

No interior destes discursos e das interrogações de Caduca, subentende-se a intenção crítica do narrador/autor, denunciando a injustiça social e o abandono do Porto Grande. É também perceptível o jogo sobre a linguagem dialógica (Bakhtine 95-101), explorando as suas potencialidades estéticas e oralizantes.

Além destes espaços, outros há que assumem um papel relevante na economia narrativa. Entre eles destaca-se a rua, onde Caduca vagueia nas noites agradáveis ("a rua é palácio dos pobres"), a taberna de Luísa Manobra, onde encontra os "rocegadores e catraeiros sem bote" e as meninas de vida. Nestes momentos nocturnos, ele mergulha na atmosfera da morna e do "drogue,"[11] para escutar Goi que toca violino, Tchuf que toca guitarra, e ouvir cantar Lela de Maninha,[12] o "Poeta da Ponta da Praia." Para ilustrar os aspectos que focámos, atente-se no seguinte excerto. Note-se as imagens e metáforas utilizadas, que além de caracterizarem o protagonista, traduzem a sua simbiose com o meio envolvente:

> Quando a baia está mansa as ondas desfazem-se na praia e o barulho vasto dos calhaus é sonoro e sacudido. É assim o sorriso de Caduca. Porque Caduca tem na boca serena e livre, calhaus secos da praia. O carvão negro suja-lhe o corpo, mas o salitre branco branqueia-lhe o rosto (...).
> Que ninguém procure Caduca no mar quando as noites são boas. Se o quiserem ver procurem-no com os seus amigos. (...) Estará com eles na rua, porque rua é palácio de pobre.[13]

Este conto constrói três espaços distintos, ligados a atmosferas também diferentes: a baía, a realidade exterior (ruas e praças) e a taberna de Luísa Manobra. Primeiramente, o leitor pode seguir o trajecto de Caduca nas profundezas da baía, nas noites de lua cheia. A descrição desta paisagem submarina reveste-se de um imaginário fantástico, no qual Caduca incarna o regresso a um certo animismo, vivendo em harmonia com os elementos naturais, cúmplices no roubo dos três bocados de carvão. Por conseguinte, constatamos a antropomorfização do mar, da lua e dos lanchões, representados por acções, sentimentos e gestos cúmplices e comoventes para com o seu protegido Caduca:

> Caduca vai devagar porque a lua cheia bóia a seu lado. (...) Ele mergulha e caminha com os pés no fundo. Vem à tona e volta a mergulhar. A praia aproxima-se. A baía aquieta-se. Os lanchões murmuram entre si murmúrios alvos de espuma.[14]

Como se pode verificar nesta passagem, o antropomorfismo, traduzido num registo poético, contribui para favorecer o *ethos* fantástico que explica a eficácia do protagonista. A baía é, aliás, uma quase personagem, porque ela própria também tem uma vida e uma expressão: nasceu com os vapores e o carvão,[15] expandiu-se com as rotas da navegação e começou a declinar com o surgimento do combustível e com a fundação dos portos de Dakar e de Las Palmas que, gradualmente, substituíram o Porto Grande no reabastecimento dos navios. Portanto, ela participou e participa dos sonhos, das alegrias e das angústias do povo do Mindelo. Ela introduz todo um sistema de mudanças qualitativas, eufóricas e disfóricas, que marcaram épocas sucessivas. A descrição da baía é completada pelo sonho de Caduca, incorporado no discurso do narrador, sob forma de uma narração da tradição oral, marcada pelo maravilhoso: a aparição de uma sereia encantada que seduz Lázaro e lhe dá três fios dourados dos seus cabelos, maravilhando todos os que puderam assistir a esta cena. A nível enunciativo, a inserção deste episódio joga sobre o efeito de variação do registo linguístico, acentuando os traços poéticos da narrativa, na nossa opinião uma das mais belas da obra.

Outra parte da acção decorre na baía, focando o trabalho dos pescadores, portanto, num ambiente realista. Caduca ajuda os pescadores a empurrar os botes para a água e com eles mantém conversas que mergulham na crise do Porto Grande e na falta de chuva. Os diálogos entre Caduca e nhô Crisóstomo, por exemplo, assim como as interrogações de Caduca sublinham, de maneira persuasiva e até irónica, o inconformismo, a denúncia da injustiça e a incúria do poder colonial, responsável pela situação de crise da baía. O recurso ao discurso directo das personagens introduz as preocupações e as realidades comuns dos habitantes do Mindelo da época, restituindo, simultaneamente, o ambiente linguístico da língua portuguesa falada, na sua variante cabo-verdiana.

O valor crítico implícito no diálogo dos pescadores salienta o papel de conscientização do leitor, como sendo um dos propósitos de um autor comprometido com os objectivos do movimento do *Suplemento Cultural* (Almada 146-149). As observações de Caduca e de nhô Crisóstomo testemunham o declínio de um espaço que afecta a sociedade e a economia do Mindelo, bem como de todo o arquipélago, originando o desemprego, desequilíbrios sociais e situações de exploração, agravados pela falta de chuva.

O percurso[16] de Caduca a caminho do centro da cidade constitui uma outra representação do espaço, descrito numa vivência quotidiana, evocativa de uma época histórica e social do Mindelo. O trajecto do protagonista pelas ruas que vão da baía aos diferentes pontos da cidade e da vida nocturna articula uma sucessão de lugares e de atmosferas sociais, nomeadamente: o espaço do cais, ligado às actividades da descarga do carvão onde se agitam os carregadores (homens e mulheres) com sacos às costas, cheios de carvão, ganhando uma miséria; as ruas frequentadas pelas meninas de vida; o largo da Alfândega e a rua de Lisboa onde pululam os estudantes do liceu; a loja de Luísa Manobra, refúgio de bebida e de música cabo-verdiana. A recorrência destes signos ilustrativos de um espaço e de um tempo, traduzidos por referências muito breves e fragmentadas, fornece o panorama do Mindelo dos anos quarenta. Brevidade e fragmentação convergem na narrativa de Gabriel Mariano, revelando a sua arte na recriação desta imagem condensada, mas viva, numa escrita que oscila entre a prosa e poesia.

Enquanto que o onirismo e o antropomorfismo humanizam o meio circundante da baía, a música envolve o espaço adstrito à taberna de Luísa Manobra, criando um clima de intimidade, de calor e de ascese que influi sobre a resistência das personagens ao sofrimento e às preocupações. Este espaço nocturno e gregário, onde afluem personagens de todas as camadas sociais, vindas de vários lugares, transforma-se num universo musical, mergulhado nas mornas, elevando a emoção e os sentimentos acima da precariedade quotidiana. Podemos verificar uma sucessão de verbos de deslocação (Borillo 131) ("vieram," "desceu," "chega," "chegou," "veio," "misturou," "aparecem") que traduzem este movimento de convergência do mundo exterior para o interior da taberna, convertido assim num espaço de (re)conforto.

Um outro espaço implicado na narrativa e eivado de simbolismo ganha particular relevo nos dois contos, na medida em que está associado à fundação de signos recorrentes nas literaturas africanas de língua portuguesa. Assim, a referência ao "Sul," feita de forma velada e alusiva, por motivos censórios, convoca o implícito político do leitor, capaz de nela reconhecer o fenómeno da emigração compulsiva. Neste único lexema, reside a evocação de um espaço longínquo e desconhecido, que se estende a toda a dura realidade das roças de S. Tomé e Príncipe e de Angola. Este espaço é sugerido ao longo da narrativa sob duas configurações antagónicas. Por um lado, enuncia um lugar de refúgio e de fuga à falta de trabalho e ao flagelo da seca e da fome, ou seja, "um meio de libertação relativamente à impossibilidade de sobreviver em Cabo Verde."[17] Por outro, denuncia, de forma implícita, o cenário do trabalho forçado e desumano nas roças, disfarçado sob a designação de "contrato,"[18] tema recorrente na produção literária de Gabriel Mariano e, igualmente, nas literaturas africanas de língua portuguesa, em particular nas de Cabo Verde, Angola e Moçambique.

O momento final, que decorre na taberna Luísa Manobra, evoca uma atmosfera tradicional associada à partida, frequente em S. Vicente, nos momentos de despedida. Eugénio Tavares e B. Leza compuseram, cada um, uma morna com o motivo "Hora di bai,"[19] perpetuando, assim, esta tradição ligada a um momento dramático.

A incorporação de fragmentos de mornas na narrativa, cantadas pela voz de Lela de Maninha, faz emergir um elemento do património literário e musical, evocando os momentos dramáticos e os espaços onde se realizavam os "bailes de despedida." Este propósito, iniciado pelos *Claridosos*, utilizado eficazmente por Baltasar Lopes em *Chiquinho*,[20] inscreve-se nos objectivos de busca das raízes culturais, conciliando-os com a inovação na criação de novas formas estético-literárias. Os enunciados "O luar nasce na boca de Lela de Maninha. Lela abre a voz para todos. E o luar ilumina todo o mundo...,"[21] reenviam metaforicamente para este aspecto.

Uma outra dimensão espacial, de natureza textual e intertextual, está relacionada com a arquitectura narrativa, reflectindo-se no processo enunciativo e na matéria significante. Podemos constatar que uma das características deste conto evidencia-se na desordem (aparente) da narração e numa certa indisciplina na organização dos discursos, fenómenos que conferem uma estrutura fragmentária e um carácter poético e oralizado ao conto, aproximando-o simultaneamente da prosa poética e das estórias da tradição oral. Este aspecto deve-se a algumas técnicas recorrentes em Gabriel Mariano, (Cristina Pacheco: 1987 e Glória Brito: 1998 e 2002), nomeadamente a inserção de fragmentos de mornas, interrogativas e repetições que, por um lado nos remetem para uma ambiência de tradição oral, por outro criam um efeito de sentido que vai ecoando, retroactivamente e profeticamente ao longo da enunciação, sublinhando as consequências trágicas da decadência do Porto Grande e da seca: a partida e a morte.

Partir implica "desespero de partir,"[22] mas também morte ("Caduca pensa que ir para o Sul é trocar a hora da morte"). Ficar pressupõe miséria e morte lenta ("esta terra está apodrecendo na ourela do mar"), mas também resistência e solidariedade para "ressuscitar nas mornas de Lela de Maninha." Caduca não parte, "vai ficar para viver." No semantismo do nome "Caduca" reside um duplo simbolismo: por um lado o efémero, a morte, mas por outro a vida e a reintegração. A nível intertextual, Caduca talvez possa ser associado à incarnação da problemática literária da anti-evasão, da recusa do espaço da "Pasárgada," poetizada por Ovídio Martins,[23] um dos elementos fundador do *Suplemento Cultural*.

Nesta perspectiva, a dimensão trágica da morte, transposta em símbolos ("luar"; "dia luminoso"), anunciada metaforicamente de forma profética, é atenuada pelos efeitos poéticos que influem na emoção do leitor ("o luar morre afogado nos olhos de Mã-Bia") e asseguram a poeticidade do conto.

O efeito de representação do espaço neste conto constrói-se numa interacção com as descrições das personagens, os ambientes familiares e culturais e a paisagem física e social exterior. Henri Mitterand (55) considera que "L'espace naît alors du regard du personnage, de ses gestes, de son écoute, de ses perceptions, qui l'authentifient et le justifient. " No entanto, mais do que representar aquelas componentes da narrativa, o que parece dominar na narração é o propósito ideológico do autor, empenhado em denunciar a exploração e incúria do regime colonial perante os dramas do seu país, e em afirmar a sua fidelidade às raízes culturais. Para tal, Gabriel Mariano cria uma nova forma de expressão que concilia a ideologia com uma prática narrativa de estrutura repetitiva e fragmentada, explorando os efeitos poéticos e os recursos sonoros e rítmicos da língua portuguesa oralizada e cabo-verdianizada.

"O rapaz doente ou a conjura": um percurso funesto

No conto "O rapaz doente ou a conjura," o autor recorre ao mesmo espaço urbano, mas variando o uso de signos interiores e exteriores, multiplicando assim os efeitos de representação dos lugares e ambientes criados na narração. As personagens que constituem o universo diegético transportam outro tipo de motivações e de dramas, conferindo, obviamente, outras propriedades e configurações à realidade espacial.

Neste conto, a personagem Júlio, afectada pela tuberculose, procura em vão a influência de D. Maninha, a fim de conseguir entrar no hospital do Mindelo. Esta doença, incurável na época em que se situam os acontecimentos do texto, deixa os pobres numa situação de extrema fragilidade, vítimas de atitudes de receio e de marginalização, sobretudo por parte do grupo social abastado. Vindo da cidade da Praia, na ilha de Santiago, Júlio desembarca no Mindelo, portador de uma carta para D. Maninha, enviada pelo seu marido, funcionário naquela ilha e seu superior hierárquico. Apesar dos esforços imediatos de D. Maninha junto do Dr. Nogueira e do Director do hospital, para internar Júlio, este confronta-se com reacções de recusa, de rejeição e até de hostilidade. Sem saída, D. Maninha e o enfermeiro concebem uma conjura e mandam-no de novo para a Praia.

O trajecto da personagem em busca de uma cura possível, introduz um olhar novo sobre o espaço urbano do Mindelo, capital do arquipélago na época, conduzindo o narrador a evocar factos ocorridos em espaços e tempos precedentes.

No decorrer da acção, que tem como pano de fundo a capital de S. Vicente, são postos em cena vários quadros espaciais urbanos, correspondendo cada um deles a variações de lugares que constroem a paisagem física e social da cidade do Mindelo, constituintes do universo narrativo de Gabriel Mariano. O leitor pode seguir, ao longo da narração, a sucessão de espaços traçados onde se imprimem os acontecimentos e as sensações: a igreja, a casa de D. Maninha, as ruas e praças, os cafés, o cinema, as tabernas, a casa do Dr. Nogueira, o hospital e o Grémio. A expressão espacial evidência, também, algumas actividades profissionais, ressaltando o carácter dissimétrico da ocupação do espaço geográfico pela escala social, composta por um leque de figuras que vão desde a prostituta ao administrador do Grémio (uma espécie de clube reservado à elite urbana), cobrindo, praticamente, toda a hierarquia da sociedade mindelense. Do mesmo modo, os temas emergentes no conto (a vulnerabilidade dos pobres com doenças incuráveis e contagiosas, a hostilidade, a hipocrisia e a fatalidade humana) assumem relevância em relação com os quadros espaciais traçados.

A dinâmica da representação do espaço joga sobre o trajecto do protagonista que, deslocando-se de um lugar para o outro, abre ao leitor a variedade de lugares e de ambientes representados. Estes aparecem-nos segundo a lógica de dois olhares, o de Júlio e o do narrador. Ao nível discursivo as transições do olhar são em geral efectuadas pelas passagens dialógicas.

O primeiro cenário reenvia para um espaço interior, perspectivado num ambiente familiar, a casa de D. Maninha, no momento em que o protagonista lhe entrega a carta e aguarda as suas ordens. As referências descritivas incidem sobre os objectos e gestos que se revestem de medo de contaminação, de precauções, de repugnância, de revolta e de olhares desconfiados, por parte de D. Maninha, e de curiosidade, de admiração e até de sensualidade, da parte de Júlio.

A descrição do quarto de D. Maninha ultrapassa o esboço, próprio do conto e da novela (Grojnowski 84), assumindo uma configuração próxima da romanesca, pela presença de pormenores sobre a decoração. Todo o espaço está impregnado de devoção, conferida pela presença de objectos religiosos ("um oratorio," "uma vela," "uma grande pintura de S. Sebastião," "imagens amarelecidas e misteriosas") e de "odor pesado de incenso" que "exala do oratório." Assim, o quarto converte-se numa espécie de prolongamento do espaço da igreja, sublinhando a ligação estreita de D. Maninha com as actividades religiosas, mas ressaltando, simultaneamente, a oposição entre as acções virtuosas e as atitudes hipócritas.

Como verificámos em "Caduca," podemos constatar que o trajecto constitui um elemento da tipologia espacial, constante na utilização dos lugares por Gabriel Mariano, levando-nos à hipótese da existência de "um esquema ou sistema especial" (Bourneuf 84). Aliás, este processo é recorrente noutros contos ("Filho Primogénito" e "Ti Lobo"). Tal como em "Caduca," algumas etapas da acção inscrevem-se no percurso de Júlio, acompanhado de D. Maninha e de Norberto, na esperança de encontrarem o Dr. Nogueira ou o director do hospital. Este itinerário simples permite associar os lugares individuais a outros socialmente marcados (o Grémio, o porto, o hospital), e fornecer vários planos representativos do espaço urbano do Mindelo na época colonial. Os lugares e ambientes são sugeridos, mais uma vez, por traços condensados e fragmentados, reenviando para as actividades portuárias, a animação das ruas e dos cafés nos dias da chegada dos marinheiros e dos estrangeiros nos barcos que atracavam no cais, a prostituição, as vendedoras de rua... Na evocação desta atmosfera exterior, as sensações visuais, sonoras e tácteis imbricam-se, fazendo ressaltar a variedade de figuras humanas que compõem o cenário: marinheiros, vendedoras, crianças, estrangeiros, polícias, prostitutas, bêbados...

O Grémio estabelece uma fronteira entre a população menos favorecida e a elite, reunida à volta de bebidas e festas, longe dos olhares alheios. Local de encontro para discussões políticas, negócios, jogo e até adultérios, o Grémio representa um espaço recorrente na literatura cabo-verdiana, associado aos contrastes sociais.

À semelhança do conto "Caduca," o narrador insere na narrativa outra variante espacial das roças de S. Tomé. As referências que reenviam para a roça Zé Maria são duplamente sintomáticas: ilustram a relação entre o passado e o presente e tecem signos que têm o seu lugar na história do país e da colonização. O discurso directo do protagonista visa testemunhar o abuso, a opressão e o sofrimento vividos neste espaço e revelar algumas tarefas do "contrato" (trabalhos forçados na lama e no capim das ruas de São Tomé sob a torreira do sol) e procedimentos (chicotadas recebidas na prisão). Este discurso é submetido às lembranças e percepções que desempenham um papel importante na memória evocativa. O uso do pretérito imperfeito do indicativo, da comparação, de frases nominais curtas e da suspensão ("O chicote de cavalo marinho queimava como fogo..."; "Trabalho duro"; "Enterrado na lama") funcionam como formas de reactualização da acção passada, tornando-a mais viva, estimulada pelas sensações desencadeadas pela recordação.

De um modo mais globalizante, a "roça" constitui um paradigma espacial que comporta uma carga afectiva, ideológica e estético-literária, estando na base de figuras e processos retóricos, actualizados pelos sucessivos movimentos literários cabo-verdianos e igualmente angolanos.

Neste texto, assume um papel peculiar um espaço delimitado: o hospital. O hospital, espaço muito específico, é o lugar da conjura, concertada entre o enfermeiro e D. Maninha, que vai decidir o destino de Júlio, ou seja, mandá-lo novamente para a Praia sem qualquer tratamento. Este lugar não merece o agrado do narrador, que focaliza apenas "o corredor deserto," um gabinete do enfermeiro frio, triste, sujo, privado de calor humano e de sentimentos. A referência a objectos não apropriados ao gabinete médico[24] ("um cinzeiro," "uma garrafa de grogue") ressoa como uma acusação à ociosidade, à negligência e à falta de probidade.

As ocorrências do "vento," "sacudindo as acácias" ou explodindo "em rajadas no corredor deserto do hospital," põem em evidência a correlação entre a impotência do homem perante a morte e as intempéries climáticas. Também o semantismo de "seco," um atributo que transita do meio natural para o ser humano (Júlio), traduz uma relação recíproca entre o homem, a natureza e os fenómenos climáticos e topográficos:

> De pé o rapaz segurava, com os dedos secos e descorados, a boina velha. (...) Os olhos sobressaltos corriam a sala toda como se um acontecimento imprevisto os tivesse de súbito surpreendido.[25]
>
> O vento era forte e sacudia de tempos a tempos as acácias secas que ladeavam o caminho.[26]

Estas analogias contribuem para acentuar a atmosfera trágica, construída no conto. Um outro autor, Manuel Lopes, poetizou de forma exemplificativa e dramática esta reciprocidade, no poema "Crioulo."[27]

Por conseguinte, o espaço pode comportar uma dimensão paradoxal, visto que em relação a ele, as personagens experimentam emoções opostas, de acordo com as circunstâncias climáticas, também opostas (a chuva e a seca). As afirmações de Manuel Lopes—"a riqueza de Cabo Verde provém da sua extrema pobreza"[28]—ressaltam o paradoxo da existência humana nestas ilhas. E Gabriel Mariano reforça esta ideia, afirmando:

> Cabo Verde é um milagre! Este povo já devia estar morto e enterrado há duzentos anos, pelo menos. Mas ele não morre! O milagre, é que apareceu nestas pequenas ilhas do Atlântico uma apetência literária, um vigor cultural que, aparentemente, não tem nenhuma razão de existir.[29]

A não razão da existência ou a existência, apesar da razão, são exemplarmente narradas em Gabriel Mariano. O espaço, como fomos assinalando, é um dos elementos justificativos das vidas que podemos testemunhar na obra do autor. Também pudemos verificar que Gabriel Mariano recorre a diferentes formas de representação espacial: o trajecto, a aglomeração, o espaço limitado interior, o espaço desdobrado e o espaço convocado pela memória... Tendo em conta que uma das características das suas narrativas reside no carácter fragmentário e repetitivo da narração, poderemos inferir que o relevo do percurso nos dois contos, efectuado no interior de um mesmo espaço (Mindelo), corresponde, por um lado, a uma necessidade de organização, de forma a assegurar a unidade das diversas componentes narrativas. Por outro, o percurso, enquanto espaço de deslocação do(s) olhar(es) (tal como a câmara no *traveling*), permite registar o espaço físico real (objectos, personagens, impressões), mas também, captar os sentidos veiculados pelas percepções sensoriais, culturais e ideológicas. Ou seja, identificar nos lugares e ambientes os signos representativos do espaço de referência.

Os contos de Gabriel Mariano ilustram em que medida a representação espacial utiliza um grande número de lugares e de que forma um mesmo lugar pode participar em várias representações espaciais e em ambientes afectivos e sociais diferentes, susceptíveis de traduzir a concepção do universo insular, e podendo participar na reconstituição histórica do arquipélago, sobretudo das ilhas de S. Vicente e S. Nicolau.

Notas

[1] Mariano, Gabriel, *Vida e Morte de João Cabafume* (Lisboa: Vega, s.d.).

[2] Fundada em 1936 por Manuel Lopes, Baltasar Lopes e Jorge Barbosa, representa a primeira manifestação da modernidade cabo-verdiana. Os dinamizadores deste movimento, gerado em torno da revista, propunham-se estudar os contextos e ambientes sociais, humanos e linguísticos da realidade local, motivados pela (re)descoberta das raízes culturais do país, até então ausentes da literatura cabo-verdiana. Foram publicados três números no primeiro ano e, após um interregno de dez anos, a revista *Claridade* retomou as sua actividade, embora de forma irregular, de 1947 a 1960, tendo publicado mais nove números.

[3] Movimento que surgiu no cenário cultural cabo-verdiano entre 1958 e 1965, constituído pela designada terceira geração de intelectuais que vai assimilar as características dos dois movimentos precedentes [*Claridade* (1936) e *Certeza* (1944)], mas propondo uma inovação no plano estético, sociológico e ideológico. Gabriel Mariano, considerado o mentor do grupo, Terêncio Anahory, Onésimo da Silveira, Jorge Pedro, Ovídio Martins, Aguinaldo da Fonseca, Virgílio Pires, entre outros, são os representantes desta geração que Luís Hopffer Almada (146) considera como a primeira ruptura em relação à *Claridade.*

[4] Mariano, Gabriel, *Cultura Caboverderana* (Lisboa: Vega, 1991).

[5] Mariano, Gabriel, *Ladeira Grande* (Lisboa: Vega, 1993).

[6] O realismo humanista evidencia-se nos primeiros romances dos fundadores da *Claridade*, sobretudo em *Chiquinho* de Baltasar Lopes, cuja linguagem e criação de figuras humanas e de contextos socioculturais remetem para textos dos escritores brasileiros Jorge Amado, José Lins do Rego, Manuel Bandeira entre outros (Manuel Ferreira 86). A afinidade entre estes escritores e a geração *Claridosa* era reconhecida a nível das temáticas idênticas: os dramas da fome e da seca, a dança e até a modulação e musicalidade próprias da variedade brasileira da língua portuguesa.

[7] Thorberg, Joseph Muntañola, "Remarques épistémologiques sur la sémiotique des lieux," *Communications, Sémiotique de l'espace* 27 (1977): 16.

[8] Ver, entre outros, os poemas "Libertação," "A Garrafa" e "Écran" in Manuel Ferreira (org.), *50 Poetas Africanos,* 2ª edição (Lisboa: Plátano Editora, 1986) 189-194.

[9] Este aspecto é visível no poema "Mãe" de Osvaldo Alcântara in *Cântico da Manhã Futura* (Linda-a-Velha: Edições ALAC, 1991), 75, no qual a analogia Mãe/Mar põe em evidência a esterilidade: "Mar sem vida no ventre."

[10] Sobre a narrativa poética em prosa ver, entre outros, Jean-Yves Tadié, *Le Récit Poétique* (Paris: PUF, 1978) e, igualmente, Dominique Combe, *Les genres littéraires* (Paris: Hachette Supérieure, 1992).

[11] Bebida típica de Cabo Verde, feita de álcool e cana de açúcar.

[12] Estes músicos foram grandes animadores das noites do Mindelo durante os anos 40/50. Goi ou Goy, nascido nos anos 20, compôs sambas e canções para as marchas do carnaval da cidade. Tocava banjo, bateria, guitarra e cavaquinho. Tchuff foi um discípulo de Francisco Xavier da Cruz—B. Leza (1905-1958), um dos primeiros compositores cabo-verdianos da morna a denunciar o sofrimento humano e a opressão colonial. A ele se deve a forma moderna da morna. Lela de Maninha foi um grande intérprete e dançarino de mornas. Sobre este assunto veja-se, entre outras, as seguintes obras: Vladimir Monteiro, *Les Musiques du Cap Vert* (Paris: Editions Chandeigne, 1998); Vasco Martins, *A Música Tradicional Cabo-Verdiana—I (A Morna)* (Praia: Cabo Verde, Instituto Cabo-Verdiano do Livro e do Disco, 1989), obra patrocinada pelo Instituto Cabo-Verdiano do Livro e do Disco, pela Direcção Geral do Património Cultural, com o apoio financeiro do FIPC—Fundo Internacional para a Promoção da Cultura—UNESCO.

[13] Op. cit., 85 e 87.

[14] Op. cit., 85-86.

[15] O primeiro depósito de Carvão foi criado em 1838 pela companhia Inglesa John Rendall. Entre 1838 e 1930 o Porto Grande e a cidade do Mindelo desenvolveram-se progressivamente, entre três culturas (africana, portuguesa e inglesa), tornando-se num grande centro comercial, cultural e de emprego do arquipélago. No entanto, a partir de 1920, a substituição do carvão pelo combustível e a fundação dos portos de Dakar e Las Palmas desviaram a rota internacional com escala no Mindelo, mergulhando o Porto Grande numa enorme crise que arrastou o desemprego e a miséria. Estes acontecimentos foram agravados ainda com a Ditadura de Salazar, a partir de 1928, e com o fenómeno da seca.

16 O percurso inscreve-se num sistema de representação espacial do qual fazem parte os itinerários, com as suas etapas e segmentos narrativos. Veja-se: Louis Marin, *Utopiques: jeux d'espaces* (Paris: Les Éditions de Minuit, 1973) 261-269; A. P. Lagopoulos, "L'image mentale de l'agglomération, " *Sémiotique de L'Espace, Communications* 27 (1977): 70.

17 Afirmações de Gabriel Mariano no seu ensaio "Hora di bai e evasionismo" in *Cultura Caboverdeana* (Lisboa: Vega, 1991) 100.

18 A propósito do recrutamento de mão-de-obra "indígena" para vários serviços públicos ou empresas agrícolas e mineiras, nas antigas Províncias Ultramarinas, veja-se, entre outros, Joaquim. M. Da Silva Cunha, *O Trabalho Indígena: Estudos de Direito Colonial* (Lisboa: Agência Geral do Ultramar, 1952); sobre as diversas formas de trabalho disfarçadas de escravatura, veja-se Pedro Ramos de Almeida, *História do Colonialismo Português em África* (Lisboa: Estampa, 1979), Vol. 2.

19 Tradição descrita por Gabriel Mariano, Op. cit., 100.

20 Baltasar Lopes, em *Chiquinho,* 6ª Edição Portuguesa (2ª fac-similada) (Linda-a-Velha: Editor África—Literatura Arte e Cultura, 1988), insere fragmentos da tradição oral e musical, bem como uma variedade de provérbios e ditos populares. Gabriel Mariano, na linha dos *claridosos,* também procedeu ao recenseamento do folclore, tendo publicado composições da tradição oral em crioulo, na revista *Claridade,* nºs 6 e 7, respectivamente em 1948 e 1949. A sua obra poética e narrativa está impregnada de marcas da tradição cultural de raiz popular e oral.

21 Op. cit., 119.

22 O processo de metaforização do "desespero de partir" é uma das problemáticas abordada por G. Mariano a nível ensaísta, distinguindo-o do "evasionismo." Veja-se: "Hora di bai e evasionismo" in *Cultura Caboverdeana* (Lisboa: Vega, 1991) 100-102. As interrogações e as repetições sucessivas e insistentes põem em evidência o desespero, a dúvida, o medo, mas também, a advertência e a não resignação, sublinhando, implicitamente, o ponto de vista crítico e acusatório do autor.

23 Veja-se os poemas "Anti-evasão" e "Flagelados do Vento Leste" in Manuel Ferreira, *No Reino de Caliban* (Lisboa: Plátano Editora, 1975) 180 e 186.

24 O léxico utilizado na ilustração deste espaço não obedece ao protocolo realista traçado por Philippe Hamon a propósito da ligação entre o local de actividade profissional e o papel dos objectos nele presentes. Veja-se: Philippe Hamon, "Un discours contraint" in *Littérature et Réalité* (Paris: Seuil, 1982) 146.

25 Op. cit., 23.

26 Op. cit., 37.

27 Poema inserido na antologia organizada por Manuel Ferreira, *No Reino de Caliban* (Lisboa: Plátano Editora, 1975) 105.

28 Afirmações feitas na entrevista com Ricardo Araújo Pereira, "Manuel Lopes, o contador de histórias" in *Jornal de Letras Artes e Ideias* (Abril 1998): 15.

29 Afirmações de Gabriel Mariano numa entrevista dada a Luís Carlos Patraquim in *Revista Razão* 26 (Novembro 1991): 35-40.

Obras Citadas

Almada, José Luís Hopffer. "La fiction capverdienne post-Claridade aspects fondamentaux de son évolution." Veiga, Manuel (org.). *Insularité et Littérature aux îles du Cap Vert.* Paris: Editions Karthala, 1997. 175-194.

Bakhtine, Mikhaïl. *Pour une esthétique du roman.* Paris: Gallimard, 1978 (1975).

Borillo, Andrée. *L'Espace et son Expression en Français.* Paris: Ohrys, 1998.

Bourneuf, Roland. "L'organisation de l'espace dans le roman." *Études Littéraires* 3 (1970): 77-94.

Brito, Glória de. "Exercice d'un langage pur et dépouillé chez Gabriel Mariano." in Actes du Colloque *Pays de La Langue, Pays de la Poésie* (Université de Pau, 27-29 Novembre 1996), (Pau L.R.L.L.R. et Editions Covedi, 1998): 171-179.

———. "O efeito das vozes no conto 'Vida e Morte de João Cabafume de Gabriel Mariano.'" *Saberes no tempo, Homenagem a Maria Henriqueta Costa Campos.* Lisboa: Colibri, 2002. 579-589.

Carvalho, Alberto Duarte. "Emigração e orfandade em *Chiquinho* de Baltasar Lopes." *Literaturas Africanas de Língua Portuguesa,* Actas do Colóquio sobre Literaturas dos Países Africanos de Língua Portuguesa (Lisboa, Julho de 1985). Lisboa: Fundação Calouste Gulbenkian, 1987. 215-229.

Ferreira, Manuel. "Consciência literária cabo-verdiana—Quatro gerações: Claridade-Certeza-Suplemento Literário-Boletim do Liceu Gil Eanes." *Estudos Ultramarinos* 4 (1959): 89-92.

França, Arnaldo. "Naissance et reconnaissance d'une littérature en prose." Veiga, Manuel (org.). *Insularité et Littérature aux îles du Cap Vert.* Paris: Editons Karthala, 1997. 119-129.

Gardies, André. *L'Espace au Cinéma.* Paris: Méridiens Klincksieck, 1993.

Grojnowski, Daniel. *Lire la Nouvelle.* Paris: Dunod, 1993.

Hall, Edward T. *La dimension cachée.* Paris: Éditions du Seuil, 1971 (1966).

Hamilton, Russel G. *Literatura africana, literatura necessária.* Vol. II. Lisboa: Edições 70, 1984.

Hamon, Philippe. "Un discours contraint." *Poétique* 16 (1973): 411-445.

Laban, Michel. *Cabo Verde encontro com escritores.* Vol. I. Porto: Fundação Eng. António de Almeida, s.d.

Mariano, Gabriel. "Inquietação e serenidade." *Estudos Ultramarinos* 3 (1959): 55-80.

———. *Cultura caboverdeana: Ensaios.* Lisboa: Vega, 1991.

Miterrand, Henri. *L'illusion réaliste.* Paris: P.U.F., 1994.

Pacheco, Maria Cristina. "As estratégias da repetição nos contos de Gabriel Mariano." *Literaturas Africanas de Língua Portuguesa.* Actas do Colóquio sobre Literaturas dos Países Africanos de Língua Portuguesa (Lisboa, Julho de 1985). Lisboa: Fundação Calouste Gulbenkian, 1987. 25-33.

Rivas, Pierre. "Insularité et déracinement dans la poésie capverdienne. " *Les Littératures Africaines de Langue Portugaise-À la recherche de l'identité individuelle et nationale.* Actes du Colloque International (Paris, 28-30 novembre 1984). Paris: Fondation Calouste Gulbenkain, 1985. 291-294.

Veiga, Manuel (org.). *Insularité et Littérature aux îles du Cap Vert.* Paris: Éditons Karthala, 1997. 113- 117.

Maria da Glória Brito é Docente na Universidade Aberta e realizou um Mestrado em Literatura e Cultura dos Países Africanos de Expressão Portuguesa pela Universidade Nova de Lisboa. A elaborar tese de doutoramento sobre o escritor cabo-verdiano Henrique Teixeira de Sousa. Artigos publicados: "A *Carta* de Pêro Vaz de Caminha e a pintura da época" em *Actas do Congresso Literatura, Cinema e outras artes, Homenagem a Ernest Hemingway e Manuel de Oliveira* (Porto, 31 de Maio a 2 de Junho) (Porto: Universidade Fernando Pessoa, 2001) 373-397; "Escrita e reescrita da História em *Mayombe*" em *Actas do 1º Congresso Internacional A Guerra Colonial: Realidade e Ficção* (Universidade Aberta, 13 a 15 de Abril) (Lisboa: Editorial Notícias, 2001) 349-359; "O efeito das vozes no conto 'Vida e Morte de João Cabafume' de Gabriel Mariano" em *Saberes no tempo, Homenagem a Maria Henriqueta Costa Campos* (Lisboa: Colibri, 2002) 579-589. E-mail: gloriabrito@netvisao.pt

Globalização, cultura e identidade em Orlanda Amarílis

Benjamin Abdala Junior

Resumo. Análise de *Cais-do-Sodré té salamansa*, de Orlanda Amarílis, no contexto da globalização neoliberal. Ao ser destacado seu caráter de uma literatura identificada com a migração, são destacados os sentidos estratégicos das articulações comunitárias (comunitarismo cultural e da literatura de gênero) que aí se verificam, que fazem face à estandardização dos produtos culturais do mercado global. Releva-se, para tanto, o estatuto híbrido de suas produções—um processo de problematização de diferenças, que não se reduz a um amálgama unívoco, conforme foi entendido pelas perspectivas autoritárias da mestiçagem, onde se inclui o pensamento do brasileiro Gilberto Freyre.

Num texto de 1989, analisamos a circulação cultural entre o Brasil, Portugal e África, tendo como motivo condutor a imagem de Pasárgada, de Manuel Bandeira. Procuramos então discutir essa figuração utópica por recorrência a Osvaldo Alcântara (pseudônimo poético de Baltasar Lopes) e a Ovídio Martins. O primeiro, com os "pés" em Cabo Verde, sonha à Bandeira com uma pasárgada que existiria em outra margem do oceano. Se o poeta brasileiro imagina um reino com um rei bonachão que lhe permitiria todas as "libertinagens" (título da coletânea do poeta brasileiro), Osvaldo Alcântara tem saudade de uma pasárgada futura que encontraria no "caminho de Viseu" *(...indo eu, indo eu,/a caminho de Viseu.*[1] Osvaldo Alcântara, repetimos, estava com os pés em Cabo Verde, mas a cabeça inclina-se para fora, para as possibilidades de se encontrar plenitude na imigração. Sua perspectiva é aquela que historicamente sempre se colocou para seu povo de migrantes e ele não deixa de ter consciência de que *esta saudade fina de Pasárgada/é um gostoso dentro do meu coração.*[2] A partir das carências de sua terra, Osvaldo Alcântara sonha com o que não tinha.

Ao contrário de Osvaldo Alcântara, Ovídio Martins—identificado com os pressupostos ideológicos da Casa dos Estudantes do Império em Lisboa—já estava insatisfeito com o reino de Pasárgada. Em oposição ao que ocorrera no sonho de Bandeira, ele não só não era amigo do rei (*Vou-me embora pra Pasárgada/Lá sou amigo do rei/Lá tenho a mulher que eu quero/Na cama que escolherei*—Apud: Idem. Ibidem. 142) como foi perseguido por sua polícia. Não conseguindo permanecer em Lisboa, foi obrigado a imigrar para a Holanda. Ovídio Martins, como Osvaldo Alcântara, sonha com o que não tinha: justamente sua terra, Cabo Verde. Se Osvaldo Alcântara olha para horizontes indefinidos do mar, Ovídio Martins adota a perspectiva inversa: procura arremessar-se ao chão (*Pedirei/Suplicarei/Chorarei/Não vou para Pasárgada/Atirar-me-ei ao chão/e prenderei nas mãos convulsas/ervas e pedras de sangue/Não vou para Pasárgada*[3]).

É dentro desse contexto que iniciamos nossas observações sobre a obra de Orlanda Amarílis, uma obra também construída fora de seu país. Motiva-nos sobretudo colocações capazes de situá-la dentro do campo de nossos estudos—os Estudos Comparados de Literaturas de Língua Portuguesa. Parece-nos importante, neste momento de globalização da economia capitalista e estandardização de produtos, relevar nossa maneira de ser, adotando perspectivas de ordem comunitária (comunitarismo lingüístico e cultural). Voltando ao contexto criado a partir de Manuel Bandeira, podemos afirmar que o olhar de Orlanda Amarílis vai igualmente na direção inversa à do poeta brasileiro. Mais: ela não aceita a perspectiva patriarcal das libertinagens de Bandeira,[4] que reduziam o amor a atos sexuais com prostitutas; sua bandeira é outra, de caráter feminista.

Servirá de motivo condutor de nosso discurso o conto "Cais do Sodré," que pertence à coletânea *Cais-do-Sodré té Salamansa,* publicada um pouco antes dos Cravos de Abril.[5] Esse conto serve de pórtico para essa coletânea e permite identificar estratégias narrativas e motivos temáticos que têm recorrência no conjunto das produções de Orlanda Amarílis. Como se sabe, após a edição dessa coletânea, Orlanda Amarílis publicou ainda os seguintes de volumes de contos: *Ilhéu dos Pássaros*[6] (1983) e *A Casa dos Mastros*[7] (1989).

Começamos com duas citações que nos servem de primeiro contexto crítico. O primeiro é o ensaio "As Mulheres-Sós de Orlanda Amarílis," de

Maria Aparecida Santilli, que integra o livro *Africanidade*.[8] Relevamos suas observações sobre a óptica feminista da escritora em *Ilhéu dos Pássaros*—perspectiva que a crítica brasileira associa também à coletânea anterior (*Cais-do-Sodré té Salamansa*). Citamos as conclusões de Maria Aparecida Santilli:

> Neste último livro de contos, confirma-se o processo de elaboração da coleção anterior da Escritora, *Cais-do-Sodré té Salamansa*, fundamentalmente organizada sobre os sulcos da memória, por convergência de pequeninas e múltiplas vertentes das recordações, canalizadas na rede de vasos comunicantes da intriga de ficção. A memória funciona, então, como sistema de estímulos para se irem abrindo as comportas da interligação de muitas caixinhas de segredo, revelando a pouco e pouco o retrato caprichoso de suas mal-amadas heroínas. Nas voltas delicadas para fundir o que "era" no que "é" caboverdiano fica delineada a solução literária "feminina" da Contista, quase como contraponto do estilo convulso, de "serpentinata" da memória de seu companheiro de letras caboverdianas, o Manuel Ferreira de *Voz de Prisão*.

A linguagem de Orlanda é ainda a das mulheres contidas, a caminho de libertarem-se do código de manifestação que a sociedade masculina ao longo dos tempos lhes impôs.[9]

Para Maria Aparecida Santilli, as *mulheres-sós* de Orlanda Amarílis—que têm no crioulo a sua forma lingüística de identificação—são personagens da literatura feminina universal. Pretendemos retomar mais adiante esse sentido das articulações do discurso de Orlanda Amarílis.

Neste rastreamento crítico inicial, é de se apontar, em seguida, o estudo "Mulheres, Ilhas Desafortunadas," de Pires Laranjeira, que serve de prefácio ao livro *A Casa dos Mastros*, de Orlanda Amarílis. Para nossos objetivos, fazemos referência ao seguinte comentário:

> Passagem para a diáspora, a grande cidade (é o local) onde se instala a sôdade onde se tecem teias da cumplicidade (desde "Cais-do-Sodré," o primeiro conto do primeiro livro, sobre um encontro, sobre a Mãe Terra) [...]. Com a diáspora por cenário se abrem os três livros de contos de Orlanda Amarílis, que logo se continuam em histórias localizadas no chão das ilhas, de outros tempos (anos 30, 40 e 50, podemos adivinhar, quando não datadas [...]). Como que a dizer: o narrador-mor, pai de sete narradores, em cada conjunto de histórias, vive na diáspora, vivendo de recordações. O narrador recorda como (quem) fala, coloquiando, oralizante, fragmentário nas

> falas (discurso sincopado, em português, com o crioulo espreitando na língua literária), fragmentando as histórias em episódios soltos, ou quase [...].[10]

Como vimos, Maria Aparecida Santilli, ao analisar o registro feminino da solidão das *mulheres-sós* em Orlanda Amarílis, localiza-o não apenas em *Ilhéu dos Pássaros:* o processo seria anterior, observável na sua primeira coletânea de contos, sobretudo em "Cais-do-Sodré." Pires Laranjeira, na referência atrás e no conjunto desse seu prefácio, enfatiza a recorrência dos temas e procedimentos discursivos, extensíveis ao conjunto da obra da contista. É de se destacar a ênfase dada ao local de onde fala o sujeito do discurso: Lisboa, um dos núcleos centrais da migração caboverdiana. A fala das *mulheres-sós* é de quem imigrou e diríamos, a partir de Pires Laranjeira, que o caráter sincopado dessa fala vem de uma situação de divisão: uma divisão no espaço (poderíamos dizer, como no título da primeira coletânea, entre "Cais-do-Sodré," local de onde parte a linha de Cascais—um dos suburbanos de Lisboa, e a praia de Salamansa, em Cabo Verde); divisão também no tempo (em que a mesmice do presente da pretensa Pasárgada opõe-se a uma singularidade—mesmo que dramática e trágica—recuperada pela memória).

Dito de outra forma, o texto de ficção de Orlanda Amarílis mostra-se bastante auto-recorrente, criando um *continuum* como se a escritora estivesse sempre escrevendo um mesmo livro, com seus narradores trazendo novas visões dos mesmos objetos ou acréscimos de histórias intercaladas. Além disso, esse *continuum* do espaço-tempo, em oposição ao insulamento das *mulheres-sós,* cria ao nível da enunciação um espaço de solidariedade. Esse recorte é manifestação do desejo da escritora, de sua vontade. Ou, se quisermos, uma configuração virtual que cria horizontes capazes de levar o escritor e seus atores a dialogarem em termos de presente com seus leitores. Dessa forma, o que poderia ser denúncia da situação da mulher caboverdiana acaba também por constituir uma forma solidária de encontro. O texto, assim, não deixa de ser manifestação utópica: uma manifestação da vontade da escritora que acredita que as coisas possam ser diferentes do que são e se seu leitor, como boa suas personagens, não podem modificar o mundo, poderão pelo menos modificar suas atitudes diante dele.

Voltemos ao conto "Cais-do-Sodré." É aí que se encontra uma das narradoras de Orlanda Amarílis, Andresa. Sua voz, repetimos, é exercida a partir de carências, não apenas aquelas recuperadas do referente Cabo Verde, mas sobretudo aquelas de quem se vê longe da terra e se encontra num "reino" frustrante. Esse reino, de características burguesas, move-se através de formas rituais tão estandardizadas quanto os seus produtos. Não se trata da *outra civilização* dos sonhos de Manuel Bandeira. É um espaço que enreda as personagens de Orlanda Amarílis, levando-as a um mundo competitivo que seria o avesso daquele sonhado pelas perspectivas libertárias que balizam o horizonte estético-ideológico da contista. Relações de solidariedade entre essas personagens, quando ocorrem, são fugazes e podem ser creditadas a manifestações de ordem comunitária que invariavelmente apontam para os signos da identidade caboverdiana.

Entre esses signos, é central a língua literária de Orlanda Amarílis, um português padrão entrecruzado pela cadência oral do crioulo, ou língua caboverdiana. São dois níveis culturais que se disputam: o da literatura, modelada por uma tradição européia milenar (secular, se fizermos um recorte ligado à formação dos estados nacionais); e o da literatura oral (ou oralitura), em que o contributo das culturas africanas é essencial. Interessante a se assinalar é que Andresa, a personagem central do conto, que se encontra na estação de Cais--do-Sodré em Lisboa, vê-se enredada de tal maneira pela língua de identidade nacional, que parece ter simbolicamente seus passos orientados por sua lógica discursiva. Numa das imagens centrais dessa narrativa, extensiva ao conjunto das produções de Orlanda Amarílis, essa personagem parece modelada pela língua, tornando-se uma atriz que expressa a sua maneira de ser enquanto produto originário de duas culturas.

Em oposição à estandardização, estamos procurando relevar marcas de identidade (individual e nacional). A identidade nacional, em Orlanda Amarílis, está nas marcas da *diferença* caboverdiana. Essa diferença, mediada pela sua linguagem artística, aponta para os signos comunitários compartilhados pela nação caboverdiana, entendida no sentido antropológico desenvolvido por Benedict Anderson em *Nação e Consciência Nacional* (São Paulo: Ática, 1989): a nação como comunidade política imaginada, em que se desconsidera a desigualdade e a exploração, isto é, as diferenças internas, em favor de um companheirismo profundo e horizontal. É uma espécie de extensão dos laços de parentesco, tendo como base um sentimento de fraternidade, sem que as pessoas se conheçam.

Mas Andresa está na estação de Cais-do-Sodré, ponto de partida e de chegada da linha de suburbana que segue paralelamente à foz do Tejo, trajetória análoga às das antigas embarcações que se dirigiam ao Atlântico. E, por trás dessa personagem, está Orlanda Amarílis. O sentido do deslocamento do trem/comboio é aquele que levaria até a praia de Salamansa? O título da coletânea de contos é *Cais-do-Sodré té Salamansa:* o *té* é da oralidade crioula e *Salamansa* é uma praia caboverdiana. Ou o suburbano levaria à região periférica de Lisboa, onde o caboverdiano é sinônimo de proletário? Tais ambigüidades, na verdade, valorizam a narrativa de Orlanda Amarílis quando são estabelecidos laços comunitários supranacionais ao lado de diferenças. A caracterização da maneira de ser caboverdiana constitui matizações equivalentes àquelas que separam regiões ou a cidade do campo.

A Ilha de São Vicente, onde se localiza a cidade de Mindelo, é a referência básica de Orlanda Amarílis. Na ambiência insular de uma cidade média, a atividade social se circunscreve e todos se conhecem. E, ao curso das conversas, configuram-se os elos de articulação da comunidade:

> Oh gente, se encontra pessoas, como ela, vindas daquelas terras de espreguiçamento e lazeira, associa-as quase sempre a uma ou outra família. Se não as conhece, bom, de certeza conheceu o pai ou o primo ou o irmão, ou ainda uma tia velha, doceira de fama, até talvez uma das criadas lá da casa. E a conversa, por esse elo, estende-se, alarga-se, num desfolhar calmo, arrastado, saboroso quase sempre.[11]

A linguagem não exclui, mas inclui, constituindo forma de integração social. Seu ritmo traz as marcas do "desfolhar calmo" da vida caboverdiana, diferentemente do que acontece na antiga metrópole. Poder-se-ia talvez afirmar que há na cultura popular de Cabo Verde (ou mesmo do Brasil) um Portugal que já não existe na capital metropolitana. Como o Brasil, Cabo Verde também possui uma cultura crioula—isto é, uma cultura formada de pedaços da cultura portuguesa e de várias culturas africanas, formando um todo mestiço não-unívoco, não-sintético, ao contrário do que acontece com povos de formação mais antiga.

Orlanda Amarílis está assim na encruzilhada entre Portugal e Cabo Verde. Suas narrativas, como "Cais-do-Sodré," pautam-se pela ênfase social na definição da identidade cultural. Em Cabo Verde, essa forma de consciência evolui de uma perspectiva regional (as produções, sobretudo as primeiras, da revista *Claridade*) para uma consciência nacional. Ou, como se apontava na crítica neo-realista, o nacional deveria fincar pé na região. Essa estratégia de identificação era avessa ao cosmopolitismo desfigurador. Por extensão, os leitores de Orlanda Amarílis têm em seus contos produtos contrapostos à estandardização da indústria cultural, que hoje, dentro da globalização neo-liberal, leva os mesmos produtos para todos os pontos do planeta. A estandardização vem de uma nova forma de imperalismo ligada ao enfraquecimento do Estado, substituído pela força da corporação multinacional. Se um dos tópicos do Neo-Realismo foi analisar a decadência diante das novas técnicas de produção, agora esse processo que se confinava mais à região de um país torna-se supranacional.

A busca da diferença não deixa, pois, de ser uma forma de defesa. Entretanto, isso não pode significar a simples volta às formas de produção anteriores, já que o conhecimento técnico também é um patrimônio coletivo. Em "Cais-do-Sodré," a narradora mostra notável conhecimento das implicações sociolingüísticas de sua linguagem artística. Não se reduz a uma perspectiva mimética na incorporação do crioulo: uma identidade, poder-se-ia entender, para trás, de características folclóricas. Sua linguagem imbrica, como dissemos, o português padrão com o crioulo, ou língua caboverdiana, com grande produtividade lingüística. Embora Orlanda Amarílis procure recuperar o passado pela memória, seu olhar volta-se para o futuro, tornando possíveis estratégias textuais que não se deixam seduzir por um passadismo folclórico, afim das ópticas neocoloniais. Constitui, ao mesmo tempo, é necessário que se ressalte, um produto cultural que têm possibilidades de colocação num mercado mais restrito. Sob esse aspecto de consciência do caráter da circulação, em que as mídias são essenciais, as produções empenhadas contemporâneas afastam-se daquelas das décadas de 30-50.

Voltando ao início do conto, podemos visualizar a personagem Andresa na estação de Cais-do-Sodré. Sua primeira reação, ao se encontrar com sua compatriota Tanha, foi se afastar. Entretanto, as funções sociais da linguagem, imbricadas na fala de Andresa, acabaram por determinar uma lógica discursiva mais forte que suas motivações conscientes. A interlocução, como forma de sociabilidade, acabou por enredar na própria fala da personagem os signos de identidade (individual e nacional). A estratégia discursiva da conversa é de domínio geral: perguntas para se levantar laços de parentesco, uma familiaridade ou fraternidade. A terra-mãe torna-se assim, desde uma distância metropolitana, uma imagem utópica de vida comunitária, contraposta às relações cotidianas da grande cidade. Conversa vai, conversa vem, Andresa acaba por descobrir a origem da interlocutora: ela era filha de Simão Filili. Essa personagem marcou parte do imaginário de Andresa, quando ela ainda era criança. Simão Filili, pelas margens da sociedade de Mindelo, foi personagem de impacto por afrontar comportamentos tradicionais. É de se citar Orlanda Amarílis, no momento em que Andresa faz essa descoberta:

> Agora sim, Andresa conseguiu mais ou menos os cordéis e sente-se à vontade. Quem poderia esquecer o homem pequenino e chupado daquela casa vermelha ali no Alto de Celarine? Só quem nunca tivesse ouvido contar histórias de gongon, histórias de correntes arrastadas na estrada da Pontinha, em noites de ventania, por artes do xuxo, ou das trupidas dos cavalos a atravessarem a morada por volta da madrugada. O povo só se lhes referia ao barulho fragoroso das patas raspando o empedrado. Andavam a pregar a tumba de nhô Vendido dizia-se. Nha Xenxa, viúva de nhô João Sena, contava, e a voz velava-se-lhe de medo [...].[12]

A procura da identidade, através da chamada "literatura oral" (ou, se se quiser, oralitura), leva o narrador a incorporar formas do imaginário popular. Em alguns momentos da obra de Orlanda Amarílis, o discurso do narrador não se distancia dos relatos das personagens, impregnando-se de referências fantásticas. Assim a identidade faz-se por dentro e não apenas através do discurso referido. E a estratégia discursiva, ao nível da efabulação, torna-se simétrica com o já indicado ao nível lingüístico.

Nessa situação narrativa que incorpora o "causo" de Simão Filili—uma história encaixada dentro do conto—é notória a religiosidade cristã da ideologia oficial, que não aceita a diferença do outro: um maçom, relegado à solidão. Nesses relatos originários da oralitura, o fantástico vem de fontes culturais crioulas, na mescla do misticismo das culturas africanas com o dos primitivos colonos portugueses que vieram ter ao arquipélago. Simão Filili, no passado, despertou medo na menina Andresa; agora, no presente da enunciação, sua figura é recuperada com empatia.

Os "causos" de Orlanda Amarílis são relatados, conforme indicamos, sobretudo por vozes femininas. À identidade da nação soma-se a do assim chamado "gênero." Não se trata apenas de representar Cabo Verde, mas de construir a "maneira de ser" das mulheres caboverdianas. Intensificam-se, então, as marcas de diferenças da "comunidade imaginada," mas parece-nos que são atenuadas aquelas desse caráter comunitário supranacional. Essa foi uma outra perspectiva do Neo-Realismo: construir um texto que viesse de uma situação concreta (econômica e social), própria de uma nação, mas que tivesse sua universalidade pela ação de fatores comunitários. Veio dessa preocupação um notável diálogo entre os artistas (literatura, cinema, artes plásticas e visuais) que participaram de forma direta ou indireta da frente popular antifascista, do período entre-guerras, e que se projetou nos primeiros anos da guerra-fria.

A perspectiva supranacional pressupunha a diferença do assim chamado "típico" de cada país ou condição social. E o típico, ao contrário dos que o confinam ao estereótipo, implicou a representação ambígüa, problemática, como pode ser observado na construção da personagem Andresa, de "Cais-do-Sodré." Aí a predicação individual, singular, da personagem central da narrativa interage—sem se reduzir—com os atributos de ordem social. Ou, conforme se dizia dentro da óptica do realismo crítico, ela se coloca como uma heroína problemática diante do mundo alienado.

Dessa forma, Orlanda Amarílis procura aquilo que lhe falta e também a suas personagens. Não obstante as carências que poderiam levá-las a um emparedamento trágico ao gosto neo-naturalista, sempre acaba restando alguma luz no horizonte. Observado de Lisboa, o insulamento da terra não deixa de ser um elemento mítico de encontro. Uma utopia registrada criticamente e que propicia o nascimento de projetos. Não um sonho abstrato, devaneio, mas um sonho diurno de quem tem convicções transformadoras. Este é um outro traço de Orlanda Amarílis: num mundo apático, de indiferença social, ela tem convicções.

Orlanda Amarílis incorpora o "papiâ" caboverdiano. As conversas costuram as narrativas, que se iniciam no Cais-do-Sodré e se dirigem aos subúrbios, uma linha vetorial que chega a Cabo Verde. A imagem da costura ou tecedura é aqui adequada para explicar o processo de composição de Orlanda Amarílis—uma produção artesanal, restrita aos papeares domésticos. Suas narradoras são sucedâneas, na escrita, dos antigos "griots" africanos. Uma dessas vozes narrativas em "Cais-do-Sodré" é Bia Antónia:

> Bia Antónia, a velha criada da casa, era quem contava estas e outras patranhas à Andresa. Depois do jantar, Bia Antónia sentava-se num caixote, perto da escada, na varanda sobranceira ao quintal. Entre duas fumaças do canhoto sempre dependurado no canto da boca, a serva desfiava um ror de histórias.[13]

A imagem de Bia Antónia com o fumo no canto da boca, é correlata à dos "griots" suburbanos do continente africano. Há, pois, comutação de papéis, como também veio a ocorrer no continente. Símbolo de identidade, essas contadoras de história preservam a memória da terra — sempre uma terra-mãe. Essa simbolização feminina leva-nos a situá-la como uma Mátria (no dizer de uma feminista, Natália Correia), em oposição à Pátria (de caráter patriarcal, masculina), identificada com o poder colonial. É interessante indicar que boa parte dos escritores do chamado Neo-Realismo (no Brasil e na África) tiveram em sua infância uma contadora de histórias, normalmente de origem negro-africana, no caso brasileiro.

O enredamento de Andresa na própria dinâmica da conversa, uma atração avassaladora que a leva a procurar os símbolos de sua identidade, ocorre independentemente de sua vontade. Ela queria preservar a distância social que a separava de seus compatriotas, mas não consegue: a função social da linguagem imprime toda uma lógica discursiva que acaba por escapar de suas intenções iniciais. Essa lógica vem de seu inconsciente e determina o processo, revelando seu ser interior que não se conforma com os estereótipos de sua conduta social em Lisboa. Seu papel é outro. Após a interlocução com Tanha, Andresa procura subterfúgios para se afastar da compatriota, embora fosse na mesma direção. Quando Tanha se afasta para tomar o trem, ela continua na estação. Vê-se, então, num banco ao lado de uma inglesa ruiva e percebe que pouco tinha a ver com ela. Não teve dúvidas em ir atrás de Tanha, para continuar suas conversas.

A identidade feminina, como se vê, caminha ao lado da identidade nacional. Era a perspectiva do Neo-Realismo. Mais: essa perspectiva associa reivindicações de gênero às sociais. Isto é, as articulações feministas subordinavam-se às sociais, da mesma forma que as de natureza étnica, tão presentes no contexto africano. Neste momento de globalização, a tendência dominante é a articulação comunitária, que envolveriam as mulheres independentemente de suas condições sociais. Há fragmentação, mas a articulação torna-se mais enfática e específica, em face do enfraquecimento dos estados nacionais. Se se afirma de forma dominante a lógica da corporação, o feminismo não deixa de ser uma resposta a ela. Entretanto, em Orlanda Amarílis continua a visão totalizadora do Neo-Realismo, com suas vinculações político-sociais ligadas diretamente à esfera do trabalho. O feminismo articulado, assim, a reivindicações mais gerais, de ordem social. Andresa, assim, não se vê identificada com a inglesa ruiva, que—apesar de mulher—era diferente dela do ponto de vista étnico e lingüístico.

A identidade individual e nacional prende-se, assim, à cultura. Não à cultura em geral, mas de como esta é apropriada às margens do sistema—outro tópico Neo-Realista. Trata-se de uma apropriação feminista e de caráter popular. O trabalho artístico de Orlanda Amarílis pauta-se justamente por essas formas de produtividade. O diferente vem do fato de que as marcas feministas é que se articulam ao social e não o contrário, como acontecia nas obras de autoria masculina. A condição social agrava uma distonia anterior, que seria de gênero. Tudo, é claro, dentro dos horizontes da nação e das questões político-sociais por ela delimitadas. Observe-se o seguinte "causo" em torno de Zinha, irmã de Tonha:

> Zinha andava doente há longos meses de uma doença esquisita. A pele virara-se baça e de cor suja. O noivo lá para Guiné e o povo murmurava. Doença assim não podia ter outra origem senão mal-feitiço feita pela amante preta de Bissau. Vocês não sabiam? Gente da Guiné fazia mal-feitiço por tudo e por nada. Também não era novidade: Qualquer rapaz solteiro costumava arranjar a sua rapariga e, muitas vezes, um ou dois filhos antes de casar com outra. Quanto à Zinha, mal-feitiço ou não, a verdade era ela estar doente. Mal-feitiço ou não, muita gente nova de Soncente morria tuberculosa e, se crianças ainda, morriam de febre tifóide, e se meninos de mama, morriam com desinteria. Então, pâ mode quê tanta tolice de boca para fora?[14]

As referências de ordem social contextualizam as de gênero, embora o ponto de observação situe-se na mulher. Nesses momentos, narradoras burguesas, como Andresa, abandonam pontos de vista de classe, aderindo à óptica de quem observa o sistema não propriamente com os "pés," mas sobretudo com a "cabeça" em Cabo Verde, como pretendia uma das personagens do caboverdiano Manuel Lopes (*Galo Cantou na Baía e Outros Contos.* 3ª. ed. Lisboa: Edições 70, 1984). É a narradora de "Cais-do-Sodré" que informa o leitor sobre essa identificação:

> Andresa relembra tudo isso com tanta minúcia como se tivessem passado dias atrás. Como se nunca se tivesse despegado da Mãe-Terra, e tivesse continuado as pegadas de nhô Simão Filili, de nhô Faia, de Antoninho Ligório, do Pitra.[15]

A adesão empática vem, pois, dentro das condições da migração. Como se sabe, há mais caboverdianos fora do que dentro de seu país. E articulações de caráter comunitário, como a das narradoras de Orlanda Amarilis, podem ser manifestações das potencialidades de articulações supranacionais onde se preservem as diferenças. O caminho suburbano aponta a direção. Para quem observa em sua perspectiva, é possível visualizar alguma luz no horizonte.

Para finalizar, parece-nos importante relevar alguns pontos indicados nesse nosso percurso:

1. As formulações utópicas que envolveram a formação da literatura cabo-verdiana, com um horizonte voltado entre o partir e o ficar, revestem-se hoje de atualidade, quando antigas fronteiras nacionais diminuem suas distâncias, mais parecendo novas formas de regionalismo. Orlanda Amarílis situa-se criticamente num dos pólos dessa tensão, mas volta-se para suas origens, procurando uma adesão empática para um Cabo Verde dos anos 30-50.

2. Sua literatura é do migrante, com a enunciação revelando tensões da atualidade lisboeta e o enunciado trazendo situações do passado de Cabo Verde. Essa recuperação, pela memória, segue padrões da estética neo-realista. Certas marcações enfáticas da exploração do homem pelo homem, ou da mulher pelo homem, que poderiam ser creditadas a uma espécie de neo-naturalismo à maneira, por exemplo, de Luís Romano, parece-nos mais afins do expressionismo. Podemos associar essas deformidades a um contexto mais amplo, dentro dos países de língua portuguesa, se parafrasearmos o são-tomense Francisco José Tenreiro em "Coração em África":

> [...] de coração em África com as mãos e os pés trambolhos disformes/e deformados como os quadros de Portinari dos estivadores do mar/e dos meninos ranhosos viciados pelas olheiras fundas das gomas de Pomar/vou cogitando na pretidão do mundo que ultrapassa a própria cor da pele/dos homens brancos amarelos negros [...].[16]

3. Essa é a perspectiva de mundialização do que se convencionou chamar em Portugal de Neo-realismo—uma corrente artística voltada para uma inserção crítica no real, e suas perspectivas de transformação. Ao contrário dos produtos estandardizados da globalização neoliberal, essa mundialização procurou, como acontece em Orlanda Amarílis, estabelecer traços de identidade comunitária, através de produtos culturais diferenciados, com marcas que apontam para singularidades individuais, regionais ou nacionais. Discutir a dialética dessas marcas identitárias, neste momento, pode ser uma das formas de se opor à globalização descaracterizadora, próprias do capitalismo "neo-selvagem", denunciado por Boaventura de Sousa Santos. Se a globalização neoliberal vale-se do enfraquecimento dos Estados Nacionais para impor a lógica da corporação multinacional e seus produtos estandardizados, a mundialização que estabelece fronteiras de cooperação e de solidariedade, aqui apontadas, mostra formas possíveis de associações comunitárias supra-

nacionais. E, com esse horizonte, nós — brasileiros, portugueses e africanos — podemos começar relevando o comum de nossas diferenças.

4. A ficção de Orlanda Amarílis, com sua óptica feminina, é também uma forma de articulação supranacional. Entretanto, sua perspectiva não se restringe aos horizontes mais cirscunscritos da chamada "literatura de gênero," porque aspira ao sentido da totalidade—uma totalidade imaginada, conforme o desejo (potencialidade subjetiva) do neo-realismo. Sua óptica, entretanto, não deixa de ser de "gênero": da maneira equivalente às produções paradigmáticas da tendência estético-ideológica neor-realista, que procura discutir o geral através do particular, a nação através da região, o coletivo através do individual, em tensões que se pretende sejam problematizadoras, Orlanda Amarílis vê seu povo de migrantes através da mulher—da adversidade de sua condição olha para uma adversidade mais geral.

5. Já se escreveu sobre o nosso tempo classificando-o como próprio de uma época de indiferença: uma pretensa democracia não como forma de respeito ao "outro," mas como ideologia da indiferença. A ficção de Orlanda Amarílis recoloca o homem no centro de suas preocupações. O "papiâ" que lhe serve de estratégia discursiva é uma forma de encontro, de aproximação. À perspectiva anômica da dispersão, solidão, individualismo, opõe a solidariedade, procurando, assim, analogicamente, a discursividade dos contadores de estórias. Assim, além de memória cultural de seu povo, sua ficção constitui produção simbólica solidária (enquanto tal, concretiza laços de solidariedade), pela intercalação de múltiplas vozes e múltiplos "causos."

Notas

[1] Apud: Abdala Junior, Benjamin, *Literatura, história e política* (São Paulo: Ática, 1988) 49.

[2] *Idem, Ibidem* 49.

[3] *Idem, Ibidem* 16.

[4] Bandeira, Manuel, *Antologia poética,* 9ª. Ed. (Rio de Janeiro: José Olympio, 1977).

[5] (Coimbra: Centelha, 1974).

[6] (Lisboa: Plátano).

[7] (Linda-a-Velha: ALAC) (Col. Africana).

[8] (São Paulo: Ática, 1985) 107-111.

[9] *Idem, Ibidem* 111.

[10] *Idem, Ibidem* 10.

[11] *Cais-do-Sodré té salamansa* 9.

[12] *Idem, Ibidem* 12-13.

[13] *Idem, Ibidem* 17.

[14] *Idem, Ibidem* 19.

[15] *Idem, Ibidem* 21.

[16] Apud: Abdala Junior, Benjamin, *Op. Cit.* 186.

Benjamin Abdala Junior, professor titular de Estudos Comparados de Literaturas de Língua Portuguesa da Faculdade de Filosofia, Letras e Ciências Humanas da Universidade de São Paulo, é membro do Comitê Assessor da Diretoria do CNPq— Conselho Nacional de Desenvolvimento Científico e Tecnológico, Vice-Presidente da CCInt—Comissão de Cooperação Internacional da Universidade de São Paulo. Entre as suas publicações, a mais recente é *Fronteiras múltiplas, identidades plurais - um ensaio sobre mestiçagem e hibridismo cultural.* Organizou *Ecos do Brasil: Eça de Queirós, leituras brasileiras e portuguesas*; *Personae: grandes personagens da literatura brasileira*; *Canudos, palavra de Deus, sonho da terra*; *Gil Vicente.*

A ficção cabo-verdiana pós-claridosa

José Luís Hopffer Cordeiro Almada

É no plano da prosa de ficção que a influência da claridosidade mais se faz sentir na literatura cabo-verdiana. Tal circunstância funda-se em múltiplas razões podendo, de entre elas, ser destacado o facto de que com a obra ficcional dos claridosos, nomeadamente com os romances *Chiquinho*, de Baltasar Lopes, *Os Flagelados do Vento Leste* e *Chuva Braba*, de Manuel Lopes, a colectânea de contos *Galo Cantou na Baía* de Manuel Lopes e as novelas de António Aurélio Gonçalves são tecidas as linhas-mestras da moderna ficção cabo-verdiana, quais sejam: a) o telurismo, enquanto tessitura literária da comunhão entre o homem cabo-verdiano e o seu meio-ambiente. Tal comunhão tem vertentes, tanto de cariz rural, como são os casos dos três primeiros romances acima referidos, como de cariz urbano, como ocorre em parte do romance *Chiquinho*, na colectânea *Galo Cantou na Baía* e, sobretudo, na ficção de António Aurélio Gonçalves; b) a abordagem do conjunto dos dramas do povo cabo-verdiano. Na verdade, com a ficção claridosa é todo o ser cabo-verdiano, que, na multiplicidade da sua existência atribulada, se torna húmus literário. Antes de mais, no que se refere às condições ecológicas e sociais da sobrevivência do cabo-verdiano. E é nesse contexto, que as chuvas, e a sua ausência, com todas as consequências nefastas consubstanciadas na tragédia das secas, das crises e das fomes, surgem como o verdadeiro barómetro do destino do Homem das ilhas e do seu modo de se apreender e aos ciclos vitais da sua existência. Outros epifenómenos da realidade cabo-verdiana, como a emigração enquanto traço emblemático da sociedade crioula, mais não são do que expressões do que acima se referiu. Quando se refere às condições ecológicas, é necessário também nelas incluir não só as caracteristicamente rurais, como as de natureza urbana. Neste contexto, surge o Porto Grande do Mindelo como o rosto mais visível dessa realidade. Demiurgo da vertente urbana dos cabo-verdianos, no plano ficcional, é também o Porto Grande, nas suas oscilações como fonte de receitas e emprego e, por isso, como factor susceptível de condicionar a vida em todas as ilhas do Arquipélago, mormente as de Barlavento, emblemático da dependência do cabo-verdiano em relação a factores que de longe o ultrapassam e com os quais ele é obrigado a conviver durante toda a sua vida, enquanto sujeito e vítima de crises permanentes.

Porque significou a construção das traves-mestras da moderna ficção caboverdiana, a claridosidade foi-se renovando por várias décadas, até mediante o labor de autores que, em outras áreas da produção literária, criaram perspectivas completamente novas. Tal é o caso, por exemplo, de Gabriel Mariano que, sendo uma das pedras basilares da nova largada da poesia cabo-verdiana, na ficção é um claridoso típico, quanto aos traços estéticos acima referidos, devendo, no entanto, ser ressalvado o forte pendor de denúncia também da sua obra ficcional. A mesma asserção pode ainda ser aplicada à grande maioria dos ficcionistas revelados durante o período colonial, quais sejam os contistas Francisco Lopes da Silva, Virgílio Pires, Teixeira de Sousa, Pedro Duarte. Interessante é que também do ponto de vista quantitativo, a obra ficcional dos claridosos sobrepõe-se de forma nítida à ficção *pós-claridosa* anterior à independência nacional. Com efeito, concomitantemente com a edição da revista *Claridade* e da obra poética e ensaística, os claridosos publicaram, até aos anos sessenta, o essencial da ficção anterior à independência nacional. Cabe assinalar que essas obras são pacificamente consideradas como constituindo as obras clássicas da literatura cabo-verdiana.

No entanto, os fenómenos da consciencialização anti-colonial e do aprofundamento do conhecimento dos meandros do ser cabo-verdiano que vinham tendo lugar desde a 2ª Guerra Mundial e que já foram referidos quando se abordou a poética cabo-verdiana pós-claridosa não poderiam permanecer alheios à criação ficcional em Cabo Verde. É neste contexto que deve ser enquadrada a publicação de *Famintos* de Luis Romano. De uma virulência extrema pelo modo como aborda de forma clara, nua e crua, o fenómeno da fome em Cabo Verde, o romance *Famintos* permanece como um caso único em Cabo Verde. Não obstante as suas nítidas deficiências no que tange à sua conformação literária, ele constitui certamente a primeira obra de denúncia total de todo o sistema colonial e de toda a economia da fome em Cabo Verde, em especial da pilhagem dos famintos pelo capital usurário no campo e do enriquecimento de alguns à custa das vítimas das estiagens. Convém salientar que tais questões são igualmente afloradas em obras como "Ti Lobo" de Gabriel Mariano, "Migração" de Pedro Duarte, "A Herança" de Virgílio Pires, ou "Chuva de Agosto" e "Resgate," de Francisco Lopes da Silva, mas estas, ainda que denotando uma maior mestria literária, nunca atingem a virulência dos *Famintos.*

Outros indícios de uma paulatina ruptura com a claridosidade, a par de fenómenos sintomáticos da sua continuidade, como o são os contos de Jorge Tolentino (por exemplo, "Brisas de Ontem," "A chefe"), Nicolau de Tope Vermelho, João Rodrigues, ou Fátima Bettencourt (na colectânea *Semear em Pó*), acontecem fundamentalmente com a publicação de obras de ficção no período posterior ao 25 de Abril de 1974. É nesse quadro que se integra o romance *Ilhéu de Contenda* de Henrique Teixeira de Sousa. O romance *Ilhéu de Contenda* é, enquanto obra de ficção, um fresco sobre a estrutura social da ilha do Fogo, nomeadamente sobre a decadência dos descendentes dos povoadores brancos e da correlativa ascenção do mestiço e do negro. Nesse romance, o autor serve-se de algumas famílias (nomeadamente, os Medina da Veiga, os Vieira da Fonseca, Anacleto Soares, entre outros) para descodificar a evolução histórica e humana da ilha do Fogo. O romance traça-nos o quadro do relacionamento entre as diferentes classes sociais como relações de dominação. Descreve-nos o poderio dos morgados, "donos de escravos às dezenas, animais às centenas, moedas de ouro aos alqueires," esclarece-nos sobre o tratamento reservado aos camponeses, enquanto objectos de exploração e desumanização. No entanto, a fase mais recente da evolução da ilha constitui o conteúdo fundamental do romance *Ilhéu de Contenda.* Essa fase é a da decadência das antigas Famílias e da ascensão de novas categorias sociais, constituídas por Negros e Mulatos. O binómio decadência-ascensão explicita-se como integrando vários factores e sendo de natureza complexa. Entre esses factores pode-se apontar a partilha dos patrimónios acumulados e a consequente desagregação do Morgadio, a degeneração física pelo casamento entre parentes consanguíneos das classes possidentes, a emigração, a instrução, a seca, a competição social e a emergência do "mundo que o mulato criou" (Gabriel Mariano). Do mesmo modo são múltiplos os símbolos presentes em *Ilhéu de Contenda,* dos quais destacamos: o sobrado enquanto espaço de identificação e reprodução das classes dominantes; a loja enquanto lugar de enriquecimento e propulsor de novas dinâmicas sociais; o "morgadio" enquanto complexo de terras, latifúndios e face visível do passado económico e social da ilha. Todos esses símbolos interpenetram-se, condicionando-se mutuamente, na sua existência e pertinência social. Assim, o morgadio e a loja constituem o sustentáculo económico do sobrado, sendo este o selo social daqueles. A queda social coincide com a mudança da posse do sobrado e a sua ocupação pelos novos potentados. A nova ascensão social coincide com a apropriação do sobrado e de toda a memória nele ínsita.

De particular importância na tessitura romanesca de *Ilhéu de Contenda* é a problemática do racismo. O mesmo é analisado como integrante do morgadio e presença actuante no relacionamento entre as diferentes classes sociais. No presente histórico do romance, o racismo actualiza-se como reacção de desespero das classes brancas dominantes face à sua queda social irreversível, ilustrável, por exemplo, no desprezo que Felisberto (personagem branca desclassificada) nutre pelo Dr. Vicente (médico mulato), apodando-o de "doutor de cabelo cuscus." No entanto, várias são as nuances que tornam a problemática do racismo mais interessante, pelos vários factores humanos que se revelam no relacionamento entre os indivíduos e as classes sociais e a natureza irreversível da mestiçagem em Cabo Verde.

Para além da abordagem do racismo, o que por si só constitui um dado novo na ficção cabo-verdiana, se nos abstrairmos do caso de *O Escravo*, de José Evaristo de Almeida, publicado no século passado, e, em menor grau, de *Famintos* de Luis Romano, o romance *Ilhéu de Contenda* representa o Cabo Verde colonial nas vésperas da independência. Os sintomas da próxima eclosão da liberdade encontram-se expressos, de forma variada: na denominação da metrópole colonial como Portugal, portanto, país, estrangeiro em relação a Cabo Verde; na crítica aberta ao Poder colonial pela sua incapacidade em promover o desenvolvimento técnico e económico do país, na denúncia da contratação dos trabalhadores para S. Tomé, na caracterização da natureza repressiva do Estado Colonial e da sua polícia política, a Pide, quando estes protagonizam a transferência-expulsão do Dr. Vicente para a Ilha da Boavista, etc.

O romance *Ilhéu de Contenda* pode ser pois considerado como um dos marcos fundamentais do segundo realismo ficcional cabo-verdiano, pelo que representa de novidade no aprofundamento da questão social iniciada com a primeira claridosidade. Aliás, Teixeira de Sousa vem consolidando tal postura com os romances *Xaguate* e *Na Ribeira de Deus*, em particular, que com *Ilhéu de Contenda*, constituem a sua anunciada trilogia sobre a formação e a evolução da sociedade cabo-verdiana, com o epicentro na Ilha do Fogo. Diga-se, aliás, em abono da verdade que Teixeira de Sousa tem sido o mais profícuo dos ficcionistas cabo-verdianos. Anteriormente, tinha ele já publicado uma colectânea de contos, de excelente recorte telúrico e social (*Contra Mar e Vento*), para, na época pós-independência, publicar os romances *Capitão de Mar e Terra*, o qual se debruça sobre os anos 30/40 na ilha de S. Vicente, a crise do Porto Grande, a formação da geração claridosa e o seu *hintergrund social*, *Djunga* bem como *Entre Duas Bandeiras*. Este último romance pretende debruçar-se sobre um facto histórico recente, a independência de Cabo Verde, e as lutas políticas e sociais que a ela conduziram. Controverso pelo que contém de valoração subjectiva de factos e actos não totalmente iluminados pela História, particularmente do protagonismo político-partidário correlativo com a problemática da Unidade Guiné-Cabo Verde, o "revolucionarismo" então em voga e a ambiguidade e o oportunismo da pequena burguesia entrincheirada nesse símbolo do Poder que era o "Grémio." *Entre Duas Bandeiras*, não deixa de desempenhar uma função pioneira e desinibidora na abordagem da história recente de Cabo Verde com as técnicas do romance histórico.

Com o seu romance *O Eleito do Sol*, Arménio Vieira, pedra fundamental da moderna poesia cabo-verdiana, transfere para a ficção a sua enorme capacidade de surpreender, de que tinha dado provas irrefutáveis na poesia. Primeiramente, porque toda a intriga do romance decorre no Antigo Egipto durante a dinastia do Faraó Amenófis XXVIII. Discorrendo sobre a atribulada vida de um escriba egípcio, o romance constitui uma verdadeira alegoria sobre as relações entre o Poder e Saber, entre a tirania e a intelectualidade. Neste sentido, *O Eleito do Sol* representa uma profunda cesura com o modo como até então se escreveu ficção em Cabo Verde, já porque rompe com o telurismo atávico dominante, já porque fugindo dos cânones tradicionais significa a transplantação da realidade profunda do Cabo Verde contemporâneo, ou melhor, de qualquer sociedade submetida a poderes autoritários e/ou totalitários (a omnipresença do Estado e dos seus agentes, os jogos palacianos do poder, o ambiente concentracionário, a miséria e a insolúvel dependência em relação aos maiorais, etc) para uma realidade aparentemente longínqua. Aparentemente, porque todo o romance é um fresco absurdo e virtual sobre as expectativas mais profundas da sociedade cabo-verdiana, quer dizer, reformas sociais profundas, maiores liberdades cívicas e relações menos cínicas entre o Poder e os cidadãos. Tanto do ponto de vista da temática, como dos recursos da linguagem utilizada representa *O Eleito do Sol* o alargamento das perspectivas da ficção cabo-verdiana pela sua fuga em relação à "hegemonia" claridosa.

Tal alargamento de perspectivas é também visível nos romances *O Meu Poeta* e *O Testamento do Sr. Napumuceno da Silva Araújo* de Germano Almeida. Neste autor, a ironia conquista foros de cidadania e cumpre todo o seu poder corrosivo de uma sociedade — aquela que continua a persistir no pós-independência — já em si anquilosada pela hipocrisia de um poder omnisciente e omnipresente. Particularmente em *O Meu Poeta* são ainda as relações entre os corredores do Poder e as crescentes reivindicações dos cidadãos por maiores direitos cívicos o núcleo fundamental do labor ficcional de Germano Almeida. Contrariamente a Arménio Vieira, é a realidade cabo-verdiana centrada na cidade do Mindelo que é apreendida no seu devir actual e nos seus detalhes comezinhos. Assim, uma extensa paleta de questões são objecto da indagação das personagens: a acomodação da pequena-burguesia em relação ao poder dominante, as relações entre os intelectuais e o poder político, as rivalidades entre as diferentes ilhas de Cabo Verde, a inserção de Cabo Verde em África, o revolucionarismo pequeno-burguês, as relações entre a língua portuguesa e a língua caboverdiana, a prostituição nos meios urbanos, a emergência e a decadência do Regime de Partido único, enfim, tudo o que, de alguma forma, preocupou os estratos urbanos da sociedade cabo-verdiana, sobretudo desde a independência nacional.

N'*O Meu Poeta* é, assim, um Cabo Verde prestes a desenvencilhar-se do Regime de Partido único e do seu cortejo de mordomias, mal-entendidos e máscaras duplas ou triplas que desfila sob os nossos olhos. Teoricamente, é um facto banal — o encerramento do café "Retiro fechado" — o catalizador de toda a intriga romanesca, de características, por vezes, nitidamente burlescas e satíricas.

De fundamental importância no actual panorama ficcional em Cabo Verde são o romance *O Estado Impenitente da Fragilidade* bem como os *Contos da Macaronésia* de G.T. Didial. Em ambas as obras uma perspectiva perfeitamente nova faz a sua aparição na ficção cabo-verdiana, designadamente a perspectiva filosófico-metafísica. Em ambas as obras de ficção, as personagens existem sobretudo como interpeladoras do destino e dos meandros que o mesmo tece nas relações entre o Transcendente e o Homem. Não interessa se essas personagens são tecnocratas cidadãos do mundo ou um pobre pai repetindo o acto de sacrifício de Abraão num dos anos de crise em Cabo Verde. O essencial é que lodo o gesto das personagens carrega em si a imponderabilidade do sagrado. É assim que nas quinze narrativas que constituem os *Contos da Macaronésia* indagações várias são afloradas. No conto de abertura, "As Inscrições," procede-se à mitificação das origens de Cabo Verde (denominado Macaronésia), situando os antepassados dos seus primeiros povoadores na Ásia Menor. Esses primeiros povoadores viriam a desaparecer, em virtude de pragas enviadas pelos deuses na sequência de lutas fraticidas entre aqueles. Nessa primeira narrativa, o autor imbrica essa primeira história da Macaronésia (Cabo Verde) e dos seus reis (Micanor e Macero) na mitologia grega e na obra de Sófocles. É esse tom renovador, tanto na temática como na linguagem, de sabor bíblico, que perpassa todos os *Contos da Macaronésia.* Problemáticas várias são trazidas à colação: a maternidade, as tensões entre o conhecimento e a ignorância, a diáspora intelectual cabo-verdiana, a sexualidade, a impotência e o adultério, a religiosidade popular, a loucura, o suicídio, o espiritismo, o gregarismo cabo-verdiano e o racismo na diáspora, a solidão, etc. Contos exemplares, pelas interpelações filosóficas neles ínsitas e pela singularidade da cosmovisão do homem cabo-verdiano, aliás, também integrantes do romance *O Estado Impenitente da Fragilidade,* eles oferecem ao seu autor um lugar exemplar e singular no panorama da ficção cabo-verdiana contemporânea. Exemplaridade e singularidade que aliás afloram na forma original como o autor conjuga metafísica e telurismo, banalidade e profundidade filosófica (como por exemplo nos contos "O Vulcão," "Feitiço de Cão," "Kleist").

Uma outra importante vertente da ficção pós-claridosa, particularmente daquela que surgiu no período posterior à independência nacional, é a que integra o real maravilhoso na tessitura ficcional. Tal vertente teve os seus primeiros indícios em Jorge Barbosa (nomeadamente com o conto "Conversa Interrompida") e Arménio Vieira (sob o pseudónimo de Silvenius) mas só conheceu momentos mais elevados e elaborados com a publicação das colectâneas de contos *A Casa dos Mastros* de Orlanda Amarílis e *Desassossego* de Fernando Monteiro. Tradicionalmente abordou a ficção cabo-verdiana seres sobrenaturais mais como produtos do imaginário infantil e personagens da literatura oral. Com as obras acima referidas, particularmente com *Desassossego,* os seres sobrenaturais ("finados," "espíritos," "Satã") tornam-se eles próprios as personagens fundamentais da intriga ficcional. Inseridas na realidade telúrica e espiritual do Homem cabo-verdiano, elas mesmas são os actores fundamentais dessa mesma realidade, ainda que absurdas pelo que representam de inverosímil quando se é conduzido por cânones de pensamento puramente racionais. No entanto, elas são profundamente verosímeis pois que se inserem numa realidade já em si absurda pela precariedade da sua existência tanto material quanto espiritual. É assim que no conto "O Contrato" da colectânea *Desassossego*, o enriquecimento repentino de um lumpem, abandonado à sua sorte, é explicado pela intervenção de seres demoníacos que, para a consecução do propósito acima referido, exigem contrapartidas fortes quais sejam a alma do beneficiário em troca de felicidade e de bens materiais. A verosimilhança de tal intriga reside no facto de tais possibilidades não serem puras projecções, mas encontrarem-se profundamente ancoradas na mentalidade do cabo-verdiano e no modo de o mesmo se relacionar com o mundo dos espíritos. A abordagem nova reside, como já foi aflorado, no facto de tais estórias serem concebidas não como produto de qualquer fantasia infantil ou supersticiosa, mas como integrando o real concreto da vida quotidiana. Se em Fernando Monteiro, o real maravilhoso e mágico tem as suas profundezas na espiritualidade rural e suburbana de Cabo Verde, particularmente da ilha de Santiago, em Orlanda Amarílis o mesmo funda-se no espiritismo urbano da ilha de S. Vicente, particularmente no chamado racionalismo cristão de forte influência brasileira.

O realismo mágico e maravilhoso é ainda patente em obras ficcionais de outros autores, como por exemplo "Chuva Nocturna," de Dionísio de Deus y Fonteana, "A Noiva" e "Púbis de Vénus" de Euricles Rodrigues, "A Cidade e o Ídolo," de José Vicente Lopes, *A Ilha Fantástica* de Germano Almeida e de forma difusa e imbricada com um certo realismo metafísico na obra de G.T. Didial (como, por exemplo, nos contos "A pergunta," "Em Antinoopolis").

Característica da literatura claridosa foi o inventar de uma nova linguagem literária, a qual consiste fundamentalmente na recriação do português-padrão, adaptando-o à língua própria dos cabo-verdianos que é o Crioulo. Se essa nova linguagem é profundamente artificiosa e puramente literária porque não corresponde a uma qualquer fala existente na realidade concreta do cabo-verdiano, ela desempenhou no entanto um notável papel pelo que significou de aproximação de uma língua estrangeira às mentalidades específicas do cabo-verdiano e de abertura da possibilidade da conquista dessa mesma língua pela maioria dos potenciais bilingues cabo-verdianos. A crioulização do Português foi uma das possíveis formas da autonomização da literatura cabo-verdiana e constitui uma das marcas mais salientes da claridosidade e um dos signos maiores da sua continuidade na ficção cabo-verdiana que a ela se seguiu. Na verdade, rara é a obra ficcional cabo-verdiana pós-claridosa que não carregue consigo essa imbricação insólita que é o português literário cabo-verdiano. Com o paulatino progredir do bilinguismo português-crioulo nas comunidades cabo-verdianas, o supra-referido português literário tende a minorar o seu grau de artificiosidade para reflectir uma realidade linguística mais ou menos patente na vida sócio-cultural dos cabo--verdianos. Cabe neste caso sublinhar o importante passo em frente nesse domínio que constitui *A Ilha Fantástica* de Germano Almeida.

Pode-se afirmar que essa obra é daquelas que mais longe foi na recriação de um português cabo-verdiano pejado de crioulismos, o que lhe confere uma nova autenticidade. Por outro lado, a fluência dos longos discursos indirectos e dos monólogos interiores, a par da indiferenciação entre as funções do narrador e das personagens consolidam essa autenticidade, que se vivifica de um telurismo típico dos meios pequenos, como o é a ilha da Boavista. Telurismo que em si conjuga a realidade comezinha dos dias de sobrevivência ao fantástico que percorre o imaginário da criança, narradora e personagem omnipresente.

Outras obras e autores podem ainda ser destacados pela sua conjugação do português e do crioulo, de uma forma assaz incomum. Tal é o caso de *Cais de Pedra* de Nuno de Miranda, de "Lázaro, o Salteador" e "Raboita de Rubom Manel" de João de Deus Lopes da Silva, de vários contos dispersos de Nicolau de Tope Vermelho, de *Vida Crioula* e *O Meu Tio Jonas* de Teobaldo Virgínio [sendo de se salientar que no caso deste autor há, por vezes, a inserção de diálogos inteiros em crioulo (ou em crioulo aportuguesado) no corpo do texto em português].

A propósito deste autor, e sobre a presente problemática, escreve Manuel Ferreira:

> A capacidade do autor para utilizar uma língua portuguesa bem amestrada, permitiu-lhe vivificá-la com os sons internos da sua outra face linguística — o Crioulo — e com ele a ternura do verbo com o qual, de quando em quando, adoça e vivifica a língua portuguesa, num jeito de caboverdianização já com larga tradição na moderna literatura caboverdiana.

Ainda segundo Manuel Ferreira, "tal policromia linguística dá à sua escrita uma expressão de solidariedade e de telúrico."

À semelhança de *Ilhéu de Contenda* de Teixeira de Sousa, de *Percurso Vulgar* de Carlos Araújo, as obras supramencionadas podem ser classificadas como integrando a literatura regenerativa cabo-verdiana, isto é, aquela que abordando o nosso passado histórico, fá-lo na perspectiva político-ideológica da actualidade, o que desde logo lhes confere uma nítida marca pós-claridosa, não só do ponto de vista cronológico, como do ponto de vista da mundivisão a elas subjacente. Em "Lázaro, o Salteador" e "Raboita de Rubom Manel," por exemplo, são contadas as histórias de personalidades e situações rurais e míticas da história de Cabo Verde. Baseadas grandemente na memória mítica do povo, tais histórias carregam consigo uma forte carga lendária, pelo que, também nestes casos, o realismo mágico joga de alguma forma o seu papel. Mas o fundamental é que elas se debruçam sobre as lutas sociais numa das ilhas mais esquecidades pela primeira ficção claridosa, que é a ilha de Santiago. Na esteira de *O Escravo* de José Evaristo de Almeida, considerado o primeiro romance de temática cabo-verdiana e o qual tem como cenário a grande ilha, é todo um passado de dissenções sociais, desarmonias raciais e culturais que vêm à tona, tendo como pano de fundo a luta mortal entre os grandes proprietários fundiários e os camponeses pobres. É notável que uma das vias fundamentais do surgimento de uma literatura pós-claridosa em Cabo Verde tem surgido da abordagem literária do passado histórico das ilhas do Morgadio, nomeadamente das ilhas do Fogo e de Santiago. Literatura pós-claridosa não no sentido da linguagem literária utilizada ou do patente telurismo, mas pela retratação de realidades novas, ainda que integrantes do passado, e por sua sustentação por concepções estético-ideológicas diferentes. As asserções acima referidas podem ser aplicadas *mutatis mutandis* ao romance *A Saga das As-Secas e das Graças de Nossenhor* de Onésimo Silveira. Claridoso em grande medida na sua abordagem da vida rural santantonense, suas vicissitudes e sua correlação umbilical com a ilha de S. Vicente, *A Saga...* traz um tom novo quando se debruça sobre a vida dos contratados cabo-verdianos em S. Tomé, seu quotidiano de sujeição aos roceiros e seus sequazes, suas relações enquanto originários de diferentes ilhas de Cabo Verde, entre si, e com os originários (também submissos) da África Negra (Moçambique, por exemplo) e com os forros (nativos livres de S. Tomé e Príncipe). A abordagem da vida dos caboverdianos em S. Tomé foi por demais empreendida na poética cabo-verdiana quer claridosa quer pós-claridosa. Na ficção, ela é rara quando pensamos numa abordagem directa. Antes de Onésimo Silveira, um dos autores que melhor logrou essa abordagem foi Maria Margarida Mascarenhas, com alguns contos constantes da sua colectânea *Levedando a Ilha*, particularmente no conto "A Viola Partida."

Aliás, cabe aqui sublinhar que a diáspora cabo-verdiana, quer para os países do "Sul-Abaixo" quer para os países europeus e americanos não tem merecido a devida atenção da ficção cabo-verdiana. Assim, no período posterior à publicação da revista *Claridade*, poucos se têm abalançado a tal função. São os casos para além dos exemplos já citados, de Nuno de Miranda, Teobaldo Virgínio com *O Meu Tio Jonas*, Daniel Benoni, com *Não Queria Ser Tambor* e *Um Caboverdiano em Moçambique*, Manuel Ferreira, com *Terra Trazida*, Orlanda Amarílis, com *Cais de Sodré Té Salamansa*, Luís Romano, com a colectânea de contos *Ilha*, Manuel Veiga, em *Oju d'Águ*, Tomé Varela da Silva, particularmente no conto "Sermas." Se a emigração constitui presença constante na vida das personagens das obras de ficção cabo-verdiana, pela permanente evocação que dela fazem e pela sua inquestionável importância para a sobrevivência dos que regressaram ou permaneceram na ilha, ela é ainda assim só escassamente abordada enquanto cenário concreto da vida dessas mesmas personagens.

De um outro quilate é a obra *Tempos da Moral moral*, de Vasco Martins. Com fortes laivos de ficção científica, tal como os "Contos de Ternala" de Oswaldo Osório, a obra conduz-nos a alguns lugares, fontes de sabedoria e de pureza, situados em África (negra e sariana) e na Europa, num contexto, — situado temporalmente no século XXI — de completa exacerbação de todos os conflitos e dramas do homem moderno (políticos, totalitários, tecnológicos, sociais, culturais e mentais). Não fosse a falta de mestria da linguagem literária utilizada, poder-se-ia dizer que *Tempos da Moral moral* é o equivalente futurista d'*O Eleito do Sol*, de Arménio Vieira. Será tal viagem futurista ainda uma forma de dissecação da eterna busca pelo caboverdiano do seu verdadeiro ser? Em *Tempos da Moral moral* (e n'*A Verdadeira Dimensão*, a outra obra romanesca de Vasco Martins) a indagação é sobretudo existencial. É também a indagação existencial a substância nuclear de *Lágrimas de Bronze* de Euricles Rodrigues. Obra ficcional destituída de personagens palpáveis pela completa dispersão do narrador, enquanto sintonia da dispersão do indivíduo no nosso tempo, *Lágrimas de Bronze* é significativa sobretudo pela utilização pioneira que empreende o seu autor do monólogo interior enquanto técnica de dissecação da psique e da dilacerada interioridade do narrador e das personagens. Narrador e personagens que às vezes são um político acometido pela loucura do poder, um poeta extasiado pelos sonhos que libertam, um par de amantes alucinados pela paixão, uma vítima ressuscitada e vivendo no mundo da amnésia, seres de um mundo surrealista, que, afinal, constitui o nosso quotidiano. Outras vezes, o narrador é um carniceiro pois que "seguir a luz da cruz é ser algoz da voz de Jesus." Ou simples ninfomaníaca, embrenhada na sua toxicodependência. O mais das vezes, são corpos perdidos no onirismo da vigília e do pesadelo. Expressão da dilaceração do ser desses entes desvairados, que são os jovens urbanos da nossa capital: narcisismo, culto do corpo em paradoxal comunhão com a toxicomania, o alcoolismo, a absoluta paixão pelo sexo, a náusea esparramando-se por esses intermináveis diálogos que consigo mesmos estabelecem. Porque "cada ser de uma cidade é uma silenciosa cidade de gritos ricocheteados nas paredes do próprio ser."

Tal *démarche* é, aliás, visível também em Rosa de Saron, uma "ficcionista gêmea" de Euricles Rodrigues ou Dina Salústio, a ficcionista cabo-verdiana mais consequente na criação de estórias-crónicas, reunidas em *Mornas Eram as Noites*.

Uma das mais importantes vertentes da actual ficção caboverdiana, pela sua exemplaridade e riqueza de consequências, é aquela escrita em língua cabo-verdiana. A escrita em língua cabo-verdiana conta já com mais de um século de História se nos ativermos aos trabalhos filológicos sobre o Crioulo escritos em Crioulo e em Português por A. de Paula Brito e aos trabalhos literários em língua cabo-verdiana do Cônego Teixeira. Essa escrita conheceu momentos de profundo recorte literário com a poesia de Eugénio Tavares e Pedro Cardoso. O trabalho destas duas grandes estrelas do firmamento crioulo teve continuidade com a produção de Sérgio Frusoni, sobretudo com o seu *Vângele Contóde de Nos Moda*, Armando Napoleão Fernandes, Jorge Barbosa, Jorge Macedo Barbosa, Luis Romano, Ovídio Martins, Felisberto Vieira Lopes (Kaoberdiano Dambará), Artur Vieira, Jorge Pedro Barbosa, Corsino Fortes, Emanuel Braga Tavares, Arménio Vieira e um bom número de literatos da novíssima geração. Como acontece com o conjunto da literatura caboverdiana, a produção em Crioulo tem maior incidência quantitativa na poesia. No domínio da prosa ela é relativamente recente. Iniciada com trabalhos de recolha da tradição oral, como no caso do trabalho pioneiro de Elsie Parsons, que procedeu, nos Estados Unidos da América, a uma vasta recolha das tradições orais da diáspora cabo-verdiana, bem como de *Negrume-Lzimparim*, de Luis Romano, ela só conhecerá o seu verdadeiro perfil, enquanto conjunto de obras de imaginação conduzidas por mentalidades modernas, nos anos que se seguem à independência nacional. Anos, diga-se de passagem, caracterizados por uma intensa luta em favor do Crioulo, enquanto língua nacional e literária. É assim, que a par do seu inestimável labor científico em prol do Crioulo, labor esse consubstanciado no ensaio linguístico *Diskrison Strutural di Língua Kabuverdianu*, na primeira *Introdução à Gramática da Língua Cabo-verdiana*, no Alfabeto do Crioulo, de base fonético-fonológica, adoptado pelo Colóquio do Mindelo (1979), no seu contributo determinante na elaboração do Alfabeto Unificado da Língua Cabo-verdiana (ALUPEC), Manuel Veiga publica na segunda metade dos anos 80, *Oju d'Agu*, o primeiro romance em língua cabo-verdiana. Romance de iniciação aos meandros da nossa língua no que ela contém de riqueza metafórica e analógica, consubstanciada em ditos, provérbios, adivinhas, reelaboração de estórias, crenças e costumes tradicionais *Oju d'Agu* é, à semelhança do moderno romance africano, uma feliz recriação da oralidade, e da espiritualidade a ela subjacente, pelas técnicas do romance moderno.

Tal integração da oralidade no corpo do romance evidencia-se, desde logo, no facto de a própria narrativa iniciar-se nos moldes das estórias tradicionais. É um velho, Palu di Djódja (Papai Grandi), que reúne as crianças e narra os destinos das várias personagens: Zé di Beba, o filho do morgado nascido em Goltarpu (Portugal) que regressa a Cabo Verde para reencontrar-se e às suas raízes; Pedrinho, o alter ego do autor e do narrador autodiegético e que representa o intelectual cabo-verdiano identificado com o seu povo, com as suas raízes e cujo percurso é aliás representativo do percurso de grande parte dos intelectuais originários de Santiago: infância no campo, estudos no seminário católico, formação teológica e universitária, crises de vocação, abandono da vocação sacerdotal e opção pela ruptura com a ala conservadora da Igreja e os seus valores; Regina, a personagem feminina, que em busca da felicidade e de si, une-se a Mamadu, um negro-africano, continental e muçulmano, conhece o *Oju d'Agu* (enquanto metáfora das origens negro-africanas do caboverdiano) e regressa definitivamente a Cabo Verde. No que respeita ao seu conteúdo, *Oju d'Agu* é assim a história da viagem iniciática das personagens (a subentender os diferentes tipos do cabo-verdiano) pelo mundo das suas origens enquanto país, e enquanto país africano. Deste modo, conflitos de matrizes várias — sociais, geracionais, culturais, religiosas, sexuais — vêm à ribalta para nos elucidar sobre o longo e por vezes doloroso percurso na constituição da nossa identidade. Deste modo, o romance *Oju d'Agu* constitui como que uma síntese de toda a história cabo-verdiana — desde a sua gênese escravocrata e latifundiária até aos primeiros anos pós-independência ? plasmada em Santiago, mas com afluentes pelas outras ilhas e pela diáspora. O romance *Oju d'Agu* constitui assim como que uma reformulação de todos os pressupostos estético-ideológicos da claridosidade, pela sua negação, por um lado, particularmente do lusotropicalismo, e pela sua complementação, por outro lado, pela inserção de toda a problemática social do morgadio, do racismo, da africanidade, de uma certa negritude crioula e de toda a ideossincrasia santiaguense na saga literária caboverdiana. E é nesse aspecto, a par do facto de ter sido integralmente escrito em Crioulo, que reside a inquestionável importância de *Oju d'Agu*. Não é pois descabida a asserção do professor Gerald Moser, segundo a qual *Oju d'Agu* é comparável, em certos aspectos, a *Pilgrim's Progress* ou a *Roots*.

A publicação do romance *Oju d'Agu*, apesar de ter sido aplaudida por uma parte importante da intelectualidade cabo-verdiana, não deixou de suscitar controvérsias as mais variadas. A primeira de entre elas foi certamente a relativa à capacidade do Crioulo em servir de veículo de produção de obras literárias de grande fôlego. A controvérsia relativa a essa primeira questão ficou agravada pelo facto de o autor de *Oju d'Agu* ter procedido, com essa sua obra, às duas experimentações equiparadas pelas mentalidades preconceituosas dos detractores do Crioulo a "pecados mortais": a) a integração total do mundo das tradições orais e da oralidade num conceito técnico de romance moderno; b) a utilização de um alfabeto, de base fonético-fonológica, na escrita do romance. Pecado mais mortal, neste último caso, quando se tem em linha de conta que alguns signos utilizados (nomeadamente os que se destinam a representar as palatais) tinham sido objecto de grande contestação. Tanto mais que a contestação era simplesmente a ponta do "iceberg" da contestação mais geral de qualquer afinidade de Cabo Verde com a África Negra e os processos literários com ela conexos.

De todo o modo, é inquestionável que a publicação de *Oju d'Agu* representa uma revolução nas letras cabo-verdianas pela grande valorização que representa para a língua cabo-verdiana e pelo seu contributo para a afinação e moldagem literária da mesma língua. Na sequência da sua publicação, alguns outros trabalhos no domínio da prosa de ficção vieram a lume. De entre eles, cabe destacar o livro de contos *Natal y Kontus* de Tomé Varela da Silva. Livro do quotidiano do Homem cabo-verdiano, e por vezes das suas franjas mais marginalizadas, o livro *Natal y Kontus* vale sobretudo pelo que significa de ousadia no tratamento literário do Crioulo e pela sua visão profundamente crítica da sociedade cabo-verdiana. Tal postura é aliás característica do seu autor. Autor de várias obras de recolha nos mais variados domínios da tradição oral, o autor notabilitou-se pela sua poesia radical, pelo seu conteúdo crítico e pela recuperação da essência morfológica e lexical da nossa língua.

Infelizmente, a prosa de ficção em Crioulo não tem conhecido o desenvolvimento que merece. Contos esparsos têm vindo, no entanto, a lume em revistas e outras publicações periódicas (como são os casos das narrativas em verso de Ano Nobo, de "Kabera Manu Dama," de Pedro Freire e "Stórias di Arvi" de Zé di Sant'y Águ), a par de inúmeros textos poéticos.

O curioso é que a maioria dos raros textos produzidos nesse domínio de quase indigência da literatura cabo-verdiana que é o teatro — a par da literatura infanto-juvenil —, (se nos abstrairmos dos textos de Jaime de Figueiredo, Francisco Fragoso e *Quem é Quem* de Maria José) foram-no em língua cabo-verdiana. Trata-se do texto dramático *Matilde — Viage di Distino*, do poeta Artur Vieira, das peças teatrais "Julgamento de Totó Montero" de Ano Nobo e "Descarado" de Donaldo Macedo, bem como da obra dramática "Spingardas di Tia Karar" de Horácio Santos, tradução da peça "Die Gewehre der Frau Karar" de Bertolt Brecht. Ainda a propósito do Crioulo, seja dito, a título de curiosidade, que um grupo de jovens, sobretudo professores, tem vindo a publicar, na Praia, uma folha cultural intitulada "Xatiadu si," integralmente redigida em cabo-verdiano e com base no ALUPEC.

Com o alargarnento do raio de acção do Crioulo para a prosa de ficção, o ensaio e o teatro, consolida-se, de algum modo, o tendencial bilinguismo cabo-verdiano e restringe-se os efeitos maléficos da diglossia. O cabo-verdiano pode, doravante, comungar dessa santíssima trindade literária, que lhe é cada vez mais própria: a literatura cabo-verdiana de língua portuguesa — a literatura cabo-verdiana de língua cabo-verdiana — a literatura oral obviamente em língua cabo-verdiana.

Obras Citadas

Almeida, Germano. *A Ilha Fantástica.* Mindelo: Ilhéu Editora, 1994.

_____. *O Meu Poeta.* Lisboa: Editorial Caminho, 1992.

_____. *O Testamento do Sr. Napumoceno da Silva Araújo.* Mindelo: Ilhéu Editora, 1990.

Almeida, José Evaristo de. *O Escravo.* Praia: ICL, 1988.

Amarílis, Orlanda. *A Casa dos Mastros.* Praia: ICL, 1988.

Araújo, Carlos. *Percurso Vulgar.* Mindelo: Ilhéu Editora, 1990.

Benoni, Daniel. *Um Caboverdiano em Moçambique.* [Cabo Verde]: Imprensa Nacional de Cabo Verde, 1994.

Bettencourt, Fátima. *Semear em Pó.* Praia: Ministério da Cultura e Comunicação Social: ICL, 1994.

Didial, G.T. *Contos da Macaronésia.* Volume I. Mindelo: Ilhéu Editora, 1994.

_____. *O Estado Impenitente da Fragilidade.* Praia: ICL, 1989.

Duarte, Dulce Almada. "*Oju d'Agu* de Manuel Veiga: uma proposta de leitura." *Voz di*

Povo. [Praia] 23 de Maio, 1987: s/p.

Ferreira, Manuel. Prefácio. *Vida Crioula* de Teobaldo Virgínio. Boston: Quality First Printing, 1993.

Fragmentos 1-10 (1987-1993).

França, Arnaldo. "Claridade et Après. Panorama de la Littérature Écrite." *Notre Librairie*, 112 (janvier-mars 1993): 31-36.

Francavilla, Roberto. *Viaggio Nella Letteratura Capoverdiana, Momenti e Problemi.* s/l: Alberto Santoro Editoré, 1994.

Heilmair, Hans-Peter. *Die Entwick1ung der Kapverdischen Literatur im Soziokulturellen Kontext.* Frankfurt am Main: TFM, Domus Editoria Europaea, 1992.

Lopes, Baltasar. *Antologia da Ficção Cabo-verdiana Contemporânea.* Praia: Edições Henriquinas, 1961.

Mariano, Gabriel. *Vida e Morte de João Cabafume.* Lisboa: Vega, 1993.

Martins, Ovídio. *Tchutchinha.* Praia: Gradefito, s.d.

Martins, Vasco. *Tempos da Moral moral.* Mindelo: Ilhéu Editora, 1993.

_____. *A Verdadeira Dimensão.* Linda-a-Velha: Edições ALAC, s.d.

Mascarenhas, Maria Margarida. *Levedando a Ilha.* Praia: ICL, 1988.

Menezes, Euclides de. *Toti Cadabra e Outras Estórias.* Praia: ICL, s.d.

Miranda, Nuno de. *Cais de Pedra.* Praia: ICL, 1989.

Monteiro, Fernando. *Desassossego.* Praia: Spleen-Edições, 1994.

Moser, Gerald. "Recensão crítica de *Oju d'Agu.*" *World Literature Today* 62.4 (Autumn 1988): s.p.

Pré-textos 0-1 (1990-1994).

Rodrigues, Euricles. *Lágrimas de Bronze.* Praia: Edição do Autor, 1990.

Rodrigues, João. *Caminhos Agrestes.* Praia: ICL, s.d.

_____. *Montes Verde-Cara.* 2ª edição. S. Vicente: Publicações Gráfica do Mindelo, Lda., 1993.

_____. *Casas e Casinhotos.* S. Vicente: Publicações Gráfica do Mindelo, Lda., s.d.

Romano, Luís. *Famintos.* Rio de Janeiro: Editôra Leitura, 1962.

_____. *Ilha.* Mindelo: Ilhéu-Editora, 1995.

Salústio, Dina. *Mornas Eram as Noites.* Praia: ICL, 1994.

Silva, T.V. da. *Natal y Kontus.* Praia: Inst. Kauberdianu di Libru, 1988.

Silveira, Onésimo. *A Saga das As-Secas e das Graças de Nossenhor.* Mem Martins, Portugal: Publicações Europa-América, 1993.

Sousa, [Henrique] Teixeira de. *Capitão de Mar e Terra.* Mem Martins, Portugal: Publicações Europa-América, 1994.

_____. *Djunga.* Mem Martins, Portugal: Publicações Europa-América, 1990.

_____. *Entre Duas Bandeiras.* Mem Martins, Portugal: Publicações Europa-América, 1994.

_____. *Ilhéu de Contenda.* Livros de bolso. Mem Martins, Portugal: Publicações Europa-América: s.d.

_____. *Na Ribeira de Deus.* Mem Martins, Portugal: Publicações Europa-América, 1993.

_____. *Xaguate.* Mem Martins, Portugal: Publicações Europa-América, 1987.

Veiga, Manuel. *Oju d'Agu.* Praia: ICL, 1987.

_____. *A Sementeira.* Lisboa: Edições ALAC, 1994.

Vieira, Arménio. *O Eleito do Sol.* Lisboa: Vega, 1993.

Vieira, Artur. *Matilde—Viage di Distino.* Rio de Janeiro: Raba, Co. Editora e Impressora Ltda., 1993.

Virgínio, Teobaldo. *O Meu Tio Jonas.* Boston: private production, 1986.

_____. *Vida Crioula.* 2ª edição. Boston: Quality First Printing, 1993.

José Luís Hopffer Cordeiro Almada é co-fundador do Movimento Pró-Cultura e da Associação dos Escritores Cabo-verdianos, director da revista *Fragmentos—Revista de Artes, Letras e Cultura* e co-fundador e co-director da Spleen Edições. Publicou: *À Sombra do Sol* (1990), *Assomada Nocturna* (1993) e *Mirabilis—De Veias ao Sol* (1998). Tem sido colaborador para várias revistas como também para as seguintes antologias: *Changing Africa: The First Literary Generation of Independent Cape Verde* de Gerald Moser (1992) e *Vozes Poéticas da Lusofonia,* organizada por Eduardo White. Utiliza os seguintes nomes literários: Zé di Sant' y Ágù, Alma Dofer, Dionísio de Deus e Fonteana, Tuna Furtado e Erasmo Cabral de Almada.

O Tema do 'Contratado' na Literatura Caboverdiana: génese e variações

Cristina Pacheco

Resumo. O presente artigo pretende—através de uma breve apreciação do contexto sócio-económico e literário de Cabo Verde, sobretudo entre os anos 30 e 60, e dos motivos que contribuiram para o aparecimento do fenómeno da contratação de caboverdianos para o trabalho nas roças de S. Tomé e Príncipe—analisar a importância da introdução desta temática, e seu(s) respectivo(s) tratamento(s), na Literatura Caboverdiana.

Em Março de 1936, data da publicação do primeiro número da revista "Claridade," na cidade do Mindelo, ilha de S. Vicente, regista-se o início de uma actividade literária conjunta no Arquipélago de Cabo Verde, isto é, uma produção mais ou menos sistemática, levada a cabo por um grupo de escritores em torno de um ideário expresso e comum, quer por colaboração directa na revista quer pela edição de textos (narrativos, poéticos, ensaísticos) que, ainda que editados individualmente, se foram inserindo no âmbito de um mesmo projecto global. Tais factos legitimam, pois, a designação atribuída a esses escritores: "Geração da 'Claridade.'"

Independentemente de sabermos que existira, antes de 1936, uma incipiente e dispersa produção escrita em Cabo Verde—da autoria de, entre outros, Pedro Cardoso, José Lopes e Eugénio Tavares—, importa vincar que é aos "claridosos" que justamente se reconhece um estatuto de pioneirismo, no que se refere ao intuito de criar uma literatura que representasse a vivência e as contingências típicas locais,[1] bem diferentes das da Metrópole e daquelas que afectavam as, ao tempo, outras colónias portuguesas. E é assim que, nos textos de Jorge Barbosa ou de Manuel Lopes ou ainda de Baltasar Lopes/ Osvaldo Alcântara, os três pilares da geração, surpreendemos os alicerces da cosmogonia caboverdeana: a dispersão insular, as secas prolongadas, a escassez e pobreza da terra, o isolamento, a omnipresença do mar, a luta quotidiana pela sobrevivência e, consequentemente, os apelos ou a necessidade de Evasão, de Partir, em permanente conflito com o amor telúrico e quase sacralizado que o caboverdeano nutre pelo seu 'pedacinho de chão,' a que, de um modo tão esforçado, dedica o seu duro e persistente trabalho diário. Por isso é um Homem estóico, firme, resistente, íntima e exteriormente religioso, apegado às tradições, à família, aquele que perpassa pelas páginas dos 'claridosos'; mas também sonhador, ansiando por novos horizontes, sentindo muitas vezes o apelo irresistível do mar, veículo de (e para) outros mundos, mesmo que, por vezes, esse mesmo mar seja visto como elemento castrador de movimentos, já que, naturalmente, transforma o caboverdiano em prisioneiro na sua própria ilha. A comprová-lo, atente-se nos seguintes versos de Jorge Barbosa:

> Ai o mar
> que nos dilata sonhos e sufoca desejos!
>
> Ai a cinta do mar
> que detém ímpetos
> ao nosso arrebatamento
> e insinua
> horizontes para lá
> do nosso isolamento!
>
> (Convite da viagem apetecida
> que se não faz.)

Um dos aspectos mais característicos da Literatura Caboverdiana, abordado quase até à exaustão por críticos e estudiosos, é a questão do Evasionismo e das diversas vertentes de que se reveste. De facto—e sem querermos esmiuçar tal problemática, embora nos seja imprescindível referi-la, dado a temática que nos propomos tratar—, é bem perceptível, quer na prosa quer na poesia, o drama principal do caboverdiano que, sentindo as suas raízes presas à terra, não consegue impedir-se de imaginar o que estará para além do mar. Terra e Mar moldaram-no desde sempre e, dado que o seu sustento lhe não é garantido pela terra, que é pobre, seria inevitável que começasse a pensar que o caminho, único, a proporcionar-lhe uma real melhoria das condições de vida estivesse na saída dessa terra, que o mesmo é dizer pela emigração; esse caminho para a saída só poderia ser marítimo. Tal drama existencial, constantemente reiterado em diferentes textos literários, faz da literatura caboverdiana um dos melhores exemplos universais de "literatura insular," o único no âmbito das literaturas africanas de língua portuguesa (já que o tópico literário da 'insularidade' se encontra praticamente ausente da literatura santomense, o outro espaço colonial geograficamente insular).

Voltando à questão evasionista, impõe-se, agora, que distingamos pelo menos duas linhas que foram sendo desenvolvidas pela Literatura—reflexo, em graus de aproximação diversos, da realidade de Cabo Verde—e que ainda não deixámos nítidas. A primeira prende-se com o sonho de partir, decorrente das agruras vivenciais experimentadas pelos caboverdianos, sonho esse que, actuando como paliativo ou "refúgio," pode nunca vir a realizar-se. A segunda linha ilustra a emigração concreta, efectuada por muitos, com as implicações práticas e psicológicas que daí advêm. Por outras palavras: uma coisa é o desejo, algo difuso e atópico, de partir para melhorar de vida ou conhecer outros lugares; outra, muito diferente, é emigrar de facto, para trabalhar num destino pré-estabelecido. Aqui chegados, parece-nos importante transcrever algumas passagens da comunicação apresentada por Luís Terry, em 1959, intitulada "O problema da emigração cabo-verdiana"[2]:

> É altura de novamente fazer o ponto e repor a rota do trabalho na matéria concreta do emigrante cabo-verdiano. A primeira pergunta que ocorre, após se ter averiguado da razão por que emigra—e essa é de carência económica estreme, quase primária—, é: para onde emigra? Sabemos que se orienta para a América do Norte e para as Américas latinas, preferentemente para a Argentina e Brasil; emigra ainda para a África Francesa, de preferência Dacar. Últimamente tem ido como serviçal para S. Tomé, em regime de contratado, o que quer dizer que regressa, embora possa ser contratado novamente.
>
> Destes casos é forçoso eliminar para o futuro a América do Norte, pois que para aí as possibilidades estão quase esgotadas. Em Providence e New Bedford, no estado de Massachussets, vivem numerosos cabo-verdianos, muitos deles já aí nascidos, mas mantendo os hábitos sociais e até o dialecto das ilhas de origem. [...] Também não interessa, como já se disse, o caso do Brasil, pelas restrições que esse país tem imposto. Quanto a Dacar, é admissível que as circunstâncias venham a

> piorar com as alterações do estatuto político aí operado. Importa, por conseguinte, restringir o exame ao caso de S. Tomé [...].

Eis, pois, num excelente resumo de Luís Terry, o ponto da situação que, em 1959, era possível fazer acerca dos destinos de emigração escolhidos pelo caboverdeano.

Relegando para mais tarde o testemunho que o surto emigratório para S. Tomé haveria de deixar nas páginas literárias (propósito final deste artigo), começaremos por verificar—para melhor contextualizarmos, depois, essa ocorrência—quais os vestígios que os outros lugares de emigração deixaram na literatura.

Sem pretendermos ser exaustivos, quase nos apetece afirmar que as referências à emigração aparecem desde o início da literatura caboverdiana. Com efeito, elas podem ser detectadas em alguns dos primeiros textos dos escritores da "Claridade," apesar de neles surgir, com mais nitidez, a tónica colocada no sonho difuso da evasão (o que motivou algumas críticas por parte das gerações literárias seguintes, que se ativeram, sobretudo, à poesia de Jorge Barbosa—que apelidaram depreciativamente de "barbosianismo"— e ao poema "Itinerário de Pasárgada," de Osvaldo Alcântara).

Ora, como dizíamos, quer os 'claridosos' quer os escritores que, a partir de 1944, estiveram na base da criação da revista "Certeza"—uma nova Geração cuja escrita revela, pela primeira vez em Cabo Verde, uma influência assinalável da ideologia marxista—, quer ainda os autores que lançaram o chamado "Suplemento Cultural" (em 1958), todos abordaram ou trataram especificamente a realidade emigratória dos caboverdianos, ainda que com perspectivas e tratamentos diferenciados. De facto, os 'claridosos' não terão feito mais do que deixar apontada a existência dessa realidade; enquanto que os homens da "Certeza" e os do "Suplemento Cultural" focalizaram ideologicamente o problema, vendo-o não apenas como decorrente das condições climatéricas e geográficas do Arquipélago mas, acima de tudo, como consequência da sua situação de colónia, abandonada e/ou explorada pela administração portuguesa que, entre outros factos, deixara decair completamente uma das principais fontes de riqueza das ilhas crioulas, a saber, o Porto Grande , de S. Vicente. Repescando um pouco ao acaso, seguem-se, pois, alguns excertos de poemas que demonstram como Jorge Barbosa, Manuel Lopes, António Nunes, Gabriel Mariano, glosaram o referido tema. Comecemos por Jorge Barbosa:

[...] *Americanos* que chegam...
Na balbúrdia do cais
há lágrimas de alegria
fugidios cristais
iluminando os olhos das mulheres...

Foguetes
estalam no ar por toda a Brava
contagiando a harmonia
de cores
e de flores
da gracílima paisagem.

E depois... lá vão
outra vez,
tristonhos, os emigrantes...

: América! Mar largo!

Amores distantes,
saudades crioulas
das mornas de Eugénio!...

Jorge Barbosa (poema "Ilhas," *Arquipélago*, 1935)

A palavra "americanos," grafada em itálico, refere-se, é claro, aos emigrantes caboverdianos que, talvez vindos de férias, visitam as respectivas famílias, regressando novamente para a América, tal como se deduz pela sequência poética. Também no início do poema "Irmão," todo ele assente no dialogismo, Jorge Barbosa evoca o grande número de caboverdianos que, contratados por baleeiros dos Estados Unidos, neles prestavam serviço, fixando-se, depois, na America : "Cruzaste Mares / na aventura da pesca da baleia, / nessas viagens para a América /de onde às vezes os navios não voltam mais." (Ambiente, 1941).

O caso do escritor Manuel Lopes é, a nosso ver, dos mais interessantes no que a esta temática diz respeito, até porque, ao escolher para um dos seus livros de poesia o título *Poemas de quem ficou* (1949)—onde, aliás, inclui um texto poético de título idêntico—, prefere enaltecer os que não emigraram, sem fazer referência, a não ser por omissão e contraste, àqueles que partiram. Esta mesma opção, vamos também encontrá-la naquele que é, quanto a nós, o seu mais belo romance, *Chuva Braba*, editado uns anos mais tarde (1956), e cujas características estéticas se filiam no mais puro neo-realismo, ainda sem tendências marxistas. Nele, o conflito sentido pela personagem principal, Mané Quim, entre partir e ficar, constitui o núcleo de todo o desenrolar da acção que, à medida que vai progredindo, mais acentua a criação da personagem como a de um caboverdiano-tipo. No caso deste romance, a hipótese de Mané Quim partir para o Brasil (e não um Brasil qualquer, mas Manaus, a principal cidade da Amazónia) é-lhe oferecida pelo seu padrinho Joquinha, lá emigrado há anos, que lhe pinta um vivo contraste entre as condições de vida em Cabo Verde (no romance, ilha de Santo Antâo)—onde a vinda das chuvas ameaça nunca se concretizar, jogando na miséria e no recurso às hipotecas de terras todos os que delas dependem para sobreviver—e a prosperidade fértil que aguarda todos os que como ele, Joquinha, decidem emigrar. Os argumentos do padrinho, perante as circunstâncias, parecem ser muito fortes; mas não para o jovem Mané Quim, demasiado preso à sua hortinha, à mãe e à rapariguinha que ama, sofrendo, por isso, hesitações e dilemas que o levam a procurar opinião e conselhos, os quais, por tão variados, apenas lhe aumentam a própria ansiedade em vez de o ajudarem a resolver-se. Do seu complexo drama se alimenta, como dissemos, todo o romance, cujo desfecho ficará a dever-se à vinda da tão desejada chuva 'braba.' A nosso ver, esta é a obra que mais claramente se ocupa da problemática da emigração no seio dos autores da "Claridade," sendo nítida a tomada de posição do narrador pela hipótese de 'ficar,' uma das razões pelas quais terá merecido um especial destaque no ensaio "Consciencialização na Literatura Caboverdiana,"[3] de Onésimo Silveira (pertencente à geração do "Suplemento Cultural"), texto que viria a tornar-se tão polémico.

Já da geração seguinte, a da "Certeza," o poeta António Nunes deixa expressos, no seu belíssimo texto "Terra," os principais destinos de emigração do caboverdiano— "Nha Chica, conte-me/ aquela história/ dos meus irmãos/ hoje perdidos/ no mundo grande/ (...) Lisboa, América/ Dakar ou Rio/ - dentro de nós/ surge esta ideia/ partir! partir! [...]" —, bem como a confissão de fé num futuro diferente: "[...] Olho estes campos,/ olho estes mares/ e sinto a Vida/ prendida à terra[...]."

De Gabriel Mariano, implicado na publicação do único número do

"Suplemento Cultural,"[4] aqui ficam excertos do poema "Carta de Longe" (do volume *12 Poemas de circunstância*, editado na Praia, em 1965):

Carta de longe lembrando
a dispersão dolorosa.
Carta de Boston América
de Jorge Pedro Barbosa.

[...] Tinha Brasil Argentina
tinha Dakar-Senegal.
América vinha primeiro
já nos obscuros caminhos.

Já nos obscuros caminhos
da encruzilhada inicial
já insinuando por perto
Brasil Dakar-Senegal.

Tinha Guiné Moçambique
Angola veio e depois
Macau Timor Venezuela
Goa Brasil São Tomé [...]

A passagem pela poesia de Gabriel Mariano coloca-nos, finalmente, na rota que pretendíamos seguir, isto é, os reflexos que conheceu, na Literatura, a emigração do caboverdiano para São Tomé. Todavia, antes de o verificar, necessário se torna esboçar alguns dados contextuais relativos a este tipo particular de emigração.

O Arquipélago de S. Tomé e Príncipe teve, para Portugal, uma enorme importância económica, sobretudo pelas suas potencialidades agrícolas, dada a fertilidade do solo e o seu privilegiado clima, equatorial. Foi a partir do século XIX, com a introdução das culturas do café e do cacau—e este viria até a ser reconhecido como o melhor do mundo!—, que começou uma nova vaga de exploração colonial nas ilhas.[5]

Ora, com a abolição da escravatura e a atitude da maioria dos santomenses, que por razões várias (internas ao arquipélago), se recusou a trabalhar nas grandes 'roças,' quase todas nas mãos de proprietários coloniais, a Administração Portuguesa resolveu socorrer-se de mão-de-obra colhida nas suas outras colónias africanas, dando-se, assim, início a um fluxo constante de emigração forçada. Não sabemos ao certo quando terá começado a ida de trabalhadores de Cabo Verde para as roças, embora possamos afirmar que nos anos 20 existiam caboverdianos a trabalhar em S. Tomé, informação que colhemos de uma obra de Carlos Benigno da Cruz[6]; mas é de supor—até pelas palavras que já transcrevemos da conferência de Luís Terry—que esse surto se terá adensado a partir dos anos 40 deste século, uma vez que, por essa altura, já os tradicionais destinos de emigração dos caboverdianos se encontravam quase inatingíveis.

Regressando à conferência de Luís Terry, vejamos algumas das suas constatações e conselhos, concernentes a este especial caso:

> [...] a mão-de-obra extra-insular em S. Tomé tem algo de chocante.
> Aquela província necessita, para uma boa valorização das suas riquezas em cacau, café e coconote, de cerca de 25.000 serviçais, e para os ter importa desde há muito de Moçambique, Angola e ultimamente de Cabo Verde. (...)
> [...] O recrutamento dos trabalhadores em Cabo Verde é indiscriminado; mais adequado seria dizer que é feito ao contrário, pois o vadio ou desempregado das cidades é o que menos se presta para o trabalho das roças. Habituado aos pequenos trabalhos de carrego, de transporte, de construção civil; viciado pela vida da cidade e habituado aos prazeres fáceis; portador de certos hábitos de vida e comportamento, sente-se completamente deslocado nos trabalhos agrícolas, que realiza mal e com descontentamento. A mudança do clima, que em S. Tomé é muito mais violento; a diferença da dieta a que se tem de sujeitar; a disciplina de trabalho ordenado que tem de aceitar e a saudade dos que deixou ao partir vão lentamente minando a sua disposição. Algumas vezes, quando compara a sua própria educação e cultura com a dos capatazes sob cujas ordens directas trabalha, não pode deixar de se sentir diminuído e humilhado. Finalmente, o completo desconhecimento, com que partiu, das condições de vida e trabalho que ia encontrar colhe-o em total despreparação.[...]
> [...] pois se trata de massa humana diferente da de Angola e Moçambique. É preferível alojá-los em casas independentes, com um terreno anexo para cultura hortícola, em que o rural cabo-verdiano é exímio. Deve-lhes ser fornecida a dieta em géneros, o que não é difícil, porque a vida tornou-os sóbrios. Milho, feijão, banha, banana e mandioca, com alguma carne e peixe seco ou fresco, são para eles condimentos de uma ementa apetecida.[7]

Pareceram-nos fulcrais esta palavras de Luís Terry—por isso a transcrição um tanto longa—, pela enorme quantidade de informações úteis que nos transmitem. É que não apenas se traça aqui o perfil do homem caboverdiano, como ainda ficamos a perceber as condições de vida que iria encontrar em S. Tomé, as razões pelas quais se sente frustrado e desconhecido, e os simples (e tão pouco exigentes, tão básicos!...) cuidados que seriam necessários para lhe garantir um mínimo de bem-estar. Mas, embora excelente o quadro pintado por Luís Terry, deveremos reforçar as tintas de um dos seus elementos: a mudança de clima. Ido de uma terra seca, onde a chuva é um bem raro e precioso, o "serviçal" caboverdiano deparava-se com um clima equatorial, de grau muito elevado de humidade permanente, o que lhe dificultava muitíssimo a adaptação física, consumindo-o de doenças—de que uma das mais graves é, como sabemos, o paludismo, de características particularmente nefastas, em S. Tomé! Essa a razão pela qual, muitas vezes, o "contratado" regressava bem doente ou, pior!, não chegava a regressar!... Notemos ainda que, ao referir-se "ao vadio e desempregado da cidade," Luís Terry aponta-os como a maioria dos que são contratados, em Cabo Verde, para irem para S. Tomé, contrariamente ao que seria mais esperado em termos de experiência e, portanto, de rentabilidade para o trabalho exigido. Este testemunho é relevante, uma vez que nos permite deduzir que os lugares mais afectados pela saída dos seus habitantes são as cidades; logo, com toda a certeza, as cidades do Mindelo (ilha de S. Vicente) e da Praia (ilha de Santiago), as mais importantes do território insular. Por outro lado, não seria de estranhar que, de entre todas, a cidade do Mindelo fosse a que mais exportaria mão-de-obra: a ilha de S. Vicente, de todo imprópria para a agricultura, possuía, em alternativa aos terrenos aráveis, o maior porto de mar do arquipélago, o chamado Porto Grande, que, em tempos mais áureos, gerara e representara uma parcela razoável da economia insular, visto estar na rota escolhida pelos principais navios e cargueiros transatlânticos; mas, por incúria da Administração Portuguesa, este acabou por entrar em declínio, quando as rotas internacionais começaram a preferir as condições oferecidas pelos portos das Ilhas Canárias, o que deixou em grandes dificuldades, como se pode imaginar, toda uma população que gravitava em torno das actividades portuárias.

Estamos, pois, agora, na posse de um mínimo de dados históricos e sociais que nos permitem perceber as razões que terão levado os autores caboverdianos a incluir esta problemática em alguns dos seus textos. Vejamos, então, ainda que através de uma breve e incompleta panorâmica, como foi tratada pela Literatura Caboverdiana a temática do "contratado."

Pelos textos de que dispomos, parece-nos não errar muito se dissermos que Baltazar Lopes foi o primeiro—e o único da Geração da "Claridade"—a focar esta questão em poesia, usando, portanto, o pseudónimo poético Osvaldo Alcântara. Fê-lo apenas em dois dos seus textos poéticos , que intitulou de "Panfleto" e "Romanceiro de S. Tomé." O primeiro, datado de Junho de 1946, é o texto de abertura do volume *Cântico da Manhã Futura*—publicado em 1986, por ocasião da comemoração dos 50 anos da revista "Claridade," e que reúne a quase totalidade da poesia deste autor.[8] Quanto ao segundo, o longo poema dividido em 8 partes, "Romanceiro de S. Tomé"—uma "dolorosa novidade poética," como se lhe refere Manuel Ferreira[9]—foi publicado, pela primeira vez, no n.º 8 da "Claridade," em Maio de 1958. Do poema "Panfleto," repescamos os seguintes versos:

> [...] Só queria saber quem foi o réu desta culpa:
> vê-lo, discriminar as suas feições,
> a cor do seu cabelo, o tamanho do seu corpo;
> denunciar a desencarnação em que ele se esconde anonimamente;
> fazer dele um substantivo concreto
> que eu pudesse apreender sob a acção tumultuosa
> de todos os meus sentidos despertos;
> vê-lo, dominá-lo com a justiça implacável
> deste "gado humano" que no vapor da carreira chegou hoje de S.Tomé,
> onde em vez da horta da casa há a "roça,"
> onde a única tranquilidade consiste
> em ser accionista com palacete em Lisboa; [...]

Eis como Osvaldo Alcântara denuncia o drama da emigração para S.Tomé, opondo o "gado humano," que o mesmo é dizer o contratado/colonizado caboverdiano, ao "accionista com palacete em Lisboa," isto é, aos colonizadores endinheirados, proprietários das roças santomenses. No entanto, ainda assim, o sujeito de enunciação tenta buscar um culpado maior do que cada um dos indivíduos colonizadores, como se estes apenas fossem agentes de um poder superior, de um sistema de que eles mesmos não seriam os responsáveis. O poema é, pois, denunciador e acusatório, mas parece ilibar, de certa forma, cada um dos homens directamente implicados, já que a crítica recai no próprio sistema colonial, encarado, na sua globalidade, como principal réu, culpado da opressão dos homens. De seguida, transcrevemos algumas passagens de um texto de Gabriel Mariano, a propósito do poema "Romanceiro de S. Tomé":

> O "Romanceiro" está estruturado em torno de três figuras, ou três símbolos: "Nicolau," "Caim" e o "Amigo." Nicolau é aquele que foi transformado em serviçal, em gado humano, em coisa, em mercadoria. Caim é o inimigo, o que subtraiu a Nicolau a sua liberdade essencial, o porta-voz daqueles que se opõem à libertação do homem. O Amigo, é o libertador.[10]

E Gabriel Mariano prossegue, citando e comentando os seguintes versos:

> Vem Amigo.
> Chicoteia outra vez, que faltam séculos
> de séculos
> para o teu reino ser achado.
>
> Olha por Nicolau.
> Os mercadores nada poderão contra ele.
> Sei que a tua espada há-de fulgurar nas
> batalhas necessárias
> e Nicolau nunca mais voltará a ser a moeda
> das riquezas de Caim.
>
> Tal como o Apóstolo Tiago, Osvaldo Alcântara poderia dizer: "Eis que o salário dos trabalhadores que ceifaram as vossas terras, que por vós foi diminuído, clama; os clamores dos que ceifaram, entraram nos ouvidos dos Senhores dos Exércitos." Reparem: "o oprimido é a fonte da prosperidade do opressor. O Libertador assume o oprimido: é a vanguarda consciente e organizada da legião dos oprimidos. A batalha a travar é, duplamente, necessária: necessária, por ser inevitável; necessária, por conduzir à libertação, do homem."[11]

Pensamos que a leitura que Gabriel Mariano propõe, destes versos de Osvaldo Alcântara, é não só interessante como acertada, respeitando, quanto a nós, as intenções de escrita do poeta visado. Mas as marcas do discurso de Gabriel Mariano transportam também um sabor ideologicamente marxista e revolucionário, que conotam a escrita literária (e não apenas a ensaística) deste autor. A verdade é que ele foi, juntamente com os seus companheiros do "Suplemento Cultural," um dos escritores que mais visaram o tema do 'contratado' na Literatura Caboverdiana. Tal facto não é de estranhar, se nos recordarmos que os anos 50 foram os que registaram uma maior fuga, enquanto último recurso de vida, de caboverdianos para S. Tomé e que 58 foi o ano em que apareceram quer o n.º único do "Suplemento Cultural" quer o n.º 8 da "Claridade," onde, como referimos, Osvaldo Alcântara publicou o seu "Romanceiro." Os discursos de uns e de outro são, no entanto, bem diferentes, talvez porque, na sua essência, encontramos gerações etárias e perspectivas muito distintas, bem como distintos e diferentes serão os objectivos a atingir pelos respectivos textos. Na verdade, é por um tom reivindicativo e agressivamente desafiador que os homens do "Suplemento Cultural" se investem do papel de acusadores do sistema colonial, fazendo da emigração forçada para S. Tomé a bandeira dessa luta empreendida pela independência das colónias, assim juntando a sua escrita interventiva à dos seus irmãos de letras de Angola, Guiné, Moçambique e até de S. Tomé e Príncipe.

Mas vejamos, então, como foram múltiplos os textos desta geração dedicados ao tema do contrato.

Mesmo que indirectamente, o ensaio de Onésimo Silveira "Consciencialização na Literatura Caboverdiana," a que já fizemos referência, enquadra-se e, simultaneamente, lança as bases organizadas desta luta conjunta. Terminando com uma espécie de palavra-de-ordem, em maiúsculas—"*ESTA É A GERAÇÃO QUE NÃO VAI PARA PASÁRGADA.*"—, o ensaio pretende contrapor a nova geração de escritores à da "Claridade," recusando o sonho da evasão, exigindo uma intervenção sócio-literária clara e reivindicando o estatuto de africanidade para Cabo Verde, em detrimento daquilo que Onésimo classifica como um "regionalismo europeu," praticado pelos claridosos. Ainda que com muitas reservas face às críticas dirigidas ao movimento claridoso e, principalmente, recusando uma génese puramente africana para um povo que é comprovadamente 'crioulo,' não podemos deixar de reconhecer que o ensaio-manifesto demonstra, quer pela argumentação quer pelos exemplos que fornece de textos da nova geração literária, ter acontecido, em Cabo Verde, uma transformação de mentalidades e de projectos, como afirma o próprio ensaísta: "A síntese de consciencialização e a totalidade de força expressiva que Ovídio Martins encerrou em 'Hora,' poema formalmente tão curto, quase pirular, mostram definitiva tomada de posição e o grau de maturidade espiritual alcançado pelo grupo que caracterizamos com a expressão 'Nova Geração.'"[12]

De Ovídio Martins, não transcreveremos o poema referido (intencionalmente escrito em crioulo!), apenas por não se enquadrar no tema do 'contratado,' mas falaremos de outros, onde esta problemática, por demais explorada poeticamente pelo autor, surge mais explícita. Compulsando a sua colectânea de 100 poemas, com o título *Gritarei, Berrarei, Matarei / Não Vou para Pasárgada,*[13] facilmente nos damos conta de um conjunto de textos que, subordinados ao título "caminho da perdição," se referem ao 'caminho' que leva a S. Tomé, o "caminho longe"— designação corrente em Cabo Verde e também título do primeiro poema do conjunto que mencionámos. Ei-lo:

Caminho longe...

Caminho obrigado
caminho trilhado
nos braços da fome

Caminho sem nome
caminho de mar
um violão a chorar

Caminho traidor
caminho da dor
ó lenta agonia

Caminho sem dia
caminho sem fé
Roças de S. Tomé

Caminho longe...[14]

Estruturado em forma de ladainha chorada, o texto é tão pungente e claro ao caracterizar esse "caminho," que nos abstemos de mais qualquer comentário, a não ser o de chamarmos a atenção para a grafia, em maiúsculas, da palavra 'Roças,' o único terceiro verso de uma estrofe em que a palavra inicial aparece dessa forma. Ainda do mesmo autor, não resistimos a transcrever os primeiros versos do poema "Alerta," dirigido a cada um dos seus conterrâneos:

Cuidado Companheiro
não te percas nos acenos da Terra-Longe
Terra-Longe tem roça
Roça tem desespero
Que as ilusões de fartura da Terra-Longe
não prendam teus passos
E sobretudo Companheiro sobretudo
não deixes que te impinjam
a mentira do contrato (...)[15]

Como podemos verificar, através deste aviso directo e claro, Ovídio Martins, neste grupo de poemas (são dez ao todo[16]), dedica uma atenção exclusiva à emigração para as roças santomenses. Seria despropositado querer, neste espaço, dedicar a cada um deles a atenção que merece; mas ser-nos-ia impossível não realçar uma curiosa ocorrência, em dois deles[17]: a evocação da figura bíblica de Caim, que, como vimos, também aparece no poema "Romanceiro de S. Tomé," de Osvaldo Alcântara. Ou é pura coincidência (justificada pela cultura religiosa que quase todo o caboverdiano da época possuía) ou, melhor ainda, trata-se de uma espécie de influência de uma linha simbólica que, usada por Osvaldo Ancântara, Ovídio Martins terá decidido convocar também, e no mesmo sentido, para o tratamento da problemática comum.

Continuando a nossa visão panorâmica, pelo menos também três poemas de Onésimo Silveira são dedicados a este tema: "Poema," "Regresso" e "Ausência"[18]; o mesmo Onésimo da Silveira transcreve—no ensaio várias vezes referido—um poema de Terêncio Anahory, também intitulado "Regresso" (que nos pinta o "retorno desejado" do contratado, a quem o sujeito de enunciação se dirige: (...) Vou contar-te histórias/ para embalar o teu sono/ Afugentar do teu pensamento// Roças, secas, sol ardente,/ Fuba,/ Terra-longe! "); e, para terminar, falaremos de um outro cultor desta temática, tanto na poesia como em textos narrativos: Gabriel Mariano. Comecemos pela poesia.

Na antologia poética *Ladeira Grande*,[19] seis dos poemas aludem ao fenómeno do contrato. Um deles é "Carta de longe," de que já transcrevemos algumas passagens, e que foca a emigração generalizada do caboverdiano, mencionando também, como verificámos, a partida para S. Tomé. Dos restantes, aqui se reproduzem alguns excertos:

"(...) Eles já chegaram. / Gerente,/ tesoureiro, / guarda-livros. // Os traidores foram recrutados / e tudo se perfez com segurança. / Compraram serviçais venderam serviçais / e a morte definiu / de novo seu caminho. (...)" - "Denúncia elementar" ;" (...) Se sabedes do contratado/ nas roças de São Tomé/ aideus aiué// Nas roças de São Tomé/ que é já o prazo saído/ aideus aiué// Que é já o prazo saído/ que é já o choro chorado/ aideus aiué (...) - "Chorar de amigo" (que, como se constata, parodia, quer pelo título quer pela estrutura escolhida, as "cantigas de amigo"—composições medievais portuguesas) ;"(...) Se boi cantasse, ó comprador de serviçais,/ seria tranquila a tua consciência/ e sereno o sono futuro dos teus filhos..// Se boi cantasse, ó nosso amigo,/ seria sem perigos/ o canto dos serviçais./ Incómodo já não seria/ o canto dos serviçais./ Molemente acabaria/ o canto dos serviçais (...)- "Boi não canta" (de tom sarcástico e ironicamente acusador) ; "Serviçal de roça/ Caboverde é longe (...) Serviçal de roça enrocada,/ equador é onde/ tua dor ecoa. // De noite alguém chora.// Choro de noite é caminho."—"De noite alguém chora ;"Caminho/ caminho longe/ ladeira de São-Tomé/ Devia ser de regresso/ devia ser e não é." — "Caminho longe" (a tónica deste texto recai, como vemos pela transcrição da última estrofe, na dor dos que acabam por não regressar à sua terra).

Se, a estes poemas incluídos em *Ladeira Grande*, juntarmos outros dois sobre o mesmo tema, coligidos por Mário de Andrade[20]—"Poema do serviçal" (onde estão patentes muitas semelhanças com o poema "Monangamba," do angolano António Jacinto) e "Comissário ad hoc" ("Capataz de escravos/ é o que tu és meu irmão comissário(...)," poema visando os angariadores de contratados e, por isso, de teor idêntico ao já citado "Boi não canta")—, ficaremos com uma ideia aproximada acerca da importância que o Gabriel Mariano-poeta atribuiu a esta problemática.

Contudo, e finalizando esta nossa abordagem, falta ainda referir a presença deste tema na prosa do Gabriel Mariano-narrador. Reportamo-nos, é claro, aos seus contos "Caduca" e "Vida e morte de João Cabafume" (título este que dá nome à antologia que reúne 9 contos do autor[21]). As personagens Caduca e João Cabafume—cada uma delas personagem principal, no conto respectivo que inspira—têm alguns aspectos em comum: masculinas, vivendo na cidade do Mindelo, ambas se recusam a aceitar a contratação para S. Tomé como resolução das suas imensas dificuldades de vida. Aparentemente mais manso e despreparado do que João Cabafume, Caduca, que nem casa tem e dorme na areia da praia, abrigado debaixo de um bote, mantém com nhô Crisóstomo, outra personagem da história, dois diálogos interessantíssimos em que, usando uma argumentação quase infantil, chega à conclusão de que

"Deus é mau," porque não manda chuva e tira os vapores da baía, fontes imprescindíveis de sobrevivência. As respostas de Nhô Crisóstomo, todavia, deixam-no a pensar:

> (...) que é que Caduca vai fazer? E os outros? Que é que os outros vão fazer? Que vão fazer os rocegadores de carvão? E os catraeiros sem bote? E as carregadoras do vais, e as meninas-de-vida? (...) Caduca pensa que ir para o Sul é apenas trocar a hora da morte. (...) Como é que não tem que fazer? Questão era ter chuva e vapor na baía? Se nunca mais cair um pingo de chuva? Se um dia vapor deixar baía para sempre? Que é que Caduca vai fazer? Que é que todos vão fazer? Nhô Crisóstomo falou que não tem trabalho. Por isso todo o mundo deu nome e vai para o Sul. Mas se ninguém saísse? Se todos de repente resolvessem ficar? Questão é fincar pé e pedir trabalho. Mas nhô Crisóstomo falou que não tem trabalho. Questão era fincar pé. Quem é doido? Caduca é doido porque Caduca não vai. Os outros são sabidos porque deram nome no escritório e vão para o Sul.

Como percebemos, é do problema crucial da sobrevivência dos habitantes mais simples e pobres da cidade do Mindelo que o autor nos quer falar. Por isso, as dificuldades são enumeradas; por isso, as perguntas constantemente se repetem e enovelam, num discurso que, propositadamente, confundem ou fazem coincidir o pensamento de Caduca com questões directas que o narrador coloca aos leitores; por isso, a única saída parece ser "ir para o Sul," embarcar para as roças de S. Tomé. Mas Caduca, embora um tanto ingénuo, acaba por concluir o mesmo que os homens da Geração do seu narrador: ir para o Sul é "apenas trocar a hora da morte," não é solução; é preciso ficar na terra, revolucionar mentalidades, exigir investimentos e, portanto, trabalho. Eis, por conseguinte, a grande mensagem deste lindíssimo conto, não muito diferente da que nos é transmitida pelo outro, *Vida e morte de João Cabafume*, em que a personagem principal também recusa a ida para o contrato.

Para resumirmos esta outra história, repetiremos aqui o que já escrevemos, quando elaborámos a "Introdução" que prefacia o volume de contos:

> Desafiador incansável do destino que "queria matá-lo de fome," João Cabafume que "não aceitava desaforo de ninguém. Nem de preto nem de branco. Nem de pobre nem de rico," altivo, de temperamento primário, cioso da sua liberdade, morreu "no meio da baía numa noite de lua cheia" quando fazia contrabando, depois de ter escapado ao contrato que o enviaria para as roças de S. Tomé, de ter

recusado a esmola de comida de D. Maninha e de ter abandonado, de forma violenta, o emprego na loja do Sr. Varanda. Lutou para sobreviver mas não foi subserviente. E enganou o destino, porque não morreu de fome."

Mas reparemos como nos é narrado o episódio em que João recusa o contrato:

(...) Albergue estava cheio. Aqueles pobres de Cristo ouviam, calados, a fala do Sr. Administrador:

— Porque é que não procuram que fazer?

— Dondê trabalho, Sr, Administrador? Porquê que o senhor não mande abrir trabalho?

Sr. Administrador olhou para João Cabafume mas não respondeu. Continuou a falar. Depois tirou da pasta uns papéis castanhos.

— Vocês têm de assinar isto se querem sair. Depois vão ter com o senhor Nogueira. No escritório da casa Gomes...

Todos botaram assinatura e saíram. Todos foram ter de Sr. Nogueira no escritório da casa Gomes. Ele andava catando gente. Por cada cabeça recebia cem escudos. Contou os homens que estavam na sua frente. O Administrador era homem de palavra. Depois falou com eles. Cada um ia receber, adiantado, setenta e cinco escudos. Tirou as notas do cofre. No dia 30 seguiriam no vapor da carreira. Setenta e cinco escudos para quem não tem pão certo é muita coisa. Só João Cabafume não recebeu.(...) Quando Sr. Administrador o chamou no seu gabinete ele disse que ninguém o podia obrigar. Sr. Administrador falou: tu assinaste contrato. João Cabafume respondeu: assinei contrato para sair do albergue. Sr. Administrador gritou: tu tens de ir. João Cabafume abriu a boca: não vou. (...) João Cabafume arrebentou-lhe a boca com duas palmadas na cara!

Eis como alguns caboverdianos—os tais "vadios e desempregados" de que fala Luís Terry—eram arrastados para o 'contrato' e como alguns, à imagem de João Cabafume, conseguiam escapar-lhe.

Com a abordagem destes dois contos de Gabriel Mariano, chegámos à recta final do que nos propusemos elaborar: contextualizando-a no quadro sócio-económico do arquipélago, esboçámos um panorama geral da importância e do tratamento literário que a existência do regime do contrato suscitou em Cabo Verde.

Notas

[1] Dizendo de outro modo, "a preocupação essencial residia na análise do processo de formação social do arquipélago e no estudo das suas raízes" IN Andrade, Mário de, "Prefácio," *Antologia Temática de Poesia Africana*, vol. I, 2ª ed (Lisboa: Sá da Costa, 1976) 5.

[2] IN *Colóquios Cabo-Verdianos* (Lisboa: Junta de Investigações do Ultramar, Centro de Estudos Políticos e Sociais, 1959) 97-113.

[3] Neste ensaio, publicado pela CEI em 1963, Onésimo Silveira dirige um violento ataque aos 'Claridosos,' por não terem patenteado, nos respectivos textos, uma análise séria dos problemas que afectavam a sociedade caboverdiana, acusando-os de cultivarem literariamente o que designou por "regionalismo europeu." Referindo-se especificamente à abordagem que fizeram do drama da evasão, diz, a determinada altura: acabaram por simplificar, arbitrariamente, este complexo problema e por oferecer uma imagem estereotipada do homem caboverdiano, renunciando conscientemente a buscar as raízes psicológicas e sociais do facto emigratório. (10) Mais adiante, distingue, então, o romance *Chuva Braba*, que apelida de romance de intenção social clara, tanto pelo criticismo pertinente à sociedade santantonense, como pela luz que seu epílogo traz à decantada questão evasionista. Esta é pela primeira vez posta, não como uma fatalidade e sim como uma razão forte, deparada a certa altura do processo geo-social do ilhéu, traduzindo uma situação cuja gravidade os outros escritores deformaram, pela implícita solicitação de fuga às raízes do problema emigratório. (14)

[4] O 2º número, pronto a sair, viria a ser proibido pela Censura.

[5] A anterior havia sido no século XVII, com a cultura da cana-de-açúcar, que veio a decair quando o Brasil se transformou num dos seus maiores produtores.

[6] Referimo-nos a *S Tomé e Príncipe: do colonialismo à independência* (Lisboa: Moraes Editores, 1975). Na obra citada se transcreve, na pág. 38, a Portaria Colonial n.º 51, de 9-6-1928, que diz especificamente respeito "aos trabalhadores oriundos da Colónia de Cabo Verde."

[7] Op. cit. 110-111. Ainda sobre as diferenças do trabalhador caboverdiano face aos oriundos das outras colónias africanas, assim como ao tratamento particular que lhe deveria ser proporcionado, aconselhamos vivamente a leitura das páginas 55-58 do livro, já referido, de Carlos Benigno da Cruz. Nessas páginas se faz a transcrição de uma Circular da "Sociedade de Emigração para S. Tomé e Príncipe," datada de Novembro de 1954, onde aparecem "recomendações quanto ao tratamento a dar aos trabalhadores daquela Província," pelo Agente Geral em Cabo Verde (texto em perfeita consonância com as opiniões e conselhos de Luís Terry). Do mesmo livro de Benigno da Cruz, deixamos aqui transcrita uma nota de rodapé da pág.23, que nos parece elucidativa acerca do número de trabalhadores 'importad' para o serviço das roças: "Em 1956, por exemplo, havia nas roças de S. Tomé 9680 angolanos, 6320 caboverdianos e 4910 moçambicanos, em regime de trabalho forçado." Note-se, dadas as proporções dos respectivos territórios de origem, o peso que significaria, para Cabo Verde, a saída de um tão grande número de emigrantes com destino a S. Tomé.

[8] No número especial da revista "Claridade" de 1986—editado na cidade da Praia pelo ICLD-, que constitui uma "Publicação Comemorativa do Cinquentenário de 'Claridade,'" aparece um artigo do escritor Arnaldo França, organizador da colectânea poética de Osvaldo Alcântara, que, intitulado 'Cântico da manhã futura—comentários,' presta alguns esclarecimentos acerca dos poemas nela incluídos, um dos quais relativos a edições anteriores de cada um deles, quando não se trate de poemas até então inéditos. Como não se indica nenhuma outra publicação do poema "Panfleto," estamos em crer que este será um dos editados pela primeira vez em *Cântico da manhã futura*, aparecendo entre parêntesis—na colectânea—aquela que terá sido a data da sua escrita: Junho de 1946.

[9] Cf. Ferreira, Manuel, *A Aventura Crioula*, 2.ª edição (aumentada) (Lisboa: Plátano

Editora, 1973) 272.

[10] Mariano, Gabriel, "Osvaldo Alcântara — o caçador de heranças ou inquietação social," IN *Cultura Caboverdeana (ensaios)*, Lisboa: Vega Ed., 1991) 176.

[11] op. cit.

[12] Op. cit. 30.

[13] Embora saibamos ter sido publicada, pela 1.ª vez, em Roterdão, em 1973, referiremos sempre as páginas da 2.ª edição, publicada no Mindelo, S. Vicente, pelo Instituto de Promoção Cultural, em 1998, de que possuímos um exemplar.

[14] Op. cit. 49.

[15] op. cit. 50.

[16] São eles, pela ordem em que figuram no livro: "caminho longe," "alerta," "serviçal," "consolança," "canta amigo," "voltarás serviçal," "a noite de s. tomé," "emigração," "aviso" e " queixume."

[17] Referimo-nos aos textos intitulados "voltarás serviçal" e "a noite de s. tomé."

[18] Deles tivemos conhecimento através de Mário de Andrade, que os coligiu para a sua *Antologia Temática de Poesia Africana*, op. cit.

[19] Mariano, Gabriel, *Ladeira Grande (Antologia poética)* (Lisboa: Vega Ed., 1993).

[20] IN *Antologia Temática de Poesia Africana*, op. cit.

[21] Mariano, Gabriel, *Vida e Morte de João Cabafume* (Lisboa: Vega Ed., s.d.) [1989].

Obras Citadas

Alcântara, Osvaldo. *Cântico da Manhã Futura.* Praia: Instituto Caboverdiano do Livro, 1986.

Andrade, Mário de. *Antologia Temática de Poesia Africana.* Lisboa: Sá da Costa, 2ª ed, 1977.

Barbosa, Jorge. *Arquipélago.* S. Vicente: Ed. 'Claridade,' 1935.

"Claridade." edição facsimilada dos 9 números da revista. Lisboa: ALAC, 1986.

"Claridade." (Publicação Comemorativa do Cinquentenário). Praia: ICLD, 1986.

Cruz, Carlos Benigno da. *S. Tomé e Príncipe: do colonialismo à Independência.* Lisboa: Moraes Editores, 1975.

Ferreira, Manuel. *A Aventura Crioula.* Lisboa: Plátano Ed., 2.ª ed. (aumentada), 1973.

_____. *No Reino de Caliban.* vol. I, Lisboa: Seara Nova, 1975.

_____. *50 Poetas Africanos.* Lisboa: Plátano Editora, 1989.

_____. Moser, Gerald. *Bibliografia das Literaturas Africanas de Expressão Portuguesa.* Lisboa: INCM, 1983.

Lopes, Manuel. *Chuva Braba.* Lisboa: Edições 70, 1982.

Mariano, Gabriel. *Cultura Caboverdeana (Ensaios).* Lisboa: Vega, 1991.

_____. *Ladeira Grande (Antologia Poética).* Lisboa: Vega, 1993

_____. *Vida e Morte de João Cabafume.* Lisboa: Vega, s.d. [1989].

Martins, Ovídio. *Gritarei, Berrarei, Matarei/ Não vou para Pasárgada.* Mindelo: Instituto de Promoção Cultural, 1998.

Pacheco, Maria Cristina. "Introdução." *Vida e Morte de João Cabafume.* Lisboa: Vega, s.d. [1989].

Silveira, Onésimo. *Consciencialização na Literatura Caboverdiana.* Lisboa: CEI, 1963.

Terry, Luís. "O problema da emigração cabo-verdiana." *Colóquios Cabo-Verdianos.* Lisboa: Junta de Investigações do Ultramar, Centro de Estudos Políticos e Sociais, 1959.

Maria Cristina Pacheco é docente de Literaturas Africanas de Expressão Portuguesa na Universidade do Porto e membro fundador do Centro de Estudos Africanos da Universidade do Porto. Tem um Mestrado com uma tese sobre Tomaz Vieira da Cruz e está na fase final de doutoramento. Entre outros artigos, publicou: "Estruturas narrativas na poesia de Agostinho Neto, António Jacinto e Viriato da Cruz," em *A Voz Igual—Ensaios sobre Agostinho Neto* (Porto: Fund. Engº António de Almeida, 1989); "Prefácio" do volume de contos de Gabriel Mariano, *Vida e Morte de João Cabafume* (Lisboa: Vega Ed., Colecção 'Palavra Africana,' n.º 1, s.d. [1989]; "Tempo de memória de tempos (uma leitura da poesia de Manuel Rui)," em Suplemento Vida & Cultura do "Jornal de Angola," 11 de Fevereiro de 1996; "Humanismo nas primeiras gerações literárias dos Países Africanos de Língua Portuguesa," em Actas do Congresso "L'Umanesimo Latino e l'Umanesimo Africano," realizado na cidade da Praia, Cabo Verde, em Janeiro de 2000. E-mail: crispacheco@clix.pt ou crispacheco@netcabo.pt

Echoes of Cape Verdean Identity: Literature and Music in the Archipelago

Simone Caputo Gomes
Translated by
Luís R. Mitras
Revised by
Mark Streeter

Abstract. This article addresses the close connection between music and literature in Cape Verde, which is able to harmonize those forces that are an index to Cape Verdean identity: bread, sound & phoneme. A choir of illustrious voices plays a melody (or a polyphonic composition) whose theme is the thirst for survival of the Cape Verdean people and the permanence of a Creole culture founded upon a symbolic national trilogy—corn, the discourse on music and literary discourse.

Entre sons de violão & viola
Sons uterinos da ilha que nasce
E consanguíneos do tambor que ama. [...]

Naquel fosfre de morna
polvra de koladera
E exploson de funaná
Corsino Fortes[1]

Taking our lead from an observation by Tomé Varela, the renowned poet and researcher of Cape Verde's oral traditions, we will be guided by his luminous intuition: the proposal to look at the relation between literature and music as an index to Cape Verdean identity. According to Varela, Daniel Spencer's composition "Nhá terra escalabróde" is characteristic of the music produced in Cape Verde:

Pureza ta morá
Na nha terra escalabróde
Na nôs morna, coladera
Funaná e batuque.[2]

Speaking of literature, it is possible to assert that Creole writers have made superb use of the discourse of national music as a means of expressing Cape Verdean identity. *Mon pays est une musique* is the echo we hear from Mário Fonseca's lyre.[3]

José Luís Hopffer Almada's poem "Colina de Pedra" ["Stone Hillside"] seems to act as a response to the song "Nhá terra escalabróde," which is evidence of the bridge that has been built between the two art forms:

ouvi este som dolente
repercutindo a saudade da minha alma
às minhas almas ancestrais
dos degredados e negreiros
A *morna* é um crepúsculo de lágrima
desta súbita e antiga recordação [...]
O *funaná* é uma remota e dolorosa saudade
de outros horizontes
e nele circulam o negro e o
negreiro no imenso rio da farsa sobre a ilha

Eia estrangeiros
ouvi ainda
o *batuque*, o *cola*, a *coladeira*,
o *landum* oh a música da *tabanka*.[4]

[I heard this sorrowful sound
reverberating with the longing of my soul
back to my ancestral souls
men banished to the isles and slave traders
The *morna* is the twilight of that shed tear
of this sudden and ancient remembrance (...)
The *funaná* is a remote and sorrowful longing
for other horizons

where the black man and the slave trader
walk together in the immense river of sham that's over the island

Ahoy foreigners
listen still to
the *batuque*, the *cola*, the *coladeira*,
the *landum* oh the music of the *tabanka*.]

Frank Tenaille, a French journalist and an expert on "world music," correctly states that "*O mais fiel bilhete de identidade de Cabo Verde é a sua música*"[5] ["Cape Verde's most faithful identity card is its music"]; he emphasizes the plurality that arose out of the configuration of what was insular with what arose as a result of syncretism. Vasco Martins, a maestro, composer, poet and novelist, describes the principal modality of Creole music as being akin to the trade winds.[6] Let us sum up his ideas.

A rich popular music arose out of the merging of European, African and South American[7] cultures; this music is represented by forms such as: the *tabanca* on the island of Santiago (ritualistic, repetitive, with sea shells blown in counterpoint, drums and brass bugles), the party rhythms of the feast of the *pilão* ["pestle" or "crusher"] on the island of Fogo (the pestle that is used to pound the corn is also used as a musical instrument), the drums of San Jõm, the mazurka and the quadrille (both of European origin) developed on the island of Santo Antão, the *coladeira* (exuberant, sensual, with hints of the *cumbia* and Afro-Cuban music), the *batuque* on the island of Santiago (the African cry, the women playing percussion on their thighs with cloths and plastic pouches), the *finason* (the lament of the slaves), the *funaná* (a hypnotic trance), the Christian chant—the *divina*—of the island of São Nicolau (four women's voices) and the nostalgic *morna* from the island of Boavista with its harmonies that are the result of musical syncretism (which originated with the Brazilian *modinha* and subsequently crossed with the *lundum*, the fado, the samba, the fox-trot and the mambo).

From the cultural point of view, and given the diversity within the islands, the Creole language, cookery, literature in the Portuguese language and music all constitute important unifying phenomena. Speaking about music, Gabriel Mariano[8] points to the unity of the archipelago in so far as the *morna*, the violin, the guitar, the *cavaquinho* [a very small guitar], and the drum are concerned.

At the first "Encontro da Música Nacional" ["Gathering of National

Music"] António Pedro Monteiro Lima pointed out, once again, that the social function of Creole music, from the traditional to the newer versions, "*é também de fixar de forma inamovível o ideal da Unidade nacional no coração de cada caboverdiano*"[9] ["is also the fixate, in a permanent form, the ideal of national Unity in the heart of each Cape Verdean citizen"].

Commonplace and characteristic scenes of miscegenation and syncretism on the islands are the festivals in honor of the saints' days.[10] Side by side with the celebration of devotion to the Catholic saint is the African "feeling," which is expressed by means of the circle formed by drummers in the main square and where pairs are *colando* [lit. "sticking together" but also performing the "cola"] under a hot and exciting rhythm, their thighs touching. The *Cola Sam Jom* seems to us like a good example of the night-time feast rocked by the "rebencadas" of the drums and by the *coladeira*; the woman are decked with necklaces of *midje iliόde* (corn). The night before, the host organizes the *pilão*, an activity accompanied by a dance when the guests pound the corn for the *xerém*.

In his poem "De boca a barlavento" ["From Mouth to Windward"], Corsino Fortes speaks of the

árvore E o arbusto
Que arrastam
As vogais e os ditongos
para dentro das violas.[11]

[tree AND shrub
That drag
The vowels and diphthongs
Inside the Spanish guitars.]

On the other hand, in his re-invention of the Cape Verdean land,[12] he inserts Spanish guitars into the poetic discourse, accompanied by the pestle/crusher and the drums. Bread (*corn*), sound (the *marulho* and the pestle/crusher) and the poem (phoneme, vowels, diphthongs) are harmonized in a trilogy of nationality—food, music and words are intertwined, to enlarge on the constituent elements of the country's symbolism:[13]

Poeta! todo o poema:
geometria de sangue & fonema

Escuto Escuta
Um pilão fala
    árvores de fruto
        ao meio do dia
E tambores
    erguem
    na colina
    Um coração de terra batida
E lon longe
Do marulho à viola fria
    Reconheço o bemol
Da mão doméstica
        Que solfeja

Mar & monção mar & matrimônio
Pão pedra palmo de terra
        Pão & patrimônio.[14]

[Poet! The entire poem:
    geometry of blood and phoneme
I listen Listen!

A pestle speaks
    fruit trees
        at midday

And drums
    rise up
    on the hillside
    A heart of beaten earth
And fa far
From the *marulho* to the cold guitar
    I recognize the flat note
Of the domestic hand
        That practices sol-fa

Sea & maritime monsoon & matrimony

Bread stone handful of land
 Bread & patrimony.]

Let us now proceed on a brief excursion, in company with those writers who have appropriated the Creole musical heritage, and who have made use of this as a way of reclaiming the singularity of their culture. Let us start with the *morna*, the one thing that binds together Cape Verdeans scattered all over the world.

To trace the history of the *morna* is a complex task, one that has occupied musicians, intellectuals and all Cape Verdeans alike. Some have emphasized the melancholy of the lower tones, the technical-musical basis of the *fado*. Eugénio Tavares, for example, used to compose his *mornas* with a Portuguese guitar; bit-by-bit, the Portuguese guitar came to be substituted by the *violão* [large guitar], the instrument of the *morna* par excellence, with its low ballads and transition chords. The similarities between the *fado* and the *morna* can perhaps be attributed to the (African) musical form that is at the origin of the *fado*, the *lundum*, assimilated in Brazil but which still persists in Cape Verde on the island of Boavista. Others, such as António Aurélio Gonçalves, look for the source of the *morna* in the chants of the female *cantadeiras* [lit. "woman singers"] who sang in solo and with a choir.

Vasco Martins maintains that even though its origin may have been lost in the mists of time, he insists that "*se a morna evoluiu, deveu-se a influências sobretudo brasileiras*"[15] ["if the *morna* evolved at all it was largely as a result of Brazilian influences"], and this is especially true of the *modinha*, on the island of Boavista. From its earlier (more syncopated) form to the way it is performed today, the journey of the *morna* has culminated in its election as the most popular song form in the archipelago.

Eugénio Tavares and the musicians Luís Rendall, Francisco Xavier da Cruz (B. Léza), Jorge Monteiro (Jótamont), Armando António Lima (Lela de Maninha), Manuel de Jesus Lopes (Manuel d'Novas) have demonstrated the exchange that exists between poetry and music in their *mornas* interpreted by Cesária, Titina, Arlinda Santos, Mité Costa, Zenaida Chantre, Celina Pereira, Tetê Alhinho, Bana, Amândio Cabral, Manecas Matos, Dudu, Djack Monteiro, Zezé di nha Reinalda, Fernando Quejas, Mário de Melo, Marino Silva, Djosinha, Voz de Cabo Verde, Tubarões, and Bulimundo, among others.

From the pre-*Claridade* days of Eugénio Tavares and Pedro Monteiro Cardoso, the authors of *Mornas, cantigas crioulas* [*Mornas, Creole Songs*]

(1932) and *Folclore Caboverdiano* [*Cape Verdean Folklore*] (1933) until our day, the musical dimension has assumed a privileged place in Cape Verdean literature.

"Mornas Passam Cantando as Crioulas Trigueiras"[16] ["Mornas Go Past Singing the Creole *Trigueiras*"] in Pedro Cardoso's *Hespérides* [*Hesperides*]. The creation of the *morna* by Toi is at the center of Manuel Lopes's tale *Galo* [Que] *Cantou na Baía* [*The Cockerel that Sang in the Bay*] (1936). Manuel Ferreira's collection of Cape Verdean short stories goes by the title of *Morna* (1948), and there is also the novel *Hora di Bai* (1962). In the nineties we have *Mornas Eram as Noites* [*Tender Were the Nights / The Mornas Were Night*] (1994) by Dina Salústio—the idea applies, also, to the protagonists of her texts.

Thus we see varied ways in which the relationship between the *morna* and literature is being developed. Let us look at some of the variations through concrete examples.

For Pedro Cardoso the "Morna" was the

> Lídima filha, pois, da Trova lusitana!
> Traduzindo a alegria e a "dor da nossa raça."
> Em ritmo polariza a Alma caboverdiana![17]
>
> [Untainted daughter, then, of the Lusitanian Ballad!
> Translating the joy and the "pain of our race."
> Its rhythm splits the Cape Verdean soul asunder!]

In Jorge Barbosa's *Arquipélago* (1941), the "Brother" identifies with the *morna* which

> parece que é o eco em tua alma
> da voz do Mar
> e da nostalgia das terras mais ao longe [...]
>
> o eco
> da voz da chuva desejada,
> o eco
> da voz interior de nós todos,
> da voz de nossa tragédia sem eco!18

[is just like echo in your soul
of the voice of the sea
and the nostalgia for distant shores (...)

the echo
of the voice of the awaited-for rain,
the echo
of the voice deep within us,
of the voice of our tragedy that has no echo!]

In his invitation to the Cape Verdean poet Daniel Filipe, who was raised in Portugal to visit the islands—an invitation extended to other Portuguese poets—Barbosa adds:

Que venham ouvir
a alma do arquipélago
cantando mornas![19]

[Come and listen
to the soul of the archipelago
singing the *mornas*!]

Manuel Ferreira is in agreement with the above when he emphasizes the collective nature of the musical dimension; he asks: "*até que ponto o homem crioulo não transferiu o seu sofrimento social para a dor da morna amorosa?*"[20] ["to what extent did not the Creole man transfer his social suffering to sorrow of the *morna* that sang of love?"]

In Ovídio Martins's poem, which celebrates the arrival of the "Chuva em Cabo Verde" ["Rain in Cape Verde"], the dancing and playing of the *morna* is at the center of the festival:

  Festa nas Ilhas
Soluçam os violinos choram os violões
nos dedos rápidos dos tocadore [...]
Nas ruas nos terreiros
  por toda banda
as mornas unem os pares

nos bailes nacionais
Mornas e sambas
mornas e marchas
mornas mornadas.[21]

[Celebration on the islands
The violins sob, the guitars cry
in the nimble fingers of their players (…)
On the streets in the squares
all over
Mornas unite dancing pairs
at the "national balls"
Mornas and *sambas*
mornas and parade music
mornas mornadas.]

With respect to what it says about the dialogue between the literary and the musical arts, "Galo Cantou [Que] na Baía," the short story that gives title to Manuel Lopes's book, can be regarded as exemplary.

As the text unfolds it also reproduces the process of gestation of a *morna* by Toi, the *morna*-maker; the central image in the text is that of a cockerel singing in the dawn. As a kind of preamble to his composition Toi the watchman proposes a "philosophy" of the *morna*, one that makes use of Western imagery:

> a morna veio do mar. Como Vénus (imagem colhida num tal Alcindo que fazia parte dum grupo literário), surgiu pura e nua das espumas do mar, e também como Vénus, é a protectora do amor, porque foi à sua sombra que os nossos avós armaram casamento e o farão também os filhos dos nossos filhos, afirmara Toi, com eloquência, num baile nacional do Tolentino.[22]

> [the *morna* came from the sea. Like Venus (the image he had gotten from a certain Alcindo who was part of a literary group) it arose pure and naked from the foam of the sea and, like Venus, it is the protectress of love because it is under her shadow that our grandparents got married and that the children of our children will get married; this is what Toi declared with such eloquence during a "national ball" at Tolentino.]

To compose his *mornas* Toi needs to be close to the sea:

Quando sinto que estou para "ter morna," procuro sombra. E sombra com mar diante. Só com mar diante...

A mesma inquietação voltou a formigar-lhe lá dentro, transformada em vagas palavras confusas e em notas de música sem sentido. Esta, não obstante, já revelava um ritmo embalado, de remo na forqueta, mas era, por enquanto, uma melopéia estranha, elementar, quase reminiscente, toada de coisa recordada, sons ainda dúbios em busca de equilíbrio [...].

De súbito estacou. Apurou os ouvidos. Suspenso assim alguns segundos entre a realidade e o sonho, escutou dentro do cérebro um chacoalhar de vozes e ecos. Toi reconheceu o atalho que, habitualmente, o levava aos ocultos tesouros. [...]

A quadra saíra assim inteirinha, de improviso. [...] Vênus nascia completa, com cabeça, tronco e membros, e alma. Declamou, cantarolando, duas, três vezes a quadra recém-nascida das ondas do mar.[23]

[When I feel "I'm getting a *morna*" I look for the shade. And shade with the sea before me. Only with the sea in front...

The same feeling of disquiet began to eat at him and it was transformed into vague and confused words and into senseless musical notes. Despite this, it already revealed a lulling rhythm of the pitchfork but, for the time being, it was a strange melody, basic, almost the tune of a memory of something he remembered, its sounds were uncertain, as if they were in search of some sort of harmony (...).

Then all of a sudden he stopped. He pricked up his ears. Lost between reality and dream for a few seconds, he heard from within his brain the agitation of voices and echoes. Toi recognized the road that usually led him to hidden treasures. (...)

The stanza came out complete, and no planning was required. (...) Venus was born complete, with a head, trunk, members—and a soul. Crooning along, two or three times he recited the stanza that had been born from the waves of the sea.]

In this description of the poetic process of giving birth to the *morna*, the tiredness associated with the effort of composing the first stanza is compounded with the difficulty of organizing the second one. It is only after the rooster has crowed and flapped its wings—a metaphor for Toi's having found his expression—that his search will have come to fruition:

> Veio mesmo do mar.—Ahn! Cantar de galo, galo canta na baía! Sonha naturalmente que está empuleirado numa árvore que balança com a aragem. Porto abandonado. É como uma casa velha, cheia de aranhas e bichinhos vagabundos. Até galo já canta na baía! Mas é poético. Se fosse rouxinol ou cotovia, como nos livros, mais poético seria. Mas não temos cotovias, temos é galo. [...] Qualquer um que o ouve cantar, fica sabendo que a manhã não tarda, o sol vem perto. Toi declama: "*Galo cantâ na baía...*" assim mesmo na língua sabe da nossa terra... [...] A segunda quadra irrompe inteirinha, numa catadupa de palavras e música:
>
> *"Já cantâ galo na baía*
> *Sol cá ta longe de somâ.*
> *Comam ta longe de Maria*
> *Scuro ta continuâ..."*
>
> Era a linha dorsal, o eixo. Era o nascimento de Vênus. Morna salgada, morna de mar.[24]
>
> [It really did come from the sea.—Ah-ha! The crowing of the cockerel, the cock crowing in the bay! Naturally, it is dreaming that it is perched on a tree held in sway by the wind. Abandoned harbor. It's like an old house, full of spiders and stray little animals. Even the cock is singing in the bay! But it is poetic. If it were a nightingale or a skylark, like it always happens in books, then it would be more poetic still. But we have no skylarks here; what we have is a cock. (...) Anyone who hears it singing will know that soon it will be morning, that the sun is close by. Toi recites: "*Galo cantâ na baía...*"—"Cock crows in the bay"—in the language of our country... (...) In a catapult of words and music the second stanza arises fully formed:
>
> *"Já cantâ galo na baía*
> *Sol cá ta longe de somâ.*
> *Comam ta longe de Maria*
> *Scuro ta continua..."*
>
> That was the backbone, the axis. It was the birth of Venus. Salty *morna*, maritime *morna.*]

Beginning to feel that he has become a rival of Eugénio Tavares in having his art so tirelessly praised by Salibânia, Toi savors the reverence of those who play *mornas*, sambas, and Brazilian *modinhas*—so recently arrived in the country with the steamers. They wait for his new creation while they drink grog and while Jack with his fine handwriting writes out the lyrics of the *morna*. And the central image of his song gains in strength and becomes more clearly defined:

> Um galo de guerra, com o seu grito de alerta, alerta está!—Sê rosto, não. Quero antes...—Cerrou as pálpebras, com raiva. Põe lá: "GALO CANTÂ NA BAÍA."[25]

> [A warring cock with its shout of alert: Alert!—No, I'd rather have... His eyes were firmly shut, in rage. He writes instead: "GALO CANTÂ NA BAÍA."]

The singing of the cockerel heralds the coming of the morning. Venus[26] is born: Toi's briny *morna*.

Let us examine in more detail the images that Manuel Lopes works around in order to produce a theory of the genesis of the *morna*. Botticelli's "Birth of Venus" (Venus as the goddess of love, beauty and conception), which is associated with the strength of Toi's creative act, appropriated the dominant ideologies of classical antiquity in pictorial form and established the norm for Renaissance beauty: humanism, harmony, ideal beauty. The Neo-platonic ideas developed in Marsilio Ficino's writing and in the poems of Poliziano, combined with certain Christian precepts, seem to be the main inspiration behind Sandro Botticelli's painting; the construction of the painting reveals a re-reading of the texts about the myths of Venus-Aphrodite emerging from the sea (*Anadiômene*) in a seashell that the Aeolian gods had taken to the beach. According to Botticelli's version—which is in agreement with the one provided by Apelles, which in turn is inspired by what Hesiod had said in his *Theogony*—Venus-Aphrodite is born out of the foam (*aphros*) in the sea, which is really a mixture of the semen and the spilled blood of Uranus (the Sky), who was castrated by his son Cronus-Saturn in a power struggle. In the Renaissance, painting the shell seems to symbolize the fertilizing and creative powers of the water.

What is important to note is that the lyricism that is present in the work of Botticelli is less concerned with action than with the adoption of a contemplative attitude, of aesthetic admiration; he is, in effect, making the apology for the beauty embodied in the figure of Venus, an emblematic representation of totalizing perfection, the image of an imaginary beauty. If we take this Venus to be a representation of the feminine condition, what stands out from it is a sort of static aesthetic autism and, consequently, an obstacle to living life fully.

We would like now to expand on these considerations by speaking about the image of the cockerel. We recall that the image is part of the collective memory of many peoples; it stands for vigilance, creativity and the resurrection, and also for the male and for power.[27] A Persian tradition that has remained, despite its having been Christianized, holds that the cockerel wakes the dawn and summons humankind to greet the sacredness of perfection. In ancient Greece, a cockerel was offered up to the god Priapus (the son of Dionysus and Aphrodite) so that men could ensure their manliness and virility.

A possible interpretation for the joining of the images of Venus (Aphrodite) and the cockerel in Manuel Lopes's short story would situate the *morna*, driven by the trade winds, in the context of the power of the masculine lyre of Toi (the Guard, the vigilant watchman, the cock), a kind of creativity that summons us to contemplate perfect beauty.

The underlying vision that is behind the appearance of the *morna* in the short story by Manuel Lopes contrasts with the way this theme is treated in more recent Cape Verdean fiction written by women. In the work of these women love and beauty stand back from the sphere of *Venustas* (or Absolute Beauty), a derivation of that absolute One embodied by Venus, and instead opt for the plurality that reality has imposed on conventions. Venus escapes from the shell.

Mornas eram as noites (1994), a collection of short stories by Dina Salústio, foregrounds how women take on the *morna* just by operating within the hermeneutics of a Cape Verdean woman's daily life: "… *de como elas se entregaram aos dias*" ["of how they gave themselves to the days of their life"] is the opening quote of the work.

Bearing in mind that we are speaking about the signs that reveal that a female perspective and the reality of woman's daily life has been incorporated in literary works written in Creole, we should recall another time—which would go from the time of the *Antologia da ficção caboverdiana* [*Anthology of Cape Verdean Fiction*], which Baltazar Lopes edited in 1960, and consisted of texts written by male authors,[28] to the two volumes of interviews carried out by Michel Laban[29] in 1992, where only Orlanda Amarílis stood beside 24 writers—when the Cape Verdean canon demonstrated little openness to female authorship.

Beginning in the nineties, women, who had been silenced in the history of literature, start painting true portraits of Creole daily life, oil paints on canvas: **women with the landscapes in the background**[30] **or landscapes with women in the background**, enabling the possibility of addressing themes that speak of women themselves and to write texts and scenes where women are the main protagonists.

In an interview that Dina Salústio granted to the writer of this article on November 12, 1994 in Praia, she spoke about her recently published book and stated that it had been born out of

> necessidade de publicar as inúmeras histórias de mulheres, histórias de vida que passam por mim [...]. Não são ficção, é cá um encontro que é verdade, um momento só. [...] Não fiz uma selecção desses textos, só o primeiro foi intencional, para querer mostrar o meu reconhecimento a estas mulheres caboverdianas que trabalham duro, que fazem o trabalho da pedra, que carregam água, que trabalham a terra, que têm a obrigação de cuidar dos filhos, de acender o lume. Quis prestar uma homenagem a esta mulher. [...] As histórias acontecem, ao sabor do vôo. Falo das mulheres intelectuais, daquelas que não são intelectuais, daquelas que não têm nenhum meio de vida escrito, falo da prostituta, falo de todas as mulheres que me dão alguma coisa, e que eu tenho alguma coisa delas. [...] Em Cabo Verde, quando nasce uma menina, ela já é uma mulher.
>
> [the need to publish the countless stories of women, those life stories that I witness (...). They are not fictional stories, it's something that happens that's true, a single moment. (...) I didn't make a selection of these texts, except for the first one, which was intentional, and that's because I wanted to give credit to these Cape Verdean women who work hard, who do a laborer's job, who fetch the water, who work the land, who have to take care of their children, light the fire. I wanted to pay homage to that kind of woman. (...) These are the kind of stories that happen. I speak about intellectual women, those that are not intellectual, I speak about those that have never been written about, I speak of the prostitute, I speak of all those women that have given me something, and those that are somehow part of me. (...) When a girl is born in Cape Verde she is already a woman.]

Her texts, like condensed plots of short films, give emphasis to the *morna*:

it appears in the title, theme and structure. "The nights were music" is a possible reading for *Mornas eram as noites.* Woman's music. But also: music of nationality and cultural identity.

A true instance of appropriating the voice and actions of women (from silence to the scream) in a Creole world, a woman's story/song about the woman in Cape Verde, *Mornas eram as noites* reveals to us a scenario of feminine complicity and curiosity, of machismo and the reconsideration of machismo (on the part of woman and on the part of man himself), of woman's freedom (either postponed or appropriated), madness, witchcraft, drunkenness, lesbianism, prostitution, adolescent or child mothers, domestic violence, child abuse and child prostitution, paedophilia, as well as other themes.

The short story "Álcool na noite" ["Alcohol at night"], either an allusion to or else the reason for the title of the book, exposes the tragic dimension to the lives of many women in Cape Verde; Cesária's *morna* (*Ó mar, Ó mar!*—O sea, O sea!) is in the background:

> A *noite* estava serenamente calma e o calor convidava a estar-se a olhar para as estrelas, preguiçosamente [...]. De lá das bandas do cemitério *uma voz canta uma morna.* Tudo normal se a voz não parecesse sair dos intestinos de algum bicho em vez de uma garganta humana, por muito desafinada que fosse. *Era de uma mulher*, reconheci com mais cuidado. Aliás, *eram as vozes de duas mulheres. A segunda faz coro* com obscenidades e a desarmonia, o desleixo transparecido e o despudor agridem os ouvidos. [...] Vêm-se aproximando. E estão bêbadas. [...] Sinto raiva. Agora posso vê-las no arco iluminado pelo candeeiro. Parecem-me jovens. [...]
> A noite não tinha mais magia. Acho que nem estrelas. [...] vou pensando, enquanto desço as escadas.
> E os passos falam vergonha, humilhação e revolta. E pena.[31]

> [The *night* was serenely calm and the heat was almost an invitation to look at the stars, indolently (...). From around the cemetery *a voice sings a morna.* There was nothing strange about this if it wasn't for the fact that the voice didn't seem to come from a human throat, no matter how out of tune it was, but seemed to erupt from within the guts of some animal. After listening more carefully I realized that voice belonged to a woman. In fact, it wasn't one but *the voices of two women. The second voice was like a dissonant chorus* spewing obscenities; the obvious sloppiness and the sexual candor offended my ears. (...) I see them coming. They are drunk. (...) I am enraged. I now see them in the arch illuminated by the streetlight. They look young. (...)

> The night had lost its magic. And I think its stars, too. (…) I'm thinking as I walk down the stairs.
> And those steps speak of shame, humiliation and outrage. And sorrow.]

Venus has refused the ideal beauty, and has taken on the imperfections and the multi-faceted riches of reality. The laughter of chickens wakes Cape Verde up as much as does the cock's crow[32] (and the sound of the drum and of *catchupa* [sic] in the frying pan). Looking at it from a woman's perspective, the *morna* goes beyond the ecstasy of creation and contemplation. It is deeply rooted, as Dina Salústio's narrative tells us, in the "*esconderijos privados*" ["private hiding-places"] of Creole society; it exposes hypocrisy and extreme situations, it brings into the open those feelings fed by the waves of the sea and the screams of the night, it helps to create a space for a social conscience, education and struggle.

Salústio's text, so full of pain at times, is the text of a woman who thinks and who writes and who, over and beyond seeking to express the intimacy of a voice, wants to give voice to all women, wants to write about the communal reflection of all women, one that takes the other into account and all the many ways he has changed. The struggle for a place in society, lyricism and humor combine in these narratives, and they produce that powerful effect of discourse: communication. Daniel Spínola maintains that Dina Salústio "*inaugura uma nova forma de comunicar e um novo modo de percepção do mundo*"[33] ["introduces a new form of communicating and a new way of perceiving the world"] in Cape Verdean fiction, one that involves readers and provides them with a new way of looking at social or existential situations which have ossified or have become stagnant.]

In chorus with Dina Salústio's "solo" is the portrait of Augusta painted by Fátima Bettencourt in *Semear em pó* [*Sowing in Dust*] (1994), a text that also explores the interaction between literary and musical discourses. The sensual maidservant exposes her passions through her song (or the "secret beat" of the *coladeiras*), which end in pregnancy and in fatherless children.

> Toda ela era energia pura, os pés descalços não paravam quietos, com os braços roliços abraçava o próprio busto num visível esforço para se conter. Irradiava dela uma chama que na época eu não soube compreender mas agora não me surpreende que se mantivesse acesa e nítida nas minhas lembranças de muitos anos atrás. […] Minha mãe, meio desconfiada de tanta alegria de viver, resmungava contra o

> conteúdo duvidoso de algumas músicas de sua preferência. Até que um dia ela não apareceu no trabalho e mandou uma prima avisar que estava passando mal por causa da gravidez. [...]
> —Logo vi que havia mouro na costa! Bem que sempre embirrei com aquela cantiga que ela não tirava da boca "*esse frio cum tem na corp ê só bô sô ê q'ta trame elê*"! Imaginem uma cantiga destas com o calor que tem feito![34]

> [She was all pure energy, her barefoot feet couldn't keep still, her rolling arms hugged her own breast in a visible effort to control herself. A flame seemed to glow out of her, one that at the time I did not understand, but now it doesn't surprise me that this flame remained clear and alive in my memories of so many years ago. (...)
> My mother, somewhat sceptical of so much joy for life, moaned about the dubious content of some of the music she liked. Until one day she didn't appear at work and sent her cousin to say she wasn't feeling too well because of the pregnancy. (...)
> "I knew there was a man lurking in the background! Well, I never could stomach that song she wouldn't stop singing, '*esse frio cum tem na corp ê só bô sô ê q'ta trame ele!* Imagine how much heat this song must have generated!"]

Masterfully, Fátima is able to combine tragedy with humor, making the social critique all the more biting:

> o homem que arranjou levou-a para Santo Antão e pô-la *a trabalhar na estrada* onde apanhou uma tuberculose. [...] Acabou morrendo, deixando o primeiro filho pois o segundo se fora por conta de uma diarreia ao sol e ao vento das estradas do Porto Novo. A minha mãe tomou conta do garoto e criou. É um dos meus irmãos adoptivos. Vive na Suécia, dedica-se à música nas horas livres, *um gosto que certamente apanhou quando boiava no útero materno.*[35]

> [the man who fixed her took her to Santo Antão and *put her to work on the road* and because of that she got TB. (...) She ended up dying, leaving her first-born behind; the second-born had already died because of some diarrhea in the sun and wind of the roads of Porto Novo. My mother took the boy in and raised him. He's one of my adopted brothers. He lives in Sweden, and in his free time he devotes himself to music, **a** *taste he had certainly acquired while he was floating in his mother's womb.*]

What we have tried to demonstrate, beginning with the opening quotation, is that music ("the womb-like sounds of an island that's born") has provided a rich wellspring for literary texts that wish to reclaim tradition and assert a Cape Verdean cultural identity.

The sound of the slave-ships celebrated in "Ritmo de Pilão" ["The Rhythm of Crusher"] by António Nunes, the whispering of people's poetry in Jorge Barbosa's "Violão" ["Guitar"], music as act of daring in "Viola partida" ["Broken Portuguese Guitar"] by Maria Margarida Mascarenhas, Zinda's aching *morna* in the story by Ivone Aída, the thrill of the *tabankas* in Canabrava's poetry, the distant sound of the original *batuque* in Vera Duarte's *O Arquipélago da Paixão*,[36] would permit us to proceed with our song, with a choir of so many different voices, echoes, indefinitely. Because...

> Na ilha do meio do Atlântico
> existe uma pequena imagem de mulher [...]
> Está em cima de um fonolito que canta quando sopram os ventos alísios.[37]
>
> [On the island in the middle of the Atlantic
> there's this small image of a woman (...)
> It's on top of a clinkstone that sings when the trade winds blow.]

Notes

[1] Fortes 1986, 31-2.

[2] Varela 60. "Purity resides / In my furrowed land / In our *morna, coladeira / Funaná* and *batuque.*

[3] Fonseca.

[4] Almada 1990, 44-45; my emphasis.

[5] Tenaille 47.

[6] Martins 1993, 44. And also 1999, 34-38.

[7] On the **circularity** of the Brazilian literary text, the *modinhas* and the Cape Verdean Carnival consider the comments made by Orlanda Amarílis 142. See also Vasco Martins 1989, 46, when he speaks of the profound influence the Brazilian *modinha* on what he calls the "*Morna preliminar*" ["preliminary morna"].

[8] Mariano 74.

[9] Lima 92.

[10] Lopes Filho 97-113.

[11] Fortes 1980, 7.

[12] Leite, A. M. "ÁRVORE & TAMBOR ou a reinvenção da terra cabo-verdiana." In Fortes 1986, 11-18.

[13] Consider corn as an element in the Cape Verdean flag.

[14] Fortes 1986, 8.

[15] Martins 21.

[16] Cardoso, P. qtd. in Ferreira 1989, 162.

[17] Ibidem 158. "Morna," a poem from *Folclore caboverdiano.*

[18] Barbosa, J. qtd. in Ferreira 1989, 166. Poem "Irmão."

[19] Barbosa 56.

[20] Ferreira 1967, 234. See also Gomes 1993, 48-49.

[21] Martins, O. qtd. in Ferreira 1989, 228-229.

[22] Lopes, M. 13.

[23] Ibidem 15-17.

[24] Ibidem 36-7. My emphasis.

[25] Ibidem 43.

[26] Recall, also, that Venus is the morning star and the star of the dawn.

[27] The cock is a symbol of power in Lusophone communities.

[28] Lopes, B.

[29] Laban, M.

[30] Research carried out at the Faculdade de Letras da Universidade Federal do Rio de Janeiro [Faculty of Arts of the Federal University of Rio de Janeiro], in the Setor de Literaturas Africanas de Língua Portuguesa [Section of African Literatures in Portuguese] (coordinated by Prof. Carmen Lucia Tindó Ribeiro Secco), from 1999 to 2001, with a resarch grant, Visitante Nível Especial A, from FAPERJ. Title: "Óleo sobre tela, mulher com paisagem ao fundo (a prosa de autoria feminina em Cabo Verde)."

[31] Salústio 46-47. My emphasis. Consider the structure of the traditional *morna* where a female soloist was accompanied by a female choir.

[32] Ibidem 40.

[33] Spínola 205.

[34] Bettencourt 34. "Secreto compasso," a short story. The emphases are mine; the text in Creole is a stanza from a traditional song; it means: "this cold I have in my body only you can take away."

[35] Ibidem 36. My emphasis.

[36] Poems by António Nunes and Jorge Barbosa, short stories by Maria Margarida Mascarenhas and Ivone Aída ("Zina ó grogue nha sina"), poems by Canabrava ("Passageiro do tempo") and Vera Duarte ("A canção do corpoamor"), respectively.

[37] Martins 1989a, 13.

Works Cited

Almada, José Luís Hopffer. *À sombra do sol.* Praia: Grafedito, 1990.

———. "O papel do milho na simbolização da identidade cultural do cabo-verdiano." *Cabo Verde: insularidade e Literatura.* Paris: Karthala, 1998. 63-80.

Amarílis, Orlanda. "O desbravar da escrita." *Literatura e História: três vozes de expressão portuguesa.* Ed. Tania Franco Carvalhal & Jane Tutikian. Porto Alegre: Editora da Universidade Federal do Rio Grande do Sul, 1999.

Barbosa, Jorge. *Jorge Barbosa: poesia inédita e dispersa.* Ed. Elsa Rodrigues dos Santos. Lisboa: ALAC, 1993.

Bettencourt, Fátima. *Semear em pó: contos.* Praia: Instituto Caboverdiano do Livro e do Disco, 1994.

Chevalier, J. & Gheerbrant, A. *Dicionário de Símbolos.* Rio de Janeiro: José Olympio, 1996.

Ferreira, Manuel. *A aventura crioula ou Cabo Verde, uma síntese étnica e cultural.* Lisboa: Ulisseia, 1967.

———. *50 poetas africanos.* Lisboa: Plátano, 1989.

Fonseca, Mário. *Mon pays est une musique, poèmes, 1984-1986.* Nouakchott: Éd. de l`auteur, 1986.

Fortes, Corsino. *Pão & fonema.* 2nd ed. Lisboa: Livraria Sá da Costa, 1980.

———. *Árvore & tambor.* 1st ed. Praia -Lisboa: Instituto Caboverdiano do Livro-Publicações Dom Quixote, 1986. Prefácio by Ana Mafalda Leite, "ÁRVORE & TAMBOR ou a reinvenção da terra cabo-verdiana."

Gomes, Simone Caputo. *Uma recuperação de raiz: Cabo Verde na obra de Daniel Filipe.* Colecção TESE. Praia: Instituto Caboverdiano do Livro e do Disco, 1993.

———. "Óleo sobre tela: mulher com paisagem ao fundo (a prosa literária de autoria feminina em Cabo Verde)." *A mulher na Literatura.* Boletim do GT. Maceió: EDUFAL/ANPOLL, 2000. 128-136.

Laban, Michel. *Encontros com Escritores.* Porto: Fundação Eng. António de Almeida, 1992.

Lima, António Pedro Monteiro. "Intercâmbio e influências musicais: o caso do kaoguiamo." *Fragmentos: Revista de Letras, Artes e Cultura.* [Praia: Movimento Pró-Cultura] 3-4 (Dec. 1988).

Lopes, Baltazar, ed. *Antologia da ficção caboverdiana contemporânea.* Praia: Imprensa Nacional, 1960.

Lopes, Manuel. *Galo cantou na baía e outros contos.* Porto: Edições 70, 1984.

Lopes Filho, João. *Cabo Verde: retalhos do quotidiano.* Lisboa: Editorial Caminho, 1995.

Mariano, Gabriel. *Cultura caboverdeana: ensaios.* Lisboa: Vega, 1991.

Martins, Vasco. *A música tradicional cabo-verdiana — I. A morna.* Praia: Direcção-Geral do Patrimônio Cultural/Instituto Caboverdiano do Livro e do Disco, 1989.

———. *Navegam os olhares com o vôo do pássaro.* Praia: Instituto Caboverdiano do Livro, 1989(a).

———. "Ventos alíseos." *Révue Noire.* [Praia: Bleu Outremer] 10 (Sept.-Nov. 1993).

———. "A música cabo-verdiana. Breve introdução." *Mar além.* [Lisboa: Mar além-GTMR-CDP] 2 (May 1999): 34-38.

Salústio, Dina. *Mornas eram as noites.* Praia: Instituto Caboverdiano do Livro e do Disco, 1994.

Secco, Carmen Lucia Tindó Ribeiro, ed. *Antologia do mar na poesia africana de língua portuguesa do século XX. Vol. II: Cabo Verde.* Rio de Janeiro: UFRJ, 1999.

Spínola, Daniel. "Mornas eram as noites." *Cabo Verde: insularidade e Literatura.* Paris: Karthala, 1998. 205-208.

Tenaille, Frank. "Saudade majeure." *Révue Noire.* [Praia: Bleu Outremer] 10 (Sept.-Nov. 1993): 47.

Varela, Tomé. "Cabo-verdianidade: uma virgindade no seio de um triângulo por penetrar." *Revista Pré-textos.* [Praia: Associação dos Escritores Cabo-verdianos] (June 1994): 59-60.

Simone Caputo Gomes is retired Adjunct Professor at the Fluminense University in Brazil. She holds a doctorate in Portuguese Language and Literature. She has published *Uma recuperação de raiz: Cabo Verde na obra de Daniel Filipe; Letras em Tese; África e Brasil: letras em laços*; and has co-authored a book of poetry, *Como se fosse música.* E-mail: simonecg@ar.microlink.com.br or simone@seleto.com

Cape Verde: People and Places. Photographs

José M. Rodrigues

The photographs shown here are the result of his travels through the ten islands of Cape Verde in 1997. Among hundreds of photos, he photographed the tomb of Eugénio Tavares on the island of Brava, the volcano of Fogo and the black floor of magma, traveling a cultural route between everyday life, music, literature and the poetry of the image.

José M. Rodrigues loves flamenco and knows better than anyone else the light of Vermeer, having lived in Holland part of his life. There he became a photographer and founded the well-known gallery *Perspektief* and the magazine that bears the same name, which were at the center of a photographic revolution in Holland. He does not see great differences between himself, light and nature. The portrait, the flavors of life, travels, trees and the stones of light from Alentejo are proofs of his fidelity to the dream. He won the Prémio Pessoa in 1999; however, well before that he had photographed the waters of the Amstel and the waters of the Cape Verdean and São Tomé and Príncipe's seas. A free-spirited and spontaneous outlook on a peculiar destiny and course of life belongs to José M. Rodrigues, an international photographer represented in the best known galleries of photography, a world traveler and a keeper of magical images.

BOUTIQUE GIZELLE
BOUTIQUE GIZELLE
CAFE LISBOA
CAFE LISBOA

Postcolonial Cape Verdean Literature/
Literatura Caboverdiana Póscolonial

Projetos literários em antologias caboverdianas

Maria Nazareth Soares Fonseca

Resumo. Este artigo afirma a importância de publicações que resgatam a produção literária dos países africanos de língua portuguesa para as pesquisas que se realizam à distância do contexto em que os textos se produzem. Tomando como referência o volume editado com os números da revista *Claridade*, em 1989, por Manuel Ferreira, e a Antologia dos novíssimos poetas caboverdianos, *Mirabilis de veias ao sol*, publicada em 1988, são ressaltadas características da literatura produzida em Cabo Verde em dois momentos históricos de importante significação.

Para os pesquisadores das literaturas africanas de língua portuguesa, que vivem distante das livrarias e editoras portuguesas ou que não têm condição de visitar com freqüência os países africanos de língua portuguesa, o acesso aos textos dos escritores africanos dá-se de forma ainda restrita e isso dificulta a investigação mais detalhada de questões que os próprios textos acentuam.

Esta realidade, vivida com freqüência por alguns pesquisadores brasileiros, obriga-os a produzir estratégias que possam contornar as dificuldades que sempre aparecem em busca de resultados mais produtivos. A carência de obras específicas de determinados autores pode ser contornada pela pesquisa do material fornecido por antologias e esse trabalho pode resultar em soluções bastante animadoras, principalmente quando se valorizam os elementos da produção do volume, as informações dadas pela seleção de autores e textos e se reflete sobre a intenção político-literária que transparece nos poemas.

O estudo das antologias revela-se, portanto, como um excelente recurso para quem investiga à distância os textos literários produzidos na África de língua portuguesa em diferentes momentos da fase anterior à independência e na do pós-independência, época em que os projetos literários assumem novos percursos, procurando revigorar conquistas já alcançadas mesmo quando a dureza da situação histórica exigia outros modos de expressão. Atualmente, os contatos mais freqüentes com as editoras portuguesas, via Internet, ajudam o pesquisador distante a ampliar o acervo de textos, mas, pelo menos no caso do Brasil, o alto preço dos livros ainda é um grande impedimento à maior circulação dos textos africanos entre os pesquisadores. O estudo das antologias continua a ser um recurso válido de acesso a uma amostragem consistente da produção poética que traz em si marcas do momento sócio-histórico da sua produção. O material das antologias propicia várias direções de pesquisa e sugere temas para uma comparação frutífera com a produção literária de outros espaços culturais.

No caso específico da literatura de Cabo Verde, as antologias organizadas por Mário Pinto de Andrade e Manuel Ferreira[1] apresentam-se como excelente material que nos possibilita não apenas o contato com diferentes feições literárias da fase anterior à independência do país, mas ainda o acesso a informações sobre ideais e idéias que, em momento de grande efervescência política, fortaleceram alguns dos movimentos literários que revelaram as ilhas ao mundo. A *Antologia temática de poesia africana*; na noite grávida de punhais (1975), organizada por Mário Pinto de Andrade, como o próprio título indica, agrupou poemas a partir de temas gerais que perpassavam as literaturas de língua portuguesa na África. A coleção *No reino de Caliban* (1997), organizada por Manuel Ferreira, particulariza as manifestações poéticas de Angola, Moçambique, Cabo Verde, São Tomé e Príncipe, áreas onde o fenômeno literário adquiriu um relevo significativo, já na fase colonialista. A antologia se organiza tentando construir um percurso literário que vai dos chamados precursores à fase imediatamente anterior ao 25 de abril de 1974, marco do término da dominação portuguesa em África.

Todavia, para me ater ao propósito que norteia este trabalho, qual seja o de reafirmar a colaboração valiosa que as antologias de poemas africanos de língua portuguesa, publicadas em diferentes fases, podem prestar principalmente àqueles pesquisadores que, distantes de Portugal e da África, insistem na investigação das literaturas africanas, assumo um recorte que me propicia discutir duas experiências bastante significativas para o estudo da literatura de Cabo Verde. Vou me referir, em primeiro lugar, ao volume que resgata a produção da revista *Claridade*, organizado por Manuel Ferreira. O volume é publicado em 1986, cinqüenta anos após o lançamento do primeiro número da revista, que nasceu na cidade do Mindelo, ilha de São Vicente. Este importante material possibilita ao investigador identificar os percursos literários traçados pelos escritores caboverdianos envolvidos com a publicação e, a partir deles, avaliar a produção literária levada à luz pela revista *Claridade,* comparando-a com a de outros movimentos literários que se desenvolviam em vários pontos da África e das Américas na mesma época. Numa fase em que o ideário colonialista instigava a produção de textos voltados à valorização do homem e da terra, definidos por processos perversos de exclusão, *Claridade* desponta, no campo literário caboverdiano, como um divisor de águas. Algumas particularidades da revista, que, segundo Manuel Lopes, um dos fundadores, não tinha um programa, embora fosse incentivada por estímulos concretos e imediatos (Lopes, apud Ferreira, 1986, p. XXX), fornecem excelente material de pesquisa, principalmente quando se compara a revista com aspectos de outras publicações que marcam o percurso literário das diferentes nações africanas de língua portuguesa.

Um fato que se destaca na revista *Claridade* é o que comprova a presença do Brasil em Cabo Verde, reconhecida por vários estudiosos e referida tanto em textos literários, quanto na Imprensa em geral. A relação afetiva, cultural e literária com o Brasil é reconhecida como estímulo a uma consciência de pertencimento e na modelagem de uma expressão literária que rompe com fórmulas gastas e preconiza a liberdade de expressão. O ardor com que os escritores modernistas brasileiros expõem o seu projeto de renovação é bem acolhido pelos escritores caboverdianos, Baltazar Lopes, Jorge Barbosa e Manoel Lopes, fundadores da revista *Claridade.* O depoimento de Jorge Barbosa é importante para testemunhar a presença brasileira em Cabo Verde:

> Influência da literatura brasileira teria havido, por certo, nos modernos escritores caboverdianos, que por essas paragens se lançaram na aventura da produção literária (...). Deles aproveitamos, pois, a descoberta e a experiência, que nos contagiaram com o seu entusiasmo de coisa nova. (Barbosa, apud Ferreira XXXI)

O escritor, dentre os vários poemas em que o Brasil e a literatura dos modernistas são referidos, apresenta-nos um endereçado a Manuel Bandeira, "Carta a Manuel Bandeira" no qual, poeticamente, recorta caminhos que ligam Cabo Verde ao Brasil, através "de sonhos e de versos," construídos "no outro lado do mesmo mar." (Barbosa, apud Ferreira 25).

Baltazar Lopes destaca a importância da leitura de romances como *Menino do Engenho* e *Bangüê,* de José Lins do Rego, *Jubiabá* e *Mar morto,* de Jorge Amado e de obras do escritor Marques Rebelo que chegavam às mãos dos escritores "em sistema de empréstimo." O mesmo escritor ressalta a emoção e o alumbramento propiciado pela leitura de poemas de Manuel Bandeira e Jorge de Lima. Em outro momento, destaca afirmações do sociólogo brasileiro, Gilberto Freyre, para reforçar o "lastro comum" existente entre as culturas do Brasil e as de Cabo Verde, principalmente porque constituídas por misturas étnicas e lingüísticas muito próximas. (Lopes, apud Ferreira 4, 15-22). Em vários poemas de escritores caboverdianos, essa proximidade de feições lingüísticas e sociológicas faz do Brasil uma terra irmã, com características semelhantes às que se mostravam em Cabo Verde.[2] As imagens do Brasil reforçam uma visão nascida do "alumbramento" dos poetas caboverdianos pela poesia brasileira que, como nos diz Manuel Ferreira (1989) era vista como "o compêndio, o modelo, (...) a fórmula sagrada" (157).

O escritor Manuel Lopes também ressalta a presença da literatura brasileira na formação de uma consciência estética "nacionalizada," motivada por um "encontro repercussivo de determinantes rácicos, (...) e por fontes quase idênticas" (Lopes, apud Ferreira XXXI). A imagem de um Brasil próximo a Cabo Verde era fortalecida pelas experiências literárias com que os modernistas brasileiros inventavam uma outra tradição: a rebeldia e a contestação de uma literatura pautada em formas rígidas e em preceitos ultrapassados. A "unidade de sentimento e de cultura" defendida por Gilberto Freyre em vários textos, inclusive em *Casa Grande e Senzala,* perpassa a reflexão de Baltazar Lopes em vários momentos da *Claridade.*

Ressalte-se, portanto, que a presença brasileira em Cabo Verde motivou a produção de uma gama de textos que conotam a incursão da literatura na leitura do ambiente físico e na invenção de mitologias que ajudavam a compor um projeto cultural nacionalista, conforme afirma Pires Laranjeira (1992). Com essa intenção, as coisas do Brasil aparecem nas páginas da revista *Claridade* e demonstram formas interessantes da ancoragem de textos brasileiros nas ilhas. Os poetas do modernismo brasileiro, por vias às vezes contraditórias, chegaram às ilhas e ajudaram a fortalecer as imagens de uma terra em que as misturas étnicas e lingüísticas apresentavam um resultado positivo. Nesse aspecto, a recepção dos textos de Gilberto Freyre em Cabo Verde—e na África portuguesa de modo geral-é material interessante de pesquisa, pois permite contrapor as diferentes leituras das idéias do sociólogo brasileiro em países africanos de língua portuguesa às que circularam no Brasil à época em que seus mais importantes livros foram publicados.

Os escritores caboverdianos, ao atestarem a presença importante de obras brasileiras na formação de uma consciência de nacionalidade literária, não desmerecem, entretanto, outros estímulos. Dentre esses estímulos, a revista portuguesa *Presença* destaca-se pelos ecos modernistas que levou a Cabo Verde. Manuel Ferreira, no item 2. do seu importante texto "O Fulgor e a esperança de uma nova idade," prefácio ao volume de 1986 que recupera os números de *Claridade*, vê a revista portuguesa como um elo entre os jovens poetas caboverdianos e os novos aspectos "da estética metropolitana." A esse respeito, é importante o testemunho do teórico:

> Em suma, é substancial o **corpus** de dados e informações escritos ou orais que iluminam a dimensão do papel fundamental da **Presença** coimbrã no projecto de mudança literária e cultural que agitou Cabo Verde nos anos 30 rumo ao seu destino histórico. (Ferreira XXVII)

A pesquisa dos dados fornecidos pela revista *Claridade* ressalta presenças exógenas na formação de uma consciência de nacionalidade em Cabo Verde, em convivência com outros elementos que contribuíram internamente para a visualização de um conjunto de preocupações e experiências comuns que fortaleciam uma forma de se estar no mundo. Politicamente, a intenção era a de "fincar os pés na terra," como afirmam os fundadores da revista; era assumir as questões específicas de cada ilha como componentes de uma cultura geral, a caboverdiana. Apreender Cabo Verde como um conjunto de relações concretas—geográficas, econômicas, sociais—fortalece o entendimento de um homem marcado pelas contradições do espaço físico e por outras que definem a situação de se estar nesse lugar. As imagens de terra acentuam a angústia marítima do ilhéu, como bem percebe Gabriel Mariano (1991), circulam nos textos da revista e expõem os modos como a literatura se vê e como ela percebe o lugar em que é produzida. A nova experiência encaminhada pela *Claridade* traduz diferentes modos de se compreender a trajetória literária das ilhas e os esforços para que a literatura pudesse nelas ganhar contornos próprios. As imagens ligadas à terra, as referências ao destino do homem caboverdiano—"Viver sempre vergado sobre a terra,/ (...) pobre/ingrata/querida"[3]—reforçam os rumos a serem assumidos por uma literatura que se afirma em Cabo Verde. Em *Claridade*, ao lado dos textos literários — poemas e contos —, proliferam reflexões sobre aspectos etno-sociais das ilhas, sobre a língua falada no arquipélago, o crioulo caboverdiano e redefine-se um espaço cultural recortado em ilhas, definido pela presença forte do mar, dados que lhe dão traços peculiares.

Anos mais tarde, os poemas da Antologia dos Novíssimos Poetas Caboverdianos; *Mirabilis de veias ao sol*, organizada por José Luís Hopffer Cordeiro Almada e publicada pela Editora Caminho, em 1991, constitui-se um novo material de produção literária. As revelações poéticas que, em inúmeras publicações, vieram à luz após o 25 de abril de 1974, revelam o ressurgimento da poesia caboverdiana em contornos temáticos, estéticos e ideológicos cultivados no pós-independência.

Dado o grande número de poetas que fazem parte da coletânea, torna-se necessário estabelecerem-se alguns norteadores para que as diferentes feições do volume possam ser avaliadas. A primeira característica que chama a atenção do leitor está na apresentação dos poemas: alguns escritos em crioulo, outros em francês e em inglês, além da grande maioria em português. Como assinala o organizador, a realidade sociolingüística vivida pelo povo das ilhas de Cabo Verde transpõe-se para a Antologia e torna-se um elemento da pluralidade que se expõe no volume.

Evidenciam-se, por outro lado, alguns dos sinais dos novos tempos literários das ilhas de Cabo Verde: a feição metalingüística encaminha uma tendência também presente em antologias de Angola e Moçambique que acolheram os textos poéticos publicados após 1974. As indagações dos poetas sobre a função da poesia nas tardias sociedades pós-coloniais alimentam o material poético a ser trabalhado por eles. A reflexão, via literatura, sobre o lugar do poeta e da poesia nos novos tempos do pós-independência, em Cabo Verde, está, por exemplo, no poema "Meus versos," de Alberto Lopes, que apresentando seu poema como porta-voz dos novos tempos e seus versos, "seivas que alimentam nova vida/ pólen de novo amor e de nova alegria", registra a tônica do período. Ao falar de si a literatura busca outros caminhos e procura delinear as feições da multiplicidade das experiências e vivências em Cabo Verde. Em vários poemas, a alusão reiterada ao novo diz bem do propósito de se perceber a liberdade conquistada como expressão de um "mundo sem cor, sem cárcere, sem limite," como bem acentua o verso de Alberto Lopes.

Já José Cabral em "Um poema para o ano dez," ao conclamar os seus pares para a construção de "um poema diferente," insiste no abandono de métricas e rimas bem comportadas e na eleição de novas formas que se façam próximas ao canto dos tempos novos.

Os ventos desses novos tempos induzem o labor poético a reconfigurar a face multifacetada de espaços onde as tentativas de experimentação de novos ritmos e formas assumem as transformações que aportaram às ilhas do arquipélago. Com a intenção de celebrar as "lusoáfricas," as ilhas onde brota a "poesia morena," Correia e Silva brinca com as possibilidades da língua portuguesa na elaboração do poema "A poesia do reverso," insistindo em aliterações e jogos de sonoridades: "tão linda a ledice lírica/vero verso e vertigem" (218). No poema, a imagem de Pasárgada relembra a evasão aflitiva dos anos de opressão e alude aos novos tempos simbolizados pelo "pássaro da paz."

Por outro lado, valorizando também recursos fônicos, Jorge Soares cria "Uma história de amor" (269-70), imprimindo velocidade aos versos que estruturam a história das "personagens" António e Julieta. Sem a preocupação de acentuar no poema uma função metalingüística explícita, Soares o elabora com a utilização de formas mais lúdicas que permitem que nele se ouça a "trova nossa," cantada por Cabral no poema "Um poema para o ano dez" (74-78).

Em vários poemas exploram-se os materiais de poesia que se vêm cultivando nos países africanos de língua portuguesa na busca de ultrapassagem de componentes marcadamente sociais. Como acentua José Luís Hopffer Almada, os percursos dos novos poetas de Cabo Verde fazem-se semelhantes à *mirabilis*, que cresce "na margem desértica do mar" (26). A imagem da planta, ao revigorar a nova poesia, disseminando-a pelos caminhos atordoados pelo sol e pela dureza dos novos tempos, reestabelece as experiências e os sentimentos individuais que se apropriam dos versos do poema. No título da coletânea, os elementos sol e mar reforçam a experiência literária propiciada pela construção poética que se faz *mirabílica*, resistente às intempéries, às agruras dos ventos e das secas, e metaforizam as novas paisagens que os poemas anunciam muitas vezes em crioulo.

Muitos poetas da coletânea, semelhantes a outros, cujos poemas estão em antologias dos novos poetas de Angola e de Moçambique, procuram retomar as questões sociais e os recursos poéticos são enfatizados como forma de se ressaltarem os traços fortes da cultura.[4] Vozes femininas deixam-se ouvir no espaço da antologia e tecem, com os recursos poéticos, o que Simone Caputo[5] denominou de "cumplicidade de fêmeas", retomando verso do poema de Dina Salústio, publicado à p. 155 da *Mirabilis de veias ao sol*. É nesse espaço de cumplicidade, de mãos dadas com o outro, que o eu-poético deixa que as palavras moldem uma dimensão feminina da vida preocupada também com a captação dos "sussurros de prazeres dolorosamente cambiados em mercado negro"[6]. Os textos poéticos permitem falar de medos e indecisões, dos cercos e das armadilhas que definem o espaço das mulheres acostumadas com a tradição da espera: "presas ao cais, esperando, submissas, os amantes, filhos e maridos que saíam para a pesca da baleia ou iam estudar em Portugal," como nos informa Carmem Tindó Secco (1999).[7]

Os "Exercícios poéticos," de Vera Duarte, transgridem os espaços demarcados e acolhem as "imagens interditas e as sensações proibidas" (518), e de algum modo procuram romper com a tradição de mulheres submissas e silenciadas. Os versos da poeta deixam-se visitar por sensações que perpassam o corpo da mulher e as letras do texto recolhem as indecisões que pontuam o medo de entregar-se ao prazer: "Ceder à paixão, deixar-me arrastar por esta força magnífica. Sentir-me feliz..." (521). Ou articulam estratégias que ajudam a sufocar as pulsações de um corpo que aspira ao prazer:

> Sublimar é palavra d´ordem. O amor e a paixão a libido e o prazer. No altar dos valores supremos. Sublimar e agora manter estóica e estupidamente secretos os diálogos que comigo mantenho contigo. (518)

Outros poetas, na Antologia *Mirabilis de veias ao sol* buscam fortalecer as tradições que recuperam a linguagem do corpo e de seus desejos. A poesia intimista se mostra no traçado de uma poética que conclama as manifestações do corpo, as imagens que traçam a geografia múltipla das ilhas e as sonoridades várias que a escrita procura recuperar. Os poemas recolhem imagens e odores das ilhas mágicas em festas imensas de cheiros. Os poetas voltam-se para o seu próprio interior e deixam emergir as inquietações que os caboverdianos vivenciam, quer no contato com a escassez de chuvas e os ventos fortes que varrem as ilhas, quer no inexorável destino que os impele a outros mundos em busca de sobrevivência. Daí a constante referência, em muitos dos poemas, à solidão, à carência de afeto e ao fardo duro legado pela geografia das ilhas.

Ao recuperar algumas tendências que já se mostravam em diferentes momentos da poesia africana de língua portuguesa, a Antologia *Mirabilis de veias ao sol* faz-se, como as demais antologias, um espaço de gestação de identidades. Os poetas-ainda que abandonem a feição marcada pelo compromisso com projetos políticos e desviem do meramente circunstancial, tão próprio da poesia de combate, dos sentidos previsíveis da urgência com que a literatura percorreu, em vários pontos da África, as trilhas abertas pelos projetos de unidade nacional-também registram o desencanto que caracterizou a época do pós-independência. Tal sentimento incita a produção de novos arranjos expostos na Antologia *Mirabilis de veias ao sol* e acentua a preocupação com o fazer poético e com a definição do lugar da literatura numa sociedade de diferentes sotaques e múltiplas colorações.

Em muitos poemas em que a escrita percorre as sonoridades do crioulo, trazendo-as para a página do livro, procura-se recuperar elementos herdados da tradição oral, visíveis em versos como "caco-lecó,/gal djá cantá,/nhôs dã nhá pó/môça robada."[8] Em outros poemas podem também ser percebidas outras articulações com a terra, com a corporeidade das ilhas, com traços da geografia de espaços "entri mar i céu" (399). A tradição da poesia participante, aos poucos, cede lugar à procura de outros rumos, ainda que a rudeza das necessidades concretas insista em exigir o compromisso do poeta com os problemas do país.

Quando se pensa nos sentidos encaminhados por um tipo de literatura que se produz atenta aos acontecimentos, cuidadosa com as tradições e memória oral, talvez seja possível identificar nesse esforço o desejo de se constituir enquanto instituição na qual se gestam alguns dos sentidos explicitados por Pierre Nora (1984), ao cunhar o conceito de "lugares de memória," para identificar funções específicas de espaços em que as sociedades modernas, impulsionadas por rápidas mudanças, imaginam organizar o passado e preservar os vestígios de sua história. A escrita literária, ao acolher os costumes e tradições, abre-se também às alterações que se vão inscrevendo nos cenários em transformação. Por isso muitos temas presentes na Mirabilis de veias ao sol são também indicadores do mal-estar dos nossos tempos porque ratificam a certeza de que só é possível reproduzir os gestos que acolhem as lembranças de manifestações coletivas que se perdem na corrente de transformações da vida contemporânea.

A reedição das revistas *Claridade*, em 1986, ao salvar do esquecimento os documentos que testemunham o esforço de uma geração para firmar os alicerces literários de uma nação em construção, propicia o contato com textos que, em sua variedade, revelam os caminhos que os escritores, os chamados claridosos, procuravam trilhar. O volume organizado por Manuel Ferreira, que também é responsável pelo excelente texto de introdução com que analisa a produção literária de gerações anteriores e posteriores à *Claridade*, assume, de certo modo, a eficácia dos arquivos. O gesto de salvar da perda irreparável o material publicado nos números da revista que vão de março de 1936 a dezembro de 1966, possibilitou aos pesquisadores vasculharem, mesmo à distância das ilhas, as referências de uma época e investigarem as reservas de memória de sociedades transformadas pela violação colonial (Nora 1984). O gesto de Manuel Ferreira aquece a frieza dos dados coletados com a paixão com que pesquisou as culturas africanas, particularmente a caboverdiana, para doar aos pesquisadores de outras épocas a efervescência de manifestações que concretizaram projetos literários que cada vez mais se distinguem uns dos outros.

É com um pouco da paixão dos colecionadores de objetos, dos organizadores de coletâneas literárias que percebemos as antologias como um material de pesquisa em que pulsa uma variedade de vozes. Na recepção dessas vozes, recuperam-se vestígios da memória que a escrita procurou perpetuar. Os gestos de leitura retomam os dados da memória, os apelos do passado já transmudados pela experiência da escrita e os inscrevem em novos atos de preservação de lembranças fertilizadoras.

Em novos arranjos, os textos fornecidos pelas coletâneas analisadas procuram dar conta dos conflitos vividos por sociedades que se localizam entre o culto de tradições e a experiência, às vezes brutal, de seu apagamento; entre as manifestações características da cultura e a inserção dos valores que a escrita arrebanha. Participam, portanto, como os de outras coletâneas e antologias literárias, das contradições dos "lugares de memória." Inseridos em produções híbridas que acolhem as perdas de grupos, as reservas de memória, precisam contar com outro tipo de capital simbólico que a exposição do material coletado aufere de públicos diferenciados. Por isso, esse material literário que se produz com a disposição de resgatar do esquecimento tendências e feições literárias que, transitando entre uma visão totalizante das literaturas africanas e outra que se liga a projetos de feição nacional, fortalece os contatos com novos públicos, com pesquisadores distantes que chegam aos textos, às vezes, sem muito conhecimento das motivações histórico-sociais que os produziram. No caso específico do pesquisador brasileiro, é sempre muito agradável ver-se refletido em muitos dos textos que as coletâneas recuperam e, através deles, poder conhecer as circunstâncias em que a literatura do Brasil esteve presente na formação literária das ex-colônias portuguesas na África e, como acentua Manuel Ferreira, "com maior expressão e profundidade" em Cabo Verde.

Notas

[1] Refiro-me, particularmente, à *Antologia temática de poesia africana; na noite grávida de punhais* (1975), organizada por Mário de Andrade e à coleção *No reino de Caliban* (1997), organizada por Manuel Ferreira.

[2] É interessante observar as imagens do Brasil que circulavam, na época, entre os escritores caboverdianos. Manuel Ferreira refere-se à diversidade de visões sobre o Brasil e, no prefácio à edição da revista *Claridade*, de 1986, alude muito adequadamente ao "mito do Brasil," nascido da percepção do país latino-americano como um "lugar onde se forjou uma nova fisionomia humana e social."

[3] Versos do poema "Irmão," de Jorge Barbosa, publicado em *Ambiente* (1941) 20.

[4] Ver, sobre as perspectivas da nova poesia de Cabo Verde, o ensaio "Mar, memória e metapoesia, na lírica caboverdiana," de Carmem Lúcia Tindó Secco (1999).

[5] Caputo (2001) 113-132.

[6] Verso do poema "Apanhar é ruim demais," de Dina Salústio, 159.

[7] Ver ensaio citado na nota 4.

[8] Versos do poema de Mário Macedo Barbosa, " Caco-lecó" [Apud Ferreira, (7) 33].

Obras Citadas

Almada, José Luís Hopffer Cordeiro, (org.). *Antologia dos novíssimos poetas cabo-verdianos; Mirabilis de veias ao sol.* Lisboa: Caminho, 1991.

Andrade, Mário Pinto de. *Antologia Temática de Poesia Africana; na noite grávida de punhais.* Lisboa: Sá da Costa Editora, 1975.

Andrade, Mário Pinto de. Tenreiro, Francisco E. (Org.). *Poesia Negra de expressão portuguesa.* (1953). Lisboa: n.p., 1982.

Ferreira, Manuel (org.). *Claridade, revista de arte e letras.* 2ª ed. Linda-a-Velha: Arte, Literatura, Arte e Cultura, 1986.

Ferreira, Manuel. "A emergência da intertextualidade afro-brasileira." *O discurso no percurso africano I.* Lisboa: Plátano Editora, 1989. 139-186.

Fonseca, Maria Nazareth. "Afrodições: voz e gestualidade na poesia africana de língua portuguesa." *Metamorfoses.* Cátedra Jorge de Sena para Estudos literários Luso-afro-brasileiros. Rio de Janeiro: UFRJ, 2000. 153-161.

_____. *Vozes femininas em afrodicções poéticas: Brasil e África portuguesa.*

Martinho, Ana Maria Mão-de-Ferro (org.). *A mulher escritora em África e na América Latina.* Évora: Editorial NUM, 1999. 173- 185.

Laranjeira, Pires. *De Letra em riste; identidade, autonomia e outras questões da literatura de Angola, Cabo Verde, Moçambique e São Tomé e Príncipe.* Porto: Edições Afrontamento, 1992.

Leite, Ana Mafalda. *Oralidades & escritas nas literaturas africanas.* Lisboa: Colibri, 1998.

Mariano, Gabriel. "Inquietação e serenidade, aspectos da insularidade na poesia de CaboVerde. *Cultura caboverdiana, ensaios.* Lisboa: Veja, 1991. 95-120.

Nora, Pierre. *Les lieux de mémoire.* Paris: Gallimard, 1984.

Secco, Carmem Lúcia Tindó Ribeiro. "Mar, memória e metapoesia na lírica caboverdiana." *Antologia do Mar na poesia africana de língua portuguesa* do séc. XX. Rio de Janeiro: Faculdade de Letras da UFRJ, 1999. 9-27.

Sepúlveda, Maria do Carmo. "Duarte: Vera poesia multifacetada no espelho Caboverdiano." *Brasil & África; letras em laços.* Sepúlveda, Maria do Carmo & Salgado, Maria Teresa, (org.). Rio de Janeiro: Atlântica, 2000. 329-347.

Maria Nazareth Soares Fonseca é Professora do Programa de Pós-graduação da Pontifícia Universidade Católica de Minas Gerais, Brasil. Entre outros artigos, publicou: "Mário Pinto de Andrade e questão das literaturas nacionais," Mata, Inocência & Padilha, Laura Cavalcante (org.), *Mário Pinto de Andrade: um intelectual na política* (Lisboa: Edições Colibri, 2000); "Afrodições: voz e gestualidade na poesia africana de língua portuguesa," *Metamorfoses* (Cátedra Jorge de Sena para Estudos literários Luso-afro-brasileiros, Faculdade de Letras/UFRJ, 2000) 153-161; "Poemas para ler e sentir," Cuti, *Sanga (Poemas)* (São Paulo: Mazza Edições 2002). 7-11. A sua área de pesquisa atual é Literaturas africanas de língua portuguesa, literatura afro-brasileira. E-mail: mfonseca@pucminas.br

"Chronicling" from the Center of the Periphery: *Estórias Contadas (Tales Told)* by Germano Almeida[1]

Russell Hamilton

Abstract. Germano Almeida, one of Lusophone Africa's and, certainly, Cape Verde's most prolific writers, is best known for *O Testamento do Sr. Napumoceno da Silva Araújo* (1989). A movie based on this first novel has received excellent reviews and delighted viewers in Europe and the United States. What has engaged moviegoers and readers alike is Almeida's talents as a teller of tales. Almeida's novels, short stories, and non-fiction contain narratives and dialogue that are replete with humor and a perceptiveness that reflects the author's unremitting quest for historical truths. What comes forth in Almeida's *estórias* is lived history and social satire recounted from an often autobiographical and editorializing perspective. Nowhere is the latter more apparent than in *Estórias Contadas* (1998), a collection of 55 *crónicas*, originally published in the Lisbon newspaper *Público*. Almeida makes clever use of the *crónica*, which, in the Portuguese-speaking world, has evolved into a unique literary genre, with elements of quotidian history and op-ed provocation. The present article focuses on several of the *crónicas* that elucidate Almeida's talent for historicizing and storying the uniqueness of Cape Verdean identity and the archipelago's paradoxically central and peripheral location in Africa, the former Portuguese empire, and the broader world.

Germano Almeida unquestionably qualifies as one of Cape Verde's and, indeed, all of postcolonial Lusophone Africa's most prolific and engaging writers. From 1989, the year in which his first major work appeared, until the present, Almeida has published nine works, including four novels, two collections of short stories, a non-fictional account, a volume of chronicles, and what might be termed a fictionalized biography.

To date Almeida's best-known work is *O Testamento do Sr. Napumoceno da Silva Araújo* (1989; *The last will and testament of Mr. Napumoceno da Silva Araújo*). It is, in fact, the film version of this premier novel that most contributes to Germano Almeida's name recognition beyond the Portuguese-speaking world. According to "Colonialism & Liberation: O Testamento do Senhor Napumoceno — Napumoceno's Will," a promotional piece appearing in the magazine *Library of African Cinema 2000*, this Cape-Verdean movie of universal appeal is "…the first truly Pan-Lusophonic film production and certainly the first to be released in North America" (17). The "Pan-Lusophonic" label derives from the fact that Francisco Manso, the film's director, is Portuguese, most of the actors are Brazilians, and the soundtrack features the singing voices of Cape Verdeans Cesária Évora, often referred to as the Barefoot Diva, and Tito Paris. Both of these vocalists have gained worldwide renown for their renditions of Cape Verde's traditional *mornas* and *coladeiras*.

In Cape Verde and the other four Lusophone African countries, as well as in Portugal and Brazil, Germano Almeida's publications, particularly his novels and short stories, continue to grow in popularity. At this point it is worth noting that with regard to the author's own distinction between his novels and short stories, during an interview published in the Lisbon newspaper *Público*, in April of 1998, Almeida commented that when he sits down to write, he doesn't necessarily have the pretension of writing a novel. In the interview Almeida averred: "Quando eu começo a escrever, pergunto-me o que é que eu vou escrever e as estórias vão saindo, é-me completamente indiferente." (3; "When I begin to write, I ask myself what it is that I'm going to write and the stories just start coming out; what they are makes no difference to me"). That is to say, it makes no difference to the author whether a short story, novella, or novel results from his writing. Telling a story or a series of stories is the author's concern, and Almeida is, indeed, a master teller of *estórias* (the latter being equivalent to "tales"). His approach to weaving tales, which, as he writes them down, sometimes evolve into novels, brings to mind the epigraph that appears in João Ubaldo Ribeiro's *Viva o Povo Brasileiro* (1984; *Long Live the Brazilian People*).[2] The epigraph that introduces this monumental novel reads: "O segredo da Verdade é o seguinte: não existem fatos, só existem histórias" ("The secret of arriving at the Truth is the following: facts do not exist, only stories exist").

As does his Brazilian counterpart, in seeking to arrive at historical truths, Germano Almeida spins imaginative tales, many of them replete with sardonic humor and social satire. As regards humor and satire, *A Família Trago* (1998; *The Trago Family*), Almeida's most recent major work, has attracted considerable critical acclaim. This fictionalized family biography or genealogical novel, set on the writer's home island of Boa Vista, has struck some readers as being autobiographical, a designation that Almeida flatly denies. He does admit, however, that the story of the patriarch nho Trago ("nho" being a creolized form of "senhor", meaning "mister" or "sir") is in large measure the story of the author's grandparents.

In much of his writings Germano Almeida reveals his penchant for the autobiographical, if not overtly in his novels then certainly so in his non-fiction. With the autobiographical component in mind, I now turn to a consideration of one of Germano Almeida's works that technically falls into the category of non-fiction. Although the title of said volume is *Estórias contadas* (1998), which translates literally as "tales told" or, more freely, as "stories already told," the work is identified as a collection of 55 *crónicas* (chronicles), each originally published in *Público*, the aforementioned Lisbon newspaper.

At this juncture I must comment on the meaning of *crónica*, as it relates to its English cognate. According to *The Random House Dictionary of the English Language*, "chronicle" has but one definition: "A chronological record of events; a history." English-speaking readers should be advised, however, that although a cognate of "chronicle," the Portuguese *crónica* has multiple denotations. Thus, upon consulting *Novo Aurélio: O Dicionário da Língua Portuguesa* we find no fewer than seven definitions. The first of these is similar to the single one found in English-language dictionaries. Without citing all of the remaining six definitions listed in *Novo Aurélio*, I do think it worthwhile to cite three of them, starting with number 3, which reads: "Pequeno conto de enredo indeterminado" ("A short short story with an indeterminate plot"). Even more pertinent with respect to Almeida's *Estórias Contadas* is definition 4, which reads: "Texto jornalístico redigido de forma livre e pessoal, e que tem como temas fatos ou idéias da atualidade, de teor artístico, político, esportivo, etc., ou simplesmente relativos à vida cotidiana" ("A journalistic text composed in a free and personal form, having as themes facts or ideas reflecting the present, and written in a style that is artistic, political, sportive, etc., or simply related to everyday life"). Finally, I cite definition 5, which seems especially relevant with respect to what the word *crónica* comes closest to denoting and connoting in the writings of the Anglo-American world: "Seção ou coluna de revista ou de jornal consagrada a um assunto especializado" ("A section or column of a magazine or newspaper devoted to a particular topic"). In Anglo-American journalistic terminology, the key word is "column," such as the syndicated columns that appear on the op-ed pages of many U.S. newspapers. I should emphasize the fact that in the Portuguese-speaking world the *crónica* has become a quasi-literary genre often originally published in newspapers.[3]

Bearing in mind, then, that in the context of the Portuguese-speaking world the *crónica* combines past history with accounts of lived or quotidian history, journalism, personal opinion, and storytelling, I turn now to a consideration of the form and content of a small, but significant sampling of the fifty-five *crónicas* originally published as the equivalent of opinion/editorial commentaries in *Público*, the Lisbon daily. The reason for opting to consider Almeida's quasi-literary, at times autobiographical tales is that individually and collectively they constitute a perceptive, often provocative, cleverly elaborated, and aesthetically pleasing representation of the historical, contemporary, and, in some ways, future place of Cape Verde as a nation-state and society in Africa, in the Portuguese-speaking world, and in the world at large. Some prospective readers might be taken aback and/or amused to see that the title of the collection's first *crónica* is "Cabo Verde é o Centro do Mundo" ("Cape Verde is the center of the world"). By the time the initially puzzled, bemused, or simply unsuspecting reader finishes the chronicle's initial three paragraphs, he or she will most likely be intrigued. After reaching the *crónica*'s final sentence, most readers will be enlightened, delighted, and intellectually stimulated.

The first-person narrator begins by informing the reader that when he was a child "...o mundo todo resumia-se à ilha da Boa Vista"(9; "...the whole world was summed up in the island of Boa Vista"), where Germano Almeida was born and raised. The chronicler/storyteller then goes on to admit that eventually maps afforded him and his classmates a "confused consciousness" of other geographical entities whose names their teachers obliged them to commit to memory. The *cronista* recalls, however, that the existence of these other lands was summed up on maps drawn on small sheets of paper that in no way compared with the "immensity" of Boa Vista island, where it could take a day's travel to go by foot or even by donkey from one village to another. When the adolescent Germano Almeida did gain definitive proof of the existence of other worlds, he still maintained that "...éramos, sem dúvida, o 'centro do mundo,' onde tudo vinha parar e morrer, desde ingleses de

Sua Majestade e judeus de Rabat, como se podia confirmar pelo pequeno cemitério, a 500 metros do túmulo de Maria, onde repousavam Isaak Ben'Oliel e seus descendentes" (11; "...we were, without a doubt, the 'center of the world,' where everything ended and died, from His Majesty's Englishmen and Jews from Rabat, as confirmed by the small cemetery, some 500 meters from the tomb of Maria, where Isaak Ben'Oliel and his descendents lay in repose"). In other words, Boa Vista was "cosmopolitan," as evidenced by the early presence of the British who passed through on their way to the Caribbean and Africa. Moreover, just as on other Cape Verde islands to which relatively large numbers of Sephardim and "new Christians" emigrated, there is a Jewish cemetery on Boa Vista.

Continuing with his boastful topophilia, or love of place, the chronicler waxes etiological when he recounts that it is said that after God made the world and distributed the riches that would sustain his children—blacks in Africa, whites in Europe, and yellows in Asia and the Americas—He noticed that his hands were soiled with bits of clay. He then vigorously shook His hands in the air to free them of the dirt. Shortly thereafter, He saw tiny islands—in other words, the pieces of clay—floating in the ocean not far from the west coast of Africa. His helpers, also noticing the islands, told God that inadvertently He had created more lands. Unfortunately, there were no riches left to distribute, and, moreover, there were no people left to inhabit the islands. Because God had no intention of creating the islands in the first place, He told His concerned assistants that no one need inhabit these tiny bits of land. When he created this etiological fable Germano Almeida no doubt had in mind a poem written in the 1930s by the classic Cape Verdean poet Jorge Barbosa and first published in his collection *Arquipélago* (1935). The first stanza of Barbosa's poem, titled "Panorama: Destroços de um Continente" ("Panorama: The flotsam and jetsam of a continent"), reads: "ilhas perdidas / no meio do mar, / esquecidas / num canto do mundo" (17; "islands lost / in the middle of the ocean / forgotten / in a corner of the world"). One of the paradoxes of traditional Cape Verdean ethos is that the archipelago is both the center of the world and a group of obscure little islands scattered on the ocean at a continent's periphery.

Continuing with his account, Almeida, giving a mischievous twist to his prose, then reports that the Portuguese, either because they were unaware of the Lord's mandate or because they purposely disregarded it, transformed Cape Verde into a entrepôt (in other words, a commercial center) for the distribution of slaves to Europe and especially the Americas. The storytelling chronicler reports that when slavery ceased to be a profitable business, the Portuguese placed the islands under the jurisdiction of provincial governors. The Lusitanian discoverers then forgot about the islands, which resulted in a neglect that, frankly and in truth, directly converges with the original divine distraction. In other words, "there were no more riches to distribute." The chronicler's sardonic intention lends a humorous twist to Cape Verde's traditional ethos when, continuing with his rather irreverent, albeit not sacrilegious, rendering of a divine presence, Almeida writes: "Mas também é muito natural que Deus tivesse em vista um outro projecto bem mais complexo e que de imediato não quis revelar aos seus colaboradores criar um laboratório experimental de miscigenação de raças e culturas e ver o que dessa miscelânea poderia sair. E saiu o homem cabo-verdiano" (12; "But it is also natural that God would have in mind another project that was much more complex and which he did not immediately wish to reveal to his collaborators: that is, to create an experimental laboratory for the mixing of races and cultures so as to determine what might emerge from this miscellany. And what emerged, was the Cape Verdean human being").

Indeed, what emerged was the first and most comprehensive Creole society in the Portuguese overseas empire and, indeed, anywhere in the colonized world. Creole in this case refers of course to racial, linguistic, and cultural hybridity. Apropos of the historical underpinnings of this phenomenon, in his book, *The Diligent: A Voyage Through the Worlds of the Slave Trade* (2002), Robert Harms assesses the process of creolization on the Cape Verde leeward island of Santiago: "The free black population on Santiago grew, and racial distinctions became blurred as Portuguese men continued to father children with their slave wives and concubines. A *mestiço* [mixed-race] community on Santiago had been recognized as early as 1582, and by 1731, Santiago counted 394 whites and 2,461 *mestiços*" (113). Harms goes on to document that when the crew of the French slave ship *Diligent* disembarked on Santiago "...the Cape Verde Islands represented a kind of cultural 'halfway house' between the society they had left behind in France and the ones they would encounter in Africa. Not only did the skin tones they observed on the island cover the full spectrum from white to black, but the cultural mixture also defied existing stereotypes. Santiago had literate black priests and illiterate white priests, and the only dynamic sector of its economy was dominated by enslaved weavers using African technology. Culturally, as well as geographically, the crew of the *Diligent* was halfway between Europe and its designated landfall in West Africa" (113). What applies to Santiago, with respect to Cape Verde's racial and cultural hybridity, applies even more to the islands of São Vicente, São Nicolau, Santo Antão, Brava, Fogo, and Boa Vista.

At the end of "Cabo Verde é o Centro do Mundo," Germano Almeida recounts an amusing anecdote that truly captures the paradox of the center and the periphery. After reminding the reader that Cape Verde gained its political independence on the 5th of July, 1975, the chronicler/storyteller recounts: "E dizia-me, há tempos, um cabo-verdiano convencido de que a data coincidia com a dos Estados Unidos da América: 'Dois grandes países: Cabo Verde e América!'" (12; "And a while back a Cape Verdean, convinced that the date [i.e., the 5th rather than the 4th of July] was the same as that of the independence of the United States, said to me: 'Two great countries: Cape Verde and America!'"). The narrator then explains that his compatriot's assertion, although rather presumptuous, when translated from the islands' creole language into Portuguese, "...perde grande parte do seu pitoresco sabor, perde mesmo toda a ingénua mas deliciosa bazofaria nacional, sobretudo porque é completamente indescritível o solene e absolutamente convincente menear de cabeça que a acompanhou." (12; "...loses much of its picturesque flavor, really loses all of its ingenuous but delicious national vanity, especially because what is totally indescribable is the solemn and absolutely convincing nod of the head that accompanied the assertion"). The narrator further observes, but also with a conscious mixture of the same delicious national vanity and solemnity he attributes to his compatriot, "[m]as é assim o cabo-verdiano: orgulhoso do centro da terra onde vive, sofre e labuta contra a permanente estiagem, os olhos no estrangeiro, o coração nas ilhas" (12; "but thus is the Cape Verdean: proud of the center of the earth where he lives, suffers, and struggles against permanent drought and where he looks, with his heart in the islands, to leaving for foreign lands"). Needless to say, the allusion is to the Cape Verdean's legendary patterns of emigration, especially to North America.

With respect to geographical location, Germano Almeida also deals with the provocative subject of identity within Cape Verde's linguistic, politico-ideological, racial, social, and cultural space. The volume's second and third chronicle-tales bear, respectively, the titles "Uma Forma de Identidade Africana" ("A form of African identity") and "Uma Perspectiva da Identidade Cabo-Verdiana" ("A perspective of Cape Verdean identity"). The form and content of both are aesthetically pleasing and substantive elaborations of historical and contemporary real and imagined truths of Cape Verde as the archetypal Creole society. They give a historian's analysis and a storyteller's verve to what Eve L. Crowley so aptly delineates in "Creoles," an entry in the *Encyclopedia of Africa South of the Sahara* (1997). In a sub-section titled "Portuguese Creoles," Crowley writes: "A scarcity of human and financial resources made miscegenation with local populations a tactical necessity for Portuguese and Afro-Portuguese trade intermediaries.... In Cape Verde, superior education, cultural proximity to the Portuguese, and physical resistance to tropical diseases made the Creole offspring of Europeans and slaves from Senegambia, Guinea, and the Gold Coast (present-day Ghana) ideal employees in Portuguese firms and administration throughout Portugal's African colonies" (380). Crowley characterizes Cape Verde's Creole inhabitants as substantially less African than their counterparts in such lands as São Tomé e Príncipe and Angola. She does counter, however, an accusatory belief held by some during the final decade or so of colonial domination when she states that "[a]lthough some Creoles of Cape Verde and Guinea-Bissau opposed independence from Portugal, most of the Creole elite were catalysts behind the armed struggle for independence..." (380). Amílcar Cabral, the Cape Verdean-Guinean statesman and liberation leader, comes immediately to mind with regard to an engagé member of the Creole elite.

In coming to terms with racial, ethnic, and national labels, in "Uma Forma de Identidade Africana," Germano Almeida evokes the late Baltasar Lopes da Silva, the renown jurist, philologist, poet, novelist, and co-founder, in the 1930s, of Cape Verde's modern literary-cultural movement. Almeida documents the intellectual preeminence of that member of the *Claridade* generation in the following terms: "...já em meados de 1967, Baltasar Lopes da Silva tinha reequacionado o problema de forma lapidar e convincente: não éramos nem africanos nem europeus, apenas cabo-verdianos" (16; "...already in mid-1967 Baltasar Lopes da Silva had 're-equationed' the problem convincingly in lapidary form: we were neither Africans nor Europeans, just Cape Verdeans"). Rather than seeking to de-Africanize Cape Verde and its inhabitants, as one might infer, Almeida instead comes to terms with the Western world's propensity to lump together with the application of a definitive label peoples from forty-seven distinctive Sub-Saharan countries. Almeida observes that "[d]a Europa conhecíamos os portugueses, os franceses, os italianos, os espanhóis, os alemães.... Mas para toda a África havia apenas a genérica expressão quase pejorativa de 'africanos...'" (17; "with respect to Europe we knew about the Portuguese, the French, the Italians, the Spanish, the Germans.... But for all of Africa there was just the generic, almost pejorative expression Africans'"). I note parenthetically that "African Held After Name Is Left in Cave," the title of a recent item, written by Philip Shenon and published in a recent issue of the *New York Times*, would appear to attest to the validity of Almeida's observation. Upon reading the text of the news item we do learn that the African in question is a Tanzanian. It is, however, unlikely that a citizen of Portugal, France, Italy, Spain, Germany, or even a lesser known country such as Andorra, would be labeled as simply a European in the title of a U.S. newspaper item.

As regards "Uma Perspectiva da Identidade Cabo-Verdiana," the narrator brings this seminal *crónica* to a close with the following avowal of nativist identity: "Claro que não apenas a cachupa, o grogue e a morna respondem pela nossa identidade, sendo embora facto que ela passa, e não poderá ser entendida, sem a constância desses elementos. Mas a tentativa de assimilação do estrangeiro pela via da crioulização não é senão uma maneira de trazer o 'outro de fora' para 'dentro de nós,' e acho que é isso que é normalmente conhecido pelo nome de 'morabeza'" (22; "Of course, not just the *cachupa*, *grogue*, and the *morna* answer to our identity, although they are realities through which that identity passes and which could not be understood without the constancy of those elements. But the attempt at the assimilation of the foreign by means of creolization is nothing more than a way of bringing the 'other outside' to 'us inside,' and I believe that that is commonly known as *morabeza*"). *Cachupa* is, of course, the archipelago's national dish, which is to Cape Verde what *feijoada* is to Brazil. *Grogue*, which derives from the English word "grog," is a rum drink that is to Cape Verde what *cachaça* is to Brazil. And certainly the *morna* is to Cape Verde what the fado is to Portugal. Finally, *morabeza* is a sui generis, reputedly untranslatable Creole term, more or less equivalent to "affability" and "amiability." In keeping with Germano Almeida's use of the term in the context of the paragraph quoted above, *morabeza* might be termed a Creole quality of hybrid adaptability. In the volume's fifth chronicle, Germano Almeida explains that *morabeza* is a word "...tão nascida da secura das nossas terras, que não das nossas gentes, que nenhum dicionário a traduz sem risco de encher páginas e páginas e mais páginas, pelo tanto que já traduz de nós em termos de afirmação cultural e demais pormenores interligados" (30; "...so born of the dryness of our lands, but not of our people, that no dictionary could translate it without the risk of filling pages, pages, and more pages, because of how much of us it translates in terms of cultural affirmation and other interrelated details"). The declaration quoted above appears in a chronicle/tale that bears the intriguing title "O Dragão do Atlântico" ("The Dragon of the Atlantic"). The chronicler explains, in this tale of identity and identification, that one day he and fellow viewers were surprised when a smiling face appeared on their television screens and a joyous voice announced that Cape Verde was indeed destined to be the "Dragon of the Atlantic." The image of the dragon derives, in this usage, from a slogan launched during the last national election in Cape Verde by an opposition political party, which promised that "...o nosso pacato arquipélago estava em breve destinado a ser o Hong Kong de África" (27; "...our tranquil archipelago was soon destined to be the Hong Kong of Africa"). In a surge of nativist and ethnic pride, the narrator reports that the collective, taking this comparison as an affront, reacted in unison: "Porquê Hong Kong se já somos Cabo Verde?" (27; "Why Hong Kong if we're already Cape Verde"). With his customary touch of collective self-deprecating humor, Almeida fashions a fetching tale of the sometimes ironic telluric and identity realities that pervade a time-honored pre-independence and now post-colonial Cape Verdean ethos.

All of the fifty-five *crónicas* brought together in *Estórias contadas* elucidate compelling social, political, and cultural matters relevant to Cape Verde and its historical and contemporary place on the planet. This overview and brief assessment seeks to record Germano Almeida's preeminence as an imaginative and perceptive *cronista* with a unique talent for historicizing and storying the Cape Verdean's unique identity and the archipelago's simultaneously central and peripheral locations in Africa as well as in the Portuguese-speaking world and beyond. Literally and figuratively, Germano Almeida reports and creates from the center of the periphery.

Notes

[1] This article is a revised version of a talk delivered on April 19, 2002 during the " Tribute to José Saramago: Contemporary Literature from the Portuguese-Speaking World," a symposium held at The John F. Kennedy Library in Boston, Massachusetts. The symposium was sponsored by the Massachusetts Foundation for the Humanities, the John F. Kennedy Library, and the Center for Portuguese Studies and Culture at the University of Massachusetts Dartmouth.

[2] The title of Ribeiro's own English translation of the novel is *An Invincible Memory* (1989).

[3] Recommended reading is the issue of *Boletim Bibliográfico Biblioteca Mário de Andrade*, 46.1-4, Janeiro a Dezembro de 1985, dedicated to the *crónica*. The journal's introductory section titled "A crônica: teoria e história do gênero," consists of three essays. Of particular interest, as regards definitions and the nature of the quasi-literary genre, is "Fragmentos sobre a Crônica," by Davi Arrigucci, Jr. *Crónicas ao Sol e à Chuva* (2002; *Chronicles in the sun and rain*) by the Angolan writer Arnaldo Santos is a volume of interest. The preface to these *crónicas*, originally published during 1992 in the Luanda newspaper *Jornal de Angola*, was authored by João Melo, another Angolan writer of considerable talent. Melo begins his provocative preface with the question: "O que é uma crónica?" (11; "What is a *crónica*?"), and as do the Brazilian literary critics in the above-cited journal, he discusses the origins and definitions of the genre.

Works Cited

Almeida, Germano. *O Testamento do Sr. Napumoceno da Silva Araújo*. São Vicente: Ilhéu Editora, 1989.

———. *O Meu Poeta*. São Vicente: Ilhéu Editora, 1990.

———. *O Dia das Calças Roladas*. Mindelo, São Vicente: Ilhéu Editora, 1992.

———. *A Ilha Fantástica*. Mindelo, São Vicente: Ilhéu Editora, 1994.

———. *Os Dois Irmãos*. Mindelo, São Vicente: Ilhéu Editora, 1995.

———. *Estórias de Dentro de Casa*. Lisboa: Editorial Caminho, 1996.

———. *A Família Trago*. Lisboa: Editorial Caminho, 1998.

———. *Estórias Contadas*. Lisboa: Editorial Caminho, 1998.

———. Entrevista. "Não tenho a pretensão de escrever romances." *Publico* 25 de Abril de 1998.

———. *Dona Pura e os Camaradas de Abril*. Colecção Caminho de Abril. Lisboa: Editorial Caminho, 1999.

Barbosa, Jorge. "Panorama: Destroços de um Continente." *Arquipélago*. São Vicente: Editorial Claridade, 1935.

Boletim Bibliográfico Biblioteca Mário de Andrade. 46.1-4 (janeiro a dezembro de 1985).

"Colonialism & Liberation: O Testamento do Senhor Napumoceno - Napumoceno's Will." *Library of African Cinema 2000*. San Francisco: California Newsreel, 2000.

"Crônica." *Novo Aurélio Século XXI: O Dicionário da Língua Portuguesa*. 1999 ed.

"Chronicle." *The Random House Dictionary of the English Language*. 1987 ed.

Crowley, Eve L. "Creoles." *Encyclopedia of Africa South of the Sahara*. 1997.

Harms, Robert. *The Diligent: A Voyage Through the Worlds of the Slave Trade*. New York: Basic Books, 2002.

Ribeiro, João Ubaldo. *Viva o Povo Brasileiro*. Rio de Janeiro: Editora Nova Fronteira, 1984.

———. *An Invincible Memory*. London: Faber, 1989.

Santos, Arnaldo. *Crónicas ao Sol e à Chuva*. Luanda: União dos Escritores Angolanos, 2002.

Shenon, Philip. "African Held After Name Is Left in Cave." *New York Times* 18 Aug. 2002, natl. ed.: A15.

Russell G. Hamilton is Professor Emeritus of Lusophone African, Brazilian, and Portuguese Literatures. After receiving his Ph.D. from Yale University, he served for twenty years as a faculty member at the University of Minnesota. In 2002 he retired from Vanderbilt University, where he had served as a faculty member for eighteen years and Dean of the Graduate School for sixteen years. The author of numerous articles and chapters on Portuguese-language literature and culture, he has published two books on Lusophone Africa. He is currently revising and updating *Literatura Africana, Literatura Necessária*, his two-volume study first issued in 1981 and 1983. E-mail: Russell.Hamilton@vanderbilt.edu

A Busca de Adélia: Narrativa Póstuma em *Testamento do Senhor Napumoceno da Silva Araújo* de Germano Almeida

Robert H. Moser

Resumo. O conto "Galeria Póstuma" do romancista brasileiro Machado de Assis levanta algumas das questões principais apresentadas neste estudo sobre o romance de Germano de Almeida, *O Testamento do Senhor Napumoceno da Silva Araújo*, nomeadamente: como é a escrita memorialista alterada quando narrada de uma perspectiva póstuma? Semelhantemente, como é que podemos reconciliar a suposta voz memorialista autêntica com a frequente voz distorcida e irónica do narrador póstumo? Como resposta a estas perguntas, este ensaio problematiza o mito do Sr. Napumoceno como um "self-made man" e, ao fazê-lo, chama atenção ao papel que o seu "testamento" e outros manuscritos autobiográficos narrados postumamente têm na subversão do relato monástico da sua vida. Ao oferecerem as suas memórias à posteridade, os memorialistas, por sua vez, ensaiam as suas próprias mortes e uma subsequente posição póstuma através do acto da escrita. No entanto, existe uma ambiguidade inerente na tentativa do narrador póstumo de inserir o presente e o passado anacronicamente num presente que virá mais tarde. Fundamentalmente, a reconstrução do Sr. Napumoceno é um esforço colectivo que envolve os conteúdos indetermináveis das suas memórias, as recordações da sua família e amigos, a manipulação de um narrador omnisciente e as inferências contínuas do leitor.

Em 1884 aparece na coleção *Histórias Sem Data* de Machado de Assis um conto intitulado "Galeria Póstuma" que aponto aqui pela proximidade à obra e tema tratados neste presente ensaio. O conto tem início com a morte inesperada de Joaquim Fidélis, deputado municipal já aposentado que, segundo o narrador, foi um homem "rico e letrado," e apreciado por todos, apesar de ser "um profundo céptico" nos seus últimos anos de vida (396). Benjamin, sobrinho lutuoso, com quem ele vivia e tratava como se fosse filho, acaba por descobrir um diário deixado pelo tio. Intrigados pelo desenterro desta fonte de segredos íntimos do tio, e ansiosos por ressuscitar a sua memória, Benjamin e um grupo de amigos chegados lêem em voz alta as primeiras páginas do diário. A primeira impressão do manuscrito confirma de facto a memória digna que cada um guarda do finado: "Grande foi a comoção dos amigos; lê-lo era ainda conservá-lo. Tão reto caráter! Tão discreto espírito!" (398).

Depois de marcar para o dia seguinte mais um encontro destinado à leitura agradável do diário, Benjamin faz as despedidas e aproveita as últimas horas da noite para ler o manuscrito sozinho. As passagens que se seguem revelam, porém, um outro homem, longe daquele que abriu tão discretamente as primeiras páginas. O sobrinho descobre na sua leitura privada o cerne do diário, "o texto primitivo e interior, a lição exacta e autêntica" em que o finado disseca os hábitos, falhas e inconsistências das mesmas pessoas que tinham carregado o seu caixão e partilhado, com prazer, da primeira leitura do diário. O tio descreve um colega como "estúpido e crédulo," outro como sendo de conversa "vulgar, polida e chôcha," enquanto o terceiro "mente com facilidade" (399-400). Espantado com esta revelação escandalosa do tio, o sobrinho incrédulo tenta evocar a versão mais dócil da sua memória:

> Evocou a figura do tio, com o olhar espirituoso e meigo, e a pilhéria grave; em lugar dessa, tão cândida e simpática, a que lhe apareceu foi a do tio morto, estendido na cama, com os olhos abertos e o lábio arregaçado. Sacudiu-a do espírito, mas a imagem ficou. Não podendo rejeitá-la, Benjamin tentou mentalmente fechar-lhe os olhos e consertar-lhe a bôca; mas depressa o fazia, como a pálpebra tornava a levantar-se, a ironia arregaçava o beiço. Já não era o homem, era o autor do manuscrito. (401)

Afinal, o diário contém poderes restaurativos, mas quem ressurge não é o tio afável e bondoso, mas o morto irónico, o "autor do manuscrito." Não este é o único caso na ficção machadiana em que um escritor assume outro tom depois da morte. A voz brutalmente franca do tio morto nos lembra o outro ironista póstumo, Brás Cubas, embora este seja, como ele próprio proclama, mais "defunto autor" do que "autor defunto." Mesmo assim, o diário em "Galeria Póstuma" levanta questões particulares ao fenômeno da narrativa póstuma como sub-gênero do memorialismo: como muda a voz memorialista quando ela é lida postumamente? Onde é que podemos situar a fronteira entre a pessoa e o "autor do manuscrito"? Até que ponto a narrativa póstuma interfere com a noção de memorialismo como um relato "verdadeiro" da vida do autor? Estas são as perguntas principais que nos interessam na análise que se seguirá com respeito ao romance *O Testamento do Senhor Napumoceno da Silva Araújo* do escritor caboverdiano Germano Almeida.

O romance de Germano Almeida começa, como sabemos, com o gesto postumamente abusivo do Senhor Napumoceno ao exigir que seus herdeiros se sentem pacientemente durante a leitura do seu "testamento" de 387 páginas, processo doloroso que durará quase quatro horas. Assumindo o papel de médium, o testamenteiro e depois outros colegas presentes, cumprem o último desejo do falecido de transmitir as suas palavras do além ao mundo terreno. Ao aproveitar esta ocasião solene, o Sr. Napumoceno também abusa do próprio gênero do testamento, pois o que ele deixa é justamente um livro de memórias que conta, supostamente, as suas intimidades nunca expressas enquanto vivo. O terceiro ato abusivo vem incorporado na sua decisão de identificar Maria da Graça, filha desconhecida, como herdeira quase universal dos seus bens, e não Carlos, o seu sobrinho e herdeiro natural. Esta rejeição leva o sobrinho a murmurar: "que se foda no inferno o velho danado!" (8). Quem é, afinal, este Sr. Napumoceno? O empresário moderado e generoso "conhecido" por todo mundo na ilha de São Vicente, ou o "autor do manuscrito" capaz de produzir um testamento dissimulado, esconder a filha ilegítima e desprezar os seus parentes mais chegados? O resto do romance procura, dentro destes parâmetros, reconciliar a sua voz póstuma com as memórias que os outros guardam de si.

Como qualquer finado, quer o Sr. Napumoceno morto quer as suas palavras póstumas são recebidos com uma mistura de respeito e desconfiança. A aparição do morto no mundo dos vivos pode ser ocasião de confiança, pois marca a interferência benevolente de um advogado celestial, ou de medo primitivo, no caso do retorno de uma alma errante. A própria palavra "defunto" funciona como uma espécie de talismã linguística no mundo católico lusófono, como nos lembra Luis da Câmara Cascudo no seu *Dicionário do Folclore Brasileiro*: "Dirigir-se ao morto pelo designativo de defunto, o finado, o falecido, é tradicional no Brasil, provindo de Portugal. É uma reminiscência viva do poder mágico e evocador do nome, susceptível de fazer retornar ao convívio humano o desaparecido" (283-284). Portanto, não é por acaso que o narrador omnisciente se refere ao Sr. Napumoceno, sobretudo, como "falecido" ou "defunto" ao longo do texto, pois atrás destas palavras esconde a identidade do homem que tanto o narrador como os personagens procuram evocar.

A ilusão oferecida pelo testamento/livro de memórias é que a pessoa autêntica seja revelada através das suas páginas. Um colega exclama que o testamento lhes ofereceu "uma nova luz sobre a vida e pessoa do ilustre extinto" e outro comenta que "a luz parecia total" (11). A palavra chave aqui é "parecia," pois descobrimos depois que há muitas omissões na sua história, e que existem outros manuscritos póstumos que esclarecem (ou confundem) o conteúdo do próprio testamento. A ambiguidade desta luz parcial é complicada pelo fato do leitor raramente ter acesso às próprias palavras do Sr. Napumoceno, porque as histórias contadas no testamento e nos cadernos são quase sempre filtradas pela narrativa do narrador omnisciente.

Outro fator complicador é que, ao escrever as suas memórias, o Sr. Napumoceno não é motivado, principalmente, pela idéia de contar todos os segredos da sua vida. A escrita do testamento e dos outros materiais memorialistas é, sobretudo, a expressão central que corresponde à busca existencial que caracterizava a última fase da sua vida: os "seus tempos de preparação espiritual" (55). A escrita, nesta busca, serve como veículo principal da sua auto-construção, enquanto os elementos cotidianos da sua chefia empresarial se tornam inconsequentes: "com Carlos nas importações, ele dedicava-se exclusivamente à meditação, preparando-se para escrever a sua vida de *self made man* " (116). Este período de reflexão é justamente o do *self made man,* no sentido do homem que se constrói, ou melhor, se reconstrói.

A maior omissão do testamento, Maria da Graça descobre, é a história do amor dele por Adélia, a moça com "olhos de uma gazela brava" e "objecto de cinco cadernos escolares de 24 páginas cada" (88, 78). No início do primeiro caderno, o Sr. Napumoceno explica o seu motivo de inclusão deste evento definidor nas suas memórias: "[...] declarou que decidira dar a conhecer à posteridade, para exemplo e edificação de quantos alguma vez o lessem, a tragédia amorosa que mais que tudo no mundo lhe arrasara a existência" (79).

O exercício de oferecer à posteridade, através da escrita, o "texto primitivo e interior" da nossa vida acaba por ser intrínseco não só à narrativa póstuma mas a toda a expressão memorialista. Mas a questão fundamental é esta: seria possível dizer que qualquer autor, quando tem seus olhos fixados na posteridade, já se projeta precocemente a uma posição póstuma? Para um "além túmulo" onde a sua consciência todavia continua? O autor consciente da potencialidade póstuma da sua escrita age, de alguma maneira, como o beato que, para cumprir uma promessa, se deita num caixão fingindo que está morto, numa procissão de enterro igualmente fingido. Semelhantemente, o memorialista ensaia a sua própria morte através do ato de escrever. Se isto for verdade podemos perguntar então se este fingimento da morte, da voz póstuma, pertence apenas aos autores com intenções deliberadamente póstumas, ou a todos os escritores? Veja-se, por exemplo, o comentário de Jeremy Tambling no seu livro *Becoming Posthumous: Life and Death in Literary and Cultural Studies* com respeito à natureza anacrônica da voz póstuma:

> The posthumous challenges a life-death distinction and the order in which that distinction is phrased; it throws chronology into disarray, when the works of long dead writers suddenly appear later, out of 'time, and it makes all writing potentially posthumous since it cannot have a punctual relation to a life of writing. (7-8)

No entanto, todos os escritores, quer seja pelos livros publicados, ou pelos manuscritos guardados na secretária, como no caso machadiano do Conselheiro Aires, deixam algo à posteridade, ou seja, compõem as suas mensagens que serão depois, através do "médium" da escrita, transmitidas do além. Além do mais, a potência póstuma destes já está garantida no ato de escrever e, portanto, os seus textos assumem um aspecto dissimulador, ensaiador da morte. É na narrativa póstuma que o escritor insere o seu presente e passado anacronicamente num presente que virá mais tarde.

Como sabemos, a dissimulação do Sr. Napumoceno não acaba na vida. Numa inversão do seu fingimento da morte enquanto vivo, os manuscritos póstumos permitem que o autor defunto ensaie a própria vida na morte. Mesmo assim, não sabemos se a vida evocada através das suas memórias é a do homem ou a do autor do manuscrito. É evidente que, quando falamos de uma narrativa póstuma, a fronteira entre o "autor defunto" e o "defunto autor" se torna mais instável. As duas posições representam a continuação da consciência após a morte, mesmo que as palavras do primeiro sejam escritas em vida. As suas mensagens, o desempenho da sua narração, as particularidades da sua voz, chegam a nós, leitores, como se fossem murmúrios espectrais ultrapassando os limites do tempo e do espaço.

A reconstrução do Sr. Napumoceno certamente está longe do mito do "self made man," fruto de uma força solitária. Ao contrário, ela é uma obra coletiva envolvendo as pesquisas da sua filha, as anedotas dos outros personagens, a manipulação constante do narrador e, claro, as inferências do próprio leitor. A riqueza do romance está justamente nas tentativas de decifrar o sentido (ou melhor, os sentidos múltiplos) das narrativas póstumas propostas pelo autor defunto.

Apesar de consistir numa bela produção, o filme (do mesmo título) acaba empobrecendo a história ao empregar o truque das cassetes gravadas com a voz do Sr. Napumoceno que Graça escuta, ao invés de ler os cadernos. Esta mudança tem o efeito de aniquilar as possibilidades de interação entre leitor e texto e de reduzir as potencialidades expressivas da narrativa.

As contribuições a esta reconstrução coletiva deixadas pelo próprio autor defunto constituem, como sabemos, pistas dissimuladoras, pois nenhum manuscrito póstumo individual conta a história inteira, antes cada um forma parte de um retrato em constante transformação. Ao invés de uma autobiografia definitiva, cândida, os seus manuscritos demonstram um universo caleidoscópico de verdades e memórias múltiplas, umas vezes complementares, outras vezes contraditórias. A busca de Graça pelas origens do pai, e a sua confusão com respeito a sua relação com ele (ela não sabe se deve chamar-lhe "falecido" ou "pai") fazem parte deste universo ambíguo. É verdade que os manuscritos detalhados permitem que ela imagine uma relação íntima entre a filha e um pai reconhecível, quase vivo:

> A pasta de couro deu a Maria da Graça uma visão quase exaustiva do homem que fora seu pai porque permitiu-lhe recriar o seu dia-a-dia do nascer ao pôr do Sol e conhecer-lhe as excentricidades e manias como se tivesse convivido com ele durante uma vida inteira. (123)

Porém, o emprego do subjuntivo ("como se tivesse") e das palavras "recriar" e "quase exaustiva" sugere que o "verdadeiro" pai continua a se esconder dela. Até ela reconhece que os cadernos abrem amplo espaço para a interpretação, ainda mais porque os trechos nunca foram datados. Com respeito ao caderno de tom mais confessional de todos, onde ele disserta sobre os seus sentimentos por Adélia, Graça procura dar uma temporalidade mais poética às expressões amorosas do pai: "A verdade, porém, é que preferiu situar o terceiro caderno nessa época com o exclusivo objetivo de justificar o pai, pensar que ter ele escrito o que sonhara e não o que acontecera na realidade" (107).

Quando não aparece nenhuma Adélia em São Vicente para receber a última ordem legatária do falecido, uma cópia do livro *Só* de António Nobre,

Graça começa a duvidar da própria existência da moça tão cobiçada pelo pai, que talvez "não existira senão na imaginação do velho" (110). Porém, os traços de Adélia sempre foram fugazes. Quando a moça lhe dá uma fotografia dela, ele confessa que "não a reconhecia naquela imagem, nada tinha da menina fugitiva que escapava à compreensão do seu espírito[...]" (91). Ela também foge dos braços do Sr. Napumoceno apenas para voltar depois, segundo ele, uma pessoa estranha, desconhecida. E o livro conclui com a imagem patética do velho, já sofrendo de demência, fazendo exclamações a uma Adélia ilusória.

Torna-se evidente que, neste romance, a figura de Adélia simboliza a memória de um passado que nos escapa eternamente ou que, talvez, nunca existisse. De uma forma semelhante, ela representa metaforicamente o desejo humano de plenitude, de se sentir "inteiro." Portanto, a busca dela é também a busca desta inteireza, tão ligeira e fútil como a evocação de apenas um Sr. Napumoceno inteiro, autêntico. No final de contas, escrevemos postumamente também na busca de Adélia, na busca desta inteireza que só vem no ato impossível de autobiografar a nossa própria morte.

Obras Citadas

Almeida, Germano. *O Testamento do Senhor Napumoceno da Silva Araújo.* Lisboa: Caminho, 1991.

Cascudo, Luis da Camara. *Dicionário do Folclore Brasileiro.* São Paulo: Itatiaia, 1998.

Assis, Joaquim Maria Machado de. *Obra Completa.* Org. Afrânio Coutinho. Vol. II. Conto e Teatro. Rio de Janeiro: José Aguilar, 1962.

Tambling, Jeremy. *Becoming Posthumous: Life and Death in Literary and Cultural Studies.* Edinburgh: Edinburgh Univ. Press, 2001.

Robert H. Moser é Professor Auxiliar de Português na Universidade da Georgia. Recentemente completou a sua tese de doutoramento intitulada *The Carnivalesque Defunto: Death and the Dead in Modern Brazilian Literature*, no Departamento de Estudos Portugueses e Brasileiros da Universidade de Brown. Também leccionou Português na Universidade de Harvard. Tem publicado sobre a literatura brasileira do século XX em *Brasil/Brazil*, *Hispania* e no próximo volume de *Representations of the Dead.* O seu trabalho sobre o historiador português Jaime Cortesão foi publicado em *Leituras: Revista da Biblioteca Nacional.* As suas áreas de pesquisa actual são: a figura do morto, a narração póstuma e as expressões de assombração e luto na literatura luso-brasileira. E-mail: rmoser@uga.edu

The Beginning of the World as We Would Like It to Have Been, or an Analysis Towards a Theory of Gender in Germano Almeida, or ...

Paula Gândara
Translated by
Luís R. Mitras
Revised by
Mark Streeter

Abstract. Germano Almeida's *Memórias de um Espírito* is able to achieve two feats. Firstly, he does justice to Machado de Assis: starting off from the similarity in titles, we are able to read Machado's work with all its traces of postmodernity—narrative fragmentation, the addressing of the reader and his inclusion in the narrative, the mixture of fiction and reality—and of a certain kind of feminine *écriture* that is revealed not only through these traces but also in his ability to give flesh to portraits of fully-rounded women. Secondly, he makes a break with the Brazilian tradition, a tradition he refers to when he shows us a universe ruled by pleasure and by an optimism based on the life of one man, the center of whose being is based on the primacy of feeling and not of reason. In Germano Almeida, irony coincides with humor and Machado de Assis's "pen of birth" is used to subvert the universe whence it came.

We would like to begin our analysis with *Memórias de um Espírito* [*A Spirit's Memories*] (2001) in order that we may, retrospectively, observe the intertextual dialogic circle created by the author—one that in a certain sense heralds the end of a certain stage in his writing—and so that we may observe a new phase in his writing, one that incorporates more recent literary-theoretical preoccupations.

It is quite clear to everyone that *As Memórias de um Espírito* cannot but evoke one of the greatest names in Brazilian literature, Machado de Assis, and, in particular, his work *Memórias Póstumas de Brás Cubas* (1880). Both characters, Brás Cubas and Alíro de Sousa, reflect on their own past. An innovator in all respects, Machado de Assis already incorporated elements of what we would today call postmodernism and there is no doubt that this author had already, in his fiction, walked all the avenues and byways of post-colonialism; it is sufficient for us to detain ourselves for a short while in "Instinto de Nacionalidade" ["The Instinct of Nationality"] (1962) so that we can see how the major thrust of his argument is appropriated by Germano Almeida more than a hundred years later, and working without the aid of a theoretical system. Machado de Assis asks for a literary independence, something that it is necessary to create, over and beyond political independence; he insists on the need for a system of self-criticism and self-analysis at a national level[1] and holds that it is necessary to continue creating a national literature with an eye for the future. We are dealing with three points that are fundamental for the comprehension of Germano Almeida's texts, which, while they do not negate the weight of history, which is already evident from the [fact that he writes in the] official language of the country, look at and make use of the literature that came before with a critical eye, especially with regards to whether it can be incorporated, developed or whether it should be side-stepped; these texts do not adopt a perspective of spurious repudiation, which would create an unreal historical vacuum, one that would give Cape Verde no basis from which to launch itself into the world. I would like to remind the reader that it is only occasionally that Germano Almeida makes use of grammatical structures borrowed from the Creole;[2] he does not have to dramatically recreate a new language. Once again, this sort of concern cannot but suggest Machado de Assis: a space of epistemological progression, one without breaks with the past but rather continuity, where language is seen as an ideological, political and socio-cultural instrument within a temporal continuum. Suffice it to recall Machado de Assis's condemnation of Gallicisms and his opinion that it is in sixteenth-century Portuguese that we may discover the future of the language: "*desentranhar dêles mil riquezas, que, à força de velhas se fazem novas* [...]. *Nem tudo tinham os antigos, nem tudo têm os modernos; com os haveres de uns e outros é que se enriquece o pecúlio comum*" ["to unearth thousands of riches which though old are made new (...). The ancients never had everything, as neither do the moderns; it is with what they had and with what we have that we may enrich the word-hoard"] (1962, 809). Compare this idea with some of the commentaries made by some of the characters in Germano Almeida: the comparison between [the characters] Natal [lit.

"Christmas"] and Caga-Vírgulas [lit. "The Shitter of Commas"], both the motive of jest and ridicule on the part of the narrator, given the first one's project of writing an *Arte de Carpir em Cabo Verde* [*The Art of Lamentation in Cape Verde*] (216) and the second one's intention of writing "*coisa inovadora, uma espécie de saga capaz de abarcar a globalidade da nossa realidade social desde os tempos das descobertas*" ["something innovative, a type of saga capable of dealing with the totality of our social reality ever since the time of the discoveries"] (159), not to mention the silliness of funeral orations, which that same character regards as essential to develop in the country and whose tradition (to paraphrase Caga-Vírgulas) harkens back to names of Brazilian origin. The truth, the narrator tells us, is that Natal "*é no aspecto literário tão chato como o Caga-Vírgulas e a única vantagem que me parece que ele tem sobre o outro é o facto de continuar a adiar para o ano seguinte todos os seus projectos de escrita*" ["in so far as his literary qualities go, he is as much of a pain as Caga-Vírgulas and the only advantage he has over the other is the fact that he continues to postpone his literary projects from year to year"] (216). These are comments that naturally remind us of those historical periods when there was a need to create a historical past and to make use of material that was indigenous to the country; for instance, the use of terms of Amerindian origin to which Machado de Assis refers and which, according to him, is necessary, although it is erroneous to suppose that it is the only element necessary with which to build a Brazilian literature. Finally, it would be somewhat pathetic on our part if we did not refer to the similarities between Machado de Assis and Germano Almeida; it would be equally pathetic if we were to imagine that Germano Almeida was somehow innocently trying to establish this theoretical-diegetic link without a specific end in mind.

However, let us not forget the initial comparative proposition that we have made use of: the development of a feminine space within a social and politico-literary kingdom traditionally closed off to women. Although space forbids us from developing this idea, we cannot but note that the development of literature written by women in Brazil (as opposed to the panorama in the rest of Latin America) was a phenomenon that, according to Judith Paine (1993), was explainable by Machado de Assis's creation of original and revolutionary female figures, within his literary universe that is. It is a universe that would have contributed, and noticeably at that, towards the emergence of an unorthodox creative environment, one where women would feel freer to produce and where, from early on, it was possible to find rounded, complex and rich female characters. The truth is that tradition determines that knowledge belongs within the sphere of rationality, which is attributed to the male, but if that which is masculine and that which is feminine are mixed in the creative results of works whose authors are male but whose characteristics point to the feminine, then this fluidity can be used to demystify the political world and power structure where only the masculine voice has a place.

It is precisely with this stance in mind that we would like to investigate the work of Germano Almeida, someone who, though living in a different world and in a context that is different in all respects to that of Machado de Assis, still needs to fight for the inclusion of the feminine in a universe that has only very slowly come to accept its inclusion, a universe that, almost always, is antagonistic to and fears the other half of humanity. On the other hand, the obvious connection that Germano Almeida's title suggests to Machado de Assis's novel is, to say the least, disconcerting. Given that, and there is ample evidence of this in his work, Almeida's critical stance towards the connection with Brazil, which serves neither literature nor the political needs of his country, what do we make of this obvious intertextual connection? It seems as if the best way to make sense of this situation is, in fact, to analyze it *ad nauseum*, which will lead us to the obvious conclusion: this connection can quite easily be understood as a large-scale parody of Machado de Assis's novel. Consider: if, on the one hand, Brás Cubas, at the moment of his death, has a woman, Virgília, beside him, and the text summons up three further women, Sabina, Eugénia and Marcela, Alírio de Sousa, on the other hand, has twelve women standing around his coffin, of which only one was not a girlfriend, and the narrative casts its net wider to deal with eight other women, of which only one did not have intimate relations with the "dead man." The excessiveness in number, and the kind of psyche that would permit such "playfulness" also has the ability to give voice to all these women—this is something Machado de Assis does not achieve, for it is always Brás Cubas who holds the reins of the narrative.

Let us observe, with more concrete examples, how Germano Almeida, under the guise of his character, transforms fiction into reality, or, more correctly stated, into another fiction, into a space where the connection with the reality of the country is so obvious that there is no way we can relegate his work to the area of pure fiction where we could ignore the social effects of this sort of writing.

The female characters in *Memórias de Um Espírito* are introduced as the narrator's wake takes place. Even though they are presented by the same narrator—"*Agora é Julinha que entra. Vem composta como de costume, serena*" ["Now it is Julinha who comes in. As always, she is composed, serene"] (115)—they quickly take command of their own stories, making the dead man's words superfluous, and they create a world of internal commentaries in which they become the actors and interpreters of their own narrative. Add this to the fact that the novel in question is in permanent dialogue with the author's other works, and it is not difficult to find a certain amount of repetition—which we could, after all, find redundant. For example, on page 27, when we are first introduced to Aninhas: Aninhas has already appeared as a character in *D. Pura e os Camaradas de Abril* [*Dona Pura and the April Comrades*] and she is the addressee of a letter written by Caga-Vírgulas in the last story in *Estórias de Dentro de Casa* [*Stories from Inside the House*], "Agravos de um Artista" ["An Artist's Wrongs"] (which in turn establishes a dialogue with a non-fictional text, "Agravos de um Artista" ["A Writer's Wrongs"], included in *Estórias Contadas* [*Recounted Tales*] [59-63], a collection of journalistic accounts). This is one of the many examples of such repetition. Now, as Susan Suleiman has told us, in her *Authoritarian Fictions, The Ideological Novel as a Literary Genre* (1983), the more redundancy we encounter in a text the greater likelihood it is that we have before us a *roman à la these* [sic], one that attempts to transmit a specific message. This message may be either transmitted directly or we may find it in specific contexts, namely that of intertextuality, whereby a story is presented as a variation of another story. What we thus have are kinds of exemplary stories in which there is a process of reduplication *ad infinitum*. We already had the occasion to conclude[3] that this characteristic of Germano Almeida's texts does not serve authoritarian purposes. Based as it is on continual and renewing desire, each repetition can be regarded as yet another attempt at ecstasy, one whereby the body of an ethical outlook would be configured with the body of the text. It is an ethical outlook that would privilege, and permanently at that, the dialogic situation, be it in the space of intimacy, which is configured in the very act of writing or creating—which would be equivalent to the sexual act—or be it in the public sphere, the sphere of speech that escapes the domination of the singular and ephemeral voice and that is recovered in a permanent dialogue with the reader. It is almost like taking the author's mental associations and what they mean in the text, and re-inventing them. The text is the author and it is worthy of interest both as a signifier and as a signified; like a parallel structure, the text belongs to the order of the individual and that of the collective.

For, if authorial plurality contributes to the devaluation of that same plurality to the detriment of the characters, these same characters, such as is the case with *O Meu Poeta* [*My Poet*] as well as in the work we are discussing, are more or less evidently authorial in category and for that reason in control of discourse. We have already ascertained that this authorial polyphony reveals itself to be the guiding principle of writing and that it is also a cultural hallmark. The authorial "I" appropriates for itself borders that are unsteady; it goes from the aforementioned position of subject to that of object, and thus it is through this polyphony that we are able to go beyond the binary structures of traditional dialogue. Polyphony reveals the contiguity that exists between the inner and outer lining of the textual and cultural space that surrounds him and which he creates and which he leaves for us as a body of writing and, also, as the desire that determines this body of writing should be integral to a *poesis* that, after all, coincides with the political vision of the work itself.

Let us accept that this intertextual repetition of characters and stories is like a representation of sensual jouissance that works towards the demolition of expectations: the text is created anew in a new text, one where the ideology and ethics of an open, borderless space remain an important idea. Thus we see how the figure of the narrator, which could easily be perceived as both suffocating and authoritarian, is transfigured, and how the typically colonial discourse of power is reworked.

On the other hand, in tandem with Lukács, the novel is the biography of a difficult individual; that is to say, the novel portrays the world he moves in, subject to its contingencies and without transcendental meaning. Now, in a world of this nature, human individuality ceases to be organic. Or, better stated, this human individuality is no longer something the individual possesses nor is it the basis of his immediate existence. Individuality is transformed into an object that is searched for: "[T]he story of the soul that goes to find itself, that seeks adventures in order to be proved and tested by them, and by proving itself, to find its own essence."[4] We have chosen this quote because it applies so obviously to the *Memórias de Um Espírito.* The text is literally about a difficult individual, an atheist, who because he does not seek to find meaning in a transcendental order uses his non-organic nature in the most ironic manner possible: after he has died and has no body, he has around himself a group of women who, they insist, are connected to him primarily through this body. A body that was used not only in aid of a certain lifestyle, but which is also like the literary text that revolves around the death of this body, bringing it back to life and preventing it from being completely forgotten, because that body is made eternal within the text and in the multiple memory of those who "usufruct" that body. In conclusion, if under these circumstances, and in agreement with Lukács, what is searched for when one writes a novel is the essence of the soul, it seems quite clear to us that he lacks all props except that of his body. Consider, for example, the final irony when Alírio is taken to the gates of death by two "*belas moças, nuas em pelota*" ["lovely naked nude lasses"] (319). Besides, according to Miguel Oliveira da Silveira in his article "Hormonas, Afectos e Razão," in the human being there exists the "*presença do outro como mistério, também do outro sexo em nós, a importância insubstituível da fruição da alteridade sexual nos nossos sentimentos e razão, do si mesmo que se transforma, pela dialéctica da alteridade, pelo acolhimento desse mesmo outro*" ["presence of the other as a mystery, and also of the other sex within us, the irreplaceable importance of the fruition of sexual otherness in our feelings and our reason, of the I that is changed through the dialectics of otherness by receiving this same other"] (23). We will in due course invoke Cixous's feminine écriture as an aid to a structural understanding of Germano Almeida. Let us make use of this quotation as a way of achieving a profound understanding not only of the way the text makes use of sexuality as an obvious part of the content but also as a way of understanding the feminine element in this work, which implies not only the right of the female to reclaim her own bodily pleasure but also the right of the female to reclaim her own space within a narrative written by a male author, something Germano Almeida evidently is. Note how the various women insist on making use of Alírio de Sousa as a body for sex. Let us take the example of Irma and all the different ways this manifests itself:

> eu, uma mulher habituada a mandar em homens e a ser obedecida por eles, conhecida entre os meus pares pela minha independência, estar aqui a chorar um macho (285)
>
> [I, a woman used to bossing men around and being obeyed by them, a woman who's known among her peers for her independence, here I am crying for a male];
>
> uma das razões que a tinha levado ao divórcio era o facto de se sentir rebaixada, e até muitas vezes conspurcada quando o marido a possuía: trepava para cima dela e despejava-se! (290)

> [one of the reasons that had driven her to divorce was the fact that she felt demeaned, and many times even defiled, when her husband possessed her: he climbed on top of her and poured it all out inside her!];
>
> Dizia que preferia aquele lugar para poder ter um melhor domínio da situação, poder controlar até ao último instante o perverso risco de ser surpreendida em flagrante delito (281)
>
> [She said she preferred that place so she could have a better command of the situation, so she could have full control over that perverse risk of being caught redhanded];
>
> E foi muito estimulante continuar o jogo de não saber quem entrava e quem saía, e de cada vez que o tinha [Alírio] e o sentia e verificava que *estava* comigo inteiro e que continuava a querer-me (287)
>
> [And it was very stimulating playing that game of not knowing who was going in and who was going out, and that each time I'd had him [Alírio] and felt him and made sure he was with me and still desired me];
>
> Especializámo-nos a fazer amor falando de história, literatura, direito, pintura, etc., até que descobri o prazer de tocá-"lo" (287)
>
> [We became experts in the act of making love by talking about history, literature, law, painting, etc., until I discovered the pleasure of touching him].

There is an issue raised in Miguel Oliveira de Silveira's text, to which we have referred, and that is that it is not possible to assess the true weight of the female biological condition in its [culturally] accepted role of subordination, or rather, it is not possible to assess the cultural importance of man's use of physical strength, because that would suggest the permanent possibility of physical and sexual abuse of woman. It seems that the several excerpts from Germano Almeida's book point in the direction of the possibility that woman can be freed of this burden and also to the fact that this possibility of freedom is intimately related to education and, finally, to the fact that it is possible, to some degree, to alter sexual roles: it is not only Irma who is in control of her own sexual pleasure but it is the sexual act itself that can turn her on only if it happens out of the bed, "*na cama, passividade completa, mesmo um certo enfado*" ["total passivity in bed, even a certain resentment"] (285). And we are not dealing with a situation where there has been a sudden inversion of the rules, one where a woman—unexpectedly, improbably, and ridiculously—holds the reins of a situation that is almost always held by the man. True-to-life, Alírio de Sousa maintains his habit of having several relationships at the same time and he is fully involved in all of them. We are not dealing with the imposition of a female harem, of an unwanted polygamy, but rather a space for genuine dialogue with several women; here the author allows space, as in the example of Irma we have analysed, to be occupied by the will and desire of this female character. He gives her space not only so that she can express her point of view but also to affirm her control at a sexual and social level, for she is also a member of the political power structure. Note how the text itself, in very similar ways to Germano Almeida's other literary texts, provides space for a disagreement of opinions and for doubts about the verisimilitude of what is being represented. What we have is that now-commonplace narrative plurality and a space where there is no absolute truth but where all the characters are given the opportunity to present their own version of the facts. It is this opportunity, which we have here in the episode cited, and which brings us closer to Alírio de Sousa's voice, completely dismantles that idea, unthinkable in patriarchal culture, that woman could be in control of a sexual situation! We are, no doubt, dealing with the space for power, but one in which both at different times admit that they have been defeated: "*Acabei finalmente por dar-me por vencido*" ["I finally admitted to myself that I'd been defeated"] (284) and "*acabei atirando a toalha ao tapete, dar-me por vencida*" ["I gave up and admitted I'd been defeated"] (287). There are no winners, nothing is imposed, there is surrender to the "other sex within us," to the jouissance of sexual otherness, the otherness of roles and the otherness of the self itself in his or her ability to take up this difference in all the different existential dimensions. Note, for example, how Irma considers that the main reason for her indifference to sex is because of an excess of interest on the part of the male—the way all men around her seem to want to approach her, and want to have sex with her, altogether ignoring the intellectual qualities she possesses—and see, also, how Alírio de Sousa offers, instead, a somewhat different version of all this:

> a Irma é uma mulher não só voluntariosa como muito inteligente. Ora, quanto a

mim, o drama principal da inteligência é ela desumanizar as pessoas e como consequência resistir à reconciliação dos diversos indivíduos que existem em cada um de nós. E tinha-me ficado evidente que a Irma sobretudo tinha vergonha daquilo que considerava as suas fraquezas, como sejam a necessidade de dar e receber carinho, gostar de meiguice, a carência dos outros, antes privilegiando a razão como a única virtude digna de se orgulhar. (291)

[Irma is not only wilful, but she is also a very intelligent woman. For me at least, what's really wrong with intelligence is that it makes people less human and makes it difficult for us to be able to reconcile all the different people that exist within each of us. It had become quite obvious to me that Irma was actually embarrassed about what she regarded as her weaknesses, like giving or receiving affection, like being tender when others are needy; instead of that she privileged her rational side as the only virtue worthy of her pride.]

These different versions serve the purpose not only of presenting the different spaces for rationalization, both feminine and masculine, they are also, by themselves, reflections about the private areas of intimate relationships. We can say that, with this work, Germano Almeida makes an epistemological break with the rest of Cape Verdean literature. This text (and the ideologies underlying the construction of this particular text can already be found, as we have already stated, in earlier books—and we cannot overemphasize the importance of *O Meu Poeta* and *A Morte do Meu Poeta*) throws some rational doubt about the need to analyze the socio-political sphere from the position of the domestic sphere and, also, the assertion that any reflection on the feminine condition has been non-existent or simply based on a masculine projection about what men wanted women to have been or to be.[5] This quotation, and the structure of the work in general, promotes—and quite exactly at that—the assertion of different projections made by some about others and about those times when they [the women] agree or disagree with the reality of the *other*. In fact, Germano Almeida is given the opportunity of going beyond feminine stereotypes, as well as the cultural conditioning upon which these stereotypes have been based. When Irma is presented to us as a woman dominated by rationality and whose fears are connected with those commonplace characteristics that throughout the centuries have been attributed to woman, Germano Almeida demystifies the prototype of a discourse based on the idea that women belong in the "natural" domain of instincts and emotions whilst men, on the other, are located at the other end, exemplary specimens of the Enlightenment that they invented and that they constructed without any regard about what could or could not have been "womanly." As we are told by Montserrat Galcerán, in her article "Naturalismo e Anti-Naturalismo em Torno da Distinção Sexo/Género," it is on the basis of this theme that today we still insist "num pretenso *instinto maternal*, aspecto específico das mulheres" (36) ["on the would-be *maternal instinct*, something specific to woman"] as a constitutive element of her identity. And we are well aware how Freud came to make a bad situation worse when he put woman on that relative plane because her penis was missing and man was at the center, and it was from him that we could build this comparison. We believe that, in very many ways, Germano Almeida is capable of making the contrast between those differences that are biological in nature and those that are socio-cultural constructions.

We can now proceed to analyze an excerpt from the novel in light of this idea of the penis—the phallus of patriarchal power that has materialized and which has now been reduced to an instrument for pleasure, not only for the man, but also for the woman:

> É que nunca tinha encontrado uma mulher que tratasse a ferramenta com um carinho tão picante, [...] metendo-a e tirando-a da boca, mordiscando-a de brincadeira, depois torcendo e largando para a ver voltar à posição erecta, ou dando-lhe breves palmadinhas, por sinal nem sempre cariciosas. Nessas ocasiões *eu zangava-me:* isto aqui é um instrumento sério, dizia-lhe, exige respeito, tratamento de primeira, carinhos leves, não pode ser tratada assim a trouxe-mouxe como tu fazes [...]. *Mas ela não ligava nenhuma* às minhas queixas, antes murmurava como se fosse *só para ela,* eu adoro isto, adoro brincar com ele. (278, negrito nosso)

> [I had never come across a woman who treated the jack-hammer with such spicy tenderness [...] putting it in her mouth, taking it out, playfully nibbling at it, and twisting it and letting go of it so that it would return to its erect position; or else she would give it a few slaps, and by the look of it they weren't always that gentle. *I'd get cross* when that happened: "This here is a serious tool," I'd say to her, "it expects some respect, first-class treatment, tender loving care; You can't treat it like this, all slapdash like you do" [...]. *But she didn't pay any attention* to my complaints; she'd mumble something like *it was for her only,* "I love playing with this

> thing, I love playing with it." (our emphasis)]

The playful aspect is strongly stressed, and playful too is the independent and self-centered attitude of this woman who, on the one hand, could easily embody the sort of male sexual fantasy that she is making advances towards, and who, on the other hand, is a woman who is very much her own madam, someone who does not mourn the fact that she does not have a penis or who lives out the frustration of her deprivation, but who instead "plays" with this penis and with this idea that represents the power of the male, a mere jack-hammer in her hands. And still on this same theme, we would like now to consider the representation of the maternal in this work.

We are told about the conjugal relations between Alírio de Sousa and Alda right at the beginning of *As Memórias*:

> Os anos seguintes foram realmente de pacato deleite, os dois tacitamente de acordo em seguir o conselho de uma tia da Alda que certa vez nos visitou: Vocês têm uma vida tão calma e harmoniosa, disse ao despedir-se, não deixem que alguma criança a venha estragar! Não deixámos. (22)

> [The years that followed were really years of laid-back delight; the two had tacitly agreed to follow the advice of an aunt of Alda's who'd visited them one day: "The two of you have such a calm and harmonious life," she said as she was leaving. "Don't let some child come and spoil it all!" We didn't let it.]

A bit of advice that came from a woman, and one which the two heed. In a scenario where the main characters are always of the female sex and who add up to nothing less than eighteen—Alda, Alma, Aninhas, D. Rosalinda, Irma, Solange, Melly, Nanda, Lena, Dala, Julinha, Tiana, Ondina, Ângela, D. Sebastiana, Lídia, Shiva, not mentioning the other women who never get to speak in the first person—it is interesting that it is only Nanda who deals with the theme of the pregnancy in a relatively long manner. There is a passing reference to another pregnancy, one that in fact terminates in an abortion on account of some malformation in the foetus, and where the woman in question, Ana, makes the following statement: "*já viste como estaria agora empatada com uma criança nos braços?*" ["have you considered how tied down I'd be if I had a child in my arms?"] (96). This is after her relationship with Manco [lit. "Cripple"] has failed; similar to what happens with Caga-Vírgulas, Manco's name reveals his disabilities. If, on the one hand, this abortion is presented to us as a blessing given the context, the possibility that Nanda might be pregnant happens in a genuinely pathetic context. Still living in Angola, Alírio de Sousa, his love affair with Nanda having run its course, literally does his duty as a friend: he makes her pregnant! She, who does not mind raising a child alone in that environment of civil war, will eventually marry a doctor who will find a solution to her infertility. Or rather, motherhood, the "natural instinct" of all women, is an object of controversy, eighteen to one! (Ana does not count in that number because she was never given a chance to take up a narrative voice.) Even for her, motherhood is something that she has to have the will to fight for and something her body craves for; she desires to have a child, even without a companion, husband or lover (were it not for the kindness of her friend, Alírio); her desire for a child obliges her to seek medical treatment, so that she can attain her aim. This pregnancy is, without a doubt, the result of Nanda imposing her "want" on the world, it is not the consequence of predestined biological and instinctual imperatives (and notice how this episode can be regarded as one of the redundancies of which we spoke!). And it is with some curiosity that we should consider how this theme is dealt with in *Memórias de Brás Cubas*: not only does the main character die obsessed with the fact that he has not left any children, throughout the text, whenever he speaks up on this topic, his perspective is radically different from that which we find in Germano Almeida. Machado de Assis's vision of life, and even of death, is pessimistic; this is totally inverted in Germano Almeida's text. In the second text people do not have children and if they do have children it is because they want to be happy; in the first text people do not have children and the only good that comes out of this is that: "não transmiti a nenhuma criatura o legado da nossa miséria" ["I did not transmit to any living creature the legacy of our misery"] (230). Alírio de Sousa is guided by the pleasure principle and the need for well-being; independently of all social prejudices, Brás Cubas is guided by these very prejudices and his well-being is determined by material gain. Consider Eugénia, who could have made him happy but who was poor and lame and whom he eventually left because he was considering political office, which meant that he had to marry Virgília, a marriage that never took place, notwithstanding the love that developed between the two of them, because Virgília was too similar to Brás Cubas and a more successful suitor came along. Consider, still, Marcela, who uses him for his money. The work of Machado de Assis portrays a universe dominated by social, political and material concerns that begin and end with a feeling of failure and sadness—we have already read the concluding sentence in the text, let us now read the dedication: "*Ao verme que primeiro roeu as frias carnes do meu cadáver dedico como saudosa lembrança estas MEMÓRIAS PÓSTUMAS*" (sic) ["It is with fondness that I dedicate these POSTHUMOUS MEMORIES to that worm who first gnawed at the cold flesh of my corpse"]. In Germano Almeida, the world is governed by the pleasures of the flesh, by the desire for the Other—never mind the age or social standing; consider, for example, Ângela, who was a prostitute and much older than Alírio de Sousa, or D. Sebastiana, portrayed to be in a loving marriage with a man much older than she is, he who is the owner of a brothel and almost incapable of having an intimate relationship with the woman he loves! If Machado de Assis dedicates his book to the worm that will gnaw at his corpse, a suggestion of pessimism at its worst, Germano Almeida, on the other hand, dedicates his book "*a todos os seus companheiros de ficção e também aos que se dignaram acompanhá-lo durante as horas do seu agitado velório*" ["to all my literary companions and also those who deigned to keep him company during his agitated wake"]. One turns his attention towards death, the other towards life, a life that, even after his death, is pregnant with beauty and desire. Actually, in destroying the idea of the death of the body, not only with the mental existence that these women conjure up for his body, but also with the way they project death onto that body that is still present and is surrounded by the bodies of beautiful women. At the same time, Germano Almeida is also destroying the binary opposition of body/soul, one that brings with it an entire set of presuppositions: the death of the subject is less important than his funeral service, where, through the presence and the voices of these women, the discourse of his body is made to speak, the primacy of desire, which now more than at any other time, finds its prop in absence, in emptiness, but which on this occasion is able to transcend it [the emptiness]. There is no doubt that here we can find—or create—a new theoretical postulate that surpasses postmodernism, especially in so far as postmodernism is unable to provide an answer: we are dealing with the death of the rational, logocentric subject, but not the death of the de-centered subject who is propped up by the libido and who, as a consequence of that, is grounded in the unconscious. The connection between this idea and the ideas proposed by feminist theories is more than obvious; if it is not obvious then we should read Adrienne Rich:

> I am convinced that there are ways of thinking that we don't yet know about. I

> take these words to mean that many women are *even now* thinking in ways which traditional intellection denies, or is unable to grasp [...]. In arguing that we have by no means yet explored or understood or biological grounding, the miracle and paradox of the female body and its spiritual and political meanings, I am really asking whether women cannot begin, at last, to *think through the body*, to connect what has been so cruelly disorganized. (192)

In other words, speaking in theoretical terms, Germano Almeida's work, especially with regards to the philosophical question of the death of the subject, does not permit us to escape from making a connection with feminism. It is our opinion that the metaphor is too facile: the death of the subject of rationality that modernity introduced and the leap towards the emptiness of the "untruths" introduced by postmodernity are closely connected to feminist discourse as a discourse of subjectivity. It is this discourse, which as we know and have seen, anchors itself in the word, in the [grammatical] first person, as a way of expressing otherness (the plurality of the various I's vying for attention in the text). Of course, the question that remains is knowing to what extent the emergence of a feminine discourse is rooted in the death of the rational male subject, and to what extent this feminist discourse is dependent on the male subject. That is to say, to what extent can Germano Almeida's feminine écriture not be regarded as an enunciation of the female political and theoretical subject? If the death of Alírio de Sousa—which is also the death of the author—is also, as we have so obviously seen, not the death of the patriarchal metaphor, but the death of the body, then the question that remains for us to ask is: what is the significance of this Cartesian death in the context of feminine écriture, at least in the manner that it was conceived by the French school, and also the weight of this project of thinking out the subject as a bodily entity in the Kingdom of Psychoanalysis which, so obviously, was the discipline that invented this whole way of looking at things when it postulated that consciousness was separate from the unconscious and when it linked the unconscious to the Kingdom of Basic Desires and, consequently, the body?

Concluding this first reading of this work, we can say that Germano Almeida is able to achieve two feats. Firstly, he does justice to Machado de Assis: starting off from the similarity in titles, we are able to read Machado's work from an extremely up-to-date perspective, one that is replete with the traces of postmodernity—narrative fragmentation, the addressing of the reader and his inclusion in the narrative, the mixture of fiction and reality ("*eu, Brás Cubas, se adotei a forma livre de um Sterne, ou de um Xavier de Maistre, não sei se lhe meti algumas rabugens de pessimismo*" ["if is true that I, Brás Cubas, have adopted the free form of, say, Sterne or Xavier de Maistre, I can't be sure I haven't added some of my own pessimistic gripes"] (21)—and of a certain kind of feminine écriture that is revealed not only through these traces but in the ability to give flesh to portraits of fully-rounded free-willed women. Secondly, he makes a break with the Brazilian tradition, a tradition he refers to when he shows us a universe ruled by the body, by pleasure, by desire, by an optimism based on the life of one man, the center of whose being was based on the primacy of feeling and not of reason. Machado de Assis's "*pena da galhofa*" ["pen of mirth"] is put in the service of melancholy and pessimism and his sense of irony is altogether lacking in humor. In Germano Almeida, irony coincides with humor and the same "*pena da galhofa*" that we find in his work subverts the universe whence it came: be it the world of *Claridade*, Brazilian realism or this text by Machado de Assis.

This in a first reading. If one were to make a more profound reading, the sort of questions we would have to ask ourselves would include the connection between postmodernism and feminism and the "novelty" of postmodernism itself. It is important to recall that many of the features of postmodernism have long been articulated by feminists: the question of gender as a social construction, the integration of marginalized discourses in the canon, non-totalization or the rigidity of the answers that are sought after, and the connection between all this and a political vision of effective action, of visible social and material consequences, space and time as fragmentary notions, the plurality of the subject and of reality. The truth is that if postmodernism has come to integrate all these presuppositions as being uniquely its own, it has done so in order that it can apparently facilitate the consequences that women can gain from them—and, since we are we talking about it, other marginalized groups, too; the problem is that in doing so postmodernism runs the risk of feminizing the universe, the universe we want to be free of the ideology of patriarchy or the simple lack of humanity in the system. Naturally, this global feminization easily falls into the same binary logic that it wanted to escape from, only this time it is not based on the difference in the sexes, but the difference of gender, one that unfortunately falls into the trap of becoming the Enlightenment *au contraire*: the primacy of feeling and the female gender. All that remains for us to do it to analyze the work of Germano Almeida from this perspective and assess the extent to which his re-invention of reality is free from these dangers.

Notes

[1] "[A] literatura caboverdeana sofre do grandessíssimo defeito de ter sido até agora uma literatura meramente descritiva. Ora a consequência disto é que os nossos escritores não estão preparados para analisar e interpretar. Eu pessoalmente penso que as pessoas no geral e as que escrevem em particular sentem que há mudanças. Mas repara que uma mudança de mentalidade [...] não é uma realidade imediatamente apreensível [...]. Porém, para o escritor [as mudanças] já deveriam sê-lo, se ele estivesse preparado para analisar, quase que para reinterpretar a realidade" (Almeida 1992, 188). ["Cape Verdean literature suffers from that grave defect of having been, until now, merely a descriptive literature. The result of this is that our writers are not equipped to analyze and interpret. Personally speaking, I think that people in general and those who write feel that there are changes in the air. But note that a change in mindset [...] is not something that is immediately apprehensible [...]. But they [the changes] should be so for writers, had they been equipped to analyze, and even reinterpret reality."] And now read Machado de Assis: "A falta de uma crítica assim é um dos maiores males que padece a nossa literatura; é mister que a análise corrija ou anime a invenção, que os pontos de doutrina e de história se investiguem, que as belezas se estudem, que os senões se apontem, que o gôsto se apure e eduque, e [a literatura brasileira] se desenvolva e caminhe aos altos destinos que a esperam" (1962, 804). ["The lack of critics is one of the worst ills of our literature; it is imperative that analyses should correct or enliven that which has been invented, that history and our belief-system should be investigated, beauty studied, the "if nots" pointed out, and taste should be refined and people should be help to acquire it, so that Brazilian literature may develop and walk towards the high destinies that await it"]—the repetition of the same preoccupations in two countries so far away from each other, not only in terms of space but by time, but which are united in a common (post-)colonial experience, which is what has created this lack of critical sense in the first place; they [these countries] have been sabotaged by an external authority that had no interest in creating a critical sense.

[2] For example: "tempos de grande sabura" (Almeida 2001, 22).

[3] We invite the reader to read two articles written by the author of this article, one published in *Revista Expressão* 5.2 (Jul-Dec), 109-116. Santa Maria: Ed. CAL-UFSM, entitled "O momento do 'crime' e uma breve contextualização: *Dois Irmãos* e *et al* de Germano Almeida"; and the other due for publication: "A Fronteira da Desconstrução: Construir Germano Almeida,"Actas do XVIII Encontro de Professores Brasileiros de Literatura Portuguesa,

[4] Lukács, *Theory of the Novel* 89. Qtd. in Suleiman 65.

[5] Observe the figure of Caga-Vírgulas, whose name is obviously derogatory, and the manner in which it is through him, once again (for we have already encountered this scene in *Estórias de Dentro de Casa*, "Agravos de um Artista"), that the supposedly traditional male and female roles are ridiculed: "*[Dizia ele que,] como seria do meu conhecimento era dos livros que qualquer marido detém, por força da sua superioridade intelectual, um poder/dever de correcção sobre a mulher*" (160) ["He told me I should know from books that any husband, by virtue of his intellectual superiority, will have power over/the right to reprimand his wife"].

Works Cited

Almeida, Germano. *O Meu Poeta.* Lisboa: Caminho, 1992.

———. *A Ilha Fantástica.* Lisboa: Caminho, 1994.

———. *Estórias de Dentro de Casa.* Lisboa: Caminho, 1996.

———. *Dois Irmãos.* Lisboa: Caminho, 1998.

———. *A Morte Do Meu Poeta.* Cabo Verde: Ilhéu Edit., 1998.

———. *Estórias Contadas.* Lisboa: Caminho, 1998.

———. *O Dia das Calças Roladas.* Lisboa: Caminho, 1999.

———. *D. Pura e Os Camaradas de Abril.* Lisboa: Caminho, 1999.

———. *As Memórias de Um Espírito.* Lisboa: Caminho, 2001.

Ferreira, Maria Luísa Ribeiro, org. *Pensar no Feminino.* Lisboa: Edições Colibri, 2001.

Galcerán, Montserrat. "Naturalismo e Anti-Naturalismo em Torno da Distinção Sexo/Género." Ferreira 35-45.

Machado de Assis. *Memórias Póstumas de Brás Cubas.* Belo Horizonte; Rio de Janeiro: Garnier, [1880].

———. "Notícia da Actual Literatura Brasileira, Instinto de Nacionalidade." *Obras Completas, III.* Rio de Janeiro: José Aguilar Ltd., 1962. 801-09.

Rich, Adrienne. *Of Woman Born.* New York: Norton, 1976.

Silveira, Miguel Oliveira da. "Hormonas, Afectos e Razão." Ferreira 21-27.

Suleiman, Susan. *Authoritarian Fictions, The Ideological Novel as a Literary Genre.* New York: Columbia UP, 1983.

Paula Gândara works at the University of Massachusetts, Amherst. She has written articles on Jorge de Sena and has co-edited a collection of articles on Jorge de Sena. She has also written a five-page article entitled "Qual Adélia?" E-mail: pgandara@spanport.umass.edu

A Cabeça Calva de Deus by Corsino Fortes: Litany & Music in Praise of Cape Verde

Ana Mafalda Leite
Translated by
Luís R. Mitras
Revised by
Mark Streeter

Abstract. This article sums up some of the major features of the three books of poetry by Corsino Fortes, which were collected in one volume entitled *A Cabeça Calva de Deus.* It emphasizes (a) the way the author's work can be seen as a continuation of the Cape Verdean literary tradition, (b) the innovative nature of his poetic language, and (c) his vocation for a kind of writing that is epic, rhetorical and sacral. It further describes the pictographic transfiguration achieved by Fortes in his poetic rendering of the cultural and historical universe that is Cape Verde.

A Cabeça Calva de Deus [*God's Bald Head*] is the name of a poetic trilogy that was begun in 1973 with the publication of *Pão & Fonema* [*Bread & Phoneme*], followed by *Árvore & Tambor* [*Tree & Drum*] in 1986, and concluded with *Pedras de Sol & Substância* [*Stones of Sun & Substance*], published in 2001. The trilogy can be read as a journey, one that begins by announcing the liberation of the country, rejoices at this newfound liberation through the sounds of celebration and rejoicing, and, finally, renders Cape Verde's sun-drenched culture into something worthy of dignity. *God's Bald Head* is a condensed image for the potential for growth of the Cape Verdean world, and also for the regeneration that must begin from the limitations of its geography, climate and soil. Forsaken by the gods in the middle of the Atlantic Ocean, the ten islands of Cape Verde, halfway between Africa, Europe and America, with the mineral nakedness of the drought, have in them that poetic and rhythmic strength of which Corsino Fortes's inaugural poetry sings in an epic and sacred tone.

The first book, *Pão & Fonema*, presents us, first of all, with a poem that functions as an initial proposition, prologue or plan of intention; this is followed by three cantos. The title functions as the synthesis or alliance of two fundamental and concrete symbols which the poet conceived of in order to reformulate the Cape Verdean universe in poetic terms. These two elements carry in them various meanings—which are developed throughout the text—and they are revealing of the main characteristics of the islands of Cape Verde.

Thus, the first element—bread—is the result of the positive combination of *rain* and *corn*, those essential components that offer a solution or way-out for a country traditionally subject to drought and hunger, and, as a result of these things, to immigration. To this initial element of growth and regeneration can be added the second element—the phoneme—which implies an access to the voice, to the word, to literacy, to culture, or, better still, to the creation of an autonomous cultural world. Phoneme is also a way of reclaiming the very act of writing and of poetic creation—*poiesis*— as a new aesthetic-cultural act within the Cape Verdean literary tradition. The two symbols that have been united (and the sign that joins them—&—makes the association clear) represent physical and spiritual food, bread for the body, a voice for the mind, food that will rescue Cape Verdeans from their worldly misfortunes. An epic poem of bread and the word, the poem can be interpreted as an offering of renewal and it is invested with the ritual force of a symbolic Eucharist.

The poetic output of those in the *Claridade* movement, which was innovative in its description of Cape Verdean themes such as the flight from the land, the diaspora, homesickness, the drought and hunger, came to be enlarged upon with newer thematic and ideological perspectives by those Cape Verdean poets writing between 1962 and 1974. This is evident, and we are citing merely a few examples, in the work of Ovídio Martins, who played an important role in developing a critique of "the flight from the country" theme, in the reappropriation of African cultural elements in the poetry of António Nunes and Onésimo da Silveira, or in Gabriel Mariano's reappraisal of traditional culture in his struggle poetry. But the kind of poetry that breaks with the past and introduces an element of renewal in Cape Verdean poetry appears, in fact, only with the poetry of Arménio Vieira, T. T. Thiofe and, essentially, with the initial publication of *Pão & Fonema* in 1974. This collection is technically innovative and its content reveals it to operate according to an altogether different ideological-thematic paradigm.

The reappraisal of the theme of "the flight from the land" takes up the second canto of this book, "Mar & Matrimónio" ["Sea & Marriage"]. The flight from the islands is seen, not as a misfortune, but rather as an attitude of searching, as a search for knowledge, as a way of achieving inner growth. In this sense it is like a rite of initiation; the intentions that lie behind this act are well suggested by the poem "De pé nú sobre o pão de amanhã" ["Barefoot over Tomorrow's Bread"]. This is the point Mesquitela Lima makes in his foreword to the work: "*O caboverdiano ao sair da terra (para assumir a atitude dinâmica) vai nu, sem nada, e caminha para o pão do futuro*" ["When Cape Verdeans leave the land (in this active and dynamic stand) they go barefoot, without anything at all, and they walk in the direction of the bread of the future"] (1974, 78). Journey and exile are things that allow the islanders, both as a community and as a nation, to see themselves in an altogether different dimension: "*Que toda a partida é alfabeto que nasce / todo o regresso é nação que soletra*" ["For every time someone leaves it's an alphabet that's reborn / every time someone returns it's the entire nation that spells out the letters"] (70).

The first canto heralds this change and newfound maturity. We witness how this change, born out of the impatience, the accumulated energy, and the strength that stirs within the breast of each Cape Verdean citizen, is ready to reveal itself like the volcano on the island of Fogo: "*Tchon de povo tchon de pedra! C'ma fogo ma pedra na vulcon de D'jar-Fogo*" (36). This potential movement—germinated of itself, and in empathy with the mineral wisdom of the islands—is precisely that silent movement that stirs both interior and exterior, the islands and the islander, intimately connected.

"Pão & Património" ["Bread & Patrimony"], the third and last canto of *Pão & Fonema*, traces a circle around the topographical features of Cape Verde. After calling upon the systolic and diastolic movements—which reveal that the aspirations at the heart of the islanders beat to the rhythm of their insularity—there is, once again, the contraction, the return, the point of departure. This return, emphasized through the presence of the adverb "agora," "*Agora povo pulso / agora pão agora poema*" ["People pulse now / bread now poem now"] (76), representing, as it does, the future liberation from colonial domination that has come **now**, this return is at the origin of the discovery of the "*nova terra dentro da terra*" ["new land inside the land"] and of a new dawn, something that is made quite explicit in the poem "Konde Palmanhã Manchê"

["When Morning Dawns"]. The return implies a re-encounter: "*Não a terra das cicatrizes / Mas a terra que cicatriza*" ["Not the land that has been scarred / But the land that heals itself"] (80)—which means that the scar on the islander, who is a symbolic kind of Ulysses, needs to be accepted or recognized as such by his beloved/the island. The island, feminine, a space that is turned back on itself, provides the sense of closure necessary for the simultaneous birth and creation of the new cosmos and, also, of the poem that it celebrates by naming: "*Oh verso livre / oh semente / oh sangue de violas & viola Não consintam / Que o tempo / Roube à minha fome / O ovo do sol que nasce / e a tábua / Do meu tabernáculo*" ["O free verse (O liberated verse) / o seed / o blood of guitars & guitar Don't permit / That time / Should steal from my hunger / The egg of the sun that's born / And the tablet / Of my tabernacle"] (93).

Thus, what we have here is the convergence between a utopian, imaginary space—one that has always been sought and sung about in Cape Verdean poetry—and the geography of the country, and also the nation. Since the days of its inception Cape Verdean literature has mapped out a mythical scenario for itself, one that Manuel Ferreira has referred to as the "*mito hesperitano ou a nostalgia do paraíso perdido*" ["Hesperidian myth or the nostalgia for the lost paradise"] (1985) and that one encounters, especially, in the works of José Lopes, Eugénio Tavares and Pedro Cardoso; that myth revolves around the idea of a legendary or magical origin for the islands (the Hesperides, Atlantis) *in illo tempore*, one that evokes the gardens of Paradise (the gardens of the Hesperides), the nostalgia for a lost paradise and a golden age. A subsequent myth that was incorporated into this earlier myth by the poets of the *Claridade* movement is the myth of "Pasárgada," fundamentally a "flight from the country" myth; this myth gives continuation to that search for an ideal space by expanding the search for a space of happiness that is evident in the first myth, a space the islands cannot provide. What *Pão & Fonema* does is to summon that mythical space/time so that it coincides with the real space/time; this other mythical country of origin—of flight, of escape—is returned to the center of the islands, and, for the first time, the space of fertilization and blessedness, the *locus-amoenus*, coincides with the motif of the nation, which has been rediscovered by the foundational myth.

Árvore & Tambor [*Tree & Drum*], the second collection, published in 1986, was the promise, "the Promised Land" of Corsino Fortes's first book, *Pão & Fonema* (1973). The first poem of the third canto in this collection explains the title in the following manner: "*Que as colinas nascem / na omo-*

plata dos homens / com um cântico na aorta / árvore & tambor & sangue" ["May the hills be born / In the shoulder-blades of men / with a canticle in the aorta / tree & drum & blood"] (75).

Thus we see that the first book already contained the second collection in gestation; and we see the obvious thread that links the first to the second. The historical imperative of re-inventing Cape Verde in epic and mythical terms remains and it is further expanded upon. The title *Árvore & Tambor* retakes the proposal of *Pão & Fonema* and enlarges on it. Out of the fragmented phoneme that reclaimed the freedom to be both word and voice comes the full sound of the drum; because it belongs within an African tradition the drum introduces a new language of identification with Africa, a language of celebratory rhythms and solidarity: "*Os homens que nasceram da Estrela da manhã / assim foram / Árvore & Tambor pela alvorada / plantar no lábio da tua porta / África: / mais uma espiga mais um livro mais uma rocha*" ["The men born out of the Morning Star / were thus formed / Tree & Drum at dawn / so as to plant on the lips of your door / Africa: / one more corn cob one more book one more rock"] (102).

The African connotations of the word "drum" are deliberately appropriated by the poet; it is a word that harkens back to the work of many other poets, the most significant one being José Craveirinha, the Mozambican poet ("*Quero ser tambor*"—"I want to be a drum"). The concept of "tree" also suggests "bread"; it is a way of using the action in order to make concrete the act: planting, building, renewing the body, the spirit, the land, the nation: "*E o espírito é árvore*" ["And the spirit is a tree"]; "*ó velho arbusto! Que foi colónia*" ["O old shrub! That was a colony once"]; "*Vem! E ergue a tua árvore / Aqui*" ["Come! And raise your tree / Here"]. (105, 106, 193)

Árvore & Tambor also works around the important symbolism of rounded forms, where the circularity of the universe that it is being created, when it acquires its own momentum, acquires also the spherical form of a cosmos. If we consider, for example, the structure of the poem, the initial "Proposição & Prólogo" ["Proposition & Prologue"] and the five cantos that follow, which together constitute the text (and the organization of this material, once again, reveals the author's vocation for epic poetry), we notice how the text ends with a final "Proposição & Prólogo" that takes up the material developed in the beginning. Any reading of the poem (and of its intentions) thus becomes circular; there has been a necessary closing off of that which has grown within the poem and of the world that it has concentrically conquered.

But the semantic field around these words and around the title does not exhaust itself with these observations we have made. One of the characteristic features of Corsino Fortes's poetry is the use of a same word in different contexts, never as mere repetition, but rather for the sake of recurrence; this, in turn, allows for the generation of new metaphors, which, as we know, revolve around an axis of equivalence. It is this axis of equivalence that throughout the poem establishes the likeness that exists between a group of words suggested by "*tambor*" ["drum"], words such as "*esfera*" ["sphere"], "*roda*" ["wheel"], "*rosto*" ["face"], "*ovo*" ["egg"], "*ventre*" ["womb"], "*útero*" ["uterus" *or* "womb"], "*umbigo*" ["navel"], or between those words suggested by "*árvore*" ["tree"], words such as "*raiz*" ["root"], "*hélice*" ["coil"], "*arbusto*" ["shrub"], "*semente*" ["seed"], "*seiva*" ["sap"], "*sangue*" ["blood"]. These semantic clusters, of which we have mentioned but a few, tend to group and regroup in the most varied of combinations, which results in the constant appearance of new images, all based around these condensed groups of symbolically-charged words. A similar umbilical growth—which coheres around the energy source of sound, which is also the source of meaning (and note how alliteration, which creates meaning through sound, is also one of the characteristic features of this poetic universe)—is revealed at the rhetorical level; it duplicates the theme of "genesis," which is developed at the level of content. Take, for instance, the poem "Ilha" ["Island"], included in "Proposição & Prólogo":

Sol & semente: raiz & relâmpago
Tambor de som
que floresce
A cabeça calva de Deus. (10)

[Sun & seed: root & lightning
Sound-creating drum
That flowers
God's bald head.]

If we exclude those words that are used to connect the elements in the sentence, we find that the poet uses merely ten words: he is thus formally drawing the map of the ten Cape Verdean islands. The first terms are terms pertaining to gestation or genesis *par excellence*, and this sense is suggested also by alliteration: "*Sol & semente*" ["Sun & seed"]. These terms are the source of the terms that follow, which continue with the gestation cycle: "raiz & relâmpago" ["root & lightning"]. These images, in turn, unleash an image that stands for sound, but instead of the word "thunder," which is what we would expect, what we have instead is the symbolic "*Tambor*" ["Drum"], the circular form of rhythm, fertilizing strength, energy. The only verb in the poem, "*floresce*" ["flowers" *or* "flourishes"], gives momentum to this process that has been set in motion, and which transforms and recreates the dryness and nakedness of the islands, itself conveyed through the alliterative image: "*A cabeça calva de Deus*" ["God's bald head"]. Thus we see how the work of renewing the face of God's earth has been initiated by human beings; but then humans are also a kind of God.

Borrowing directly from the divine gesture in Genesis, the first canto, "De manhã! Os Tambores Amam A Chama Da Palavra Mão" ["In the morning! The Drums Love the Flame of the Word Hand"] re-invents the creation of the islands, its mythical birth, not in some distant past, but in a time that renews itself and begins all over again. Thus the phrase "De manhã!," which is repeated in the form of a litany throughout the text, almost as though it were a magical incantation, establishes this idea of something that was founded, of leaving the chaos in the direction of the light and of a new order: "*De Manhã! as ilhas / da minha pátria nascem grávidas / com o arco-íris / na menina do olho*" (111) ["In the morning! the islands / of my mother-country are born pregnant / with the rainbow / in the gleam of the eye (*or* in the beloved)"].

Still in this same poem, the author continues to work around the anti-"flight from the country" theme that he had first rehearsed in *Pão & Fonema*, but now the call for people to return to the country is formulated as a constant and continuous appeal. This is because they would be participating in the reconstruction of the new nation, something that demands of all the children of the islands the repetition of that same mythical gesture of Genesis:

Vem! simples & Redondo
pelo sol pela gema
E pela dor do ovo que o povo fecundou
As colinas aguardam pela mão
o gomo da tua herança
E pelo ventre de Bia
A Cimboa
dará

terra
terra nua
terra virgem
À árvore da tua parabola. (190)

[Come! simple & rounded
through the sun through the yolk
And through the agonies of the egg that people had fertilized
The hillsides await your hand
the bud of your inheritance
And through Bia's womb
Cimboa
will give
land
naked land
virgin land
To the tree of your parable.]

The birth ritual is thus accomplished, and it all begins at "*uma hora zero*" ["a zero hour"], the moment when the old colony becomes this new nation, this eminently sun-drenched land; this first canto suggests all the colors of this new sunscape, beginning with yellow and going through to the colors of the rainbow; these colors are combined and recombined as though he were an alchemist: everything is transmuted, the furrowed nature of the islands and even those features that suggest shortage and hunger, such as, for example, the goat and the volcano: "*o vulcão é força / a ilha é semente / o mar é músculo / a cabra é ouro*" ["the volcano is strength / the island is a seed / the sea is a muscle / the goat is golden"]. Gestation, in turns, acquires feminine attributes, and the poem is literally dotted with multiple references of this kind: "*os sons uterinos da ilha que nasce*" ["the womb-like sounds of an island that's born"] (111); "*o sol desce / velho & jovem / E ajoelha-se à porta das maternidades*" ["the sun comes down / ancient & young / And kneels at the door of maternity hospitals"] (116).

The poem reveals itself to be an "*acto de cultura*" ["act of culture"]—an allusion to the title of one of the other poems (a title that, in turn, suggests the famous sentence by Amílcar Cabral, "*Toda a revolução é um acto de cultura*" ["Every revolution is an act of culture"])—insofar as it suggests change through renewal and fulfils its role of being "*a expressão dinâmica de um caos inicial*" ["the dynamic expression of an original chaos"] because it transforms the island, language, love and the human being into things that exists within a cosmic order: "*Como o som cresce na fruta! na árvore está o tambor / E contra a erosão: a política de sedução*" ["Like sound growing within the fruit! the tree is within the drum / And against soil erosion: the politics of seduction"] (179).

"Hoje Chovia A Chuva Que Não Chove" ["Today it Rained the Rain that Doesn't Rain"], a poem from Canto III, suggests that after genesis comes fertility. It does not cease to rain in the poem, the entire alphabet, from A to Z, rains down on the poem—so that it will rain, too, in Cape Verde, a land where the drought driven in from the Sahel is what is most natural to the country and, consequently, the great poetic theme in the literature of that country. This symbolic "deluge" is a blessing of renewal (thus inverting the Biblical meaning of the term, where the deluge was brought on as a punishment) and the promise that the islands will fulfill their "tree" ["*árvore*"]: "*O povo / chove no povoado a sua chuva de séculos / E a goela das ribeiras / incha-se De aplausos / Que a chuva / é podium / na maratona das nossas artérias*" ["People / Rain down their centuries-old rain on the town / And the throat of the riversides / swells up in applause / For the rain / is the podium / in the marathon of our arteries"] (128) . The entire Canto III is a delirium of poetic word-play and rhetorical joy. The scarce rain—"*Chove pulga & ponto: sangue & vírgula*" ["It rains down fleas and periods (full stops): blood & commas"] (133)—acquires, by means of the rhetorical tropes of hyperbole and synecdoche, the dimension of a gigantic raindrop through which we can see, as though through a microscope, the islands in miniature: this glass dome full of water that was so often dreamed about. The world is reinvented in an inverse order, and the magnitude of the hyperbole is associated with the pregnancy of the world that is to be born: "*Mas no olho vítreo da gota / uma cabra dança e outra coxeia / Ambas arrastam Entre as patas / Um eclipse de sol / No rosto oblongo da gota / As ilhas são cabras / as cabras são ilhas / com úberes na Via Láctea*" ["But in the glassy eye of the raindrop / a goat dances and another one limps / Both drag between their paws / An eclipse of the sun / In the oblong countenance of the raindrop / The islands are goats / the goats are islands / with udders in the Milky Way"]. In this universe the roles are reversed, they are subject to change, and the elements are rendered equivalent to each other: an island for a goat, a goat for an island. The real is continually subject to change, and metamorphosis leads directly to personification:

what is abstract acquires life, and what is inanimate acquires a form that is concrete. In this world that is about to be born, a world that is both placenta and the mother's womb, everything is pulsating and works towards acquiring multiple and unexpected dimension: "*E de pé o arquipélago ganha vela / porto & terra / De hélices nas raízes*" ["As it arises the archipelago acquires sail / harbour & land / Coils on the roots"]; "*Por vezes o deserto chocalha nos ossos o seu esqueleto de gotas*" ["At times the desert jingles in the bones of its skeleton made of raindrops"]; "*E as ilhas soerguem-se / pelo arquipélago das patas / E vão / De cratera em cratera / Erguer / na boca das sementes / A força contida nos vulcões*" ["And the islands are lifted up / By the archipelago of the paws / And they go / From crater to crater / Raising / in the mouth of seeds / The strength that's inside volcanoes"] (131, 132).

Canto III, "O Pescador O Peixe E A Sua Península" ["The Fisherman the Fish and His Peninsula"], presents us with the first anonymous heroes who inhabit and work in this newly created world. Now that the island has been re-created, regenerated by the symbolic deluge, it is time to portray humans and their labor. In the sea "*a terra é arável*" ["the land can also be ploughed"] and the fisherman's toil is an often-forgotten daily epic struggle of awesome dimensions. Land and sea combine in preparing terrain favorable for work: "*Além! no podium do mar largo / os cetáceos são olhos que saltam saltos de solidão / E se apaixonam / Ao longo da costa / Pelo ombro da ilha Que de longe balouça*" ["Beyond! in the podium of the wide sea / the cetaceans are eyes that leap at the leaps in solitude / And they fall in love / all along the coastline / With the shoulder of the island that swirls in the distance"] (145). Sacred and ritual, the fisherman's trade unites the island with its natural environment, the sea; they are brought together fraternally, and bound in a relationship of mutual dependence and respect: "*Quando a ilha é sacerdote / E o mar é catedral / E o poente! oração / Que se ergue / Entre o mar E o seu cardume / O anzol aproxima-se do ofício / Como o céu da boca / Entre a hóstia e a comunhão*" ["When the island is a priest / And the sea is a cathedral / And the sunset! a prayer / That rises up / Between the sea and its shoal / The fishhook is like a trade / Like the roof of the mouth / That's between the host and the Eucharist"] (146).

The second poem of Canto III, "*Onde Mora A Viola Do Artesão*" ["Where the Guitar of the Artisan Resides"], explores the regenerative processes of memory and narrates those historical events that have paved the way for this present cosmogony. It is necessarily retrospective and pedagogic: "*Ali! as narinas de meu pai / Sofreram o sopro / E a forja redonda / Do carvão de cruz &*

caos" ["There! my father's nostrils / They suffered the breath / And the rounded forge / Of the Cross of coal & chaos"]; "*Além! sob o silêncio do tambor de Deus / Dentes d'Europa / vendiam o pão d'África à fome das Américas*" ["Beyond! under the silence of God's drum / The teeth of Europe / Sold the bread of Africa to the hunger of the Americas"] (154). In a similar account, the artisan who forges a new world from the same rock—"*Quando as rochas / dão têmpera & aço / Ao corpo da vida*" ["When the rocks / give temper & steel / To life's body"] (153)—redeems the time and space that had existed before with his word/fire, and he re-inscribes them in the poem. The powerful hand of this descendant of that mythological blacksmith produces a new weapon, a new shield, the incandescent word—"*E da cicatriz da mão / brotam raízes / Que vicejam a memória dos séculos*" ["And from the scar on his hand / Spring up roots / That germinate with the memory of centuries"] (131)—one that carries within itself the map of History: slavery, forced labor, deportation, poverty, etc.

The predominant emphasis of the last canto is an appeal for Cape Verdeans to return and to help reconstruct their country. As we have mentioned above, the poem "Tempo De Ser Ovo Ovo De Ser Tempo" ["Time To Be an Egg Egg To Be Time"] presents itself as a space that is ready to be inhabited; it brings the call for people to return back to the inaugural time. The island is female, given that it is she who bears this new cosmos, and it is she who, seductively, incites her lover to return—consider in this regard the poem "*Cantiga de Amigo*" [lit. "A Song to a Friend," a medieval verse form]: "*Já te sinto! aqui / Como um coração que bate à porta da sua morada / Mas vem! / pelos afluentes de ti / pela nascente & nascentes / Do teu corpo inteiro / E inunda-me! meu território*" ["I can feel you already! here / Like a heart that knocks on the door of where it resides / But come! / through the tributaries of your self / through the spring & springs / With your whole body / And flood me! my territory"] (198, 199)—her lover who is the emigrant, an imaginary Ulysses. The first poems portrays, then, the figure of a man and the figure of a woman: they stand in for that original couple that populated and nourished the world. "*Mestiço & mestiça*" ["Mulatto & Mulatta"], the poem that follows, takes this idea a step further, towards marriage and the birth of those cultural signs that are so specific to the archipelago.

Thus, the idea of the nation that awaits the return of the prodigal son is reworked in "A Fome de Ambrósio" ["Ambrósio's Hunger"]. The allusion to the well-known poem by Gabriel Mariano, "Capitão Ambrósio" ["Captain

Ambrósio"], is used to re-inscribe a new motif, that of "*a bandeira negra da fome*" ["the black flag of hunger"] (187), and transforms it into "*pão sobre o forno*" ["bread on the oven"]. This intertextual dialogue allows the Captain to be reborn for a future of plenty that is prepared for him, one when the Promised Land will flourish. There is also the poem "Lestada De Lés A Lés" ["The East Wind from One Side to Other"], which is a re-reading of Ovídio Martins's "Flagelados do Vento Leste" ["Flagellated by the East Wind"]—a poem whose title and theme were themselves borrowed from a novel by Manuel Lopes, one of the key works by that Cape Verdean novelist who was so much part of the *Claridade* movement. The poem by Corsino Fortes alludes to the previous poem, in order to negate it: "*Mesmo sendo! Já não somos / Os flagelados do vento leste /* [...] */ Que o digam / os braços do povo no povoado / E os tambores de pão / de pedra & pólen*" ["Even if we are! We no longer are / Those flagellated by the east wind / [...] / Let the arms / of people in town say it out / And the drums of bread / Of stone & pollen"] (202). An important reformulation of the great themes of Cape Verdean poetry is thus introduced, not only insofar as it is critical of those who mourn the "flight from the country," but because it suggests that "Pasárgada" can be discovered within the archipelago; also, it take cognisance of the fact that people can fight back despite the "flagellations" of natural phenomena, and credit should be given to the possibility of transformation: "*Aqui! onde / A seca é arma E a fome! desafio / A ilha é vida e a secura! vivência / E alta / negra! a estrela traga / A bandeira branca / Da nossa guerra / Entre céu & terra*" ["Here! where / The drought is a weapon and hunger! a challenge / The island is life and the dry season! existence / It is high / black! let the star bring / The white flag / Of our battle / Between land & sky"] (201, 204).

It is in the sequence of this new proposition that the tribute to António Nunes can be read as a necessary homage. In "Bom-Dia! António Nunes" ["Good Morning! António Nunes"] Corsino Fortes invites the said person to participate in the joy of the change that has been carried out. António Nunes also symbolizes that "tomorrow" that has became today, the day when the land has come into the inheritance of its own people: "*É teu António! o umbigo do mundo / onde / a força do teu suor desagua / E da ilha! / o cristal do tempo*" ["It's yours, António! the navel of the world / where / the strength of your sweat finds its outlet / And the island! / the crystal of time"] (194). We cannot but refer to that beautiful poem in Creole, "Golpe D'Estode Na Paraise." And even though it is the only poem in the book that is written entirely in Creole, there are also stanzas or parts of stanzas that are written in this language. This is evidence of the author's poetic bilingualism; he is an innovator in the one language as much as he is in the other.

The third collection, *Pedras de Sol & Substância* [*Stones of Sun & Substance*], ends the trilogy that had been announced by the very first poem and, like the other two collections, it is organized around three cantos that are preceded by a Proposition. Here we read of a insular landscape that has been forgotten and left to its own devices; it is described in figurative terms: "*Uma pedra no deserto + um dragoeiro / Um anjo da guarda ! no útero da paisagem / Não ! na ilha*" ["A stone in the desert + a dragon tree / A guardian angel! in the womb of the landscape / No! on the island"] (207).

The title calls upon the irradiating strength of the sun-baked stone, which is on fire—"*o olho da cabra sobre o olho da terra / Como é belo o fogo! da flor da secura*" ["the eye of the goat over the eye of the land / How beautiful is the fire! of the flower of the dry season"]—and subject to transformation, as though through alchemy; all the different versions of the myth of Sisyphus are reworked in this patient and mineral vigor that makes human beings equal in nature to the land and allows them to overcome the limitations of their soil-based inheritance:

Toda palavra é útero de sete pedras
E
Toda a pedra é um poeta bissexto
Leva quatro anos de pudor
E quarenta & tantos de paixão
Para inundar o deserto da estiagem
Com o dilúvio de chama que bebe
Nas crateras do jazz & batuque da esperança. (207)

[Every word is a womb with seven stones
And
Every stone is a leap-year poet
He gets four years for *pudeur*
And forty or so for passion
So he can flood the desert of the drought
With the deluge of flame that he drinks from
In the craters of jazz & the *batuque* of hope.]

The poem "Rotcha Scribida" ["Rock Written On"], about a rock with markings thousands of years old, is almost an archaeological study of the primeval origins of the archipelago; the words registered on the stones of the enigmatic rocks of São Nicolau acquire poetic force of a sacred tablet of commandments, or of a heritage. The sacred character of these markings invites the narrator of this poem to give continuation to the prophetic and sacred writing by a hand and head that engender and regenerate its cosmos, an image that coheres around the image of *God's Bald Head*: "*Ó bíblia de murmúrio / na tua semântica / De sal ! sangue & paradoxo / Ó universo de mil sons / Que circulam / Pela maternidade / Do versículo que nos une / Na tua chama / Na tua lava / No teu tambor inanarrável*" ["O Bible of whisperings / in your semantics / Of salt! blood & paradox / O universe of a thousand sounds / That circle around / Maternity hospitals / Of the stanza that unites us / In your flame / In your lava / In your inexpressible drum"] (223).

The first canto, "Sol & Substância" ["Sun & Substance"], also includes the poem "A Cesariana dos Três Continentes" ["The Cesarean Operation Performed on Three Continents"], where the geographical and cultural origins of the archipelago are narrated, the ten "*umbigos de pedra*" ["belly-buttons of stone"] (222) that arose out of the merging of many cultures. Turning his attention to roots, and the symbols of resistance and the historical inheritance, he further dedicates a poem to the dragon tree [*Dracaena draco*]: it is a tree that confirms that drought on the island can also be fertile, it suggests a kind of survival that has lasted thousands of years: the singular destiny with which the islander can identify: "*Da rocha ao rosto que me deste / Do rosto à raiz que te dou / Florescem no teu tronco / O crâneo de Deus + o fogo do povo / Que nos abraça! Como / Se o arquipélago já não fosse / A tua Ordem / E as ilhas + ilheus! A tua Regra*" ["From the rock to the face you have given me / From the face to the root I give you / Sprout from your trunk / The skull of God + the fire of people / That embrace us! As though / The archipelago were no longer / your monastic Order / And the islands + islanders! Your Rule"] (227).

The poem "*Na Morna! Na Mazurca O Trompete da Evasão*" ["In the *Morna*! In the *Mazurka* the Trumpet of Those Who Flee the Land"] a historical roll-call is made of the various musical traditions that the country inherited and reformulated; different dance rhythms are named, and traditional Cape Verdean musical customs are poetically acted out in a choreography of lines of verses spread over the page, conveyed in a sinuous, mobile and broken rhythm:

A morna! o finançon nos conduz
ao frigórifico da cultura
das terras do fim do mundo
À guerra da pobreza
No metrónomo do batuque
E ao dente de ouro da tabanca
No mestruo das salinas
À coladeira & funaná
na erupção do funacol
E ao rondô que renova o passo
como quem baila o landum
E ao kolá kolá
da morança e da melancolia
que salte & bate
bate & une
As coxas d'Africa às ancas da Macaronésia. (239)

[The *morna*! the *finançon* leads us
to the refrigerator of the culture
of lands at the end of the earth
To war against poverty
In the metronome of the *batuque*
And the *tabanca*'s gold tooth
In the *mestruo* of the salt-pans
To the *coladeira* & *funaná*
that erupt in the *funacol*
And to the *rondô* that renews the step
for those who dance the *landum*
And to the *kolá kolá*
of the hamlet and so the melancholy
leap & beat
beat & unite
The thighs of Africa to the buttocks of Macaronesia.]

The cultural rainbow of the archipelago is revealed throughout this collection. This is also done by means of the pictorial chromaticity of the lithographs of São Filipe, where the painters Luisa Queirós Figueira and Manuel

Figueira are an integral part of the images in those poems written about the traditional festivals of the city of São Filipe on the Island of Fogo; further on still, in another set of poems, the same sort of thing is done with the work of the painter Tchalé Figueira. The lithographs, made over a period of seven days, the number of days of the creation, celebrate the vigor of the horse races and of the festival customs; this is done by evoking the different kinds of pomp and celebration used during each of the days of the festival: "*À frente da bandeira / Parlamentavam os cavalos / E só depois os cavaleiros / E os festeiros / Abriam no coração da ilha / 'O vulcão da festa que se festeja*" ["The horses parleyed / In front of the flag / And it was only then that the horse-riders / And the festival-goers / Opened that *volcano of the festivities that are celebrated* / inside the heart of the island"] (245)

The figure of the writer António Aurélio Gonçalves is granted another set of poems, poems that in the manner of an elegy or ode reconstruct his human and intellectual trajectory, and where references to the stories and novellas of this distinguished Cape Verdean writer are not lacking: "*Do Liceu Velho as lições do mestre continuam: ano & dia / Lembro-me. O oceano da voz balouça vários mundos nas / nossas cabeças; isto é, o verbo desloca nos nossos / crâneos um navio de longo curso. E nós: o arco-íris do / casco, a proa dos mastros & bandeira dos tripulantes em / viagem*" ["The lessons by the master in the *Liceu Velho* (Old Lyceum *or* Old Seconday School) still continue: year & day / I recall. The ocean's voice made several worlds dangle over / our heads; that is, the word brings to our / skulls voyaging ships. And we: the rainbow of the / cranium, the prow of the masts & flag of the crew on / a voyage"] (301). Another figure that is present in these poems is Germano de Almeida, not only on account of his literary qualities, but also as a public and political figure.

The different threads that constitute the political history of the country are also suggested in several poems. One of the texts, "Uma Espiga de Milho na Boca do Parlamento" ["A Corn Cob in Parliament's Mouth"] evokes the important figure of Abílio Duarte. The names of others singers, poets and composers of the *morna*, names such those of Eugénio Tavares, Manuel de Novas, Ana Procópio, B. Lêza, wisely make the link between traditional and literary cultures; the work of these people invades the poems with the rhythms derived from a Creole tradition, one where the merging of forms, and where poetry's close involvement with music resulted in that marriage that gave birth to that unique musical form that is the *morna*: "*O hino! como morna / E o funaná! como bandeira / E das trovas d'Eugénio / E das noveletas d'Aurélio / Pedras caíam / Pedras batiam na B. Lêza da pátria*" ["O hymn! like a *morna* / And the *funaná*! like a flag / And the songs of Eugénio / And the romances of Aurélio / Stone would fall / Stones would beat to the B. Lêza (a homophone of "beauty") of the nation"] (282).

It is worth pointing out that in the poetry of Corsino Fortes there are always two levels of "appeal." One consists in "naming," the other in "invoking," and this second one reveals a trajectory that is one of action. At the same time that the cosmos is getting "named," created, it is also "invoked." The main vocative forms employed in this poetic universe are those of invocation and exclamation:

> E na verdade! na verdade vos digo
> Se a ilha é menor
> que a palma da mão do habitante
> Se o arquipélago é menor
> que a planta do pé da multidão
> A boca alarga & engendra colinas
> na terra primitiva
> A língua ergue & engorda planaltos
> nas salinas de massapé
> E o espírito multiplica os oceanos do interior
> Ao encontro do ovo & ovação d'aldeia olímpica
> E dos corpos que cosem
> os bocados dispersos
> Do continente redondo da alma. (272)

> [And in truth! in truth I tell you
> If the island is smaller
> than the palm of the hand of the one who resides in it
> If the archipelago is smaller
> than the sole of the foot of the crowd
> A mouth enlarges upon & engenders hills
> over the primitive land
> Language raises up & it fattens plateaux
> on the salt pans of the black soil
> And the spirit multiplies the oceans within
> When it finds the egg & ovation of the Olympic village

And the bodies that stitch together
those scattered bits
Of the rounded continent of the soul.]

Invocation, the first, the more direct form of the vocative, is the privileged mode of appeal. In the classical sense of the term it is a type of oration, such as the poets of old composed when they entreated the muse to aid them, and it is this that gives the text an epic grandeur. Exclamation is content to call up, in a much more discreet manner, an emotion. At any rate, in the case of one as much as in the other, their importance for the poetry of *God's Bald Head* resides, on the one hand, in the demarcation of the rhythm and scansion within the text, and, on the other hand, insofar as it is a homage to the human voice and to recitation, it can be received as something of an auditory nature, something that is imbued with the persuasive and rhetorical strength contained in the poem. The force and the capacity of conviction of the poetic word are thus rendered unmistakable and strangely suggestive.

The sun-driven substance of this most recent book—*Pedras de Sol & Substância*—translates itself into the persistence of the symbol of the stone, the stone of identity, recognizable in the bloom and splendor of the multiple cultural creations of the country, and the recognition that the origins of the country are African-American and Western, diversified, subject to the successive layers that have created Creole culture.

God's Bald Head is offered up to the reader/listener as a trilogy about the origins of the country and as an epic poem of the country's history; what Corsino Fortes's most recent book in essence reveals are archaeological and cultural facets to these origins; he does this by singing, over three cantos, the sun-drenched substance of creativity in all its varied manifestations, musical, pictorial, literary, political, that makes ductile the mineral hardness of the islands through the gentle and nostalgic movements of the *morna*, or the measured beat of the *rondó*, or the agitated and harmonious rhythms of the ancient mazurka or the *funaná*.

Works Cited

Fortes, Corsino. *A Cabeça Calva de Deus.* Lisboa: D. Quixote, 2001.

Ferreira, Manuel. "O mito hesperitano ou a nostalgia do paraíso perdido." *Les Littératures Africaines de langue Portugaise.* Paris: F. C. Gulbenkian, 1985. 241-250.

Lima, Mesquitela. Posfácio. "*Pão & Fonema* ou a Odisseia de um Povo." *Pão & Fonema.* Lisboa: Sá da Costa, 1980.

Ana Mafalda Leite is a Professor at the University of Lisbon. She specializes in African Literature. She has published *A poética de José Craveirinha* (Vega, 1990), *Modalização Épica nas Literaturas Africanas* (Vega, 1996), *Oralidades & Escritas nas Literaturas Africanas* (Colibri, 1998) and has co-authored *The Postcolonial Literature of Lusophone Africa* (Hurst, 1996). E-mail: analeite@mail.telepac.pt

Under the Aegis of Antigone: The Tragic Dimension of Lyrical Poetry in *O Arquipélago da Paixão* by Vera Duarte

Carmen Lúcia Tindó Ribeiro Secco
Translated by Luís R. Mitras
Revised by Mark Streeter

Abstract. Drawing inspiration from the strength of *Antigone*, an allegory for the incommensurable tragic dimension in which a female is also capable of partaking, Vera Duarte's *poiesis*, in giving a voice throughout to a female lyrical subject, proceeds to draw up a critical inventory of the passions, the dramas, the whips and scorns of fate experienced not only by women, but also by the poets and by the people of Cape Verde.

Não nasci para o ódio, apenas para o amor.
[I was not born for hatred, merely for love.]
—Sophocles, *Antigone*

1. The Teeming of Passions...

Fechemos as cloacas fétidas da cidade e deixemos inebriarem-se os ares de recendidos perfumes estivais. É o preço da liberdade. Palmeiras ao sol e longas praias de areia molhada a manterem desperto o fervilhar anímico das paixões. A voz da libido. Em toda a sua violência incontrolável.

[Let us close the rank sewers of the city and let us become inebriated with the air of perfumes exhaled by the summer. It is the price of freedom. Palm trees in the sun and long beaches with moist sand will keep alive the psychic teeming of passions. The voice of the libido. In all its uncontrollable violence.]
—Vera Duarte, *Amanhã Amadrugada*

In her fine preface to Vera Duarte's *O Arquipélago da Paixão*, Simone Caputo Gomes, the Brazilian scholar and specialist on Cape Verdean literature, writes that the work fulfills a "*projeto que contempla os níveis existencial, nacional e universal, sob o signo da Paixão. Paixão que domina e liberta, paixão do eu, paixão do outro, paixão-mulher; Paixão do Arquipélago, Arquipélago de Paixão*"[1] ["an endeavor that works at various levels, existential, national and universal, all under the sign of Passion. Passion that can dominate and liberate, passion of the 'I,' passion for the other, woman-passion; Passion for the Archipelago, Archipelago of Passion"].

Our reading will also look at the multiple facets and senses of passion in Vera Duarte's poetic discourse, but it will concentrate on an analysis of the tragic dimension in this poetry, that is to say, insofar as this poetry "*coloca o ser humano em questão*" ["puts into question the human being"].

Ever since her first book, *Amanhã Amadrugada* [*Dawned Tomorrow*] (1993), Vera Duarte has tried to delve into the inner depths of the female universe, and has tried to liberate those passions that have been repressed in the unconscious of most Cape Verdean women. The author's poetry needs to be read in the context of the kind of literature produced in Cape Verde between 1990 and 2000, a literature marked by a certain disenchantment. Her poetry is included in *Mirabilis: de Veias ao Sol* [*Mirabilis: With its Veins in the Sun*], an anthology edited by José Luís Hopffer Almada and dealing with "*poética caboverdiana*" ["Cape Verdean poetry"] produced after the 25th of April [Revolution]. The failure to carry out the promises of social justice in the period after independence generated a certain amount of discouragement among Cape Verdeans, and this discouragement crept into the literary world. However, these literati took inspiration from the *mirabilis* [*mirabilis* = wondrous or marvellous], a plant that can withstand drought in a desert; a new generation appearing in the 1990s took to calling itself "*mirabílica.*" The poetic intention of these people was to resist "*aos maus ventos literários*" ["the bad literary winds"], and, with this in mind, they produced a number of critical reflections about the present state of the archipelago:

> Fustigada pelos ventos (da incompreensão!), pelo sol (da hipocrisia!), pelos tempos vários do mau tempo literário, desse tempo querendo-se vegetação literária. No deserto, cresce a geração mirabílica, feita signo na margem desértica do mar. De veias ao sol. As veias da indagação. As veias alagadas da terra das estradas, da poeira do dia-a-dia, do massapé dos campos, do lixo dos caminhos suburbanos, do

desespero recoberto de moscas, baratas e outros vermes. As veias loucas do mar, do marítimo lirismo dos dias afogados nos ciúmes dos montes. As veias, veias de vida, de morte, de desespero, das quatro estações místicas do que se medita no refúgio do silêncio. Veias do camponês e da enxada neste coito de séculos com a terra. Ao sol, hipócrita por entre a bruma e os cerros. Sol, signo de luz. Sol que ilumina. Sol que queima e ofusca o caminhar. Sol dependurado da perseverança secular. Mirabilis—de veias ao sol. Geração mirabílica indagando o sol. "No Deserto cresce a Mirabilis."[2]

[Lashed by the winds (of incomprehension!), by the sun (of hypocrisy!), by the several kinds of literary bad weather, they expect literary vegetation from this weather. But the *mirabílica* generation blooms in the desert; it has been made into a sign in the desert that lies on the edge of the sea. With its veins in the sun. The veins of inquiry. The veins swelled-up with soil from the roads, the dust of our day-to-day, the black soil of the fields, the garbage from the pathways in the urban areas, from the despair all covered in flies, cockroaches and worms. The crazy veins of the sea, of the maritime lyricism of days drowned out in jealousies up on the hills. The veins, veins of life, of death, of despair, of the four mystical seasons about which we meditate when we take refuge in silence. The veins of the peasant and the hoe that, for centuries, has performed coitus with the soil. Under the sun, a hypocrite somewhere between the fog and the hills. Sun, sign of light. Sun that gives light. Sun that burns and whose glare makes it difficult to walk. Sun hanging up above with the perseverance of centuries. *Mirabilis*—with its veins in the sun. The generation of the *Mirabilis* questioning the sun. "In the desert grows the *Mirabilis*."]

Vera Duarte is someone who stands out among the poetic voices of this generation; she has insisted on the right of women to have access to the eroticism of their bodies and of discourse, thus establishing a lyrical universe marked by the "*cumplicidade das fêmeas*" ["complicity of females"],[3] one where woman longs to be the mistress of her own desire:

[...] choro da dor de me saber mulher feita não para amar mas para ser amada. Choro porque sou e amo. [...] Sinto-me escravizada, tiranizada, violentada. E meu ser nascido livre se revolta. [...] Por isso quero desvendar os universos proibidos e purificar-me.[4]

> [(...) I cry in pain at the knowledge that I am woman who is made for loving but not to be loved. I cry because of what I am and because I love (...) I feel enslaved, tyrannized, raped. And what was born within me is outraged (...). That's why I want to unmask the forbidden universes and to purify myself.]

With this *poiesis* that challenges the submission of women, the lyrical "I" breaks up the idea of the "*cais da saudade*" ["the quayside of homesickness *or* longing"][5]—or "cais da ***sôdade***" in Creole—that has always been used to keep Cape Verdean women in their places, back at home, on the islands. Taking a narrative tone, the poetic subject delves into a kind of poetry that is confessional and autobiographical, one that establishes the writing as "*escrita de mulher*."[6] It is the kind of writing that rebels against the long wait of the "*mulheres-sós de Cabo Verde*" ["the Cape Verdean women who are all alone"][7]—this is how it was described by Prof. Maria Aparecida Santilli in her critique of Cape Verdean machismo.

In the poems included in *Amanhã Amadrugada* the lyrical voice—in the feminine—is not found on land, but is floating in the immense sea, symbol of her memory and the collective imagination of her people:

> [...] eu penetrava no mar, um mar verde e lodento que se me escorregava debaixo dos pés e me causava náuseas. com [*sic*] a água pela cintura e os braços em arco, passava por entre os barcos de minhas viagens de antanho, marinheiro descobridor do mundo [...].[8]

> [(...) I wallowed deeper into the sea, a green and muddy sea that was slipped under my feet and I was filled with nausea. With water at my waist and my arms heaved up in an arch, I journeyed among the ship of my bygone days, a seafarer discovering the world.]

She is thus able to accomplish a journey to her own source of origin. The sea is the place where Cape Verdeans seek to discover their identity, but it is also a space for existential freedom where feminine poetry may be discovered. It is a kind of poetry in dialogue, in search of a lover and a reader, and where the lines of poetry, as if in a continual coitus, allow the libido to overspill and sprout from the very act of producing a reading that opens itself to metalinguistic considerations: "*Para que servem as palavras? Para flutuar, perdida à mercê delas?*" ["What's the use of words? To float, lost, at their beck and call?"].[9] The woman poet wants to be the mistress not only of her body, but also the mistress of language—and this is because she has taken cognizance of the fact that she can think about the world and herself only if she has control over words.

In this first book of Vera's, the woman poet still finds herself reeling under the effects of the uncontrollable discovery of her own desires; she is driven by the drives of that "*fervilhar anímico das paixões*" ["psychic teeming of passions"] that await a tomorrow pregnant with the freedom of the dreamed dawns....

In *O Arquipélago da Paixão*, even though the lyrical subject—in the feminine—continues her song about the liberation of woman, she looks at her own passions and those of the archipelago with a greater maturity; she seeks not the "*fervilhar anímico das paixões*," but the plenitude of Eros. Like Antigone, she seeks Love, and not hate.

2. In the web of Páthos [παϑος, sickness]

> Castração é perda, é falta, é limite imposto à onipotência do desejo.[10]
>
> [Castration is a loss, it is a lack, it is a limit imposed on the omnipotence of desire.]
>
> —Maria Rita Kehl

The figure of Antigone becomes an alter-ego of the feminine poetic voice in *O Arquipélago da Paixão* from the very beginning; in the dedication chosen for the book, she takes on as her own the emblematic rebelliousness of this Greek heroine of Sophocles; passions are an integral dimension of her own *poiesis*. Drinking deep from *páthos*, the essence of the tragic attitude in the face of existence, the lyrical "I" questions not only the desires and the suffering of the woman poet, but also the anguish of Cape Verdean women in general and the social pains of the people in the archipelago.

We shall begin our analysis by reminding ourselves that passions are intimately related to the tragic. Etymologically, the word "passion" comes from the [Late] Latin *passio, passionis*, meaning both *suplício* [torture, death], as in the Passion of Christ, and *affectus*[11] [*adfectus*, feeling]. The word belongs in same semantic field as the Greek *páthos*, and it refers as much to the moral dilemmas that summon up tragedies as to the pains of love[12] that make lovers prisoners of their own feelings.

In the days of classical antiquity the two philosophies of the passion were very much opposed to each other:[13] for Aristotle, seemingly the more condescending of the two, passion was an impulse, an element basic to humans and their *praxis*; Platonic Stoicism, on the other hand, conceived passion in terms of ascetics, something men could purify themselves of. There is an obvious split in this second conception between reason and passion; in this sense passion would be regarded as a "*desvario*" ["folly"], as "*cegueira*" ["blindness"] and as "*loucura*" ["madness"]. Insofar as "passions" drive human beings towards irreconcilable conflicts of a social or existential nature, they are the basis of all tragedies. It was not for nothing that Plato regarded these "passions" as too dangerous, and banished them from his ideal Republic.[14] For a long time the *passionnel* was associated with what is pathological, with addiction and sin. Tragedy, conditioned as it was by the Stoic vision, was converted into a moral example for the atonement of human guilt when it had infringed on the laws of the gods.

A new conception of the tragic emerges, however, with the tragedies of Sophocles. Tragedy now begins to deal with man's own solitude. The heroes in the work of Sophocles are no longer subject to divine dictates. Their actions and behavior can longer be explained by the determinism of a destiny engineered by the gods. *Agon* [ΑΓΩΝ, a contest], *Páthos* [sickness]—the essence of this new kind of tragedy—expresses the conflict between characters whose vices and virtues are fully human. Although the gods are still present, they do not intervene in forming the opinions and feelings of humans. Men are alone with their passions and need to demonstrate skill and courage in order to face their own existence. Sophocles's *Antigone* is an example of one of these strong characters. Even as a woman, which Greek society at the time regarded as an inferior being, she fights with great nobility to preserve the sacred values of her dynasty; because she was not permitted to provide a tomb worthy for her brother's body she preferred, instead, to be buried alive. In this act of transgressing the laws of the State, Antigone rises up as the symbol of a rebellious, feminine oratory, this in a Greece where the *Logos* was preeminently masculine.

Inspired as it is by the strength of this Greek heroine, an allegory for the incommensurable tragic dimension in which a female is also capable of partaking, Vera Duarte's *poiesis*, in granting voice throughout to a female lyrical subject, proceeds to draw up a critical inventory of the passions, the dramas, the whips and scorns of fate experienced not only by women, but also by the poets and by the people of Cape Verde.

The poetic journey of *O Arquipélago da Paixão* begins with a taking cognizance of a *páthos* that renders woman passive in the face of a passion that makes her despair, blinds her and makes her dependent on the lover. The "paratext" of the inscription—which sheds light on this journey by the lyrical subject—makes an intertextual connection between Vera's poetry and the inheritance from the *Claridade* movement, especially the insularity of which Jorge Barbosa had sung: "*Eu trago dentro de mim um pássaro fechado* [...]. *Bate asas—quer voar!—em ânsias desmedidas* [...]" ["I carry within me a bird with its wings tightly shut (...). It beats its wings—it wants to fly!—in its anguish that has no end (...)"].[15] The desire to escape comes up against the fact that she will never be free to emigrate to Love, as it were. Feeling a sense of disquiet, the woman poet does not allow herself to take flight, but remains imprisoned in her waiting, imprisoned by the bitter taste of the betrayal: "*ai pobre de mim traída / ai pobre de mim deixada*" ["Aye, poor me, betrayed / Aye, poor me, abandoned"]. Made to feel inferior, she takes pity on herself, the sort of thing that is performed by the chorus in a Greek tragedy. But when she faces up to the abandonment of her own solitude, she accepts the tragic sense of the human condition—when it is female—and questions the foolishness of this kind of passion that drains her of all her strength and robs her of her happiness:

> Mas cansei-me de meus gemidos
> E de meus olhos consumidos pela mágoa
> Deuses, ouvi a minha súplica
> Arrebatai a minha alma
> Para que despedaçada ela se liberte.[16]
>
> [But soon I tired of my wailings
> And of my eyes consumed by sorrow
> Gods, hear my cry
> Take my soul from me
> So, once broken, it will be freed.]

When she begins questioning the *sôdade* [*saudade*] that has been forced on Cape Verdean women for centuries, tying them down to the quay, where they would wait for their companions forever travelling to distant countries, the lyrical voice in the "Primeiro Caderno" ["First Notebook"] comes to the lucid understanding that the absence of the lover ended up tearing her soul. Her clarity of thought regarding this split in herself—which occurs as a result of the distance separating her from her lover—makes her feel a strange sensation, one that makes her question the passivity of her own waiting. Subverting, as she does, the theme of the "flight from the land," so frequent in the poetry produced earlier, the woman poet longs for one thing:

> [...] que este longe sem regresso
> possa varrer a dor
> e trazer de novo a vida
> no sorriso de outro amor.[17]
>
> [(...) may this distance that has no return
> sweep away the pain
> and bring life back
> in the smile of another beloved.]

Despite these new objectives, the lyrical "I" still finds herself besieged by the labyrinthine intricacies of a passion that is castrating of her own female identity. It is then that she invokes "*um coração guerreiro*" ["a heart that fights"]; she clamors after the example of other strong women—Sappho, Queen Ginga [Jinga], Mother Teresa[18]—who, like Antigone, would not allow themselves to be humiliated. Thus it is that the woman poet acknowledges the losses and frustrations that "*a paixão insensata*" ["foolish passion"] had submitted her to. However, passions that are "*desvairadas*" ["deranged"] can become the source of her liberation, because the anguish, the hurt, and the feeling of disquiet she had been subject to, can all become profound agents of change, a change towards questioning her own existence. This is in fact what occurs with the lyrical subject—written in the feminine—whose passions, at the same time that the they tear her apart, push her towards self-knowledge and in search of a love that will liberate her.

3. The Plenitude of Eros

> [...] o amor, por muito tempo e pela vida afora, é solidão, isolamento cada vez mais intenso e profundo. [...] O amor é uma ocasião sublime para o indivíduo amadurecer, tornar-se algo por si mesmo, tornar-se um mundo para si, por causa de um outro ser [...].[19]
>
> [(...) in loving, we freed ourselves from the loved one, and, quivering, endured: / as the arrow endures the string, to become, in the gathering out-leap, / something more than itself? For staying is nowhere. (trans. J. B. Leishman)]
>
> —Rainer Maria Rilke

In the "Segundo Caderno" ["Second Notebook"], the lyrical subject goes beyond her condition as a submissive woman who has been subjugated by the misfortunes of life. She overcomes her feelings of self-pity and the sensual joy within her that has been repressed is allowed to blossom. Not longer feeling inferior to her lover, she has become her own mistress and she declares:

> Mas hoje
> Dona dos meus jardins
> Livre e insubmissa
> Ajoelho-me a teus pés
> Em sinal d'amor e liberdade.20
>
> [But today
> The mistress of my own gardens
> Free and unyielding
> I kneel at your feet
> As a sign of love and freedom.]

Freed from a passion that is wholly narcissistic, the woman poet steps inside the sphere of Eros, in search of the plenitude of love that, once it has encountered the other, will spawn all the possibilities in poetry. No longer

> a poesia produzida pelas frustrações da paixão, mas a poesia da paixão. A transformação dos desejos que não podem se concretizar na paixão amorosa no desejo de

> outra coisa que a poesia (no sentido lato, não apenas no sentido da produção de poemas) pode realizar.[21]
>
> [the poetry produced by the frustrations of passion, but the poetry of passion. The transformation of desires that cannot be attained in the passionate love affair—in the desire for something else—and which poetry (in the broad sense of term, not only in the sense of producing poems) can accomplish.]

The lyrical "I" takes stock of the fact that her sorrows and letdowns are greater than those of her people. She looks at what is around her and understands that the social model is in crisis. Clearly seeing that the dawn that had been announced at the time of independence was not a full dawn—after the initial euphoria all that remained "*foi o gosto amargo das desilusões*" ["was the bitter taste of disillusionment"][22]—she introduces her thoughts on politics into her art and poetry. She then makes an inventory of other kinds of passions: the ones to do with social sufferings, not only in Cape Verde, but also in another parts of the world. Aware that the present days are lacking in utopian ideals, the dearth of the old hopes that had stirred the revolutionary movements on behalf of freedom, the lyrical "I" invokes the memory of those times and of the resistance heroes who had fought against several kinds of oppression:

> Quero poder ouvir
> para sempre
> as canções heróicas
> que deram som às revoluções
> [.....................]
> quero poder
> por meus pés
> cruzar ares
> cruzar mares
> conhecer gentes
> cantar independências
> e tudo que cheirar liberdade
> [.....................]
> Que me importa se
> —no fim—
> ela (ainda) não foi possível

o que quero ter nos braços
é a idéia de a Ter
e poder cantar abril
[....................]
quando tudo o que restou
foi o gosto amargo das desilusões.[23]

[I want to able to hear
always
the heroic songs
that gave sound to revolutions
[....................]
I want to be able
to step on my feet
to breathe different airs
to cross the seas
to meet different people
to sing of independence
and all that smells of freedom
[....................]
What does it matter if
—in the long run—
it is (still) not possible
what I want to hold in my arms
is the idea of having it
and to be able to sing of April
[....................]
when all that remains
was that bitter taste of disillusionment.]

In the clef note of passion, the woman finally admits to enjoying her own pleasure. She becomes, then, mistress not only of her own body, but also of her lover's body; she commandeers all the love games in a type of "*corpoamor*" ["bodylove"] with the language of poetry itself. And it is in this fever of despair that she acquires a better knowledge of herself and the world. The bodies of those who love are thus linked, and the objective distance that positivist history has erected between reason and passion is dissolved. These, merged in one single body, are evidence that the subject can also be rational—and this is especially true insofar as human beings can be fully whole only when they feel passion:

> O amor sublime não abre mão da paixão, mas sabe transformar o impossível da paixão em possibilidade de troca simbólica. É quando o outro fala comigo, é quando dois universos simbólicos se tocam, se interpenetram, frutificam, se potencializam, é nesse caso que a paixão pode se tornar aliada do amor.[24]
>
> [Sublime love does not open the hand of passion, but knows how to transform any impossible passion into the possibility of a symbolic exchange. It is when the other talks to me, it is when two symbolic universes encounter each other, interpenetrate, fertilize each other, discover their potential, it is then that passion may become the ally of love.]

It is the discovery of this that leads the lyrical "I" to reflect on the other kinds of passion, among which are those that involve the social suffering of the people of Cape Verde:

> Quero sim
> que um ódio desmesurado se acumule
> e meu coração bata descompassado
> a cada genocídio acontecido
> pela guerra, pela fome, pela sida
>
> Quero sim
> que a solidariedade me chame
> imperativa
> quando as crianças
> mancas
>   aleijadas
>   famintas
>   esfarrapadas
>   despojos de guerras sem glória
> barrarem todos os caminhos.[25]
>
> [Yes, I want
> boundless hatred to accumulate

and my heart to beat out of measure
at each genocide that has occurred
as a result of war, hunger, AIDS

Yes, I want
solidarity to call me
imperative
when children
crippled
    disabled
        famished
            ragged
the spoils of a war for which there is no glory
will bar the way to everyone.]

Existing on a par with the disillusionment and the disenchantment is the belief on the part of the subject of the poetry—even though she is aware that society has changed—in justice and bravery, best exemplified by Antigone and Queen Ginga [Jinga, the Angolan warrior-queen]. In a text that makes intertextual references to the well-known poem by the poet Ovídio Martins, a text where he resists the idea of "leaving the country," she, too, says, that she does not want to emigrate; she thus makes a break with the idea of insularity that has always imprisoned Cape Verdeans:

Desvendando o segredo do amor
quero permanecer na ilha
[.....................]
Não quero mais partir!

De malas desfeitas
quebrarei na ilha
a prisão das ilhas
e voarei para lá do horizonte
com os pés fincados na areia [...].[26]

[As I begin to understand the secret of the love
I want to remain on the island

[....................]
I no longer want to leave!

With my suitcases unpacked
It's from this island that I'll break down
The prison of the islands
And I'll fly to the far-ends of the horizon
My feet firmly planted on the sand (...).]

The conquest of this love that is full and free allows the lyrical subject to reflect, both politically and poetically, not only on her role as a female, but on the sub-human conditions of the poor in the archipelago.

4. The Critical Inventory of Passions

> Pensar a paixão é, pois, uma exigência. [...] Sendo fonte de prazer ou angústia, alegria ou tristeza, desejo ou padecimento, as paixões, em qualquer uma dessas formas, pode ser sempre uma afirmação de liberdade.[27]
>
> [To think of passion is, therefore, a demand. (...) Being as it is a source of pleasure or anguish, happiness or sadness, desire or suffering, passion, in any one of these forms, can always be an affirmation of freedom.]
>
> —Adauto Novaes

In the "Terceiro Caderno" ["Third Notebook"], where she uses a more relaxed lyrical form that, visually at least, looks more like prose, the enunciator of the poetic discourse proceeds to make an inventory of the kinds of sadness and sorrow suffered by the people of Cape Verde. She begins by focusing on the day-to-day poverty of children, who live wrapped in the acrid smell of the sea and of despair. Her gesture of solidarity with these children is an intertextual reference to the Brazilian poet, Manuel Bandeira; she offers them "*Estrela da Manhã*" ["Star of the Morning"],[28] a metaphor for those dreams that are still to come with the dawn. She also enters into dialogue with Cape Verdean authors, among them Manuel Lopes, Jorge Barbosa, Baltazar Lopes, and António Aurélio Gonçalves; she has to rethink the dialectics of "*do partir e do ficar*" ["staying or going"] which have marked the soul of Cape Verdeans; she questions the burden of women with faces burnt by the sun who sell fish so that they can support all those countless children with unknown fathers; she discusses the importance of the rain for that dry universe that suffers from periodic droughts. Calling on the political conscience of a poet like Manuel Alegre and the sensitivity of someone like Florbela Espanca, she dreams of a "*mundo ao avesso*" ["an inside-out world"][29] that can satisfy her "*sede de infinito*" ["thirst for the infinite"][30] justice and freedom.

5. Steering Feelings: Fragments from a Cartography of Love...

> Dialogando com a razão, as paixões não se extinguem, mas se tornam por assim dizer menos nebulosas, mais sólidas, mais materiais: chegam à consciência de si enquanto paixões.[31]
>
> [When they enter into dialogue with reason, passions are not extinguished, but they become, as it were, less nebulous, more solid, more material: they take cognizance of the fact that they are passions.]
>
> —Sérgio Paulo Rouanet

In the "Quarto Caderno" ["Fourth Notebook"], the lyrical subject—who writes in the feminine—after having discovered a balance in her own subjective experience, a balance woven by the dialogue between reason and passion, steers through various feelings and estrangements, love and hate, and takes stock of that for which she is to blame and of what can be blamed on society—the collective. What she in effect does is to make a critique of the morality that, in general, the world uses to hem in passions. As she unmasks the prejudices that complicate human emotions, she makes problematic the oppression that has imprisoned men as though they were birds in cages. She focuses on crimes of passion that ruin lives fettered by the ties of submission. As she uncoils the webs of passions she also brings into question the ideas of jealousy, spite, and envy in relation "*à outra*" ["to the other"], the one in the love triangle who is always discriminated against, and socially condemned for being the one who usurped the wife's place. She also discusses more sublime sentiments such as friendship and love. Finally, in "Juízo Final" ["Final Judgement"], she comes to understand that life and passions are transitory, made up of "*material incandescente e precário*" ["material that is incandescent and precarious"].[32] Through this act of learning of love and through the constant questioning of existence and society, she sees herself, like so many others in the archipelago, as a woman and as a Cape Verdean. The image of the "*pássaro vermelho*" ["red bird"][33] that flies away from her in the direction of the loved one is a metaphor for the plenitude of a love that, aware of the exhaustion provoked by the intensity of passions, seeks to follow the more gentle routes that her heart has mapped out. Having liberated herself of the anguish, the solitude and the lamentation that breeds jealousy, of emotions and petty resentments, the woman poet is whole again and has attained the liberated stature of someone like Antigone. She comes to understand that she was not born for hatred, but for love. A love that is unencumbered and free, one whose tragic dimension allows her to step inside the domains of Eros and inside the heart of the poetry of passion.

Notes

1 Gomes 2001, 7.

2 Almada, Apresentação 26-27.

3 Gomes 1993, 63.

4 Duarte 1993, 40.

5 Duarte 1993, 40.

6 Duarte 1993, 40.

7 Santilli 1985, 107.

8 Duarte 1993, 54.

9 Duarte 1993, 38.

10 Kehl 477.

11 Torrinha 609.

12 Nascentes 544.

13 Lebrun 28.

14 Lesky 23.

15 Duarte 2001, 33.

16 Duarte 2001, 38.

17 Duarte 2001, 39.

18 Duarte 2001, 42.

19 Rilke, qtd. in Novaes 371.

20 Duarte 2001, 58.

21 Kehl 484.

22 Duarte 2001, 61.

[23] Duarte 2001, 60-61.

[24] Kehl 484.

[25] Duarte 2001, 62-63.

[26] Duarte 2001, 64-65.

[27] Novaes 11-12.

[28] Duarte 2001, 81.

[29] Duarte 2001, 86.

[30] Duarte 2001, 87.

[31] Rouanet 448.

[32] Duarte 2001, 99.

[33] Duarte 2001, 98.

Works Cited

Almada, José Luís Hopffer, org. *Mirabilis de veias ao sol: antologia dos novíssimos poetas caboverdianos.* Lisboa: Caminho e Instituto Caboverdiano do Livro, 1991.

Duarte, Vera. *Amanhã amadrugada.* Lisboa; Praia: Vega; Instituto Caboverdiano do Livro e do Disco - ICLD, 1993.

———. *O Arquipélago da paixão.* Mindelo: Edições Artiletra, 2001.

Ferreira, Manuel. *Aventura crioula.*3ª. ed. Lisboa: Plátano, 1985.

Gomes, Simone Caputo. "A poesia Africana de Língua Portuguesa em Voz de Mulher." *Cadernos da UFF* 8 (1993): 61-72.

———. "Ainda e sobretudo a Paixão." Prefácio. Duarte, *O Arquipélago da paixão* 7-24.

———. *Percurso da poesia de Cabo Verde até a atualidade.* Atas do I Seminário das Literaturas Africanas. Org. Carmen Lucia Tindó Secco. Rio de Janeiro: UFRJ, Faculdade de Letras, 1996. 61-71.

Kehl, Maria Rita. "A psicanálise e o domínio das paixões." Novaes 469-496.

Laban, Michel. *Encontro com escritores. Cabo Verde.* 2 vols. Porto: Fundação Eng. António de Almeida, 1989.

Laranjeira, Pires. *Literaturas africanas de expressão portuguesa.* Lisboa: Universidade Aberta, 1995.

Lebrun, Gerard. "O conceito de Paixão." Novaes 17-33.

Leite, Ana Mafalda. Posfácio. Fortes, Corsino. *A Cabeça calva de Deus.* Lisboa: Dom Quixote, 2001. 293-302.

———. *A Modalização épica nas literaturas africanas.* Lisboa: Vega, 1996.

Lesky, Albin. *A tragédia grega.* São Paulo: Editora Perspectiva, 1971.

Mariano, Gabriel. *Cultura caboverdeana. Ensaios.* Lisboa: Vega, 1991.

Nascentes, Antenor. *Dicionário etimológico resumido.* Rio de Janeiro: Instituto Nacional do Livro - INL; Ministério da Educação e Cultura - MEC, 1966.

Novaes, Adauto, org. *Os sentidos da paixão.* São Paulo: Companhia das Letras, 1987.

Rouanet, Sérgio Paulo. "Razão e Paixão." Novaes 437-467.

Torrinha, Francisco. *Dicionário latino-português.* 3ª. ed. Porto: Ed. Maránus, 1945.

Veiga, Manuel. *Cabo Verde: insularidade e literatura.* Paris: Ed. Karthala, 1998.

Carmen Lucia Tindó Sécco teaches African Literatures in Portuguese at the University of Rio de Janeiro. She holds a doctorate in vernacular languages. She has published *Morte e prazer em João do Rio; Além da idade da razão; Guia bibliográfico das literaturas africanas em bibliotecas do RJ*; and *Antologias do mar na poesia africana.* E-mail: carmenlt.trp@terra.com.br

Language Politics

Literacy in Post-Colonial Cape Verde

Donaldo Macedo

A major pitfall in post-colonial Cape Verde is the almost total lack of understanding of the importance of language in the construction of human subjectivities. Although the literature during the struggle for independence correctly stressed the need to valorize and appreciate our cultural differences as a process for all Capeverdeans to come to voice, the underlying assumption is that the celebration of our culture would take place in Portuguese, a language that may provide most Capeverdeans with the experience of subordination. In this paper I discuss the issue of language and its role in the reconstruction of post-independent Cape Verde, particularly the role of language in the reproduction of Portuguese colonial values through the educational system. In fact, most Capeverdeans who courageously fought against Portuguese colonialism remain, paradoxically, colonized with respect to the question of language. Most Capeverdeans, without saying so, assume that education and other aspects of civic life in Cape Verde can take place effectively through Portuguese only. Such an assumption neglects to appreciate how Portuguese, as a dominant language, even in a somewhat multilingual country, may continue to devalue Capeverdeans and their culture. In other words, one cannot celebrate one's cultural values through the very dominant language that devalues, in many ways, the cultural experiences of different cultural groups. Capeverdean leaders and educators need to understand that language is the only means through which one comes to consciousness. In this article I provide a critical analysis of the politics of language and its role in the reproduction of colonial values in Cape Verde. The reproduction of the colonial values also prevent even progressive Capeverdeans from accepting and embracing the virtues of bilingual education as eloquently argued by Zeynep F. Beykont, among others.

With the exception of a small number of critical thinkers, most Capeverdeans have simply failed to undertake the necessary critical analysis of the politics of language and its role in education and civic life. The dearth of critical work concerning the ideological construction of language and its cultural manifestation is due, primarily, to two fundamental factors: 1) the teaching of Portuguese as an end in itself and 2) the lack of political clarity among Capeverdean leaders who, in turn, prevent (sometimes unknowingly) even the most committed Capeverdean educators from understanding the neo-colonial language policy that informs and shapes educational programs in Cape Verde.

Although the political rhetoric right after the independence promised to give Capeverdeans cultural voice, most political leaders, particularly those educated in colonial schools, were unable to fracture the colonial yoke as far as the issue of language was concerned. These leaders failed to realize that their national goal to achieve cultural independence from Portugal was insidiously being undermined by a process of valorizing the Capeverdean culture through the use of Portuguese, a language that historically served as a weapon to devalue, demonize, and dehumanize Capeverdeans. That is, by refusing to totally allow the Capeverdeans's minds to be decolonized, these leaders understood little about how the Portuguese language, as a colonial language, is able to subordinate and alienate members of the Capeverdean culture who are struggling to have a cultural voice. In addition, the use of Portuguese as the dominant language in cultural, educational, and civic life in Cape Verde not only eclipses real opportunities for the development of cultural independence and solidarity but it also hides the privilege and paternalism prevalent among the *petit bourgeoisie* class responsible for language and educational policies. It is the same paternalism that is often encoded as: "We need to give Capeverdeans voice." First of all, we need to become keenly aware that voice is not something to be given by those in power. In addition, voice cannot be given in the very Portuguese language that keeps the Capeverdean language submerged. Voice requires struggle and the understanding of both possibilities and limitations. The most leaders and educators can do is to create structures that would enable submerged voices to emerge. It is not a gift. Voice is a human right. It is a democratic right.

Against a landscape of increased neo-colonialism in Cape Verde, I doubt very much that the continued use of Portuguese only in education and other important aspects of civic life will enable Capeverdeans to critically understand how the imposed use of Portuguese together with neo-liberal policies construct, shape, and maintain the cruel reality of neo-colonial dependence. I also doubt that the present educational experience in Cape Verde can equip Capeverdeans with the necessary critical tools to understand how language is often used to ideologically construct realities that veil the raw racism that devalue, disconfirm, and poison other cultural identities. Even within the progressive sector of the Capeverdean society, most individuals fail to understand the neo-colonialist ideology that informs the language debate in Cape Verde to the extent that leaders and educators almost always structure their arguments within a reductionistic view of language.

If we analyze closely the ideology that informs and shapes the present debate over the role of the Capeverdean language in education, we can begin to see and understand that the ideological principles that sustain the Capeverdean language debate are consonant with the structures and mechanisms of a colonial ideology designed to devalue the cultural capital and values of the colonized.

It is only through a full understanding of our colonial legacy that we can begin to comprehend the complexity of our bilingualism in Cape Verde. For most linguistic subordinate speakers in colonized territories, their bilingualism is not characterized by the ability to speak two languages. There is a radical difference between a dominant speaker learning a second language and a subordinate speaker acquiring the dominant language. While the former involves the addition of a second language to one's linguistic repertoire, the latter usually provides the subordinate speaker with the experience of subordination in speaking both his or her language which is devalued by the dominant values and the dominant language that he or she has learned, often under coercive conditions. Both the colonized context and the asymmetrical power relations with respect to language use in Cape Verde create, on the one hand, a form of forced bilingualism and, on the other, what Albert Memmi appropriately calls a linguistic drama:

> In the colonial context, bilingualism is necessary. It is a condition for all culture, all communication and all progress. But while the colonial bilinguist is saved from being walled in, he suffers a cultural catastrophe which is never completely overcome.
> The difference between native language and cultural language is not peculiar to the colonized, but colonial bilingualism cannot be compared to just any linguis-

> tic dualism. Possession of two languages is not merely a matter of having two tools, but actually means participation in two physical and cultural realms. Here, the two worlds symbolized and conveyed by the two tongues are in conflict; they are those of the colonizer and the colonized.
>
> Furthermore, the colonized's mother tongue, that which is sustained by his feelings, emotions, and dreams, that in which his tenderness and wonder are expressed, thus that which holds the greatest emotional impact, is precisely the one which is the least valued. It has no stature in the country or in the concept of peoples. If he wants to obtain a job, make a place for himself, exist in the community and the world, he must first bow to the language of his masters. In the linguistic conflict within the colonized, his mother tongue is that which is crushed. He himself sets about discarding this infirm language, hiding it from the sight of strangers. In short, colonial bilingualism is neither a purely bilingual situation, in which an indigenous tongue coexists with a purist's language (both belonging to the same world of feeling), nor a simple polyglot richness benefiting from an extra but relatively neuter alphabet; it is a linguistic drama. (107)

Unfortunately, the tragedy of our Capeverdean linguistic drama is ill understood by policy makers, particularly among literacy experts who are responsible for the education of those who are often victims of their policies. Within the last decade, literacy has taken on new importance as an issue among educators. Sadly, the debate that has emerged has tended to recycle old assumptions and values regarding the meaning and usefulness of literacy. The notion that literacy is simply a matter of learning the standard language still informs the vast majority of literacy programs, and manifests its logic in the renewed emphasis on technical reading and writing skills.

I want to propose in this article that literacy cannot be viewed as simply the development of skills aimed at acquiring the dominant standard language. This view sustains a notion of ideology that systematically disconfirms rather than makes meaningful the cultural experiences of the subordinate linguistic groups who are, by and large, the objects of its policies. For the notion of literacy to become meaningful, it has to be situated within a theory of cultural production and viewed as an integral part of the way in which people produce, transform, and reproduce meaning. Literacy must be seen as a medium that constitutes and affirms the historical and existential moments of lived experience that produce a subordinate or a lived culture. Hence, it is an eminently political phenomenon, and it must be analyzed within the context of a theory of power relations and an understanding of social and cultural reproduction and production. By "cultural reproduction" I refer to collective experiences that function in the interest of the colonizer, rather than in the interest of the oppressed groups that are the object of its policies. I use "cultural production" to refer to specific groups of people producing, mediating, and confirming the mutual ideological elements that emerge from and reaffirm their daily lived experiences. In this case, such experiences are rooted in the interests of individual and collective self-determination.

This theoretical posture underlies my examination of how the public school systems in the Republic of Cape Verde have developed educational policies aimed at stamping out a very high illiteracy rate inherited from colonialist Portugal. These policies are designed to eradicate the colonial educational legacy, which had as its major tenet the total de-Africanization of Capeverdeans. As Paulo Freire succinctly points out, colonial education

> was discriminatory, mediocre, and based on verbalism. It could not contribute anything to national reconstruction because it was not constituted for this purpose.[...] Schooling was antidemocratic in its methods, in its content, and in its objectives. Divorced from the reality of the country, it was, for this very reason, a school for a minority, and thus against the majority. (13-14)

Before the independence of Cape Verde in 1975, schools functioned as political sites in which class, gender, and racial inequities were both produced and reproduced. In essence, the colonial educational structure seemed to inculcate the Capeverdean natives with myths and beliefs which denied and belittled their lived experiences, their history, their culture, and their language. The schools were seen as purifying fountains where Capeverdeans could be saved from their deep-rooted ignorance, their "savage" culture, and their bastardized language which, according to some Portuguese scholars, was a corrupted form of Portuguese "without grammatical rules (they can't ever be applied)" (Caetano 349). Consequently, as Freire points out, "[t]his system could not help but reproduce in children and youth the profile that the colonial ideology itself had created for them, namely that of inferior beings, lacking in all ability" (14).

On the one hand, schooling in Cape Verde served the purpose of deculturating the natives while on the other hand, it acculturated them into a predefined colonial model. Schools in this mold functioned "as part of an ideological state apparatus designed to secure the ideological and social reproduction of capital and its institutions whose interests are rooted in the dynamics of capital accumulation and the reproduction of the labor force" (Giroux). This educated labor force in Cape Verde was composed mainly of low-level functionaries whose major tasks were the promotion and maintenance of the status quo. Their role took on a new and important dimension when they were used as intermediaries to further colonize other Portuguese possessions in Africa. Thus, colonial schools were successful to the extent that they created a *petit-bourgeois* class of functionaries who had internalized the belief that they had become "white" or "black with white souls," and were therefore superior to Africans who still practiced what was viewed as barbaric culture.

The assimilation process in Cape Verde penetrated the deepest level of consciousness, especially in the bourgeoisie class. For instance, with respect to becoming "white," I am reminded of an anecdote about a black Capeverdean so preoccupied with his blackness that he paid a well-respected white Capeverdean to issue him a decree proclaiming him white. The man jokingly wrote for him on a piece of paper *Dja'n branco dja*, meaning *I have thereby been declared white.*

After independence and in the reconstruction of a new society in Cape Verde, schools have assumed as their major task the "decolonization of mentality," as it is termed by Aristides Pereira, and which Amilcar Cabral called the "re-Africanization of mentality." It is clear that both Pereira and Cabral were well aware of the need to create a school system in which a new mentality cleansed of all vestiges of colonialism would be formulated: a school system that would allow Capeverdeans to appropriate their history, their culture, and their language. A school system where, according to Freire

> It was imperative to reformulate the programs of geography, history and the Portuguese language, changing all the reading texts that were so heavily impregnated with colonialist ideology. It was an absolute priority that [...] students should study their own geography and not that of Portugal, the inlets of the sea and not Rio Tejo. It was urgent that they study their history, the history of the resistance of their people to the invader and the struggle for their liberation which gave them back the right to make their own history, and not the history of the kings of Portugal and the intrigues of the court. (20)

Freire's proposal to incorporate a radical pedagogy in Capeverdean schools has met a lukewarm reception in Cape Verde. I want to argue that the suspicion of Capeverdean educators is deeply rooted in the language issue (Capeverdean vs. Portuguese) and has led to the creation of a neo-colonialist literacy campaign under the superficially radical slogan of eliminating illiteracy in Cape Verde. The difficulties of reappropriating Capeverdean culture have been magnified by the fact that the means for such struggle has been the language of the colonizers. I want to argue also that the present literacy campaign in Cape Verde concerns itself mainly with the creation of functional literates in the Portuguese language. No longer based on the cultural capital of subordinate Capeverdeans, the program has fallen prey to positivistic and instrumental approaches to literacy concerned mainly with the mechanical acquisition of Portuguese language skills (Bourdieu and Passeron).

Before my discussion of the politics of an emancipatory literacy program in Cape Verde, I want to discuss the various approaches to literacy. First, I will briefly discuss those approaches which are derived from a positivistic school and are linked to the process of cultural reproduction. Then, I will analyze the role of language in the reproduction process. Finally, I will argue that the only literacy approach which would be consistent with the construction of a new Capeverdean society is one rooted in the dynamics of cultural production and informed by a radical pedagogy. That is, the literacy program that is needed is one that will affirm and allow Capeverdeans to re-create their history, culture, and language and that will, at the same time, help lead those assimilated Capeverdeans who perceive themselves to be captive to the colonial ideology to "commit class suicide" (Freire).

APPROACHES TO LITERACY

Almost without exception, traditional approaches to literacy have been deeply *ingrained* in a positivistic method of inquiry. In effect this has resulted in an epistemological stance in which scientific rigor and methodological refinement are celebrated while "theory and knowledge are subordinated to the imperatives of efficiency and technical mastery, and history is reduced to a minor footnote in the priorities of 'empirical' scientific inquiry" (Giroux). In general, this approach abstracts methodological issues from their ideological contexts and consequently ignores the interrelationship between the socio-political structures of a society and the act of reading. In part, the exclusion of social and political dimensions from the practice of reading gives rise to an ideology of cultural reproduction, one which views readers as "objects." As Freire has aptly stated, it is "as though their conscious bodies were simply empty, waiting to be flied by that word" from the teacher (72). Although it is important to analyze how ideologies inform various reading traditions, in this essay I will limit my discussion to a brief analysis of the most important approaches to literacy, linking them to either cultural reproduction or cultural production.

The Academic Approach to Reading

The purpose assigned to reading in the academic tradition is two-fold. First, the rationale for this approach "derives from classical definitions of the well educated man-thoroughly grounded in the classics, articulate in spoken and written expression, actively engaged in intellectual pursuits" (Walmsley 78). This approach to reading has primarily served the interests of the elite classes. In this case, reading is viewed as the acquisition of predefined forms of knowledge, and is organized around the study of Latin and Greek amid the mastery of the great classical works. Second, since it would be unrealistic to expect the vast majority of society to meet such high standards, reading was redefined as the acquisition of reading skills, decoding skills, vocabulary development, and so on. This second rationale served to legitimize a dual approach to reading: one level for the ruling class and another for the dispossessed majority. According to Giroux "this second notion is geared primarily to working class students whose cultural capital is considered less compatible, and thus inferior in terms of complexity and value, with the knowledge and values of the dominant class." This two-fold academic approach to reading is inherently alienating in nature. On the one hand, it ignores the life experience, the history, and the language practice of students. On the other hand, it overemphasizes the mastery and understanding of classical literature and the use of literary materials as "vehicles for exercises in comprehension (literal and interpretative), vocabulary development and word identification skills" (Walmsley 80). Thus, literacy in this sense is stripped of its socio-political dimensions; it functions, in fact, to reproduce dominant values and meaning. It does not contribute in any meaningful way to the appropriation of working-class history, culture, and language.

The Utilitarian Approach to Reading

The major goal of the utilitarian approach is to produce readers who meet the basic reading requirements of contemporary society. In spite of its progressive appeal, such an approach emphasizes the mechanical learning of reading skills while sacrificing the critical analysis of the social and political order which generates the need for reading in the first place. This position has led to the development of "functional literates," groomed primarily to meet the requirements of our ever more complex technological society. Such a view is not simply characteristic of the advanced industrialized countries of the West; even within the Third World, utilitarian literacy has been championed as a vehicle for economic betterment, access to jobs, and increase of the productivity level. As it is clearly stated by UNESCO,

> literacy programs should preferably be linked with economic priorities [. … They] must impart not only reading and writing, but also professional and technical knowledge, thereby leading to a fuller participation of adults in economic life. (97)

This notion of literacy has been enthusiastically incorporated as a major goal by the Back-to-Basics proponents of reading. It has also contributed to the development of nearly packaged reading programs which are presented as the solution to difficulties students experience in reading job application forms, tax forms, advertisement literature, sales catalogs, labels, and the like. In general, the utilitarian approach views literacy as meeting the basic reading demand of an industrialized society. As Giroux points out, literacy within this perspective is geared to make adults more productive workers and citizens within a given society. In spite of its appeal to economic mobility, functional literacy reduces the concept of literacy and the pedagogy in which it is suited to the pragmatic requirements of capital; consequently, the notions of critical thinking, culture and power disappear under the imperatives of the labor process and the need for capital accumulation.

Cognitive Development Approach to Reading

While the academic and utilitarian approaches to reading emphasize the mastery of reading skills and view the readers as "objects," the cognitive development model stresses the construction of meaning whereby readers engage in a dialectical interaction between themselves and the objective world. Although the acquisition of literacy skills is viewed as an important task in this approach, the salient feature is how people construct meaning through problem-solving processes. Comprehension of the text is relegated to a position of lesser importance in favor of the development of new cognitive structures which can enable students to move from simple to highly complex reading tasks. This reading process is highly influenced by the early work of John Dewey and has been shaped in terms of the development of Piagetian cognitive structures. Under the cognitive development model, reading is seen as an intellectual process, "through a series of fixed, value-free, and universal stages of development" (Walmsley 82). The cognitive development model thus avoids criticism of the academic and utilitarian views of reading and fails to consider the content of what is read. Instead, it emphasizes a process which allows students to analyze and critique issues raised in the text with an increasing level of complexity. This approach, however, is rarely concerned with questions of cultural reproduction. Since students's cultural capital, i.e., their life experience, history, and language, is ignored, they are rarely able to engage "through critical reflection, regarding their own practical experience and the ends that motivate them in order, in the end, to organize the findings, and thus to replace mere opinion about facts with an increasingly rigorous understanding of their significance" (Freire 25).

The Romantic Approach to Reading

Like the cognitive development model, the romantic approach is based on an interactionist approach with a major focus on the construction of meaning; however, the romantic approach views meaning as being generated by the reader and not occurring in the interaction between reader and author via text. The romantic mode greatly emphasizes the affective and sees reading as the fulfillment of self and a joyful experience. One writer praises the intimate reliving of fresh views of personality and life implicit in the work of literature; the pleasure and release of tensions that may flow from such an experience … the deepening and broadening of sensitivity to the sensuous quality and emotional impact of day-to-day living (Rosenblatt 37-38).

In essence, the romantic approach to reading presents a counterpoint to the authoritarian modes of pedagogy which view readers as "objects." However, this seemingly liberal approach to literacy fails to make problematic class conflict, gender, or racial inequalities. Furthermore, the romantic model completely ignores the cultural capital of subordinate groups and assumes that all people have the same access to reading, or that reading is part of the cultural capital of all people. This failure to address questions of cultural capital or various structural inequalities means that the romantic model tends to reproduce the cultural capital of the dominant class, to which reading is intimately tied. It is presumptuous and naive to expect a student from the working class, confronted and victimized by myriad disadvantages, to find joy and self-affirmation through reading alone. But more important is the failure of the romantic tradition to link reading to the asymmetrical relations of power within the dominant society, relations of power that not only define and legitimatize certain approaches to reading but also disempower certain groups by excluding them from such a process.

I have argued thus far that all of these approaches to literacy have failed to provide a theoretical model for empowering historical agents with the logic of individual and collective self-determination. While these approaches may differ in their basic assumptions about literacy, they all share one common feature: they all ignore the role of language as a major force in the construction of human subjectivities. That is, they ignore the way in which language may either confirm or disconfirm the life histories and experiences of the people who use it. This becomes more clear in my analysis of the role of language in Capeverdean literacy programs.

THE ROLE OF LANGUAGE IN CAPEVERDEAN LITERACY

The Capeverdean literacy programs have been plagued by constant debate over whether the language of instruction should be the native Capeverdean language or the official Portuguese language. Such debate, however, hides issues of a more serious nature which are rarely raised. This is in line with Antonio Gramsci's argument that,

> Each time that in one way or another, the question of language comes to the fore, that signifies that a series of other problems is about to emerge, the formation and enlarging of the ruling class, the necessity to establish more "intimate" and sure relations between the ruling groups and the national popular masses, that is, the reorganization of cultural hegemony. (52)

Gramsci's argument illuminates the issue underlying the debates over language in Cape Verde, where there is still no agreement as to whether the native language is really just a dialect of Portuguese. Capeverdean educators repeatedly use the lack of orthographic uniformity for the Capeverdean language to justify their present policy of using Portuguese as the only medium of reading instruction. They raise the question of which dialect such an orthography should be based on. However, the most common argument is that Portuguese language has international status and therefore guarantees upward mobility for the Portuguese-educated Capeverdeans.

The sad reality is that while education in Portuguese provides access to positions of political and economic power for the high echelon of Capeverdean society, it screens out the majority of the masses who fail to learn Portuguese well enough to acquire the necessary literacy level for social, economic, and political advancement. By offering a literacy program conducted in the language of the colonizers with the aim of reappropriating the Capeverdean culture, these educators have, in fact, developed new manipulative strategies that support the maintenance of Portuguese cultural dominance. What is hidden in the language debate in Cape Verde is possibly a resistance to re-Africanization, or perhaps a subtle refusal on the part of the assimilated Capeverdeans to "commit class suicide."

The pedagogical and political implications of using Portuguese as the only medium of instruction in Capeverdean literacy programs are far-reaching and yet largely ignored. The reading programs in Cape Verde often contradict a fundamental principle of reading, namely that students learn to read faster and with better comprehension when taught in their native tongue. The immediate recognition of familiar words and experiences enhances the development of a positive self-concept in children who are somewhat insecure about the status of their language and culture. For this reason, and to be consistent with the plan to construct a new society in Cape Verde free from vestiges of colonialism, a Capeverdean literacy program should be based on the rationale that such a program must be rooted in the cultural capital of subordinate Capeverdeans and have as its point of departure the Capeverdean language.

Capeverdean educators must develop radical pedagogical structures which provide students with the opportunity to use their own reality as a basis of literacy. This includes, obviously, the Capeverdean language they bring to the classroom. To do otherwise is to deny Capeverdean students the rights that lie at the core of the notion of an emancipatory literacy. The failure to base a literacy program on the Capeverdean language means that oppositional forces can neutralize the efforts of Capeverdean educators and political leaders to achieve decolonization. Capeverdean educators and political leaders must recognize that

> Language is inevitably one of the major preoccupations of a society which, liberating itself from colonialism and refusing to be drawn into neo-colonialism searches

> for its own recreation. In the struggle to recreate a society, the reconquest by the people of their own world becomes a fundamental factor. (Kenneth)

It is of paramount importance that the incorporation of the Capeverdean language as the primary language of instruction in literacy be given top priority. It is through their own language that Capeverdeans will be able to reconstruct their history and their culture.

The debate over whether the Capeverdean language is a dialect of Portuguese, a simplification of Portuguese, or a valid language, and whether it is a restricted or elaborated language, points to the issue of whether Portuguese is in fact a superior language. In a more important sense these linguistic categories rest on the technical question of whether the Capeverdean language is a valid and rule-governed system. Despite synchronic and diachronic analyses of the Capeverdean language (Macedo, "Conceptualizing," "Capeverdean") the fact still remains that the Capeverdean language continues in a stigmatized and subordinate position. I want to argue that the Capeverdean language has to be understood within the theoretical framework that generates it. Put another way, the ultimate meaning and value of the Capeverdean language are not to be found by determining how systematic and rule-governed it is. We know that already. Its real meaning has to be understood through the assumptions that govern it, and it has to be understood via the social, political, and ideological relations to which it points. Generally speaking, the issue of systematicness and validity often hides the true role of language in the maintenance of the values and interests of the dominant class. In other words, the issue of systematicness and validity becomes a mask that obfuscates questions about the social, political, and ideological order within which the Capeverdean language exists.

If an emancipatory literacy program is to be developed in Cape Verde, in which readers become "subjects" rather than "objects," Capeverdean educators must understand the productive quality of language. Donald puts it this way:

> I take language to be productive rather than reflective of social reality. This means calling into question the assumption that we, as speaking subjects, simply use language to organize and express our ideas and experiences. On the contrary, language is one of the most important social practices through which we come to experience ourselves as subjects [....] My point here is that once we get beyond the idea of language as no more than a medium of communication, as a tool equally

> and neutrally available to all parties in cultural exchanges, then we can begin to examine language both as a practice of signification and also as a site for cultural struggle and as a mechanism which produces antagonistic relations between different social groups. (44)

It is to the antagonistic relationship between the Capeverdean and Portuguese speakers that I want to turn now. The antagonistic nature of the Capeverdean language has never been fully explored. In order to more clearly discuss this issue of antagonism, I will use Donald's distinction between *oppressed* language and *repressed* language. Using Donald's categories, the "negative" way of posing the Capeverdean language question is to view it in terms of *oppression*—that is, seeing the Capeverdean language as "lacking" the Portuguese features which usually serve as a point of reference for the Capeverdean language. By far the most common questions concerning the Capeverdean language are posed from the *oppression* perspective. The alternative view of the Capeverdean language is that it is *repressed* in the Portuguese language. In this view, Capeverdean as a repressed language could, if spoken, challenge the privileged Portuguese linguistic dominance. Capeverdean educators have failed to recognize the "positive" promise and antagonistic nature of the Capeverdean language. It is precisely on these dimensions that educators must concentrate to bring forth an emancipatory literacy program which will demystify the Portuguese language and the old assumptions about its inherent superiority. Capeverdean educators must develop an emancipatory literacy program informed by a radical pedagogy so that the Capeverdean language will cease to provide its speakers the experience of subordination and, moreover, may be brandished as a weapon of resistance to the dominance of the Portuguese language.

EMANCIPATORY LITERACY IN CAPE VERDE

In maintaining a certain coherence with the revolutionary plan to reconstruct a new society in Cape Verde, Capeverdean educators and political leaders saw the need to create a new school grounded in "a new educational praxis, expressing different concepts of education consonant with the plan for the society as a whole" (Freire 13). In order for this to happen, the first step was to identify the objectives of the inherited colonial education. Next, it was necessary to analyze how the methods used by the colonial schools functioned, legitimizing the dominant values and meanings, and at the same time disconfirming the history, culture, and language practices of the majority of Capeverdeans. The new school, so it was argued, must also be informed by a radical pedagogy, which would make "concrete such values as solidarity, social responsibility, creativity, discipline in the service of the common good, vigilance and critical spirit—values by which PAIGC has been forged through the whole liberation process" (Freire 43).

An important feature of the new educational plan in post-independence Cape Verde was the development of a literacy program rooted in an emancipatory ideology, where readers become "subjects" rather than mere "objects." The new literacy program needed to move away from traditional approaches which emphasize the acquisition of mechanical skills while divorcing reading from its ideological and historical contexts. In attempting to meet this goal, it purposely rejected the conservative principles embedded in the approaches to literacy I have discussed previously. Unfortunately, the new literacy program unknowingly reproduced one common feature of those approaches by ignoring the important relation between language and the cultural capital of the people whom the literacy program was aimed at. The result has been the development of a literacy campaign whose basic assumptions are at odds with the revolutionary spirit that launched it. The new literacy program was largely based on Freire's notion of emancipatory literacy in which literacy is viewed "as one of the major vehicles by which 'oppressed' people are able to participate in the sociohistorical transformation of their society" (Walmsley 84). In this view, literacy programs should be tied not only to mechanical learning of reading skills but, additionally, to a critical understanding of the overall goals for national reconstruction. Thus, the readers's development of a critical comprehension of the text, and the sociohistorical context to which it refers, become an important factor in Freire's notion of literacy. As he points out,

> The act of learning to read and write, in this instance, is a creative act that involves a critical comprehension of reality. The knowledge of earlier knowledge, gained by the learners as a result of analyzing praxis in its social context, opens to them the possibility of new knowledge. The new knowledge, reveals the reason for being behind the facts, thus demythologizing the false interpretations of these same facts. And so, there is now no more separation between thought-language and objective reality. The reading of a text now demands a reading within the social context to which it refers. (Freire 24)

Literacy, in this sense, is grounded in a critical reflection on the cultural capital of the oppressed. It becomes a vehicle by which the oppressed are equipped with the necessary tools to reappropriate their history, culture, and language practices. It is, thus, a way to enable the oppressed to reclaim "those historical and existential experiences that are devalued in everyday life by the dominant culture [...] in order to be both validated and critically understood" (Giroux).

The theories underlying Freire's emancipatory literacy have been, in principle, wholeheartedly embraced by Capeverdean educators. However, I must argue that, in practice, the middle class, especially teachers trained by the colonial schools, has not been able to play a radical pedagogical role. These educators have failed to analyze and understand the ways in which the colonizers used the Portuguese language to maintain class division, thereby keeping subordinate Capeverdeans in their proper place. I am reminded now of a friend in Cape Verde who, having intellectually embraced the revolutionary cause, is unable to perceive himself as still being emotionally "captive" to the colonial ideology. But when I asked him which language he most often uses in the office, he quickly answered, "Portuguese, of course—it is the only way to keep my subordinates in their place. If I speak Capeverdean, they don't respect me."

This view of language in Cape Verde is illustrative of the extent to which Capeverdeans are held "captive" by the dominant ideology, which devalues their own language. Not surprisingly, many progressive educators and leaders fail to recognize and understand the importance of their native language in the development of an emancipatory literacy. As I have mentioned before, literacy programs in Cape Verde are conducted in Portuguese, the language of the colonizer. The continued use of Portuguese as the sole vehicle of literacy in Cape Verde will only guarantee that the future leaders will be the sons and daughters of the ruling class.

In essence, progressive educators sometimes not only fail to recognize the positive promise of the students's language, but they systematically undermine the principles of an emancipatory literacy by conducting literacy programs in the dominant colonial language. The result is that the learning of reading skills in the dominant colonial language will not enable subordinate students to acquire the critical tools "to awaken and liberate them from their mystified and distorted view of the world" (226). Educators must understand the all-encompassing role that the dominant colonial language has played in this mystification and distortion process. They must also recognize the antagonistic nature of the subordinate language and its potential challenge to the mystification of the dominant colonial language superiority. Finally, they must develop a literacy program based on the theory of cultural production. In other words, subordinate students must become actors in the reconstruction process of a new society.

Literacy can only be emancipatory and critical to the extent that it is conducted in the language of the people. It is through the native language that students name their world and begin to establish a dialectical relationship with the dominant class in the process of transforming the social and political structures that imprison them in their silenced culture. Thus, a person is literate to the extent that he or she is able to use language for social and political reconstruction. The use of the dominant colonial language only (Portuguese in the case of Cape Verde) weakens the possibilities for subordinate students to engage in dialectical encounters with the dominant class. Literacy conducted in the dominant colonial language empowers the ruling class by sustaining the status quo. This elite model of education creates intellectualists and technocrats rather than intellectuals. In short, literacy conducted in Portuguese only in Cape Verde is alienating to subordinate Capeverdean students, since it denies them the fundamental tools for reflection, critical thinking, and social interaction. Without the cultivation of the Capeverdean language, and robbed of the opportunity for reflection and critical thinking, subordinate Capeverdean students find themselves unable to re-create their culture and history. Without the reappropriation of their cultural capital, which includes the Capeverdean language, the reconstruction of a new society in Cape Verde free from the yoke of colonialism can hardly be a reality.

Works Cited

Beykont, Zeynep F., ed. *Lifting Every Voice: Pedagogy and Politics of Bilingualism.* Cambridge, Mass.: Harvard Education Publishing Group, 2000.

Bourdieu, Pierre and Jean-Claude Passeron. *Reproduction in Education, Society, and Culture.* Beverly Hills: Sage, 1977.

Caetano, J. *Boletim da Sociedade de Geografia.* 3rd ser., n.d.: n. pag.

Donald, J. *Language, Literacy and Schooling.* London: Open University Press, 1982.

Freire, Paulo. *Pedagogy in Process.* New York: Seabury Press, 1978.

Giroux, Henry A. *Theory and Resistance in Education: A Pedagogy for the Opposition.* South Hadley, Mass.: J.E. Bergin Publishers, 2000.

Gramsci, Antonio. *Selections from Prison Notebooks.* Ed. and trans. Quinten Hoare Geoffrey Smith. New York: International Publishers, 1971.

Kenneth, John. "The sociology of Pierre Bourdieu." *Educational Review* 25.3 (1973): 237-249.

Macedo, Donaldo. "Conceptualizing Bilingual Education for Capeverdeans in the United States." Second National Portuguese Conference, Providence, Rhode Island, 1977.

Macedo, Donaldo. "Capeverdean Orthography Development in the United States." In *National Language Planning and Treatment.* Ed. Richard Wood. Texas: University of Texas Press, 1982. n. pag.

Memmi, Albert. *The Colonizer and the Colonized.* Trans. Howard Greenfeld. Boston: Beacon Press, 1967.

Rosenblatt, L. "The Enriching Values of Reading." In *Reading in an Age of Mass Communication.* Ed. William S. Gray. New York: Appleton-Century Crofts, 1949. n. pag.

UNESCO. *An Asian Model of Educational Development: Perspectives for 1965-1980.* Paris: UNESCO, 1966.

Walmsley, Shawn A. "On the Purpose and Content of Secondary Reading Programs: Educational Ideological Perspectives." *Curriculum Inquiry* 11.1 (1981): 73-93.

Donaldo Macedo is professor of English and Distinguished Professor of Liberal Arts and Education at the University of Massachusetts Boston. He has published extensively in the areas of linguistics, critical literacy, and bilingual and multicultural education. His publications include *Literacy: Reading the Word and the World* (with Paulo Freire, 1987), *Literacies of Power: What Americans Are Not Allowed to Know* (1994), *Chomsky on Miseducation* (with Noam Chomsky, 2000) and *Ideology Matters* (co-authored with Paulo Freire, forthcoming). E-mail: donaldo.macedo@umab.edu

Bibliographic Appendices/
Apêndices Bibliográficos

A Literatura Caboverdiana: hipóteses de periodização e apêndices bibliográficos

M. Brito-Semedo

Hipóteses de periodização

Durante um período de pouco mais de um século (1856-1975), as diferentes gerações de elite intelectual produziram uma prática e elaboraram um discurso, de carácter ideológico, rasteado na imprensa periódica publicada em Cabo Verde, conducentes à construção de uma identidade nacional crioula e que se revelam como indicadores de que o processo estava em curso.

Este processo tem a sua sustentação em duas dimensões que se sobrepõem e se complementam—uma dimensão *cultural* e uma dimensão *política*. Difícil é saber, contudo, quando se passa da dimensão cultural à dimensão política ou quando começa uma e termina outra, de tal forma estão ligados entre si, confirmando os fortes vínculos existentes em Cabo Verde entre a literatura e a política.

A dimensão cultural, que compreende a emergência de um *sentimento nativista*, enquanto portadores dos valores culturais próprios, passa para uma *consciência regionalista* e chega a uma *afirmação nacionalista*. A dimensão política, que teria começado como uma *reclamação* de um estatuto de igualdade em relação ao português reinól da metrópole, progride para a *reivindicação* da diferenciação regional dentro da filosofia de um Portugal "uno e indivisível" protagonizado pelo Estado Novo, culminando na *exigência* de uma autonomia política de Cabo Verde no concerto das nações.

Considerando a intercepção ou a sobreposição dessas dimensões propomos uma organização da produção jornalística e literária cabo-verdiana, até ao momento da independência nacional em três grandes períodos, cada um deles constituído por duas fases,[1] sendo os dois primeiros antes da independência nacional e o outro depois da independência.[2]

A ideia de base defendida desde os anos quarenta por Eduíno Brito (S. Vicente, 1923-), Arnaldo França (Santiago, 1925-), António Aurélio Gonçalves (S. Vicente, 1901-1984) e pelo próprio Manuel Ferreira (Leiria, 1917-1992)[3] é a de a *Claridade—revista de arte e letras* (S. Vicente, 1936-1960) ser a divisora das águas dessa periodização, girando tudo o resto em função dessa revista e do movimento literário por ela originada.

Com base num maior conhecimento do primeiro período, adquirido através da pesquisa dos periódicos da época, propomos uma nova organização, mais equilibrada e de maior valorização, sendo cada um deles constituído por duas fases. Assim:

PERÍODO DO CABO-VERDIANISMO (1842-1936)

Os aspectos estético-formais e temáticos que caracterizam este período são os do Neoclassicismo (1756-1825) e do Romantismo (1825-1865) Português, particularmente da última fase deste, o ultra-romantismo, cultivados tardiamente em Cabo Verde.

Este período de produção jornalística e literária é por nós classificado de *cabo-verdianismo*,[4] por analogia com africanismo, já que o enunciado dos textos reproduzidos não reflecte, *grosso modo*, o real social cabo-verdiano, embora a produção fosse feita por "filhos das ilhas," por oposição às outras colónias onde, na mesma época, havia uma produção realizada essencialmente por portugueses europeus radicados.

Não era, todavia, de se esperar que fosse de outra maneira e que nos homens dessa época houvesse uma concepção clara das funções político-sociais e culturais que uma literatura poderia desempenhar. "Esses notáveis Poetas viveram no seu tempo e para o seu tempo e escreveram segundo o rumo poético da sua época. Ilustraram como puderam a sua e nossa terra," defendia José Lopes em 1952.[5]

Paradoxalmente, este é também o início da valorização da língua crioula e a sua elevação a estatuto de língua literária. Distinguimos neste período do Cabo-verdianismo duas fases: a dos *Primórdios* e a da *Crioulidade:*

Fase dos Primórdios

Estabelece-se que esta fase tenha surgido com a instalação do prelo, em 1842, embora se creia se possa ter iniciado antes.[6] É a fase do nascimento da imprensa e do lançamento das bases da literatura cabo-verdiana com a publicação dos primeiros textos literários. Evidenciam-se nomes como os de Antónia Gertrudes Pusich Amado (S. Nicolau, 1805-1883)—o primeiro poeta ultramarino a ver os seus versos incluídos no *Almanach de Lembranças* (Lisboa, 1851-1932) e a primeira mulher a dedicar-se ao jornalismo em Portugal—Guilherme da Cunha Dantas (Brava, 1849-1888), Joaquim Maria Augusto Barreto (Brava, 1854-1878), Luiz Medina e Vasconcellos (Praia, 1855-1891), Maria Luiza de Senna Barcellos, "Africana" (Brava, ?-1893) e Gertrudes Ferreira Lima, "Humilde Camponesa" (Santo Antão, ? -1915).

Fase da Crioulidade

Esta fase, que se localiza nos inícios de novecentos, é marcada pela exaltação dos valores crioulos e é integrada, principalmente por antigos estudantes do *Seminario-Lyceu* de S. Nicolau, fundado em 1866. Destacam-se Eugénio Tavares (Brava, 1861-1930),[7] Luiz Loff de Vasconcellos (Brava, ? -1923), Januário Leite (Santo Antão, 1865-1930), José Lopes da Silva (S. Nicolau, 1872-1962), António Corsino Lopes da Silva (Santo Antão, 1883-1944), Félix Lopes da Silva (i.e. Guilherme Ernesto) (Santo Antão, 1889-1967) e Pedro Monteiro Cardoso ("Afro") (Fogo, 1890-1942).

PERÍODO DA CABO-VERDIANIDADE (1936-1975)

Os aspectos estético-formais que predominam neste período são as mesmas das do Modernismo Português (1927-1940) e Brasileiro, com temáticas próprias do Realismo, por influência do modelo brasileiro (entre 1930 e 1945/50, *grosso modo*), e do Neo-realismo, seguindo o modelo português (1940-1950).

Aplica-se aqui o conceito de *cabo-verdianidade* por semelhança aos de africanidade, angolanidade e moçambicanidade, no contexto de África, Angola e Moçambique, respectivamente, porque o enunciado dos textos produzidos já reflecte o real cabo-verdiano e aquilo que o identifica, e ao mesmo tempo o distingue, socio-culturalmente como povo. O início deste novo período é marcado pelo surgimento da revista *Claridade—revista de arte e letras* (S. Vicente, 1936-1960), cujo nome passou a designar uma geração de autores e uma nova forma de fazer literatura.

Ao longo deste período foram surgindo, em torno de uma revista ou de uma folha literária — são os casos da *Claridade* (S. Vicente, 1936), da *Certeza* (S. Vicente, 1944), do *Suplemento Cultural* (Praia, 1958) e do *Seló* (S. Vicente, 1962)—gerações que se congregaram à volta de um projecto político--literário que, de uma certa forma, são o resultado do contexto histórico e social e do avanço ideológico vivido por cada uma delas.

Em 1963 Gabriel Mariano era de opinião que esse ciclo *claridoso* ainda não se tinha fechado.[8] Aliás, posição essa muito depois reforçada e alargada por Baltasar Lopes em 1986—"o movimento claridoso continua, com a mesma impregnação cívica, servido por outros processos."[9] De facto, só em 1974/75, nos prenúncios da independência nacional, é que veio a aparecer a indicação do surgimento de uma literatura fora dos moldes da *Claridade*, com Corsino Fortes (S. Vicente, 1933-) e João Varela ("Timóteo Tio Tiofe") (S. Vicente, 1937-), respectivamente, com *Pão & Fonema* (1974) e *O Primeiro Livro de Notcha* (1975), de conteúdo mais simbolista e universalista.

Consideramos existir igualmente neste período da Cabo-verdianidade duas fases: a do *Regionalismo* e a do *Nacionalismo.*

Fase do Regionalismo

Esta fase despontou em 1936 com o propósito de "fincar os pés na terra"[10] das ilhas e concretiza-se na publicação da revista *Claridade.* Destacam-se figuras de proa como Baltasar Lopes da Silva (S. Nicolau, 1907-1989), Jorge Barbosa (Praia, 1902-1971), Manuel Lopes (S. Vicente, 1907-), António Aurélio Gonçalves (S. Vicente, 1901-1984), Félix Monteiro (S. Vicente, 1909-2002), Sérgio Frusoni (S. Vicente, 1901-1975), António Nunes (Santiago, 1917-1951), Henrique Teixeira de Sousa (Fogo, 1919-) e Arnaldo França (Santiago, 1925-).

Fase do Nacionalismo

Esta é uma fase em que se passa a usar a literatura como arma de combate na construção de uma nova pátria, fase essa que é iniciada pelo grupo "Nova Largada," com a publicação do "Suplemento Cultural" ao *Cabo Verde—Boletim de Propaganda e Informação*, em 1958. Destacam-se, entre outros, Aguinaldo Fonseca (S. Vicente, 1922-), Gabriel Mariano (S. Nicolau, 1928-2002), Ovídio Martins (S. Vicente, 1928-1999), Terêncio Anahory (Boa Vista, 1932-2000) e os que os seguiram, como Corsino Fortes (S. Vicente, 1933-), Onésimo Silveira (S. Vicente, 1935), Felisberto Vieira Lopes ("Kaoberdiano Dambará") (Santiago, 1937-), Oswaldo Osório (S. Vicente, 1939-), Mário Fonseca (Santiago, 1939-) e Arménio Vieira (Santiago, 1941).

PERÍODO DO UNIVERSALISMO (1975-)

Vivemos sob o signo deste novo período onde convivem duas gerações de difícil delimitação pela ligação estabelecida entre si, daí não considerarmos fases, à semelhança do que fizemos nos períodos anteriores mas a *Geração dos Consagrados* (1975-1986) e a *Geração dos Iniciados* (1986-).

Geração dos Consagrados

Esta geração teve uma grande predominância no período entre 1975 e 1986. Contudo, a sua actividade literária, que vinha de trás, iria acompanhar a geração dos mais novos e caracterizar-se pelo signo da continuidade.

São de destacar: Teixeira de Sousa, Onésimo Silveira, Orlanda Amarílis, Luís Romano, Teobaldo Virgínio, "G. T. Didial" (i.e. João Varela), e João Rodrigues, a nível da ficção; Corsino Fortes, "Timóteo T. Tiofe" (i.e. João Varela), Oswaldo Osório, Arménio Vieira, Mário Fonseca e João Rodrigues, a nível da poesia; António Carreira, Manuel Ferreira[11] e Oswaldo Osório, a nível dos estudos e ensaios; Donaldo Pereira Macedo, "Kuame Kondé" [i.e. Francisco Fragoso], Oswaldo Osório, Arménio Vieira e Artur Vieira, a nível do teatro.

Geração da Independência

Esta geração surgiu a partir de 1975, com pouco mais de uma vintena de novos escritores que têm vindo a amadurecer e a afirmar-se no panorama literário das ilhas. Tem uma actuação destacável, particularmente a partir de 1986, e conta com mais de uma trintena de livros publicados. Caracteriza-se pelos signo da continuidade e da renovação, ensaiando uma nova estética e uma temática mais intimista e universalista.

De destacar: Germano Almeida, Manuel Veiga, Vasco Martins—revelados na fase anterior e agora confirmados—Jorge Tolentino, José Vicente Lopes, Dina Salústio, Fernando Monteiro, Fátima Bettencourt, "António de Névada" (i.e. António Brito Neves)—novas revelações, sendo a maior parte delas com obra publicada, a nível da ficção; Oliveira Barros, Jorge Carlos Fonseca, Sukre d'Sal (i.e. Francisco António Tomar), Vera Duarte, Vasco Martins, Marino Verdeano Raimundo (i.e. Aristides Raimundo Lima)—revelados na fase anterior e agora confirmados—David Hopffer Almada, Tomé Varela da Silva, Jorge Tolentino, José Vicente Lopes, José Luís Hopffer Almada, "Valentinous Velhinho" (i.e. Valdemar Rodrigues Velhinho), "Euricles Rodrigues" (i.e. Daniel Euricles Rodrigues Spínola), Mário Lúcio Sousa, Filinto Elísio (Correia e Silva), "António de Névada" (i.e. António

Brito Neves)—novas revelações e já com obras publicadas, a nível da poesia; Eduardo Cardoso e Manuel Veiga, Daniel Spínola, José Vicente Lopes, José Luís Hopffer Almada e M. Brito-Semedo, a nível dos estudos e ensaios; e "Maria José" (pseudónimo de que nunca se soube o nome verdadeiro),[12] a nível do teatro.

CONCLUSÃO

Ressalva-se que a passagem de um período ou de uma fase para outra etapa para outra não terá sido tão marcante, abrupta e datada, como aqui o apresentamos, nem tão nítida que excluísse a anterior, mas havendo momentos de sobreposição. De acordo com esta concepção, a periodização literária e jornalística é uma formação cumulativa por níveis, cada um deles construído sobre os anteriores e estabelecendo os alicerces para o desenvolvimento dos que lhe sobrevêm.

Notas

1 Esta hipótese de classificação foi inicialmente defendida por nós, ainda que de forma menos elaborada, no artigo "A Produção Literária Cabo-verdiana no Período Pós-Independência," IN *Cultura—Revista de Investigação Cultural e de Pensamento,* N.º 2 (Praia, Julho de 1998) 150-167.

2 T. T. Tiofe (1985:309-315), tomando como referência a data da publicação da *Claridade,* considera haver quatro períodos (do ponto de vista sociológico) e duas fases (do ponto de vista estético) para a poesia cabo-verdiana: o 1º período que vai de 1936 a 1956, correspondendo à prospecção e identificação da cabo-verdianidade; o 2º período, entre 1950 e 1962, que se caracteriza pelo desencanto social, o "desejo de matar a morte," sendo também "a época 'di briga cu diabu' das roças"; o 3º período, de 1963 a pouco depois de 1975, que se caracteriza pelo cantalutismo; e o 4º e último período, que se inicia em 1981, sendo o período actual, de "procura de inefável identidade." Pires Laranjeira (1995:180-185), por sua vez, defende para a literatura cabo-verdiana seis períodos. A saber: 1º período, das origens até 1925, a que chama de Iniciação; 2º período, de 1926 a 1935, Hesperitano; 3º período, que principia no ano de 1936 e vai até 1957, da Cabo-verdianidade; 4º período, indo 1958 a 1965, de Cabo-verdianitude; 5º período, entre 1966 e 1982, do Universalismo; e 6º Período, de 1983 à actualidade, de Consolidação.

3 Conferir, respectivamente, "Jorge Barbosa e a Poesia Caboverdeana," de Eduíno Brito, IN *Certeza,* N.º 2, (S. Vicente, Junho de 1944); *Notas Sobre Poesia Cabo-verdiana* (Praia, 1962) 11-12, de Arnaldo França; e "As Origens da Literatura Cabo-verdiana," de António Aurélio Gonçalves, agora IN *Ensaios e Outros Escritos* (Praia-S. Vicente, 1998) 109-119; e *A Aventura Crioula,* de Manuel Ferreira (Lisboa, 1985) 229-320.

4 Os termos *Cabo-verdianismo* e *Cabo-verdianidade* foram tomados por empréstimo de Manuel Ferreira, IN *A Aventura Crioula* (Lisboa, 1985), que os usa com este mesmo sentido. Por outro lado, somos de opinião que a classificação até aqui adoptada—"Pré-Claridoso," "Claridoso" e "Pós-Claridoso"—não é a mais adequada já que é feita em função da *Claridade.*

[5] José Lopes, "Ainda os Nossos Poetas," IN *Cabo Verde*—Boletim de Propaganda e Informação, N.º 36 (Praia, Setembro de 1952) 10.

[6] Ao que tudo indica, os primeiros escritores foram os Quinhentistas André Alvares d'Almada e André Donelha. *Cf.* Conferência Proferida pelo Comandante Avelino Teixeira da Mota, "Dois Escritores Quinhentistas de Cabo verde, André Alvares de Almada e André Dornelas (Séc. XVI-XVII)," IN *Boletim Cultural, Suplemento* (Luanda, Novembro, 1970).

[7] Para Jorge Barbosa, "ninguém como Eugénio Tavares viveu tão intensamente pela sua terra. Ninguém pode medir-se com Êle no grau atingido do *caboverdianismo*," *in Notícias de Cabo Verde*, N.º 6 (S. Vicente, de Maio de 1931) 2.

[8] Gabriel Mariano, "O Ciclo Claridoso Ainda não se Fechou," IN *Cabo Verde—Boletim de Propaganda e Informação*, N.º 13/15 (Praia, Outubro a Dezembro de 1963) 8-11.

[9] "Depoimento de Baltasar Lopes e Manuel Lopes," IN *Claridade—revista de arte e letras*, Edição fac-similada, 1986, XV.

[10] Manuel Lopes, "O Programa da Claridade Era Fincar os Pés na Terra Cabo-verdiana," IN *Cabo Verde— Boletim de Propaganda e Informação*, N.º 121 (Praia, Outubro de 1959).

[11] Manuel Ferreira é considerado um "caso especial de um escritor português que, tendo conhecido a fundo a realidade cabo-verdiana, decidiu [...] dar a conhecer tal realidade através de vários escritos." IN T. T. Tiofe, "Primeira epístola ao meu irmão António: a propósito de *O primeiro livro de Notcha*," IN *África—Literatura, Arte e Cultura*, N.º 3, Jan-Mar de 1979, 271-279.

[12] José Hopffer Almada garante ser o autor Flávio Moreira, um jovem natural de Santa Catarina que se suicidou tempos depois.

Apêndices cronológicos: escritores, obras e jornais do pós-independência

Escritores e obras

Almada, David Hopffer. Poeta (n. Santa Catarina, 19.12.1945. Jurista)
Canto a Cabo Verde (Praia, 1988)

Almada, José Luís Hopffer. Poeta e Ensaísta (n. 1960, Santa Catarina. Jurista)
A Sombra do Sol I e II (Praia, 1990)
Mirábilis de Veias ao Sol. Antologia dos Novíssimos Poetas Cabo-verdianos (Praia, 1991)
Assomada Nocturna (Praia, 1993)

Almeida, Germano. Ficcionista (n. Boa Vista, 31.07.1945. Jurista)
Testamento do Sr. Napumoceno da Silva Araújo (Mindelo, 1989)
Meu Poeta (Mindelo, 1990)
O Dia das Calças Roladas (Mindelo, 1992)
A Ilha Fantástica (Mindelo, 1994)
Os Dois Irmãos (Mindelo, 1995)
Estórias de Dentro de Casa (Mindelo, 1996)
A Família Trago (Mindelo, 1998)
Estórias Contadas (Mindelo, 1998)
Dona Pura e os Camaradas de Abril (Mindelo, 1999)
As Memórias de Um Espírito (Mindelo, 2001)

Almeida, Sara. Ficcionista (n. Lisboa, Portugal ?. Professora de Línguas)
Depois Telefono (Praia, 1993)

Araújo, Carlos. Ficcionista (n. Paúl, Santo Antão, 1950. Engenheiro Electrotécnico)
Percurso Vulgar (Mindelo, 1990)

Na Corda Bamba (Mindelo, ?)
Vendaval (Mindelo, ?)

Barbosa, Carlos Alberto. Poeta (n. S. Vicente, 1.05.1947. Técn. Comercial)
Vinti Sintidu Letradu na Kriolu (Praia, 1984)
Son di ViraSon (Praia, 1997)
Chão Terra Maiamo (Praia, 2001)

Barreto, Leopoldina. Ficcionista (n. S. Nicolau, ?)
Monte Gordo (Praia, 1997)

Bettencourt, Fátima. Ficcionista (n. Santo Antão, 16.02.1938. Prof. e Jornalista)
Semear em Pó (Praia, 1994)
A Cruz do Rufino (Praia, 1996), Infanto-juvenil
Um Certo Olhar... (Praia, 2001), Crónicas

Brito, Margarida, Ensaísta (n. Boa Vista, 11.06.1956. Professora)
Os Instrumentos Musicais em Cabo Verde (Praia, 1998)

Brito-Semedo, M. Ensaísta (n. Mindelo, S. Vicente, 01.05.1952. Professor)
Caboverdianamente Ensaiando, Vol. I e II (Mindelo, 1995 e 1998)
A Morna-Balada. O Legado de Renato Cardoso (Praia, 1999)

Cardoso, Eduardo Augusto. Ensaísta (n. Mindelo, S. Vicente, 05.1955. Linguista)
Crioulo da Ilha de S. Nicolau (Lisboa, 1990)

Cruz, Eutrópio Lima da. Ficcionista (n. Boa Vista, ?. Musicólogo)
Perkurse de Sul d'Ilha (Praia, 1999)

Duarte, Vera. Poeta. (n. Mindelo, S. Vicente, 02.10.1952. Jurista)
Amanhã Amadrugada (Praia/Lisboa, 1993)
Arquipélago da Paixão (Praia, 2001)

Fernandes, Ivone. Ficcionista (n. ?)
Vidas Vividas (S. Vicente, 1990)
Futcera ta Cende na Rotcha (S. Vicente, 2000)

Ferreira, Armindo. Ficcionista (n. Guiné ?. Engenheiro Civil)
O Passaporte (Praia, 2002)

Ferreira, Hermínia Curado. Ficcionista (n. ? Professora)
Histórias de Encantar Praia, 2000)

Ferreira, Ondina. Ficcionista (n. ?. Professora)
Amor nas Ilhas e Outras Paragens (Mindelo, 2001)

Figueira, Tchalé. Poeta (n. S. Vicente, 1952. Artista Plástico)
Onde os Sentimentos se Encontram (Praia, 1998)
O Azul e a Luz (Praia, 2002)

Fonseca, Jorge Carlos. Poeta (n. S. Vicente, 20.10.1950. Jurista)
Silêncio Acusado de Alta Traição e de Incitamento ao Mau Hálito Geral (Praia, 1995)

Lima, António Germano. Ensaísta (n. Boa Vista, ? Pedagogo)
Boa Vist —Ilha de Capitães (Praia, 1997)

Lima, Humberto. Ensaísta (n. S. Vicente, ? Historiador)
Um Bes Tinha Nhu Lobu ku Xibinhu (Praia, 2000)

Lopes, José Vicente. Poeta e Ensaísta (n. S. Vicente, 02.10.1959. Jornalista)
Cabo Verde. Os Bastidores da Independência (Praia, 1996)
Os Desatinos de Caldeira Marques (Praia, 2000)

Lopes, Eugénio. Poeta (n. ?)
Saudade Perdida (Praia, 1993)

Azul Apesar da Noite como te Vejo (Praia, 2002)

Lopes, Leão. Ficiconista (n. Santo Antão, ? Artista Plástico)
Blimundo (Praia, 1997), Infanto-juvenil
Unine (Praia, 1998), Infanto-juvenil

Martins, Vasco. Poeta e Ficcionista (n. Lisboa, 12.07.56. Compositor Musical)
Universo da Ilha (Praia, 1986)
Navegam os Olhares com o Vôo dos Pássaros (Praia, 1989)
A Verdadeira Dimensão (Praia, 1990)
Tempos da Moral Moral (Praia, 1993)

Matos, Mário da Silva. Ficcionista (n. S. Vicente, ?-2000. Enfermeiro)
Contos e Factos (Mindelo, 2000)

Monteiro, César. Ensaísta (n. Santo Antão, ? Sociólogo)
Recomposição do Espaço Social Cabo-verdiano (Praia, 2001)

Monteiro, Fernando. Ficcionista (n. Praia, Santiago, 1951. Jornalista)
Desassossego (Praia, 1994)

Monteiro, Vladimir. Ensaísta (n. Senegal ?. Jornalista)
Portugal Crioulo (Praia, 1995)
Les Musiques du Cap-Vert (Praia, 1998)

Névada, António de. Poeta e Ficcionista (n. S. Vicente, 1974. Engenheiro)
Acto Primeiro ou o Desígnio das Paixões (Praia, 1993)

Pereira, Daniel. Ensaísta (n. S. Vicente, ?. Historiador e Diplomata)
A Situação da Ilha de Santiago no Primeiro Quartel do Século XVIII (Praia, 1984)
Estudos da História de Cabo Verde (Praia, 1986)
Marcos Cronológicos da Cidade Velha (Praia, 1988)

Pereira, Marilene. Ficcionista (n. Brasil, ?. Jornalista)
O Bentinho Traquinas (Praia, 2000)

Pina, Arsénio de. Ficcionista (n. ? Médico)
Fid'Kadon (Mindelo, ?)
Uli-Me Li (Mindelo, 1999)
Você Falou em Economia de Bazar (Mindelo, 2000)
Mania de Pensar (Mindelo, 2001)

Queirós, Isabel. Ficcionista (n. Portugal, ?. Artista Plástico)
Saarac — O Último Gafanhoto do Deserto (Praia, 1998), Infanto-juvenil

Rodrigues, Euricles. Poeta e Ficcionista (ver Daniel Spínola)
Lágrimas de Bronze (Praia, 1990)
Na Kantar di Sol (Praia, 1991)
Vítreas Labaredas: Poemas e Canções — 1992 (Praia 1992)
Adon & Eva (Praia, 2000)

Rodrigues,, Moacyr. Ensaísta (n. S. Vicente, ? Professor)
A Morna da Literatura Tradicional (Praia, 1996), Co-autor
Festas de Romaria — Festas Juninas (Mindelo, 1997)

Salústio, Dina. Poeta e Ficcionista (n. Santo Antão, 27.03.1941. Assistente Social)
Mornas eram as Noites (Praia, 1994)
A Louca de Serrano (Praia, 1998)
A Estrelinha Tlim Tlim (Praia, 2000), Infanto-Juvenil

Semedo, José Maria. Ensaísta (n. Praia, ? Geógrafo)
Cabo Verde — O Ciclo Ritual das Festividades da Tabanca (Praia, 1997), Co-autor

Silva, António Leão Correia e (n. Santo Antão, 1963. Sociólogo e Historiador)

Histórias de um Sahel Insular (Praia, 1995)
Nos Tempos do Porto Grande do Mindelo (Praia, 2000)

Silva, Filinto Elísio. Poeta e Cronista (n. Praia, Santiago, 24.01.1961. Biblioteconomista)
Do Lado de Cá da Rosa (Praia, 1995)
O Prato do Dia (Praia, 2001)
O Inferno do Riso (Praia, 2001)

Silva, Jorge Soares. Ficcionista (n. S. Vicente, ?)
A Família do Chibim (Praia, 1995), Infanto-juvenil

Silva, Tomé Varela da. Poeta e Ensaísta (n. Órgãos, Santiago, 19.12.1950. Filósofo)
Finaçon di Nha Nássia Gomi (Praia, 1985)
Kumunhon d'Afrika: Onti, Osi, Manan (Praia, 1986)
Kardisantus (Praia, 1987)
Na Boca Noti (Praia, 1987)
Natal y Kontus (Praia, 1988)
Nha Bibinha Cabral (Praia, 1988)
Escada de Luz (Praia, 1989)
Nha Guida Mendi (Praia, 1990)
Tempu di Tempu (Praia, 1992)
Komparaçon di Konbersu (Praia, ?)
Na Altar di Nha Petu (Praia, 1997)
Força di Amor (Praia, 1999)
Nha Caminhu (Praia, 2000)

Sousa, Mário Lúcio. Poeta (n. Tarrafal, Santiago, 21.10.1964. Jurista)
Nascimento de um Mundo (Praia, 1991)
Sob os Signos da Luz (Praia, 1993)
Para nunca mais falarmos de amor (Mindelo, 1999)

Spínola, Daniel. Ensaísta. (n. Ribeira da Barca, Santiago, 11.04.1962. Prof. E Jornalista)
Três Obras Poéticas da Contemporaneidade Caboverdeana (Praia, 1990)

Tolentino, Luís. Poeta (n. Mindelo, S. Vicente, 16.10.1949. *Designer* Gráfico).
Terra Gritante (Praia, 1983)

Varela, José Maria. Cronista (n. Praia, ? Jornalista)
69 Cenas de Humor (Praia, 2001)

Veiga, Manuel. Ensaísta e Ficcionista. (n. Santa Catarina, Santiago, 27.03.1948.Linguista)
Diskrison Strutural di Língua Kauberdianu (Praia, 1982)
Odju d'Agu (Praia, 1987)
A Sementeira (Praia, 1994)
Introdução à Gramática: O Crioulo de Cabo Verde (Praia, 1995)
Le créole du Cap-Vert (Praia, 2000)

Velhinho, Valentinous. Poeta e Cronista (i.e. Valdemar Valentino Velhinho Rodrigues, n. Calheta, Santiago, 29.05.1961. Jornalista Cultural)
Relâmpagos em Terra (Mindelo, 1995)
Adeus Loucura Adeus (Mindelo, 1997)
No Ponto do Rebuçado (Mindelo, 2001)

Jornais

Da Primeira República (1975-1990)

Voz di Povo (Praia, 1975-1992)

Terra Nova (S. Vicente, 1975-)

Tribuna (Praia, 1984-1991)
Raízes (Praia, 1977-1984)
Ponto & Vírgula, Revista de Intercâmbio Cultural (Mindelo, 1983-1987)
Fragmentos, Revista de Letras, Arte e Cultura (Praia, 1987-)
Notícias (S. Vicente, 1987-1992)
Sopinha do Alfabeto (Praia, 1991)
Magma (Fogo, 1988-1990)
Seiva (Praia, 1986-1989)
Azágua (S. Vicente, 1990)
Opinião (Praia, 1990-1991).

Da Segunda República (1990-2001)
A Semana (Praia, 1991-)
Agaviva (S. Vicente, 1991-1992)
Artiletra (S. Vicente, 1991-)
Montanha (S. Vicente, 1991)
Mantenha (Praia, 1991-1993);
Pré-Textos, Ideias & Cultura (Praia, 1991-)
Ekhos do Paúl (Praia, 1991-)
Novo Jornal de Cabo Verde (1992-1998)
Correio Quinze (Praia, 1994-1997)
Já (S. Vicente, 1995-1996)
O País (Praia, 1995-1996)
Cultura, Revista de Investigação Cultural e de Pensamento (Praia, 1997-)
Direito e Cidadania (Praia, 1997-)
Horizonte (Praia, 1998-).

M. Brito-Semedo é doutorando em Antropologia na Universidade Nova de Lisboa. É membro fundador da Associação de Escritores Cabo-verdianos (AEC). Participou, entre outros, no Simpósio Internacional sobre a Cultura e a Literatura Cabo-verdianas, em comemoração ao 50º Aniversário da fundação da "Claridade," S. Vicente, Novembro de 1986. É autor de *A Morna-Balada, O Legado de Renato Cardoso* (Praia, 1999) (Estudo Poético e Sociológico das Baladas), *Caboverdianamente Ensaiando,* Vol. I e II (S. Vicente, 1995 e 1998) (Ensaios sobre a Literatura Cabo-verdiana).

Writing and Music/Escrita e Música

Na morna! Na marzurca o trompete da evasão

Corsino Fortes

I

O trompete chegava
Assim! farto de fome & faminto de fartura
Aos quatro mercados do dia
De palha & peixe De roupa & verdura

Houve sempre esta demanda
 entre o milho e o feijão
Que na ilha
As maternidades são úteros que emigram
E nos olhos da criança nasce
                    cresce
                    o elogio da evasão

Rosto! se evadires antes
Os membros emigrarão depois
Do poço! as mãos do êxodo
Da vida! os pés errantes
E se na ida! a memória
Das lavas nos ilumina
As falésias abrirão crânios adentro
O sino de quantas paróquias

Emigrante! aquele
        que leva no estômago
Uma ribeira de pedras soltas...
Ribeira que morre antes
        para nascer depois
Entre
    a erecção do Monte Clara
        E
    as pernas de Pico d'Antónia

Todo o emigrante é um coreógrafo
Que leva na ópera de metal & osso
Os acrobatas de "Pedra Rolada"
E sendo arquitecto! toda a mão que emigra
A ilha é telha! cada vez mais
            telha
            no tecto do mundo

II

Não! o trompete diria

Quando somos vulcões em viagem
O céu abre nas nossas cabeças
        a flor de quantas crateras...
Se o mar
        no fogo das artérias é terra arável
            Isto é

Da erosão! nasce o rosto
Da evasão! nasce o homem
E mais que primo & primas
Menos que gémeo & gémeas
Rebeldes! a órbita e o mundo crescem
Na raiz do labor que perdura
Entre a dor e a diástole da canção

Mensageira! da renovada parábola
para a Liberdade das estátuas
Para as mãos de Cristo no Corcovado
E para as rugas do Monte Cara
Que pesa & sopesa
a nudez da montanha no ombro de Bia + a
pedra verde do mito
Na sua gramática do silêncio
Na sua cratera oca de vocábulos

III

Ó lestada de ser homem E mulher do harmatão
Ó rapsódia dos ventos d'aquém & além
Ventos que balançam o "erg" do equinócio
Quebrando a tíbia e a matriz dos dedos
Na morabeza da moção atlântica
Se
a erosão é fogo no motor da evasão
A morna! o finançom nos conduz
ao frigorífico da cultura
das terras do fim do mundo
À guerra da pobreza
No metrónomo do batuque
E ao dente de ouro da tabanca
No mênstruo das salinas
À coladeira & funaná
na erupção do funacol
E ao rondó que renova o passo
como quem baila o landum
E ao kolá kolá
da morança e da melancolia
que salte & bate
bate & une
As coxas d'África às ancas da Macaronésia

E dão
o grão a hóstia o jazz
Da(s) nossa(s) genealogia(s)
E dançam & tecem
na virilha dos continentes
o seu pano inconsútil
E constroem
a catedral do ego
com
a ressaca das raízes abruptas

IV

Seferis! para que o Outono se reconheça
Na primavera do retorno
Cabo Verde viaja! viaja sempre
Pelo umbigo & ventre da sua proa
Redonda! porque
Toda a lava que emigra
pela ribeira da vida
Toda a erupção que evade
do vulcão da vida
Regressa! regressam antes da partida

✦

Assim foi
Antes & depois do 7.° dia
A erupção de sol & substância
que vai solta
Nas sementes & árvores
Das ribeiras
que vão & vêm
Assim
fartas de fome & famintas de fartura

Corsino Fortes é licenciado em direito. É Professor e Embaixador. Uma das vozes poéticas mais significativas da literatura caboverdiana contemporânea. Colaborou na revista *Claridade, Cabo Verde e África.* Representado e traduzido em várias antologias. Publicou *Pão & Fonema* (1974), *Árvore & Tambor* (1986), *A Cabeça Calva de Deus* (2000).

from *O Testamento do Sr. Napumoceno da Silva Araújo* (1989)

Germano Almeida
Translated by
Luís R. Mitras
Revised by Mark Streeter

At the time, Mr. Napumoceno was working as deputy manager at J. Baptista Ltd., and rumor had it that the partners were constantly pestering him to acquire some of the shares in the company and to take over the management of it with a salary four times higher than he was then getting. But it was also said that he always turned down the offer, saying that he wasn't cut out for such responsibility, etc. But what was said in whispers was that once he was a manager he wouldn't be able to pull the tricks that everyone knew about. However, the truth of the matter is such that a few years later he left the company to set up his own business, Araújo Ltd.—Import-Export. Notwithstanding the fact that he was the sole owner of the company he had the word "Limited" added to its name, and the gossip that went around town said that his "limit" was the share he had taken from Baptista, and that no one could tell whether this was great or small. But right from the beginning Mr. Napumoceno revealed himself to be an extremely astute businessman—or else a man as lucky as the devil. It happened that because his warehouse was located in the Salinas area he very often had to go there under the blazing sun of August, and by foot at that, since he didn't have a car and, in fact, didn't even know how to drive. That's why he decided to buy himself an umbrella. He searched in every shop and corner store but it was in vain. There wasn't a single umbrella on sale and he had to make do with a cork cap, which was singularly unpractical as an appendage; being the polite man that he was, he was forever lifting his cap to greet those people to whom he had to show a certain respect, which meant that he had to run the risk of getting wind on his forehead, or catching a cold, or something worse. It was precisely this market deficiency that he complained about to a traveling salesman when they met on the street, after he had uncovered his head to greet the other, that is. But the man laughed broadly and said, "If you want I'll order you, not one, but dozens. Hundreds, if you want. That should be no reason for you to be upset." Now it so happened that Mr. Napumoceno was preparing to place an order with this gentleman and, almost as a joke, though quite aware this wasn't anything other than an unnecessary outlay of capital, he added a request for 1000 umbrellas. He knew that in the best case scenario he would sell about 10 a year but that at least the market would be served; it would put an end to the scandal of a person searching all of Mindelo for an umbrella and not finding a single one.

Yet, a few days later, when he received the traveling salesman's invoice it was a stroke of luck that he didn't have a heart attack. Ten thousand umbrellas, in a country where they are used as parasols because unhappily it never rains! He would not admit that he had written an extra zero on the order form and for that reason he felt insulted by the traveling salesman who had taken advantage of his friendship. He sat down at once to write out an enraged letter: "How can you, Sir, continue to regard the firm Araújo, Ltd. as one of your clients after an outrage of this nature that…" but tore up the letter and took himself to the post office because only an urgent telegram would relieve him of his rage; he wrote out SIR UNHAPPY MANNER CARRIED OUT OUR DEAL, but he tore that up, asked for another form, merely wrote out I AM LOST FOR WORDS TO EXPRESS MY DISAPPOINTMENT COMMA FULL LETTER TO FOLLOW PERIOD, left, noticed that Mr. Paiva Português was calling out to him, said "shit" between his teeth but smiled at him anyway and told him of his troubles. Mr. Paiva, who was a man for whom there were no problems that could not be solved, suggested that Mr. Napumoceno should try and sell his parasols or umbrellas, for either term would do, on the other islands. Or even in Africa! It would be interesting if Cape Verde were to begin exporting umbrellas to the other Portuguese provinces. But that solution did not please Mr. Napumoceno and that's why, when they said goodbye, in order to console him for his woes, Mr. Paiva prophesied that it would rain that year and that he would end up selling all his stock. "What a story! What a man!" said Mr. Napumoceno, exasperated. "This country is cursed; nothing will get the rain to come down." He walked away in the direction of the warehouse. He had left the shop assistant to do some small jobs, things sufficient to protect the merchandise from the sun until they were put away. He had decided, right from the get-go, that he was a wholesaler. He wanted nothing to do with shops, grocery stores, counters and putting up with people, be they staff or be they clients. He was more than tired of having to deal with the nonsense of clients who didn't know what they wanted and with having to sort out problems to do with ill-trained staff. It was for that reason that he had decided that he and the shop assistant would be more than enough to guarantee the proper running of the company. He, Napumoceno, would make the contacts and the boy would run the errands, for moving about is something youths generally like. The merchandise would be stocked in the warehouse and sold directly to retailers, and the quantity depended on the relative strengths of these clients, but always in boxes, bags or bales. And while he gave instructions to the boy about where to place the goods, for he wanted to leave some space in front of the warehouse for a future office, he was mentally drafting another letter to the traveling salesman, a tough, almost offensive, letter that would make the man feel as humiliated as he, Napumoceno, felt. He thought: "Sir…" but he scratched that out: To hell with Sir! What he deserves is: You son of a bitch, you snake in the grass, you cheapskate crook forcing a small tradesman at the beginning of his career to be stuck with ten thousand umbrellas that won't get sold, not even at the rate of 5 a year. Unfairness and deceit are not strong enough words to express the dishonest manner in which you, Sir, have treated me. You, Sir, have deliberately ignored the good relations of loyalty that are implicit in the transactions between businessmen, or be it, the principles of mutual trust and confidence. In sending me an order for ten thousand umbrellas you, Sir, cannot but be aware that you have obliged me to make an extremely high outlay of capital that will be locked up until the goods have perished, for I do not foresee having sales of these goods at a rate higher than 5 units per annum. I repeat: if there is no reasonable explanation for this excessive number or if there is no action sufficient to repair the damages that you, Sir, have caused me, our future relations, be they professional or be they personal, cannot but be conducted on the basis of absolute mistrust, harmful for any type of understanding, the more so because I shall be forced to relate to my fellow businessmen that your lack of honesty disfavors carrying out even the most insignificant of transactions with you, Sir.…

The invoice had arrived on the first day, the insolent and threatening letter dispatched on the second day, registered and with a delivery note, and on the third day the ship with the umbrellas sailed into the bay. Fortunately in those days there were no air links or even regular steamships and the mailbag left when chance took it. Because the ship laid anchor in the morning and close to midday it began to rain. First it was a light and gentle drizzle, but persistent nevertheless, which made the radio announcer at the local radio station give out the news that in São Vicente it was raining torrentially. But this drizzly rain lasted the whole afternoon and the whole night—the sky was permanently overcast and threatening heavier showers—and so the next morning Mr. Napumoceno was quick to try and get his merchandise through customs, always with this drizzle falling, and because they were already in October, by tradition a month when it sometimes rained, and merely as a way of being at ease with his conscience, he had it announced through the radio that the firm Araújo, Ltd. had received a small batch of umbrellas and these were available for local tradesman at his warehouse located at Largo das Salinas. It was with no surprise that, the next day, he watched as 1000 umbrellas left the warehouse, which covered the cost of 5000. Still, it was only three days later, after he had placed 6000 umbrellas in the market, that it dawned on him that it wasn't worth it to offend his friend, the traveling salesman, for such a petty reason and took himself to the post office, he himself with an umbrella, and filled out a form (Model 3, Variant C7) requesting the return of his correspondence and returned to the warehouse; he smiled with happiness when he went past a certain "Rua de Lisboa" and saw the whole street jam-packed with umbrellas. When he arrived back at the warehouse he found there was an order for another 2000.

The rain continued to fall down, gentle and calm, and at peak hour the streets would be transformed into black clouds, rising and falling, and everyone would be laughing with joy, and the announcers on the radio would be playing with the idea of the rain and umbrellas: *Protect yourself from the rain with the Best umbrella; for only the rain is better than the Best.* And for eight days the rain continued to fall in the same beautiful and useful manner, drenching the ground, the houses, the streets. And when the last batch of 500 left the warehouse, Mr. Napumoceno had sparkling wine served to all those who were present at the Royal; he said he was celebrating the departure of the ten thousand.

In his will he admitted that the business had been a stroke of good luck; it was done by mistake and through an accident, because, some time afterwards, as he was going through his things, he discovered the order form and he saw for himself that the extra zero in his request had been his mistake. Yet, when he had the glass in his hand at the Royal, he boasted about his commercial scent, that instinct that had made him foresee that it would rain that year and the great deal he had just made.

Germano Almeida holds a *Licenciatura* in Law. He was founder and co-director of the magazine *Ponto & Vírgula* (1983-87). He made his debút in fiction with *O Testamento do Sr. Napomuceno da Silva Araújo* (1989) and has published many books that have been translated into various languages.

Apeiron

Vasco Martins
Translated by
Luis R. Mitras
Revised by
Mark Streeter

ApEiRoN, music for electronic sound sources, percussion and sound design: The first steps towards the composition

In 1998 I commissioned the architect Anildo Silva to build me a Roman-Etruscan arch over a limestone terrain that was filled with underwater fossils and petrified trees. The choice of place was based on artistic intuition and a feeling for positive telluric forces.

The arch faces east, in the direction of the rising of the sun, and on the 1st of January of every year the sun rises in the center of the arch. The arch was inaugurated on the 21st of June, the day of the summer solstice, a date that for thousands of years has been a ritualistic one, and one that is still visibly part of the human unconscious: consider, for example, the June festivals in Cape Verde that have to do with the land and fertility. The arch was given the name of **ApEiRoN**.

ApEiRoN

The concept of ***ApEiRoN*** is a very ancient one; it harkens back to Greece and to the pre-Socratic philosopher Anaximander. In those days philosophers observed nature; intuitive beings, they were, in essence, poets. With their open-minded souls they began to understand the world. That is how Anaximander got around to creating the concept of Apeiron, which means "indefinite" or, even, "invisible."

It took a year to compose the music: the artist is the recipient of cosmic forces and he conveys what he has learnt. This comes into close union with the philosophies of the beginning of the universe proclaimed by Indian mysticism:

In the beginning was the Sound, represented by the word "om" (as opposed to the Judaeo-Christian philosophies, which speak of the Word). This primordial sound is disseminated throughout the whole of the universe (which coincides with the recent discovery of the "white noise" that exists everywhere in the Cosmos, and which was discovered by an American scientist in the 1950s: it is the primordial sound of the Big Bang and it is more than 15 billion years old).

In ancient Indian philosophy there were two kinds of sound:

Anahata: those vibrations that man cannot hear

Ahata: normal sound

Musicians and composers with a mystical inclination may, in a certain sense, be the recipients of such *anahata* vibrations; by means of their intuition and meditation and by making an effort to perceive those sounds, they may even transform it into normal sound, *ahata.*

Everything Vibrates

Planet earth itself produces a vibration that has been calculated at 1/31,556,925.9747 Hz. As we know, the human ear can hear only from 16 Hz up to more or less 22,000 Hz. If we multiply this very low frequency by 32 we obtain 136.10 Hz, which is the mystical note used in Buddhist temples, which they call *Sadja*, and which is situated between C# and D (bass). The songs of the Buddhist monks in their hidden plateaus in Tibet have made a perceptible connection with planet Earth and, consequently, with the Cosmos.

Two "drones" were used, one in A, the other in D.

Three "loops" were also used, and these were mainly based on the ancient Greek Lydian scale.

But the more invisible, more secret motivations behind the construction of the arch, one for which there is no formulation according to some method, belongs to the world of metaphysics and to the deepest recesses of the soul. Of these we shall not speak. Over-interpretation can destroy the poetry that is intrinsic to it and sometimes it is only to another being that we owe an explanation.

Tone colors used

Textures from: psycho-sonic synthesizers, ritual Chinese flute, ghuzen (a guitar-like Chinese instrument), "whistling piano," strings, etc.

For percussion: "udus" from Nigeria, "floor-toms," cymbals, Tabanka seashells, Tibetan bell, "djembê," etc.

All in all, more than 30 different tone colors [*timbres*] were used.

Two seashells are used in **ApEiRoN**: one which has been "baptized" by the "Tabanka da Várzea" on the island of Santiago, and the other made in São Vicente and "baptized" by the sea around the Baía das Gatas. It is an oceanic instrument and, according to Pierre Schaffner, it is the instrument that gave birth to wind instruments. In certain age-old oriental philosophies the seashell is a symbol of creation.

The use of the seashell in **ApEiRoN** is necessary on account of its oceanic tone color and it is also a calling from outside time.

Poetry is alive in the environment north of Praia

Yellow flowers in the dunes that seem to have grown out of nothing and that flower only in February, limestone rocks, rare water-springs, sea-birds, common plants, the breathing of the ocean, rocks from primordial lava, "ouedes" (the desert river-beds of brooks)…

These environmental features contributed to the creation of **ApEiRoN**; all in all: the arch symbolizes the vertical union between the land and the cosmos and the need for sublimation and for love. The environment all around is that of Cape Verde, in its natural strength that goes beyond men, in the strength that is intrinsic to it. At night the stars illuminate Praia; or else it is the moon, which is born in the distant horizon, in the east or in the northeast.

The *Morna*, or the ambience of the *Morna* as a Cape Verdean reference

The *Morna* is the source of inspiration of **ApEiRoN**. Some basic principles were established: soul (a subjective notion, but one that is inherent to any musical form that has attained a synthesis of the musical personality of a people).

The rhythm is supplied by pre-established sequences, in counterpoint. The harmonies operate above. There is a kind of static movement. In their turn, the percussion instruments, the "udu" or the "djembê" or the cymbals, produce the rhythmic cells and "loops." The melody is constructed and simple, almost minimalist; there is space for improvisation.

The mountain-scape as random musical reference

The mountains surrounding the **ApEiRoN** arch are beautiful, solid, furrowed, and full of the power of the earth. These are rocks older than 300 million years. If we trace the lines from the summits of the mountains we have the outline of a random music, one which has been used in the "atmospheric" parts (excluding "the desert atmosphere," where Berber scales from Mauritania are used) and in the "spiral-wise oceanic movements" theme.

ApEiRoN is a musical metaphysical necessity, the attempt to make a cosmic connection through the music.

Already Pythagoras had divided music into the following types:

Music made with instruments
Music created within men
The music of the spheres

Every night the stars communicate the great mystery of creation and how it remains unfathomable.

Note (an aside, but an integral part of the rest; not a justification but a reflection):

I don't know why some people question electronic instruments. It is true that there is a certain vogue for what is acoustic, a return to roots (as if that were possible! The Universe is on the move all the time...), and an ecological spirit of the "long live the ox-wagon" type. But these people, these inflexible critics, have in their homes electronic music players to listen to their CDs; they travel by plane, they communicate by means of cellular phones and through the internet, they make use of multimedia.

An instrument is an instrument, so long as it serves to create music and make substantial what is insubstantial.

Music is sufficient: it embraces the world, brings out the profundities, it reaches deep into what is metaphysical, it creates worlds, it gives food to the spirit, it gives strength, sublimates, calms down; it is life; it is sufficient to offer what there is to offer; it encapsulates the universe, it communicates with men and with the gods within them or outside of them.

Vasco Martins is an ethnomusicologist who studied in France, a composer, poet and novelist with many published novels, among them *Tempos da Moral Moral* (1993). He also has published poetry and an essay about the *Morna*, as well as a vast discography with more than ten titles.

Reviews/ Recensões

José Vicente Lopes. *Cabo Verde: Os Bastidores da Independência.* Praia — Mindelo, Instituto Camões/ Centro Cultural Português, 1996.

David Brookshaw

Compared to the mainland countries of Mozambique, Angola and even Guinea-Bissau, the recent history of Cape Verde has not attracted very much academic scrutiny, which is surprising given its unique independence process and its early political links with Guinea-Bissau under the banner of one political party, the African Party for the Independence of Guinea and Cape Verde (PAIGC). There are, of course, exceptions. Colm Foy's now dated analysis of the country's Marxist regime and programmes (*Cape Verde: Politics, Economy and Society* — 1988) focuses relatively little on the tensions at the heart of the liberation movement. Similarly, Basil Davidson's *The Fortunate Isles: a Study in African Transformation* (1989) is inevitably inflected by the idealism gained from the author's close personal association with Amílcar Cabral and the PAICG/PAICV leadership of the first fifteen years of independence, most notably Aristides Pereira. Richard Lobban's *Cape Verde: Crioulo Colony to Independent Nation* (1995) conveys similar sympathies for those who brought Cape Verde to independence, but benefits from the changes that occurred in the early 1990s, and is a subtler, more nuanced interpretation of the development of this island state in the context of its traditional position as an economic and cultural entrepôt between Europe and West Africa.

The above are general studies and, of course, particularly useful for those who do not understand Portuguese. For those with a knowledge of the language, José Vicente Lopes's monumental work, *Cabo Verde: Os Bastidores da Independência* not only plugs a huge gap in our knowledge of Cape Verde's political history and the fortunes of its major personalities between the 1950s and 1981, but also slays one or two sacred cows along the way. Rather than a historical study in the traditional, academic sense, Lopes's book is an exhaustive piece of investigative journalism, during the making of which the author undertook extensive archival work and interviewed many well-known figures, as well as a range of lesser players. Nor does he limit himself purely to politicians, for there are useful and informative incursions into literary and cultural debates, most notably that over the role of the *Claridade* movement in defining Cape Verdean literature, and the polemic surrounding Creole in the aftermath of independence. The opinions of Lopes's interviewees are reproduced, often competing and conflicting with each other. Lopes, who is himself one of Cape Verde's foremost journalists, limits himself to periodic reflections, inviting us to pick our own path through the undergrowth of truths and half-truths. The effect is that of a polyphonic narrative that makes history come alive. Like characters in a novel, the witnesses to events reappear during the course of the narrative, to cast their judgement again and again on matters viewed through the prism of memory. At the same time, the relative absence of a judgemental omniscient narrator makes the account of Cape Verde's recent history more vivid and complex than more traditional, ideologically biased accounts, with their tendency to assume that all colonial administrators were venal and all freedom fighters morally unblemished. Most historical accounts, for example, of the assassination of Amílcar Cabral in 1973 take it as a given that it was the work of the Portuguese secret police, a last desperate attempt to forestall the inevitable military defeat facing the colonial army in Portuguese Guinea. *Os Bastidores* neither denies nor supports this notion. What it does is to place Cabral's charismatic leadership within a local context, in which there were rivalries within the nationalist movement itself, opportunists on the fringes, petty jealousies and surprising examples of megalomania, which even include Cabral's "host" the Conakry Guinean dictator, Sekou Touré, for whom the presence of such a prestigious liberation leader not only threatened to reduce him to playing second fiddle but potentially shattered his own regional ambitions for a "Greater Guinea."

Although the research begins in 1910, with the advent of the first Portuguese Republic and ends in 1981, particular emphasis is placed upon the first five years of Cape Verde's independence from Portugal (1975-80) because, in the words of the author, it was during this time that the structures that still characterize Cape Verde today were put in place, and because, after nearly twenty years of independence, it was easier for his interviewees to look back on the events of those five crucial years dispassionately. It was during that period that the newly independent republics of Cape Verde and Guinea-Bissau lived an unlikely betrothal under the banner of one political party that aspired to the eventual union of the two countries. Much attention has been placed on the 1980 coup in Bissau that brought this union to an end. Traditionally, it has been assumed that "Nino" Vieira's "movement of readjustment"—the ousting of the regime of the first president, Luís Cabral - was due to the latent hostility of the Guineans against the Cape Verdean leadership of the PAIGC. Lopes's investigation presents, once again, a much more complex view of events. Irrespective of those Cape Verdeans (especially in the windward group) who desired some sort of continued association with Portugal, there was a certain amount of friction between the young radicals who returned from Lisbon, influenced by revolutionary ideologies culled from books and proponents of the notion of "continuous revolution," and the PAIGC leadership in Cape Verde, which consisted largely of people who had participated in the guerrilla war on the mainland, and which adopted a cautious and pragmatic approach, in contrast again to the more militaristic sibling government of the PAIGC in Bissau. By the time of Vieira's coup, there is little doubt that, in spite of the crocodile tears shed over the separation by the Cape Verdean branch of the party, there was little love lost between Bissau and the more cosmopolitan, well schooled and relatively liberal Cape Verdeans in Praia. Once again, Lopes's panoply of protagonists reflect upon the intricacies of the events of those five years.

In spite of the author's intention to place particular emphasis on the period leading up to 1981, and the founding of the PAICV (Cape Verde's successor to the PAIGC), we must not forget that the book was only published in 1996, and that it was designed to recall the pioneering years of Cape Verdean independence at a time when democratic change and free elections had transformed the country from a one-party state into a parliamentary democracy. Moreover, although it cannot be doubted that the demise of the Soviet Union and analogous events of 1989 must have played some part in this political transformation, Lopes's study also demonstrates that the potential for democratic change was unleashed by the events of 1980, as evidenced by a growing movement of disenchantment among a younger generation of Cape Verdeans during the 1980s. Indeed, it could be argued that Vieira's coup in Guinea-Bissau freed Cape Verde from its "socialist revolutionary" African status, returning it to its traditionally more pragmatic vocation. Perhaps the most lasting epitaph to that generation of post-independence leaders is its idealism. In the words of one politician of the period commenting on the economic policies of one of his more quixotic colleagues, who dreamed of a cement works in the archipelago at a time when there was an international glut, and a shipyard at a time when shipbuilding was in crisis, "one needs to dream to get things done, but one needs to keep one's feet on the ground too." On balance, history will show that Cape Verdeans managed to tread a fine line between these two Cervantine extremes.

David Brookshaw is Professor of Luso-Brazilian Studies at the University of Bristol, England. He is a specialist in colonial and postcolonial literary discourse and has written widely on Brazilian and Lusophone African literatures. He has also translated works by African writers into English, most notably the work of Mia Couto. His latest book is *Perceptions of China in Modern Portuguese Literature - Border Gates* (Edwin Mellen Press, 2002).

Arménio Vieira. *No Inferno*. Lisboa: Editorial Caminho, 2001.

Naomi James Sutcliffe de Moraes

What do you get when you cross Dante's *Inferno* with *Robinson Crusoe*? *Romeo and Juliet*! *No Inferno* also interweaves poetry, stage drama and prose throughout.

Arménio Vieira's second novel, recently published in Portugal by Editorial Caminho, is an homage to the Western Canon. The novel contains one reference after another to classics in English, French, Spanish, and Russian—sometimes with helpful footnotes when Arménio thought it was necessary. The main character has a photographic memory and seems weighted down by the presence of all these words in his head. The words of others inhibit him from exercising his own creativity.

The work begins with a writer being forced to write a novel. The next passage—the beginning of the novel, finds the main character, Leopold, locked inside a house and forced to write a novel to obtain his release. Additionally, he has no memory of his past or how he came to be there. Leopold's name then changes to Robinson "because it was time to change the character's name." He slowly comes to realize he is Cape Verdean through some shards of memory (shades of *A la recherche du temps perdu*), but they are presented more as facts than deep insights into the character's personality or culture.

The rest of the work is a series of dreams, short stories written by Robinson in his attempt to write himself out of captivity, chats with the Devil and ambiguous passages that could be any of the three.

We vertiginously fall deeper and deeper into the sub-texts, as Alice fell down the rabbit hole until, in the end, the structure disintegrates—leaving us wondering what the principal frame of reference really was. The book is self-referencing in that both Arménio and the writer character are trying to write a novel and the effect is not, shall we say, novelistic. Robinson, inside the writer's story, is also trying to write a novel and can only write short stories.

What is really exciting is that Arménio seems to have broken away from the undertow of the Claridade movement of the 1930s. The popular Claridade themes (drought, starvation, immigration, etc.), considered as defining Cape Verdean writers up to the current generation, are almost completely absent. Arménio takes Germano Almeida's innovation one step further, as the plot takes place outside of Cape Verde and references to traditional themes are symbolic if at all.

The Robinson Crusoe theme and the house/prison far from civilization are indicative of the isolation of the islands and how they become a prison for many during droughts. The omnipresent explicit and implicit references to foreign literature show the influence the many sailing vessels had on Cape Verdean culture. The predominance of these references compared to Portuguese or even Cape Verdean ones is telling. Cape Verdean literature has become a literature to be reckoned with on an international level.

Naomi James Sutcliffe de Moraes is a PhD student in Comparative Lusophone Literature at the University of São Paulo, Brazil. Her research interests are: contemporary Cape Verdean and Brazilian Literatures, with emphasis on Germano Almeida and Arménio Vieira. She has published articles on technical translation and the teaching of translation, and also translates fiction, plays and screenplays from Portuguese to English. E-mail: naomi@lps.usp.br

Clifford E. Landers. *Literary Translation: A Practical Guide*. Clevedon, UK: Multilingual Matters, 2001.

Inês da Silva Paulino

To translate, or not to translate? This is one of the difficult questions that would-be translators have to answer or have answered on their own. For (almost) everything else, there is Clifford E. Landers's first guide on translation, *Literary Translation: A Practical Guide.* Landers, a professor of Political Science at New Jersey City University and the English translator of at least thirteen novels by renowned Brazilian authors, such as Rubem Fonseca, Jorge Amado and Rachel Queiroz, shares his experience as a literary translator in this pragmatic guide. Clifford E. Landers's sourcebook surveys the field in only three but thorough sections: "The Fundamentals," "Techniques of Translation" and "The Working Translator."

In "The Fundamentals," Landers introduces the literary translation environment by guiding the reader from the beginning to the end of the translation process with suggestions ranging from the decision to do literary translation to publishing. Inherent throughout this process is his realistic but encouraging outlook that literary translation is hard work. Nevertheless, those who accept the challenge will reap the exhilaration of contributing to the fulfilling creative process that constitutes translation. Furthermore, one will also play a role in the transculturization of literary works that might not otherwise reach foreign audiences, as is the case with Landers's own translation of the short story, "Night Drive," by Ruben Fonseca, transcribed at the beginning of this first section.

Theory aside, for "it is the act of translating that makes you a translator," (13) in "Techniques of Translation," Landers, the "practitioner," (49) states his positions on the importance of tone, resistance and register in achieving fluency, a requisite for good literary translations. Other topics are the usage of vocabulary non-existent in the target language, the mistranslation of common words or the incorrect use of frequent words. He also discusses the handling of the difficult issues of pornography and profanity.

Furthermore, the author describes techniques for revision and proofreading, using color-coded text and paper, as well as for publishing. He also discusses the importance of the potential author/translator relationship. Clifford Landers's practical touches are indeed laudable.

From the old, to the new high-tech CD-ROM and on-line dictionaries, to an eclectic collection of other reference materials, in "The Working Translator," Landers surveys his bookcase(s) and shares his list of reference materials (five-and-a-half page bibliography). New and experienced translators will want to add them to their libraries. His discussion of the use of dictionaries is particularly insightful. He also shares ideas on making the most out of the working environment. Taxes and contracts, including copyright issues, are two technicalities that the author briefly, but thoroughly, also introduces. He especially dedicates several pages to tax deductible topics. He also gives consoling but professional advice on how to handle rejection, bad reviews and dishonored contracts. On a more aesthetic note, Landers's translation of the short story, "Blind Justice," by Moacyr Scliar, another renowned Brazilian author, again demonstrates his "love affair with words" (7) in the final pages of the section.

Landers's direct and, at times, humorous writing style makes reading this guide an enjoyable experience. The diagrams of a "literary translator's brain," (46) the 12 commandments of literary translation, a sample table for organizing submissions to publishers, a sample contract and a literary translation ethics quiz are included in the illustrations and appendix, which are very appropriate complements to the readable prose.

"Techniques" is especially a useful reference section for all literary translators. As such, translators of fiction, poetry, non-fiction, theater and children's literature, will find a plethora of suggestions for their fields. The author's explanations are usually so thorough that sporadic brief solutions do not quench the reader's thirst for lengthier explanations.

Translation students of any combination of languages will also find this book a great contribution to their field of study. Although passages in French, Spanish, German and even English are included, those from Brazilian Portuguese to English dominate the text. Thus, translators from Portuguese will especially find this guide very useful.

Furthermore, the combination of minimal theory and the abundance of pragmatic discussions found in this sourcebook enrich the translation studies *genre* in general. A brief search on the Internet shows the respect that *Literary Translation* has gained in academia. Translation studies programs, in both the United States and abroad, have added the guide as a pedagogical tool to both undergraduate and graduate reading lists.

Translation, especially literary translation, is very rewarding. However, it can be solitary and its multifaceted characteristic confusing. Not any more!

This well-rounded guide is the novice's consultation manual and the expert's translation insider. Clifford Landers's *Literary Translation: A Practical Guide* must be read and *re-read* as one progresses along the distinct steps recurrent in the art of translation.

Inês da Silva Paulino holds a bachelor's degree in Portuguese and Political Science from the University of Massachusetts Dartmouth. She has done technical translations and is currently working on her first literary translation. E-mail: Copoleite@aol.com

Review Essays/Recensões-ensaios

Lição de crônica: *Um certo olhar* de Fátima Bettencourt sobre o mundo caboverdiano

Simone Caputo Gomes

Sobre Fátima Bettencourt. *Um certo olhar.*
Praia: Instituto da Biblioteca Nacional-Direcção do Livro, 2001.

"A crônica, portanto, é uma *tenda* de cigano enquanto consciência da nossa transitoriedade; no entanto é *casa*—e bem sólida até—quando reunida em livro, onde se percebe com maior nitidez a busca de coerência no traçado da vida, a fim de torná-la mais gratificante e, somente assim, mais perene." Os ecos das palavras saudosas de Jorge de Sá, um dos mais assíduos estudiosos da crônica no Brasil, resumem a impressão que nos causa, de início, *Um certo olhar* de Fátima Bettencourt. Professora, jornalista, locutora, produtora, apresentadora de programas radiofônicos, contista (*Semear em pó.* Instituto Caboverdiano do Livro e do Disco, 1994), Fátima, natural de Santo Antão (1938), vem reunir sua colaboração regular na imprensa, de 1992 a 1997, na coletânea de crônicas que ora apresentamos.

Sabemos que o jornal e a revista conferem à cronista a missão de colocar a vida no exíguo espaço da narrativa curta; a crônica herda do periódico a precariedade e a efemeridade. Ao eternizar suas crônicas em livro, a autora seleciona textos, atribui-lhes uma seqüência cronológica e temática capaz de mostrar ao leitor um mosaico antes fragmentado nas páginas dos periódicos. A construção dos tipos (retratos) e a focalização dos acontecimentos compõem o painel de um tempo (Cronos) e de uma sociedade. Assim a "tenda" se torna "casa."

Reunindo em volume suas crônicas publicadas em alguns dos principais periódicos de Cabo Verde, como A *Semana*, *Novo Jornal de Cabo Verde*, *Horizonte* (jornais), *Artiletra* e *Cultura* (revistas), Fátima Bettencourt vai resgatar o valor sociológico da crônica na construção do painel da sociedade crioula dos anos noventa, dando relevo ao pitoresco, ao acidental, ao banal, ao aparentemente irrisório do seu quotidiano. Na simplicidade reside a beleza da sua crônica.

"Afinal o que me inspira é o nosso quotidiano de vivências simples e não os momentos de solene intimismo em que, sòzinha, olhando a folha em branco, lucubro que nada vale a pena" (crônica "Angústia").

No exercício da crônica—esta "conversa fiada" com o leitor, como dizia Vinícius de Moraes—o prosador do quotidiano busca fundo na sua imaginação um fato qualquer, de preferência colhido no noticiário matutino ou da véspera, em que possa com suas artimanhas injetar sangue novo. Na prosa do dia-a-dia, misto de jornalismo e Literatura, a busca do pitoresco permite ao cronista capturar o lado engraçado das coisas, fazendo do riso ou da ironia estratégias para examinar determinadas contradições da sociedade. O humor possibilita a recuperação da capacidade crítica, enquanto o leitor se diverte.

Um certo olhar de Fátima Bettencourt, desde o título, nos dá a medida de um painel que se estrutura a partir de um ângulo, agudo: a cronista não é "mulher de medos" ("Navegador solitário"). A partir de um olhar crítico, vai pintando retratos e cenas com palavras, desvendando a gênese de sua coluna no jornal A *Semana* (*Rostos e palavras*) e do seu próprio texto literário:

> o impulso que leva as coisas a se corporizarem em palavra escrita, quer se escrevam páginas imortais ou levíssimas crônicas. (...) E porque, afinal, são as palavras que se colocam, umas com as outras, as responsáveis por tudo, ela está no título genérico da coluna. É com elas que ganhamos o pão nosso de dia-sim-dia-não, com elas reclamamos porque não é de dia-sim-dia-sim, com elas vivemos, sofremos, lutamos, nos comunicamos, amamos, odiamos(...).
>
> Quanto aos *rostos*, eu sei que o leitor está à espera de uma boa justificação, uma história bem contada, nada, suponho, como aquilo que tenho para dizer.
>
> O rosto é tudo, são os seres humanos, os que conheço ou sei de ouvido ou imaginação, são os bons e os maus, os públicos e os anónimos, os transparentes e os ocultos, os da miséria e os da bonança, os da vingança e os do perdão, os da coragem e os do desânimo, os que vivem apenas nas lembranças e na saudade e os que, nebulosos, já caem no esquecimento. Quantos rostos guardamos numa vida em estranha e progressiva colecção? (...) colecções únicas, preciosas e, por vezes, muito perturbadoras" ("Angústia", Grifos da autora).

De fatos e feitos da vida emocionalmente despertados pela concentração pode também surgir a crônica, deflagrando num instante uma visão da essência, revestida do cômico ou da tragicidade. Para Rubem Braga, como aqui, a verdade da crônica é o instante: os pequenos momentos permitem entrever a condição humana. É fundamental que o cronista se defina num tempo e num espaço, compondo uma cronologia esclarecedora da sua relação com os seres e objetos.

Além disto, a crônica precisa atingir o máximo de matizes com o mínimo de elementos, em virtude de sua economia estrutural, pelo limite de espaço que ocupa no periódico.

O trabalho de Fátima Bettencourt neste *Um certo olhar* marca, a par da busca constante do resgate da tradição (já evidenciada no seu conto premiado, "Vovô," que dá início a *Semear em pó*), o tempo e o espaço social em que se insere. Observemos.

A coletânea de crônicas estrutura-se de forma circular, caminhando das "Origens" às raízes, em "Avô, tataravô e outros que não sei nomear"—a última crônica do livro citando a primeira. Nos dois textos a cronista reflete sobre questões de identidade e de assunção das raízes negras com humor cáustico, evidenciando aquele seu "olhar de um modo especial" para um quadro ou situação. Na crônica "Origens" reflete:

> Temos, via de regra, orgulho excessivo na nossa costela lusitana, francesa, italiana, inglesa e outras. As restantes costelas, todas vindas directamente do Continente Africano, ficam numa nebulosa indefinida, confinada a uma silêncio total, ninguém delas toma conhecimento, o acordo é tácito, não há denúncias, pesquisas muito menos, e dos avós negros nem novas nem notícias. (...) Bem que podíamos assumir as duas raízes: a negra e a europeia. Mas não, ninguém procura, ninguém quer saber.

E acrescenta, na crônica "Avô, tataravô e outros que não sei nomear":

> Sempre admirei um escritor afro-americano que teve a coragem de partir em busca das suas raízes negras e onde todos esperavam um enorme insucesso, para espanto de todos, foi o contrário. O livro, intitulado RAÍZES, que descreve a homérica tarefa, imortalizou o autor e se transformou em estandarte dos negros de todo o mundo.(...) Nestas nossas ilhas achadas desertas e durante muitos anos interposto do comércio escravo, nas mãos de traficantes, negreiros e bandoleiros, proliferou uma mestiçagem desenfreada, mas registo que é bom, muito pouco. Se nem dos avós brancos damos conta certa, que será dos negros?

A crônica "Do Mindelo com amor" retrata as suas vivências crioulas, os sentimentos que a cidade, a ilha e sua gente despertaram na escritora, com a coloquialidade de uma conversa amável:

> Mindelo vai a pouco e pouco tornando-se um estado de espírito. Baixa uma paz sobre mim quando piso este chão e ando pelas ruas, parando metro a metro, para um abraço, uma conversa amável, às vezes um alô apenas. É a *minha cidade* que

me abre os braços e o coração *e me sinto no colo mesmo da minha mãe,* acalentada e confortada, em perfeita comunhão com todos e comigo mesma.
Filha adoptiva, é como se tivesse dado coices nas suas entranhas, tenho uma dívida impagável para com *esta cidade, esta ilha, estes montes pelados, esta gente indómita.* Eu sei que ela está paradona, estagnada, morta, mas as suas tardes continuam cálidas, as suas noites plenas de magia, e aquele toque de *morabeza* permanece intacto nas suas gentes que, às vezes, se levantam sem saber se verão o sol baixar no *Monte Cara* antes de pôrem uma panela de-riba-de-lume. *O cati-cati de cada dia,* sempre difícil, mas não a ponto de perderem o riso bom, *o requebro do andar, a piada inesperada, o dito picante, a graça infinita.* (...)
Bela amante adormecida(...) Quem semeará teus bairros de lares-oficinas, escolas-empresas e abrigará *teus velhos, teus loucos, teus meninos sózinhos, teus artistas, tuas prostitutas ainda com a boneca escondida no travesseiro*?" (Grifos nossos).

A cidade e os velhos, guardiães da cultura, resistem à globalização, a um tempo que insiste em desfigurar suas faces:

Uma zona histórica com seus sobrados, varandas de ferro, casinhas de meia-porta onde *velhas de cachimbo se sentam para contar estórias aos netos* impacientes na hora da televisão que os acaba levando, deixando a velha sozinha a derramar o seu olhar mortiço sobre as agressões que sofre a sua morada.(...) A cidade cresceu, vive apressada, não repara em nada, passa voando(...). ("A Cidade")

Mas o trágico da cena, pela advertência crítica que dirige o olhar para a importância da manutenção da cultura, ainda permite esperança e a utopia:

não vou mais encolher-me para não roçar a mão estendida do mendigo; não vou evitar o boteco da esquina onde corpos gentis de adolescentes se leiloam; não vou enjoar-me com o cheiro de 'erva' que inunda um recanto mal iluminado; não vou ver as ruas ficando desertas, as pessoas com medo de passear na Marginal nas noites quentes, os velhos parados olhando o mar, os jovens à toa, de braços caídos, a desesperança e o tédio cercando a ilha. Aí sim, vai ser bom pisar teu chão. ("Do Mindelo com amor")

Os quadros pintados por Fátima Bettencourt, por "Atalhos, veredas, caminhos de cabra" (título de outra crônica), nos possibilitam, como disse José Saramago [*Caboverdiando,* crônica, *Jornal de Letras* 731 (14 de Outubro de 1998): 28-29], "ver a terra e conhecer as pessoas, tremer de comoção real. Cabo Verde fabrica o seu próprio chão, inventa a sua própria água, repete dia a dia a criação do mundo./Porém, se uma simples pessoa não cabe numa crónica, como caberiam um povo e um país?"

Assim a *tenda* se tornou *casa*. E a casa caboverdiana ganhou mundo.

A lição de crônica que Fátima Bettencourt nos dá neste volume, o seu amor ao examinar o quotidiano caboverdiano e o "toque crioulo" certamente não cabem em nosso pequeno texto. Vão muito além, ao encontro do leitor, no espaço mágico da comunicação.

Simone Caputo Gomes é Professora Adjunta reformada na Universidade Fluminense no Brasil. É doutorada em Língua e Literatura Portuguesa. Publicou *Uma recuperação de raiz: Cabo Verde na obra de Daniel Filipe*; *Letras em Tese*; *África e Brasil: letras em laços*, e foi co-autora de um livro de poesia, *Como se fosse música*. E-mail: simonecg@ar.microlink.com.br ou simone@seleto.com

Light and Obscurity in *Tropical Truth*

Dário Borim Jr.

on Caetano Veloso.

Tropical Truth: A Story of Music and Revolution in Brazil.

Translated by Isabel de Sena. Edited by Barbara Einzig.

New York: Alfred A. Knopf, 2002.

One of the greatest champions of the cultural movement known as *tropicália* or *tropicalismo*, Caetano Veloso has been, since the mid-1960s, an artist whose thoughts and creations have influenced dozens of styles of music and various other forms of art, such as poetry, acting, and film-making. His compositions and performances bear such a mighty sense of uniqueness and sophistication that his profile as a musician or an intellectual affords no single definition (even that of *tropicalista*). If music has always been a dexterous mediator through different sectors of society, as anthropologist Hermano Vianna, in *The Mystery of Samba*, has cunningly pointed out, Veloso does this job more effectively than any other singer-songwriter in Brazil or, perhaps, much of the world, ever. Originally released in Portuguese in 1997 as *Verdade tropical* (with no subtitle) by São Paulo's acclaimed Companhia das Letras, and recently published in English (October 2002) by internationally famous Alfred A. Knoff, *Tropical Truth: A Story of Music and Revolution in Brazil* shows us, above all, how Veloso, an artist from outside the dominating centers of international mass culture, perceives and reacts to the baffling intricacies of art, philosophy, politics, and social behavior, through creative work and polemical commentaries.

A long piece of English prose with an insider's insight into the complex and multifaceted cultural movement called *tropicalismo* was overdue in the United States and Canada, despite the excellent academic research volumes launched by Christopher Dunn, Randal Johnson and Charles Perrone in the last two years (*Brutality Garden, Studies in Latin American Popular Culture,* and *Brazilian Popular Music and Globalization*). Other musicians, intellectuals and non-mainstream music lovers in this country have regarded Veloso as hipster or high-art icon since David Byrne's 1989 release of an anthological CD called *Beleza Tropical.* The Tropicalists in general (including Gilberto Gil, Tom Zé and Os Mutantes) have been construed by the well-informed in contemporary music as the late 1960s precursors of the most visible trend in world music in the late 1990s: the creative blending of music styles from all eras and all corners of the Globe. Critic Jon Pareles, for instance, contends that finally North-Americans are receptive to this trend, whereas "Brazilians were twenty years ahead of their time, from the United States perspective. They were mixing and matching things. They were taking from outside and drawing from their roots."

The New York Times critic adds that people growing up now are plugged into the Internet "and *tropicália* was like the original Internet. You can go surfing on *tropicália* and you can hear rock, you can hear reggae, you can hear all the Brazilian kinds of music." Pareles then concludes: "It makes sense now because our attention is so chopped off and fragmented, and far-reaching at the same time. *Tropicália* was ahead of all this." Other critics corroborate Pareles' view. The Tropicalists' "collagist approach to history, region, genre and nationality—not to mention their thoroughly contemporary idea of being at once local and global—have become as commonplace today as the nearest laptop," writes Paul de Barros, a jazz critic for *The Seattle Times.*

While *Alegria, alegria,* Veloso's first book (a collection of short prose pieces and poetry published 25 years ago), remains basically unknown anywhere on the face of the Earth, his second volume has been reviewed throughout Brazil and the United States with varied opinions: from flying colors to a considerable degree of negative criticism and controversy. After all, this is not any novelty, since polemics and provocations are nothing from which the Bahian writer shies away in his country or abroad. They have been recurrent phenomena ever since he took his first steps on Rio de Janeiro stages, in 1967.

Reactions to *Verdade tropical* in Brazil can be divided into three basic categories, according to Liv Sovik, from Universidade Federal da Bahia: those that accept Veloso's importance and write laudatory reviews; those that admit *tropicalismo* as watershed but criticise its results and the book itself; and "a small number that use the occasion to reflect on themes of Brazilian culture" (4). The first group, adds Sovik, includes assessments that regard *Verdade tropical* as a reference book "to join the fan literature that reproduces quotations from interviews and articles by him" (4). The second one focuses on the present and "attempt to reveal the reasons for the consensus and aura of power that surround Caetano" (4). The third group ponders over *Verdade tropical*'s arguments in favor of Brazil's important role in the map of the world's cultures. Such reviewers insert Veloso's critical legacy into that rich tradition of identity discourses developed by Gilberto Freyre, Sérgio Buarque de Holanda, and Oswald de Andrade (5-6).

Since October, 2002, *Tropical Truth* has received excellent appraisals in the United States, but almost all of them have something to say about its readability problems. It is a formidable book, "even a vexing one at times," contends Gerald Marzorati, the editorial director of *The Times Magazine*. To him, this weakness has less to do with the translation than with the editing. Readers "only casually familiar with Brazilian music," adds Marzorati, "will find the narrative by turns too thin on context or too thick with it." Perhaps some of the harshest criticism of *Tropical Truth* comes from Bondo Wyszpolski, from the *Easy Reader*, a weekly newspaper based in the South Bay of southern California, and *Brazzil*, a Los Angeles-based printed and web-based magazine that often provides a wide international audience with serious, well-written pieces on Brazilian music. *Tropical Truth* is not a terribly compelling book, writes Wyszpolski: "The passion we find in the music here seems lacking, nor is there anything approaching the lilt and the rhythm of his greatest compositions." Wyszpolski's reaction is, in part, one of the two forms of unmatched expectations that Veloso himself feared. According to the singer-songwriter, people who liked music would find too much of a complicated book in *Tropical Truth*; and people who liked books would get discouraged by the excessive space reserved to pop music in it (8-9).

Several critics, including Marzorati, assume that most problems with *Tropical Truth* result from the translator's and/or editor's flaws. For the reader who is also capable of reading the English and Portuguese versions of the text, the critics' assumption becomes partially unsustainable, especially if they are attributing translation issues to Isabel de Sena alone, and, likewise, editing deficiencies to nobody but Barbara Einzig. Any translator is faced with two major choices: to create the new text as objective and clear as possible, according to the reader's point-of-view, or make the writing run as faithfully as possible to the author's original aesthetic vision. Translation jobs may also mix both attempts at various ratios of preference. As far as the translation and editing processes of *Tropical Truth* are concerned, there seems to be a somewhat unbalanced mix of both choices, but to ascribe faults and merits to specific names would probably be an impossible task, since the translated text must have been touched by very many hands (including those of the author himself, who is well versed in English). To make the matter even more complex, the original text itself is a "translation" of sorts. The book, commissioned by New York editors in 1991 (after Veloso published an article on Carmen Miranda, in *The New York Times*), is clearly written for an international audience. Furthermore, the Portuguese text is not devoid of obvious editing flaws. (By the way, how many would have dared to openly confront self-assured Veloso on this issue?)

One is tempted to wonder, therefore, how much input into the English translation and editing might have come from the author himself. On the one hand, it is fair to say that a great number of sentences remain just as long, obscure and labyrinthine as they are in Portuguese. On the other hand, the official translator and editor may be the ones responsible for splitting and, to some extent, improving the clarity and cohesion of sentences and chapters (or whatever we may want call the individually titled segments of the book). One of the longest sentences in *Verdade tropical* appears in its first chapter, "Elvis e Marilyn." In the Portuguese version, the sentence speaks of samba and bossa nova for nothing less than 36 lines without a period (35-36). In the English-translated version, the chapter itself is split into three, and the content of that extra-long sentence spreads out into eight shorter ones at the onset of a new chapter entitled "Bossa Nova" (22). While many translated paragraphs remain as long as their Portuguese counterparts, almost all chapters in *Tropical Truth* display white spaces that are not present in *Verdade tropical.* There are also other marks of positive editorial changes. The division of the original text into four uneven parts (with 3, 15, 1, and 7 chapters each) has been eradicated. The differences between the two versions also include the two sections of black-and-white photographs and a glossary of Portuguese /Brazilian terms; all this is added to the English edition.

It is curious to note that a hint of Veloso's hand in the process of editing actually emerges in the note of "Agradecimento," in the Portuguese version, and in "Acknowledgments," its English correlative. At first the author thanks Cristiana Lavigne, who read his "increasingly intractable fragments" and would, then, "point out connections, make editorial suggestions, and in so doing she rekindled the hope" that he could write a book (*Tropical Truth* ix). The next word of gratitude goes to well-known editor and writer Rubem Fonseca, who read the manuscript in its "organized form, made encouraging remarks [...] and suggested (in fact imposed) three cuts, short and precise like the sentences that have made him famous" (ix). Veloso then confesses that two of the instructions were immediately followed to the letter; "the other—after much hesitation—only in part" (ix). Maybe the English version's early cuts have something to do with the part of Fonseca's suggestions that was previously declined. At any rate, in both versions of his introduction Veloso is candid about his own style, or his "tendency toward digression and ellipsis that confounds my thinking, my conversations, and my writing" (*Tropical Truth* 8).

In sum, the ongoing controversy over *Tropical Truth* is much less focused on content than form, and one may argue that the book's shortcomings are mainly two. First, it displays rather long and confusing sentences, especially on its first 93 pages. Second, there are too many fragments of cultural information that either need further explanation or overexpose the reader to too many contexts and unknown names.

The positive reception of Veloso's book in the United States, in turn, reiterates the notion that there is much intellectual wit, cultural knowledge, and historical significance to it. What *Tropical Truth* misses in terms of orderly chronology, says Will Hermes of *The Village Voice*, "it makes up for in charm and smarts. Even when he veers into an academic thicket, you're happy to follow, like the moments in a great bar conversation that let you fondle your drink stirrer or admire the speaker's mouth." The Bahian, explains Mike Quinn, "weaves a captivating tale of artistic evolution alongside an important moral: The arts are just as political and inflammatory as any 'serious' social issue, and an artist with conviction and depth has to be enormously strong to stay true to his or her ideals" (Tropical).

For Gerald Marzorati, if one approaches it as one might "an adventurous Caetano album—that is, as an unconventional work combining autobiography, cultural criticism, deep musical wisdom and original, sweet riffs—the book is rather extraordinary." In terms of autobiography, for instance, "Narcissus on Vacation" (the chapter on Veloso's prison experience) stands out. Swift and precise language conveys the power of honest self-criticism, a well-balanced tone of suspense, and the opportunity for unabashed intimacy with the author's plight without a drop of sentimentality.

As it happens to most memoirs penned by poets, musicians and other artists, *Tropical Truth* sheds light on the contexts and motivations behind the creation of many of Veloso's works. This is the case of classic tunes like "Irene" and "Terra". The former, a concrete musical poem of ironic joy, was written within the confines of a dark and dirty cell in Rio de Janeiro (250-251). The latter, a marvelous piece of cubist contours, was composed several years later, but in direct connection with the memories of such appalling jail circumstances. One day Dedé, Veloso's first wife, brought him the weekly magazine *Manchete* with photos of the Earth taken from outer space:

> These were the first in which the entire globe was visible, and there was a strong emotion provoked by the confirmation of what we had until then known only through deduction and abstract representation. I considered the irony of my situation: a prisoner in a tiny cell, I looked in admiration at images of the whole planet, seen from the wide open of space. (249-250)

With regards to musical and cultural criticism at large, the list of topics brilliantly discussed is enormous. African diaspora, concrete poetry, cultural cannibalism, existentialism, globalization, music styles in/of Brazil and abroad, national identity, pragmatic philosophy, sebastianism, and vanguard cinema are but a few of them. One of the major contributions, though, is the priceless insight into the features and meanings of *tropicalismo* from the chapter entitled "Anthropophagy." Just like his lyrics and recorded interviews, Veloso's prose highlights a peculiar way of looking at every aspect of living or every detail of cultural behavior and representation. Combining logic and symbolism through a partially Nietzschean and a partially carnivalesque mode of operation, he will disclose a plurality of ironic or otherwise provocative images of the same issue, even if such an approach may cause him to sound cryptic or contradictory. He contends, for example, that in *tropicalismo*

> there is a tendency to make Brazil exotic as much for the tourists as for Brazilians. No doubt even I myself reject what seem to me ridiculous attempts to neutralize the strangeness of this Catholic tropical monster, in the hunt for the crumbs of ordinary international respectability. Of course I recognize that a headdress of bananas is not particularly useful when used by a nuclear physicist or a classicist born in Brazil. But "Brazil" can liberate the creative energies that will enable the proliferation of research (or the invention of new disciplines) only if Brazil refuses to feel intimidated by itself, and if it places its narcissistic pleasure above sensible submission to the international order. (159)

The late arrival of *Tropical Truth* in English (five years past its release in Brazil) must be celebrated, even if the writing of such a lengthy and complex piece had to be done from scratch (suggesting the phenomenal scope of

Veloso's memory), on the road and, quite often, through the small hours at a hotel room, after exhausting stage performances. It was perhaps a price that Veloso had to pay, then (and the readers, now, in the unedited course of his prose), so that more of his music could be written and performed at the same time he wrote the book of his life. After all, it was worth it, as many of us would agree with Mike Quinn: "Brazil's Caetano Veloso is one of the world's most accomplished and conscious pop artists. Anywhere. Period" (Omaggio).

Whether in a tropicalist language of evasive imagery or in a supposed pursuit of global truth about his art and his era, Veloso's occasionally chaotic and anarchist prose defies all purist labels and all Cartesian sensibilities. While ranging from personal memoir to cultural history, media analysis, philosophical inquiry, literary theory, or popular music and cinema criticism, *Tropical Truth*'s assets undoubtedly compensate for its apparent lack of contextual congruity and syntactic clarity. Caetano Veloso's newest release in English is indeed not music, but food for thought and social awareness; it is not an analytical thesis, but a priceless tool for understanding music and culture. Love it *and* do not leave it just because of some obscurity in your path through *Tropical Truth*. Even in its shadowy passages one may find scattered bits or hidden pots of precious enlightenment.

Works Cited

Dunn, Christopher. *Brutality Garden: Tropicália and the Emergence of a Brazilian Counterculture.* Chapel Hill, NC/London: University of North Carlina Press, 2001.

Hermes, Will. "Brazilian Waxes." *The Village Voice* Sept 25-Oct 1, 2002. http://www.villagevoice.com, 29 September, 2002.

Johnson, Randal, ed. *Studies in Latin American Popular Culture* 19 (2000).

Marzorati, Gerald. "Tropical Truth: A Story of Music and Revolution in Brazil." http://www.NYTimes.com, 29 November 2002.

Pareles, Jon. Interview w. Nelson Motta. *Manhattan Connection.* TBN-NY/GLOBOSAT, 1999.

Perrone, Charles, and Christopher Dunn, eds. *Brazilian Popular Music & Globalization.* Gainesville, FL: University of Florida Press, 2001.

Quinn, Mike. "Omaggio a Tropicalista." *The Austin Chronicle Sheet Music* 22, 7 (18 October, 2002).http://www.austinchronicle.com/issues/dispatch/2002-10-18/music_feature4.html, 2 December, 2002.

_____. "Tropical Truth: A Story of Music and Revolution in Brazil." *The Austin Chronicle Sheet Music* 22, 7 (18 October, 2002). http://www.austinchronicle.com/issues/dispatch/2002-10-18/music_feature5.html, 2 December, 2002.

Sovik, Liv. "Tropical Truth: A Reading of Contemporary Debate on Tropicália." http://136.142.158.105/LASA98/SOVIK.PDF, 15 December, 2002.

Veloso, Caetano. *Alegria, alegria.* Ed. Waly Salomão. Rio de Janeiro: Pedra Q Ronca, 1977.

_____. *Tropical Truth: A Story of Music and Revolution in Brazil.* Trans. Isabel de Sena. Ed.

Barbara Einzig. New York: Alfred A. Knopf, 2002.

_____. *Verdade tropical.* São Paulo: Companhia das Letras, 1997.

Vianna, Hermano. *The Mystery of Samba: Popular Music and National Identity in Brazil.* Ed. and trans. John Charles Chasteen. Chapel Hill, NC/London: University of North Carolina Press, 1999.

Wyszpolski, Bondo. "Brave Unknown World." *Brazzil* December 2002: 5.

Dário Borim Jr. is professor, translator, creative writer, and FM radio programmer. He instructs in Portuguese, Luso-Brazilian literature, cinema, and music at UMass Dartmouth. *Paisagens humanas* (Ed. Papiro), a collection of his *crônicas* and short stories, came out in December 2002. *Perplexidades: Raça, sexo e outras questões sociopolíticas no discurso cultural brasileiro* (EdUFF) is due in 2003. Borim's writings have also appeared in various journals, including *Brasil/Brazil*, *Luso-Brazilian Review*, and *Hispania;* as well as in thematic anthologies, such as *Poéticas da diversidade* (Ed. UFMG), *Bodies and Biases: Issues of Sexualities in Hispanic Cultures* (Univ. of Minn. Press), and *Latin American Writers on Gay and Lesbian Themes* (Greenwood Press). He hosts a weekly radio show dedicated to Lusophone music on www.wsmu.org. E-mail: dborim@umassd.edu

Other Articles/Outros Artigos

Figura Naturae: Religion, Nature, and the Self in Miguel Torga's *Diário*

Hannes Schneider

Abstract. In Torga's *Diário*, the discourse of theology sometimes curiously intersects with the record of apparently personal experience. This is particularly evident in the references to nature. Operating as a hermeneutic device, these instances of discourse interference provide a model of reading that seems to question, or even to suspend, the supposed referentiality of the genre. The provocation of the *Diário*, moreover, lies not only in the notorious reinvestment of Christian beliefs, which turn into an idiosyncratic worship of nature, but in the implied configuring of the diaristic "I" by means of a perversion of christological and exegetical patterns. This unprecedented and rather outré self-fashioning of a 20th century author's persona, however, is ingeniously camouflaged with the pervasive topoi of identity crisis inherent in the genre and, therefore, has often passed unnoticed so far.

Tomado à letra, é nauseabundo!
Mas será que poderá tomar-se à letra?[1]

I.

If Torga's *Diário* has primarily been considered to refer rather unequivocally to actual events, ranging from the most intimate feelings to the events of greatest significance in 20th century history, the rhetorical craft and figurative features of the diaristic discourse have not been investigated thus far.[2] The question, then, that I would like to raise in this paper is not what specific *tranche de vie* Torga refers to, but rather: how is this reference configured, and what is thereby involved beyond simple referentiality?[3]

In fact, rather than presenting life in the raw,[4] some entries, though somehow apparently grounded in factual experience, are deliberately structured around theological notions, or even superimposed upon by biblical plots and deeply informed by hermeneutical patterns of meaning. Thus removed, to a certain extent, from their embeddedness in "real life," or their immediate referentiality, these passages, although of minor occurrence to be sure, nevertheless yield a semantic surplus that allows the *Diário* to develop all the more fully.

Focusing on the entries referring to nature, especially those with regard to the sea, I propose a close reading of a crucial passage where the sheer record of facts and the discourse of biblical hermeneutics clearly intersect. Beyond simple referentiality, here the diaristic "I" tries to make sense of nature as well as of its relationship to it, and, last but not least, of its own self. Before attempting to explore further this interplay of religion, nature, and the self, however, it would seem beneficial to examine in brief the general pattern of the references to nature in the *Diário*.

II.

Far from being faithful depictions of the Portuguese countryside—and a lot of critics, indeed, have been satisfied to read them as if their only truth lay in objective mimesis—these descriptive inserts, despite their apparent referentiality and regardless of the differences between them, objectify Torga's regressive desire for an emotional and even physical identification with nature. Given the number and variety of thematizations of nature in the *Diário* (such as panoramic views, contemplation of individual objects, or descriptions serving as a background for apparently major themes), the following is a rather condensed overview, seeking primarily to lay stress upon some basic traits these passages have in common.

Torga's "empathizing" with nature develops, roughly speaking, in three stages: in the first stage, the natural sphere—as, for instance, a snow-covered slope, a precipice, or a quivering leaf—is linked with the viewer's emotional state, so that he finally identifies himself metaphorically with nature[5] to such an extent, in fact, that the "I," feeling a kind of "centrifugação do espírito" ([3]VIII: 41), completely loses his identity and passively becomes a mere surface, or a transparent screen, onto which the phenomenal world is projected:

> Deixo-me levar passivamente pelas rodas do carro, que percorre a serra em todas as direcções. Dou aos olhos plena liberdade sensorial, sem lhes pedir conta da qua-

> lidade das sensações recebidas. Abandono-me à volúpia dum encontro meramente físico com a realidade. Fragas, matas, rios e ribeiros, tudo entra em mim como a luz pelas vidraças. Entra e cabe. Não há imagens no mundo que saciem a pura transparência. ([1]X: 34)

The immediately following sentence, "Nada entendo, e nada quero entender," enacts the second stage of Torga's identification with nature by disclosing its utterly irrational or regressive impulse. The "empathizing" with nature obviously aims at losing the intellectual, emotional, and sensory faculties of the individual: "Não ler, nem escrever, nem pensar, nem amar, nem sofrer, nem sentir sequer. Estar assim deitado como estou em cima duma fraga, estúpido como ela e amorfo como ela" ([3]VII: 178-9). By physically imitating and imaginatively projecting himself into an object of nature (e.g. a rock), Torga seems to extinguish gradually the awareness of embodiment and individuality in order to regress to the natural sphere.[6] This is particularly evident in a poem emblematically entitled "Mimetismo," where the "I" empathizes with a "trunk" "lost" in a "dense forest," relapsing thereby into an "inert," "mute" and "anonymous," or "vegetable," form of existence:

> Sou mais um caule na floresta densa.
> Um tronco de preguiça vertical.
> Inerte, muda e anónima presença,
> Perdido no silêncio vegetal. ([3]VII: 31)

The third stage of identification, then, is precisely this state of fulfillment—called, e.g., "paz" ([1]X: 34), "Nirvana" ([3]VII: 25), or "plenitude" ([4]II: 72)—in which individuality becomes totally extinct by being wholly absorbed into nature. Paradoxically, losing one's identity and (self-)awareness by "empathizing" with nature involves, according to Torga, an acute form of (self-)consciousness: "Atingir na identificação inconsciente com a natureza a única consciência profunda que dela e de si pode ter" ([1]X: 34). The boundary between this kind of "profound consciousness" and the dullness of death, however, is blurred.[7]

III.

Thus far, I have traced the basic pattern of identification with and regression to the phenomenal world recurrently unfolded in Torga's descriptions of natural settings. Let us now turn to the theological-hermeneutical development of this pattern. In this regard, the entries referring to journeys to the Portuguese seacoast provide compelling examples pointing simultaneously to a different, revised understanding of Torga's often discussed notion of "telurismo."[8]

Perhaps even more than the inland scenes that have been adduced so far, the sea is, in Torga's understanding, an ideal *point de départ* for an "empathic" identification with nature, since its water corresponds materially, or isotonically, and by the way of its tidal "pulsating", to man's biochemical composition and physiological organization respectively: "Talvez por estar ainda dentro de nós, salgado, a pulsar nas artérias, com vagas e marés" ([2]XII: 156). Again, this "empathic" stance here is linked with an utterly regressive move, for the sea-water is referred to as "líquido amniótico" and hence metaphorically identified with the fetal fluid: The immersing into the sea is thus to relapse into an intrauterine existence; by plunging into the water, the bather becomes an embryo in the womb.[9] Just as the emotional identification experienced *vis-à-vis* the inland scenery of the Gerês Mountains culminated in a phylogenically remote state of mind ("E sinto paz. [...] Paz que o homem primitivo certamente já experimentou" [[3]VII: 178-9]), so the sea, here, ontogenically, "[...] proporciona ao homem o regresso à sua primitiva decência" ([2]XII: 156). As significant as his emphasis on identification and regression is Torga's use of such terms as "litúrgico," "limpo," "purificação," and "baptizado," describing the transformational power that affects him in plainly religious terms, most of which we tend to associate unanimously with baptism.[10]

IV.

The link between Torga's experience on the seashore and notions of religion, especially baptism, can be seen even more clearly in an entry from the first volume of the *Diário* written in Nazaré on July 2, 1940. Here Torga explicitly draws on the body simile of Saint Paul's first letter to the Corinthians, thereby inviting the reader to make a most promising structural comparison of his text with its biblical source:

> Chegou a hora do banho. Entrei no seio do formigueiro de gente que fervilhava dentro de água, *humanidade até pouco hostil e individual, e agora milagrosamente fraterna e solidária.* [...] *Como se uma benção os tivesse irmanado, eram todos um corpo só diante da mesma onda.* E eu pus-me a pensar na força gregária que tem o mar. Na força gregária que provoca, afinal, qualquer poder adverso. ([7]I: 157; my italics)

As mentioned above, this bathing scene is clearly set against the background of baptism: The crowd of "hostile individuals" bathing in the sea and thereby "miraculously" becoming "one body" ("um corpo") unmistakably recall the equally heterogeneous and even conflicting Corinthian community that, too, was joined "into one body" ("in unum corpus," I Cor. 12:13) precisely through baptism.

The principle governing the transition from Saint Paul's letter to Torga's diary entry is, predictably, that of secularization, or, in rhetorical terms, literalization: "baptizare" is perceived etymologically as "to immerse" or "to bathe"; the water associated figuratively with the Holy Spirit "we have been all made to drink" ("et omnes unum Spiritum potati sumus," I Cor 12:13) is changed into the real water of the sea; the spiritual "Body" in the Pauline allegory, i.e. the *Corpus Christi mysticum*, is replaced by the worldly conception of "humanity," which, however, is not joined "in the one, i.e. Holy Spirit," ("in uno Spiritu,"), but instead by "fraternity" and "solidarity." On the other hand, the only gesture that is explicitly reminiscent of the underlying sacramental subtext, namely "benção," is significantly shifted to the level of comparison and hence neutralized: "*Como se* uma benção os tivesse irmanado [...]" (my italics). In contrast to the covenant founded in communion, wherein the flesh and blood of Christ are consumed together, Torga here seems to form a kind of "New Covenant," likewise founded in communion, or "comunhão"—as Torga repeatedly calls the contact with nature[11]—, i.e., in the common sensual experience of the same natural phenomenon: "diante da mesma onda."

This all, I think, is exceedingly obvious. I would draw, however, the attention to the shift from the figurative, but yet "potable," water associated with the Holy Spirit in I Cor. 12:13 to the definitely undrinkable and literal sea-water in Torga's account. The source of this particular detail, I will argue, is the phrase "baptizati sunt [...] in mari" ("they were baptized in the sea," I Cor. 10:2) used by Saint Paul earlier in the same letter referring to the Old Testament event of the Israelite's crossing of the Red Sea under the leadership of Moses.

It may be objected that Torga (and let us suppose he was telling the truth) actually was on the beach that day, the sea being thus, to be sure, a more suitable theme presenting itself. Nevertheless, I believe that the fact that the sweet and spiritual water of I Cor. 12:13 is replaced by the literal and salty sea-water cannot be dismissed so easily as merely mimetic, for this would mean to undercut the rhetorical or figurative feature of this thoroughly intertextual passage, however "realistic" or even downright "autobiographic" it might appear. Therefore, it may not be purely coincidental that in a passage apparently referring as a whole to the baptismal narrative of I Cor. 12:13 is found an element pointing to the narrative of the Israelite's crossing of the Red Sea; much less, if we take into account the fact that precisely this narrative, namely Exod. 14, is generally considered the "type" of baptism, that is to say that the Israelite's crossing of the Red Sea, seen from the viewpoint of biblical hermeneutics, precedes and foreshadows Christ's baptism in the River Jordan which in turn supersedes and surpasses the Old Testament event. This has already and for the first time been suggested by Saint Paul by saying twice that the Israelite's experience happened to them "typologically" or, as the Vulgate puts it, "in figura" (I Cor. 10:6 and 11, for the Greek "typoi," or "typikos"). The question, however, remains, why should Torga mingle two biblical passages from the Old and the New Testaments, respectively, traditionally juxtaposed by typological exegesis, and, what is more, why should he superimpose these passages of the Sacred Scripture upon his own quite profane bathing experience?

The basis for conjoining these two biblical passages as well as for blending them with Torga's own experience, appears, I believe, to be hermeneutic, rather than mimetic. In fact, there can be no doubt that some kind of typological relationship is intended.[12] In order to do so, Torga, on the one hand, aligns himself with the biblical history that progresses hierarchically towards redemption according to the promise/fulfillment model provided by typological exegesis, while, on the other hand, extending this hermeneutical pattern beyond the narrow relationship between the Old and the New Testaments to which it was originally confined. In other words, Torga establishes a kind of three-stage typological relationship connecting (1) the Israelite's crossing of the Red Sea, (2) Christ's baptism in the River Jordan, or baptism "in the one Spirit," and (3) his own bathing experience in the Atlantic Ocean on July 2, 1940. But instead of merely repeating and imitating what has—seen from a typological viewpoint—already been fulfilled in Christ, Torga, on the contrary, deliberately thwarts the slightest idea of an *imitatio Christi*: first, by crudely literalizing the baptismal narrative of I Cor. 12:13; second, by turning the sweet water into sea-water. A minor incident, to be sure, apparently grounded in objective mimesis, but one that carefully coincides with baptism's Old Testament type, the Israelite's "baptism in the sea." Torga thus seems to put the literal or Old Testament element, i.e. the salty water of the Red Sea, above the spiritual or New Testament element, i.e. the sweet and potable water of the River Jordan, thereby operating a reversal of the clear-cut typological hierarchy established by Saint Paul. And, third, the power that reactualizes the biblical event(s) in the present time is no more the Holy Spirit, as in the conception of typological exegesis; the "hermeneutical bridge" connecting the three events is none other than the sensual contact with water, or nature *tout court.*

In summary, the incident on the beach at Nazaré—whose very place name, quite apart from its reference to the Portuguese seaside town, is clearly a kind of Christological pun[13]—is, for all of its apparent banality or supposed mimetic referentiality, a careful dramatization of baptism, blatantly reducing it to its literal level. Moreover, the bathing—or shall I say baptismal?—scene is not only a thoroughly literal reenactment of baptism, but it is also the site of an utterly unorthodox, revisionist reading of Saint Paul's *Ad Corinthios I* and its implied hermeneutical model. It seems tempting, now, to conclude that Torga here, in the fullest typological sense of the word, aims at superseding and surpassing, i.e. "fulfilling," the New Testament baptism by tracing it back, paradoxically, to its Old Testament type: the "baptism in the sea." It remains difficult, however, to decide on the basis of the *Diário* alone whether this audacious reversing of a prominent Christian theme is a mere mocking mimicry, i.e. a negativizing process,[14] or whether it is a tremendously aggressive appropriation that subverts and collapses *Heilsgeschichte* in order to establish a new religion that, in contrast to Christianity (while deeply informed by it), "não nega nem degrada a natureza" ([3]III: 77), thereby bearing witness to a "divinidade fundamentada na verdade feiticeira das coisas."[15]

V.

Before concluding this brief note, I would like to revert to the regressive identification with natural phenomena in order to show how Torga links his relationship to nature with theological-hermeneutical patterns. Indeed, the "empathizing" with nature embodies the belief that man and nature have some necessary organic relationship; the underlying logic of this emotional and physical identification is an allegory, which, typologically speaking, aims at establishing a "perfect harmony," thereby revealing Torga to be a "figure" of nature: "[...] uma sintonia total com a natureza natural de que me sempre senti figuração humana" ([1]XVI: 10). Just as the sea-water, for instance, is made up of water and minerals and is constantly moved by the regular rise and fall of the tide, the human body, representing nature on a small scale, is equally composed primarily of water and minerals and is constantly pulsating with the rhythmic circulation of the blood (cf. [2]XII: 156, quoted above; cf. also [7]I: 159, quoted in note 9). Conversely, the beating heart is extended to the macrocosmic scale and used as a metaphor for the tidal sea repeatedly referred to as "coração do mundo" (see, e.g., [7]I: 143, 155, 159, and [1]X: 98). Likewise, Torga undergoes a kind of "petrificação emotiva" ([1]XI: 137), for example, when he intentionally becomes obtuse like the rock he is lying on ("estúpido como ela [i.e. *a fraga*]," [[3]VII: 179]); he even becomes similar to it in shape: "e amorfo como ela."[16]

Thus, Torga's emotional and physical identification with nature which makes him both lose the awareness of embodiment and individuality while, paradoxically, effecting or bearing out his true identity as *figura Naturae*, is point by point drawn not only on Christian notions implying a kind of change (namely of identity, or of man's relationship to God), such as baptism, communion, or transfiguration, but also on the theological-hermeneutical pattern of typology or allegory. It is surely in this deliberate misreading of religious patterns that the key to Torga's concept of nature and the individual's relationship to it lies. In addition, the intersecting of religious patterns and personal experiences forming Torga's diaristic discourse offers an opportunity, though not in this paper, to elicit further Torga's method of configuring and presenting the self and, hence, to take a new approach to the *Diário.*

Notes

I would like to thank: Isabel Inácio, who, from the very beginning, commented on various drafts and versions of this paper; and Barbara Vinken, who generously brought about an unexpected turn at the end. I am also grateful to Anne B. Mesch and Helen Wiesen for their help in tuning up my English, though I am, of course, fully responsible for all remaining errors and inaccuracies.

[1] Freire (1990: 68), with reference to *Diário* [3]VI: 23 ("Na mesquita de Córdova"). All references to the *Diário* are to the edition in XVI volumes published by the author (Coimbra: [1-7]1941-93); the superscript number indicates the respective print or edition used.

[2] For a survey on critical studies directed to the *Diário*, see the relevant papers published in *Aqui, neste lugar e nesta hora* (1994) as well as in Fagundes, ed. (1997). See also Rocha (1990; 1992: 225-34) and, more recently, Monteiro (2000). For earlier criticism, see the judicious remarks by Mourão-Ferreira (1978: 7-9).

[3] Cf. Lepecki (1988) who seems to suggest a compatible approach to that taken here.

[4] See, for instance, [3]VII: 10 and [2]IX: 101, where Torga pretends to absolute sincerity and authenticity, while other statements clearly undermine this claim (see, e.g., [7]I: 28 and 76, [3]III:

172, [3]V: 85, [2]XII: 107). On this question, see especially Monteiro (1994). For the problem raised by the publishing as well as the revising, i.e. rewriting, of the *Diário* in subsequent editions, see the remarks by Rocha (1977: 105, note 1), Reis (1997: 319, note 7), and Sapega (1997: 415).

[5] See [4]II: 72: "Falar duma encosta coberta de neve sem ter a alma branca também, retratar uma folha sem tremer como ela, olhar um abismo sem fundura nos olhos, é para mim o mesmo que gostar sem língua, ou cantar sem voz. Vivo a natureza integrado nela. De tal modo que chego a sentir-me, em certas ocasiões, pedra, orvalho, flor ou nevoeiro."

[6] Cf. also the poem "Repouso" in [2]IX: 82: "Paz das alturas, evasão furtiva / Da inquietação rasteira. [...] *Um pequeno descanso refratário / De ser homem./* Pousei o meu carrego" (my italics).

[7] The integration of oneself into nature, psychically as well as physically, leads to a higher form of life (see, e.g., [2]IX: 156-7), but it is also equated to death ([3]IV: 45; [3]VI: 61). Such is the case especially in the entries referring to the sea, which is presented as "cemitério ideal," "grande túmulo" ([3]V: 16), or as "Sepultura sonora" ([3]V: 21) wherein the "I" is passively "floating," but also as "líquida ternura," which "transfigures" the "I" into a "floating" "imagem perfeita da vida" ([2]XII: 132; cf. ibid. 158).

[8] "Telurismo," i.e., Torga's closeness to the earth or, more exactly, his worship of the Mother Earth, is touched upon almost everywhere in the *estudos torguianos.* Most obsessively, Lopes (1975: 47; 1978: 55-61; 1984: 138, 142-3; 1993: 7 and *passim*; 1997: 373) has argued that, for Torga, *terra* is strictly opposed to *mar*, but I do not see how this conclusion can result from what is said in the texts; nor does Stegagno Picchio (see her critical remarks in 1994: 418). Cf. also Clemente (1997: 108-16) quoting Torga: "Os que falam do meu telurismo, nem de longe imaginam o fascínio que sinto pelas ondas. Nasci, de facto, em terra firme. Mas sou anfíbio [...]" ([1]XV: 52). Indeed, Torga's "telurismo" embraces both the land and the sea: "Quando pela primeira vez na meninice o vi [viz. *o mar*] em Leça, se não preteri o Marão nativo, ancorei-o em água salgada. E fiquei com duas referências cósmicas na vida. [...] O meu telurismo é oceânico" ([1]XIV: 200-1; cf. also "Visita," [7]I: 143). Hence, Torga puts *Mãe-Terra* (cf. [4]II: 73) and the "Deus líquido e azul" ([4]II: 182), i.e. the sea, side by side; the difference between them, however, is slight: "Transita-se bem da montanha para o mar. Não há quebras na respiração. Enche-se a alma da mesma amplitude e da mesma pureza. Todas as coisas grandes são, na verdade, irmãs" ([3]VIII: 153). Finally, *terra, mar*, and mankind are linked together in a "santíssima trindade, quase tão poderosa como a da doutrina" ([4]II: 180).

[9] Cf. Lopes (1997: 373), who conjectures that for Torga "a terra, essa, é o útero onde a vida nasce" (cf. 375). This argument, however, seems to depend on Mircea Eliade's concept of *regressus ad uterum*, namely into that of *Terre Mère* (developed in his *Aspects du mythe* and quoted by Lopes 1993: 27), rather than on a thorough examination of Torga's texts. In contrast to Lopes, one can argue with Torga that "embora a terra seja ainda capaz de manter a vida, a parte do mundo onde ela nasce, e onde a ciência terá de ir procurá-la, se quiser surpreendê-la no seu primeiro alento, é nele [i.e. *no mar*]. Que o mar é em última análise o coração do mundo. Que pulsa, que geme, só por ser como o nosso: fonte e consciência biológica de tudo" ([7]I: 158-9).

[10] This change of identity is also called "transfiguração" (see, for instance, [3]VIII: 86, [2]IX: 157, [2]XII: 132, 152 and 158).

[11] See, for instance, [7]I: 24, [2]XII: 134, [1]XVI: 10, or [2]IX: 156-7: "E sempre que, à custa de esforço e porfia, consigo, como há pouco na serra, unir, digamos, *o meu corpo e o meu sangue ao corpo e ao sangue da natureza*, a perfeita *comunhão* que se realiza e a estranha metamorfose que daí resulta exigem o nome sagrado de transfiguração" (my italics).

[12] David-Peyre (1976: 306) points to a similar "fusion étonnante de l'Ancien et du Nouveau Testament" in Torga's *O outro livro de Job*. Likewise, Martinho (1997: 40) remarks that in *Abismo*, too, "se combinam o Velho e o Novo Testamento." Neither David-Peyre, nor Martinho, however, raise any explanation of this phenomenon. Whether the underlying logic in these texts is also typology is a question that is beyond the scope of the present study. Cf. in addition the

conto "Jesus" in Torga's *Bichos*: Here Torga establishes a typological relationship between Joseph of Egypt (explicitly referred to by the narrator), Jesus (the New Testament figure of Joseph alluded to by the *conto*'s title, which is presumed to be also the name of the protagonist, i.e. a boy who, like Joseph, takes care of sheep), and Torga's self (by drawing on a crucial episode of his "autobiographic romance," *A criação do mundo*, in which the father urges the son to leave home in order to go either to Brazil or to the seminary). The literal level of the *conto*, i.e. Jesus's discovery of a nest and the naïve relation of this event to his parents, is thus harshly opposed to its allegorical level, i.e., the implicit threat of Jesus being "sold" or expelled from his family and home, or his "nest," in Nazaré. The analysis of this *conto* would be the subject of another article.

13 Cf. also the pun on Nazaré/Nazareth in "Jesus" (see note 12).

14 Such is the general tenor of the Catholic critiques. See the reviews of the *Diário* in the Jesuitical journal *Brotéria*: Maia (1949; 1956; 1960; 1965; 1977; 1984), Garcia (1970), and da Silva (1973). Also see the studies of the Franciscan Augusto ([2]1997: 18-31, 79-129) as well as of the Jesuit Freire (1990: 52-71, 105-20, and 171-2). Cf. also the diatribes against the Catholic criticism in [3]III: 160-3, [3]VII: 12-3, and [3]VIII: 137-8. The image of Torga in the Catholic criticism (and vice versa) has not been investigated so far.

15 On the reversing and subverting of Christian themes, see also Lopes (1984: 141-2; 1993: 36, 88-92).

16 Cf. also [1]X: 65. An additional meaning of this emotional and even physical "petrification" can be derived, if we consider the fact that Torga's "religion" is written and engraved in stones, viz. in a "catecismo pagão nas fragas" ([1]XI: 176). This echoes clearly II Cor. 3:7, "ministratio [...] deformata in lapidibus," while significantly leaving out the crucial word "mortis" (ibid.). Torga's petrification, then, appears to be a reification of the Israelites "blinding" when reading the Old Testament (cf. II Cor. 3:14: "sed obtusi sunt sensus eorum [...] in lectione veteris testamenti"). It is interesting now to note that the Latin phrase "obtusi sunt" ("they blinded, became dull or blunt") corresponds to the Greek "eporothe," which means precisely "they hardened, or petrified." Thus, Torga's "telurismo" and the pertinent stone imagery seem to be deeply informed by the "petrifying" law covenant that leads to death (as opposed to the grace covenant of the New Testament, which gives life), rather than by the rocks of his "transmontane" native place.

Works Cited

Aqui, neste lugar e nesta hora. Actas do Primeiro Congresso Internacional sobre Miguel Torga. Porto: Universidade Fernando Pessoa, 1994.

Augusto, Armindo. *Miguel Torga: O drama de existir.* 2nd ed. [1960]. Chaves: Tartaruga, 1997.

Clemente, Alice R. "Natureza e poesia em Miguel Torga." Fagundes 101-117.

David-Peyre, Yvonne. "Miguel Torga et l'Ancien Testament à travers *O outro livro de Job.*" *Arquivos do Centro Cultural Português* 10 (1976): 301-336.

Fagundes, Francisco Cota, ed. *"Sou um homem de granito:" Miguel Torga e seu compromisso.* Selecção das comunicações apresentadas no Colóquio Internacional sobre Miguel Torga, realizado na Universidade de Massachusetts, em Amherst, em Outubro de 1992. Lisboa: Salamandra, 1997.

Freire, António. *Lendo Miguel Torga.* Porto: Edições Salesianas, 1990.

Garcia, Mário. "Review of *Diário* X." *Brotéria* 90 (1970): 100-104.

Lepecki, Maria Lúcia. "Miguel Torga: *Diário XIII*: O homem, o tempo, a terra." *Sobreimpressões: Estudos de literatura portuguesa e africana.* Lisboa: Caminho, 1988. 137-144.

Lopes, Teresa Rita. "Além, aqui e aquém em Miguel Torga: Análise de *Vicente.*" *Colóquio Letras* 25 (1975): 34-49.

———. "Ao princípio era a terra: A (des?)propósito do teatro de Torga." *Colóquio Letras* 43 (1978): 51-61.

———. "L'office pour 'un Dieu de Terre'." *Le roman portugais contemporain.* Actes du Colloque Paris, 24-27 Octobre 1979. Paris: Fondation Calouste Gulbenkian/Centre Culturel Portugais, 1984. 131-152.

———.*Miguel Torga: Ofícios a "um deus de terra."* Rio Tinto: Asa, 1993.

———. "Torga e a portugalidade." Fagundes 369-382.

Maia, João. "Na rasa lei do chão [Review of *Diário* IV]." *Brotéria* 49 (1949): 141-144.

———. "Um diário íntimo [Review of *Diário* VII]." *Brotéria* 63 (1956): 586-589.

———. "Review of *Diário* VIII." *Brotéria* 70 (1960): 459-462.

———. "Review of *Diário* IX." *Brotéria* 80 (1965): 85-87.

———. "Review of *Diário* XII." *Brotéria* 105 (1977): 393-396.

———. "Review of *Diário* XIII." *Brotéria* 118 (1984): 340-342.

Martinho, Fernando J. B. "Miguel Torga e a Bíblia: O caso de *O outro livro de Job.*" Fagundes 37-50.

Monteiro, Maria da Assunção F. Morais. "Unidade e alteridade no *Diário* torguiano." *Aqui, neste lugar e nesta hora* 343-352.

———."Le journal de Miguel Torga: Un reflet du monde en fin-de-siècle." *Genres as Repositories of Cultural Memory.* Vol. 5 of the Proceedings of the 15th Congress of the International Comparative Literature Association "Literature as Cultural Memory," Leiden, 16-22 August 1997. Hendrik van Gorp, Ulla Musarra-Schroeder, eds. Amsterdam, Atlanta, GA: Rodopi, 2000. 367-382.

Mourão-Ferreira, David. "Poética e poesia no *Diário* de Miguel Torga." *Colóquio Letras* 43 (1978): 7-19.

Reis, Carlos. "Discurso diarístico e discurso histórico: Os três primeiros volumes da criação do *Diário.*" Fagundes 307-319.

Rocha, Clara Crabbé. *O espaço autobiográfico em Miguel Torga.* Coimbra: Almedina, 1977.

———. "O *Diário* de Miguel Torga." *Nova Renascença* 10 (1990): 29-34.

———. *Máscaras de Narciso: Estudos sobre a literatura autobiográfica em Portugal.* Coimbra: Almedina, 1992.

Sapega, Ellen W. "O 25 de Abril nos *Diários* de Miguel Torga: Reflexões sobre o sujeito na história." Fagundes 413-423.

Silva, Ribeiro da. "Review of *Diário* XI." *Brotéria* 97 (1973): 334-339.

Stegagno Picchio, Luciana. "Entre Douro e Mondego: A metáfora fluvial em Miguel Torga." *Aqui, neste lugar e nesta hora* 413-420.

Torga, Miguel. *Diário* I-XVI. Coimbra: Published by the author. 1-7 1941-1993.

Hannes Schneider is a doctoral candidate and research assistant in the Department of Romance Philology at the University of Hamburg (Germany), where he currently teaches Old French literature. He holds an MA degree in Romance Philology and German Studies from the University of Heidelberg (Germany), and received a one-year scholarship to study at Lyon III (France). Presently, he is preparing a dissertation on the Old French *Narcisus*, on which he has recently published an article in the journal *Archiv für das Studium der neueren Sprachen und Literaturen 238* (2001).

Revising the Record in Lusophone Historical Drama

Bonnie S. Wasserman

Abstract. This article analyzes Lusophone historical drama written during the 1960s-1970s in Brazil and Portugal. After commenting on the contributions of Bertolt Brecht, Enrique Buenaventura and Antonin Artaud to the Lusophone stage, I demonstrate how playwrights such as Augusto Boal, Gianfrancesco Guarnieri, Bernardo Santareno, and Alfredo Dias Gomes adapted dramatic techniques to rewriting oppressive periods of history such as the Inquisition and slavery. I conclude that for the Lusophone playwrights, the events of the past were analogous to contemporary repression under the Salazar regime and the Brazilian military dictatorship.

Historical drama is a sub-genre of theatre that dates back millennia. The earliest plays with historical themes were written by Greek and Roman dramatists, including Aeschylus, Phrynichus, and Seneca. Over the centuries innumerable playwrights have tried their hand at the craft of recreating historical situations and personalities for the stage. Among the most notable are Shakespeare and Ben Johnson of Elizabethan England and Lope de Vega and Calderón of Golden Age Spain. Yet, no matter what time period or national theater involved, it can be said that there is usually a direct correlation between the history selected and the period in which the drama was written. As Herbert Lindenberger writes in *Historical Drama: The Relation of Literature and Reality*, "The continuity between past and present is a central assertion in history plays of all times and styles" (6). Though the historical drama may treat a period of time long passed, there is some link with the current day. Audiences watching the drama are usually able to identify the similarities between the past and present through the portrayal of familiar situations and characters. Oftentimes, though not always as in the case of Shakespeare's Roman plays, playwrights draw from events that have occurred in their own countries. Episodes in national histories that have a connection to the current era thus tend to be the most commonly used material for historical dramas because the audience is more familiar with its own history than with that of other nations.

Many playwrights employ historical themes in their work as a way in which to comment on the socio-economic and political systems of their day. Rather than staging their political views outright and attracting the attention of censors, the composers of historical dramas use a more subtle and oftentimes cryptic approach of presenting analogous situations to make their point. This, however, does not always work, as witnessed by the numerous cases of censorship and even harsher forms of punishment for criticizing the establishment.

In the adaptation of history for the stage playwrights also imbue their own perspectives of the past. Any interpreter of history, whether he or she is a historian or playwright, infuses a personal viewpoint regardless of the rigor of his or her research methodology. In his work on the writing of history Hayden White affirms that ideology influences the recording of history, just as in any other narrative. He postulates that ideology cannot be removed from the interpretation of history, for "every representation of the past has specifiable ideological implications" (*Tropics of Discourse* 69). Furthermore, for White, facts or events do not in and of themselves make the story but rather how they are put together. It is the historian who "makes his story by including some events and excluding others, by stressing some and subordinating others" (*Metahistory* 6). Playwrights composing historical drama revise the historical record by emphasizing certain aspects and offering perspectives that are sometimes different from the official version of history. In *Theatre of Crisis: Drama and Politics in Latin America*, Diana Taylor explores how playwrights such as Enrique Buenaventura of Colombia questions the authorized rendition of the past by including a variety of events, outlooks, and versions that are usually not considered. By doing so he attempts to "inscribe and make audible the voices that have traditionally been kept out of Colombian History, voices of the victims, the victimizers, the participants or collaborators who make up the infernal world of his plays" (186).

In the case of two Lusophone countries a number of historical dramas were written in the 1960s and 1970s. It was during this time that a military regime seized power in Brazil, and Portugal was under the decades-old control of the Salazar government. Opposition groups in both countries were severely repressed and the arts were harshly censored. Of the various art forms, the ruling powers were most concerned with theater. Because theater necessarily brings together groups of people, it was feared that the masses could easily be stirred towards revolt. Furthermore, there was the possibility that performers would improvise onstage and read lines not already approved by the censors in advance. After the 1964 *coup d'état* and following the implementation of Institutional Act Number Five (AI-5) of 1968, which increased the censorship of artistic activity, it became very difficult to write and produce Brazilian theater. Both text and performance were subject to censorship—the text could be prohibited either officially or unofficially by being *engavetado* ("put in the drawer"), and performances were subject to cancellation at the last minute (Damasceno 116). An example of the latter is the case of *Calabar: O elogio da traição*, by Chico Buarque and Ruy Guerra. Days before the opening night, the censorship bureau cancelled the production indefinitely, leading to the loss of money and time of those involved in its creation.

In order to address these conditions and offer a critique of their governments, Lusophone playwrights looked to the past for similar periods of oppression and found them in the examples of slavery and the Inquisition. Portugal was very much involved in the slave trade from the time it first arrived in Sub-Saharan Africa and over the course of four centuries, transported millions of slaves to work in Brazil and the Caribbean. The second institution, the Inquisition, was created by the Roman Catholic Church to root out those who had lapsed in their Catholic faith or who belonged to other confessions. Though it had its origin in Rome, the Inquisition is particularly associated with Spain and Portugal, where it existed officially in the latter country until the nineteenth century. During the Inquisition, tens of thousands of people in Portugal and its colonies were brought before tribunals to defend themselves against charges of heretical acts such as spreading Judaism and witchcraft. Many were punished with sentences that ranged in severity from imprisonment to execution at the stake. Because of their brutality and overall significance in the history of Portugal and Brazil, these two events were used as metaphors for political repression in the modern era.

In their dramatization of slavery and the Inquisition, Lusophone playwrights drew from the work of others such as Bertolt Brecht, Enrique Buenaventura and Antonin Artaud. Of the three, Brecht had a tremendous impact. According to Lorena B. Ellis in her book *Brecht's Reception in Brazil* (1995), "Brecht's influence on Latin American theater not only brought a revolution in the aesthetic sense as it did in Europe, but also it caused sociopolitical awareness" (21). Portuguese-speaking playwrights identified themselves with Brecht's "Marxist-based analysis of social relations" (Counsell 80). The German playwright and theorist was committed to breaking down the existent bourgeois nature of theater, which did not reveal the underlying socioeconomic forces, and in transforming it to "show his audiences the true nature of society, thereby empowering them to change it" (Counsell 81). In order to do this he developed a new form of theater, which he labeled Epic theater. Epic theater was intended to elicit a critical rather than sympathetic response from the audience. John Willet explains that, "The essential point of [E]pic theater is perhaps that it appeals less to the feelings than to the spectator's reason" (23). Some of the various forms of Epic theater include the *Verfremdung*, or the alienation effect (A-effect), the use of film and music, and *Gestus*. The alienation affect sought to break the spectators' concentration on the "reality" onstage with distracting signs and labels, causing them to view the performance more objectively. Film projections were included in Brechtian theater to incorporate material that the playwright wanted the spectators to consider *while* viewing the stage performance. Indeed, according to Willet, Brecht viewed film as "a new, gigantic actor that helped to narrate events" (78). Music was also used in an entirely different fashion from earlier theater; instead of being added to merely entertain, the lyrics of songs brought up serious social and political issues. In *The Threepenny Opera* (1928), for example, the musical pieces "had the immediacy of a ballad, (and) were of a reflective and moralizing nature" (Willet 85). One of the most influencial Brechtian techniques was that of *Gestus*, an encoding gesture that embodied social relations. Brecht believed that the gestures that actors made, both subtle, as in facial expressions, and more obvious, as in arm movements, represented social interactions and class distinctions (Counsell 86). With *Gestus*, movements onstage took on an entirely different meaning for they revealed socioeconomic and political attitudes. How an actor stood and what he or she did with his or her body divulged information regarding social class. Overall, Brecht placed great emphasis on the didactic possibilities of theater. He was convinced that audiences needed to be taught and that theater was "a means of teaching and transforming his society" (Willet 75). He devised

Lehrstücke or "instruction pieces" for audiences to learn from, for his ultimate goal was that they change society.

Another European playwright who greatly influenced the Lusophone stage was Antonin Artaud. Artaud was a theatrical director who developed the "Theatre of Cruelty." As Bradby elucidates, the characteristics of this type of theater are "violence, sexuality, and the eruption of dramatic violence outside of the safe confines of the stage" (39). In *Theater and its Double*, a collection of essays published in 1938, Artaud postulates that

> [t]he image of a crime presented in the requisite theatrical conditions is something infinitely more terrible for the spirit than the same crime when actually committed. (85)

Because theater is not "real," the re-creation of violent scenes is disturbing in that they are performed specifically for a live audience. Each move and gesture is choreographed for the stage with a "visual language" of objects, gestures and movements (Artaud 90). In the historical dramas written in Brazil and Portugal during the 1960s and 1970s, there are many instances of violence—both physical and verbal. This reflected both the oppressive themes of history that were being represented onstage and convergently, the greater repression in society.

The third playwright and theorist who greatly influenced Lusophone historical drama was the already mentioned Enrique Buenaventura of Colombia. Born in 1925 Buenaventura founded the Teatro Escuela de Calí and wrote dozens of dramas. In many of his plays Buenaventura used a collage effect of unifying various pieces of information to offer a more inclusive perspective on history. Like Brecht, Buenaventura was committed to consciousness-raising and social change through the use of theater.

One of the first Brazilian theater groups that began experimenting with these forms of theater was the Teatro de Arena. Founded in São Paulo in 1953, the innovative theater in the round company was committed to encouraging popular participation in the theater and broadening its audiences to the lower and middle classes. Teatro de Arena first began staging works of foreign playwrights such as Tennessee Williams but later focused exclusively on original dramas by Brazilian playwrights such as Gianfrancesco Guarnieri. Augusto Boal explains that "This phase coincided with political nationalism, with the flourishing of industry in São Paulo, with the foundation of prizing everything that is national. At this time the Bossa Nova and the New Cinema were also born" (*Theatre of the Oppressed* 162). Guarnieri's *Eles não usam black-tie* (1958) was one of the first successful plays produced by the group. It examined class differences in Brazilian society and the struggle of *favela* or shantytown dwellers in Rio. By the early 1960s Teatro de Arena became more active in making theater a locus for "political expression and mobilization for political action" (Damasceno 66). Because of their political involvement, a number of Arena participants such as Oduvaldo Vianna Filho and Augusto Boal were imprisoned and tortured.

After the 1964 *coup d'état* that brought a military regime to power, Teatro de Arena began staging plays that would challenge the military regime and its concept of Brazil. These plays drew from stories of Brazil's past that would provide a corollary to the current repressive situation. History was re-written and retold with an emphasis on giving voice to the vanquished. Rather than privileging the conquerors, thereby reinforcing the state-sponsored version of history, Arena sought to portray in a new light those who had been defeated. The intention was to encourage those outside the power structure, such as the Brazilian Left and working class, to continue their struggle.

Arena conta Zumbi was the first of a series of plays by the Teatro de Arena that was both historical and revolutionary. In it, playwrights Augusto Boal and Gianfrancesco Guarnieri adapted the story of Palmares from a book called *Ganga Zumba* (1962) by João Felício dos Santos (Campos 71). Palmares was the maroon community that existed in the hinterland of Pernambuco; During the seventeenth century runaway slaves under the leadership of Zambi formed the agricultural-based community. Palmares was so successful that it numbered nearly 20,000 inhabitants and had extensive trading networks with neighboring non-slave villages. Fearing widespread slave revolt and departure as well as a powerful autonomous nation, the governor of Pernambuco demanded its destruction. In the end it took nearly five decades and thousands of men to defeat Palmares. Since its demise, Palmares remains in the national consciousness as a symbol of resistance to domination.

Arena tells its version of Palmares in a two-act musical, which features a "cantador" or narrator that is played by different actors. According to Boal in *Theatre of the Oppressed*, "All the actors were grouped into a single category of narrators; the spectacle ceased to be realized from the point of view of each character and came to be narrated by a team" (170). In Act I, slaves are treated brutally and encourage each other to run away to Palmares. There, under the leadership of Zambi, they work hard to become a productive agricultural community. The Palmarinos, or inhabitants of Palmares, sell their products to neighboring white villages. The peaceful relations between the two communities do not last, as the former landowners begin to complain about their loss of goods (i.e. the slaves) and encourage the once friendly neighboring whites to cut off relations with the former slaves. Before long the governor orders Palmares destroyed and in Act II, after a series of unsuccessful assaults, the whites ultimately annihilate Palmares. Before its destruction, though, Ganga Zumba, the grandson of Zambi, is born and becomes leader of Palmares. Zambi responds to the impending end of Palmares in a statement reminiscent of Bertolt Brecht's poem, "To Those Born Later" (ca. 1930).

In *Arena conta Zumbi* the playwrights creatively rewrite history, using myth and other less-than-exact documentation. The opening lines of the drama explain how the play was constructed.

> Estudamos documentos
> coisa escrita, assinada,
> mas deixamos o coração
> fazer a peça animada. [...]
> Há lenda e há mais lenda
> Há verdade e há mentira,
> de tudo pegamos um pouco
> mas de forma que servira. (12)

In this segment the playwrights describe how they researched written documents but let their hearts write down the story. They question the truthfulness of recorded history and challenge the information given by those in authority. Instead of privileging those who destroyed Palmares, the playwrights provide a different perspective—that of the former slaves. In this way *Arena conta Zumbi* sends the message that those outside the power structure, such as the Brazilian Left and the working class, should be heard.

Throughout *Arena conta Zumbi* there is a strong critique of capitalism in twentieth-century Brazil. This is made in several ways. First, slavery in the historical drama is depicted as inhumane and brutal. In Act I slaves are bought and sold at markets just like other salable goods. There is a market scene in which a merchant tries to sell his chattel:

> MERCADOR. Olha o negro recém-chegado. Magote novo,
> macho e fêmea em perfeito estado de conservação.

> Só vendo moço e com forças. Pra serviço de menos empenho tem os mais fracos e combalidos, pela metade do cobrado. Quinze mil réis o são, sete mil e quinhentos os tropiados. Escravo angolano purinho. Olha o escravo recém-chegado, magote novo, macho e fêmea. (19-20)

Like livestock, the slaves are described in terms of their physical prowess and the work they can perform. They are seen not as human beings but rather as commercial items that can be used and abused.

As property the slave is treated cruelly. In *Arena conta Zumbi* there are several episodes in which the heartless treatment of slaves is graphically described. In one scene actors recite a list of the types of instruments used to punish slaves while in Brechtian fashion a screen above them shows slides of the torture instruments. This depiction of torture is effective in making the audience visualize the multiple ways in which the slave was coerced into working. By portraying how the slaves were sold like livestock and mistreated with instruments of torture, the playwrights are also making a commentary about the contemporary period. Working conditions in the factories and farms of 1960s Brazil were poor and the worker had little recourse of appeal due to the tight restrictions on unions and other organizations. The business elite held the working class in "economic bondage" regarding them as replaceable and forcing them to work long hours for little pay.

In *Arena conta Zumbi*, the playwrights provide a solution for their politically and economically torn nation in the form of a utopia. The definition of a utopia is "a place, state, or condition ideally perfect in respect of politics, laws, customs and conditions" ("Utopia" 485). Since a utopia necessarily implies an "ideally perfect" place, it cannot exist in reality. Yet the hope for a better situation or future is one that the playwrights wish to impart upon the audience. The dramatized Palmares is featured as a workers' utopia—a classless society where freed slaves relish their freedom and work hard. This is a vision for a Brazil of the future in which—after the equal distribution of wealth and land—people could live side by side in freedom and peace. Palmares is thus featured as productive because the former slaves are happy to work for themselves instead of a slaveowner. This contentment with their new socio-economic status is reinforced with music and song.

> Trabalha, trabalha irmão.
> Trabalha, trabalha, de coração.
> Palmares tá grande, Palmares cresceu,
> com a força do braço do negro
> que sabe o que é seu. (40)

The lyrics of this song reinforce the cry for equal distribution of land and wealth in Brazil. Before the 1964 coup, attempts were made on the part of the left-wing political parties to address the issue of land reform. Once the military came to power, all inroads were brushed aside and most of the land in Brazil—especially in the Northeast—continued to remain in the hands of a few powerful families.

Like all utopias, however, Palmares cannot last and in the end the Donos das Sesmarias or white landowners and others team up to destroy it. Nevertheless, the hope brought about by its very existence and lasting power—well over a century—is an example for those who struggle against oppression in the present day. When Zambi hands the kingdom of Palmares over to his grandson Ganga Zumba at the end of Act II, he recites lines that are a loose translation of Bertolt Brecht's poem, "To Those Born Later:

> Eu vivi nas cidades no tempo das desordem. Eu vivi no meio da minha gente no tempo da revolta. [...] Assim passei os tempo que me deram pra viver. A voz da minha gente se levantou e minha voz junto com a dela. Minha voz não pode muito mas gritá eu bem gritei. Tenho certeza que os dono dessas terra e sesmaria ficaria mais contente se não ouvisse a minha voz [...]. (75-76)

In this statement Zambi describes how he lived in a time of turmoil and raised his voice along with that of his people. He knows that his actions did not please the rich landowners and the former slaveowners but that did not stop him. Regardless of the outcome, it is worthwhile and necessary to stand up to oppression. The inclusion of this poem in *Arena conta Zumbi* reflects how important the German writer's influence was both on the play and the Brazilian Arena theater group in general. It also expresses how the playwrights viewed themselves—as part of the opposition movement that rebelled against the status quo.

The end of the play illustrates that fighting oppression is not in vain. According to Robert Anderson: "Significantly, Zumbi is not killed in the final battle of the play. His final self-sacrifice is implied in the hopeless battle at the end. Zumbi never dies, just like the legend that he spawned" (21). Zumbi transcends Death and is raised to divine status. His *apotheosis* and legacy continued as a lesson and inspiration for subsequent generations of slaves until abolition in 1888. For Brazil, the political repression at the hands of the military would last until 1985, when democracy was restored. In the case of economic oppression, though, the disparity between rich and poor continues to grow.

Whereas *Arena conta Zumbi* focuses its critique on the socio-economic system of Brazil through its portrayal of slavery, the historical dramas about the Inquisition attract attention to other aspects of life under dictatorship such as the limitations placed upon freedom of expression and the imprisonment and torture of those in the opposition. In *O Santo Inquérito* and *O Judeu*, playwrights Dias Gomes and Bernardo Santareno draw an analogy between the political dissident of modern day Lusophone countries and the Jew or *cristão novo* or New Christian. Over the centuries Jews were viewed as the "Other" within society and discriminated against because they held a different belief system. The playwrights associated this oppression with that of the political dissident who was considered a menace to society, imprisoned, and "disappeared" for his or her political convictions. The playwrights were also personally familiar with repression in their respective countries. Bernardo Santareno was jailed by the PIDE, the Portuguese secret police on more than one occasion. Alfredo Dias Gomes (b. 1922), knew many people who were imprisoned by the military regime and spent some time in exile for his own safety.

The two dramas about the Inquisition vary greatly in content and style. *O Santo Inquérito* focuses on the life of Branca Dias and some of her family members. As Dias Gomes affirms in the preface entitled "O que sabemos e o que pensamos das personagens": "Parece fora de qualquer dúvida que Branca Dias, realmente, existiu e foi vítima da Inquisição"(16). That is not entirely the case. There are scholars such as Anita Novinsky, an expert on the Inquisition in Brazil, who question the existence of Branca Dias.[1] Whether she actually lived or not is not an issue for the play because of the fact that her story is famous. This demonstrates the importance of an incident or personality in a historical drama being well-known. Indeed, Lindenberger extrapolates that "What matters to a modern audience [...] is not the historical accuracy of the fable, but the fact that, whether historical or mythical, the matter is 'publicly known'" (2). Since the story of Branca Dias is recognized throughout Brazil, especially in the Northeast, the audience can relate to her as a historical figure.

Dias Gomes dramatizes Branca's life in a two-act play set in 1750 in the state of Paraíba, Brazil. The characters include Branca's father (Simão Dias), her fiancé Augusto Coutinho, Padre Bernardo, and various members of the Inquisition. Act I begins with the Inquisitional trial of Branca Dias in which Padre Bernardo describes Branca's heretic crimes to the Visitador and the Notário. Next, there is a flashback scene to the first meeting of Branca and Padre Bernardo when the young woman saved the Padre from drowning. It is then that Padre Bernardo becomes fascinated with Branca's opinions about God and religion, leading him to conclude that Branca needs his help to rid her of heretic beliefs and practices. Soon, Branca's entire family comes under suspicion and her father Simão is interrogated about the family's New Christian ancestry. Act II begins with Branca in prison, wondering what is happening to her. She is repeatedly interrogated by the Visitador and Padre Bernardo. Her fiancé Augusto is also imprisoned and tortured in an attempt to make him testify against Branca. He dies during a torture session and Branca accuses her father of not trying to save him. At the end of the drama Branca refuses to renounce her beliefs and is sentenced to death. The final scene depicts Branca's execution in an *auto-da-fé*.

There is no doubt regarding the existence of the main character of *O Judeu*—Antônio José da Silva. Da Silva, or "The Jew" as he was known, was born in 1705 in Rio de Janeiro and brought to Portugal at an early age when his mother was summoned before the Inquisition under charges of practicing Judaism. He studied Law at the Universidade de Coimbra before moving to Lisbon to become a playwright. The playwright's life ended tragically in 1739 when he was executed by the Inquisition. Even after his death, da Silva's plays were presented in Portuguese theaters. Among his more famous plays are *Vida do Grande D. Quixote de La Mancha e do Gordo Sancho Pança* (1733), *Anfitrião ou Júpiter e Alcema* (1736), and *Guerras do Alecrim e da Manjerona* (1737). In these and other satirical dramas Antônio José da Silva was known for his use of puppets and his critique of the excesses of the upper classes.

In his portrayal of Antônio José da Silva's life Bernardo Santareno weaves together in collage format numerous excerpts from various texts, including letters from figures of the time, Inquisitional testimony and selections from António José da Silva's plays. The drama is divided into three acts and the action takes place in a number of locations including Lisbon and Coimbra, where António José da Silva is a law student. Act I begins with an *auto-da-fé* in which a Padre Pregador, or preacher, attacks the Jews. The audience is at first addressed as if it were part of the masses watching the event before several actors come onstage to take the role of spectators. Next, the Cavaleiro de Oliveira appears as a narrator and comments on the *auto-da-fé* and the Inquisitional process. Throughout the drama this historical figure who lived in London as an exile explains the similarities between the period being performed and the twentieth century. He describes how difficult it is for António José da Silva to study law at Coimbra. Because of the garment that he is ordered to wear by the Inquisition he is tormented by students, especially the fearsome Estudante Pálido. In Act II Antônio José da Silva meets and marries his cousin Leonor in the home of his mother Lourença Coutinho. At the end of the act there is a segment from António José da Silva's *Vida do Grande Dom Quixote_de La Mancha e do Gordo Sancho Pança.* Act III begins with Lourença Coutinho's nightmare of the destruction of the Jewish people. There are projected images of the gas chambers of the Holocaust as a voice reads the names of concentration camps. Near the end of Act III António José is taken away after having been denounced by the Escrava Negra. He is interrogated, tortured, and eventually confesses. In the last scene there is an *auto-da-fé* in which António José da Silva is led to the pyre as people scream and the Padre Secular describes his sentence.

In each drama the playwrights try to emphasize the reasons why the protagonists attract the unwanted attention of the Inquisitional authorities and relate it to the present day. In *O Santo Inquérito* it is Branca's worldview that puts her at odds with the Inquisition. Branca naively discusses her ideas about God and religion with Padre Bernardo after she saves him from drowning in Act I:

> BRANCA. O mais importante é que eu sinto a presença de Deus em todas as coisas que me dão prazer. No vento que me fustiga os cabelos, quando ando a cavalo. Na água do rio, que me acaricia o corpo, quando vou me banhar. No corpo de Augusto, quando roça no meu, como sem querer. Ou num bom prato de carne-seca, bem apimentado, com muita farofa [...]. (30)

Branca's view of God is not punitive nor coercive but rather simplistic and sensual. Branca feels God's love all around her—in the wind, the water, her fiancé's body, etc. It is precisely Branca's sensuality and her open feelings of love that most disturb Padre Bernardo. When Branca later describes how she once swam in the nude on a hot summer's night, the Padre is even more disquieted.

Throughout *O Santo Inquérito* there are frequent references to Branca's nudity and nocturnal river bathing. These begin in Act I, Scene 1, when Padre Bernardo declares, "Ela está nua" at the end of his opening statement to the tribunal (30). Though she has clothing on, the priest cannot or will not see it. During one of her interrogations she describes bathing in the river one night when she couldn't sleep. The Padre presses her to admit that her fiancé, Augusto, watched her bathing, yet it is the Padre who becomes the voyeur. He cannot keep the thought of the young woman swimming from his mind. The repeated references to Branca's nudity in the *O Santo Inquérito* and the Padre's reaction to it symbolize how disruptive sexuality can be to societies rigorously attached to conservative values. Indeed the military regime conceived of Brazil as a conservative, traditional, Roman Catholic country. Open sexuality was contrary to this ideal because in essence it involves the most basic freedom—freedom over one's mind and body. Under dictatorship the body and the mind are governed by an outside power that puts constraints on thoughts and actions. Arthur Miller, the author of a historical drama about the Salem witch trials theorizes that there is a link between sexuality and politics. "[B]elow its concern with justice the play evokes a lethal brew of illicit sexuality, fear of the supernatural, and political manipulation, a combination not unfamiliar these days" (164). For this reason, Branca's symbolic nudity is emblematic of personal autonomy—a concept that is problematic to traditional authority.

In *O Judeu* António José da Silva also has different ideas about life. He is interested in practicing his art as a playwright and does not understand nor appreciate the limitations being placed on him because he is of New Christian heritage. The New Christians were Jews and descendants of Jews who were forced to convert to Christianity. Because da Silva himself does not practice Judaism, he does not want to be labeled as one. In an exchange with his wife Leonor he describes how he sees himself:

> ANTÓNIO JOSÉ. Eu sou tão-só um homem. Nem mais, nem
> menos. Nem raro de espírito, nem singular de
> corpo. Um homem; um qualquer. Tu, uma mulher sem
> marcas; uma no meio das gentes. Esta é a verdade.
> A verdade! (132-133)

António José da Silva cannot escape being called a Jew and feels that the label "Jew" personifies hatred. It is Leonor who reminds him that regardless of how he sees himself, the outside society and the powerful Inquisition in particular view him as a Jew. Santareno is well aware that racial and religious labels such as "Jew" or "heretic" are a social construct and create a societal expectation for that person to become what he or she is considered to be by others. In Portugal under Salazar, those who differed in opinion with official government policies were considered subversives. This included all those who protested the restrictions placed upon freedom of expression. In addition to the extreme censorship of the arts, public gatherings were not allowed and the open discussion of politics was strongly prohibited.

For those who did not abide by the strict policies of the dictatorships there was the possibility of imprisonment and even harsher punishment. This is analogized in the plays about the Inquisition. In *O Santo Inquérito* there are several scenes in which Branca is in a jail cell, lamenting her predicament. There are also several references to torture. In Act II the Visitador demands that Augusto Coutinho be brought out before Branca. The audience is not shown what happened to Augusto, but from his wounds it is apparent that he has been tortured. Even though the actual torture session is not depicted, portraying the end result of it is effective in making the audience feel uncomfortable. According to John Fraser in *Violence in the Arts*:

> If one is made to feel uncomfortable, it is because one is confronted with facts that one hadn't known, or hadn't thought carefully enough about, or is still reluctant to feel intensely about. (47)

Being visually confronted with evidence that young people like Augusto are being harmed is shocking and disturbing. The inclusion of such a scene is there to make audience members realize that a gross abuse of power is taking place around them and that they should do something about it. To reinforce the institutionalization of torture there is the dialogue between the Visitador and the Guarda. When the Visitador finds out that Augusto fainted after only fifteen minutes of torture even though the maximum allowed is an hour he declares that the guards should not have been so rough for:

> VISITADOR. A finalidade da tortura é apenas obter a verdade [...]. (Dias Gomes 98)

The Visitador's strict tone reveals a certain "by-the-book" enforcement of the rules regarding eliciting confessions. It also signifies a larger organization that is behind the use of torture. The allusion to clear guidelines in the torture of prisoners during the Inquisition to elicit information is also found in the twentieth century. According to Joan Dassin in *Torture in Brazil*: "The official proceedings of political trials held in military courts indicate that the authorities were fully aware of the routine use of torture during preliminary inquests, and that evidence produced under torture was considered valid in the courtroom" (x). During the military regime the authorities not only knew about the employment of torture methods to elicit information, but approved of it by using such methods in cases against the accused in courts.

In *O Judeu*, there are even more explicit scenes of torture. For example, in Act III the "*tratos de polé*" or pulley are re-enacted. The stage directions indicate how António José is hung by his arms, then dropped violently toward the ground only to be jerked upward again, straining his limbs and muscles. Watching this scene of torture is not only revolting to the audience but also to those who participate in the torture. After watching the scene and hearing António José confess, the stage directions call for the 1º Inquisidor to angrily stare at his superior, the Inquisidor Mor, turn his back and leave the room. In so doing he refuses to collaborate in a cruel and unjust institution. This reaction sets an example for the audience to follow in not supporting nor participating in present-day political repression.

A similar message of non-compliance with the system is offered in *O Santo Inquérito*. Simão has just told his daughter that Augusto has died during a torture session rather than implicate her. He describes how Augusto finally succumbed while hanging from his ankles. After hearing that her fiancé has perished, Branca asks her father why he did not do anything to help Augusto. He responds that although he thought about lowering the rope he didn't.

> SIMÃO. Eles têm leis muito severas para aqueles que
> ajudam os hereges. Eu já estava com a minha
> situação resolvida, ia ser posto em liberdade...
> BRANCA. Bastava um gesto...
> SIMÃO. E o que me custaria esse gesto? Um homem deve
> pesar bem suas atitudes, e não agir ao primeiro
> impulso. Eu podia ter tido o mesmo destino que
> ele. Era ou não era muito pior? (115)

After hearing from her father that Augusto is dead, Branca reacts with shock and at first blames "eles," or the Inquisition, for Augusto's death. Then she questions her father's actions and learns that he could have done something to save Augusto's life, but did not so as not to compromise his own. Branca wants to know why Simão did not offer a *gesto*, or gesture to help save Augusto. In a Brechtian sense the *gesto* or *gestus* as implied by Branca is symbolic of involvement. Simão, like many people of Dias Gomes's day, did not want to become involved in the stand against the dictatorship for fear of risking his own life. Branca in turn blames her father for being an accomplice to the death of Augusto and, symbolically, for the continuance of the military regime in Brazil. She says:

> BRANCA. O senhor é tão culpado quanto eles.
> SIMÃO. Não, ninguém pode ser culpado de um ato para o qual não contribuiu de forma alguma.
> BRANCA. O senhor contribuiu.
> SIMÃO. Não matei, não executei, não participei de nada!
> BRANCA. Silenciou. (117)

Though Simão tries to distance himself from Augusto's death, Branca finds him responsible for not saying anything. Even his denial that he did not kill, order or participate is rebuked with his daughter's statement that he was silent. For Branca, silence means complicity. She continues with, "Quem cala, colabora" meaning, literally, that whoever fails to speak, collaborates. With these three words Dias Gomes points an accusatory finger at those in the audience and in Brazilian society at large who do not rise up and protest what is happening in their country. The playwright is making a plea for action against the regime of his day on the part of the erstwhile "silent majority."

For playwrights writing under dictatorship, the historical drama proved to be an effective tool in which to address issues such as socio-economic inequality, the repression of civil rights and the imprisonment and torture of political dissidents. By going back to the past, Brazilian and Portuguese playwrights found their inspiration in actual episodes of history. Because their intent was to critique the regimes in power, Augusto Boal, Alfedo Dias Gomes, Gianfrancesco Guarnieri, and Bernardo Santareno put their own take on the past—privileging some material and perspectives over others.

They employed techniques derived from the theater of others, namely, Brecht, Artaud, and Buenaventura and adapted them to their own stage. The playwrights were extremely committed to educating the public as to what was happening around them with the hope that they would do something to change the political system. In terms of avoiding the censors, the two Brazilian plays studied suffered only minor cuts and were produced shortly after being written. It was not until 1968 when the A-I 5 Institutional Act No. 5 was in place that censorship laws became more stringent and similar productions were forbidden. *O Judeu* did not fare as well. Banned from the stage, the play was first performed in 1981—fifteen years after it was written, and sadly, a year after Santareno's untimely death. In a most ironic and perhaps fitting turn of events, the performance took place in the Teatro D. Maria/Casa de Garrett, located atop the ruins of Palácio Estaus, the headquarters of the Inquisition. In a symbolic way, the verdict against Antônio José da Silva and the thousands who were persecuted during the Inquisition was overturned. Since the return to democracy in Portugal in 1974 and in Brazil in 1985, there have been fewer historical dramas produced. Especially in Brazil, the relative lack of political constraints on artistic expression has made the covert use of history as seen in the dramas analyzed in this talk less necessary.

Notes

[1] In an interview Anita Novinsky stated that there is no reliable proof that Branca Dias actually existed.

Works Cited

Anderson, Robert. "The Muses of Chaos and Destruction in *Arena Conta Zumbi.*" *Latin American Theatre Review* 29.2 (1996): 15-28.

Artaud, Antonin. *The Theater and its Double.* New York: Grove Press, 1958.

Boal, Augusto. *Theatre of the Oppressed.* Trans. Charles A. and Maria Odilia Leal McBride. New York: Theatre Communications Group, 1985.

Bradby, David. "Artaud Antonin." *The Cambridge Guide to Theatre.* Ed. Martin Banham. New edition. Cambridge: Cambridge UP, 1995.

Buarque de Hollanda, Chico and Ruy Guerra. *Calabar: O elogio da traição.* 20th ed. Rio de Janeiro: Civilização Brasileira, 1973.

Campos, Cláudia de Arruda. *Zumbi, Tiradentes, e outras histórias contadas pelo Arena.* São Paulo: EDUSP/Perspectiva, 1988.

Counsell, Colin. *Signs of Performance: An Introduction to Twentieth-Century Theatre.* London and New York: Routledge, 1996.

Damasceno, Leslie H. *Cultural Space and Theatrical Conventions in the Works of Oduvaldo Vianna Filho.* Detroit: Wayne State UP, 1996.

Dassin, Joan, ed. Introduction. *Torture in Brazil.* Trans. Jaime Wright. New York: Vintage, 1986. ix-xix.

Dias Gomes, Alfredo. *O Santo Inquérito.* 8th ed. Rio de Janeiro: Civilização Brasileira, 1984.

Ellis, Lorena B. *Brecht's Reception in Brazil.* New York: Peter Lang, 1995.

Fraser, John. *Violence in the Arts.* Cambridge: Cambridge UP, 1974.

Lindenberger, Herbert. *Historical Drama: The Relation of Literature and Reality.* Chicago and London: U Chicago P, 1975.

Miller, Arthur. "Why I wrote *The Crucible.*" *New Yorker* 21-28 Oct. 1996: 158-160.

Novinsky, Anita. Personal interview. 14 June 1997.

Santareno, Bernardo. *O Judeu: Narrativa Dramática em Três Actos.* Lisboa: Ática, 1966.

Taylor, Diana. *Theatre of Crisis: Drama and Politics in Latin America.* Lexington, KY: U of Kentucky P, 1991.

"Utopia." *The Compact Edition of the Oxford English Dictionary.* Vol. II. P-Z. New York: Oxford UP, 1971. 485.

White, Hayden. *Metahistory, The Historical Imagination in Nineteenth-Century Europe.* Baltimore and London: Johns Hopkins UP, 1973.

———. *Tropics of Discourse: Essays in Cultural Criticism.* Baltimore and London: Johns Hopkins UP, 1978.

Willet, John. *The Theatre of Bertolt Brecht: A Study from Eight Aspects.* New York: New Directions, 1959.

Bonnie S. Wasserman teaches Portuguese and coordinates proficiency testing in foreign languages at New York University. She received a doctorate in Portuguese from the University of Wisconsin-Madison. Her current research interests include historical drama and Lusophone-African literature. E-mail: bonwass@yahoo.com

Representations of East Timor in the Poetry of Ruy Cinatti: Colonial Rule under Crossfire

Reinaldo Francisco Silva

Abstract. Informed by current postcolonial discourse, this article highlights Cinatti's position on Portuguese colonial rule in East Timor, while shedding additional light on its economic, cultural, and ethnic abuses. Realizing, shortly after the revolution, that his warnings about the future of the territory were to no avail, he ceased to write about East Timor. To his dismay, the Portuguese and their politicians were completely enraptured by the taste of freedom, unmindful of Indonesia's readiness to step in for another period of colonial rule and annexation of the territory.

In one of the most influential works in postcolonial studies, *The Location of Culture*, Homi K. Bhabha has noted that the objective of colonial discourse is to "construe the colonized as a population of degenerate types on the basis of racial origin, in order to justify conquest and to establish systems of administration and instruction" (70). This is the political and ideological apparatus that Ruy Cinatti (1915-1986) wishes to attack in his poems about East Timor, now collected in *Ruy Cinatti: Obra Poética*, published in Lisbon, in 1992. Like Bhabha, Cinatti unmasks the Portuguese colonial administration's dealings with the natives of East Timor as based on "relations of power/knowledge," where the colonizer resorts to "those terrifying stereotypes of savagery, cannibalism, lust and anarchy which are the signal points of identification and alienation, scenes of fear and desire, in colonial texts" (Bhabha 72). Although Cinatti worked for the colonial administration in

East Timor, he did not endorse the régime's political agenda and practices. Having spent a number of years in this territory as a free-lance botanist and speleologist, Ruy Cinatti wrote poems about East Timor that not only attest to his deep knowledge of the native culture and tradition, but also express his respect and admiration for its inhabitants. With self-imposed censorship necessary for the purposes of survival, Portuguese writers avoided criticizing as much as possible the political régime openly. Such is not the case with some of Cinatti's poems written before the Portuguese democratic revolution of April 25, 1974. In specific passages, they contain a criticism of the Portuguese grip on East Timor. Within a body of poems that celebrates the beauty and natural wonders of East Timor lies a caustic voice that denounces colonial privileges. Such an approach, however, undermines Gayatri Chakravorty Spivak's perception of colonial texts as centering on the "literary representations of the dominant" culture and how it interacts with its minor, colonized subjects. In these texts, Spivak contends that reality is filtered through the eyes and prejudices of the writer from the said dominant culture. Such is not the case with Cinatti. An observer of colonial excesses, Cinatti takes sides with those who are victimized by the ideological and political colonial model that Bhabha describes in the work quoted above.

In another classic of postcolonial studies, *Culture and Imperialism*, Edward Said has defined imperialism as a process that involves "thinking about, settling on, controlling land that you do not possess, that is distant, that is lived on and owned by others. For all kinds of reasons it attracts some people and often involves untold misery for others" (5). As we shall see further on in our discussion, Cinatti's poems shed much light on the dynamics of a dominant culture and how it imposes itself on the colonized and oppressed. Without the rhetorical tools now available in postcolonial discourse, Cinatti's poems are a substantiation of Said's definition of imperialism and colonialism. Imperialism, Said claims,

> means the practice, the theory, and the attitudes of a dominating metropolitan centre ruling a distant territory; 'colonialism', which is almost always a consequence of imperialism, is the implanting of settlements on distant territory. [...] 'Empire is a relationship, formal or informal, in which one state controls the effective political sovereignty of another political society. It can be achieved by force, by political collaboration, by economic, social, or cultural dependence. (8)

Informed by current postcolonial discourse, the goal of this essay is to highlight Cinatti's position on Portuguese colonial rule in East Timor, while shedding additional information on its economic, cultural, and ethnic abuses. Realizing, shortly after the democratic revolution in Portugal, that his warnings about the future of the territory were to no avail, Cinatti's poetic output about East Timor suddenly dried up. To his dismay, the Portuguese and their politicians were completely enraptured by the celebration of their freedom, unmindful of Indonesia's readiness to step in. Before delving into these matters, it is important to provide a sketch of Cinatti the man, his fondness for the territory, as well as the ways in which his poetic output has been assessed by literary critics.

Ruy Cinatti Vaz Monteiro Gomes was born in London on March 8, 1915. At the time, his maternal grandfather, Mr. Demétrio Cinatti, was the appointed Portuguese consul in the United Kingdom. The poet often stated that he could trace his Italian and Chinese blood to this side of the family. At the early age of two, the child and his mother traveled to Springfield, New Jersey to rejoin his father. At the time, Portugal was experiencing economic hardships because of the instability prompted by the Republican revolution of October 5, 1910, which brought an end to monarchical rule. At the time, the United States of America looked more promising to his jobless father. In his discussion of Cinatti's poems that reflects the poet's restlessness and strong desire for traveling, Ruy Belo claims that this led "him to Timor today and to Oxford the very next" (146; my translation). It is possible, I believe, to trace such personal characteristics as far back as his childhood, stemming from economic conditions and the circumstances of life. Perhaps the most devastating experience in his life was his mother's death when he was only two years of age, shortly after returning from America. At first, he was raised by his maternal grandparents and, later on, by his paternal grandparents. In the meantime, his father remained in the United States, where he re-married an American woman named Flora Stern. Afterwards, they all settled down in Portugal and Cinatti joined them and his half-sister, Amelia. Over the years, the alienation between father and son widened as the son failed to live up to the academic and professional expectations of his authoritarian father. Cinatti, to his father's dismay, had always expressed a longing for distant islands, preferably in the exotic South Sea. His dream finally came true on July 27, 1946, when he set foot for the very first time in East Timor. He would be joining the staff of the colonial administration since he had received an appointment as the secretary to the governor. Immediately upon arrival, Cinatti confessed that he had "fallen in love with Timor" (Stilwell 175; my translation), but he also encountered an island that had been completely destroyed by the Japanese during World War II.[1]

Through time, Cinatti attempts to convince the governor and the administration that the basis for mutual understanding is respect for the native culture. All to no avail. With academic training in botany and agriculture received at the Instituto Superior de Agronomia in Lisbon and anthropology at Oxford University, Cinatti simply detested his appointment. It did not leave him with much time to interact with the Timorese, learn more about their culture, collect minerals and plants, or even to research the economic potential of the island for agriculture and forestry. As he delved more and more into the local traditions, Cinatti made the acquaintance of several Timorese, eventually coming to the conclusion that they were, in fact, people with real problems and not the exotic, carefree figures he had read about in the travel literature of his adolescent years. As Stilwell has noted, further evidence of his respect and admiration for the Timorese can be seen in his letter to Óscar Ruas, the governor of Timor, where Cinatti reiterates his disapproval of the administration's authoritarian and violent behavior towards the natives (Stilwell 190-91). To him, the people of East Timor are far more important than the economic exploitation of the island, including its sandalwood forests and other natural resources. An uncomfortable voice for the régime to listen to for a time, Cinatti may be seen as a postcolonial critic *avant la lettre* since he anticipates what contemporary postcolonial critics such as Homi Bhabha, Gayatri Spivak, Edward Said, Robert Young, and Ato Quayson have outlined in their discussion of colonial practices and abuses. A Timorese, Cinatti argues,

> is an adult with a mind of his own, someone with a strong sense of responsibility and a well-defined social personality. I am neither interested in perceiving him as a case of survival nor do I consider his traditions as mere objects of curiosity. Despite being a more primitive people compared to us, and lacking in technological resources, this is neither evidence of childishness on the social scale nor lack of a psychological density. (qtd. in Stilwell 197; my translation)

Although Cinatti was working for the colonial administration, his outspokenness was not much appreciated and he often became the target of several attempts at silencing and retaliation.

Critical assessment of Cinatti's work is divided. While several scholars have noted some strengths in his poetry, they shy away from ranking it as anywhere comparable to that of, for example, Fernando Pessoa or other poets of his time or age. Only a very restricted number of scholars have found his writings worth praising. In the article alluded to earlier, Ruy Belo analyzed the nomadic and evocative imprint of Cinatti's poems and concluded at the end that there is something missing in his poetic skill. Cinatti's epigraph in *O Livro do Nómada meu Amigo*, taken from Ezra Pound, is, Belo argues, very suggestive: "It doesn't matter which leg of your table you make first, so long as the table has four legs and will stand up solidly when you have finished it" (qtd. in Belo 147). His poetic work, Belo concluded, is "still short of at least one leg" (152). Whereas his poetic skill is not the most commendable, I believe his ideas and castigation of colonial excesses are, as I will try to show, admirable.

Assessing Cinatti's first volume of poems, *Nós Não Somos Deste Mundo*, Adolfo Casais Monteiro contends that it is still too early to discern the ways in which Cinatti's poetry will develop. The volume in question, he argues, is the work of a poet who is still "very young" (287; my translation). In a rather caustic tone, Monteiro asks whether Cinatti "should have looked to prose as the instrument through which to communicate to us what fails to be labeled as poetry" (288; my translation).

Jorge de Sena, one of his closest friends, who resided in the United States and made a career as a teacher at the Universities of California and Wisconsin and as a prolific writer, viewed Cinatti as possessing a "quite original personality, where the Orient and the West" converged into the same person. Unfortunately, he cannot help calling Cinatti's poetic style "adolescent" (207-8).

In the preface to *Ruy Cinatti: Obra Poética*, the best edition of Cinatti's collected poems, Fernando Pinto do Amaral aims for a more favorable assessment of Cinatti's poems. He draws our attention to aspects that have been overlooked, such as the various phases in Cinatti's career, his themes, his restlessness of temper and how it marks his poems, his criticism of colonial rule in East Timor, and his Catholic fervor. Noting that the critical reception, at times, has not been very enthusiastic, Amaral argues that this was

> influenced by various factors, some not of a truly literary nature, but, instead, stemming from a certain marginality that Cinatti embraced throughout his life, publishing his work in lesser-known presses or in restricted author's editions, in addi-

> tion to refusing straightforward interaction with the dominant groups (for example, at the political level, whether those from the régime or from the opposition). Other reasons for the difficulty in accepting his poetry, thus, lie in stylistic reasons, since the type of craft adopted by Cinatti (especially after the fifties, and even much earlier) did not match the one that the national lyrical taste had gotten used to. His frequent choice of a not very fluid and relatively abrupt syntax—with sudden jerks into unpredictable directions—as well as a prosodic rhythm that is rather irregular and elliptical, did not help much to enlarge the readership of this not-much-of-a-perfectionist-poet, who kept on writing profusely and, for that very same reason, does not hesitate to give little importance to stylistic and formal details [...] preferring, by all means, to safeguard his faithfulness to his initial impulses—that is, to inspiration—the spontaneity imprinted in each one of his poems. (14; my translation)

Joaquim Manuel Magalhães has focused on the role of memory in the poetry of Cinatti in at least two works. Unlike previous scholars, he has written more favorable impressions of Cinatti's poems. In *Os Dois Crepúsculos*, Magalhães refers to him as "the voice of this major poet of ours" (46; my translation). One of the major strengths in Cinatti's poems, I believe, lies in his portrayal of East Timor. When denouncing colonial abuses, celebrating the island's natural wonders, or praising the benignity of its people, Cinatti's voice is at its most appealing, thought-provoking, and contemporary.

That Cinatti criticized Portuguese colonial rule in East Timor is a given, but what was its underlying political philosophy? In what ways does it contrast, for example, with British colonialism? And which group of Portuguese colonizers is he, in fact, criticizing? As Peter Stilwell has argued,

> historically, at the administrative level, Portugal had always known how to make amends for the economic and military weaknesses as well as for the distance separating it from East Timor. While taking advantage of the fact that the local ethnic groups possessed relatively sophisticated cultures, it had established with them relationships based on respect and participation rather than dominance. It is Cinatti who explains this in *Arquitectura Timorense*. (180; my translation)

Cinatti explains in this posthumously published work that, in the seventeenth and eighteenth centuries, for example, the Timorese could send back a governor they disliked to the Portuguese Viceroy stationed in India. In

1702, António Coelho Guerreiro, the first governor of Timor, conferred upon the Timorese nobility titles such as *Don* and military titles such as lieutenant and colonel. Stilwell further adds that in the twentieth century, the Timorese plebeians had been freed from their

> feudal dependence and had forbidden the practices of enslavement among the local ethnic groups [...]. In 1946, contrary to what happened in the Dutch colonies in the South Sea, the Timorese viewed the Portuguese presence and the return of its administration as desirable. On the other hand, the example of numerous Portuguese who had left Portugal before World War II was seen as positive. They knew how to settle down in the territory and integrate themselves in the local way of life—such had been the case of Manuel Viegas Carrascalão, who had married a Timorese princess, or Pedro Belmonte, whose house Cinatti often called upon; he, too, was married to a Timorese woman. (180; my translation)

While economics—that is, money, riches, financial gain and exploitation—are at the heart of colonialism, sexual benefits are marginal although, no doubt, appreciated too. Marriages such as these, however, were strongly discouraged in, for example, the British colonial model. Although sexual desire is an undeniable reality of colonialism, as Robert Young has shown in *Colonial Desire: Hybridity in Theory, Culture and Race*, hybrid marriages were considered socially degrading according to British standards. Even in the United States, where the dialectics of dominant vs. margins is prevalent in the colonial pattern, slave narratives such as Harriet A. Jacobs's *Incidents in the Life of a Slave Girl* highlight the dominant, white slaveholder's sexual exploitation of his black female slaves. In this narrative, the conventions of mid-nineteenth-century America do not allow the master to file for a divorce and wed his black female slave. Moreover, such an option would have never crossed Dr. Flint's mind. And yet he had fathered a few mulattos with Linda Brent. In the Portuguese colonial situation, hybrid marriages were tolerated and, at times, encouraged, not only for the sake of mutual understanding, but also for a more thorough control of the colonial possession.

This ambiance of mutual understanding in East Timor, however, came to an end when the older colonial administration was replaced by employees from the "Portuguese colonies in Africa with no experience of the Portuguese colonial tradition in Timor [and who] had adopted attitudes and introduced practices that repelled the governor's young Secretary [Cinatti]" (Stilwell 180;

my translation). In a letter dated February 27, 1952 addressed to Serpa Rosa (at the time, the governor appointed to East Timor), Cinatti listed the atrocities, violence, gradual disappearance, imprisonment, and the poor quality of the food given to the natives. The famous statement, "You already know, Sirs. Whoever mistreats a native, mistreats me," which Cinatti uttered during a local wedding banquet, dates from this period (qtd. in Stilwell 181; my translation). While Cinatti does not view these administrators as adopting racist attitudes, he considers them, nonetheless, criminals due to their authoritarianism, abuse of power, and overall lack of understanding of Timorese native culture.

Having dealt with this important preliminary material, we shall now look at some of Cinatti's poems so as to ascertain his unique, first-hand poetic account of the abuses inflicted on the natives and the land by those administrators who had come from Africa. In poems such as "Timor," where he compares the island to a sensuous woman whom he wishes to possess because he loves her profoundly, he writes:

> Antes sejas consumida
> pela paixão dos que te adoram,
> mulher-ilha!
>
> Sedes de anjos na "tuaca,"
> da minha língua ao teu seio,
> vida minha!
> [................................]
> Ilha, ilha, meu amor,
> foste minha moradia,
> meu tesouro!
>
> A minha segunda Mátria
> na minha vida insolúvel.
> Pátria: Deus! (481)

In the poem, "Huato-Buílico, Etc.," East Timor is compared to an edenic paradise where spring-like weather prevails all the year round. This edenic bliss, however, is in constant jeopardy due to the colonizer's greed. One of East Timor's most precious natural resources, its sandalwood tree forests, are being chopped down, as Cinatti reminds us in "Parâmetro Ecológico":

Onde passei havia florestas
há tantos anos [...].
Hoje, a paisagem é um deserto
De caules nus.

Ninguém me distende o esclarecer
de tal desengano.
Havia florestas, um crescer
sobrehumano.
Pedras e troncos isolados,
Assistem sós.
[................................]
Um Podocarpus
vestígio de arvoredo
outrora extenso e imponente, solitário hoje.
Tamanha ausência
supõe anos de fogo arrepiando
montes circundantes.
Um Podocarpus,
sacralizado pelos Timorenses...
é testemunho
para os viajantes.
Meu gesto lento de fotografia
atesta cegueira aos governantes,
que olhando o que vêem ousam dizer:
Foi sempre assim!

A Natureza, que é manjar dos vivos,
responde por mim.
Onde havia florestas há só capim
e fome que a os vivos arrebata! (520-21)

In this poem, Cinatti is criticizing the colonial administration's carelessness and lack of a reforestry plan. Whether it is fire or economic exploitation, the administration is insensitive to environmental matters such as erosion, issues that Cinatti draws our attention to in the notes he provides for this poem (Cinatti 552-53). In "As Camenassas de Díli," the natural beauty of Timor, symbolized by its flower gardens, is being destroyed by the colonizer's frenzy to impose the artifacts of modern civilization:

> Eram tão delicadas [...]. Mas a bruta,
> imbecil, canhestra,
> mentecapta alcateia
> de homens ciosos sem qualquer ideia,
> tomou posse de Díli-jardim,
> arrancou árvores, desviou ribeiras,
> transformou a cidade
> num deserto de casas sem memória,
> sem corolas caindo sobre a estrada. (262)

Because of such ecological disasters, over the years, the bay of Díli has been flooded by torrents of alluvium as Cinatti has shown in "Assoreamento da Baía de Díli."

The "scenes of fear" perpetuated by the colonizers and that Bhabha alludes to in *The Location of Culture* are reflected in the poem "Segunda Meditação":

> Sete homens morreram com sete
> balas plas costas.
> [......................................]
> Os outros, algemados, circulavam,
> em volta de um pião,
> que, transformado em bicho, os enrolava
>
> no seu chicote,
> à unha os atirava até morderem
> o chão.
> [......................................]
> Um homem gritava:
> Eu vi a marca
> de uma bota cardada.
> [......................................]
> Os homens não rodopiavam,

não, como piões.
Caíam, levantavam-se, ,caíam,
Chicoteados [...]. (274-75)

As mentioned earlier, the ones responsible for this violent behavior are the colonial administrators who had come from Africa. Cinatti, in particular, abhorred them because of their sadistic, violent behavior, as the references to the whip, handcuffs, and bruises in this poem substantiate. In addition, they also delighted in disrespectful practices such as the ones described in "Cemitérios de Díli e Outros de Timor":

São cemitérios de Díli,
Santa Cruz—os outros não
são mais do que nomes hoje
lembrados por alguns velhos
que viram ossos a lume
pisados pela Administração— [...]. (540-41)

The poem, "Manatuto é a Vila. Lacló—a Ribeira" is, this reader believes, a good example of how Cinatti portrays colonial excess. Instead of devoting an entire poem to the abuse at stake, Cinatti voices his criticism within a poem describing the landscape in East Timor. The poem in question focuses primarily on a stream and the fields of rice, but within lies a brief—yet important—allusion to a colonizer's manipulation of his authority in exchange for what he considers his sexual rights:

Santo que é coronel.
Tem direitos, tem deveres.
Os timorenses da vila,
dão-lhe tudo, até mulher [...]. (278)

Postcolonial theorists such as Young maintain that "colonialism was always locked into the machine of desire [...]. Nineteenth-century theories of race did not just consist of essentializing differentiations between self and other: they were also about a fascination with people having sex—interminable, adulterating, aleatory, illicit, inter-racial sex" (181). This sexual encounter with the ethnic other is not framed within the conventions of a colonial marriage celebrated between a white colonizer and a native woman. Instead, it is lustful and coercive, as bell hooks has contended in *Black Looks: Race and Representation.* Sexual fantasies directed at the dark ethnic other, hooks argues, have loomed in the imagination of white supremacists and colonizers:

> Cultural taboos around sexuality and desire are transgressed and made explicit as the media bombards folks with a message of difference no longer based on the white supremacist assumption that "blondes have more fun." The "real fun" is to be had by bringing to the surface all those "nasty" unconscious fantasies and longings about contact with the Other embedded in the secret (not so secret) deep structure of white supremacy. In many ways it is a contemporary revival of interest in the "primitive" [...]. To make one's self vulnerable to the seduction of difference, to seek an encounter with the Other, does not require that one relinquish forever one's mainstream positionality. When race and ethnicity become commodified as resources for pleasure, the culture of specific groups, as well as the bodies of individuals, can be seen as constituting an alternative playground where members of dominating races, genders, sexual practices affirm their power- over in intimate relations with the Other. (21- 23)

It is unlikely that Cinatti had such heterosexual longings, however, given his homoerotic nature.

In section forty-five of *Para Uma Corografia Emotiva de Timor (1946-1972),* Cinatti portrays the governor as an intimidating individual and mindless of the native's needs:

> Governador, não!—Astucioso
> tiranete,
> com maneiras de inocente.
> Mente oposta ao realmente
> Verdadeiro.
>
> Na Fazenda, dele sabiam
> ser pior que um fazendário.
> "Um lápis, senhores, um lápis,
> custa mais que muita tinta!"
>
> Chamavam-lhe "figo seco"

os das "mil e quatrocentas."
Os chinas diziam, cautos:
"Vale só meia gasosa."

Terra devastada.
Gente esfomeada.
Lei escamoteada
Com vagares de cínico.

Quem puder desminta
este falatório
tão mal figurado
preito a um falecido. (505)

While the governor is depicted as a tyrant and a liar, he was also a miser who delighted in the natives' starvation and the exploitation of Timor's natural resources. "Propósito Inadiável" further illustrates Cinatti's position on the economic exploitation of the natives by the Portuguese colonizers. Unquestioning and with a sense of resignation, they accept their fate with a smile on their lips:

O que magoa é ver o pobre
timorense esquálido beber
água do pântano,
onde se escoam lixos,
comer poeira
e saudar-me, quando
rodo na estrada,
deus ocioso [...]. (264)

In the poem "Em Fatu-ahi" Cinatti depicts Díli as a dirty and unpleasant city. This is, in part, due to the colonizer's neglect of local construction practices. Instead of adopting local architectural knowledge, they build replicas of houses and buildings in Portugal, which are, in essence, inadequate for the local climate. Cinatti can only hope for the sea's assistance in washing away what he considers a complete eyesore:

Quero dizer

que quando chegam deitam fora as crenças,
o pouco, talvez melhor, do que traziam.
Depois, a valer, tripudiam
até mais não poder, constroem casas,
maculam a baía,
até ficar parvinhos, mas
prepotentes.
Que o mar a invada,
esse o meu desejo, inunde as casas,
arrume as casas, destrua a imunda
palhaçada urbana, urbanizada
arquitectura
errada até à náusea.
Que o mar a salgue,
desenhe uma estrutura que se entenda,
afim da natureza:
ruas estreitas e largas, sinuosas
como os veios d'água;
jardins, ou praças, torneados, lagos
em vez de pântano-pseudo;
ruas direitas, o quanto baste, apenas,
para que seja consciente a lógica;
e casas para viver,
climaticamente imaginadas,
como as timorenses,
sentidas pelos homens que lá vivem,
cidade sem pés nem cabeça,
que nela suam, mijam, mas resistem
fundo na vida. (270)

"Um Património Sonegado" criticizes those members of the colonial administration who took advantage of their position of authority and influence to steal the churches and their works of art. It also criticizes the administration's complicity, inattentiveness, and, at times, stupidity as the following example illustrates:

Derreteram bronze

de peças históricas
para moldar eixos
de camionetas.
[........................]
Património intacto
ao longo de séculos
foi-se numa década
por caminhos ínvios.
[........................]
Perdeu-os a História,
sorve-os a Política!

São braços quebrados
de Cristo na cruz
o que em Timor fica.
Item, o diabo
que complica as vidas...
Património a saque,
Lealdades findas [...]. (519)

Cinatti sheds further light on this issue when comparing the island of Timor as a whole, that is, the Indonesian side as well as the Portuguese territory:

> As strange as it may seem, traces of the Portuguese presence are much stronger in the Indonesian part, that is, in the former Dutch section, because things were well kept there. In the Portuguese part, the military, the administrators, etc. stole everything: Luso-Indian statues from the seventeenth and eighteenth centuries, ivory faces and hands, gold-enameled wooden altars, Chinese porcelain, all of which was obtained through the commerce of sandalwood with China. Especially after 1960, by those Portuguese who had read a few anthropology books and who had been struck by the appealing prices quoted in collector's catalogs [...]. I saw a statue of ivory and another one of Our Lady of the Conception, of Luso-Indian make, being exchanged for another one of Our Lady of Fátima made of plastic, one of those that looks like a music-box [...] along with five hundred escudos into the bargain! (qtd. in Stilwell 301; my translation)

All of these poems attest to Cinatti's love and admiration for East Timor.

As the Portuguese democratic revolution was already under way, Cinatti's poetry about East Timor became imbued with a sense of evil things to happen in Timor. This feeling of foreboding can be grasped in, for example, "Premonição," written on June 30, 1974 and "Vaticínio," written the day before. In the latter, the poetic voice points out that Timor shall never be despoiled by a revolution that has left the territory to fend for itself (476). In both poems, Cinatti is drawing our attention to the confusing political situation in Portugal as well as the abandonment of its overseas colonies during the process of transition and independence. Cinatti fears for the future of East Timor since the Portuguese and their politicians were thoroughly engrossed by the democratic revolution. Stilwell points out that, as early as March of 1954, Cinatti had warned the Portuguese authorities about East Timor continuing to "look very appealing to Indonesia" (qtd. in Stilwell 216; my translation).

In "Programação," Cinatti focuses on the argument that was taking shape in Portugal after the revolution, namely the view that it was not worth bothering with this territory since it had very little to offer economically:

> Depois dos vinte e cinco de Abril
> nada mudou
> porque os homens não mudam de um dia para o outro.
> E assim assisto
> —examplo, o de Timor no qual me sinto—
> à mesma económica postura
> de que Timor
> de nada vale
> e que portanto qualquer tipo serve
> p'ra Timor governar por mais uns anos.
>
> Eu digo não! (476)

The poem "Protesto" further stresses the poet's dismay with another argument that prevailed in some political circles. Certain politicians said it did not really matter if the Indonesians occupied the territory. As a matter of fact, it would be a blessing since it was one less matter to worry about:

> Não é o dinheiro que lá gasto,
> mal gasto,

que magoa.
O que magoa é ouvir um responsável
dizer que Timor é um luxo
e portanto (por outras palavras)
que vão pró diabo
ou para a Indonésia os Timorenses [...]. (477)

The political situation in Portugal became even more confusing during the Summer of 1975 (usually referred to as the "Verão Quente," or Burning Summer) and the subsequent months, with Communists in control of the country. "The political situation was dangerously heading in the direction of a civil war and instability was affecting the central government's ability to take action" (Stilwell 373; my translation). The Indonesians took advantage of this opportunity to invade the city of Díli on December 7, 1975.

We have all learned about the violence, the gradual extinction of a people, a territory in economic shambles, cultural and linguistic imperialism, political imprisonments and mass murders during the Indonesian occupation, which lasted for about a quarter of a century, eventually ending in the apocalyptic month of September of 1999 after the Timorese had been allowed to cast their ballots for independence. The Timorese are now experiencing what Leela Gandhi describes as the "desire to forget the colonial past. [...] Postcolonial amnesia," she claims, "is symptomatic of the urge for historical self-invention or the need to make a new start—to erase painful memories of colonial subordination" (4). Whereas the East Timorese are eager to forget Portuguese colonialism, the desire to do so with that of Indonesia is much stronger.

As I hope this article has shown, Cinatti criticized the Portuguese colonial administration, but the Indonesian occupation and the atrocities it committed in less than twenty-five years will linger much longer in the minds of the people of East Timor. After all, the Timorese are more willing to forgive the Portuguese for their abuses during their colonial rule—which Cinatti so eloquently wrote about—than the bloodshed and extermination perpetuated by the Indonesians. Their choice of Portuguese for their official language is, without a doubt, meaningful. Moreover, Nobel Prize winners José Ramos Horta and D. Ximenes Belo have stressed the role of Portugal in keeping the East Timorese cause alive during Indonesian occupation. With diplomatic, financial, educational, and military support now in effect, Portugal is trying to redeem its colonial record—and assume its historical responsibilities—towards East Timor. And if there is an afterlife as Cinatti believed, one may imagine him in heavenly bliss, smiling at the winds of change now sweeping through East Timor, proud of the country he was born in even if the former administration had exploited and abused the people and the territory he had loved so much.

Notes

[1] We may now argue that this episode foreshadows the Indonesian devastation of East Timor in the aftermath of the Timorese vote for independence in late August of 1999. Whether it was the Japanese retaliation, the Indonesian invasion, or centuries of Portuguese colonial rule, the ill-fated people of East Timor have known no other reality than hardship, suffering, destruction, and oppression.

Works Cited

Amaral, Fernando Pinto do (ed). *Ruy Cinatti: Obra Poética.* Lisboa: Imprensa Nacional-Casa da Moeda, 1992.

Belo, Ruy. *Obra Poética de Ruy Belo.* Ed. Joaquim Manuel Magalhães and Maria Jorge Vilar de Figueiredo. Vol. 3. Lisboa: Editorial Presença, 1984.

Bhabha, Homi K. *The Location of Culture.* London and New York: Routledge, 1994.

Gandhi, Leela. *Postcolonial Theory: A Critical Introduction.* Edinburgh: Edinburgh UP, 1998.

Hooks, Bell. *Black Looks: Race and Representation.* Boston: South End, 1992.

Magalhães, Joaquim Manuel. *Os Dois Crepúsculos: Sobre Poesia Portuguesa Actual e Outras Crónicas.* Lisboa: A Regra do Jogo, 1981.

———. *Um Pouco da Morte.* Lisboa: Editorial Presença, 1989.

Monteiro, Adolfo Casais. *A Poesia Portuguesa Contemporânea.* Lisboa: Livraria Sá da Costa, 1977.

Said, Edward W. *Culture and Imperialism.* London: Vintage, 1994.

Sena, Jorge de. *Líricas Portuguesas.* Vol. 1. Lisboa: Edições 70, 1984.

Spivak, Gayatri Chakravorty. *A Critique of Postcolonial Reason: Toward a History of the Vanishing Present.* Cambridge, MA and London: Harvard UP, 1999.

Stilwell, Peter. *A Condição Humana em Ruy Cinatti.* Lisboa: Editorial Presença, 1995.

Young, Robert J. C. *Colonial Desire: Hybridity in Theory, Culture and Race.* London and New York: Routledge, 1996.

Reinaldo Francisco Silva holds a Ph.D. degree in English and American Literature from New York University and is a faculty member at the Department of Languages and Cultures, University of Aveiro. He is currently revising his dissertation, *Representations of* *the Portuguese in American Literature*, for publication. In addition to teaching American authors from the Realist and Naturalist periods, he also teaches contemporary ethnic fiction, with a strong emphasis on Portuguese-American writers. His publication record includes, for example, the following articles: "The Corrosive Glance from Above: Social Darwinism, Racial Hierarchy, and the Portuguese in Frank Norris's *The Octopus*" in *Frank Norris Studies*; "Representations of the Portuguese in Jack London's *The Valley of the Moon*" in *Re-Viewing Race and Ethnicity in American Texts*; and "'The 'Gees': Herman Melville's Quarrel with Racism" in the Proceedings of the 2000 International Comparative Literature Association Conference.

Prefácio do livro *East Timor: Bitter Paradise*, de Elaine Briere

Noam Chomsky

Tradução de Rita Alves

Resumo. Este artigo oferece-nos uma visão crítica da posição tomada pelas potências ocidentais em relação ao caso de Timor-Leste. Cúmplices no silêncio, essas potências deixaram que uma situação de autêntico terror se arrastasse, atingindo níveis que desafiam a imaginação. Pior que o silêncio é, contudo, o apoio (a tais atrocidades) por ele camuflado e a recusa à intervenção, a qual acaba por chegar, tardiamente, num filantropismo hipócrita. Trata-se de um artigo fundamental para a compreensão do comportamento político na defesa dos interesses internos, denunciando o caso particular de Timor-Leste.

Quando os Estados Unidos da América faziam planos para a ordem global, que viria a ganhar forma após a Segunda Guerra Mundial, não se esqueceram da pequena colónia portuguesa de Timor-Leste. Sumner Welles, Primeiro-Conselheiro de Roosevelt, comentou que deveria ser concedida a independência a Timor-Leste—mas "isso levaria uns mil anos, com certeza." O cinismo acentuou-se com as proezas de guerra dos timorenses. Dez por cento da população perdera a vida defendendo umas poucas centenas de comandos australianos que permaneceram em Timor-Leste depois da invasão dos japoneses. James Dunn, um grande especialista australiano em assuntos de Timor-Leste, descreve esta questão como "uma das grandes catástrofes da Segunda Guerra Mundial." Proporcionalmente à população, o caso representa também uma das contribuições mais extraordinárias para o esforço de guerra dos Aliados. A coragem e sacrifício dos timorenses talvez tenham salvado a Austrália de uma invasão, cujas consequências poderiam ter sido dramáticas.

Em 1975 os timorenses receberam um prémio. A invasão indonésia de Dezembro, precedida de incursões desde Outubro, foi antecipada pelas potências ocidentais. Em Agosto, o embaixador australiano em Jacarta, Richard Woolcott, aconselhou Camberra, através de uma linha secreta, a apoiar a invasão indonésia pendente, uma vez que um acordo em relação às reservas de petróleo do *Timor Gap* seria mais proveitoso com a Indonésia "do que com Portugal ou com Timor independente." Adoptando a postura do "realismo kissingeriano," Woolcott defendia ainda que a Austrália deveria tomar "uma posição pragmática em detrimento de uma posição de princípios." "É disso afinal que se trata o interesse nacional e a política externa," acrescentou.

Woolcott estava completamente certo acerca da política externa e do realismo kissingeriano; estava também certo quanto ao interesse nacional, se usarmos o termo no sentido técnico, onde a relação com os interesses da nação é apenas acidental (frequentemente nociva) mas reflecte de forma muito aproximada os interesses presumíveis do poder interno. Esta última observação acerca das sociedades ocidentais é tão velha como a crítica de Adam Smith aos "principais arquitectos" da política na Inglaterra do seu tempo, esses "comerciantes e fabricantes" que só queriam saber se os seus próprios interesses "eram atendidos ao pormenor," não importando o quão "penosas" pudessem ser as consequências para os outros grupos, incluindo a nação inglesa. Um motivo de peso para o sigilo governamental é o reconhecimento do facto de que o que se faz em nome do "interesse nacional" não será tolerado pela população; a "posição pragmática" de Woolcott é um bom exemplo disso.

Washington seguia também, sem surpresa, o rumo do realismo kissingeriano. O embaixador norte-americano em Jacarta tinha informado Woolcott de que ele tinha "ordem do próprio Kissinger para não se envolver em discussões sobre Timor com os indonésios." Chegara à conclusão de que os EUA deveriam "deixar que as coisas tomassem o seu próprio rumo" sem o envolvimento dos EUA — com a excepção do fornecimento à Indonésia de noventa por cento do armamento da mesma, cujo uso se restringia à defesa, com base num acordo solene. Kissinger e o Presidente Ford autorizaram a invasão em segredo e, sob a protecção de um embargo de armas, aumentaram rapidamente a circulação das mesmas, incluindo equipamento anti-guerrilha letal. O Conselho de Segurança das Nações Unidas condenou a agressão da Indonésia e ordenou que a mesma se retirasse imediatamente. Os EUA aliaram-se formalmente a esta decisão, facto sem grande importância, como veio a explicar uns anos mais tarde nas suas memórias o embaixador dos EUA nas Nações Unidas, Daniel Patrick Moynihan. Seguindo as directivas do Ministério dos Negócios Estrangeiros norte-americano, Moynihan orgulhou-se de ter assegurado a "total ineficácia" da ONU em qualquer acção que esta quisesse levar adiante contra a invasão e os consequentes massacres, dos quais ele estava plenamente consciente. Embora estes tenham sido, sem dúvida, os actos mais significativos da carreira de Moynihan em termos de consequências humanitárias, foram completamente omitidos nos louvores que lhe foram dirigidos pelos distintos intelectuais aquando da sua saída do Senado em 1999. Tais actos nem sequer diminuíram a sua reputação enquanto voz solitária e corajosa em apelo ao respeito pelo direito internacional.

Talvez faça sentido que o Ocidente tivesse respondido desta maneira àquele que deverá ter sido o pior massacre em termos populacionais depois do Holocausto. Apenas dez anos antes, o Presidente Suharto chegara ao poder na Indonésia, altura em que ocorria um "massacre arrepiante de enorme escala" (*New York Times*), comparado pela CIA com os crimes de Hitler, Estaline e Mao. Os factos, sem ocultação dos pontos essenciais, deram origem a uma euforia desmedida entre a generalidade dos sectores de elite, incluindo o da comunicação social, assim como ao enaltecimento de Washington por não ter dado muita importância ao seu próprio papel com o intuito de não prejudicar os "indonésios moderados" que tinham chegado ao poder, o que abriu as portas do país para a exploração dos seus valiosos recursos.

Por volta de 1978, as operações indonésias em Timor-Leste estavam muito próximas de atingir os níveis do genocídio. O Presidente Carter acelerou a circulação de armas, recorrendo mesmo a Israel, cliente de Washington, para escapar às restrições do Congresso relativamente ao envio de aviões a jacto. A Grã-Bretanha entrou na corrida, tornando-se rapidamente no maior fornecedor de armas da Indonésia. A França juntou-se também, garantindo defender a Indonésia das críticas nos fóruns internacionais, fornecendo-a, ao mesmo tempo, com aeronaves militares e equipamento para a produção de armas. Conscientes da oportunidade, também outros tiraram partido do terror e das atrocidades cometidas em Timor-Leste.

Apesar da cobertura dos acontecimentos ser limitada e enganosa, os factos mais básicos podiam ser descobertos. Eram, no entanto, muito pouco interessantes para merecer a atenção das elites ocidentais, comparando com a tarefa muito mais urgente de professar o enorme choque provocado pelos crimes dos inimigos oficiais na Indochina do pós-guerra. Deslizes casuais na silenciosa cumplicidade com atrocidades terríveis chegaram, por vezes, a provocar uma reacção: o aborrecimento. Stanley Karnow, respeitável especialista em assuntos asiáticos e correspondente internacional, falou em nome de muitos quando informou uma publicação jornalística de renome que ele próprio ainda não tinha conseguido ler um dos poucos relatórios de imprensa existentes (o qual excluía o papel dos EUA, o que seria, obviamente, a informação mais importante). "Apenas ainda não tive tempo," explicou, "não teve nada a ver comigo." Aquilo que "tem a ver connosco" são os crimes dos outros, não os nossos, os quais poderíamos mitigar ou terminar com o simples retirar da nossa participação — uma característica bem comum na história intelectual.

O registo é austero e, por isso, suprimido quase na totalidade, não sendo um candidato provável às memórias históricas. Ensina realmente bastante sobre o *realismo* que orienta o planeamento político e a cultura intelectual da qual dependem os seus êxitos.

A supressão e a evasão não se devem à distância de Timor-Leste; desculpa, aliás, grotesca em qualquer dos casos. A cobertura dos acontecimentos era substancial antes da invasão indonésia, reflectindo as preocupações de Washington relativamente à queda do fascismo português e o destino das suas posses imperiais. Assim que a Indonésia resolveu o problema através da invasão e massacres, a atenção diminuiu, chegando a atingir virtualmente o valor zero em 1978, altura em que as atrocidades e o número de mortos atingiam os seus valores mais altos. Em África, qualquer possibilidade de independência significativa para as ex-colónias portuguesas era ameaçada pelas intervenções da África do Sul, apoiadas pela dupla EUA/Reino Unido, que custaram a vida a um milhão e meio de pessoas e causaram estragos de sessenta mil milhões de dólares, e isto só durante os anos da "acção de construção" reaganiana, de acordo com os dados de uma investigação efectuada por um Grupo de Trabalho Inter-Agências da ONU. No sudeste asiático a Indonésia comportou-se de igual modo. Em ambos os casos a cobertura jornalística e o interesse das elites abrandava quando o número de atrocidades aumentava e a ameaça de independência se dissipava.

No caso de Timor-Leste, o objectivo da auto-determinação apoiado pelas Nações Unidas (e mais tarde pelo Tribunal Internacional de Justiça) parecia irremediavelmente inatingível tendo em conta a constelação de forças: um povo minúsculo e esquecido, que se confrontava com a impiedosa violência indonésia totalmente apoiada pela super-potência reinante e os seus aliados, e com meios de atingir o público ocidental barrado pela auto-censura, com a excepção dos casos da Austrália e Portugal, onde havia informação abundante e oposição popular activa, apesar dos esforços do governo australiano para esconder a parte feia da história. Ben Kiernan, especialista australiano em assuntos do sudeste asiático, actualmente a leccionar na Universidade de Yale, relata o seguinte:

> Nas montanhas escarpadas, com um pequeno rádio montado no dorso de um burro, as guerrilhas pró-independência da Fretilin transmitiam escassas notícias do território fechado. Para apaziguar Jacarta, o governo australiano tentou bloquear as transmissões através do mar de Arafura. A polícia confiscou o transreceptor, que era operado por um timorense em Darwin. Um grupo constituído por esquerdistas australianos, trabalhadores das docas, timorenses e aborígenes montaram um transreceptor móvel. Durante três anos foram-se deslocando pelas margens do interior australiano, comunicando com a resistência e tornando pública a tragédia. A Polícia Federal fez uma busca no Território do Norte mas foram incapazes de acabar com a ligação de rádio.

Também noutros locais, a informação começou lentamente a passar, pelo menos para algumas partes do público, e os protestos, que entretanto também tinham começado, ganharam alguma projecção. No entanto, apesar do trabalho de activistas dedicados, jovens na sua maioria e tão poucos que poderiam ser facilmente listados, o impacto foi demasiado leve para dissuadir a participação numa outra "grande catástrofe," esta ainda pior do que aquela pela qual o Japão tinha sido responsável. O Japão, aliás, honrava as suas dívidas de forma generosa, ao fornecer o crucial apoio diplomático e económico aos agressores indonésios.

Em 1979, a Austrália torna-se a única potência ocidental a conceder o reconhecimento de direito da anexação de Timor-Leste pela Indonésia em 1976. Um factor crucial foi, presumivelmente, o interesse do petróleo, enfatizado por Woolcott na véspera da invasão. Em 1989 foi assinado um tratado entre a Austrália e a Indonésia para roubar o petróleo de Timor-Leste, posto em prática imediatamente a seguir ao massacre de Díli, onde foram mortos centenas de timorenses. Como amargamente noticiou a imprensa australiana, o tratado foi o primeiro instrumento internacional que reconheceu oficialmente os direitos da Indonésia na "Província Indonésia de Timor-Leste," não oferecendo nada aos seus habitantes.

O massacre de Díli não foi fácil de suprimir. Foi filmado por um fotojornalista britânico e transmitido na Grã-Bretanha. Além disso, dois jornalistas americanos, Alan Nairn e Amy Goodman, quase foram mortos. Não é coisa que se faça, tendo originado, assim, aquilo que já é costume quando se cometem erros deste tipo: uma comissão de investigação que aplicou sentenças leves a funcionários de estatuto inferior, absolvendo os responsáveis. Também originou restrições do Congresso relativamente à venda de armas americanas e ao treino de oficiais militares indonésios, às quais Clinton se conseguiu evadir através de algumas manobras intricadas que irritaram o Congresso mas que não suscitaram outras reacções.

Por essa altura, desenvolvera-se em alguns países grupos substanciais de solidariedade, que começavam a ter a sua influência; outra razão para o massacre de Díli não poder ser facilmente ignorado. Foi a este respeito que o maravilhoso trabalho de fotografia de Elaine Briere, para não falar do seu activismo intenso, teve efeitos de tão grande alcance. Nada nos confrontou com a dimensão humana destas tragédias terríveis de forma mais eficaz e poderosa. É uma contribuição duradoura e não menos importante perante as outras tarefas, todas de grande seriedade, que se seguiriam.

Apesar destes desenvolvimentos, todos eles bem-vindos, o sistema não se alterou. Enquanto supervisionava o processo contínuo da obliteração de Timor-Leste e compilava um dos piores registos de direitos humanos dos finais do século vinte na própria Indonésia, o Presidente Suharto continuava "um dos nossos," como foi descrito pela administração Clinton em 1995, quando Suharto foi convidado a visitar Washington. Também outros louvaram o seu desígnio "benigno," "moderação" e bom trabalho na generalidade. Assim continuaram as coisas até 1998, quando Suharto cometeu alguns crimes a sério: começou a arrastar a execução das ordens rígidas do FMI e visivelmente a perder o controlo a favor de forças populares pró-democráticas. Em Maio, a Ministra dos Negócios Estrangeiros norte-americana, Madeleine Albright, informa-o de que era já tempo para "uma transição democrática." Poucas horas mais tarde, Suharto transfere a autoridade formal para B. J. Habibie, o vice-presidente escolhido por ele. Os eventos não tiveram, obviamente, uma simples relação causa-efeito, mas simbolizam as relações que vigoravam, como se viria a demonstrar, de forma bem mais dramática, em meados de Setembro de 1999.

Para surpresa de todos, Habibie autorizou um referendo. As Forças Armadas (ABRI, actualmente TNI) tinham, no entanto, outras ideias. Nos finais de 1998, os serviços secretos australianos — e, com certeza, os serviços secretos americanos e britânicos — estavam bem cientes de que novas forças indonésias estavam a desembarcar, incluindo unidades de comando do Kopassus treinadas nos EUA, célebres pela sua brutalidade, e que as mesmas estavam a organizar forças paramilitares locais ("milícias") a quem iriam, segundo as palavras do especialista dos serviços secretos australianos Desmond Ball, "subcontratar" a violência — uma técnica clássica para procurar obter "meios plausíveis" para negar atrocidades. O objectivo era assegurar que o resultado de um possível referendo fosse "o certo."

Por volta do início de 1999 estavam em curso vários massacres e os altos oficias das TNI deixavam claro que pior iria acontecer se a intimidação pelo terror não fosse suficiente. Os EUA e a Grã-Bretanha mantinham o seu apoio; nos EUA — um silêncio virtual. A imprensa nem sequer referiu as resoluções unânimes do Senado de Junho de 1999, que apelavam à Administração Clinton que "intensificasse os seus esforços" — os quais eram indetectáveis — "para persuadir o Governo e as Forças Armadas da Indonésia" a acabar com as milícias. Como resposta, o Ministério dos Negócios Estrangeiros norte-americano repetiu a doutrina oficial — "as Forças Armadas indonésias são responsáveis por ter as milícias sob controlo" — as mesmas milícias que organizavam e chefiavam, facto de que os serviços secretos do Ministério dos Negócios Estrangeiros estavam certamente a par; bastaria ler a imprensa estrangeira, além de que estavam a ser utilizados meios de vigilância do mais alto-nível. Washington não tinha, no entanto, a responsabilidade de reduzir a sua participação nas contínuas atrocidades das TNI. O número de mortos definia-se em milhares antes do referendo de 30 de Agosto, de acordo com fontes da Igreja e John Taylor, na sua reconhecida história da luta timorense pela independência.

Cinco dias antes do referendo, o Pentágono terminou "um treino para os EUA e a Indonésia direccionado para actividades de ajuda humanitária e de emergência." O anúncio oficial foi feito ao mesmo tempo que se iniciava o episódio seguinte do terror em massa, mas não causou qualquer vergonha nem levantou nenhuma reacção, uma vez que (como de costume) não foi noticiado.

A 30 de Agosto, num acto de coragem, perante o qual falham as palavras, os timorenses votaram massivamente a favor da independência. As TNI levaram imediatamente a cabo os seus planos para a destruição virtual do território. Os EUA observaram em silêncio. No dia 8 de Setembro, bastante depois da maior parte do país ter sido destruída e a população brutalmente expulsa, o Ministro da Defesa, William Cohen, repetiu a explicação oficial relativa à incapacidade dos EUA de acabar com os crimes em que continuavam a participar: a segurança interna de Timor-Leste "é da responsabilidade do Governo da Indonésia e nós não queremos retirar-lhe essa responsabilidade." Continuava a prevalecer o "realismo kissingeriano." Tal como explicou um alto diplomata em Jacarta no mesmo dia, "importa a Indonésia, Timor-Leste não." "Timor-Leste é uma carta fora do baralho neste jogo," em retórica oficial.

Sob pressão interna e internacional intensa, os cálculos pragmáticos mudaram — um alto oficial do governo concluiu: "Há uma carta muito boa chamada Austrália e é com ela que temos que jogar." Quando Clinton informou os Generais de que o jogo tinha chegado ao fim, retiraram-se rapidamente, permitindo que uma força de imposição de paz (INTERFET) da ONU liderada pela Austrália entrasse no território sem oposição. Os comandantes das TNI declararam até ao último minuto, com muita persuasão, que nunca tal iriam fazer. Mais uma vez aprendemos uma lição muito clara sobre onde fica o poder e sobre o que teria sido necessário para acabar com os horrores de um quarto de século, os quais em nenhum momento conheceram qualquer intervenção — apenas o afastamento de participação crucial. Essa lição é também inaceitável e, por isso, suprimida. O que aconteceu realmente foi que nós fechámos os olhos e não interviemos para tentar acabar com as atrocidades, e quando finalmente demos por elas, levámos a cabo um nobre exercício de "intervenção humanitária."

Clinton apresentou a versão aprovada nas suas próprias palavras: "Não me parece que a América nem nenhum dos outros países estivesse suficientemente sensível ao princípio... nem durante muito tempo antes de 1999, recuando até aos anos setenta, até ao sofrimento do povo de Timor-Leste," mas "quando se me tornou óbvio o que se estava realmente a passar... tentei certificar-me de que estávamos com a política certa." O discernimento surgiu algures entre o dia oito e onze de Setembro de 1999, quando Washington se apercebeu da carta no baralho juntamente com outras pressões: uma carta que importava, e que não era o povo de Timor-Leste. Os "EUA nunca tentaram sancionar ou apoiar a opressão em Timor-Leste" — isto enquanto forneciam apoio militar e diplomático crucial para essa "opressão," continuando a fazê-lo até ao último paroxismo da fúria. Mas, como disse Clinton, com boas razões para o fazer, não devemos "olhar para trás."

A Grã-Bretanha, sendo de compreensão um pouco lenta, continuou a enviar aviões *Hawk* para a Indonésia depois da INTERFET estar no terreno há vários dias, duas semanas depois da União Europeia ter decretado um embargo e duas semanas depois da Força Aérea Indonésia ter alinhado os *Hawks* britânicos "preparando-se para qualquer intromissão aérea vinda do estrangeiro na parte este do território indonésio, especialmente em Timor-Leste." Robin Cook, Ministro dos Negócios Estrangeiros, autor da "política externa ética" do Partido Trabalhista, justificou-se apoiando-se no facto do governo "ter o dever de manter uma indústria de defesa forte, a qual representa uma parte estratégica da nossa base industrial," tal como nos EUA.

A próxima "responsabilidade" era ignorar o destino amargo dos refugiados deslocados para o Timor Ocidental indonésio e os apelos dos timorenses, da ONU, e das forças de imposição de paz no sentido de serem enviados investigadores para fazerem o estudo dos acontecimentos. O contraste com o Kosovo era ao mesmo tempo particularmente notável. Num instante, o Kosovo ficou inundado de investigadores forenses para se tentar encontrar provas de crimes sérvios cometidos após o bombardeamento da OTAN, segundo a lógica curiosa, que passa sem se questionar, que tais crimes fornecem a justificação para o ataque, do qual eles foram a consequência antecipada. Clinton também pediu que o já limitado apoio à INTERFET fosse reduzido. Um Tribunal Internacional é inadmissível, mais uma vez ao contrário do Kosovo, onde Milosevic é acusado durante o período dos bombardeamentos, segundo os relatórios dos serviços secretos da dupla EUA/Reino Unido sobre os seus crimes, cometidos depois do início dos bombardeamentos (praticamente sem excepções).

Não é difícil compreender as razões para esta reacção diferencial. Os crimes só são crimes quando podem ser atribuídos a algum inimigo oficial. Caso contrário, são, no máximo, erros de omissão, falhas compreensíveis num nobre cadastro.

A vitória do povo de Timor-Leste é uma grande façanha. É difícil apontar um precedente histórico. Deveria estimular a humildade e a dedicação. Os timorenses têm tarefas gigantescas à sua frente: os problemas imediatos de sobrevivência e de encontrar uma maneira de viver uns com os outros e com o seu vizinho poderoso e ameaçador, sempre na sombra das grandes potências.

Nós também temos tarefas a cumprir, mas bem mais fáceis. A primeira é encarar o passado com honestidade, atribuir as responsabilidades a quem as deve, não poupando ninguém, nem nos importando se o dedo for apontado a pouca distância de casa. Uma tarefa mais urgente é o pagamento dos enormes prejuízos de guerra como uma forma de tentar compensar o que fizemos, pelo menos em alguma medida.

Além disso, dever-nos-íamos inspirar no triunfo dos timorenses para irmos mais além: olhar mais de perto para as origens de uma "posição pragmática em detrimento de uma posição de princípios; é disso afinal que se trata o interesse nacional e a política externa," segundo os "principais arquitectos" da política. E olhar também para as consequências que saltam à vista em muitas partes do mundo. Deveríamos, decididamente, mais do que tudo, "olhar para trás," rejeitando as insistências de Clinton, e daí aprender a "olhar para a frente" e agir de modo a não provocar novas tragédias a pessoas que sofrem, mas antes promover e alimentar a esperança delas num mundo melhor.

© 2002 Noam Chomsky. Artigo a publicar no livro de Elaine Brier, *East Timor: Bitter Paradise.* Toronto: Between the Lines, 2003. URL: www.btlbooks.com

Noam Chomsky, linguista norte-americano, é professor do Massachusetts Institute of Technology (MIT) desde 1954. De família judaica de origem russa, depois de se dedicar ao estudo do hebreu, abriu um novo paradigma na história da Linguística ao chamar a atenção para o aspecto da "criatividade" da linguagem, formulando o que chamou "gramática generativa transformacional." Considera, na linha da filosofia racionalista, as estruturas linguísticas como universais inatos. Conhecido no mundo inteiro pelo seu activismo político, Chomsky escreveu mais de trinta livros sobre a política norte-americana de "intervencionismo" no mundo em desenvolvimento e o papel dos grandes media na propaganda desta política. É também um velho "guerreiro" da causa de Timor-Leste; acompanhou e denunciou, desde a primeira hora, o envolvimento directo dos Estados Unidos e o seu apoio ao Governo de Suharto. Em 1979 escreveu *A Guerra Escondida em Timor-Leste*, uma viagem impiedosa pela política dos EUA face a Jacarta desde o fim da II Guerra Mundial. E-mail: chomsky@mit.edu

Rita Alves é finalista do curso de Línguas e Literaturas Modernas, variante Estudos Ingleses e Alemães—Ramo de Tradução (Inglês-Português-Inglês) na Faculdade de Letras da Universidade do Porto. Em 2000/2001 fez parte de um programa de intercâmbio universitário na Universidade de Mainz (FASK Germersheim), Alemanha, onde continuou a estudar a língua e cultura alemãs. Estagiou como tradutora no Center for Portuguese Studies and Culture na Universidade de Massachusetts Dartmouth, nos Estados Unidos no Outono de 2002. E-mail: rcalves@sapo.pt

Literaturas Africanas de Expressão Portuguesa — Uma História em Curso

Ana Mafalda Leite

A disciplina anual de *Literaturas Africanas de Expressão Portuguesa* foi tornada disciplina curricular obrigatória, apesar de já existir como opção na Faculdade de Letras de Lisboa e nas Faculdades de Letras portuguesas desde a Reforma dos Cursos de Línguas e Literaturas Modernas oficializada pelo decreto nº53/78.

Por seu turno, as disciplinas de *Literaturas Africanas de Expressão Portuguesa I* (anual) e *II* (semestral) foram contempladas no curriculum da Licenciatura em Línguas e Literaturas Modernas, variante de Estudos Portugueses, como disciplinas obrigatórias—e como opção para os outros cursos de L.L.M., por decreto do Governo nº75/84 de 27 de Novembro.

A primeira Universidade a introduzir a leccionação desta disciplina foi a de Lisboa tendo Manuel Ferreira inaugurado na Faculdade de Letras o ensino desta área literária em 1975. Posteriormente, a cadeira foi introduzida por Salvato Trigo na Universidade do Porto no ano lectivo de 1976-77. Mário António F. de Oliveira iniciou pouco depois a docência da disciplina na Universidade Nova de Lisboa. Por seu turno, a Universidade de Coimbra foi o quarto estabelecimento de ensino universitário a instituir a disciplina em 1980-81.[1]

Coube-nos acompanhar de perto o crescimento gradual de uma cadeira, primitivamente opcional, com média de oito a quinze alunos, até ao momento de instituição da sua obrigatoriedade curricular em Estudos Portugueses contemplando, em conjunto com a Literatura Brasileira,[2] novas áreas literárias da língua portuguesa.

Não deixa de ser importante fazer esta análise retrospectiva, quando hoje leccionamos duas turmas de *Literaturas Africanas de Expressão Portuguesa I*, com média de quarenta estudantes em cada uma delas. No entanto, o progressivo crescimento desta área curricular não trouxe ainda todas as modificações e condições necessárias, por motivos que mais adiante vamos passar a expôr, para uma prática de ensino que possibilite verdadeiramente colocar em paralelo a sua prática com a de uma outra literatura, com maior longevidade e tradição de ensino como, por exemplo, a portuguesa ou a francesa.

Saliente-se que a expressão "*literaturas emergentes*"[3] ganha todo o sentido neste quadro prospectivo de instituição curricular e prática docente se tomarmos em linha de conta que até 1974—passaram, entretanto, vinte e quatro anos—esta área era integrada na "literatura ultramarina" e amalgamava produções literárias, oriundas das então diversas colónias portuguesas. O primeiro prémio atribuído a um autor africano de língua portuguesa - ao angolano Luandino Vieira com a sua obra *Luuanda* em 1964—, foi da iniciativa de uma instituição literária portuguesa, a Sociedade Portuguesa de Autores.

Quando em 1975, na Universidade Eduardo Mondlane em Moçambique, - que então frequentava como estudante do segundo ano—, se iniciou a revisão curricular, os estudos críticos da literatura moçambicana e o conhecimento desta literatura, enquanto tal, estavam praticamente no seu início.[4]

Significa então que a prática docente da nossa área se iniciou quase em simultâneo ao próprio processo de reflexão crítica e teórica sobre as cinco novas literaturas, ligadas a Portugal pela história da colonização portuguesa e por muitos outros laços culturais e humanos resultantes desse facto. Os primeiros elementos de trabalho para o ensino destas literaturas, ou seja, grande parte dos textos literários e das obras mais significativas, começam, também, apenas a partir desse momento, a ser editados.

Há por assim dizer uma situação de quase "novidade" absoluta e de criação progressiva, tanto no campo editorial como no do ensino, da instrumentação necessária—a bibliografia activa[5] e a bibliografia passiva—para o conhecimento, estudo e ensino das cinco novas literaturas africanas de expressão portuguesa. Semelhante situação, por paradoxal que possa parecer, é, no entanto, aquela que acompanhámos e praticámos desde o início da nossa actividade docente.

Não deixa de ser relevante, por exemplo, salientar alguma interferência ideológica e política nos primeiros anos de ensino destas matérias. E também uma certa indefinição sobre o estatuto literário ou não literário de certas obras, fruto de circunstancialismos históricos, como é o caso , por exemplo, da produção escrita e designada por "literatura de combate." A necessidade e a urgência em criar e instituir o "corpus" literário destas novas literaturas, de o institucionalizar, levou, naturalmente, durante os primeiros anos, a uma certa indefinição do "literário" no âmbito destas disciplinas.[6]

É no entanto de um esforço concertado entre a prática editorial , a prática docente e a investigação universitária—que privilegia o estudo das obras enquanto matéria literária, situando-as na rede comparada das literaturas de língua portuguesa e africanas em outras línguas—que vão surgir alguns dos elementos bibliográficos fundamentais para o actual ensino das literaturas africanas.

Coube-nos a honra e a dificuldade, em conjunto com outros colegas,[7] de fazermos as primeiras dissertações, as pesquisas, de leccionarmos e participarmos em projectos editoriais, desenvolvendo simultaneamente actividade crítica. Conscientes de que da seriedade do nosso trabalho resultaria uma parte da seriedade e da dignificação de uma área de estudos literários, a das literaturas africanas de língua portuguesa.

Questões relativas ao ensino da disciplina de Literaturas Africanas de Expressão Portuguesa

Os países africanos de expressão portuguesa não têm em Portugal as suas literaturas contempladas nos currículos obrigatórios do Ensino Secundário. Tal facto não confere ao aluno, que se matricula em Línguas e Literaturas Modernas, a possibilidade de um conhecimento e informação básicos, que entrem num quadro de uma preparação geral mais ou menos consolidada, capaz de criar um horizonte de apetência e compreensão significativos.

A situação mais ou menos generalizada do aluno que se matricula no segundo ano do Curso de Estudos Portugueses na cadeira de *Literaturas Africanas de Expressão Portuguesa I* é a de um relativo desconhecimento não só das literaturas africanas, como da realidade africana em geral. A primeira dificuldade começa em situar geograficamente os países; a segunda em relembrar, ou saber, com precisão, a conexão histórica de Portugal com aqueles países, nomeadamente o conhecimento da história da colonização, os momentos mais decisivos que tiveram lugar no século passado com a ocupação territorial, ou os principais acontecimentos que levaram ao início da guerra colonial e da luta armada de libertação. Esta falta de elementos, relativa a uma cronologia histórica recente, torna-se patente em relação a outras informações sobre a África pré-colonial.

Tendo em conta esta situação que tende a agravar-se no decorrer dos anos, porque as gerações mais novas perderam o contacto[8] que, antes, possuíam através de familiares ou da experiência de amigos que tinham estado em

África, torna-se necessário ao docente fazer uma introdução a vários aspectos relativos à cultura e história africanas, de modo a poder contextualizar as especificidades destas áreas literárias e de modo a permitir a leitura analítica de heranças e tradições culturais, referências históricas, que os textos literários africanos trazem em si inscritas.

Por outro lado, a designação curricular da disciplina *Literaturas Africanas de Expressão Portuguesa*—que tem sido questionada pelo uso do termo "expressão"[9]—, abrange, numa indiferenciada totalidade, cinco diferentes literaturas que, apesar de um elo comum de colonização histórica, têm percursos individualizados, a maioria delas desde meados do século XIX.

A constatação deste facto permite salientar que o estudo rigoroso de três destas literaturas, as mais significativas em produção literária e antiguidade, como é o caso da Literatura Angolana, da Literatura Caboverdiana e da Literatura Moçambicana, exigiria a sua autonomização disciplinar. Jacinto do Prado Coelho em *A Originalidade da Literatura Portuguesa* afirma que "A vinculação da literatura à nacionalidade é que nos obriga a reconhecer como sistemas autónomos, apesar de servidos pela mesma língua, literaturas como a portuguesa, a brasileira, a angolana, a moçambicana, a caboverdiana, e a procurar nos temas, nas formas, no estilo de cada uma delas, as marcas distintivas duma experiência colectiva única."[10]

Curricularmente isso já acontece nas Universidades ou instituições superiores dos países africanos de língua portuguesa, como é o caso da Universidade Eduardo Mondlane ou da Universidade Pedagógica,[11] em Moçambique, onde é oferecida a disciplina de *Literatura Moçambicana*, e ainda no Instituto Superior de Educação da Praia, em Cabo Verde, onde a *Literatura Caboverdiana* funciona como disciplina curricular, independentemente da cadeira de *Literaturas Africanas de Expressão Portuguesa.*

O natural comentário que suscitam estas observações é o de que tal facto acontece porque no país de origem a literatura nacional forçosamente teria de constituir objecto de pesquisa e de ensino individualizados. Todavia, parece-nos argumento insuficiente para continuar a legitimar a existência de uma cadeira com uma designação—e um *corpus*—ainda marcados, quer queiramos quer não, pelo signo da colonialidade e pela tradição imperial.[12]

Semelhante reflexão não tem qualquer intuito anti-institucional ou polémico. Resulta da nossa prática de ensino ao longo destes últimos dez anos de uma disciplina que comporta uma complexidade de informação relativa a diferentes áreas do saber —antropologia, etnologia, história, literatura oral, teoria literária, literatura comparada, literaturas africanas em outras línguas— ao mesmo tempo que acumula, num mesmo tronco comum, cinco diferentes literaturas com processos individualizantes muito marcados.[13] Nomeadamente, juntam-se nas *Literaturas Africanas de Expressão Portuguesa* três literaturas continentais (a angolana, a guineense e a moçambicana) a par de duas insulares (a caboverdiana e a santomense) cujas origens e desenvolvimento, por razões de ordem histórica e cultural, são distintas e específicas.

Textos fundamentais não editados em livro e ausência de bibliografias sistematizadas

Outro dos aspectos que se torna problemático na docência da disciplina de *Literaturas Africanas de Expressão Portuguesa* tem a ver com o a dificuldade de acesso aos materiais necessários para a sua leccionação, ou seja, mais concretamente, em conseguir os textos literários fundamentais para o ensino.

Se por um lado uma das justificações que promove o ensino conjunto destas Literaturas passa pelo vínculo comum à colonização, à praxis colonial e ao modo de exercício dessa praxis, por outro é esse mesmo passado que de certo modo explica a ausência editorial destas cinco literaturas. É facto admitido que o colonialismo não favoreceu ou incrementou o desenvolvimento editorial das literaturas africanas. Se, por um lado, o próprio sistema teve necessidade de implantar nas então colónias, em meados do século passado, a imprensa e, mais tardiamente, o ensino liceal[14] e quase apenas no fim da época colonial, o ensino universitário, factores que contribuiriam para o desenvolvimento das literaturas africanas, por outro, a acção da censura, que ganha uma latitude extremada em especial a partir da década de sessenta—altura em que começa a guerra colonial—, contribui exactamente para o efeito inverso.

A situação editorial em Portugal das literaturas africanas de expressão portuguesa até 1974, ano da revolução portuguesa, resume-se praticamente a uma actividade quase clandestina e de difícil acesso no mercado editorial ao leitor interessado. Para além das publicações da Casa dos Estudantes do Império, em edições limitadas e quase familiares, de antologias e de algumas obras de autores também promovidas pela C.E.I., o panorama editorial não seria realmente aliciante para quem quisesse conhecer ou investigar estas áreas literárias. Alfredo Margarido que teve papel importante neste processo editorial da C.E.I publicou vários ensaios e artigos que, no entanto, só vieram a ser editados em livro já em 1980[15].

Em relação à bibliografia passiva, os dois volumes de Hernani Cidade, *A Literatura Portuguesa e a Expansão Ultramarina*,[16] publicados em 1963 e

1964, o primeiro dedicado aos séculos XV e XVI e o segundo aos séculos XVII e XVIII, não chegam sequer a tocar no assunto, dada a limitação cronológica por um lado, e por outro os objectivos do trabalho, relacionados em especial com a literatura portuguesa.

Outra obra, de cariz diferente, da autoria de Amândio César, *Parágrafos de Literatura Ultramarina*, publicada em 1967, é uma obra marcada politicamente pela época, que reúne artigos vários, em registo mais ou menos jornalístico, e com intuitos críticos apologéticos. Também de Amândio César são as antologias do conto ultramarino publicadas em 1969.[17] O enquadramento ideológico da época não permitiu a realização de trabalhos consequentes na área da historiografia, da ensaística e da crítica literárias.[18]

Os trabalhos mais interessantes, publicados em grande parte pela Agência Geral das Colónias, ou em edições ligadas à Igreja, situam-se no domínio da literatura oral e dos estudos antropológicos, ou em outras áreas que não têm a ver com este nosso trabalho. O artigo "Ultramar na Literatura Portuguesa," incluído no *Dicionário de Literatura* — dirigido por Jacinto do Prado Coelho[19]—com dois artigos assinados por José Osório de Oliveira e João Pedro de Andrade, inclui uma bibliografia de praticamente todas as obras editadas em Portugal e nas então colónias sobre a literatura designada nessa época por "ultramarina" e tem a utilidade de nos mostrar a incipiência crítica e ensaística sobre as obras dos autores africanos e, ao mesmo tempo, a escassez editorial de obras literárias.

Após as independências e no pós 25 de Abril houve um esforço significativo no sentido de dar a conhecer, via edição, estas novas literaturas. A prática mais comum e quase imediata foi a edição de antologias, tendo Manuel Ferreira desempenhado um papel importante neste campo ao promover a edição dos *Caliban*.[2] Mário Pinto de Andrade por seu turno fez publicar em 1975 as Antologias Temáticas de poesia africana de expressão portuguesa.[21]

Em 1977, as Edições 70 promovem a edição da tese de doutoramento de Russell Hamilton que é a primeira tentativa historiográfica literária acerca das literaturas africanas; é essa mesma editora que, com a participação da União dos Escritores Angolanos—de que era Presidente na altura José Luandino Vieira—, faz a edição de uma parte significativa das obras literárias de autores angolanos, permitindo a reedição de obras do século XIX como, por exemplo, *Espontaneidades da Minha Alma* de José da Silva Maia Ferreira e *Nga Mutúri* de Alfredo Troni, com estudos introdutórios de especialistas como Gerald Moser e Mário António de Oliveira. No início da década de oitenta é também criada uma colecção de Autores Moçambicanos pelas Edições 70, mas que não chega a ultrapassar os dez títulos.

Manuel Ferreira funda, entretanto, uma editora, África Editora, mais tarde ALAC, que promove a publicação de uma revista, *África*—dedicada ao estudo das literaturas africanas—e de livros de alguns autores africanos, bem como uma colecção denominada "Para a História das Literaturas Africanas de Expressão Portuguesa." Devido em parte à sua prática docente universitária Manuel Ferreira estava consciente da urgente necessidade de material bibliográfico, nomeadamente da edição e da reedição de obras literárias, fundamentais para serem incluídas nas bibliografias dos programas e poderem ser lidos os textos, a matéria prima, tal como da edição de obras ensaísticas que pudessem acompanhar o estudo das obras literárias. É na sequência destas preocupações que surge, em 1983, a primeira Bibliografia (bilingue, em português e inglês) das Literaturas Africanas de Expressão Portuguesa, organizada em conjunto por Manuel Ferreira e Gerald Moser.[22]

A primeira tese de doutoramento em *Literaturas Africanas de Expressão Portuguesa* é apresentada na Faculdade de Letras do Porto em 1980, sobre a obra de Luandino Vieira, por Salvato Trigo, e este trabalho pioneiro, teoricamente fundamentado e abrindo pistas bibliográficas para diversificadas áreas de estudos africanos (oratura, linguística, antropologia, história), inaugura uma nova fase de reflexão sobre as literaturas africanas.

Nesse ano inicia-se na Faculdade de Letras de Lisboa o primeiro Mestrado em "Literaturas Brasileira e Africanas de Língua Portuguesa," organizado por Fernando Cristóvão e Manuel Ferreira—que eu frequentei como aluna—e surgem a partir de 1984 as primeiras teses de Mestrado na área,[23] que irão constituir alguns dos alicerces teóricos e bases de reflexão mais aprofundada sobre as literaturas nacionais. É também no decorrer da década de oitenta que são organizados alguns dos colóquios internacionais mais significativos sobre a área de Literaturas Africanas de Expressão Portuguesa e as Actas resultantes vieram a tornar-se documentos bibliográficos indispensáveis.[24]

Apesar de nos últimos anos haver uma maior diversificação na edição das obras de autores africanos, muito do material necessário continua por editar e algumas das antologias e estudos de enquadramento destas literaturas esgotaram e não voltaram a ser reeditadas.[25] Semelhante situação é limitativa para quem, como nós, necessita de material bibliográfico abrangente para leccionar uma cadeira como a de *Literaturas Africanas de Expressão Portuguesa.*

Dado o seu carácter introdutório, a disciplina que visa abranger as literaturas africanas desde o seu nascimento até à fase das independências e ainda fazer uma amostragem dos novos rumos das literaturas nacionais. Por tal motivo tem de recorrer a diversificada utilização de obras literárias e de suporte teórico bibliográfico e, muitas dessas obras não existem no mercado, algumas nunca chegaram a ser sequer editadas, como é o caso da poesia de Rui de Noronha,[26] da poesia de Noémia de Sousa em Moçambique, dos textos de Pedro Cardoso ou de outros escritores caboverdianos do século XIX, e de diversos escritores angolanos do século passado.

Ausência de Histórias das Literaturas Nacionais

> "L'histoire de la littérature c'est un objet essentiellement scolaire, qui n'éxiste précisément que par son enseignement"(R. Barthes) [27]

Roland Barthes dá uma resposta peremptória à questão sobre as razões da escrita e da existência das histórias da literatura. São obras que servem o ensino e a história literária, e antes do mais um utensílio de ensino, um meio de transmissão de conhecimentos que tem utilidade pedagógica.[28]

Os sistemas de ensino são uma das instâncias importantes na validação institucional da literatura. A escolaridade obrigatória criou expectativas de uma integração cultural, em que a leitura supostamente deve ocupar lugar de destaque. A essa escolaridade é inerente uma preocupação com o ensino da língua, que se apoia com frequência na literatura, na medida em que nela procura textos que se consideram como linguisticamente exemplares e também representativos de uma identidade cultural que se pretende apurar.

Esta questão prende-se com uma outra que é a do "cânone." Em termos genéricos o cânone pode definir-se como " elenco de autores e obras incluídos em cursos básicos e cursos de literaturas, por se acreditar que representam o legado cultural de um país."[29] Nesta medida, os programas escolares e universitários são documentos com força normativa e testemunhos de uma consciência cultural e nacional que procura afirmar-se como legítima.[30]

A este respeito afirma Jacques Dubois: "*On dit que la littérature était ce qui s'enseignait. Disons tout au moins qu'elle est ce qui s'enseigne comme littérature. C'est l'école qui contribue le plus fortement à intégrer les pratiques littéraires dans un ensemble de normes. A cet égard, elle fait un peu plus que conserver et que célébrer les oeuvres du passé, car elle les introduit dans la logique d'un système qui projette nécessairement ses principes et ses catégories sur les productions du présent* (...)."[31]

As histórias literárias, as antologias, os manuais de ensino da literatura, os livros de ensaio literário e de divulgação crítica, como revistas de especialidade, são elementos fundamentais que estabelecem a continuidade e a herança de uma tradição. Também a formação de ordem pedagógica é reprodutora de uma certa ordem social e cultural e contribui para promover a instituição da literatura e do cânone. O cânone permite também a formação do gosto literário, o seu apuramento, pluralização e naturalmente a sua questionação.

No caso do ensino das literaturas africanas de expressão portuguesa estas questões são ainda problemáticas. Nos países africanos de língua portuguesa, os manuais escolares passaram por várias fases de elaboração, e inclusivé de clara feição e comprometimento ideológicos, e estarão ainda longe, porventura, de poder oferecer bases seguras para o estabelecimento de um cânone. Por outro lado, não existe ainda a pesquisa e o suporte historiográfico literário necessários para uma selecção definitiva, ainda que a transitoriedade do material bibliográfico existente possa servir de solução temporária.

Com aproximadamente um século e meio de existência, as literaturas africanas de expressão portuguesa encontram-se, de certo modo, ainda numa fase de instituição. Faltam-nos as histórias das literaturas nacionais e grande parte da investigação necessária para a sua concretização, nomeadamente no que diz respeito ao século passado. Faltam-nos ainda as antologias actualizadas[32] e a edição de obras de autores, a sistematização e ordenação cronológica consequente, o enquadramento histórico simultâneo, de modo ao investigador poder entender uma evolução literária e ordenar os factores constituintes de uma periodologia.

Da bibliografia mais recente respeitante à área historiográfica há a salientar a publicação do manual de *Literaturas Africanas de Expressão Portuguesa* da autoria de Pires Laranjeira, com a colaboração restrita para os temas pontuais de Cabo Verde de Elsa Rodrigues dos Santos e para a Literatura Santomense de Inocência Mata. Apesar do esforço que este trabalho representa e da sua utilidade como apoio bibliográfico—uma vez que procura dar "uma visão panorâmica, nos capítulos introdutórios a cada país, de tipo cronológico, didáctico; de apresentação de aspectos gerais e particulares (história literária, escritores , obras, temas), nos capítulos que não analisam uma obra de leitura obrigatória" [33]—, não é ainda este o caminho para se ultrapassarem os vazios de investigação literária historiográfica. Com efeito, parece-nos que este trabalho de certo modo mantém a tradição "imperial" da abrangência de um conhecimento das cinco literaturas que, no momento actual, para a sua efectiva e capaz realização, necessita da colaboração de especialistas de várias áreas (história, literatura oral, antropologia), e nomeadamente de equipes de investigadores para cada uma das literaturas.

Clément Moisan na sua obra *Qu'est-ce que l'histoire littéraire?* explica-nos que "l'histoire littéraire est de plus en plus l'affaire des chercheurs (universitaires) qui sont des spécialistes de périodes de plus en plus restreintes dans le temps de l'histoire et des théoriciens appartenant à toutes sortes de disciplines littéraires et non littéraires."[34]

Também a publicação do livro *The Postcolonial Literature of Lusophone Africa*, outro elemento bibliográfico recentemente publicado,[35] vem apenas sistematizar a produção literária e a bibliografia produzida nas diferentes literaturas nacionais desde as independências até 1994.

O século XIX está ainda a ser campo de pesquisa e de investigação na Literatura Caboverdiana. Arnaldo França no seu artigo "Panorama da Literatura Caboverdiana[36] assinala uma diversidade de autores e obras que permitirão redefinir a periodologia e a prospecção da herança literária deste século, com o surgimento do movimento da "Claridade," em 1936. No caso da Literatura Moçambicana a situação é relativamente idêntica. Após pesquisa de Ilídio Rocha,[37] que anunciou e situou a existência do primeiro poeta moçambicano, e através de pistas dadas pelo historiador António Sopa, Manuel Ferreira publicou um importante trabalho de pesquisa em que trouxe novos dados bibliográficos sobre o escritor pioneiro Campos de Oliveira,[38] que viveu em meados do século passado em Moçambique. No intervalo que vai da sua existência até ao princípio deste século, as informações são inconclusas ainda não suficientemente documentadas. Embora se saiba que há material literário por desbravar, e pesquisa aturada a fazer, a fim de se repôr um enquadramento cronológico do surgimento desta literatura, ainda não foi realizada.[39]

A situação é apesar de tudo diferente no caso da Literatura Angolana, havendo mais material disponível, não só no campo editorial, como também na área ensaística—e saliente-se o papel fundamental da obra historiográfica de Mário António Fernandes de Oliveira[40]—, em Introduções e Roteiros da Literatura,[41] e ainda com a contribuição de importantes trabalhos vindos da área da História, nomeadamente da autoria de Carlos Pacheco,[42] que situam o surgimento da primeira obra literária publicada em Angola, *Espontaneidades da Minha Alma—Álbum dedicado às Senhoras Africanas*, de José da Silva Maia Ferreira

Outros ensaios da sua autoria como o artigo, "Leituras e Bibliotecas em Angola na primeira metade do século XIX"[43] permitem situar os elos entre o surgimento da literatura e os condicionalismos culturais da sociedade angolana da época, mas não estão ainda, no entanto, suficientemente delineados todos os percursos. Saliente-se a respeito do caso da história literária angolana, o artigo de Alberto de Carvalho "A propósito de uma Historiografia Angolana,"[44] em que se problematizam alguns dos trabalhos feitos neste domínio.

Para uma avaliação mais ou menos correcta das novas gerações literárias é fundamental a prospecção do passado e da herança recebida, aceite ou não, valorizada ou não. Como nos ensina Jacques Dubois: "*Il n'est pas de texte qui ne se compose en référence à une tradition et à une norme, reproduisant ainsi un grand Texte. De plus, le produit d'écriture ne prend sa réalité et son sens qu'à partir du moment où il est reçu, lu et parlé, même si c'est par un groupe restreint. Sous ces deux aspects déjà , la création cesse d'apparaître comme l'affaire d'un seul.*"[45]

A especificidade de cada uma das literaturas nacionais radica também nessa memória, por enquanto ainda só parcialmente visível, do século XIX. Por outro lado, o surgimento das literaturas africanas é em simultâneo momento de (in)definição e de partilha com a literatura do país colonizador; verificar as épocas em que as fronteiras ainda se tocam, ou a partilha simultânea de autores por duas literaturas,[46] ou ainda as relações aparentemente disjuntivas e ao mesmo tempo, em certos casos, mais fluidas, entre o desabrochar da ficção africana e o desenvolvimento da literatura colonial, são aspectos que é necessário desenvolver teoricamente e prospectar com a maior seriedade e rigor em cada uma das literaturas nacionais.

Notas

[1] A Universidade de Évora iniciou a actividade da cadeira no ano lectivo de 1988-89; a Universidade do Minho em 1990-91; a Universidade Católica de Braga em 1993-94; e a Universidade Católica de Lisboa em 1996-97.

[2] Fernando Cristóvão foi um dos professores que mais se empenhou pela proposta de revisão curricular de Estudos Portugueses, tendo em vista a revalorização da literatura brasileira, mas em simultâneo atento à necessidade de desenvolver os estudos literários africanos. Cf. "Seis sugestões para um intercâmbio a haver" in *II Congresso dos Escritores Portugueses* (Lisboa: Associação Portuguesa de Escritores, 1982) 175.

[3] Cf. Salvato Trigo, "A Emergência das Literaturas Africanas de Expressão Portuguesa e a Literatura Brasileira," in *Ensaios de Literatura Comparada Afro-Luso-Brasileira* (Lisboa: Vega, 1990).

[4] Algumas das publicações críticas mais significativas como, por exemplo, a publicação da revista *Caliban* teve lugar entre 1971 e 72, o volume *Poesia de Moçambique* (com ensaios sobre

a poesia de Rui Knopfli, Grabato Dias e José Craveirinha*)* e *A Crónica dos Anos da Peste* de Eugénio Lisboa foram publicados apenas em 1973; por seu turno a publicação de *Karingana Wa Karingana* de José Craveirinha, por exemplo, teve lugar apenas em 1974. A revisão curricular e a actualização dos programas da Faculdade de Letras da Universidade Eduardo Mondlane iniciou-se em 1974, mas apenas em 1978 a disciplina de *Literaturas Africanas* passa a fazer parte da licenciatura em Linguística.

[5] As antologias poéticas—reveladoras dos autores e fazendo uma amostragem dos seus textos—,acerca dos cinco países começam a ser editadas a partir de 1975.

[6] Leia-se a este respeito, e sobre a literatura moçambicana, o artigo de Luís Bernardo Honwana,

"Papel, lugar e função do escritor" in *Tempo*, 22-11-81: "O pronunciamento da poesia de circunstância, justificado pela sua carga de libertação, pela sua função catártica, enfim pelo seu interesse político, implicitou o retraimento da Literatura Outra, de tal modo que à independência não correspondeu, como seria de esperar, um ressurgimento literário. E é facto que a erupção poética que se verificou desde o Governo de Transição apresenta ine ludível uma componente de xenofobia que acrescentada à redefinição da nacionalidade de mitos escritores até há pouco tidos como moçambicanos, justifica um sentimento de suspeição em relação à literatura (...)."

[7] Manuel Ferreira introduziu o ensino das Literaturas Africanas na Universidade Portuguesa no pós 25 de Abril. Embora na prática tenha sido Mário António Fernandes de Oliveira que, tendo-se licenciado no antigo ISCSPU e tendo feito parte do núcleo de estudantes africanos desse Instituto, iniciou, o estudo destas literaturas, nomeadamente por via do ensaio. Salvato Trigo, no Porto, fez a primeira tese de doutoramento na área sobre a obra de Luandino Vieira e publicou vários ensaios importantes, nomeadmente sobre a literatura angolana. Na Universidade Eduardo Mondlane-Maputo, Maria de Lourdes Cortez inicia uma actividade importante na dinamização da Literatura Moçambicana; mais tarde Lourenço do Rosário, via Coimbra, realiza o doutoramento na área da Literatura Oral, e Fátima Mendonça pesquisa e publica o primeiro livro de estudos sobre a Literatura Moçambicana. Na Faculdade de Letras de Lisboa surge o primeiro núcleo significativo de investigadores e docentes da área: Alberto de Carvalho, Ana Mafalda Leite, Pires Laranjeira, Elsa Rodrigues dos Santos, Inocência Mata e Carlos Espírito Santo. No Brasil a área é introduzida pelos ensaios de Fernando Mourão na Universidade de S.Paulo e posteriormente pelos trabalhos de Maria Aparecida Santilli e de Benjamin Abdala Júnior. Saliente-se, também no Brasil, o papel fundamental desenvolvido pelo jornalista João Alves das Neves no jornal *O Estado de S.Paulo.* Nos Estados Unidos os estudos pioneiros de Gerald Moser e mais tarde de Russell Hamilton trouxeram importante reforço bibliográfico a esta área de estudos literários já no fim da década de sessenta, no entanto a tese de Hamilton só foi traduzida e actualizada em 1977.

[8] Com excepção evidentemente para os alunos africanos que frequentam a disciplina mas que são normalmente em número muito reduzido.

[9] Alfredo Margarido coloca à discussão esta designação em *As Literaturas das Nações Africanas de Língua Portuguesa (*Lisboa: A Regra do Jogo, 1980) 8-9. Ver também Manuel Ferreira, "Dependência e individalidade nas literaturas africanas de língua portuguesa," in *O Discurso no Percurso Africano I* (Lisboa: Plátano Editora, 1989) 29.

[10] Jacinto do Prado Coelho, *A Originalidade da Literatura Portuguesa* (Lisboa: Icalp, 1977) 12.

[11] Eu própria fui autora de um programa de Literatura Moçambicana para a docência que pratiquei da cadeira na Universidade Pedagógica em 1990. Soube, com alguma satisfação, o ano passado, que esse programa está na base da organização da cadeira.

[12] Lourenço do Rosário refere—a propósito da designação englobante de "Literaturas Africanas de Expressão Portuguesa" que aparece nos planos das licenciaturas das universidades

portuguesas—"o carácter aparentemente aleatório de como se constituía o eventual corpus dessas literaturas siamesas não permitia vislumbrar senão a sua vinculação umbilical à herança colonial do ex-império recém desaparecido fisicamente, mas permanecendo nas mentes dos cidadãos, testemunhando que a proposta de ruptura, se foi consumada, ao nível político, com a constituição de tantos estados soberanos, na literatura, os passos eram ainda dados conforme o ritmo do passado recente, em que vislumbramos a permanência de uma certa ideia de unidade cultural resultante de um mesmo passado histórico." in *Singularidades-Estudos Africanos* (Lisboa: Universidade Lusófona, 1997) 75.

13 Há porventura soluções para orientar a organização da disciplina de outra maneira, sendo necessário, no entanto, incluir sempre a parte relativa às questões culturais introdutórias. No Departamento de Estudos Portugueses do King's College, em Londres, por exemplo, é oferecida aos alunos uma solução interessante em termos curriculares pela possibilidade de, semestralmente, optarem por uma destas três literaturas nacionais, que vão sendo oferecidas alternadamente

14 Não está ainda realizada a investigação sistematizada acerca do papel do ensino nas então colónias portuguesas, embora haja bibliografia sobre assunto.

15 Alfredo Margarido, *Estudos sobre Literaturas das Nações Africanas de Língua Portuguesa* (Lisboa: A Regra do Jogo, 1980).

16 Hernani Cidade, *A Literatura Portuguesa e a Expansão Ultramarina, I e II* (Coimbra: Arménio Amado Editor, 1963 e 1964).

17 Saliente-se que a designação de "literatura ultramarina" abrangia as produções literárias de todos os territórios ultramarinos, incluindo Goa, Macau e Timor, e não apenas as então colónias africanas. Amândio César, *Contos Portugueses do Ultramar* 1º e 2º volumes (Porto: Portucalense Editora, 1969). Uma anterior antologia tinha sido publicada por Forjaz Trigueiros (2 vols.) em 1962-63. Amândio César publicou ainda os *Novos Parágrafos de Literatura Ultramarina.*

18 Com excepções para alguns ensaios, como por exemplo, os de Mário António F.Oliveira e os de Gabriel Mariano.

19 "Ultramar na Literatura Portuguesa" in *Dicionário de Literatura* (Porto: Figueirinhas, 1978), 4ºvol, 3º ed.

20 Mário Pinto de Andrade, *Antologia Temática da Poesia Africana I e II* (Lisboa: Sá da Costa, 1975).

21 Russell Hamilton, *Literatura Africana Literatura Necessária I- Angola* (Lisboa: Edições 70, 1981); *Literatura Africana Literatura Necessária II- Moçambique, Cabo Verde, Guiné-Bissau, São Tomé e Princípe* (Lisboa: Edições 70, 1983). Estas obras são resultado da escrita e alargamento da tese de doutoramento, originalmente publicada em 1975 (University of Minnesota) com o título *Voices from an Empire: A history o Afro-Portuguese Literature.*

22 Gerald Moser e Manuel Ferreira, *Bibliografia das Literaturas Africanas de Expressão Portugesa* (Lisboa: INCM, 1983).

23 Saliente-se as dissertações de Elsa Rodrigues dos Santos (Literatura Caboverdiana: Jorge Barbosa), Inocência Mata (Emergência da Literatura Santomense), Pires Laranjeira (Literatura Santomense: Francisco José Tenreiro) e de Ana Mafalda Leite (Literatura Moçambicana: José Craveirinha). Mais tarde, outras teses virão a surgir, também em outras Universidades, e gostaria de destacar na área da Literatura Moçambicana o valioso contributo das teses de Gilberto Matusse , Francisco Noa (U. Nova) e de Almiro Lobo (U. de Lisboa).

24 Saliente-se em especial as publicações, de referência indispensável, resultantes dos três principais colóquios sobre esta área literária: AAVV, *X Encontro de Professores Universitários Brasileiros de Literatura Portuguesa/ I Colóquuio Luso*-Brasileiro de *Professores Universitários de Literaturas Africanas de Expressão Portuguesa,* Lisboa, Instituto de Cultura Brasileira,

Universidade de Lisboa, 1984; AAVV, *Les Littératures Africaines de Langue Portugaise*, Actes du Colloque International, Paris, Centre Culturel Portugais, Fondation Calouste Gulbenkian, 1985; AAVV, *Literaturas Africanas de Língua Portuguesa*, Lisboa, Acarte, Fundação Calouste Gulbenkian, 1987.

[25] É o caso dos dois volumes *Literaturas Africanas de Expressão Portuguesa* de Manuel Ferreira, editados pelo Icalp, dos volumes de Russell Hamilton, das Antologias Temáticas de Mário de Andrade, de algumas das antologias, organizadas por Manuel Ferreira, *No Reino de Caliban.*

[26] Cf. o artigo de Francisco Sousa Neves, "A poesia de Rui de Noronha" in *África,* nº1, Julho 1978.

[27] In Doubrovsky et Todorov, *L'Enseignement de la Littérature* (Paris: Plon, 1969) 170.

[28] Apesar de todas as questões teóricas levantadas nos últimos anos—cf. Clément Moisan, *Qu'est-ce que l'Histoire Liitteraire?* (Paris: Puf, 1987) ou Marshall Brown (ed.), *The Uses of Literary History* (North Carolina: Duke Unoiversity Press, 1995)—em torno do conceito de história da literatura e de história literária, na área de estudos literários africanos de expressão portuguesa é mais do que fundamental escrevê-las e publicá-las.

[29] In Carlos Reis, *O Conhecimento da Literatura* (Coimbra: Almedina, 1995) 71.

[30] Frank Kermode afirma a propósito do cânone que "quer pensemos nos cânones como susceptíveis de objecção, porque formados ao acaso, para servir uns interesses à custa de outros, quer suponhamos que os conteúdos dos cânones são intencionalmente escolhidos, não pode haver dúvida de que não encontrámos modo de ordenar o nosso pensamento acerca da história da literatura e da arte, sem o recurso a eles," Apud Carlos Reis, *O Conhecimento da Literatura* (Coimbra: Almedina, 1995) 73.

[31] Jacques Dubois, *L'Institution de La Littérature* (Bruxelles : Ed. Labor, 1983) 99.

[32] Não existe por exemplo no domínio da ficção africana de expressão portuguesa a publicação, em Portugal,—e que eu saiba também não nos países africanos—de nenhuma antologia desde 1972. Com efeito, foram da autoria de Amândio César as últimas antologias publicadas, designadas como sendo "do conto Ultramarino."

[33] Pires Laranjeira, *Literaturas Africanas de Expressão Portuguesa* (Lisboa: Universidade Aberta, 1995) 17.

[34] Clément Moisan, *Qu'est-ce que l'histoire liittéraire?* (Paris: PUF,1987) 238.

[35] Patrick Chabal (ed.), *The Postcolonial Literature of Lusophone Africa* (London: Hurst, 1996). O livro pretende sistematizar a produção literária que teve lugar nas literaturas nacionais no período de 1975 a 94, e dar continuação ao trabalho de Russell Hamilton, que originalmente editado em língua inglesa, se deteve na época das independências. Está organizado pelas cinco literaturas nacionais, tendo sido distribuído o trabalho por cinco investigadores desta área de estudos: Moçambique-Patrick Chabal; Angola-Ana Mafalda Leite; Guiné-Biissau-Moema Parente Augel; Cabo Verde-David Brookshaw; S.Tomé e Príncipe-Caroline Shaw. Esta obra está a ser traduzida e será editada em português com a actualização bibliográfica necessária.

[36] Arnaldo França, "Panorama da Literatura Caboverdiana," in *Vértice* nº55, Julho-Agosto 1993.

[37] Ilídio Rocha, "Sobre as origens de uma Literatura africana de expressão portuguesa: raízes e consciencialização" (1984) in *Les Littératures Africaines de Langue Portugaise* (Paris: Fundação Calouste Gulbenkian, 1985) (publ.) 407.

[38] Manuel Ferreira, *Campos de Oliveira—mancebo e trovador* (Lisboa: INCM, 1984).

[39] Saliente-se no entanto os trabalhos realizados por Fátima Mendonça, professora da Universidade Eduardo Mondlane, que têm contribuído para o esclarecimento e organização periodológica da literatura produzida neste século.

[40] Mário António Fernandes de Oliveira, *Reler África* (Coimbra: Instituto de Antropolgia, 1990); Mário António Fernandes de Oliveira, *A Formação da Literatura Angolana (1851-1950)* (Lisboa: INCM, 1997).

[41] Carlos Ervedosa, *Roteiro da Literatura Angolana* (Luanda, União dos Escritores, 1979), 2ª ed.; Salvato Trigo, *Introdução à Literatura Angolana de Expressão Portuguesa* (Porto, Brasília Editora, 1977); Salvato Trigo, *A Poética da Geração da Mensagem* (Porto: Brasília Editora, 1979); Fernado Augusto Albuquerque Mourão, *A Sociedade Angolana através da Literatura* (São Paulo: Editora Ática, 1978); José Carlos Venâncio, *Uma Perspectiva Etnológica da Literatura Angolana* (Lisboa: Ulmeiro, 1987); José Carlos Venâncio, *Literatura versus Sociedade* (Lisboa: Veja, 1992); Costa Andrade, *Literatura Angolana (opiniões)* (Lisboa: Ed. 70, 1980).

[42] Carlos Pacheco, *José da Silva Maia Ferreira. O Homem e a sua Época* (Luanda: UEA, 1990); *José da Silva Maia Ferreira—novas achegas para a sua biografia* (Luanda: UEA, 1992); "O Nativismo na poesia de José da Silva Maia Ferreira" in *Nacionalismo e Regionalismo nas Literaturas Lusófonas* (Lisboa: Ed. Cosmos, 1997).

[43] Carlos Pacheco, "Leituras e Bibliotecas em Angola na primeira metade do século XIX," in *Vértice* nº55, Julho-Agosto 1993.

[44] Alberto de Carvalho, "A Propósito de Uma Historiografia Angolana," in *Vértice* nº55, Julho-Agosto 1993.

[45] Jacques Dubois, *L'Institution de La Littérature* (Bruxelles: Editions Labor, 1983) 81.

[46] Nas "Reflexões Preliminares" da *História da Literatura Portuguesa* da autoria de Óscar Lopes e António José Saraiva (17 ed.) os autores levantam vários problemas relativos aos contornos da nacionalidade literária, que se podem detectar também nas Literaturas Africanas e que nos parecem da maior pertinência:" *(...) também se deve ter em conta: o critério da autonomia política nacional. Assim, apesar de o domínio linguístico português abranger o Brasil, não há dúvida que a literatura brasileira adquiriu características diferenciais, relacionadas com a progressiva diferenciação brasileira; e, como seria difícil, se não mesmo impossível, apontar uma divisória intrínseca, o mais razoável será deixar de incluir no nosso estudo da literatura portuguesa as obras de autoria brasileira posteriores à data da proclamação da independência desse país, embora a isso se oponha a intimidade de certas relações que chegam a pôr problemas de nacionalidade dos autores (caso de Gonçalves Crespo). Os autores radicados no Brasil anteriormente a essa data serão ainda objecto do nosso estudo; conquanto também julguemos legítimo encartá-los, a eles e até a obras de metropolitanos que viveram no Brasil (caso de Tomás António Gonzaga), sob o ponto de vista de formação da consciência nacional e literária brasileira.* O mesmo acontece com a Literatura dos países africanos de língua oficial portuguesa, nos seus vários graus de autonomia cultural. *E é por razão semelhante que, ao tratarmos da escola trovadoresca de língua galaico-portuguesa, que deu os primeiros passos de diferenciação da nossa literatura escrita, nós incluímos autores de naturalidade não portuguesa, quer galegos como João Airas de Santiago, quer castelhanos como Afonso, o Sábio, cuja corte foi tão importante para essa escola*" (1996: 12).

Issues of *Portuguese Literary & Cultural Studies*

Portuguese Literary & Cultural Studies 1
Fronteiras/Borders.

Portuguese Literary & Cultural Studies 2
Lídia Jorge in other words / por outras palavras.
Guest Editor: Cláudia Pazos Alonso, Oxford University

Portuguese Literary & Cultural Studies 3
Pessoa's Alberto Caeiro.

Portuguese Literary & Cultural Studies 4/5
Brazil 2001. A Revisionary History of Brazilian Literature and Culture.
Guest Editor: João Cezar de Castro Rocha, Universidade do Estado do Rio de Janeiro

Portuguese Literary & Cultural Studies 6
On Saramago.
Guest Editor: Anna Klobucka, University of Georgia

Portuguese Literary & Cultural Studies 8
Cape Verde: Language, Literature & Music.
Guest Editor: Ana Mafalda Leite, Universidade de Lisboa

Portuguese Literary & Cultural Studies 9
Post-Imperial Camões.
Guest Editor: João Ricardo Figueiredo, Universidade de Lisboa

Forthcoming
Portuguese Literary & Cultural Studies 7
Contemporary Portuguese Poetry.

Portuguese Literary & Cultural Studies 10
Mozambique.
Guest Editor: Phillip Rothwell, Rutgers University, New Brunswick

Portuguese Literary & Cultural Studies 11
Vitorino Nemésio.
Guest Editor: Francisco C. Fagundes, University of Massachusetts Amherst

Portuguese Literary & Cultural Studies 12
Facts and Fictions of António Lobo Antunes.

Adamastor Book Series

Eduardo Lourenço. *Chaos and Splendor and Other Essays.*
Edited by Carlos Veloso, New York University
ISBN: 0972256113

Forthcoming

Transdisciplinary Readings of Garrett's Travels in My Homeland.
Edited by Victor J. Mendes

The Later Eça Revisited.
Edited by Frank F. Sousa

Eça de Queirós. *The Relic.*
Trans. Aubrey F.G. Bell. Preface by Harold Bloom

Camões. *Sonnets and Other Poems.*
Translated by Richard Zenith

Fernando Gil and Helder Macedo.
The Traveling Eye: Retrospection, Vision, and Prophecy in Portuguese Renaissance.

Uprooted from One's Own Land: An Anthology of Brazilian Essays.
Edited by João Cezar de Castro Rocha,
Universidade do Estado do Rio de Janeiro

Maria Alzira Seixo, Universidade de Lisboa
António Lobo Antunes. The Art of the Novel.

Portuguese Language Textbooks Series

Francisco Cota Fagundes. *Um Passo Mais No Português Moderno: Gramática Avançada, Leituras, Composição e Vocabulário.*

Portuguese in the Americas Series

Portuguese-Americans and Contemporary Civic Culture in Massachusetts. Edited by Clyde Barrow, Center for Policy Analysis, University of Massachusetts Dartmouth.
ISBN: 0972256105

Charles Reis Felix. *Through a Portagee Gate.*
ISBN: 0972254148

Jerry R. Williams. *Portuguese Immigration from the Azores to the United States.* 2nd edition. Edited with preface by Andrea Klimt.

Alfred Lewis. *Sixty Acres and a Barn: A Novel.*

Donald Warrin. *The Portuguese and Cape Verdeans in American Whaling.*

The University of Massachusetts Dartmouth

Center for Portuguese Studies and Culture

Founded in 1996 by a group of faculty from four different colleges, the University of Massachusetts Dartmouth Center for Portuguese Studies and Culture is a multidisciplinary international studies and outreach unit dedicated to the study of the language, literatures and cultures of the Portuguese-speaking world. The Center is designed to be the liaison between the University of Massachusetts Dartmouth and other institutions involved in Portuguese studies both in the United States and abroad. The Center aims to develop pedagogical materials to aid in teaching and learning the Portuguese language and cultures at all levels of education, and also supports the development and dissemination of knowledge regarding the Portuguese-speaking communities in the United States. The Center for Portuguese Studies and Culture promotes outreach efforts in areas such as, but not limited to, the arts, education, economic development, health and politics related to the Portuguese-speaking communities in the Commonwealth of Massachusetts and throughout the United States.

The Center for Portuguese Studies and Culture includes the Summer Program in Portuguese, which was founded in 1994. This program has become the largest of its kind in the United States, with over 100 students from 10 different states in 2002. The Center also launched the Summer Program in Portuguese for Children in 2000. In the same year, the Center led the effort to create a separate Department of Portuguese, which was created in 2001. In fall 2002 the Department had 325 students and 46 majors. And in fall 2001, the Center led the way to the development of the Hélio and Amélia Pedroso/Luso-American Foundation Endowed Chair in Portuguese Studies. Prof. Donald Warrin of the University of California, Berkeley, a renowned expert on Portuguese-American Literature and History, occupied the Chair in Spring 2003. He will publish a book-length manuscript on the Portuguese and Cape Verdeans in American whaling in the Portuguese in the Americas Series, in 2005.

In 1998, the Center launched the semiannual peer-reviewed scholarly journal, *Portuguese Literary & Cultural Studies*, which has published essays by such eminent scholars as Harold Bloom, Hans Ulrich Gumbrecht and Luiz Costa Lima. PLCS has been very positively reviewed in the *Times Literary Supplement* of London (November 8, 2002). Recently the Center for Portuguese Studies and Culture launched three new series of publications: the Portuguese in the Americas Series (the first volume, *Portuguese-Americans and Contemporary Civic Culture in Massachusetts* was published in January 2003); the Adamastor Book Series (the first volume *Chaos and Splendor and Other Essays* by Eduardo Lourenço, Portugal's most celebrated cultural critic, was published in January 2003); and the Portuguese Language Textbook Series, whose inaugural volume is *Um Passo Mais no Português Moderno: Gramática Avançada, Leituras e Composição* by Francisco Cota Fagundes.

The Center also sponsors and organizes colloquia, concerts, art exhibitions, dance performances and theatrical productions, in addition to visits by distinguished authors and critics. With the Center's support José Saramago, the 1998 Nobel Laureate for Literature, was awarded an honorary degree in 1999 and returned to UMD in 2002 to be the keynote speaker in a similar ceremony for Harold Bloom, America's premier man of letters. In the same month of April 2002, the Center co-organized and co-sponsored events with José Saramago at the prestigious New York Public Library Bartos Forum (Prof. Bloom presented Saramago) and the John F. Kennedy Library, the latter in partnership with the Massachusetts Foundation for the Humanities. In fall 2002 the Center hosted Dr. José Ramos-Horta, Foreign Minister of East Timor and the 1996 Nobel Laureate for Peace. In April 2001, theCenter organized a colloquium and launching of an issue of *Portuguese Literary & Cultural Studies*, subtitled "Brazil 2001," at the Library of Congress in Washington, DC.

Future projects include the publication of studies on the Portuguese-American communities and the further development of the Portuguese-American Archives, located in the University Library Special Collections. In addition, the Department of Portuguese is currently developing a Graduate Program in Portuguese Studies to be launched in fall 2004. Finally, the Center and Department are working together to develop a scholarship program to promote the study of Portuguese at the undergraduate and graduate levels.

The varied activities of the Center for Portuguese Studies and Culture have been made possible by the commitment and generosity of numerous supporters. A gift from Frank B. Sousa, Chairman of the UMD Foundation Board of Directors, enabled the launching of the summer program, and subsequent major grants from the Luso-American Foundationof Lisbon and the Government of Portugal contributed significantly to the development of the Center for Portuguese Studies and Culture and the Department of Portuguese. Other grants from the Camões Institute and the Calouste Gulbenkian Foundation have supported the Summer Program in Portuguese and the organization of international coloquia. Portuguese studies at UMass Dartmouth have also benefited from the generous financial support of Anthony Andrade, Dennis Rezendes, the Citizens Financial Group, and the Portuguese-American legislative delegation in the State House of the Commonwealth of Massachusetts, led by State Representative Robert Correia. The Hélio and Amélia Pedroso/Luso-American Foundation Endowed Chair in Portuguese Studies was made possible by the generous support of Luis Pedroso, the Luso-American Foundation, Anthony Andrade, Maria Dulce Furman, Frank B. Sousa and Manuel Fernando Neto.

Portuguese Literary & Cultural Studies Subscription
Center for Portuguese Studies and Culture
University of Massachusetts Dartmouth
North Dartmouth, MA 02747 USA
Tel. (508) 999 9270 Fax (508) 999 9272 E-Mail greis@umassd.edu

Name

Address

City **State** **Zip**

Country

☐ **Annual Individual Subscription $ 40 (2 issues)**
☐ **Annual Institutional Subscription $80 (2 issues)**
☐ **Single Issue $25 (Issue Number __)**
Outside of the USA add $12.00 for shipping and handling

Payment enclosed
☐ **Check** ☐ **Visa** ☐ **Mastercard**

Credit Card Number **Expiration Date**

Signature **Date**

Notes

Notes